# Collins Student Atlas

## MAP SKILLS

| | |
|---|---|
| iii | Map symbols and Map types |
| iv | Graphs and Statistics |
| 1 | Latitude and Longitude |
| 2 | Scale |
| 3 | Projections |
| 4 | Aerial photographs |
| 5 | Introducing GIS |
| 6 | Satellite images |

## UNITED KINGDOM

| | |
|---|---|
| 7 | UK and Ireland |
| 8–9 | Southeast England |
| 10–11 | Wales and Southwest England |
| 12–13 | Northern England |
| 14–15 | Northern Ireland and Southern Scotland |
| 16–17 | Northern Scotland |
| 18 | Ireland |
| 19 | Satellite Image |
| 20–21 | Political |
| 22 | Relief |
| 23 | Geology |
| 24–25 | Climate |
| 26 | Agriculture and Forestry |
| 27 | Agriculture and Fishing |
| 28 | Industry |
| 29 | Energy |
| 30–31 | Population and Migration |
| 32 | Transport |
| 33 | Tourism |

## EUROPE

| | |
|---|---|
| 34 | Relief |
| 35 | Political |
| 36 | Climate |
| 37 | Tourism |
| 38 | Economic Activity |
| 39 | European Union |
| 40 | Population |
| 41 | Cities |
| 42 | Netherlands, Belgium and Luxembourg |
| 43 | Scandinavia |
| 44 | France |
| 45 | Spain and Portugal |
| 46–47 | Central Europe |
| 48–49 | Mediterranean Basin |
| 50–51 | Southeast Europe |
| 52–53 | Eastern Europe |
| 54–55 | Russia |

## NORTH AMERICA

| | |
|---|---|
| 56 | Relief |
| 57 | Political |
| 58 | Climate |
| 59 | Natural Hazards |
| 60–61 | Canada |
| 62–63 | United States of America |
| 64 | USA: Population |
| 65 | USA: Economy |
| 66–67 | Mexico and the Caribbean |

## SOUTH AMERICA

| | |
|---|---|
| 68 | Relief |
| 69 | Political |
| 70 | Climate |
| 71 | Economy and Population |
| 72–73 | South America |
| 74 | Brazil: Population |
| 75 | Brazil: Migration, Economy and Trade |
| 76–77 | Brazil: Deforestation |

## AFRICA

| | |
|---|---|
| 78 | Relief |
| 79 | Political |
| 80 | Climate |
| 81 | Land Use |
| 82 | Population and Wealth |
| 83 | Southern Africa |
| 84–85 | Northern Africa |

## ASIA

| | |
|---|---|
| 86 | Relief |
| 87 | Political |
| 88–89 | Climate |
| 90–91 | Population and Cities |
| 92 | Land Use |
| 93 | Middle East: Oil and Gas |
| 94–95 | Middle East |
| 96 | Pakistan, India, Bangladesh and Myanmar |
| 97 | India and Bangladesh: Population |
| 98–99 | China |
| 100 | China: Population |
| 101 | China: Land Use and Trade |
| 102–103 | Southeast Asia |
| 104 | Japan: Relief and Land Use |
| 105 | Japan: Economic Activity, Population and Tectonics |

| | |
|---|---|
| | ...d Climate |
| 107 | Political and Climate |
| 108–109 | Australia and New Zealand |
| 110 | Australia: Land Use, People and Natural Hazards |
| 111 | Australia: Minerals and Manufacturing |
| 112 | Arctic Ocean and Antarctica |

## WORLD

| | |
|---|---|
| 113 | International Organizations |
| 114–115 | Political |
| 116–117 | Relief |
| 118–119 | Tectonics |
| 120–121 | Climatic Systems |
| 122–123 | Climatic Regions |
| 124–125 | Climate Statistics |
| 126–127 | Biomes, Soils and Soil Erosion |
| 128 | Agriculture |
| 129 | Inequalities |
| 130–131 | Population |
| 132 | Urbanization |
| 133 | Migration |
| 134 | Birth Rate, Death Rate and Infant Mortality Rate |
| 135 | Life Expectancy, Literacy and Doctors |
| 136 | HDI, Access to Safe Water and Nutrition |
| 137 | HIV, Poverty and Aid |
| 138–139 | Environmental Issues |
| 140–141 | Climate Change |
| 142 | Fuel Production and Energy |
| 143 | GNI, Employment and Trade |
| 144–145 | Ecological Footprint |
| 146–147 | Tourism |
| 148 | Communications |
| 149 | Air Transport |

## WORLD STATISTICS

| | |
|---|---|
| 150–157 | Country Statistics |
| 158–163 | Regional Indicators |
| 164–179 | Dictionary of Geographical terms |
| 180–204 | Index |

Published by Collins
An imprint of HarperCollins Publishers
Westerhill Road
Bishopbriggs
Glasgow G64 2QT
www.harpercollins.co.uk

HarperCollins Publishers
1st Floor, Watermarque Building, Ringsend Road, Dublin 4, Ireland

Seventh edition 2021

A catalogue record for this book is available from the British Library.

ISBN 978-0-00-843024-5  (HB)  10 9 8 7 6 5 4 3 2
ISBN 978-0-00-843023-8  (PB)  10 9 8 7 6 5 4 3 2

Printed by GPS Group, Slovenia

**MIX**
Paper from
responsible sources
**FSC™ C007454**

FSC
www.fsc.org

This book is produced from independently certified
FSC™ paper to ensure responsible forest management.

For more information visit: www.harpercollins.co.uk/green

All mapping in this atlas is generated from Collins Bartholomew digital databases.
Collins Bartholomew, the UK's leading independent geographical information supplier,
can provide a digital, custom, and premium mapping service to a variety of markets.
For further information, e-mail: collinsbartholomew@harpercollins.co.uk
or visit our website at: www.collinsbartholomew.com

If you would like to comment on any aspect of this book,
please contact us at the above address or online.

www.collins.co.uk
e-mail: collinsmaps@harpercollins.co.uk

## Acknowledgements

Agriculture and Horticulture Development Board, UK
Airports Council International
Australian Government
Bathymetric data: The GEBCO Digital Atlas, published by the British Oceanographic Data Centre
  on behalf of IOC and IHO, 1994
BP Statistical Review of World Energy
Brazilian Institute of Geography and Statistics
British Geological Survey
Climate Change Vulnerability Index, 2020 © Verisk Maplecroft
Dartmouth Flood Observatory, USA
Global Footprint Network National Footprint Accounts, 2017 (http://data.footprintnetwork.org)
Intergovernmental Panel on Climate Change
International Telecommunication Union
IUCN Red List of Threatened Species™
Met Office, UK
NI Forest Service Copyright
Office for National Statistics, UK
UK Government (gov.uk) – public sector information licensed under the Open Government Licence v3.0
UN Commodity Trade Statistics
UN Department of Economic and Social Affairs, Population Division
UN Development Programme
UNESCO World Heritage Centre
UN Food and Agriculture Organization
UNHCR (UN Refugee Agency)
US Bureau of Labor Statistics
US Census Bureau
US Energy Information Administration
USGS Earthquake Hazards Program
USGS Mineral Resources Program
World Bank Group
World Resources Institute
World Tourism Organization

## Image credits

**p4** Richard Cooke/Alamy Stock Photo (vertical), A.P.S. (UK)/Alamy Stock Photo (oblique); **p5** MODIS Rapid Response
Team, NASA/GSFC (Alps satellite image); **p6** NASA Earth Observatory (Hurricane Sandy), NOAA Remote Sensing Division
(New Jersey), NASA/Science Photo Library (Lake Chad); **p19** Planet Observer/Science Photo Library; **p25** daulon/
Shutterstock (Greenhouse gases diagram); **p59** NASA/NOAA GOES Project; **p76-77** NASA/Earth Observatory;
**p91** NASA/Ron Beck, USGS Eros Data Center Satellite Systems Branch; **p132** NASA Earth Observatory;
**p149** NASA Johnson Space Center

## Map symbols

ymbols are used, in the form of points, lines
· areas, on maps to show the location of
nd information about specific features.
he colour and size of a symbol can give
ı indication of the type of feature and its
·lative size.
he meaning of map symbols is explained in
· key shown on each page. Symbols used on
·ference maps are shown here.

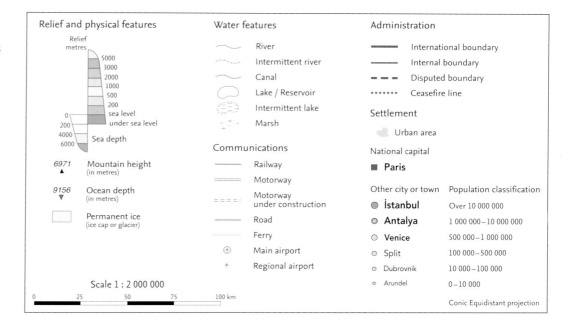

Relief and physical features

Relief metres
5000
3000
2000
1000
500
200
sea level
under sea level

Sea depth

6971 ▲ Mountain height (in metres)

9156 ▼ Ocean depth (in metres)

Permanent ice (ice cap or glacier)

Scale 1 : 2 000 000

0   25   50   75   100 km

Water features

∼ River
∼ Intermittent river
∼ Canal
Lake / Reservoir
Intermittent lake
Marsh

Communications

Railway
Motorway
Motorway under construction
Road
Ferry
⊕ Main airport
✈ Regional airport

Administration

International boundary
Internal boundary
Disputed boundary
Ceasefire line

Settlement

Urban area

National capital

■ Paris

| Other city or town | Population classification |
| --- | --- |
| ◉ İstanbul | Over 10 000 000 |
| ◉ Antalya | 1 000 000 – 10 000 000 |
| ○ Venice | 500 000 – 1 000 000 |
| ○ Split | 100 000 – 500 000 |
| ○ Dubrovnik | 10 000 – 100 000 |
| ○ Arundel | 0 – 10 000 |

Conic Equidistant projection

## Map types

any types of map are included in the atlas to show different information. The type of map,
; symbols and colours are carefully selected to show the theme of each map and to make
em easy to understand. The main types of map used are explained below.

**plitical maps** provide an overview of the
ze, location and boundaries of countries
a specific area, such as a continent.
ploured squares indicate national capitals.
ploured circles represent other cities
· towns.

**Physical or relief maps** use colour to show
oceans, seas, rivers, lakes and the height of
the land. The names and heights of major
landforms are also indicated.

**Reference maps** bring together the
information provided in the two types
of map described on the left. They show
relief and physical features as well as
country borders, major cities and towns,
roads, railways and airports.

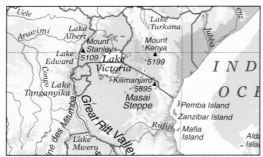

Extract from page 78

Extract from page 98

ract from page 69

**stribution maps** use different colours,
mbols, or shading to show the location and
stribution of natural or man-made features.
this map, symbols indicate the distribution
the world's largest cities.

**Graduated colour maps** use colours or
shading to show a topic or theme and a
measure of its intensity. Generally, the
highest values are shaded with the darkest
colours. In this map, colours are used to show
the number of internet users per 100 people.

**Isoline maps** use thin lines to show the
distribution of a feature. An isoline passes
through places of the same value. Isolines
may show features such as temperature
(isotherm), air pressure (isobar) or height of
land (contour). The value of the line is usually
written on it. On either side of the line the
value will be higher or lower.

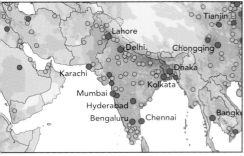

ract from page 131

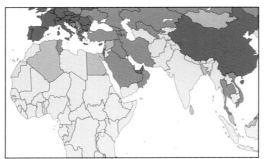

Extract from page 148

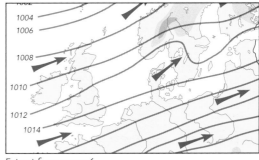

Extract from page 36

# Graphs and Statistics

Graphs are a visual way of presenting statistical information.
There are different kinds of graphs in this atlas.
Some graphs are designed to present a particular
kind of information.

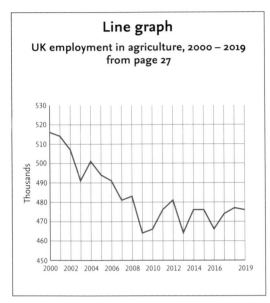

## Line graph

### UK employment in agriculture, 2000 – 2019
### from page 27

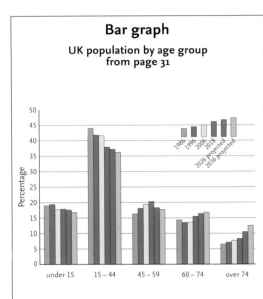

## Bar graph

### UK population by age group
### from page 31

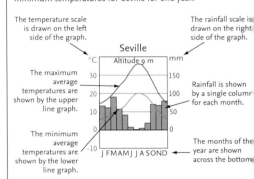

## Climate graph
### from page 36

A climate graph contains information about the average yearly temperatures and average yearly rainfall for a particular location. The graph below shows the average maximum and minimum temperatures for Seville for one year.

The temperature scale is drawn on the left side of the graph.

The rainfall scale is drawn on the right side of the graph.

The maximum average temperatures are shown by the upper line graph.

Rainfall is shown by a single column for each month.

The minimum average temperatures are shown by the lower line graph.

The months of the year are shown across the bottom.

A climate graph for Seville in Spain

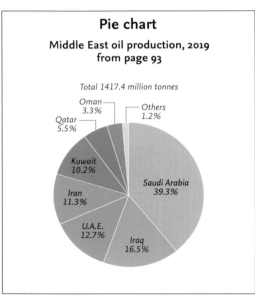

## Pie chart

### Middle East oil production, 2019
### from page 93

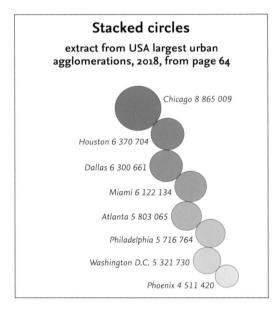

## Stacked circles

### extract from USA largest urban agglomerations, 2018, from page 64

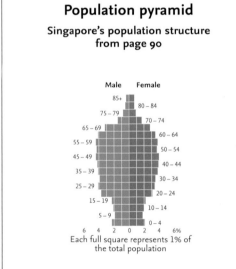

## Population pyramid

### Singapore's population structure
### from page 90

Each full square represents 1% of the total population

---

Throughout this atlas there are sets of statistics presented as tables showing values or indicators related to the themes covered on a map spread.

Climate statistics, population statistics, country indicators, trade values etc are just some of the tables found throughout the atlas.

### Population by country, 2019

| Country | Population (thousands) | Density (persons per sq km) |
|---|---|---|
| England | 56 287 | 432 |
| Wales | 3153 | 152 |
| Scotland | 5463 | 69 |
| Northern Ireland | 1894 | 139 |
| United Kingdom | 66 797 | 274 |

### Top 5 largest urban agglomerations, 2018

| Urban agglomeration | Population |
|---|---|
| **Tōkyō** Japan | 37 393 129 |
| **Delhi** India | 30 290 936 |
| **Shanghai** China | 27 058 479 |
| **Dhaka** Bangladesh | 21 005 860 |
| **Beijing** China | 20 462 610 |

| Vancouver | Jan | Feb | Mar | Apr | May | Jun | Jul | Aug | Sep | Oct | Nov | Dec |
|---|---|---|---|---|---|---|---|---|---|---|---|---|
| Temperature - max. (°C) | 5 | 7 | 10 | 14 | 18 | 21 | 23 | 23 | 18 | 14 | 9 | 6 |
| Temperature - min. (°C) | 0 | 1 | 3 | 4 | 8 | 11 | 12 | 12 | 9 | 7 | 4 | 2 |
| Rainfall - (mm) | 218 | 147 | 127 | 84 | 71 | 64 | 31 | 43 | 91 | 147 | 211 | 224 |

| Flag | Country | Capital city | Population total 2019 | Density persons per sq km 2019 | Birth rate per 1000 population 2018 |
|---|---|---|---|---|---|
| | St Vincent and the Grenadines | Kingstown | 110 593 | 284 | 14 |
| | Samoa | Apia | 197 093 | 69 | 24 |
| | San Marino | San Marino | 33 864 | 555 | 7 |
| | São Tomé and Príncipe | São Tomé | 215 048 | 223 | 32 |

## Latitude

Latitude is distance, measured in degrees, north and south of the Equator. Lines of latitude circle the globe in an east-west direction. The distance between lines of latitude is always the same. They are also known as parallels of latitude. Because the circumference of Earth gets smaller toward the poles, the lines of latitude are shorter nearer the poles.

## Longitude

Longitude is distance, measured in degrees, east and west of the Greenwich Meridian (prime meridian). Lines of longitude join the poles in a north-south direction. Because the lines join the poles, they are always the same length, but are farthest apart at the Equator and closest together at the poles. These lines are also called meridians of longitude.

## Finding places

When lines of latitude and longitude are drawn on a map, they form a grid, which looks like a pattern of squares. This pattern is used to find places on a map. Latitude is always stated before longitude (e.g. 42°N 78°W).

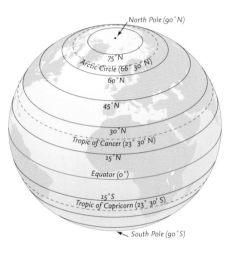

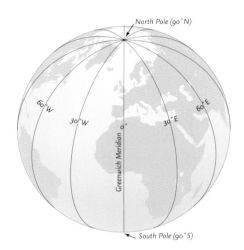

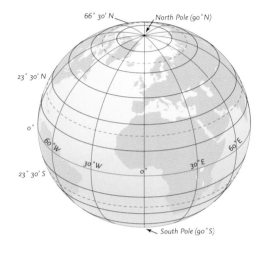

All lines of latitude have numbers between 0° and 90° and a direction, either north or south of the Equator. The Equator is at 0° latitude. The North Pole is at 90° north and the South Pole is at 90° south. The 'tilt' of Earth has given particular importance to some lines of latitude. They include:
- the Arctic Circle at 66° 30' north
- the Antarctic Circle at 66° 30' south
- the Tropic of Cancer at 23° 30' north
- the Tropic of Capricorn at 23° 30' south

The Equator also divides the Earth into two halves. The northern half, north of the Equator, is the **Northern Hemisphere**. The southern half, south of the Equator, is the **Southern Hemisphere**.

Longitude begins along the Greenwich Meridian (prime meridian), at 0°, in London, England. On the opposite side of Earth is the 180° meridian, which is the International Date Line. To the west of the prime meridian are Canada, the United States, and Brazil; to the east of the prime meridian are Germany, India and China. All lines of longitude have numbers between 0° and 180° and a direction, either east or west of the prime meridian.

The Greenwich Meridian and the International Date Line can also be used to divide the world into two halves. The half to the west of the Greenwich Meridian is the **Western Hemisphere**. The half to the east of the Greenwich Meridian is the **Eastern Hemisphere**.

By stating latitude and then longitude of a place, it becomes much easier to find. On the map (below) point A is easy to find as it is exactly latitude 58° north of the Equator and longitude 4° west of the Greenwich Meridian (58°N 4°W).

To be even more accurate in locating a place, each degree of latitude and longitude can also be divided into smaller units called **minutes** ('). There are 60 minutes in each degree. On the map (below) Halkirk is one half (or 30/60ths) of the way past latitude 58°N, and one-half (or 30/60ths) of the way past longitude 3°W. Its latitude is therefore 58 degrees 30 minutes north and its longitude is 3 degrees 30 minutes west. This can be shortened to 58°30'N 3°30'W. Latitude and longitude for all the places and features named on the maps are included in the index.

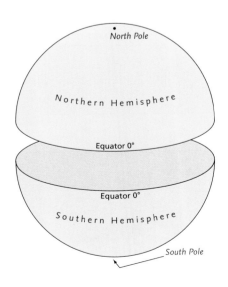

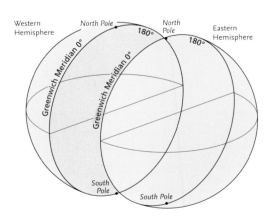

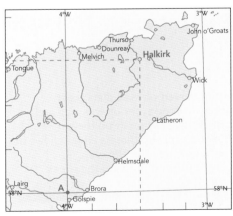

# Scale

## Scale

To draw a map of any part of the world, the area must be reduced, or 'scaled down,' to the size of a page in this atlas, a foldable road map, or a topographic map. The scale of the map indicates the amount by which an area has been reduced.

The scale of a map can also be used to determine the actual distance between two or more places or the actual size of an area on a map. The scale indicates the relationship between distances on the map and distances on the ground.

## Ways of describing scale

**Word scale**: You can describe the scale in words e.g. one centimetre on the map represents 100 kilometres on the ground.

**Line scale**: A line with the scale marked on it is an easy way to compare distances on the map with distances on the ground.

**Ratio scale**: This method uses numbers to compare distances on the map with distances on the ground, e.g. 1:40 000 000. This means that one centimetre on the map represents 40 million centimetres on the ground. This number is too large to mean much to most people, so we convert centimetres to kilometres by dividing by 100 000 which equals 400 kilometres.

## Scale and map information

The scale of a map affects how much information the map can show.

As the area shown on a map becomes larger, the amount of detail and accuracy of the map becomes less and less.

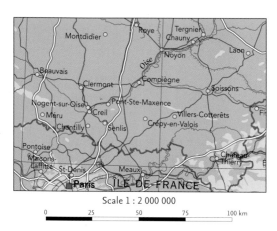

Scale 1 : 2 000 000

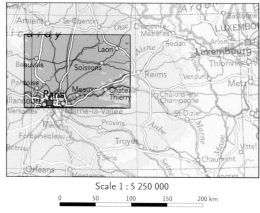

Scale 1 : 5 250 000

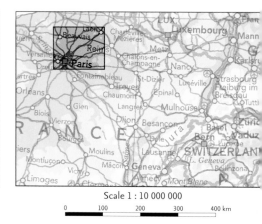

Scale 1 : 10 000 000

## Measuring distance

The instructions below show you how to determine how far apart places are on a map, then using the line scale, to determine the actual distance on the ground.

### Measuring straight-line distances:
1. place the edge of a sheet of paper on the two places on a map,
2. on the paper, place a mark at each of the two places,
3. place the paper on the line scale,
4. measure the distance on the ground using the scale.

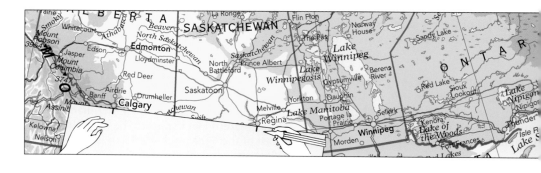

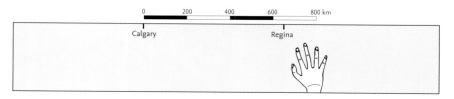

### Measuring curved or road distances:
1. place a sheet of paper on the map and mark off the start point on the paper,
2. move the paper so that its edge follows the bends and curves on the map,
3. mark off the end point on the sheet of paper,
4. place the paper on the line scale and read the actual distance following a road or railroad.

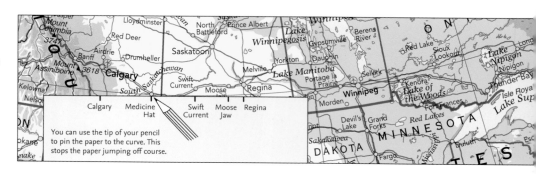

epresenting a spherical Earth as a flat map has presented a
umber of challenges for map makers. A map projection is a way
 showing the Earth's surface on a flat piece of paper. There are
any types of map projections. None of them shows the Earth
th perfect accuracy. All map projections distort either:
ea, direction, shape or distance.

## lindrical projections

lindrical projections are constructed by
ojecting the surface of the globe or sphere
arth) onto a cylinder that just touches the
tside edges of that globe. Two examples of
lindrical projections are Mercator and Times.

**ercator Projection** (see pages 102–103
r an example of this projection)

e Mercator cylindrical projection is useful for
eas near the equator and to about 15 degrees
rth or south of the equator, where distortion
 shape is minimal. The projection is useful
r navigation, since directions are plotted as
aight lines.

## Conic projections

Conic projections are constructed by projecting
the surface of a globe or sphere (Earth) onto a
cone that just touches the outside edges of
that globe. Examples of conic projections are
Conic Equidistant and Albers Equal Area Conic.

**Conic Equidistant Projection** (see pages 54–55
for an example of this projection)

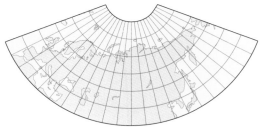

Conic projections are best suited for areas
between 30° and 60° north and south of the
equator when the east–west distance is greater
than the north–south distance (such as Canada
and Europe). The meridians are straight and
spaced at equal intervals.

## Azimuthal projections

Azimuthal projections are constructed by
projecting the surface of the globe or sphere
(Earth) onto a flat surface that touches the
globe at one point only. Some examples of
azimuthal projections are Lambert Azimuthal
Equal Area and Polar Stereographic.

**Polar Stereographic Projection** (see page 112
for an example of this projection)

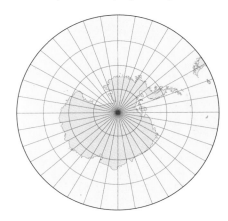

Azimuthal projections are useful for areas that
have similar east–west and north–south
dimensions such as Antarctica and Australia.

**kert IV** (see pages 116–117 for an example
 this projection)

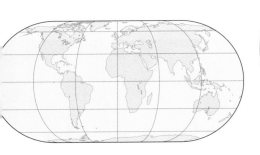

kert IV is an equal area projection. Equal
ea projections are useful for world thematic
aps where it is important to show the correct
lative sizes of continental areas. Eckert IV has
straight central meridian but all others are
rved, which helps suggest the spherical
ture of the Earth.

**Lambert Conformal** (see pages 60–61 for an
example of this projection)

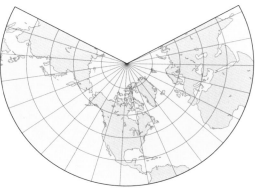

Lambert's Conformal Conic projection
maintains an exact scale along one or two
standard parallels (lines of latitude). Angles
between locations on the surface of the
Earth are correctly shown. Therefore, it is used
for aeronautical charts and large scale
topographic maps in many countries. It is also
used to map areas with a greater east–west
than north–south extent.

**Lambert Azimuthal Equal Area** (see pages
108–109 for an example of this projection)

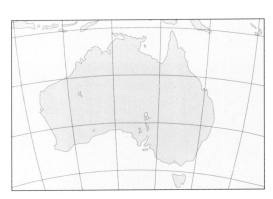

This projection is useful for areas that have
similar east–west and north–south dimensions
such as Australia.

# Aerial photographs

Aerial photographs are images of the land usually taken from an aeroplane. There are two kinds of aerial photographs, vertical aerial photographs and oblique aerial photographs.

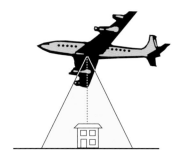

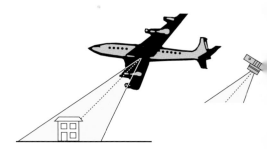

Camera position for a vertical aerial photograph

Camera position for an oblique aerial photograph

Vertical aerial photographs are taken from a digital camera fixed under an aeroplane. The camera points straight down at the ground. Objects are shown from above and may be difficult to identify.

Vertical aerial photographs show the same view of the land as a large scale map. Cartographers use vertical aerial photographs to help them make 1 : 50 000 topographic maps.

A vertical aerial photograph of Whitby, North Yorkshire

Oblique aerial photographs are taken from a camera that is positioned at an angle to the ground. Objects are more easily recognised in oblique aerial photographs. There are two kinds of oblique aerial photographs: high angle and low angle oblique

aerial photographs. A high angle aerial photograph shows a large area of land. The horizon is usually visible. In low angle aerial photographs the horizon is not visible. The area of land shown is usually much smaller.

A low angle oblique aerial photograph of the same area of Whitby, North Yorkshire

## GIS concepts

GIS is a set of tools that can be used to collect, store, retrieve, modify and display spatial data. Spatial data can come from a variety of sources including existing maps, satellite imagery, aerial photographs or data collected from GPS (Global Positioning System) surveys.

GIS links this information to its real world location and can display this in a series of layers which you can then choose to turn off and on or to combine using a computer.

GIS can work with spatial information in three ways.
- As a map made up of a collection of layers containing symbols. The illustration on the right shows a number of GIS layers.
- As geographic information called a database, stored on a computer.
- As a set of tools that create new datasets using existing stored geographic data.

## Uses of GIS

GIS can be used in many ways to help solve problems, identify patterns, make decisions and plan development. A local government for example might want to build a new business area in a settlement. A GIS would be able to provide information on: the numbers of people who live in the area, transport routes, the average income of the population, and the kinds of goods people buy. A GIS could also be used to identify the number of houses built on a flood plain. This information could inform emergency planning or the relocation of the houses.

## GIS terms

**Spatial data:** Spatial data describes the location and shape of features. You can see these features on a map or on a computer screen.

**Attribute data:** Attribute data describes or adds information about a feature, such as: population numbers, names of places, climate statistics. Attribute data may be stored in tables or as text within a GIS. Attribute data is made up of both raster and vector data.

**Vector data:** Represents map features as points, lines and area, e.g. mountain peaks, rivers, settlements.

**Raster data:** Represents map features as cells in a grid. Points, lines and areas can also be stored as cells of a grid. A satellite image is an example of raster data.

  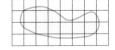

### GIS layers

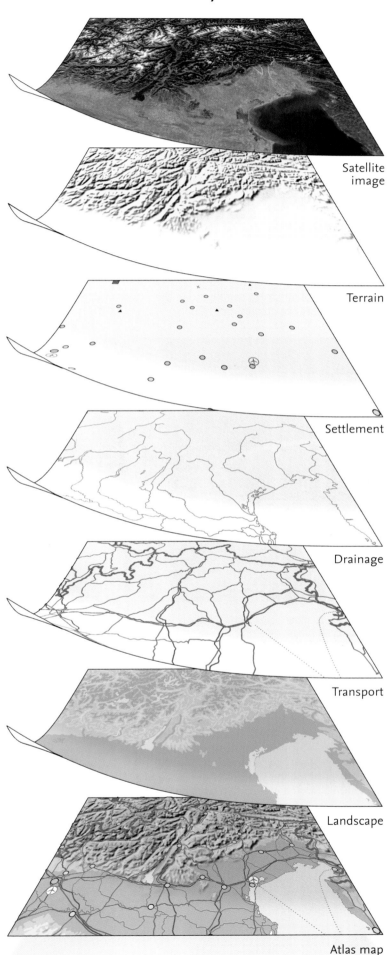

Satellite image

Terrain

Settlement

Drainage

Transport

Landscape

Atlas map

An example of different layers that can be stored and used in a GIS.

# Satellite images

## Satellite images

Images captured by a large number of Earth-observing satellites provide unique views of the Earth. The science of gathering and interpreting such images is known as remote sensing. Geographers use images taken from high above the Earth to determine patterns, trends and basic characteristics of the Earth's surface. Satellites are fitted with different kinds of scanners or sensors to gather information about the Earth. The most well known satellites are Landsat and SPOT.

Satellite sensors detect electromagnetic radiation – X-rays, ultraviolet light, visible colours and microwave signals. This data can be processed to provide information on soils, land use, geology, pollution and weather patterns.

## Natural disasters

Satellite images have many uses. One use is comparing two images to examine how conditions have changed over time. Satellite images taken before and after a natural event such as a flood or a violent storm can illustrate the extent of damage and help emergency planning.

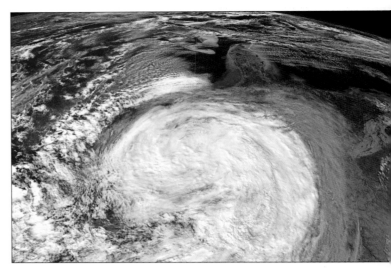

A satellite image showing Hurricane Sandy over northeastern USA, in 2012. Satellite images help people to prepare for approaching natural disasters such as cyclones and floods. Weather scientists use satellite images to help them forecast the weather.

In October 2012, the effects of Hurricane Sandy caused extensive damage and loss of life in the Caribbean and eastern USA. The two satellite images above show part of the town of Mantoloking on the New Jersey coast before (left image) and after (right image) the storm struck.

## Climate change

Satellite images taken over time can be used to identify the effects of climate change. For example, a series of satellite images can show how far ice sheets have retreated, or how the shorelines of lakes and seas have changed in a certain time period.

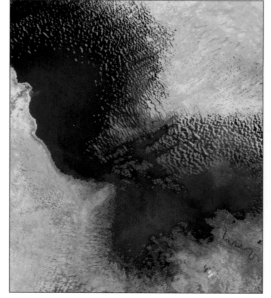 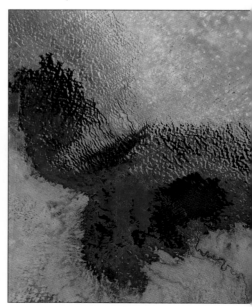

Satellite imagery showing the reduction in size of Lake Chad between 1973 (left) and 2007 (right).

Water features
~ River
Lake / Reservoir

Administration
Boundaries
International
Internal

Settlement
Cities and towns in order of size
National capital
■ London
Administrative capital
■ Belfast
Other city or town
● Glasgow
○ Liverpool
○ Swansea

Scale 1 : 4 500 000
0     50     100 km
Conic Equidistant projection

ATLANTIC
OCEAN

Shetland
Islands

Orkney
Islands

Outer Hebrides

SCOTLAND

Aberdeen

Dundee

Glasgow    Edinburgh

North
Sea

NORTHERN
IRELAND    Belfast

Isle of Man
(British Crown
Dependency)

Newcastle
upon Tyne    Sunderland

Middlesbrough

Irish Sea

IRELAND

Dublin

York    Kingston
upon Hull

Blackpool    Bradford    Leeds
Preston   Blackburn
Bolton         Huddersfield
Manchester  Oldham    Rotherham
Liverpool  St Helens
Birkenhead  Stockport  Sheffield
ENGLAND
Stoke-on-Trent
Derby    Nottingham

Norwich

Telford         Leicester    Peterborough
Walsall
Wolverhampton  Sutton Coldfield    Cambridge
Dudley  Birmingham
West        Coventry    Ipswich
Bromwich           Northampton    Colchester
Milton Keynes
Gloucester               Luton    Southend-on-Sea
Oxford  Watford
Swansea  Newport  Swindon  Slough  London
Cardiff         Reading
Bristol              Woking    Crawley

Cork

WALES

Celtic Sea

Southampton  Portsmouth  Brighton
Exeter  Poole         Worthing  Eastbourne
Bournemouth

Plymouth

English Channel

FRANCE

Channel Islands
(British Crown
Dependency)

12°  A  10°  B  8°  C  6°  D  4°  E  2°  F  0°  G  2°  H

10°  8°  6°  4°  0°  2°

**Relief and physical features**

Relief
metres
1000
500
200
100
sea level
0
50
100
200
under sea level

1085 ▲ Mountain height (in metres)

**Water features**
~ River
Canal
Lake / Reservoir

**Communications**
Railway
Motorway
Road
Car ferry
⊕ Main airport
✈ Regional airport

**Administration**
Boundaries
International
Internal

**Settlement**
Urban area

Cities and towns in order of size
National capital | Other city or town
■ London | ◉ Birmingham
| ◉ Bristol
| ◎ Oxford
| ◌ Colchester
| ○ Wantage

Scale 1 : 1 200 000
0  10  20  30  40 km
Conic Equidistant projection

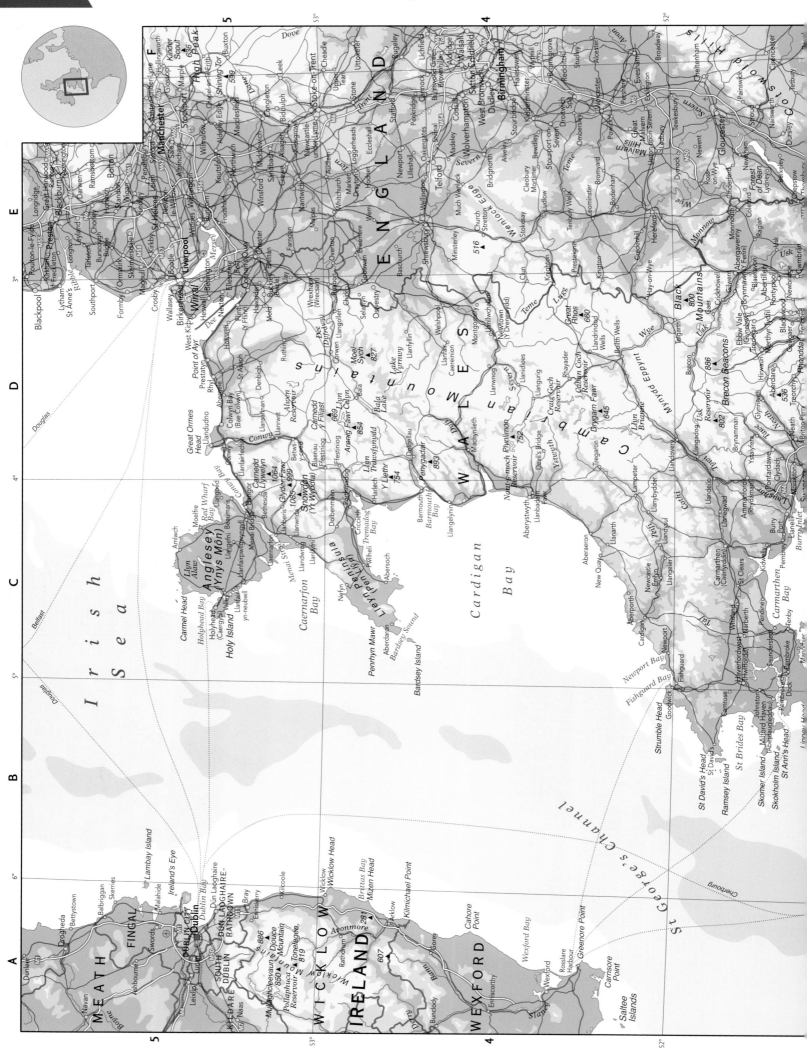

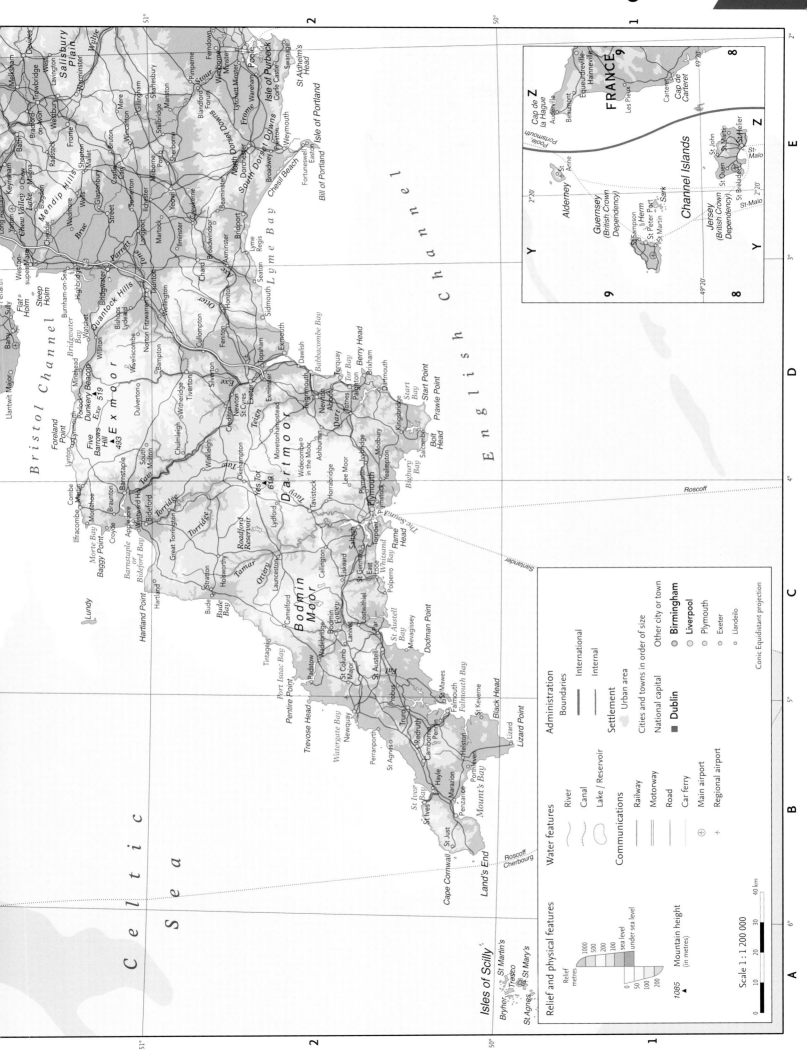

**Isles of Scilly**

Bryher
St Martin's
Tresco
St Agnes
St Mary's

*Celtic Sea*

*Bristol Channel*

Land's End
Cape Cornwall
St Just

Penzance
Marazion
Mount's Bay
Porthleven
Hayle
St Ives
St Ives Bay
Lizard
Lizard Point
Helston
St Keverne
Black Head
Camborne
Penryn
Falmouth
Falmouth Bay
St Mawes
Redruth
Truro
Probus
Perranporth
St Agnes
Newquay
Watergate Bay
Mevagissey
St Austell
St Austell Bay
Probus
Dodman Point
Bodmin Moor
Bodmin
Fowey
Par
Lostwithiel
Lanivet
St Columb Major
Wadebridge
Padstow
Trevose Head
Pentire Point
Polperro
Looe
Liskeard
Callington
St Germans
East Looe
Port Isaac Bay
Tintagel
Camelford
Launceston
Holsworthy
Stratton
Bude
Bude Bay
Hartland
Hartland Point
Lundy

*Communications*

Railway
Motorway
Road
Car ferry
Main airport
Regional airport

*Water features*

River
Canal
Lake / Reservoir

*Relief and physical features*

Relief metres
1000
500
200
100
50
0
sea level
under sea level

1085 ▲ Mountain height (in metres)

Scale 1 : 1 200 000

0   10   20   30   40 km

*Administration*
Boundaries
International
Internal

*Settlement*
Urban area
Cities and towns in order of size
National capital  ■ **Dublin**
● **Birmingham**
◉ **Liverpool**
○ Plymouth
○ Exeter
○ Llandeilo   Other city or town

Conic Equidistant projection

Barnstaple or Bideford Bay
Bideford
Appledore
Westward Ho!
Northam
Braunton
Croyde
Baggy Point
Morte Point
Morte Bay
Ilfracombe
Combe Martin
Lynmouth
Lynton
Foreland Point
Minehead
Porlock
Watchet
Williton
Dunkery Beacon
Exe 519 ▲
*Exmoor*
Five Barrows Hill
493 ▲
South Molton
Chulmleigh
Winkleigh
Great Torrington
*Torridge*
Okehampton
Yes Tor 619 ▲
*Dartmoor*
Lydford
Tavistock
Lee Moor
Lydbridge
Horrabridge
Yelverton
Plympton
Plymouth
Plymstock
Saltash
Torpoint
Rame Head
Whitsand Bay
East Whitsand
The Sound
Santander
Roscoff
Cawsand

*English Channel*

Roadford Reservoir
North Tawton
Crediton
Newton St Cyres
*Exe*
Exeter
Silverton
Cullompton
Tiverton
Witheridge
*Teign*
Moretonhampstead
Widecombe in the Moor
Ashburton
Bovey Tracey
Newton Abbot
*Dart*
Totnes
Paignton
Torquay
Tor Bay
Babbacombe Bay
Teignmouth
Dawlish
Starcross
Exmouth
Topsham
Exminster
Brixham
Berry Head
Dartmouth
Salcombe
Kingsbridge
Modbury
Bigbury Bay
Bolt Head
Bolt Tail
Prawle Point
Start Point
Start Bay

Wellington
Bampton
Bishops Lydeard
*Quantock Hills*
Bridgwater
Bridgwater Bay
Burnham-on-Sea
Highbridge
Steep Holm
Flat Holm
Sully
Barry
Llantwit Major
*Bristol Channel*

Weston-super-Mare
Long Ashton
Yatton
Chew Valley Lake
Chew Magna
Keynsham
Bath
Bradford-on-Avon
Trowbridge
Westbury
Warminster
Frome
Radstock
Shepton Mallet
Wells
*Mendip Hills*
Cheddar
Wedmore
*Brue*
Glastonbury
Street
Somerton
Langport
Ilchester
Martock
Yeovil
Crewkerne
Ilminster
Chard
Axminster
Honiton
Feniton
Sidmouth
Seaton
Lyme Regis
*Lyme Bay*
Bridport
Broadwindsor
Beaminster
Sherborne
*North Dorset Downs*
Dorchester
*South Dorset Downs*
Broadwey
Weymouth
Easton
Fortuneswell
*Bill of Portland*
*Isle of Portland*
Preston
Chesil Beach
Wareham
Poole
*Isle of Purbeck*
Corfe Castle
St Aldhelm's Head
Swanage
Wimborne Minster
Ferndown
Wool
Lytchett Minster
Bere Regis
Blandford Forum
Pimperne
*Stour*
Sturminster Newton
Stalbridge
Gillingham
Shaftesbury
Mere
Bruton
Wincanton
Castle Cary
Wilton

*Salisbury Plain*
*Wylye*
Wilton
Warminster
Devizes
Melksham
Lavington
West Lavington

Taunton
Norton Fitzwarren
*Tone*
*Parrett*
*Otter*
*Axe*

Petersfield

**Channel Islands**

*Alderney* (British Crown Dependency)
Cap de la Hague
Les Pieux
Equeurdreville-Hainneville
Beaumont
Carteret
Cap de Carteret
Audeville
St. Anne
*Guernsey* (British Crown Dependency)
Herm
Sampson
St Peter Port
St Martin
Sark
*Jersey* (British Crown Dependency)
St Ouen
St John
St Helier
St Brelade
St Martin
St-Malo
**FRANCE**

Roscoff
Cherbourg
Poole
Portsmouth

Y   Z
9
8

A

B

C

D

6°

5°

4°

3°

**Bute**
Rothesay
Sound of Bute
Great Cumbrae
Largs
**Glasgow** Coatbridge
Johnstone
Barrhead
Whitburn
West Calder
Bilston
Bonnyrigg
Gorebridge
Penicuik
Pentland Hills

Gigha
Claonaig
Lochranza
Millport
Paisley
Beith
Newton Mearns
Hamilton
Motherwell
Wishaw
Carluke

Kintyre
Kilbrannan Sound
Goat Fell
874
Arran
Brodick
Lamlash
Ardrossan
Saltcoats
Kilwinning
Stewarton
East Kilbride
Strathaven
Lanark
Rigside
Tinto
707
Biggar
Peebles
Galashiels
Melrose

Machrihanish
Campbeltown
Troon
Prestwick
Ayr
Mauchline
Muirkirk
Douglas
Abington
Selkirk
Ettrick Forest

Mull of Kintyre
Sanda Island
Firth of Clyde
Culzean Bay
Dalrymple
New Cumnock
Kirkconnel
Sanquhar
Ballencleuch Law
691
Moffat
Teviothead
Hart Fell
808
Hawick

North Channel
Rathlin Island
Benbane Head
Fair Head
Ailsa Craig
Girvan
Dailly
Loch Doon
Corserine
Merrick 843 813
St John's Town of Dalry
Thornhill
Lochmaben
M74
Langholm
Newcastleton

4

Ballycastle
Knocklayd 517
Cushendall
Garron Point
Ballantrae
Milleur Point
Stinchar
Moniaive
Dumfries
Annan
Lockerbie
Ecclefechan
Longtown

55°
Trostan 554
Carnlough
Glenarm
Kirkcolm
Cairnryan
Newton Stewart
New Galloway 711
Castle Douglas
Dalbeattie
Criffel 569
Kirkbean
Annan
Gretna

NORTHERN
Larne
Islandmagee
The Rhins of Galloway
Loch Ryan
Stranraer
Glenluce
Gatehouse of Fleet
Kirkcudbright
Solway Firth
Carlisle
Thursby
Wigton

IRELAND
Belfast
Whitehead
Portpatrick
Wigtown
Luce Bay
Wigtown Bay
Abbey Head
Maryport
Aspatria

3

Lake District

Isle of Man
(British Crown Dependency)
Point of Ayre
Andreas
Ramsey Bay
Maughold Head
Skiddaw 931
Bassenthwaite L.
Keswick
Derwent Water
Helvellyn 949
Ullswater

Isle of Man
Kirk Michael
Ramsey
Snaefell 621
Peel
Laxey
Clay Head
Onchan
Douglas
Port Erin
Calf of Man
Castletown

54°

LOUTH
Dundalk Bay
Dunany Point
Clogher Head

Irish Sea

MEATH
IRELAND
FINGAL
DUBLIN

2

Dublin
Dublin Bay

SOUTH DUBLIN
DÚN LAOGHAIRE-RATHDOWN
Bray

Carmel Head
Amlwch
Llyn Alaw
Anglesey (Ynys Môn)
Great Ormes Head
Point of Ayr
Wirral
Liverpool

WICKLOW
Djouce Mountain 886
Tonelagee 819

Snowdon (Yr Wyddfa)
WALES

53°
Wicklow
Wicklow Head

A

B

C

D

6°

5°

4°

3°

Eyemouth
Chirnside
Berwick-upon-Tweed
*Tweed*
law
*stream*
Holy
Island
*Farne
Islands*
North
Sunderland
Belford
Wooler
The
Cheviot
▲815
*Breamish*
Glanton
Longhoughton
Rothbury
Alnwick
Amble
Otterburn
Longhorsley
Bellingham
Ashington
Newbiggin-by-the-Sea
Morpeth
Bedlington
Blyth
Stannington
Cramlington
Seaton Delaval
Ponteland
Whitley Bay
North Tyne
Gosforth
Tynemouth
Haydon
Bridge
Corbridge
Gateshead
North
Shields
South Shields
Hexham
Newcastle upon Tyne
*Tyne*
Allendale Town
Washington
Sunderland
*Derwent
Reservoir*
Consett
Stanley
Chester-le-Street
Seaham
Houghton le Spring
A194(M)
Crook
Durham
Easington
Wolsingham
Peterlee
*Wear*
Spennymoor
Wingate
Bishop Auckland
Ferryhill
Hartlepool
Shildon
*Tees Bay*
Newton Aycliffe
Greatham
ddleton in Teesdale
Billingham
Redcar
-in-
Barnard Castle
Darlington
Stockton-
on-Tees
South
Bank
Brotton
oir
Middlesbrough
Guisborough
Hinderwell
Kirkby
Stephen
Bowes
*Greta*
Middleton
St George
Yarm
Thornaby-
on-Tees
Whitby
gh Seat
▲710
Richmond
Catterick
Stokesley
Hutton
Rudby
Sleights
*Cleveland Hills*
Round
Hill
▲454
E N G L A N D
Northallerton
*Hambleton Hills*
*North York Moors*
Burniston
*Wensleydale*
Leyburn
Bedale
Scalby
Scarborough
Hawes
*Ure*
Thirsk
Helmsley
Kirkbymoorside
Pickering
Eastfield
*Langstrothdale
Chase*
*Rye*
*Vale of Pickering*
Seamer
Filey
Pen-y-
Ghent
▲694
Great
Whernside
▲703
Ripon
*Derwent*
Hunmanby
Flamborough
*Flamborough Head*
Grassington
Boroughbridge
Easingwold
Malton
Norton
*Ribble*
Settle
Hetton
*Vale of York*
*Ouse*
Bridlington
*Bridlington
Bay*
Skipton
Knaresborough
Haxby
Driffield
oldswick
ndle Hill
▲557
Colne
Grassington
Harrogate
Spofforth
*Nidd*
York
Stamford Bridge
A1(M)
Hornsea
Nelson
Keighley
Ilkley
Otley
Wetherby
Fulford
Pocklington
Brandesburton
adiham
Bingley
Shipley
*Wharfe*
Boston Spa
Tadcaster
A1(M)
Selby
*Derwent*
Market
Weighton
Leven
Accrington
Halifax
Pudsey
Leeds
Aberford
A1
Holme-on-
Spalding-Moor
North
Cave
Beverley
Aldbrough
burn
Bradford
Morley
Garforth
South
Cave
Anlaby
M65
M606
Batley
Castleford
Knottingley
Howden
Brough
Bilton
*Holderness*
Todmorden
M62
Dewsbury
Wakefield
Pontefract
Shaith
*Ouse*
Kingston
upon Hull
Withernsea
awtenstall
Littleborough
Hatfield
Thorne
Goole
Winterton
Barton-
upon-Humber
Patrington
M60
Huddersfield
Honley
Darton
South
Kirkby
Adwick
le Street
Bentley
Crowle
Scunthorpe
*Mouth of the Humber*
Spurn Head
Rochdale
Haywood
Royton
Meltham
Holmfirth
M1
Barnsley
M180
Immingham
Grimsby
Oldham
Ashton-
under-Lyne
*Black Hill*
▲582
Wombwell
Doncaster
Epworth
M181
Bottesford
Brigg
Cleethorpes
Pandlebury
Hollingworth
Glossop
*Margery Hill*
▲546
Chapeltown
*Dearne*
Mexborough
Rossington
Kirton in
Lindsey
Caistor
Tetney
Manchester
M67
*Kinder
Scout*
Derwent
Reservoir
Rotherham
*Trent*
Gainsborough
Lacel
North
Somercotes
Marple
Ladybower
Reservoir
Sheffield
Maltby
A1(M)
Beckingham
Market
Rasen
Louth
Stockport
*High Peak*
Aughton
South
Anston
Blyth
Mablethorpe
ilmslow
*Shining Tor*
▲599
*Kinder Scout*
636
Moorwith
Worksop
Retford
(East Retford)
Saxilby
Dunholme
*Lincolnshire Wolds*
Wragby
Alford
Alderley Edge
Buxton
Chapel-en-
le-Frith
Dronfield
Staveley
Tuxford
Lincoln
Heighington
Horncastle
Spilsby
Burgh le Marsh
Skegness
Macclesfield
*Dane*
Chesterfield
Creswell
Bolsover
Meden
North Hykeham
Waddington
Woodhall Spa
Ingoldmells
Congleton
Clay Cross
Market Warsop
Metheringham
Coningsby
*East
Fen*
Wainfleet
All Saints
Biddulph
Leek
Matlock
*Sherwood
Forest*
Billinghay
Wrangle
ager
Kidsgrove
Wirksworth
Alfreton
Sutton in Ashfield
Kirkby in Ashfield
Southwell
Newark-on-Trent
*West
Fen*
Sibsey
Old Leake
Stoke-on-Trent
*Dove*
Ambergate
Ripley
Hucknall
*Trent*
Sleaford
Heckington
*Holland
Fen*
Boston
Cheadle
Belper
Heanor
Long
Bennington
Swineshead
*The
Wash*
Sheringham
el-Lyme
Upper
Tean
Ashbourne
Ilkeston
Eastwood
Great
Gonerby
Hunstanton
Holt
Nottingham
Great
Goherby
Grantham
Sutterton
Burnham
Market
Wells-next-
the-Sea
Cromer
Derby
Bingham
West Bridgford
Heacham
Docking

North
Sea

*Greenwich (Prime) Meridian*

IJmuiden

Rotterdam, Zeebrugge

### Relief and physical features

Relief
metres
1000
500
200
100
0 sea level
50
100 under sea level
200

1085 ▲ Mountain height
(in metres)

### Water features

~ River
~ Canal
⬭ Lake / Reservoir

### Communications

— Railway
═ Motorway
= = = Motorway
under construction
— Road
······ Car ferry
⊕ Main airport
✈ Regional airport

### Administration

Boundaries
━━ International
── Internal

### Settlement

▨ Urban area

Cities and towns in order of size

National capital
■ Dublin

Other city or town
◉ Manchester
◯ Liverpool
◯ Bradford
◦ Carlisle
₀ Keswick

Scale 1 : 1 200 000

0  10  20  30  40 km

Conic Equidistant projection

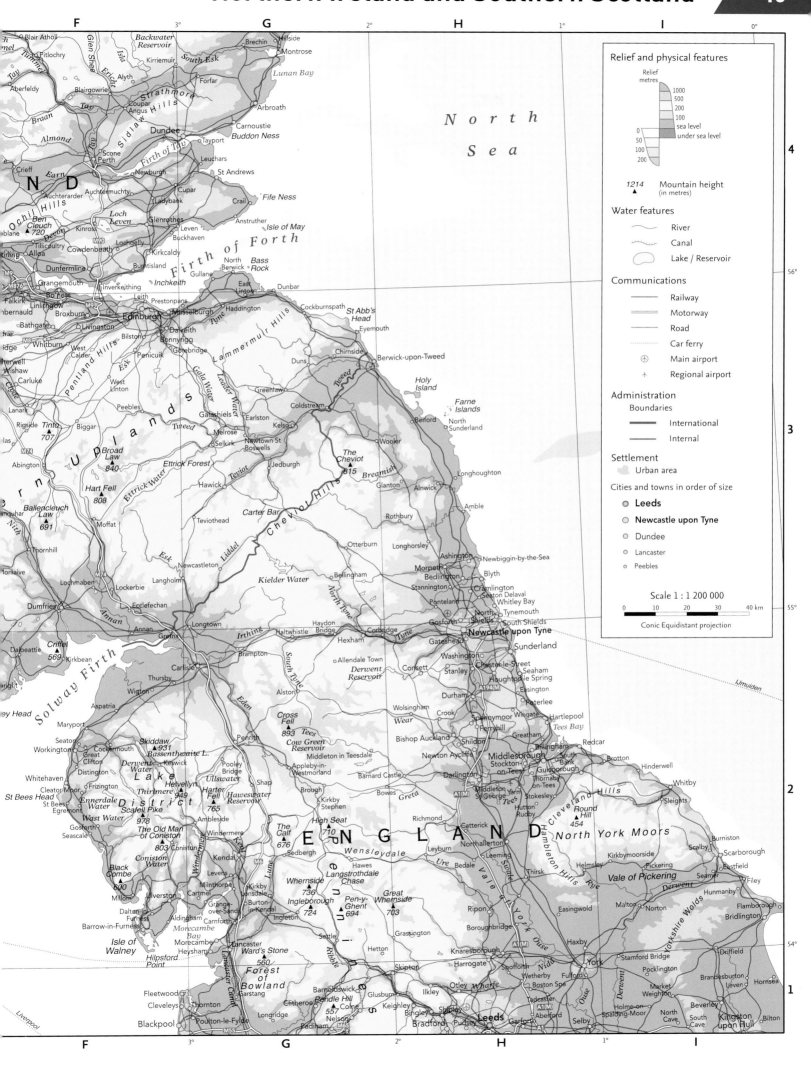

Relief and physical features

Relief metres
1000
500
200
100
0 sea level
50
100 under sea level
200

▲1214 Mountain height (in metres)

Water features

~~~ River
~~~ Canal
⬭ Lake / Reservoir

Communications

━━━ Railway
═══ Motorway
─── Road
····· Car ferry
⊕ Main airport
✈ Regional airport

Administration

Boundaries
━━━ International
─── Internal

Settlement

Urban area

Cities and towns in order of size

◉ Leeds
◎ Newcastle upon Tyne
○ Dundee
◌ Lancaster
· Peebles

Scale 1 : 1 200 000

0   10   20   30   40 km

Conic Equidistant projection

## Legend

**Relief and physical features**

Relief metres
1000
500
200
100
0 sea level
under sea level
50
100
200

▲ 1345 Mountain height (in metres)

**Water features**

～ River
～ Canal
Lake / Reservoir

**Communications**

—— Railway
—— Road
......... Car ferry
⊕ Main airport
✈ Regional airport

**Settlement**

Urban area

Cities and towns in order of size
◉ Aberdeen
◎ Inverness
○ Kirkwall

Scale 1 : 1 200 000

0 10 20 30 40 km

Conic Equidistant projection

---

ATLANTIC OCEAN

Cape Wrath
Kinlochbervie
Loch Inchard
Loch Laxford
Handa Island
Scourie
Foinave ▲ 915
Point of Stoer
Loch Assynt
Lochinver
Canisp ▲ 846
Ben Ass
Cul Mòr ▲ 849
Qui... ▲ 998
Loch Lurgainn

Rona

Butt of Lewis
Port of Ness
Muirneag ▲ 248
Tolsta Head
Isle of Lewis
West Loch Roag
Great Bernera
Callanish
Stornoway
Broad Bay
Eye Peninsula
Flannan Isles
Mealasta Island
Loch Langavat
Scarp
Tirga Mòr ▲ 679
Clisham ▲ 799
North Harris
Kebock Head
Taransay
Tarbert
South Harris
Loch Langavat
Scalpay
Rodel
Pabbay
Berneray
Boreray
St Kilda
Sound of Harris

Outer Hebrides

The Minch

Rubha Coigeach
Summer Isles
Loch Lurgainn
Ullapool
Loch Broom
Greenstone Point
Rubha Reidh
Gruinard Bay
An Teallach ▲ 1062
Fionn Loch
Beinn Dearg ▲ 1084
Gairloch
Gair Loch
Loch Maree
Sgurr Mòr ▲ 1110
Loch Fannich

WESTER ROSS

Shiant Islands

Little Minch

Rubha Hunish
Loch Snizort
Uig
Loch Dunvegan
The Storr ▲ 719
Sound of Raasay
Rona
Torridon
Shieldaig
Loch Torridon

North Uist
Lochmaddy
Sound of Monach
Monach Islands
Benbecula
Balivanich

Skye
L. Bracadale
Portree
Raasay
Inner Sound
Sound of Raasay
Carn Eighe ▲ 1183
Loch Monar

South Uist

The Cuillin
Sgurr Alasdair ▲ 993
Blaven ▲ 928
Scalpay
Kyle of Lochalsh
A'Chralaig ▲ 1120
Loch Cluanie
Glen Mor

Lochboisdale
Soay
Loch Eishort
Cuillin Sound
Ardvasar
Sound of Sleat
Ladhar Bheinn ▲ 1020
Loch Hourn
Loch Quoich
Loch Garry
Loch Loyne
Glen Garry

Eriskay
Sound of Barra
Canna
Rum
Arisaig
Loch Morar
Mallaig
Loch Beoraid
Loch Arkaig
Loch Lochy

Barra
Vatersay
Castlebay
Eigg
Sound of Arisaig
Loch Shiel
Sgurr Dhomhnuill ▲ 888
Fort William
Ben Nevis ▲ 1345
Stob C... Claur ▲ 117

Pabbay
Sandray
Muck
Eilean Shona
Loch Beoraid
Loch Leven
Kinlochl...

Mingulay
Berneray
Point of Ardnamurchan
Morvern
Loch Arienas
Loch Linnhe
Glen Coe
Bidean nam Bian ▲ 1150
Meal Bhuir... ▲ 1108
Ra...

Coll
Tobermory
Mull
Tiree

F
G
H
I
4°
3°
2°
1°
Mull Head
Papa Westray
North Ronaldsay
Noup Head
The North Sound
North Ronaldsay Firth
Westray
Eday
Sanday
Westray Firth
Loth
Sanday Sound
Brough Head
Rousay
Egilsay
Stronsay
Birsay
Stronsay Firth
Orkney Islands
Loch of Harray
Shapinsay
Auskerry
Finstown
Wide Firth
Lerwick
Loch of Stenness
Stromness
Mainland
Kirkwall
Gritley
Ward Hill
479
Scapa Flow
Copinsay
Hoy
Flotta
Burray
St Margaret's Hope
South Walls
South Ronaldsay
Burwick
Brough Ness
Pentland Firth
Pentland Skerries
Dunnet Head
Island of Stroma
Thurso Bay
Dunnet Bay
John o'Groats
Duncansby Head
Strathy Point
Dounreay
Thurso
Loch Heilen
Melvich
Halkirk
Loch Watten
Sinclair's Bay
Tongue
Naver
Halladale
Wick
CAITHNESS
Loch Loyal
Thurso
Latheron
Klibreck
961
Loch Rimsdale
HERLAND
Helmsdale
Shin
Helmsdale
Brora
Lairg
Brora
Golspie
Bonar Bridge
Dornoch
Dornoch Firth
Tarbat Ness
Tain
R
Balintore
Moray Firth
Loch Glass
Invergordon
Nigg Bay
Cromarty
Cromarty Firth
Black Isle
Fortrose
Nairn
Conon Bridge
Moray Firth
Beauly Firth
Inverness
Nairn
Burghead
Lossiemouth
Kinloss
Elgin
Forres
Lossie
Portknockie
Buckie
Portsoy
Cullen
Fochabers
Knock Hill
430
Macduff
Banff
Troup Head
Fraserburgh
Loch of Strathbeg
Rattray Head
Crimond
Deveron
Aberchirder
Turriff
New Pitsligo
North Ugie
Mintlaw
Peterhead
Boddam
Cruden Bay
Isla
Keith
Rothes
Dufftown
(Charlestown of Aberlour)
Deveron
Huntly
STRATHBOGIE
Ythan
Findhorn
Spey
Strathspey
Grantown-on-Spey
Hills of Cromdale
Insch
Urie
Bogie
Ellon
Oldmeldrum
Inverurie
Don
Kemnay
Kintore
Dyce
Aberdeen
Westhill
Carn Mòr
804
Geal Charn
821
TLAND
Ness
Aviemore
Cairn Gorm
1245
Cairngorm Mts
Avon
Don
Carn Dearg
945
Kingussie
Spey
Ben Macdui
1309
Cairn Toul
1291
Newtonmore
Aboyne
Dee
Portlethen
Banchory
Newtonhill
Braemar
Dee
Ballater
Mount Keen
939
Lochnagar
1155
Stonehaven
Grampian Mountains
Beinn Dearg
1008
Carn nan Gabhar
1121
Forest of Atholl
Mayar
928
North Esk
Inverbervie
Water of Saughs
Laurencekirk
Loch Ericht
Loch Errochty
Loch Garry
Blair Atholl
Glen Shee
Backwater Reservoir
South Esk
Brechin
Hillside
Loch Tummel
Tummel
Pitlochry
Isla
Montrose
Kirriemuir
Loch Rannoch
Schiehallion
1083
Tay
Aberfeldy
Ericht
Alyth
Forfar
Lunan Bay
Lyon
Blairgowrie
Strathmore
Arbroath
North Sea
Lerwick
Kirkwall
Aberdeen
Herma Ness
Unst
Baltasound
Point of Fethaland
Isbister
Yell Sound
Yell
Fetlar
Ronas Hill
450
Esha Ness
Hillswick
Toft
Out Skerries
St Magnus Bay
Mainland
Muckle Roe
Voe
Whalsay
Papa Stour
Melby
Walls
Shetland Islands
Bressay
Lerwick
Isle of Noss
Scalloway
Foula
Burra
60°
Mousa
Sumburgh
Sumburgh Head
Fair Isle
59°
58°
57°
1
2
3
4
5

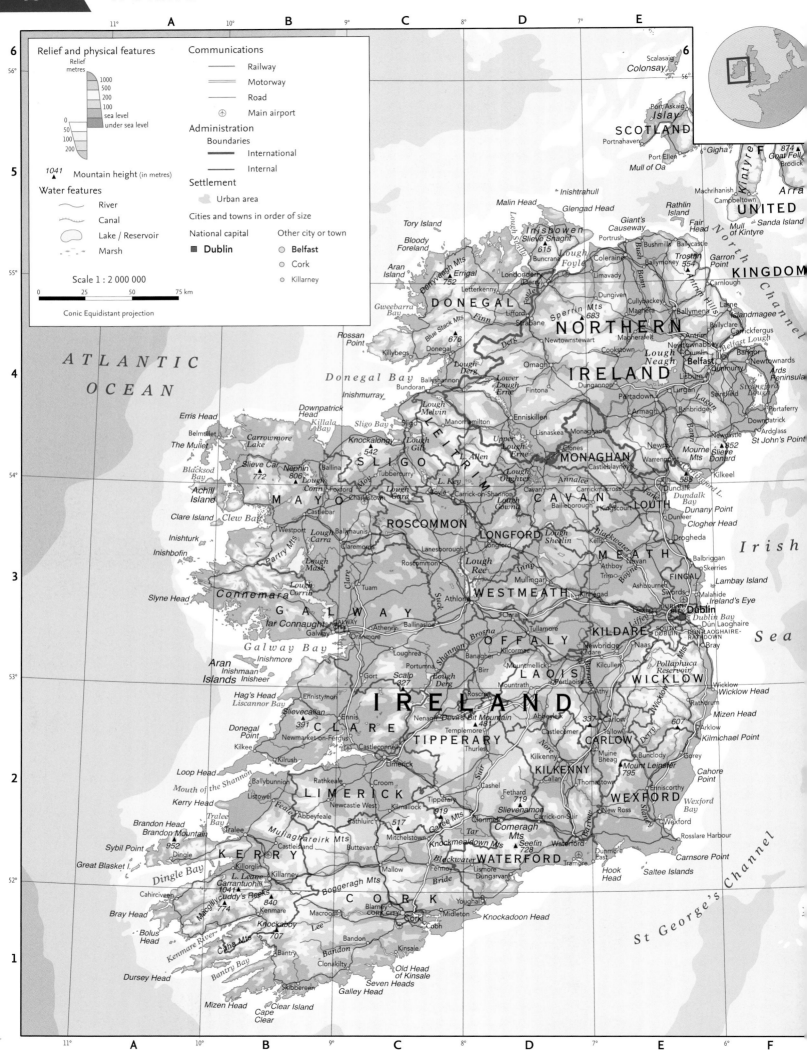

**Relief and physical features**

Relief metres
1000
500
200
100
sea level
0
50
100
under sea level
200

▲ 1041 Mountain height (in metres)

**Water features**
~ River
~ Canal
⬭ Lake / Reservoir
~ Marsh

Scale 1 : 2 000 000

0    25    50    75 km

Conic Equidistant projection

**Communications**
Railway
Motorway
Road
⊕ Main airport

**Administration**
Boundaries
International
Internal

**Settlement**
▨ Urban area
Cities and towns in order of size
National capital       Other city or town
■ Dublin               ● Belfast
                       ○ Cork
                       ○ Killarney

① Snow-covered mountains in Scotland.

② The dark green areas are coniferous forests.

③ Mountains covered with heather and poor grass.

④ Large parts of Ireland are covered in rich grassland, shown in green.

⑤ Much of the land in the UK is used for agriculture. This is why so much of the image shows greens and browns.

⑥ Areas of grey represent built-up areas.

## United Kingdom

SCOTLAND

Edinburgh

ENGLAND

London

WALES

Cardiff

Belfast

NORTHERN
IRELAND

IRELAND

FRANCE

## West Central Scotland

NORTH
LANARKSHIRE

Motherwell

Kirkintilloch

EAST
DUNBARTON-
SHIRE

Dumbarton

GLASGOW
CITY

Glasgow

Giffnock

EAST
RENFREW-
SHIRE

WEST
DUNBARTON-
SHIRE

Paisley

RENFREWSHIRE

Greenock

INVERCLYDE

## East Central Scotland

Haddington

EAST
LOTHIAN

Dalkeith

MIDLOTHIAN

Edinburgh

CITY OF
EDINBURGH

Livingston

WEST
LOTHIAN

CLACKMANNAN-
SHIRE

Alloa

FALKIRK

Falkirk

## Key

**Administration**

Boundaries

International

National

Administrative

Settlement

■ Capital city

○ Administrative centre

Scale 1 : 3 000 000

0   25   50   75   100 km

Conic Equidistant projection

SHETLAND
ISLANDS

Lerwick

ORKNEY
ISLANDS

Kirkwall

Stornoway

NA H-EILEANAN SIAR
(WESTERN ISLES)

HIGHLAND

Inverness

MORAY

Elgin

ABERDEEN-
SHIRE

ABERDEEN CITY

Aberdeen

SCOTLAND

PERTH &
KINROSS

Perth

ANGUS

Forfar

DUNDEE CITY

Dundee

FIFE

Glenrothes

EAST
LOTHIAN

Haddington

Edinburgh

Dalkeith

MIDLOTHIAN

STIRLING

Stirling

Alloa

Kirkintilloch

Glasgow

Paisley

RENFREWSHIRE

Dumbarton

Greenock

Livingston

Motherwell

Hamilton

SOUTH
LANARKSHIRE

EAST
AYRSHIRE

Irvine

Kilmarnock

Ayr

NORTH
AYRSHIRE

SOUTH
AYRSHIRE

ARGYLL
AND BUTE

Lochgilphead

SCOTTISH
BORDERS

Newtown
St Boswells

NORTHUMBERLAND

Morpeth

CAUSEWAY COAST

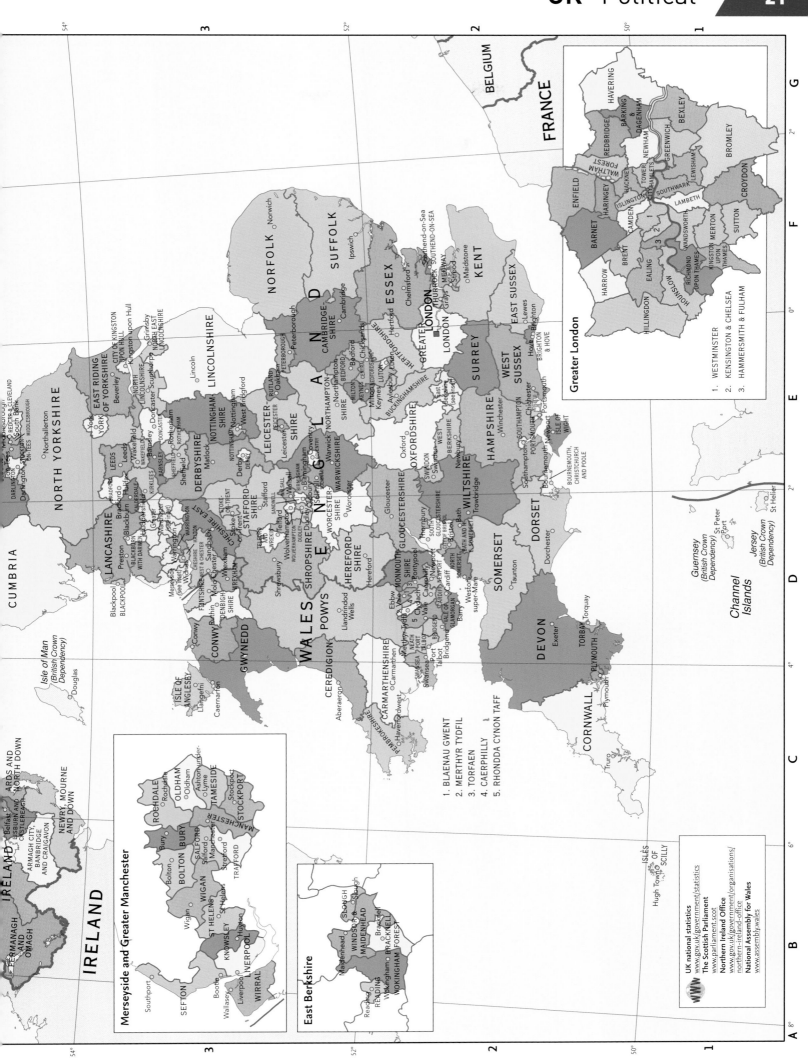

BELGIUM

FRANCE

**Greater London**

GREATER LONDON

ENFIELD
BARNET
HARROW
HILLINGDON
EALING
HOUNSLOW
RICHMOND UPON THAMES
KINGSTON UPON THAMES
MERTON
SUTTON
CROYDON
BROMLEY
BEXLEY
GREENWICH
LEWISHAM
SOUTHWARK
LAMBETH
WANDSWORTH
HARINGEY
HARINGEY
HACKNEY
ISLINGTON
CAMDEN
BRENT
WALTHAM FOREST
REDBRIDGE
HAVERING
BARKING & DAGENHAM
NEWHAM
TOWER HAMLETS
LONDON

1. WESTMINSTER
2. KENSINGTON & CHELSEA
3. HAMMERSMITH & FULHAM

IRELAND

ARDS AND NORTH DOWN
NEWRY, MOURNE AND DOWN
LISBURN AND CASTLEREAGH
Belfast
ARMAGH CITY, BANBRIDGE AND CRAIGAVON
FERMANAGH AND OMAGH

**Merseyside and Greater Manchester**

ROCHDALE
Rochdale
OLDHAM
Oldham
Ashton-under-Lyme
TAMESIDE
BURY
Bury
BOLTON
Bolton
SALFORD
Salford
MANCHESTER
Manchester
Stretford
TRAFFORD
Stockport
STOCKPORT
WIGAN
Wigan
ST HELENS
St Helens
KNOWSLEY
Huyton
LIVERPOOL
Liverpool
WIRRAL
Wallasey
Bootle
SEFTON
Southport

**East Berkshire**

SLOUGH
Slough
Maidenhead
WINDSOR & MAIDENHEAD
BRACKNELL FOREST
Bracknell
WOKINGHAM
Wokingham
Reading
READING

CUMBRIA
Isle of Man (British Crown Dependency)
Douglas

NORTH YORKSHIRE
Middlesbrough
REDCAR & CLEVELAND
STOCKTON-ON-TEES
South Bank
MIDDLESBROUGH
DARLINGTON
Darlington
Northallerton
EAST RIDING OF YORKSHIRE
CITY OF KINGSTON UPON HULL
Beverley
Kingston upon Hull
Grimsby
NORTH EAST LINCOLNSHIRE
NORTH LINCOLNSHIRE
Scunthorpe
York
YORK
Leeds
LEEDS
BRADFORD
Bradford
Halifax
CALDERDALE
KIRKLEES
WAKEFIELD
Wakefield
Barnsley
BARNSLEY
Doncaster
DONCASTER
ROTHERHAM
Rotherham
SHEFFIELD
Sheffield
Lincoln
LINCOLNSHIRE

LANCASHIRE
Blackpool
BLACKPOOL
Preston
Blackburn
BLACKBURN WITH DARWEN
Bolton
Bury
Rochdale
Oldham
Wigan
Merseyside (See Inset)
WARRINGTON
Warrington
Widnes
CHESHIRE WEST AND CHESTER
Chester
CHESHIRE EAST
Crewe

CONWY
Conwy
DENBIGHSHIRE
Ruthin
FLINTSHIRE
Mold
WREXHAM
Wrexham
Caernarfon
GWYNEDD
ISLE OF ANGLESEY
Llangefni

DERBYSHIRE
Matlock
Derby
DERBY
NOTTINGHAMSHIRE
Nottingham
NOTTINGHAM
STAFFORDSHIRE
Stafford
STOKE-ON-TRENT
Stoke-on-Trent
TELFORD & WREKIN
Telford
SHROPSHIRE
Shrewsbury
Wolverhampton
WOLVERHAMPTON
WALSALL
Walsall
DUDLEY
Dudley
SANDWELL
BIRMINGHAM
Birmingham
SOLIHULL
COVENTRY
Coventry
WARWICKSHIRE
Warwick
WORCESTERSHIRE
Worcester
HEREFORDSHIRE
Hereford

LEICESTERSHIRE
Leicester
LEICESTER
RUTLAND
Oakham
WEST BRIDGFORD

NORFOLK
Norwich

SUFFOLK
Ipswich

CAMBRIDGESHIRE
Peterborough
PETERBOROUGH
Cambridge

LINCOLNSHIRE

NORTHAMPTONSHIRE
Northampton
BEDFORD
Bedford
MILTON KEYNES
Milton Keynes
CENTRAL BEDFORDSHIRE
LUTON
Luton

ENGLAND

WALES

POWYS
Llandrindod Wells
CEREDIGION
Aberaeron
PEMBROKESHIRE
Haverfordwest
CARMARTHENSHIRE
Carmarthen
SWANSEA
Swansea
NEATH PORT TALBOT
Port Talbot
BRIDGEND
Bridgend
VALE OF GLAMORGAN
Barry
CARDIFF
Cardiff
NEWPORT
Newport
MONMOUTHSHIRE
1. BLAENAU GWENT
2. MERTHYR TYDFIL
3. TORFAEN
4. CAERPHILLY
5. RHONDDA CYNON TAFF

GLOUCESTERSHIRE
Gloucester
Thornbury
SOUTH GLOUCESTERSHIRE
BRISTOL
CITY OF BRISTOL
NORTH SOMERSET
Weston-super-Mare
BATH AND NORTH EAST SOMERSET
Bath
SOMERSET
Taunton

OXFORDSHIRE
Oxford
BUCKINGHAMSHIRE
Aylesbury
HERTFORDSHIRE
Hertford
BEDFORDSHIRE

GREATER LONDON
LONDON
THURROCK
Grays
MEDWAY
Strood
Maidstone
KENT

ESSEX
Chelmsford
Southend-on-Sea
SOUTHEND-ON-SEA

SURREY

WEST SUSSEX
Chichester

EAST SUSSEX
Lewes
Brighton
BRIGHTON & HOVE
Hove

HAMPSHIRE
Winchester
SOUTHAMPTON
Southampton
PORTSMOUTH
Portsmouth
ISLE OF WIGHT
Newport

BERKSHIRE
Newbury
WILTSHIRE
Trowbridge
SWINDON
Swindon

DORSET
Dorchester
BOURNEMOUTH, CHRISTCHURCH AND POOLE

DEVON
Exeter
TORBAY
Torquay

CORNWALL
Truro
PLYMOUTH
Plymouth

ISLES OF SCILLY
Hugh Town

Channel Islands
Guernsey (British Crown Dependency)
St Peter Port
Jersey (British Crown Dependency)
St Helier

**WWW** **UK national statistics** www.gov.uk/government/statistics
**The Scottish Parliament** www.parliament.scot
**Northern Ireland Office** www.gov.uk/government/organisations/northern-ireland-office
**National Assembly for Wales** www.assembly.wales

**Relief and physical features**

Relief
metres

1000
500
200
100
sea level
under sea level

0
50
100
200

1345 ▲ Mountain height
(in metres)

**Water features**

~~~ River

~~~ Canal

⬭ Lake / Reservoir

Scale 1 : 4 500 000

0        50        100 km

Conic Equidistant projection

ATLANTIC
OCEAN

Shetland
Islands

Unst
Yell  Fetlar
Whalsay
Foula  Mainland  Bressay

Sumburgh
Head

Fair Isle

North
Sea

Westray  Sanday
Orkney  Stronsay
Islands  Mainland
Hoy  South
Strathy  Pentland  Ronaldsay
Point  Firth  Duncansby Head

Butt of Lewis
Cape Wrath

Isle of
Lewis
North Harris
Clisham
799
South
Harris
North
Uist

St Kilda

Outer Hebrides

The Minch

Loch
Shin

Thurso

Dornoch Firth

Loch
Broom  Moray Firth

Rattray
Head

Skye
The Cuillin
993

South
Uist

Barra  Rum

Little Minch

Inner Hebrides

Coll

Tiree

North West Highlands

Ben
Nevis
1345

Ben
More
966

Loch
Ness

Cairngorm Mts
Ben Macdui
1309
Loch  Dee
Awe

Loch
Lomond

Ben Lawers
1214  Loch
Tay

Spey  Deveron

Don

Grampian Mountains

Tay

Firth of Lorn

Jura

Loch Fyne

Firth of Tay

Forth

Ochil Hills

Firth of Forth

St Abb's Head

Islay

Mull of Oa

Goat Fell
874
Arran

Rathlin
Island

Mull of
Kintyre

Firth of Clyde

Clyde

Ayr

Merrick
843

Southern Uplands

Tweed

Cheviot Hills

Holy Island

Errigal
752

Rossan
Point

Malin
Head

Foyle

Antrim Hills

Bann

Lough
Neagh

North Channel

Mull of
Galloway

Nith

Solway Firth

St Bees
Head

The Pennines

Eden

Tyne

Tees

North York
Moors

Derwent

Flamborough Head

Erris
Head

Donegal Bay

Lower
Lough
Erne  Blackwater

Lagan

Scafell
Pike
978  Lake
District

Wharfe

Spurn Head

Lough
Conn

Achill
Island

Clew Bay

Lough
Mask

Erne

Inny

Upper
Lough Erne

Mourne
Mts  Slieve
852  Donard

Calf of Man

Dundalk Bay

Isle
of Man

Isle of
Walney

Morecambe Bay

Ribble

Mouth of the Humber

Ouse

Slyne
Head

Lough
Corrib

Suck

Lough
Ree

Boyne

Irish Sea

Mersey  High Peak
Kinder Scout
636

Witham

The
Wash

Wensum

Aran Islands

Galway Bay

Brosna

Anglesey

Great Ormes
Head

Trent

Norfolk
Broads

Galway Bay

Lough
Derg

Liffey

Lugnaquilla
Mtn
926

Nore

Wicklow Mts

Holy Island

Caernarfon
Bay

Snowdon
1085

Dee

Cambrian Mountains

Severn

Avon

Welland

The Fens

Great Ouse

Cam

Little Ouse

Waveney

Loop
Head

Shannon

Barrow

Wicklow Head

Chelmer

Sybil Point

Dingle B.

Carrantuohill
1041

Galtee Mts
Blackwater

Lee

Suir

Carnsore
Point

St George's Channel

Strumble
Head

Cardigan
Bay

Teifi

Wye

Black
Mountains
886
Brecon
Beacons

Cotswold Hills

Thames

Chiltern Hills

Thames

Isle of
Sheppey

North Downs

Dursey
Head

Cape
Clear

Knockadoon
Head

St David's
Head

St Govan's
Head

Carmarthen Bay

Worms
Head

Bristol Channel

Lundy

Celtic Sea

Hartland Point

Exmoor

Mendip Hills

Avon

Salisbury
Plain

New
Forest

Avon  Test

The Solent

Leith Hill
294

South Downs

Dungeness

Beachy Head

Tamar

Yes Tor
619
Dartmoor

Exe

Lyme Bay

Stour

Bodmin
Moor

Bill of
Portland

Isle of
Wight

Land's End

Start Point

English Channel

Somme

Isles of Scilly

Lizard Point

Alderney

Channel Islands

Guernsey  Sark

Jersey

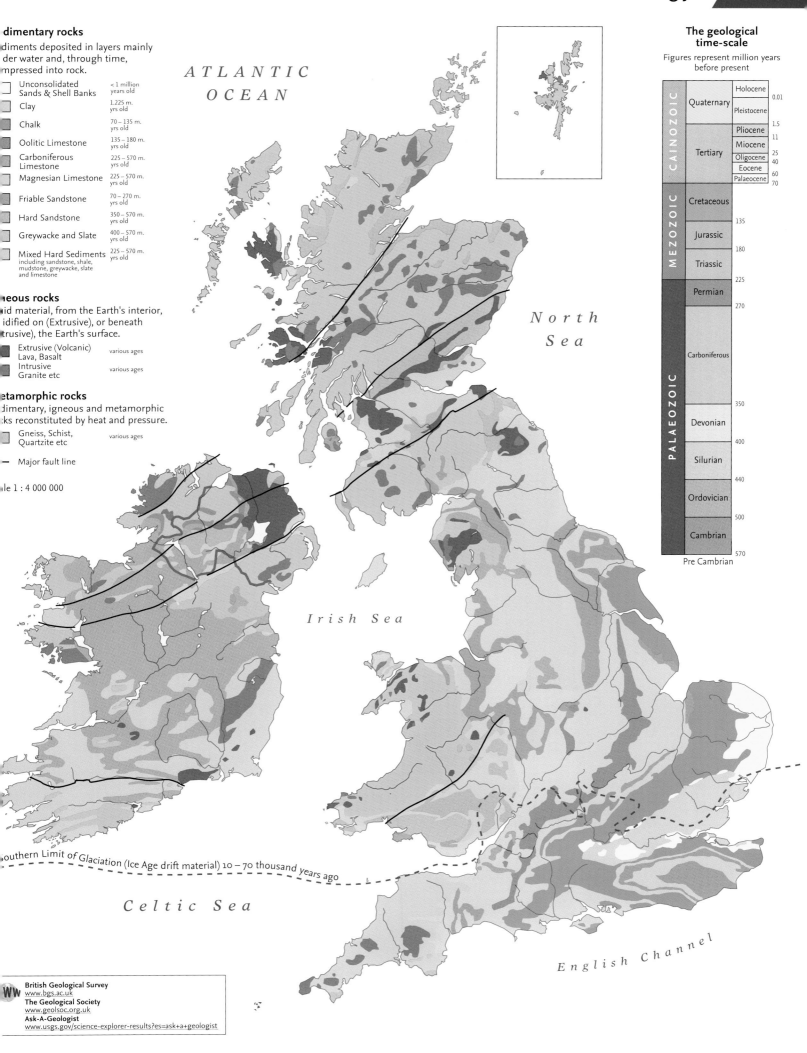

## Sedimentary rocks

Sediments deposited in layers mainly under water and, through time, compressed into rock.

| | | |
|---|---|---|
| | Unconsolidated Sands & Shell Banks | < 1 million years old |
| | Clay | 1.225 m. yrs old |
| | Chalk | 70 – 135 m. yrs old |
| | Oolitic Limestone | 135 – 180 m. yrs old |
| | Carboniferous Limestone | 225 – 570 m. yrs old |
| | Magnesian Limestone | 225 – 570 m. yrs old |
| | Friable Sandstone | 70 – 270 m. yrs old |
| | Hard Sandstone | 350 – 570 m. yrs old |
| | Greywacke and Slate | 400 – 570 m. yrs old |
| | Mixed Hard Sediments including sandstone, shale, mudstone, greywacke, slate and limestone | 225 – 570 m. yrs old |

## Igneous rocks

Solid material, from the Earth's interior, solidified on (Extrusive), or beneath (Intrusive), the Earth's surface.

| | | |
|---|---|---|
| | Extrusive (Volcanic) Lava, Basalt | various ages |
| | Intrusive Granite etc | various ages |

## Metamorphic rocks

Sedimentary, igneous and metamorphic rocks reconstituted by heat and pressure.

| | | |
|---|---|---|
| | Gneiss, Schist, Quartzite etc | various ages |
| — | Major fault line | |

Scale 1 : 4 000 000

*ATLANTIC OCEAN*

*North Sea*

*Irish Sea*

*Celtic Sea*

*English Channel*

Southern Limit of Glaciation (Ice Age drift material) 10 – 70 thousand years ago

### The geological time-scale

Figures represent million years before present

| Era | Period | Epoch | |
|---|---|---|---|
| CAINOZOIC | Quaternary | Holocene | 0.01 |
| | | Pleistocene | |
| | Tertiary | Pliocene | 1.5 |
| | | Miocene | 11 |
| | | Oligocene | 25 |
| | | Eocene | 40 / 60 |
| | | Palaeocene | 70 |
| MEZOZOIC | Cretaceous | | |
| | Jurassic | | 135 |
| | Triassic | | 180 |
| PALAEOZOIC | Permian | | 225 |
| | Carboniferous | | 270 |
| | Devonian | | 350 |
| | Silurian | | 400 |
| | Ordovician | | 440 |
| | Cambrian | | 500 / 570 |

Pre Cambrian

WW British Geological Survey
www.bgs.ac.uk
The Geological Society
www.geolsoc.org.uk
Ask-A-Geologist
www.usgs.gov/science-explorer-results?es=ask+a+geologist

# UK Climate

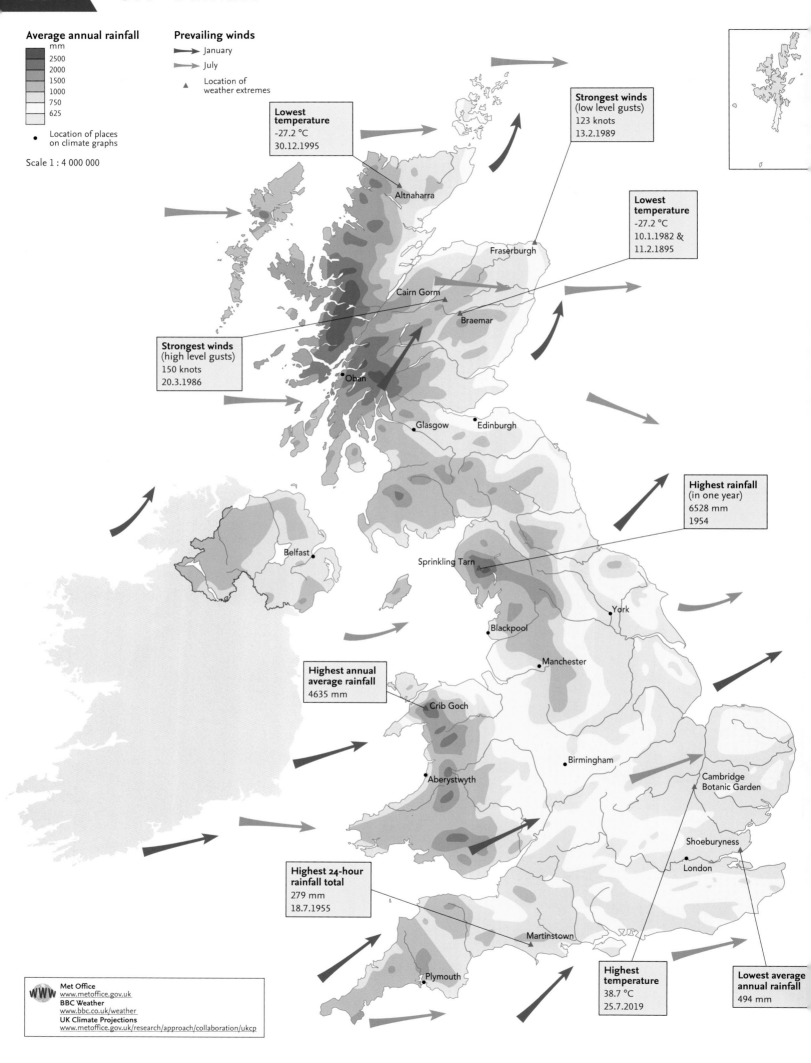

**Average annual rainfall**

mm
2500
2000
1500
1000
750
625

• Location of places on climate graphs

Scale 1 : 4 000 000

**Prevailing winds**

→ January
→ July
▲ Location of weather extremes

**Lowest temperature**
-27.2 °C
30.12.1995

**Strongest winds** (low level gusts)
123 knots
13.2.1989

**Lowest temperature**
-27.2 °C
10.1.1982 &
11.2.1895

**Strongest winds** (high level gusts)
150 knots
20.3.1986

**Highest rainfall** (in one year)
6528 mm
1954

**Highest annual average rainfall**
4635 mm

**Highest 24-hour rainfall total**
279 mm
18.7.1955

**Highest temperature**
38.7 °C
25.7.2019

**Lowest average annual rainfall**
494 mm

Altnaharra
Fraserburgh
Cairn Gorm
Braemar
Oban
Glasgow
Edinburgh
Belfast
Sprinkling Tarn
York
Blackpool
Manchester
Crib Goch
Birmingham
Aberystwyth
Cambridge Botanic Garden
Shoeburyness
London
Martinstown
Plymouth

WWW Met Office
www.metoffice.gov.uk
BBC Weather
www.bbc.co.uk/weather
UK Climate Projections
www.metoffice.gov.uk/research/approach/collaboration/ukcp

## January temperature

°C
6
4
2
0

**Currents**
→ Warm
→ Cold

Scale 1 : 12 000 000

## July temperature

°C
16
14
12
10

**Currents**
→ Warm
→ Cold

Scale 1 : 12 000 000

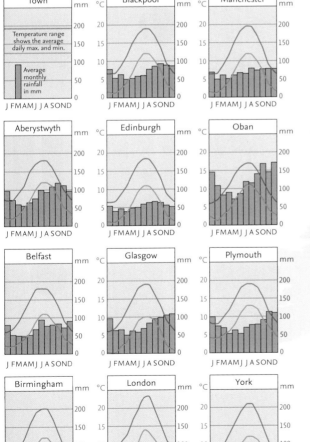

## Climate graphs

| Town | mm | °C |
|---|---|---|
| Temperature range shows the average daily max. and min. | 200 | 20 |
| | 150 | 15 |
| | 100 | 10 |
| Average monthly rainfall in mm | 50 | 5 |
| | 0 | 0 |
| J F M A M J J A S O N D | | |

Blackpool

Manchester

Aberystwyth

Edinburgh

Oban

Belfast

Glasgow

Plymouth

Birmingham

London

York

## Rainfall change

Percentage change 1919 – 2019

over 20
10 – 20
5 – 10
0 – 5
-10 – 0
-15 – -10

Scale 1 : 12 000 000

SCOTLAND N

SCOTLAND E

SCOTLAND W

NORTHERN IRELAND

ENGLAND E & NE

ENGLAND NW/ WALES N

MIDLANDS

EAST ANGLIA

ENGLAND SW/ WALES S

ENGLAND SE/ CENTRAL S

## Climate change

The Earth's climate has changed on many timescales in response to natural factors.

### The Sun drives our climate

1. Most sunlight passes through the atmosphere and warms the Earth.

2. Infrared radiation is given off by the Earth. Most IR escapes through outer space and cools the Earth.

3. But some IR is trapped by gases in the air and this reduces the cooling effect.

This is known as the greenhouse effect.

The gases responsible for this are called greenhouse gases. These include:

 $CO_2$ Carbon Dioxide

 $CH_4$ Methane

 $O_3$ Ozone

 $H_2O$ Water vapour

 $N_2O$ Nitrus Oxide

Greenhouse gases are so effective at keeping the Earth warm that any changes will affect the Earth's temperature.

### A changing climate

In the last century our climate has started to change rapidly. How can we tell if these changes are natural or down to us?

### What factors cause a warming of our climate?

 More energy from the sun.

 Large natural events e.g. El Nino.

 Increased greenhouse gases.

There is evidence that the majority of warming seen over the last 100 years is due to increased amounts of greenhouse gases in the atmosphere

Greenhouse gases occur naturally but human activities have increased the amount of carbon dioxide, methane and some others.

 Burning of fossil fuels such as coal, gas and oil.

 Changes in land use such as clearing forests for crop production.

 Carbon dioxide concentrations have increased by around 40% since 1750.

There is a natural carbon cycle in our climate. The increase in $CO_2$ in the atmosphere cannot be explained by this alone.

# UK Agriculture and Forestry

## Wheat

Production, 2016
(thousand tonnes)

- over 2000
- 1000 – 1999
- 500 – 999
- 0 – 499

Scale 1 : 12 000 000

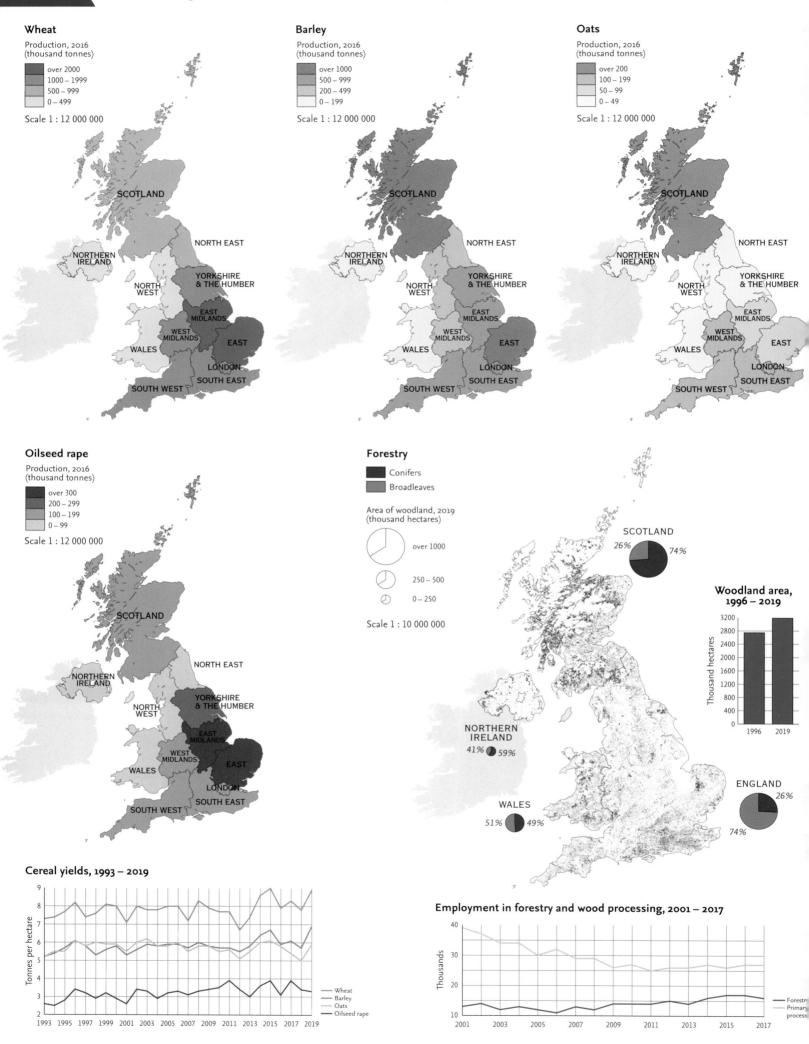

SCOTLAND

NORTHERN IRELAND

NORTH EAST

NORTH WEST

YORKSHIRE & THE HUMBER

EAST MIDLANDS

WEST MIDLANDS

EAST

WALES

LONDON

SOUTH WEST

SOUTH EAST

## Barley

Production, 2016
(thousand tonnes)

- over 1000
- 500 – 999
- 200 – 499
- 0 – 199

Scale 1 : 12 000 000

SCOTLAND

NORTHERN IRELAND

NORTH EAST

NORTH WEST

YORKSHIRE & THE HUMBER

EAST MIDLANDS

WEST MIDLANDS

EAST

WALES

LONDON

SOUTH WEST

SOUTH EAST

## Oats

Production, 2016
(thousand tonnes)

- over 200
- 100 – 199
- 50 – 99
- 0 – 49

Scale 1 : 12 000 000

SCOTLAND

NORTHERN IRELAND

NORTH EAST

NORTH WEST

YORKSHIRE & THE HUMBER

EAST MIDLANDS

WEST MIDLANDS

EAST

WALES

LONDON

SOUTH WEST

SOUTH EAST

## Oilseed rape

Production, 2016
(thousand tonnes)

- over 300
- 200 – 299
- 100 – 199
- 0 – 99

Scale 1 : 12 000 000

SCOTLAND

NORTHERN IRELAND

NORTH EAST

NORTH WEST

YORKSHIRE & THE HUMBER

EAST MIDLANDS

WEST MIDLANDS

EAST

WALES

LONDON

SOUTH WEST

SOUTH EAST

## Forestry

- Conifers
- Broadleaves

Area of woodland, 2019
(thousand hectares)

- over 1000
- 250 – 500
- 0 – 250

Scale 1 : 10 000 000

SCOTLAND
26%  74%

NORTHERN IRELAND
41%  59%

WALES
51%  49%

ENGLAND
26%
74%

### Woodland area, 1996 – 2019

Thousand hectares

3200
2800
2400
2000
1600
1200
800
400
0

1996   2019

## Cereal yields, 1993 – 2019

Tonnes per hectare

9
8
7
6
5
4
3
2

1993 1995 1997 1999 2001 2003 2005 2007 2009 2011 2013 2015 2017 2019

- Wheat
- Barley
- Oats
- Oilseed rape

## Employment in forestry and wood processing, 2001 – 2017

Thousands

40
30
20
10

2001   2003   2005   2007   2009   2011   2013   2015   2017

- Forestry
- Primary processing

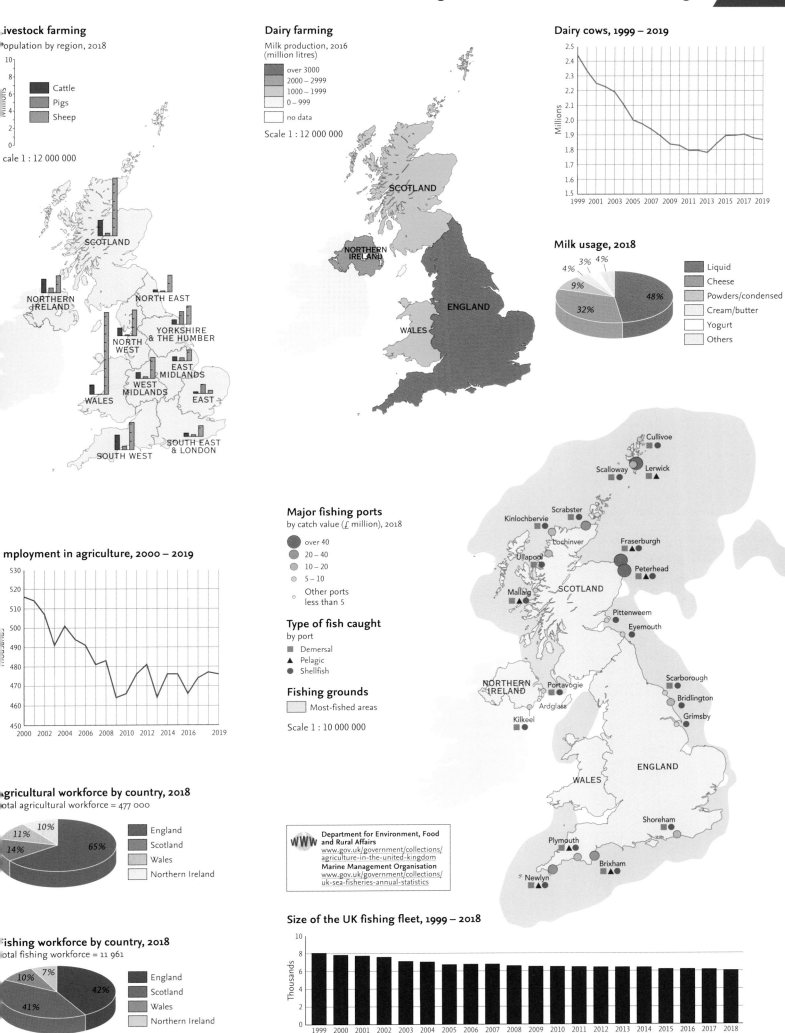

## Livestock farming
Population by region, 2018

- Cattle
- Pigs
- Sheep

Scale 1 : 12 000 000

SCOTLAND
NORTHERN IRELAND
NORTH EAST
YORKSHIRE & THE HUMBER
NORTH WEST
EAST MIDLANDS
WEST MIDLANDS
WALES
EAST
SOUTH EAST & LONDON
SOUTH WEST

## Dairy farming
Milk production, 2016 (million litres)

- over 3000
- 2000 – 2999
- 1000 – 1999
- 0 – 999
- no data

Scale 1 : 12 000 000

SCOTLAND
NORTHERN IRELAND
ENGLAND
WALES

## Dairy cows, 1999 – 2019

Millions

## Milk usage, 2018

- Liquid 48%
- Cheese 32%
- Powders/condensed 9%
- Cream/butter 4%
- Yogurt 3%
- Others 4%

## Employment in agriculture, 2000 – 2019

## Agricultural workforce by country, 2018
Total agricultural workforce = 477 000

- England 65%
- Scotland 14%
- Wales 11%
- Northern Ireland 10%

## Fishing workforce by country, 2018
Total fishing workforce = 11 961

- England 42%
- Scotland 41%
- Wales 10%
- Northern Ireland 7%

## Major fishing ports
by catch value (£ million), 2018

- over 40
- 20 – 40
- 10 – 20
- 5 – 10
- Other ports less than 5

## Type of fish caught
by port

- ■ Demersal
- ▲ Pelagic
- ● Shellfish

## Fishing grounds

- Most-fished areas

Scale 1 : 10 000 000

Cullivoe
Scalloway
Lerwick
Scrabster
Kinlochbervie
Lochinver
Ullapool
Fraserburgh
Peterhead
Mallaig
SCOTLAND
Pittenweem
Eyemouth
NORTHERN IRELAND
Portavogie
Ardglass
Kilkeel
Scarborough
Bridlington
Grimsby
ENGLAND
WALES
Shoreham
Plymouth
Brixham
Newlyn

**WWW** Department for Environment, Food and Rural Affairs
www.gov.uk/government/collections/ agriculture-in-the-united-kingdom
Marine Management Organisation
www.gov.uk/government/collections/ uk-sea-fisheries-annual-statistics

## Size of the UK fishing fleet, 1999 – 2018

Thousands

## Employment by economic sector, 2020

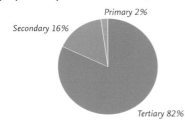

Primary 2%
Secondary 16%
Tertiary 82%

## Primary employment by industry sector, 2020

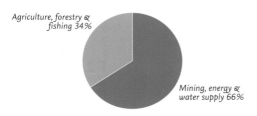

Agriculture, forestry & fishing 34%
Mining, energy & water supply 66%

## Secondary employment by industry sector, 2020

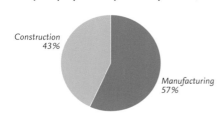

Construction 43%
Manufacturing 57%

## Tertiary employment by industry sector, 2020

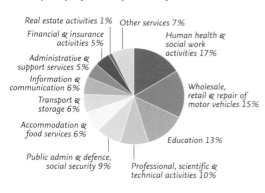

Real estate activities 1%
Other services 7%
Financial & insurance activities 5%
Human health & social work activities 17%
Administrative & support services 5%
Information & communication 6%
Wholesale, retail & repair of motor vehicles 15%
Transport & storage 6%
Accommodation & food services 6%
Education 13%
Public admin & defence, social security 9%
Professional, scientific & technical activities 10%

## Unemployment, 2002 – 2019

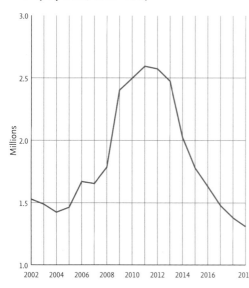

Millions
3.0
2.5
2.0
1.5
1.0
2002  2004  2006  2008  2010  2012  2014  2016  2019

## Agriculture, forestry and fishing

Employment compared to national average (index value 1.0), 2015

over 1.5
1.0 – 1.5
0.5 – 1.0
less than 0.5
no data

Scale 1 : 14 000 000

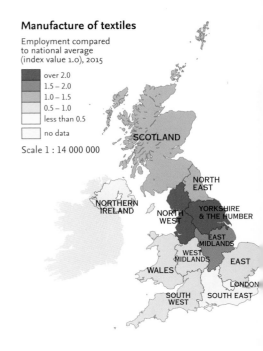

## Manufacture of chemicals and chemical products

Employment compared to national average (index value 1.0), 2015

over 2.0
1.5 – 2.0
1.0 – 1.5
0.5 – 1.0
less than 0.5
no data

Scale 1 : 14 000 000

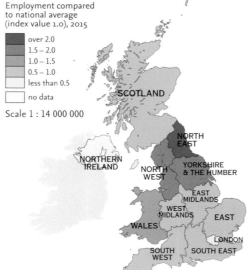

## Manufacture of motor vehicles, trailers and semi-trailers

Employment compared to national average (index value 1.0), 2015

over 2.0
1.5 – 2.0
1.0 – 1.5
0.5 – 1.0
less than 0.5
no data

Scale 1 : 14 000 000

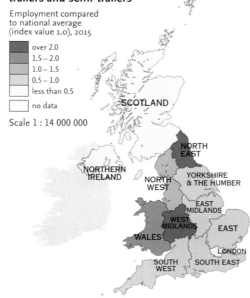

## Manufacture of textiles

Employment compared to national average (index value 1.0), 2015

over 2.0
1.5 – 2.0
1.0 – 1.5
0.5 – 1.0
less than 0.5
no data

Scale 1 : 14 000 000

## Manufacture of computer, electronic and optical products

Employment compared to national average (index value 1.0), 2015

over 1.5
1.0 – 1.5
0.5 – 1.0
less than 0.5
no data

Scale 1 : 14 000 000

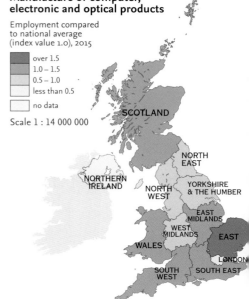

## Financial service activities, except insurance and pension funding

Employment compared to national average (index value 1.0), 2015

over 2.0
1.5 – 2.0
1.0 – 1.5
0.5 – 1.0
less than 0.5
no data

Scale 1 : 14 000 000

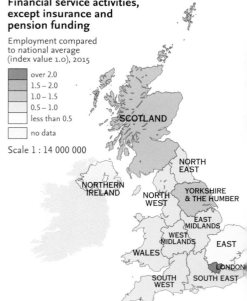

## Energy production and consumption, 2000 – 2019

Million tonnes of oil equivalent

Production
Consumption

300
250
200
150
100
2000 2002 2004 2006 2008 2010 2012 2014 2016 2019

## Energy resources

- Coalfield (not all producing)
- Oilfield
- Gasfield
- Oil pipeline
- Gas pipeline
- Gas pipeline from oilfield
- □ Oil pipeline terminal
- □ Gas pipeline terminal
- □ Oil/gas pipelines terminal
- ◇ Oil refinery

Scale 1 : 7 000 000

## Electricity generation

- ■ Pumped storage hydro-electric (400MW or over)
- □ Other hydro-electric (25MW or over)
- ■ Coal powered (400MW or over)
- ■ Gas powered (400MW or over)
- ■ Coal/gas powered (400MW or over)
- ■ Coal/biomass powered (400MW or over)
- ■ Biomass or waste powered (40MW or over)
- △ Nuclear
- ▲ Wind farm (400MW or over)
- △ Wind farm (50 – 400MW)
- △ Wave/tidal
- △ Geothermal aquifer
- ● Solar (50MW or over)

Scale 1 : 8 000 000

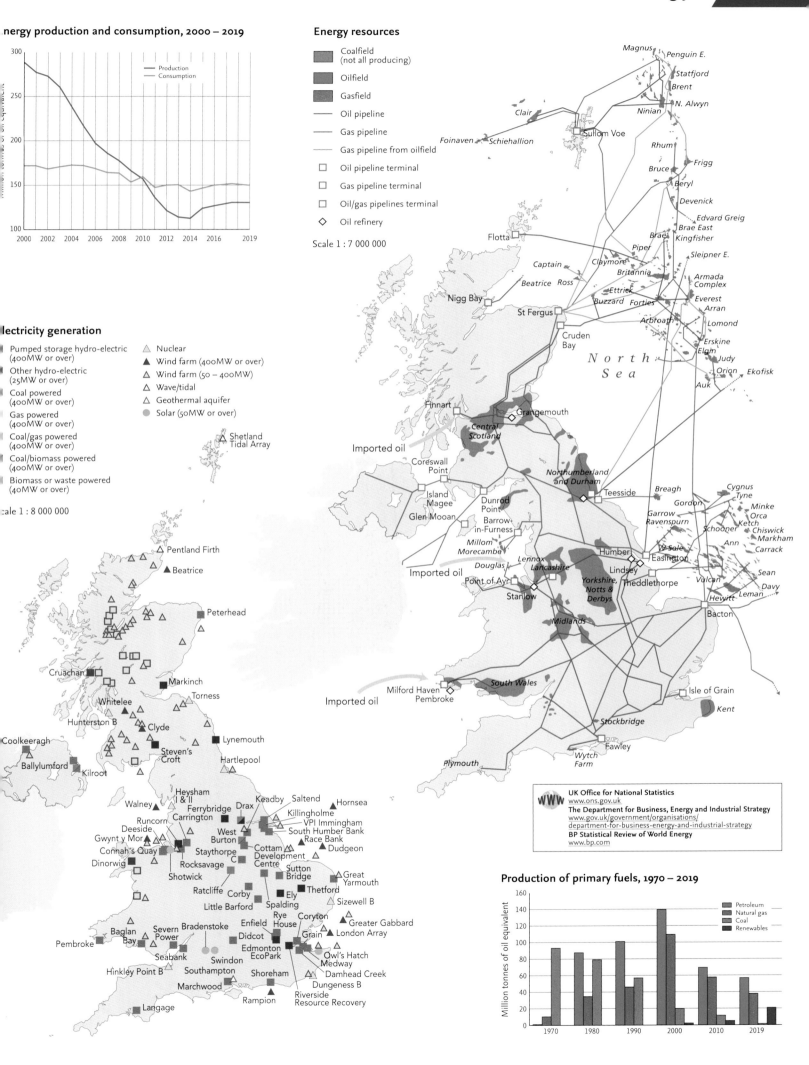

WWW UK Office for National Statistics
www.ons.gov.uk
The Department for Business, Energy and Industrial Strategy
www.gov.uk/government/organisations/
department-for-business-energy-and-industrial-strategy
BP Statistical Review of World Energy
www.bp.com

## Production of primary fuels, 1970 – 2019

Million tonnes of oil equivalent

Petroleum
Natural gas
Coal
Renewables

160
140
120
100
80
60
40
20
0
1970 1980 1990 2000 2010 2019

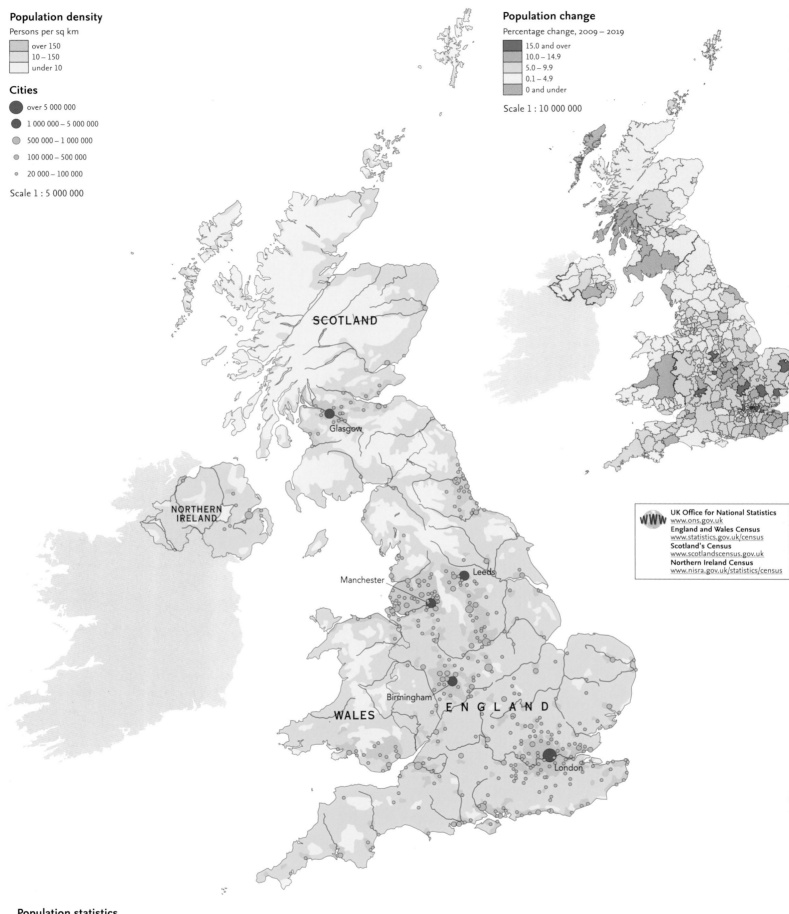

**Population density**

Persons per sq km

- over 150
- 10 – 150
- under 10

**Cities**

- over 5 000 000
- 1 000 000 – 5 000 000
- 500 000 – 1 000 000
- 100 000 – 500 000
- 20 000 – 100 000

Scale 1 : 5 000 000

**Population change**

Percentage change, 2009 – 2019

- 15.0 and over
- 10.0 – 14.9
- 5.0 – 9.9
- 0.1 – 4.9
- 0 and under

Scale 1 : 10 000 000

SCOTLAND

Glasgow

NORTHERN IRELAND

Leeds

Manchester

Birmingham

ENGLAND

WALES

London

**www** UK Office for National Statistics
www.ons.gov.uk
**England and Wales Census**
www.statistics.gov.uk/census
**Scotland's Census**
www.scotlandscensus.gov.uk
**Northern Ireland Census**
www.nisra.gov.uk/statistics/census

**Population statistics**

| Life expectancy | Birth rate | Death rate | Infant mortality | Unemployment rate | Not in education or employment |
|---|---|---|---|---|---|
| **81** years | **1.1%** 11.0 per 1000 people | **0.9%** 9.3 per 1000 people | **0.4%** 3.9 per 1000 live births | **3.8%** of workforce | **11.1%** of 16-24 year olds |

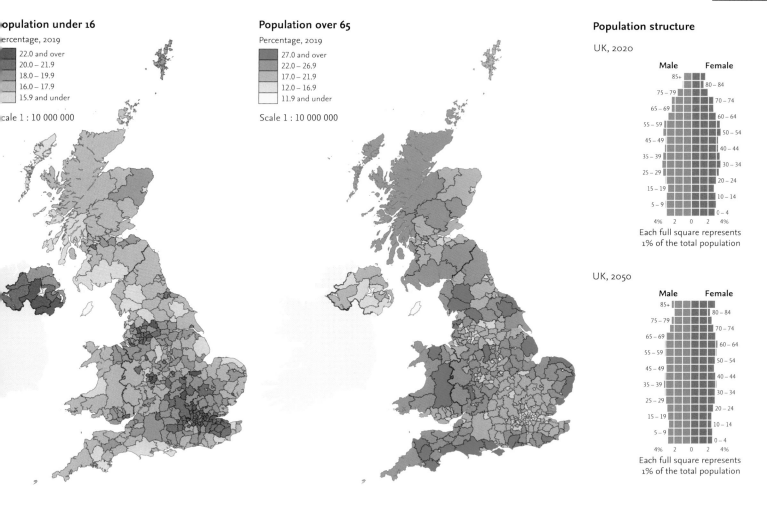

## opulation under 16

ercentage, 2019

- 22.0 and over
- 20.0 – 21.9
- 18.0 – 19.9
- 16.0 – 17.9
- 15.9 and under

cale 1 : 10 000 000

## Population over 65

Percentage, 2019

- 27.0 and over
- 22.0 – 26.9
- 17.0 – 21.9
- 12.0 – 16.9
- 11.9 and under

Scale 1 : 10 000 000

## Population structure

UK, 2020

Male    Female

85+
80 – 84
75 – 79
70 – 74
65 – 69
60 – 64
55 – 59
50 – 54
45 – 49
40 – 44
35 – 39
30 – 34
25 – 29
20 – 24
15 – 19
10 – 14
5 – 9
0 – 4

4%  2  0  2  4%

Each full square represents
1% of the total population

UK, 2050

Male    Female

85+
80 – 84
75 – 79
70 – 74
65 – 69
60 – 64
55 – 59
50 – 54
45 – 49
40 – 44
35 – 39
30 – 34
25 – 29
20 – 24
15 – 19
10 – 14
5 – 9

4%  2  0  2  4%

Each full square represents
1% of the total population

## ternal migration

umber of people moving, 2019

- Moving into area
- Moving out of area

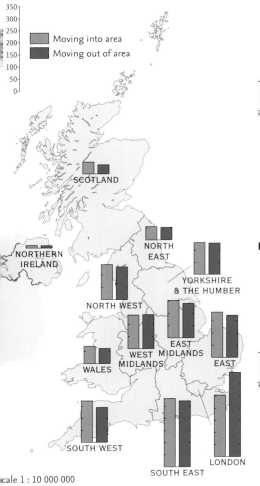

SCOTLAND

NORTHERN
IRELAND

NORTH
EAST

YORKSHIRE
& THE HUMBER

NORTH WEST

EAST
MIDLANDS

WEST
MIDLANDS

WALES

EAST

SOUTH WEST

LONDON

SOUTH EAST

cale 1 : 10 000 000

## Reasons for immigration, 2010 – 2019

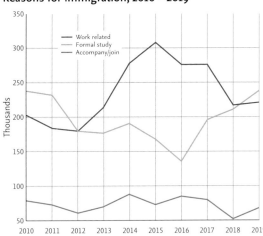

- Work related
- Formal study
- Accompany/join

Thousands

2010 2011 2012 2013 2014 2015 2016 2017 2018 2019

## International migration, 2010 – 2019

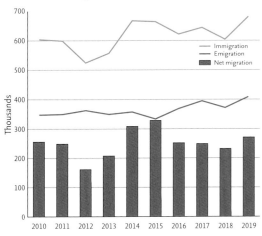

- Immigration
- Emigration
- Net migration

Thousands

2010 2011 2012 2013 2014 2015 2016 2017 2018 2019

## Population by ethnic group, 2016

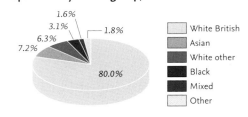

- 1.6%
- 3.1%
- 1.8%
- 6.3%
- 7.2%
- 80.0%

- White British
- Asian
- White other
- Black
- Mixed
- Other

## Population by country, 2019

| Country | Population (thousands) | Density (persons per sq km) |
|---|---|---|
| England | 56 287 | 432 |
| Wales | 3153 | 152 |
| Scotland | 5463 | 69 |
| Northern Ireland | 1894 | 139 |
| **United Kingdom** | **66 797** | **274** |

## Population by age group

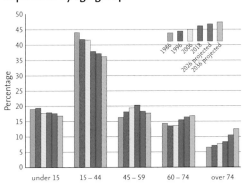

Percentage

- 1986
- 1996
- 2006
- 2018
- 2026 projected
- 2036 projected

under 15    15 – 44    45 – 59    60 – 74    over 74

# UK Transport

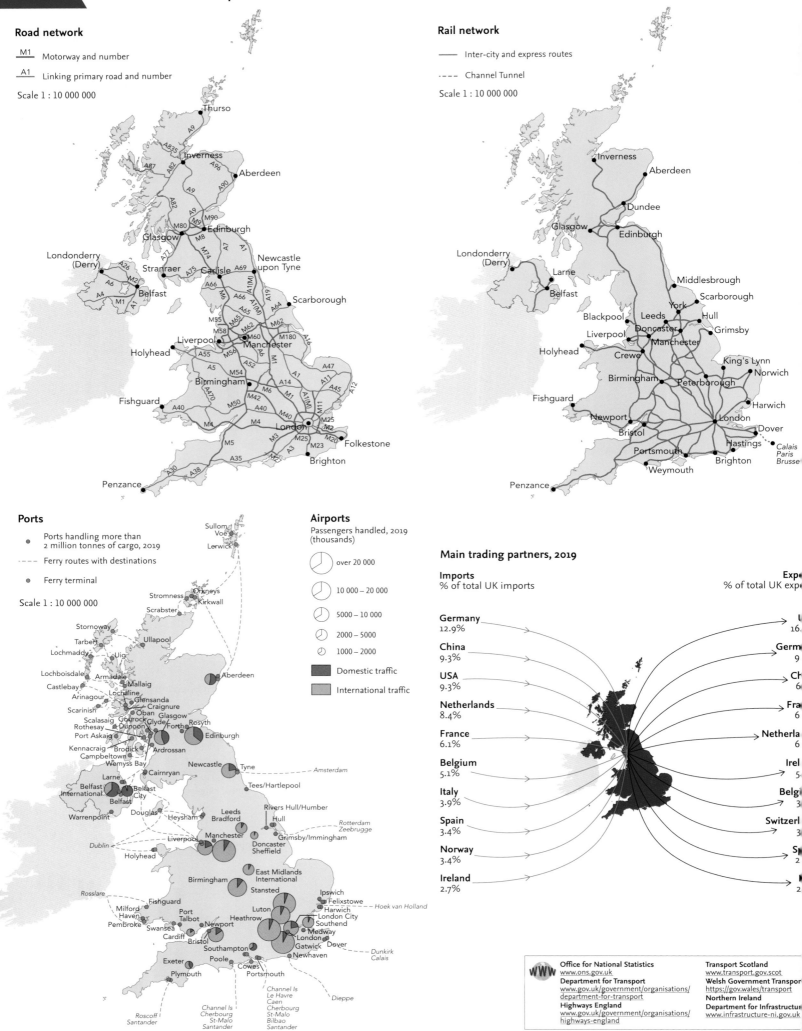

## Road network

M1   Motorway and number

A1   Linking primary road and number

Scale 1 : 10 000 000

Thurso, A9, A835, Inverness, A96, Aberdeen, A87, A82, A9, A90, A82, A9, A7, M90, M80, M9, Edinburgh, A7, Glasgow, M8, M74, A7, Londonderry (Derry), A26, Stranraer, A75, Carlisle, A69, Newcastle upon Tyne, A6, Belfast, A4, M1, A1, A66, A66, A1(M), A19, A64, Scarborough, A1, A52, Holyhead, A55, M55, M58, M62, M60, Liverpool, M56, M62, M180, Manchester, A6, A52, M1, A1, A47, Fishguard, A5, M54, Birmingham, A14, A11, A45, A12, A470, M50, A40, M6, A1(M), M11, A40, M40, A40, M4, M4, London, M1, A1(M), M2, M5, M3, M25, M20, Folkestone, A35, A3, M23, Brighton, A30, A38, Penzance

## Rail network

— Inter-city and express routes

---- Channel Tunnel

Scale 1 : 10 000 000

Inverness, Aberdeen, Dundee, Glasgow, Edinburgh, Londonderry (Derry), Larne, Belfast, Middlesbrough, York, Scarborough, Blackpool, Leeds, Hull, Liverpool, Doncaster, Grimsby, Holyhead, Crewe, Manchester, King's Lynn, Norwich, Birmingham, Peterborough, Fishguard, Harwich, Newport, London, Bristol, Dover, Portsmouth, Hastings, Calais Paris Brusse, Weymouth, Brighton, Penzance

## Ports

• Ports handling more than 2 million tonnes of cargo, 2019

---- Ferry routes with destinations

● Ferry terminal

Scale 1 : 10 000 000

Sullom Voe, Lerwick, Stromness, Orkneys, Kirkwall, Scrabster, Stornoway, Tarbert, Ullapool, Lochmaddy, Uig, Lochboisdale, Armadale, Mallaig, Aberdeen, Castlebay, Lochaline, Glensanda, Arinagour, Oban, Craignure, Scarinish, Scalasaig, Gourock, Glasgow, Rothesay, Clyde, Edinburgh, Port Askaig, Dunoon, Forth, Rosyth, Kennacraig, Brodick, Ardrossan, Campbeltown, Wemyss Bay, Newcastle, Tyne, Amsterdam, Belfast International, Cairnryan, Tees/Hartlepool, Larne, Belfast City, Belfast, Leeds Bradford, Rivers Hull/Humber, Douglas, Heysham, Hull, Warrenpoint, Liverpool, Manchester, Rotterdam Zeebrugge, Dublin, Holyhead, Doncaster Sheffield, Grimsby/Immingham, Birmingham, East Midlands International, Rosslare, Stansted, Ipswich, Fishguard, Felixstowe, Harwich, Milford Haven, Port Talbot, Luton, Heathrow, London City, Hoek van Holland, Pembroke, Swansea, Newport, Southend, Cardiff, Bristol, Medway, London, Gatwick, Dover, Southampton, Newhaven, Dunkirk Calais, Exeter, Poole, Plymouth, Cowes, Portsmouth, Channel Is Le Havre Caen Cherbourg St-Malo Bilbao Santander, Dieppe, Roscoff Santander, Channel Is Cherbourg St-Malo Santander

## Airports

Passengers handled, 2019 (thousands)

- over 20 000
- 10 000 – 20 000
- 5000 – 10 000
- 2000 – 5000
- 1000 – 2000

■ Domestic traffic

■ International traffic

## Main trading partners, 2019

**Imports**
% of total UK imports

**Germany** 12.9%
**China** 9.3%
**USA** 9.3%
**Netherlands** 8.4%
**France** 6.1%
**Belgium** 5.1%
**Italy** 3.9%
**Spain** 3.4%
**Norway** 3.4%
**Ireland** 2.7%

**Exp**
% of total UK exp

U
16.

Germ
9

Ch
6

Fra
6

Netherla
6

Irel
5

Belg
3

Switzerl
3

S
2

2

WWW   **Office for National Statistics** www.ons.gov.uk

**Department for Transport** www.gov.uk/government/organisations/department-for-transport

**Highways England** www.gov.uk/government/organisations/highways-england

**Transport Scotland** www.transport.gov.scot

**Welsh Government Transpor** https://gov.wales/transport

**Northern Ireland Department for Infrastructur** www.infrastructure-ni.gov.uk

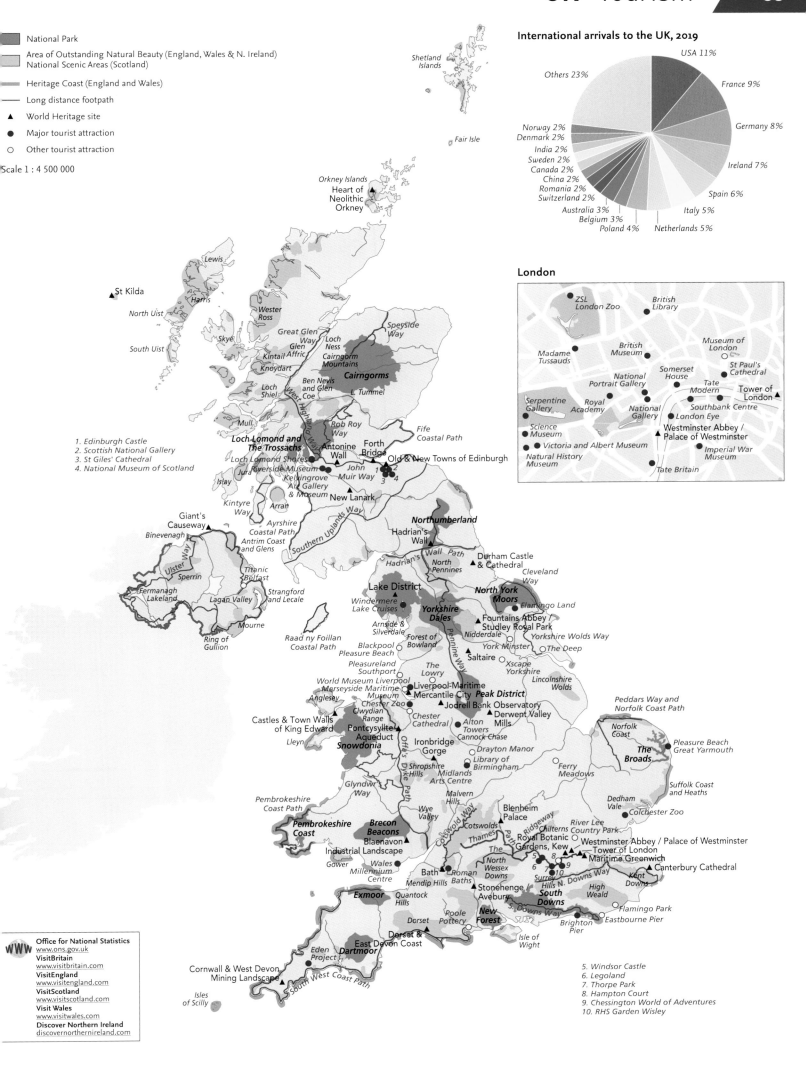

**Legend:**
- National Park
- Area of Outstanding Natural Beauty (England, Wales & N. Ireland)
- National Scenic Areas (Scotland)
- Heritage Coast (England and Wales)
- Long distance footpath
- ▲ World Heritage site
- ● Major tourist attraction
- ○ Other tourist attraction

Scale 1 : 4 500 000

**International arrivals to the UK, 2019**
- USA 11%
- France 9%
- Germany 8%
- Ireland 7%
- Spain 6%
- Italy 5%
- Netherlands 5%
- Poland 4%
- Belgium 3%
- Australia 3%
- Switzerland 2%
- Romania 2%
- China 2%
- Canada 2%
- Sweden 2%
- India 2%
- Denmark 2%
- Norway 2%
- Others 23%

**Edinburgh (numbered list):**
1. Edinburgh Castle
2. Scottish National Gallery
3. St Giles' Cathedral
4. National Museum of Scotland

**London area (numbered list):**
5. Windsor Castle
6. Legoland
7. Thorpe Park
8. Hampton Court
9. Chessington World of Adventures
10. RHS Garden Wisley

**Office for National Statistics**
www.ons.gov.uk
**VisitBritain**
www.visitbritain.com
**VisitEngland**
www.visitengland.com
**VisitScotland**
www.visitscotland.com
**Visit Wales**
www.visitwales.com
**Discover Northern Ireland**
discovernorthernireland.com

A  30°  B  20°  C  10°  D  0°  E  10°  F  20°  G  30°  H  40°  I  50°  J  60°  K  70°  L

Jan Mayen

Barents Sea

**Denmark Strait**

Ostrov Kolguyev

Gora Narodnaya 1895

Arctic Circle

Handflói

Iceland 1833 Snæfell

Fontur

North Cape
Sørøya

Cheskaya Guba

Poluostrov Kanin

Usa

Pechora

5

Faxaflói

Vatnajökull

Lofoten Vesterålen

Inarijärvi

Lapland

Kola Peninsula

White Sea

Mezen

Vychegda

Pechora

Ural Mountains

Vestfjorden

Northern Dvina

N o r w e g i a n   S e a

Luleälven

Kemijoki

60°

Faroe Islands

Scandinavia

Indalsälven

Umeälven

Gulf of Bothnia

Lake Onega

Lake Ladoga

ATLANTIC

Shetland

Rockall

Orkney

Outer Hebrides

Ben Nevis 1343

North Sea

Malåren

Hiiumaa
Saaremaa

Vänern

Gotland

Baltic Sea

Gulf of Riga

Lake Peipus

Rybinskoye Vodokhranilishche

Kuybyshevskoye Vodokhranilishche

Volga

4

OCEAN

Malin Head

Donegal Bay

Galway Bay

Ireland

Shannon

Irish Sea

Pennines

Vättern

Öland

Valdai Hills

Volga Upland

Cape Clear

Great Britain

Snowdon 1085

St George's Channel

The Wash

Jutland

Zealand
Fyn

Bornholm

North European Plain

Pripet Marshes

Central Russian Upland

Volga

50°

Land's End

Isles of Scilly

English Channel

Channel Islands

Strait of Dover

Frisian Islands

IJsselmeer

Weser

Elbe

Vistula

Oder

Warta

Bug

Kyyivs'ke Vodoskhovyshche

Don

Dnieper

Maas

Rhine

Elbe

Erzgebirge

Sudety

Tsimlyanskoye Vodokhranilishche

Don

Brittany

Loire

Seine

Marne

Ardennes

Moselle

Taunus

Bohemian Forest

Danube

Dniester

3

Bay of Biscay

Seine

Vienne

Allier

Saône

Jura

Rhine

Lake Constance

Inn

Danube

Lake Balaton

Carpathian Mts

Dniester

Sea of Azov

Caspian

Cape Finisterre

Puy de Sancy 1885

Gironde

Mont Blanc 4810

A L P S

Großglockner 3798

Matterhorn 4478

Po

Hungarian Plain

Transylvanian Alps

Mures

Danube

Crimea

Stavropol'skaya Vozvyshennost'

Cantabrian Mts

Massif Central

Rhône

Gulf of Gascony

Gulf of Lions

Côte d'Azur

Gulf of Genoa

Ligurian Sea

Apennines

Adriatic Sea

Dinaric Alps

Sava

Morava

Balkan Mts

Danube

Black Sea

Caucasus

El'brus 5642

Pyrenees

Aneto 3404

Douro

Duero

Ebro

Corsica

Strait of Bonifacio

Balearic Sea

Golfo de Valencia

Balearic Is
Minorca

Tagus

Sierra Morena

Guadalquivir

Ibiza

Majorca

Sardinia

Vesuvius 1281

Turrhenian Sea

G. of Taranto

Rhodope Mts

Pindus Mts

Mt Olympus 2911

Corfu

Aegean Sea

Evvoia

Sea of Marmara

ASIA

Cabo de São Vicente

Sierra Nevada

Strait of Gibraltar

M e d i t e r r a n e a n   S e a

Sicily Mount Etna 3323

Ionian Sea

Zakynthos

Dodecanese

Naxos

Rhodes

Kythira

C. Passero

Crete

AFRICA

**Relief and physical features**

| Relief metres | |
|---|---|
| | 5000 |
| | 3000 |
| | 2000 |
| | 1000 |
| | 500 |
| | 200 |
| 0 | sea level |
| 200 | under sea level |
| 4000 | |
| 6000 | |

▲ 5642  Mountain height (in metres)

Permanent ice (ice cap or glacier)

Scale 1 : 25 000 000

0  250  500 km

Conic Equidistant projection

0°  E  10°  F  20°  G  30°  H  40°  I

**Cross-section**

line of cross-section

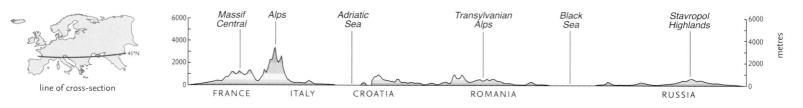

Massif Central  Alps  Adriatic Sea  Transylvanian Alps  Black Sea  Stavropol Highlands

6000  4000  2000

FRANCE  ITALY  CROATIA  ROMANIA  RUSSIA

6000  4000  2000  metres

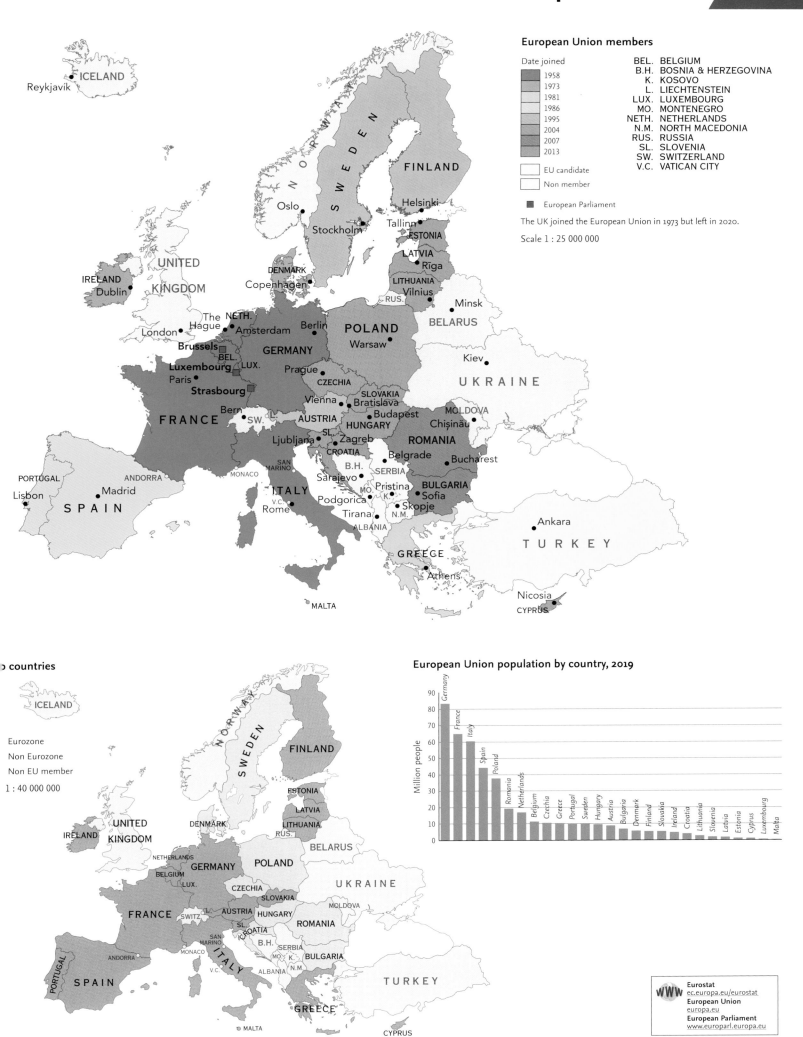

**Population per sq km**

- over 500
- 251 – 500
- 101 – 250
- 26 – 100
- 1 – 25
- less than 1

Scale 1 : 25 000 000

ICELAND

N O R W A Y

S W E D E N

FINLAND

ESTONIA

RUSSIA

LATVIA

LITHUANIA

RUS.

BELARUS

DENMARK

IRELAND

UNITED KINGDOM

NETHERLANDS

BELGIUM

LUX.

GERMANY

POLAND

UKRAINE

CZECHIA

SLOVAKIA

FRANCE

SWITZ.

AUSTRIA

HUNGARY

MOL.

SL.

CROATIA

ROMANIA

B.H.

SERBIA

ANDORRA

MON.

KOS.

BULGARIA

PORTUGAL

SPAIN

ITALY

ALBANIA

N.M.

TURKEY

GREECE

MALTA

**WWW** EUROSTAT
ec.europa.eu/eurostat/
**United Nations Population Division**
www.un.org/development/desa/pd

**Population under 15, 2019**

Percentage of total population

- over 20
- 17 – 20
- 16 – 16.9
- 15 – 15.9
- 13 – 14.9
- No data

Scale 1 : 45 000 000

**Population 65 and over, 20**

Percentage of total population

- over 22
- 20 – 22
- 18 – 19.9
- 15 – 17.9
- 8 – 14.9
- No data

Scale 1 : 45 000 00

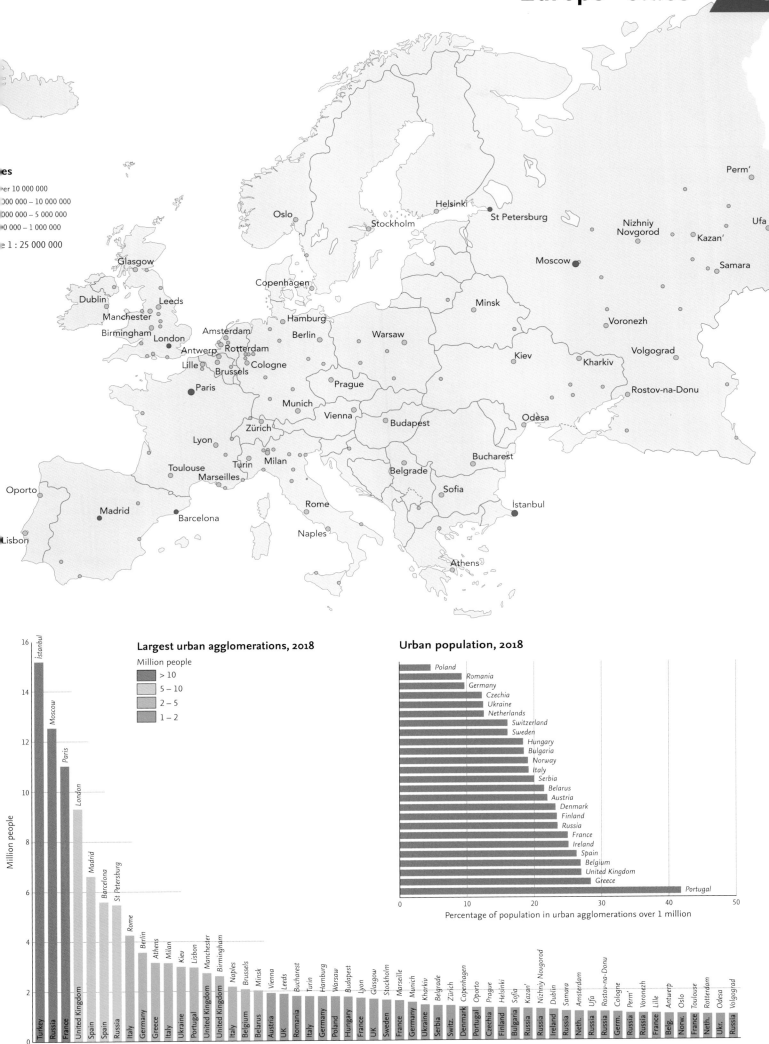

**Relief and physical features**

Relief metres

5000
3000
2000
1000
500
200
sea level
0
200
under sea level
4000
6000

▲ 818  Mountain height
        (in metres)

Permanent ice
(ice cap or glacier)

**Water features**

〜〜 River

〜〜 Canal

⬭ Lake / Reservoir

Marsh

**Communications**

——— Railway

═══ Motorway

- - - - Motorway under
        construction

——— Road

⊕ Main airport

**Administration**

Boundaries

━━━ International

——— Internal

**Settlement**

Urban area

Cities and towns in order of size

National capital

■ Brussels

● Lille

● Saarbrücken

○ Ghent

○ Leuven

Scale 1 : 2 000 000

0   25   50   75   100 km

Conic Equidistant projection

Scale 1 : 7 500 000

Conic Equidistant projection

**Relief and physical features**

Relief metres
5000
3000
2000
1000
500
200
0 sea level
200 under sea level
4000
6000

▲ 3718  Mountain height (in metres)

**Water features**

~ River
~ Intermittent river
~ Canal
Lake / Reservoir
Marsh

**Communications**

Railway
Motorway
Motorway under construction
Road
⊕ Main airport

**Administration**

Boundaries
International

**Settlement**

Cities and towns in order of size

National capital
■ Madrid

Other city or town
○ Barcelona
○ Seville
○ Pamplona
○ Benidorm

Scale 1 : 5 250 000

0  50  100  150  200 km

Lambert Conformal Conic projection

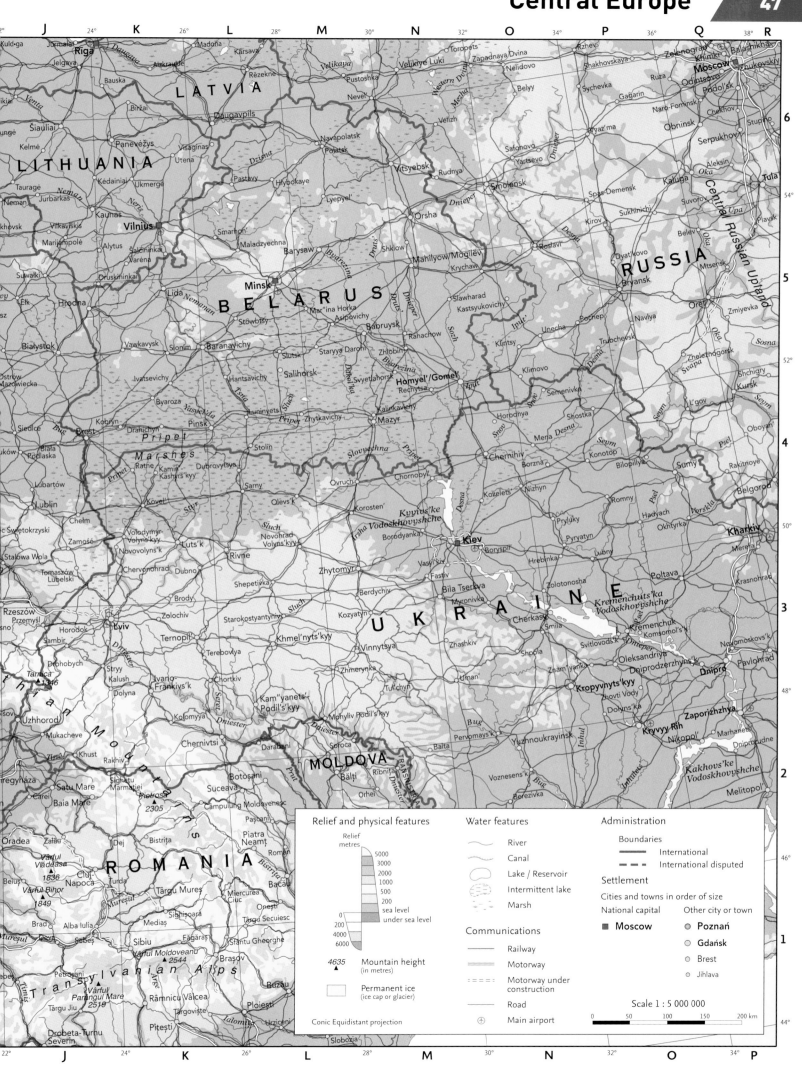

**Relief and physical features**

Relief metres

5000
3000
2000
1000
500
200
sea level
under sea level
200
4000
6000

4635 ▲ Mountain height (in metres)

Permanent ice (ice cap or glacier)

Conic Equidistant projection

**Water features**

River
Canal
Lake / Reservoir
Intermittent lake
Marsh

**Communications**

Railway
Motorway
Motorway under construction
Road
⊕ Main airport

**Administration**

Boundaries

International
International disputed

Settlement

Cities and towns in order of size

National capital          Other city or town

■ Moscow          ◉ Poznań
                   ◉ Gdańsk
                   ◉ Brest
                   ◦ Jihlava

Scale 1 : 5 000 000

0    50    100    150    200 km

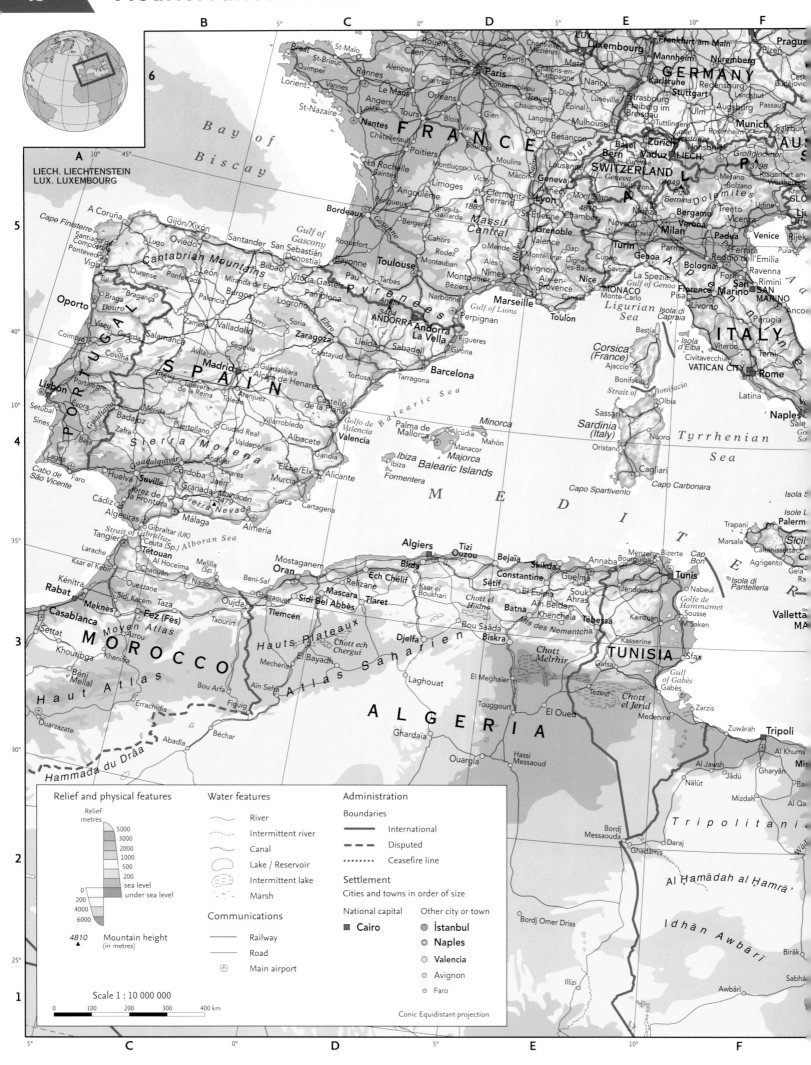

LIECH. LIECHTENSTEIN
LUX. LUXEMBOURG

Bay of Biscay

**FRANCE**

**GERMANY**

**SWITZERLAND**

A L P S

**PORTUGAL**

**SPAIN**

Cantabrian Mountains

Pyrenees

**ANDORRA** Andorra La Vella

Sierra Morena

Sierra Nevada

Gulf of Gascony

Gulf of Lions

Ligurian Sea

Corsica (France)

Sardinia (Italy)

**ITALY**

**VATICAN CITY** **Rome**

Tyrrhenian Sea

Balearic Sea

Balearic Islands

M E D I T E R R A N E A N   S E A

**MOROCCO**

Moyen Atlas

Haut Atlas

Atlas Saharien

Hauts Plateaux

**ALGERIA**

**TUNISIA**

Gulf of Gabès

Tripolitania

Al Ḥamādah al Ḥamrā'

Idhān Awbārī

Strait of Gibraltar

Alboran Sea

Algiers

**Tunis**

**Tripoli**

Relief and physical features

Relief metres
5000
3000
2000
1000
500
200
sea level
under sea level
0
200
4000
6000

4810 ▲ Mountain height (in metres)

Water features

～ River
- - - Intermittent river
≋ Canal
⬯ Lake / Reservoir
⬯ Intermittent lake
⬯ Marsh

Communications

— Railway
— Road
⊕ Main airport

Administration

Boundaries
——— International
- - - Disputed
· · · · Ceasefire line

Settlement
Cities and towns in order of size

National capital
■ Cairo

Other city or town
● İstanbul
● Naples
○ Valencia
○ Avignon
○ Faro

Scale 1 : 10 000 000

0   100   200   300   400 km

Conic Equidistant projection

## Relief and physical features

Relief metres

5000
3000
2000
1000
500
200
sea level
under sea level

0
200
4000
6000

▲ 3917  Mountain height
(in metres)

## Water features

~~~~~~~ River

~~~~~~~ Intermittent river

~~~~~~~ Canal

Lake / Reservoir

Intermittent lake

Marsh

## Communications

Railway

Motorway

====== Motorway under
construction

Road

⊕ Main airport

## Administration

Boundaries

International

- - - Disputed

········ Ceasefire line

## Settlement

Cities and towns in order of size

National capital          Other city or town

■ Athens                  ● İstanbul

                          ● Bursa

                          ○ Krasnodar

                          ○ Split

                          ∘ Dubrovnik

Scale 1 : 5 000 000

0        50      100     150 km

Conic Equidistant projection

**UKRAINE**

Odesa
Bilhorod-Dnistrovs'kyy
Artsyz
Tatarbunary
Bolhrad
İzmayıl
Tulcea
Babadag
Danube Delta
Sulina
Constanța
Mangalia
Kavarna
Nos Kaliakra
MOLDOVA

Skadovs'k
Armyans'k
Krasnoperekops'k
Novooleksiyivka
Henichens'k
Primorsko-Akhtarsk
Timashëysk
Khadyzhensk
Psebay

**CRIMEA**
Administered by Russia

Chornomors'ke
Yevpatoriya
Sevastopol'
Simferopol'
Yalta
Feodosiya
Sudak
Dzhankoy
Nyzhn'ohirs'kyy

Kerch
Temryuk
Anapa
Krymsk
Novorossiysk
Tuapse

*Sea of Azov*

**RUSSIA**

Slavyansk-na-Kubani
Kubań
Krasnodar
Tshchikskoye Vodokhranilishche

Sochi
Gagra
Sokhumi

**GEORGIA**

*Caucasus*

*B l a c k    S e a*

Bosporus
ada Burnu

Sinop
İnebolu
Bafra
Samsun
Terme
Rize
Trabzon
Giresun
Ordu

Zonguldak
Bartın
Karabük
Kastamonu
Boyabat
Vezirköprü
Merzifon
Niksar
Kelkit
Şebinkarahisar
Bayburt
Gümüşhane

İstanbul
Sarıyer
Beykoz
Kadıköy
Kartal
Ereğli
Kandıra
Adapazarı
Düzce
Bolu
Gerede
Tosya
Osmancık
Amasya
Turhal
Tokat
Suşehri
Zara
Erzincan

*Anadolu Dağları*

Yalova
Gölcük
Geyve
Göynük
Beypazarı
Çankırı
Çorum
Yeşilırmak
Yıldızeli
Sivas
Kızıl Dağı ▲3025

Bursa
Uludağ ▲2493
Bilecik
İnegöl
Bozüyük
Köroğlu Tepesi ▲2400
Mudurnu
Etimesgut
Keçiören
Ankara
Çankaya
Kalecik
Yozgat
Akdağmadeni
Kangal
Divriği
Tunceli

Kemalpaşa
Sakarya
Eskişehir
Polatlı
Kırıkkale
Delice
Boğazlıyan
Şarkışla
Arapgir
*Keban Barajı*

Porsuk
Kütahya
Tavşanlı
Sivrihisar
Sakarya
Kaman
Kırşehir
Kızılırmak
Pınarbaşı
Elazığ

Simav
Demirci
Eski Gediz
Uşak
Emirdağ
Yunak
Şereflikoçhisar
Avanos
Nevşehir
Kayseri
Erciyes Dağı ▲3917
Malatya
Ergani

**T U R K E Y**
*A n a t o l i a*

Gediz
Banaz
Afyonkarahisar
Sandıklı
Akşehir
Cihanbeyli
*Lake Tuz*
Aksaray
Göksun
Elbistan
Adıyaman
Siverek

Alaşehir
Çivril
Gelincik Dağı ▲2799
Eğirdir Gölü
Bor
Niğde
Demirkazık Tepe ▲3756
Kahramanmaraş
*Atatürk Barajı*

Nazilli
İhlı
Dinar
Eğridir
Beyşehir Gölü
Konya
Karapınar
Ereğli
Medetsiz Tepe ▲3524
Kozan
Ceyhan
Gaziantep
Nizip
Şanlıurfa

Denizli
Burdur
Isparta
Beyşehir
Seydişehir
Kadirli
Osmaniye
Kilis
Birecik
Akçakale

Yatağan
Geyik Dağ ▲2877
Karaman
Ceyhan
Tarsus
Adana
Osmaniye
İskenderun
*Euphrates*
Viranşehir

Marmaris
Korkuteli
Serik
Mersin
Kırıkhan
*Balīkh*

Dalaman
Elmalı ▲3073
Manavgat
Ermenek
Mut
Erdemli
*İskenderun Körfezi*
Antakya
İdlib
Ma'arrat ath Thawrah
Ar Raqqah

Fethiye
Antalya
*Antalya Körfezi*
Alanya
Silifke
Anamur
Samandağ
Latakia
Jablah
Bāniyās
*Buhayrat al Asad*
Ar Raqqah

Kaş
*Taurus Mountains*
*Rhodes*
ndos

Rhodes

Cape Apostolos Andreas
Aigialousa
Kyrenia
Nicosia
Famagusta
Latakia
Jablah
Bāniyās

Cape Arnauti
Administered as Northern Cyprus

**CYPRUS**
Olympos ▲1951
Polis
Paphos
Limassol
Larnaca

Tripoli
Zahlé
Beirut
**LEBANON**
Qornet es Saouda ▲3088
Al Qaryatayn
Sab' Ābār
An Nabk

**S Y R I A**
Hamāh
Homs
Ţarţūs
Tadmur
*J. an Nuşayrīyah*

*S E A*

30° 32° 34° 36° 38°

H I J K L M N

7 6 5 4 3 2 1

44° 42° 40° 38° 36° 34°

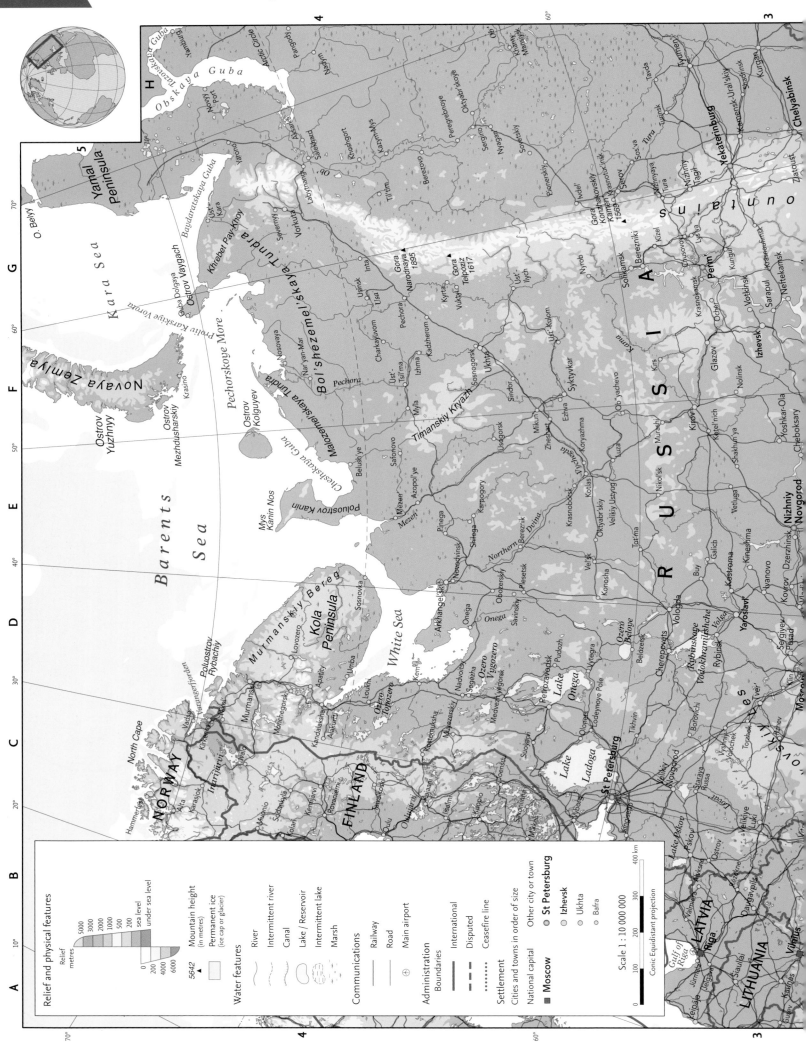

**Relief and physical features**

Relief
metres

5000
3000
2000
1000
500
200
sea level
under sea level

5642 ▲ Mountain height
(in metres)

Permanent ice
(ice cap or glacier)

0
200
4000
6000

**Water features**

River

Intermittent river

Canal

Lake / Reservoir

Intermittent lake

Marsh

**Communications**

Railway

Road

⊕ Main airport

**Administration**

Boundaries

International

Disputed

Ceasefire line

**Settlement**

Cities and towns in order of size

National capital

Other city or town

■ Moscow          ● St Petersburg

● Izhevsk

○ Ukhta

○ Bafra

Scale 1 : 10 000 000

0   100   200   300   400 km

Conic Equidistant projection

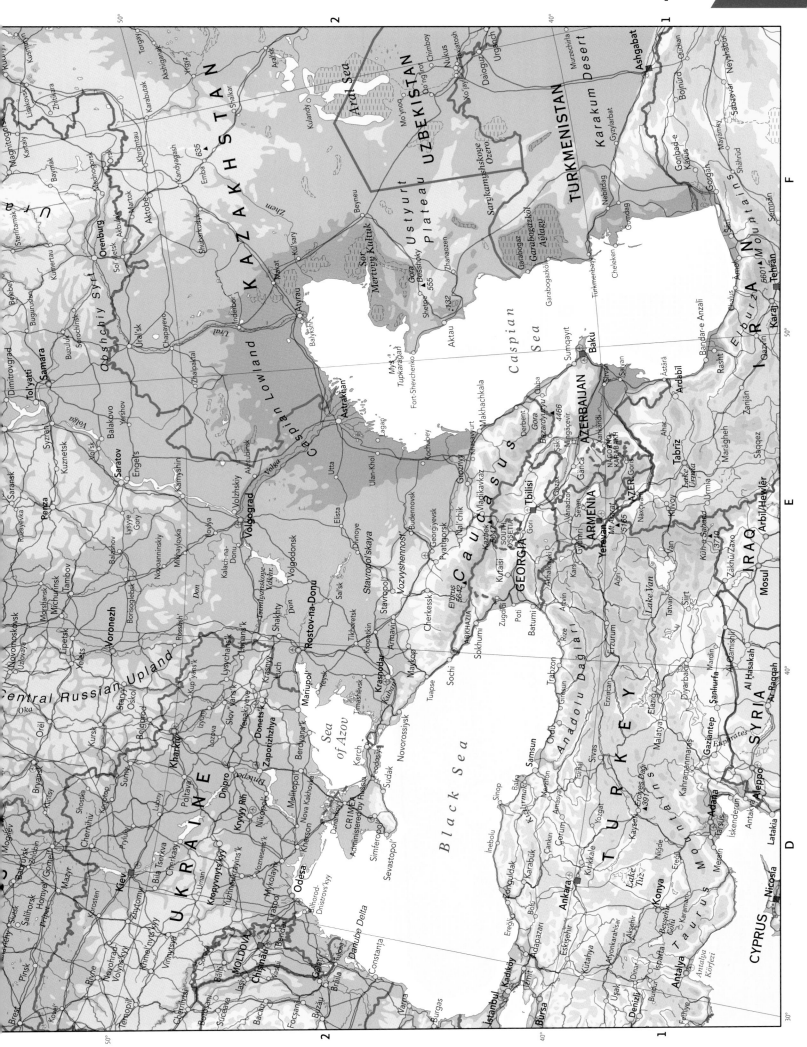

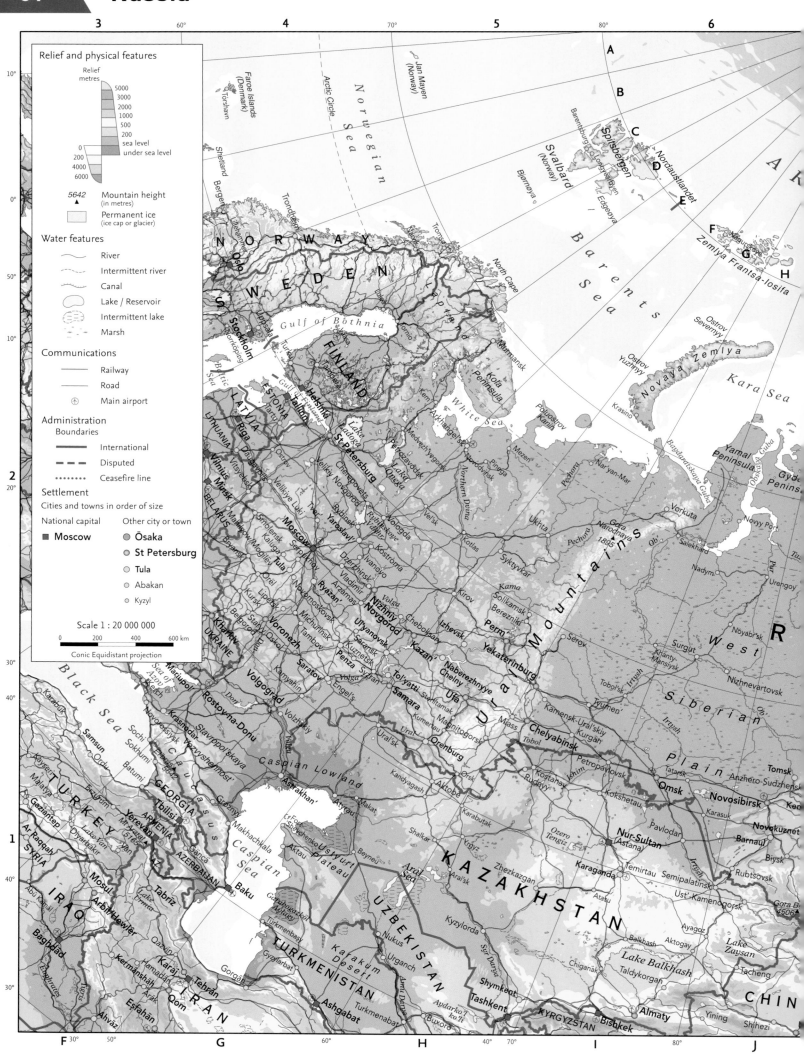

**Relief and physical features**

Relief
metres
5000
3000
2000
1000
500
200
0 sea level
200
4000 under sea level
6000

▲ 5642 Mountain height (in metres)

Permanent ice (ice cap or glacier)

**Water features**

~~~ River
- - - Intermittent river
Canal
Lake / Reservoir
Intermittent lake
Marsh

**Communications**

Railway
Road
⊕ Main airport

**Administration**

Boundaries
International
- - - Disputed
······ Ceasefire line

**Settlement**

Cities and towns in order of size

National capital        Other city or town
■ Moscow                ◉ Ōsaka
                        ◉ St Petersburg
                        ◉ Tula
                        ○ Abakan
                        ○ Kyzyl

Scale 1 : 20 000 000

0    200    400    600 km

Conic Equidistant projection

U.S.A.

ARCTIC OCEAN

Ostrov Komsomolets
Ostrov Oktyabr'skoy Revolyutsii
Ostrov Bol'shevik
Severnaya Zemlya
Proliv Vil'kitskogo

New Siberian Islands
Ostrov Novaya Sibir'
Ostrov Kotel'nyy
Ostrov Bol'shoy Lyakhovskiy

Wrangel Island
Proliv Longa
Chukchi Sea
Bering Strait
Point Hope
Arctic Circle
Seward Peninsula
Kotzebue
Chukotskiy Poluostrov
St Lawrence Island
St Matthew I.

East Siberian Sea
Laptev Sea
Yanskiy Zaliv

Taymyr Peninsula
Gory Byrranga
Ozero Taymyr
Khatangskiy Zaliv
West Siberian Lowland
Olenekskiy Zaliv
Ust'-Olenek
Olenek
Tiksi
Bulun
Popigay
Anabar
Khatanga
Kheta
Kotuy

Belaya
Uelen
Anadyr'
Egvekinot
Anadyrskiy Zaliv
Bering Sea

Ambarchik
Malyy Anyuy
Bol'shoy Anyuy
Kolyma
Srednekolymsk
Omolon
Kazach'ye

Yana
Verkhoyansk
Adycha
Mama
Gora Pobeda 3003
Khrebet Cherskogo
Indigirka
Seymchan
Oymyakon
Ol'skukchan
Strelka
Palatka
Magadan

Khrebet Kolymskiy
Kamenskoye
Penzhinskaya
Gizhiga
Zaliv Shelikhova
Palana
Koryakskiy Khrebet
Velikaya
Olyutorskiy Zaliv
Karaginskiy Zaliv
Ust'-Kamchatsk

Gory Kamen' 1678
'ril'sk
Ozero ...antauskoye
Tembenchi

Olenek
Muna
Lena
Vilyuy

Siberia
Central
Siberian
Plateau

RUSSIA
SSIA

Vilyuy
Verkhnevilyuysk
Markha
Nyurba
Nyuba
Yakutsk
Aldan
Maya
Ust'-Maya
Allakh-Yun'

Khrebet Dzhugdzhur
Okhotsk
Ayan
Shantarskiye Ostrova
Okha
Uda
Amgun'
Amur
Aleksandrovsk-Sakhalinskiy

Sea of Okhotsk

Kamchatka
Sopka Klyuchevskaya 4750
Kamchatka Peninsula
Petropavlovsk-Kamchatskiy
Ozernovskiy
Severo-Kuril'sk

Paskamennaya Tunguska
Chunya
Tura
Taymura
Angara

Chernyshevskiy
Mirnyy
Olekminsk
Lensk
Olekma
Lena
Vitim
Vilyuy
Lena
Uchur

Stanovoy Khrebet
Tynda
Zeya
Skovorodino
Amur
Svobodnyy
Blagoveshchensk
Komsomol'sk na-Amure
Khabarovsk

Sakhalin
Tatarskiy Proliv
Sakhalinskiy
Poronaysk
Udegorsk
Yuzhno-Sakhalinsk
Korsakov

Kuril Islands
Kuril'sk
Administered by Russia Claimed by Japan
Nakkanai

Krasnoyarsk
Nizhneudinsk
Abakan
nyy Sayan
Vostochnyy Sayan
Kyzyl
Kansk
Bratsk
Ust'-Ilimsk
Ust'-Kut
Lake Baikal
Kachug
Usol'ye-Sibirskoye
Irkutsk
Ulan-Ude
Kyakhta
Hövsgöl Nuur
Uvs Nuur

Yablonovyy Khrebet
Chita
Sretensk
Karymskoye
Borzya
Argun'
Hulun Buir
Hulun Nur

Stanovoy Khrebet
Bei'an
Yichun
Jiamusi
Jixi
Lake Khanka
Ussuriysk
Amur
Sikhote-Alin'
Vladivostok
Nakhodka

Hokkaido
Asahikawa
Asahi-dake 2290
Sapporo
Hakodate
Aomori
Akita

Ulan Bator
Bayan-Uul
Choybalsan
Da Hinggan Ling
Qiqihar
Ulanhot
MANCHURIA
Daqing
Harbin
Mudanjiang
Jilin
Yanji
Ch'ŏngjin
Kimch'aek

MONGOLIA
Altay
Bayanhongor
Arvayheer
Xilinhot
Gobi
Chifeng
Shenyang
Fushun
Anshan
Dandong
CHINA
Tongliao
Changchun
NORTH KOREA
P'yŏngyang

Sea of Japan (East Sea)

JAPAN
Sendai
Niigata
Tokyo
Yokohama
Nagoya
Kyoto
Osaka
Hachinohe

90° 80° 70° 60°
100° 110° 120° 130° 140° 160° 170° 180° 170° 160° 150°

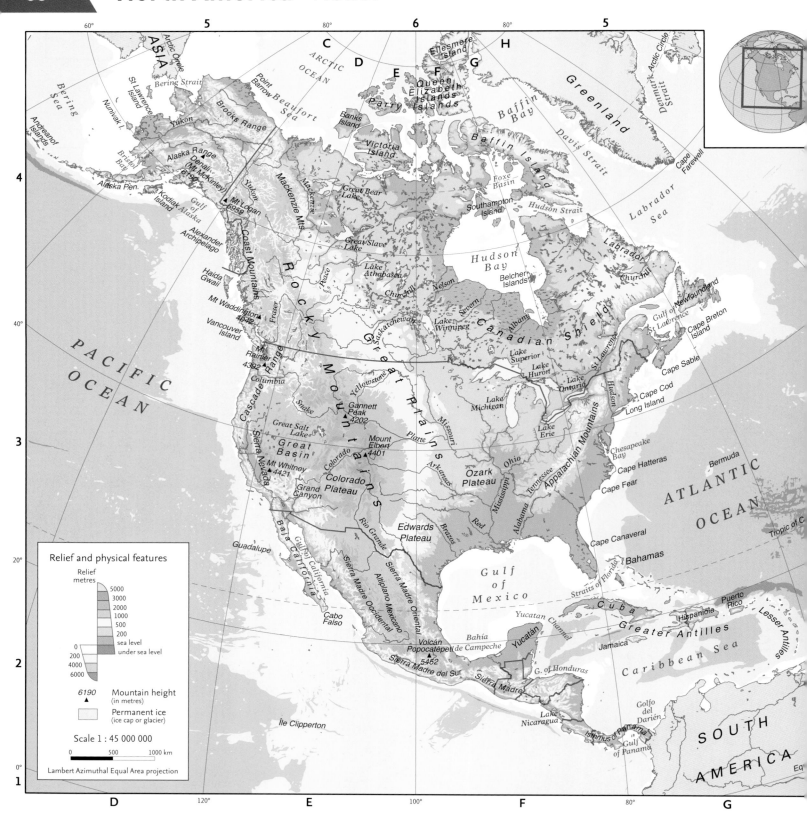

**Relief and physical features**

Relief
metres

5000
3000
2000
1000
500
200
0 sea level
200 under sea level
4000
6000

*6190* Mountain height
(in metres)

Permanent ice
(ice cap or glacier)

Scale 1 : 45 000 000

0        500        1000 km

Lambert Azimuthal Equal Area projection

ASIA
Arctic Circle
Bering Strait
ARCTIC OCEAN
Beaufort Sea
Point Barrow
Banks Island
Parry Islands
Queen Elizabeth Islands
Ellesmere Island
Greenland
Denmark Strait
Arctic Circle
Cape Farewell
Victoria Island
Baffin Bay
Davis Strait
Bering Sea
St Lawrence Island
Nunivak I.
Andreanof Islands
Yukon
Brooks Range
Mackenzie Mts
Foxe Basin
Baffin Island
Great Bear Lake
Labrador Sea
Alaska Range
Denali (Mt McKinley) 6190
Mt Logan 5959
Gulf of Alaska
Alaska Pen.
Bristol Bay
Kodiak Island
Alexander Archipelago
Coast Mountains
Yukon
Great Slave Lake
Mackenzie
Peace
Hudson Strait
Southampton Island
Belcher Islands
Labrador
Churchill
Cape Breton Island
Haida Gwai
Mt Waddington 4042
Fraser
R O C K Y   M O U N T A I N S
Lake Athabasca
Churchill
Nelson
Saskatchewan
C a n a d i a n   S h i e l d
Severn
Albany
Hudson Bay
Gulf of Newfoundland
St Lawrence
Vancouver Island
Columbia
Cascade Range
Mt Rainier 4392
Snake
G r e a t   P l a i n s
Yellowstone
Lake Winnipeg
Lake Superior
Lake Huron
St Lawrence
Hudson
Cape Sable
Cape Cod
Long Island
Great Salt Lake
Gannett Peak 4202
Missouri
Lake Michigan
Lake Ontario
Lake Erie
Chesapeake Bay
Bermuda
Sierra Nevada
Mt Whitney 4421
Great Basin
Colorado
Mount Elbert 4401
Platte
Ohio
Appalachian Mountains
Cape Hatteras
ATLANTIC OCEAN
Colorado Plateau
Grand Canyon
Arkansas
Ozark Plateau
Tennessee
Cape Fear
PACIFIC OCEAN
Baja California
Guadalupe
Rio Grande
Edwards Plateau
Brazos
Red
Mississippi
Alabama
Cape Canaveral
Tropic of C
Gulf of California
Sierra Madre Occidental
Sierra Madre Oriental
Gulf of Mexico
Bahamas
Cabo Falso
Altiplano Mexicano
Volcán Popocatépetl 5452
Bahía de Campeche
Yucatán
Cuba
Straits of Florida
Yucatan Channel
Greater Antilles
Hispaniola
Jamaica
Puerto Rico
Lesser Antilles
Sierra Madre del Sur
Sierra Madre
G. of Honduras
Caribbean Sea
Île Clipperton
Lake Nicaragua
Golfo del Darién
Isthmus of Panama
Gulf of Panama
SOUTH AMERICA
Eq

**Cross-section**

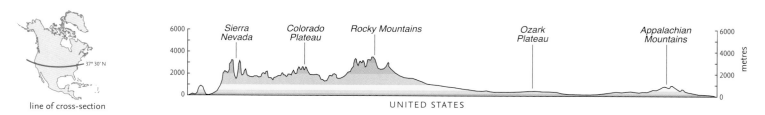

line of cross-section

37° 30' N

metres

6000
4000
2000
0

Sierra Nevada
Colorado Plateau
Rocky Mountains
Ozark Plateau
Appalachian Mountains

UNITED STATES

6000
4000
2000
0
metres

ATLANTIC OCEAN

Caribbean Sea

Greater Antilles

Lesser Antilles

THE BAHAMAS

CUBA

JAMAICA

HAITI

DOMINICAN REPUBLIC

PUERTO RICO (USA)

FLORIDA

GEORGIA

SOUTH CAROLINA

COLOMBIA

VENEZUELA

PANAMA

COSTA RICA

BRAZIL

Castries
ST LUCIA
Scale 1 : 2 000 000

BARBADOS
Bridgetown
Scale 1 : 2 000 000

TRINIDAD AND TOBAGO
Port of Spain
Scale 1 : 2 500 000

B 80° C 60° D 40° E

*Caribbean Sea*
Punta Gallinas    Curaçao    Windward Is
Golfo del
Darién
Isthmus of Panama
L. Maracaibo    Trinidad
Orinoco
Delta
4    Llanos    Orinoco
I. del Coco    Mt Roraima    Guiana Highlands
2810
Meta    Esequibo
Guaviare
Volcán    Pico de Neblina    Mouths of
I. de Malpelo    Caquetá    2995    the Amazon
Cotopaxi
5896    Ilha de
Equator    Japurá    Marajó    Equ
6263    Amazon
Islas    Chimborazo    Negro    Amazon
Galápagos    G. de Guayaquil    Fernando
Marañón    Juruá    de Noronha
Tapajós    Xingu    C. de São Roque
Pta Negra    Selvas    Madeira
Purus    Araguaia    Parnaíba
Nevado de    Tocantins    Brazilian
Huascarán    3
6768    São Francisco    Highlands
L. Titicaca
Lago de    2797
Poopó    Aguilhas    I. da Trindade    Is Martin Va
Negras
Altiplano    Tropic of Capri
Tropic of Capricorn    Gran Chaco    20°
Islas Desventuradas    Paraguay
6893
Cerro Ojos    Paraná
del Salado    Uruguay
Archipiélago    6961    Pampas    ATLANTIC
Juan Fernández    Cerro    Parana
2    Aconcagua    Río de la Plata    OCEAN

P A C I F I C

O C E A N

A n d e s
Cordillera Occidental
Cordillera Central
Cordillera Oriental
Cordillera Central
Cordillera Oriental
Cordillera Occidental
Atacama Desert

Golfo San Matías
Isla de
Chiloé    Golfo de San Jorge
40°
Patagonia    Falkland Is
Bahía
Grande
Str. of
Magellan
South Georgia
1    Tierra
del Fuego
Cape Horn    South
Sandwich Is

120° A 100° B 80° C 60° D 40° E 20° F

### Relief and physical features

Relief
metres
5000
3000
2000
1000
500
200
sea level
0
under sea level
200
4000
6000

6961 ▲ Mountain height
(in metres)

Permanent ice
(ice cap or glacier)

Scale 1 : 40 000 000

0    400    800    1200 km

Lambert Azimuthal Equal Area projection

## Cross-section

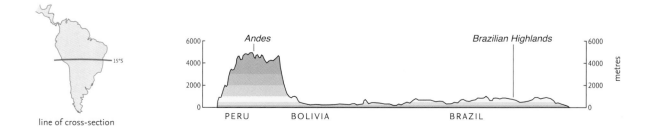

line of cross-section

Andes    Brazilian Highlands
6000    6000
4000    4000
2000    2000    metres

PERU    BOLIVIA    BRAZIL

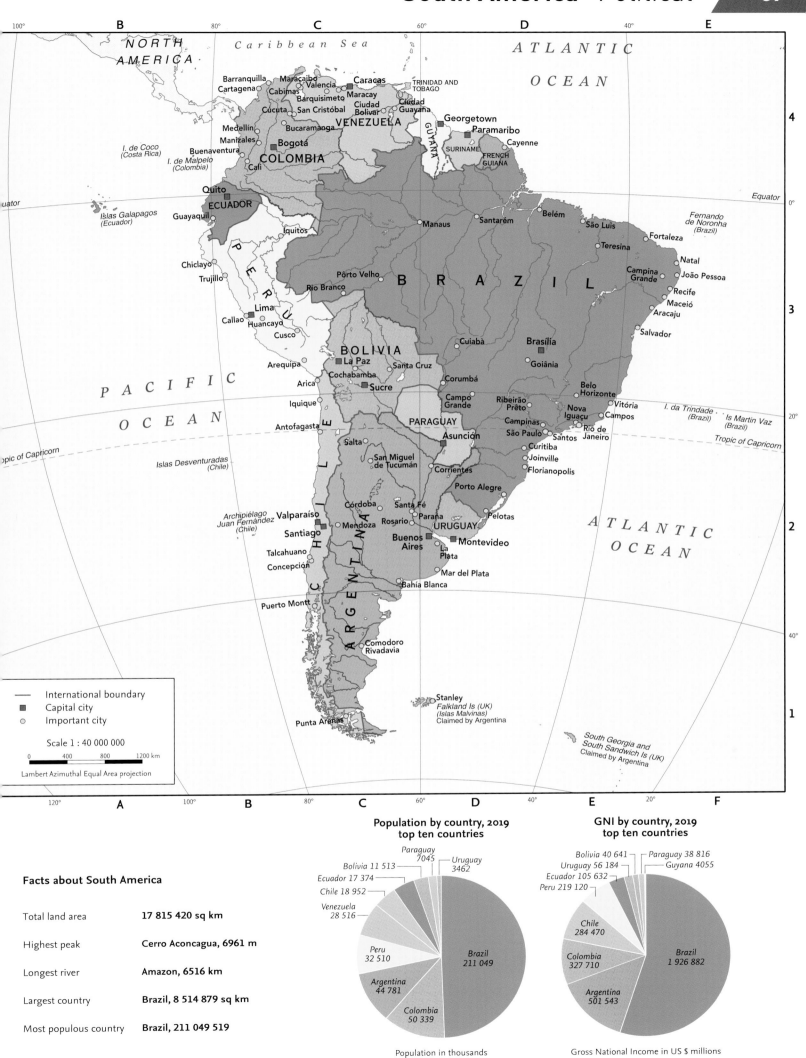

100°    B    80°    C    60°    D    40°    E

*Caribbean Sea*    *ATLANTIC*

*NORTH*    *OCEAN*
*AMERICA*

Barranquilla    Maracaibo
Cartagena    Valencia    **Caracas**    TRINIDAD AND
    Cabimas    Barquisimeto    Maracay    TOBAGO
Cúcuta    San Cristóbal    Ciudad
    Bucaramanga    **VENEZUELA**    Bolívar    Ciudad
Medellín        Guayana    **Georgetown**
Manizales    **Bogotá**        **Paramaribo**
Buenaventura    **COLOMBIA**    **GUYANA**    SURINAME    Cayenne
*I. de Coco*        FRENCH
*(Costa Rica)*    Cali        GUIANA
*I. de Malpelo*
*(Colombia)*    **Quito**    Equator
    **ECUADOR**
Guayaquil    Manaus    Santarém    Belém    São Luís    *Fernando*
*Islas Galápagos*    Iquitos        *de Noronha*
*(Ecuador)*    Chiclayo            *(Brazil)*
    Trujillo    Pôrto    B  R  A  Z  I  L    Teresina
*PACIFIC*    Rio Branco    Velho        Campina    Natal
    **Lima**    Huancayo        Grande    João Pessoa
    Callao    Cusco            Recife
*OCEAN*    Arequipa    **BOLIVIA**    Brasília    Maceió
    Arica    **La Paz**    Cuiabá        Aracaju
    Cochabamba    Santa Cruz    Goiânia    Salvador
Iquique    **Sucre**    Corumbá
    Antofagasta    Campo    Belo    *I. da Trindade*  *Is Martin Vaz*
*Islas Desventuradas*    Grande    Ribeirão    Horizonte    *(Brazil)*    *(Brazil)*
*(Chile)*    **PARAGUAY**    Prêto    Nova    Vitória
    Salta    Campinas    Iguaçu    Campos
    San Miguel    **Asunción**    São Paulo    Rio de
Tropic of Capricorn    de Tucumán        Santos    Janeiro    Tropic of Capricorn
    Corrientes    Curitiba
*Archipiélago*        Joinville
*Juan Fernández*    Córdoba    Porto Alegre    Florianópolis
*(Chile)*  **Valparaíso**    Santa Fé
    **Santiago**    Mendoza    Rosario    Paraná    Pelotas    *ATLANTIC*
    Talcahuano    **Buenos**    **URUGUAY**
    Concepción    **Aires**    La    **Montevideo**    *OCEAN*
        Plata
        Mar del Plata
    Puerto Montt    Bahía Blanca

    **ARGENTINA**

    Comodoro
    Rivadavia

Legend:
— International boundary
■ Capital city
○ Important city

Scale 1 : 40 000 000
0    400    800    1200 km

Lambert Azimuthal Equal Area projection

    Stanley
    *Falkland Is (UK)*
    *(Islas Malvinas)*
    Claimed by Argentina

    *South Georgia and*
    *South Sandwich Is (UK)*
    Claimed by Argentina

Punta Arenas

120°    A    100°    B    80°    C    60°    D    40°    E    20°    F

## Facts about South America

| | |
|---|---|
| Total land area | **17 815 420 sq km** |
| Highest peak | **Cerro Aconcagua, 6961 m** |
| Longest river | **Amazon, 6516 km** |
| Largest country | **Brazil, 8 514 879 sq km** |
| Most populous country | **Brazil, 211 049 519** |

### Population by country, 2019
### top ten countries

Paraguay 7045
Uruguay 3462
Bolivia 11 513
Ecuador 17 374
Chile 18 952
Venezuela 28 516
Peru 32 510
Argentina 44 781
Colombia 50 339
Brazil 211 049

Population in thousands

### GNI by country, 2019
### top ten countries

Bolivia 40 641
Uruguay 56 184
Ecuador 105 632
Paraguay 38 816
Guyana 4055
Peru 219 120
Chile 284 470
Colombia 327 710
Argentina 501 543
Brazil 1 926 882

Gross National Income in US $ millions

# South America Climate

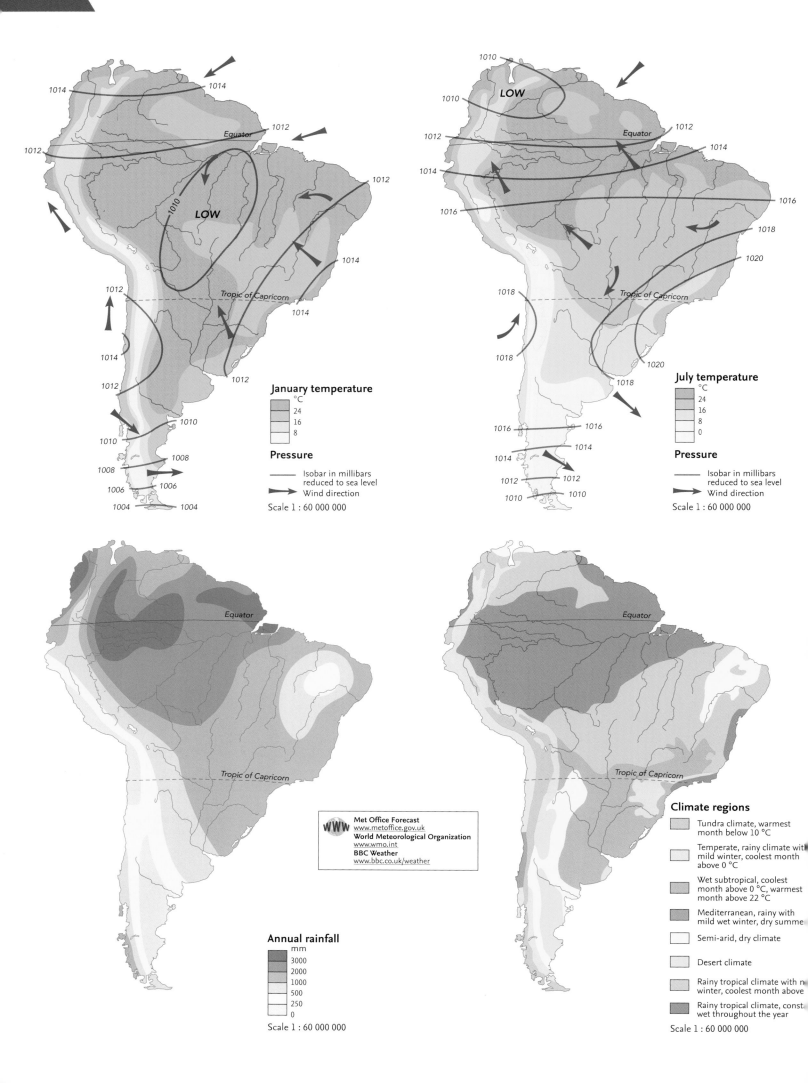

**January temperature**
°C
24
16
8

**Pressure**

——— Isobar in millibars reduced to sea level

➤ Wind direction

Scale 1 : 60 000 000

**July temperature**
°C
24
16
8
0

**Pressure**

——— Isobar in millibars reduced to sea level

➤ Wind direction

Scale 1 : 60 000 000

www **Met Office Forecast**
www.metoffice.gov.uk
**World Meteorological Organization**
www.wmo.int
**BBC Weather**
www.bbc.co.uk/weather

**Annual rainfall**
mm
3000
2000
1000
500
250
0

Scale 1 : 60 000 000

**Climate regions**

☐ Tundra climate, warmest month below 10 °C

☐ Temperate, rainy climate with mild winter, coolest month above 0 °C

☐ Wet subtropical, coolest month above 0 °C, warmest month above 22 °C

☐ Mediterranean, rainy with mild wet winter, dry summer

☐ Semi-arid, dry climate

☐ Desert climate

☐ Rainy tropical climate with winter, coolest month above

☐ Rainy tropical climate, constant wet throughout the year

Scale 1 : 60 000 000

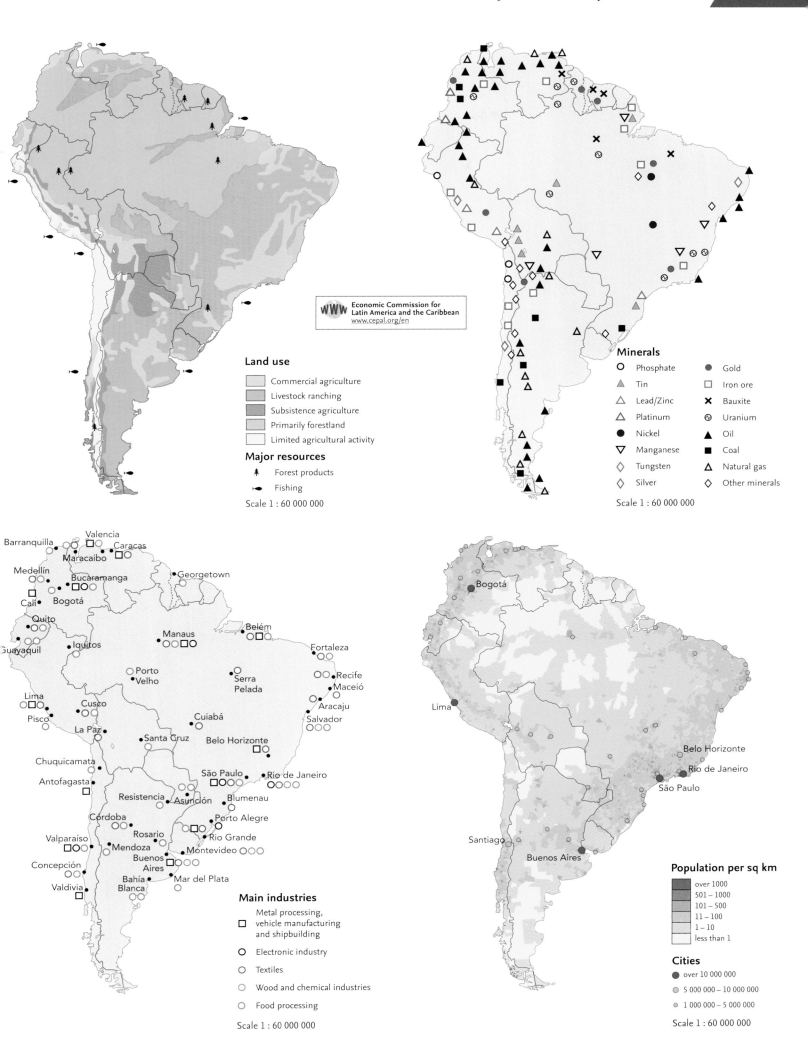

Economic Commission for
Latin America and the Caribbean
www.cepal.org/en

## Land use

- Commercial agriculture
- Livestock ranching
- Subsistence agriculture
- Primarily forestland
- Limited agricultural activity

### Major resources

- ♣ Forest products
- ◄ Fishing

Scale 1 : 60 000 000

## Minerals

- ○ Phosphate
- ▲ Tin
- △ Lead/Zinc
- △ Platinum
- ● Nickel
- ▽ Manganese
- ◇ Tungsten
- ◇ Silver

- ● Gold
- □ Iron ore
- ✕ Bauxite
- ⊗ Uranium
- ▲ Oil
- ■ Coal
- △ Natural gas
- ◇ Other minerals

Scale 1 : 60 000 000

Barranquilla
Valencia
Caracas
Maracaibo
Medellín
Bucaramanga
Georgetown
Cali
Bogotá
Quito
Belém
Manaus
Guayaquil
Iquitos
Fortaleza
Porto Velho
Serra Pelada
Recife
Maceió
Lima
Cusco
Aracaju
Pisco
Salvador
La Paz
Santa Cruz
Cuiabá
Belo Horizonte
Chuquicamata
Antofagasta
São Paulo
Rio de Janeiro
Resistencia
Asunción
Blumenau
Córdoba
Porto Alegre
Valparaíso
Rosario
Rio Grande
Mendoza
Montevideo
Concepción
Buenos Aires
Valdivia
Bahía Blanca
Mar del Plata

## Main industries

- □ Metal processing, vehicle manufacturing and shipbuilding
- ○ Electronic industry
- ○ Textiles
- ○ Wood and chemical industries
- ○ Food processing

Scale 1 : 60 000 000

Bogotá
Lima
Belo Horizonte
Rio de Janeiro
São Paulo
Santiago
Buenos Aires

## Population per sq km

- over 1000
- 501 – 1000
- 101 – 500
- 11 – 100
- 1 – 10
- less than 1

### Cities

- ● over 10 000 000
- ● 5 000 000 – 10 000 000
- ○ 1 000 000 – 5 000 000

Scale 1 : 60 000 000

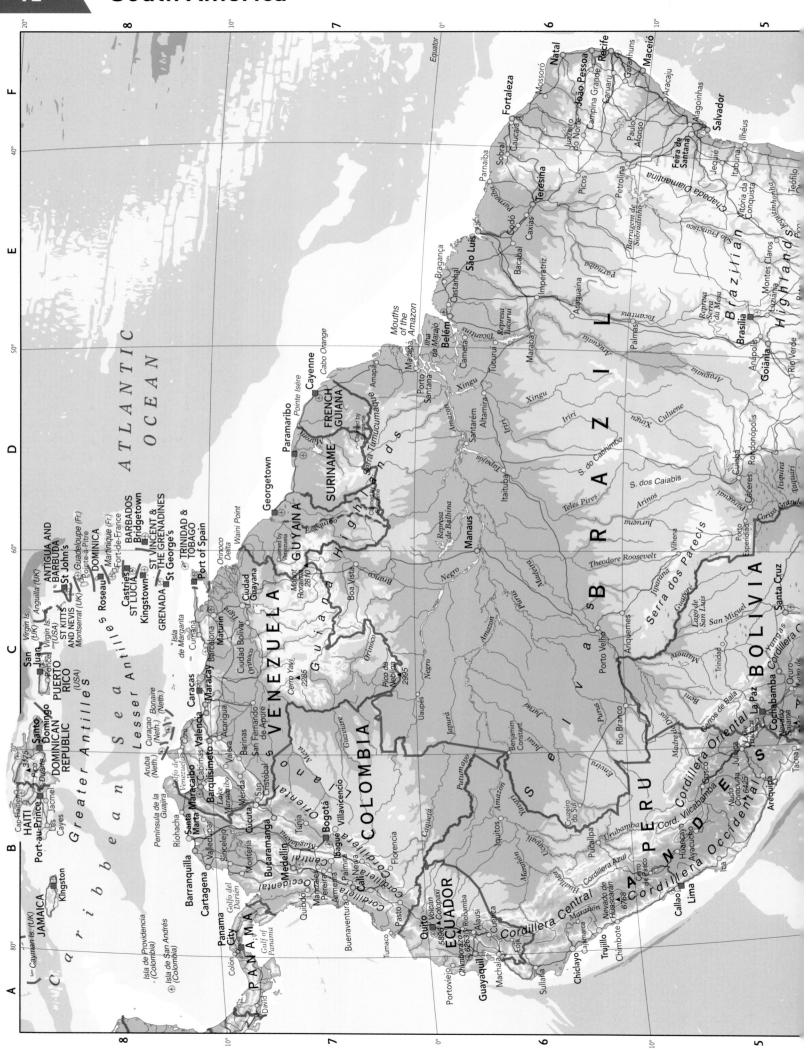

ATLANTIC OCEAN

Caribbean Sea

Greater Antilles

Lesser Antilles

Equator

20°
10°
0°
10°

80°
70°
60°
50°

**JAMAICA**
Cayman Is. (UK)
Kingston

Cap-Haïtien
**HAITI**
Port-au-Prince
Les Cayes
Jacmel

**DOMINICAN REPUBLIC**
Santo Domingo
3175 Pico Duarte

San Juan
Ponce
**PUERTO RICO** (USA)
Virgin Is. (UK)
Virgin Is. (USA)
Anguilla (UK)

**ANTIGUA AND BARBUDA**
St John's
**ST KITTS AND NEVIS**
Montserrat (UK)
Guadeloupe (Fr.)
Pointe-à-Pitre
**DOMINICA**
Roseau
Martinique (Fr.)
Fort-de-France
**ST LUCIA**
Castries
**BARBADOS**
Bridgetown
**ST VINCENT & THE GRENADINES**
Kingstown
**GRENADA**
St George's
**TRINIDAD & TOBAGO**
Port of Spain

Isla de Providencia (Colombia)
Isla de San Andrés (Colombia)

Colón
David
**PANAMA**
Panama City
Gulf of Panama
Golfo del Darién

Barranquilla
Cartagena
Santa Marta
**Maracaibo**
Riohacha
Peninsula de la Guajira
Aruba (Neth.)
Curaçao (Neth.)
Bonaire (Neth.)

Valledupar
Sincelejo
Montería
Lake Maracaibo
Golfo de Venezuela
Cabimas
Valencia
Barquisimeto
Valera
Mérida
San Cristóbal
Cúcuta
Bucaramanga
Tunja
**Maracay**
**Caracas**
Barcelona
Cumaná
Isla de Margarita
Maturín
**VENEZUELA**
Acarigua
Barinas
San Fernando de Apure
Ciudad Bolívar
Ciudad Guayana
Orinoco
Orinoco Delta
Waini Point
**Georgetown**
**GUYANA**
**SURINAME**
**Paramaribo**
**FRENCH GUIANA**
**Cayenne**
Pointe Isère
Cabo Orange

Mount Roraima 2810
Cerro Yavi 2285
Pico da Neblina 2995
Claimed by Venezuela
Claimed by Suriname
Claimed by Suriname

Quibdó
Manizales
Pereira
Armenia
Ibagué
Medellín
**Bogotá**
Villavicencio
**COLOMBIA**
Neiva
Cali
Palmira
Florencia
Cordillera Occidental
Cordillera Central
Cordillera Oriental
Llanos Orientales
Meta
Guaviare
Vaupés
Guainía

Buenaventura
Pasto
Tumaco
**ECUADOR**
**Quito**
Volcán Cotopaxi 5896
Chimborazo 6263
Portoviejo
Manta
**Guayaquil**
Machala
Sullana
Cuenca
Riobamba
Alausí

Amazon
Putumayo
Caquetá
Japurá
Iquitos
Cruzeiro do Sul
Pucallpa
Marañón
Ucayali
Huánuco
Chiclayo
Trujillo
Chimbote
Callao
**Lima**
**PERU**
Nevado de Huascarán 6768
Nevado Coropuna 6425
Cusco
Ayacucho
Arequipa
Cord. Vilcabamba
Cordillera Occidental
Cordillera Central
Cordillera Oriental
Juliaca
Tacna

Natal
João Pessoa
Recife
Maceió
Aracaju
**Salvador**
Mossoró
Campina Grande
Caruaru
Garanhuns
Alagoinhas
Ilhéus
Jequié
Itabuna
Teófilo
**Fortaleza**
Sobral
Caucaiá
Juazeiro do Norte
Picos
Petrolina
Crateús
**Teresina**
Parnaíba
Caxias
Codó
Bacabal
Imperatriz
**São Luís**
Castanhal
Bragança
**Belém**
Cametá
Tucuruí
Marabá
Santana
Macapá
Porto Santana
Ilha de Marajó
Mouths of the Amazon
Amapá

Jequié
Vitória da Conquista
Montes Claros
Ituiaba
Anápolis
**Brasília**
**Goiânia**
Rio Verde
Represa de Sobradinho
Barragem de Sobradinho
São Francisco
Chapada Diamantina
Brazilian Highlands
Serra da Mesa

Imperatriz
Araguaína
Palmas
Represa de Tucuruí
Tocantins
Araguaia
Xingu
Xingu
Iriri
Altamira
Itaituba
Santarém
Tapajós
S. do Cachimbo
S. dos Caiabis
Culuene
Teles Pires
Arinos
Juruena
Theodore Roosevelt
Serra dos Parecis
Guaporé
Jiparaná
Porto Velho
Ariquemes
Vilhena
Rondonópolis
Cuiabá
Cáceres
Iténez
Itiquira
Coxim Grande
Pantanal

**BRAZIL**
Selvas

**Manaus**
Represa de Balbina
Negro
Branco
Boa Vista
Uaupés
Amazon
Negro
Madeira
Purus
Juruá
Purus
Benjamin Constant
Javari
Madre de Dios
Beni
Mamoré
Rio Branco
Trinidad
Lago de San Miguel
San Miguel
Santa Cruz
Cochabamba
**La Paz**
**BOLIVIA**
Oruro
Sucre
Potosí
Cordillera Oriental
Cordillera Occidental
Cerros de Bala
Titicaca
Nudo Coropuna

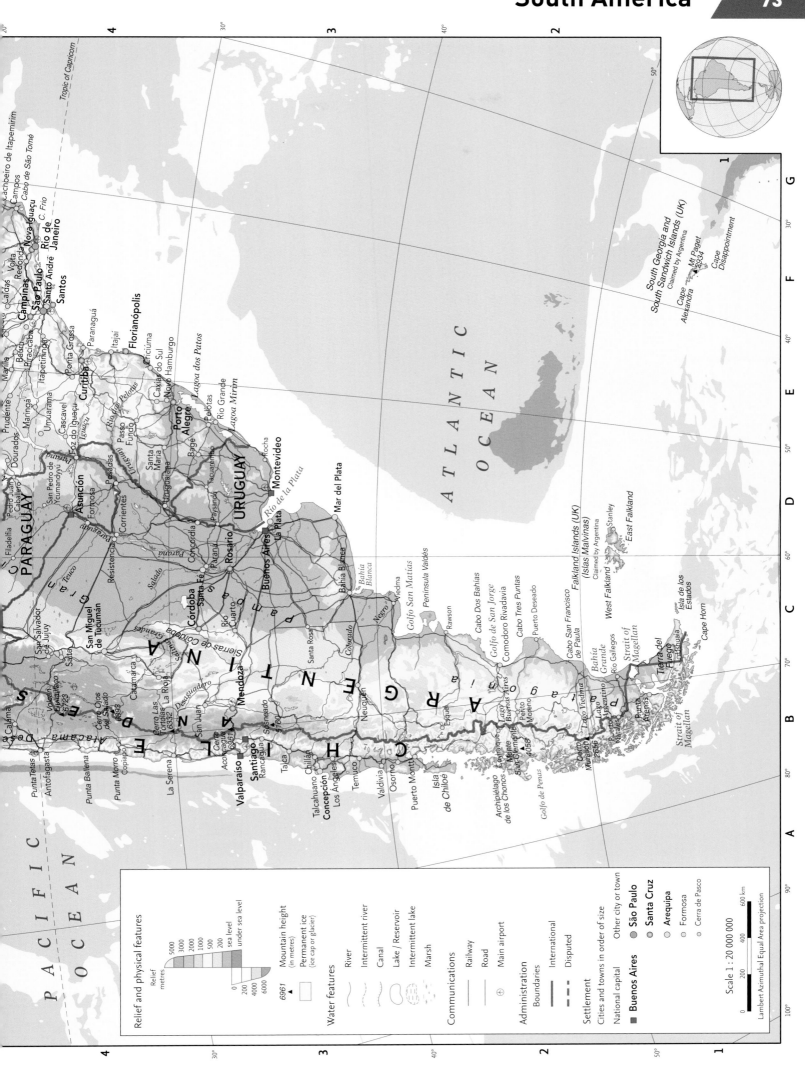

**Relief and physical features**

Relief
metres

5000
3000
2000
1000
500
200
sea level
under sea level

0
200
4000
6000

6961 ▲ Mountain height
(in metres)

Permanent ice
(ice cap or glacier)

**Water features**

River
Intermittent river
Canal
Lake / Reservoir
Intermittent lake
Marsh

**Communications**

Railway
Road
⊕ Main airport

**Administration**

Boundaries
International
Disputed

**Settlement**

Cities and towns in order of size

National capital

■ Buenos Aires   ● São Paulo
● Santa Cruz
● Arequipa
○ Formosa
○ Cerra de Pasco

Other city or town

Scale 1 : 20 000 000

0    200    400    600 km

Lambert Azimuthal Equal Area projection

PACIFIC OCEAN

ATLANTIC OCEAN

PARAGUAY

URUGUAY

ARGENTINA

Tropic of Capricorn

São Paulo
Santos
Santo André
Campinas
Rio de Janeiro
Nova Iguaçu
C. Frio
Cabo de São Tomé
Cacheoiro de Itapemirim
Campos
Volta Redonda
Caldas

Curitiba
Florianópolis
Paranaguá
Itajaí
Criciúma
Ponta Grossa
Porto Alegre
Caxias do Sul
Novo Hamburgo
Pelotas
Rio Grande
Lagoa dos Patos
Lagoa Mirim

Asunción
Formosa
Corrientes
Resistencia
Posadas
Santa Maria
Passo Fundo
Bagé
Uruguaiana
Tacuarembó
Paysandú
Concordia
Paraná
Santa Fé
Rosario
Buenos Aires
La Plata
Montevideo
Rocha
Mar del Plata

Río de la Plata

San Miguel de Tucumán
Córdoba
Catamarca
La Rioja
San Juan
Mendoza
San Luis
Río Cuarto
Santa Rosa
Sierras de Córdoba

Valparaíso
Santiago
Rancagua
Talca
Chillán
Concepción
Talcahuano
Los Ángeles
Temuco
Valdivia
Osorno
Puerto Montt
Isla de Chiloé

Cerro Aconcagua 6961
Cerro Tupungato 6552

Bahía Blanca
Viedma
Golfo San Matías
Península Valdés
Rawson
Cabo Dos Bahías
Golfo de San Jorge
Comodoro Rivadavia
Cabo Tres Puntas
Puerto Deseado
Cabo San Francisco de Paula
Bahía Grande
Río Gallegos
Strait of Magellan
Punta Arenas
Puerto Natales
Tierra del Fuego
Ushuaia
Isla de los Estados
Cape Horn

Lago Buenos Aires
Lago Viedma
Lago Argentino
Perito Moreno

Falkland Islands (UK)
(Islas Malvinas)
Claimed by Argentina
West Falkland
East Falkland
Stanley

South Georgia and
South Sandwich Islands (UK)
Claimed by Argentina
Cape Alexandra
M Paget 2934
Cape Disappointment

# **Brazil** Population

www Brazilian Institute of Geography and Statistics
www.ibge.gov.br/en

**Population per sq km**

- over 50
- 11 – 50
- 1 – 10
- less than 1

**Cities**

- ● over 10 000 000
- ● 5 000 000 – 10 000 000
- ○ 1 000 000 – 5 000 000
- ○ 500 000 – 1 000 000
- ○ 100 000 – 500 000

Scale 1 : 35 000 000

## Population growth, 2000 – 2060

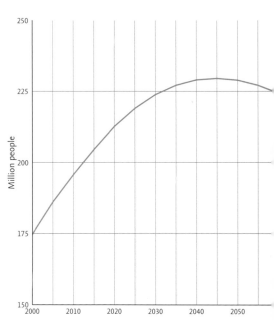

## Urban and rural population, 1940 – 2019

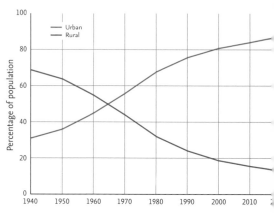

## Largest urban agglomerations, 2018

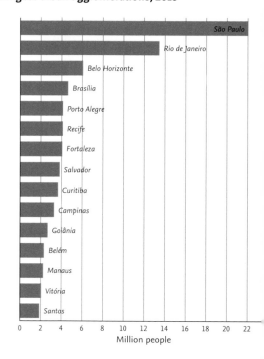

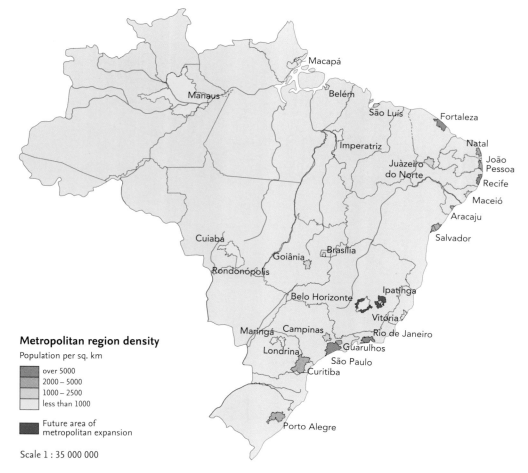

**Metropolitan region density**

Population per sq. km

- over 5000
- 2000 – 5000
- 1000 – 2500
- less than 1000

- Future area of metropolitan expansion

Scale 1 : 35 000 000

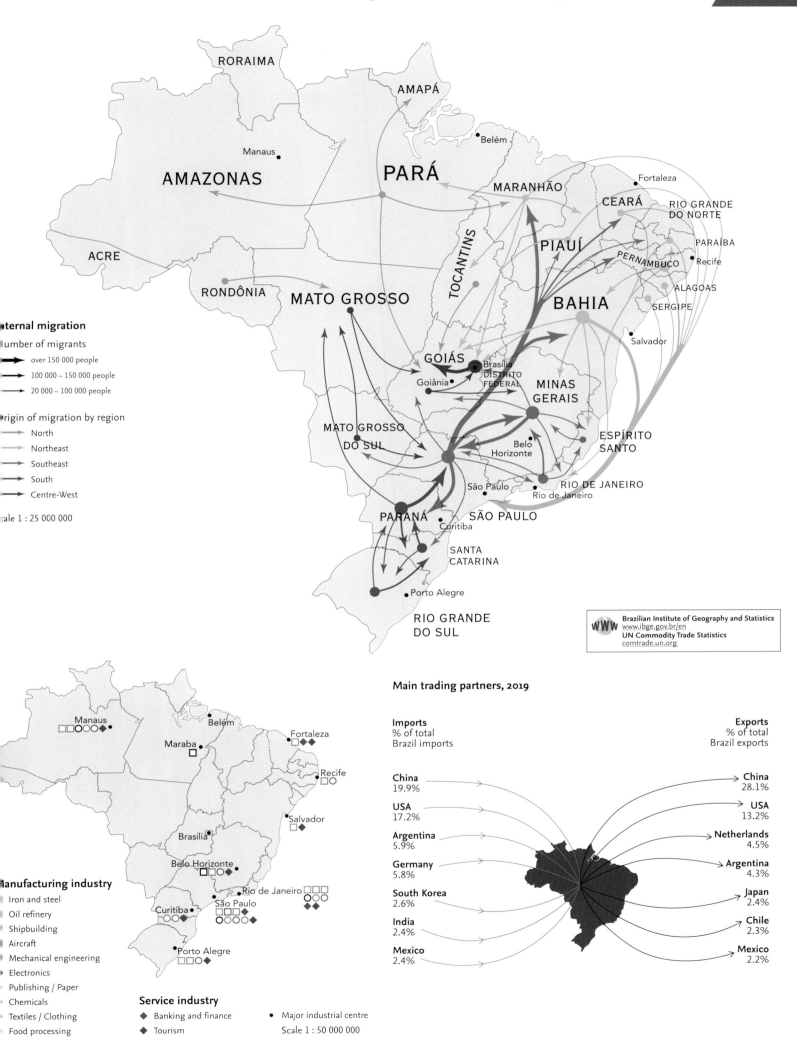

RORAIMA

AMAPÁ

• Belém

Manaus •

**AMAZONAS**

**PARÁ**

Fortaleza •

MARANHÃO

CEARÁ

RIO GRANDE
DO NORTE

ACRE

PIAUÍ

PARAÍBA

PERNAMBUCO

Recife •

RONDÔNIA •

**MATO GROSSO**

TOCANTINS

**BAHIA**

ALAGOAS

SERGIPE

**Internal migration**

**Number of migrants**

→ over 150 000 people

→ 100 000 – 150 000 people

→ 20 000 – 100 000 people

**Origin of migration by region**

→ North

→ Northeast

→ Southeast

→ South

→ Centre-West

Scale 1 : 25 000 000

GOIÁS

Brasília
DISTRITO
FEDERAL

Goiânia •

**MINAS
GERAIS**

Salvador •

ESPÍRITO
SANTO

**MATO GROSSO
DO SUL**

Belo •
Horizonte

São Paulo •

RIO DE JANEIRO

Rio de Janeiro

**PARANÁ**

Curitiba •

**SÃO PAULO**

SANTA
CATARINA

• Porto Alegre

RIO GRANDE
DO SUL

WWW **Brazilian Institute of Geography and Statistics**
www.ibge.gov.br/en
**UN Commodity Trade Statistics**
comtrade.un.org

**Main trading partners, 2019**

**Imports**
% of total
Brazil imports

**Exports**
% of total
Brazil exports

| | |
|---|---|
| **China** 19.9% | **China** 28.1% |
| **USA** 17.2% | **USA** 13.2% |
| **Argentina** 5.9% | **Netherlands** 4.5% |
| **Germany** 5.8% | **Argentina** 4.3% |
| **South Korea** 2.6% | **Japan** 2.4% |
| **India** 2.4% | **Chile** 2.3% |
| **Mexico** 2.4% | **Mexico** 2.2% |

Manaus
□□○○○◆ •

• Belém

Fortaleza
□◆◆

Maraba •
□

Recife
□○

Salvador
□◆

Brasília •

Belo Horizonte •
□○□◆

Rio de Janeiro □□□
○○○
◆◆

**Manufacturing industry**

Iron and steel

Oil refinery

Shipbuilding

Aircraft

Mechanical engineering

Electronics

Publishing / Paper

Chemicals

Textiles / Clothing

Food processing

Curitiba •
○○○◆

São Paulo •
□□□◆
○○○○◆

• Porto Alegre
□□○◆

**Service industry**

◆ Banking and finance

◆ Tourism

• Major industrial centre

Scale 1 : 50 000 000

Part of the Amazon rainforest in Rhôndonia, Brazil. The straight lines in the forest show where whole blocks of trees have been cut down.

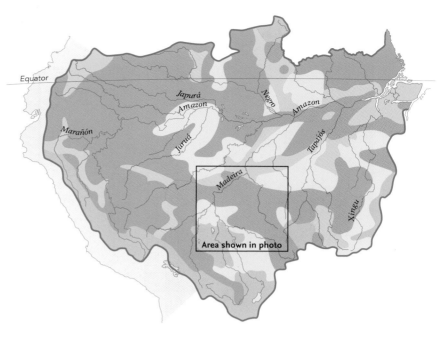

## State of the Amazon rainforest

**Rainforest**

| | |
|---|---|
| ▨ | Deforested by 2009 |
| ▨ | High threat of deforestation |
| ☐ | Medium threat of deforestation |
| ▨ | Low threat of deforestation |

**Other vegetation**

| | |
|---|---|
| ▨ | Grassland or woodland |
| ☐ | No data |
| —— | Boundary of Amazon Basin rainforest |

Scale 1 : 35 000 000

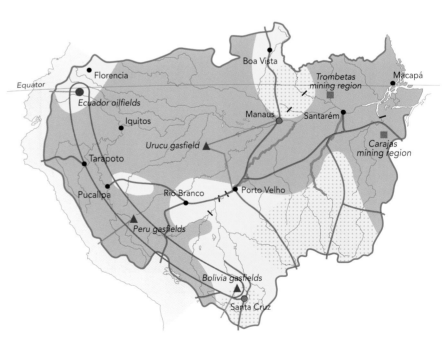

## Threats to the Amazon rainforest

**Extractive industry**

● Oilfield
▲ Gasfield
■ Mining region

—— Main highway
—I— Major dam
—— Industrial waterway
—— Pipeline
—— Boundary of Western Amazon zone of oil and gas development

**Main population centres**

● over 1 000 000
● 100 000 – 500 000

**Area of agricultural expansion**

☐ Pasture for extensive cattle ranching

▨ Extensive cropping: for stock feed (soybeans, sorghum, maize), industrial crops (oil palm, sunflower, cotton) and biofuels (sugar cane, maize)

Scale 1 : 35 000 000

A S I A

E U R O P E

*Mediterranean Sea*

Gulf of Gabes

Gulf of Sirte

Madeira

Canary Islands

Jebel Toubkal 4167 Atlas Mountains

Suez Canal
Sinai

Qattara Depression

*Libyan Desert*

Nile

Lake Nasser

Nubian Desert

Tropic of Cancer

S A H A R A

Hoggar
Mont Tahat 2918

Plateau du Djado
Tibesti
Emi Koussi 3415

Mt Gréboun 1944
Massif de l'Aïr

Bodélé

Darfur
Jebel Marra 3088

Red Sea

Gulf of Aden

Ras Dejen 4620
Lake Tana

Cape Verde
Santo Antão
Boa Vista
Fogo
Santiago

El Djouf

Niger

Lake Chad

Chari

Ethiopian Highlands

Tropic of Ca

Sénégal
Gambia

S      a      h      e      l

Fouta Djallon

Bani
Black Volta
White Volta

Niger

Jos Plateau

Benue

Sudd

Blue Nile
Gezira
White Nile
Atbara

Lake Volta

Benue

Cameroon Highlands

Logone

Wabe Shebele/Wenz

Cape Palmas

Bight of Benin
Gulf of Guinea

Mont Cameroun 4095
Bioko

Níger

Lake Turkana

Príncipe
São Tomé

Sangha
Ubangi

Congo

Aruwimi

Lake Albert

Mount Stanley 5109
Lake Edward

Mount Kenya 5199

Jubba

Equator

A T L A N T I C
O C E A N

Congo Basin

Kasai

Kwilu

Congo
Lake Tanganyika

Lake Victoria

Kilimanjaro 5895
Masai Steppe

I N D I A N

O C E A N

Equ

Ascension

Cuango

Cuanza

Chaîne des Mitumba

Lake Mweru

Great Rift Valley

Pemba Island
Zanzibar Island
Mafia Island

Rufiji

St Helena

Bié Plateau
Huíla Plateau

Cubango

Muchinga Mts
Luangwa

Lake Nyasa

Comoro Islands

Aldabra Islands

Cunene

Namib Desert

Etosha Pan

Zambezi
Victoria Falls

Lake Kariba
Zambezi
Matabele Upland

Save

Mozambique Channel

Madagascar

Réunic

Makgadikgadi

Kalahari Desert

Limpopo

Tropic of Capr

Orange

Vaal

Thabana Ntlenyana 3482
Drakensberg

Great Karoo

Cape of Good Hope

Cape Agulhas

**Relief and physical features**

Relief
metres
5000
3000
2000
1000
500
200
sea level
under sea level
0
200
4000
6000

▲ 5895   Mountain height (in metres)

Scale 1 : 42 000 000

0     500     1000 km

Lambert Azimuthal Equal Area projection

**Cross-section**

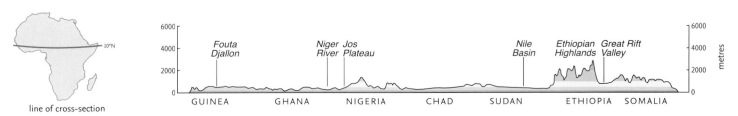

line of cross-section

10°N

6000
4000
2000
0

Fouta Djallon

Niger River
Jos Plateau

Nile Basin

Ethiopian Highlands
Great Rift Valley

6000
4000
2000
0

metres

GUINEA     GHANA     NIGERIA     CHAD     SUDAN     ETHIOPIA     SOMALIA

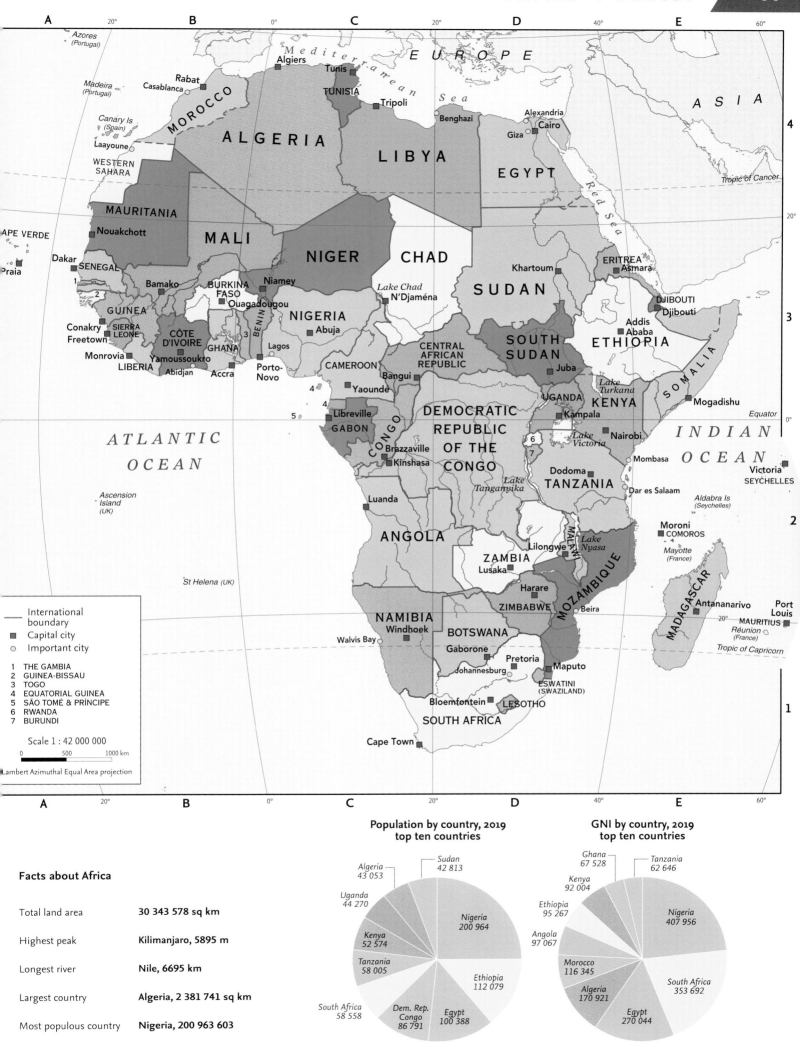

## Facts about Africa

| | |
|---|---|
| Total land area | **30 343 578 sq km** |
| Highest peak | **Kilimanjaro, 5895 m** |
| Longest river | **Nile, 6695 km** |
| Largest country | **Algeria, 2 381 741 sq km** |
| Most populous country | **Nigeria, 200 963 603** |

### Population by country, 2019
top ten countries

Sudan 42 813
Algeria 43 053
Uganda 44 270
Kenya 52 574
Tanzania 58 005
South Africa 58 558
Dem. Rep. Congo 86 791
Egypt 100 388
Ethiopia 112 079
Nigeria 200 964

Population in thousands

### GNI by country, 2019
top ten countries

Ghana 67 528
Tanzania 62 646
Kenya 92 004
Ethiopia 95 267
Angola 97 067
Morocco 116 345
Algeria 170 921
Egypt 270 044
South Africa 353 692
Nigeria 407 956

Gross National Income in US $ millions

### Map legend

— International boundary
■ Capital city
○ Important city

1 THE GAMBIA
2 GUINEA-BISSAU
3 TOGO
4 EQUATORIAL GUINEA
5 SÃO TOMÉ & PRÍNCIPE
6 RWANDA
7 BURUNDI

Scale 1 : 42 000 000

0    500    1000 km

Lambert Azimuthal Equal Area projection

# Africa Climate

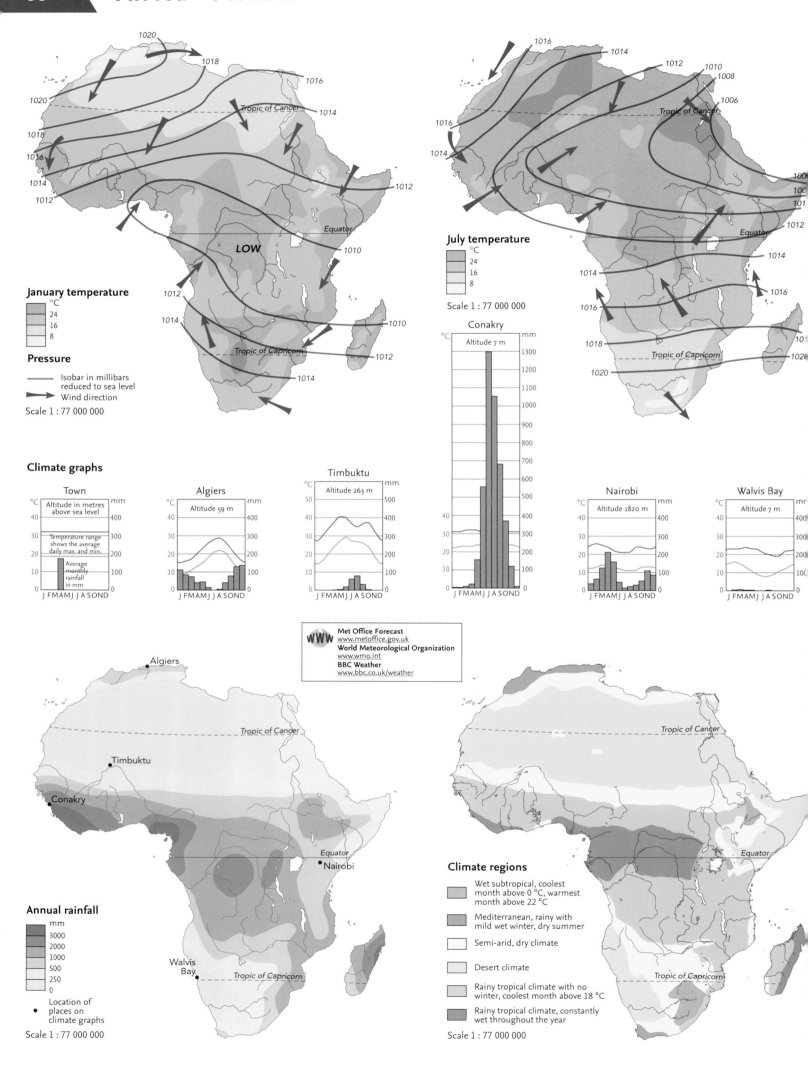

**January temperature**
°C
24
16
8

**Pressure**
— Isobar in millibars reduced to sea level
➤ Wind direction

Scale 1 : 77 000 000

1020
1018
1016
1014
1012
Tropic of Cancer
1016
1014
1012
Equator
**LOW**
1012
1014
Tropic of Capricorn
1012
1010
1014

**July temperature**
°C
24
16
8

Scale 1 : 77 000 000

1016
1014
1012
1010
1008
Tropic of Cancer
1006
1016
1014
Equator
1012
1014
1016
1018
1020
Tropic of Capricorn

**Climate graphs**

Town
°C | Altitude in metres above sea level | mm
40 | | 400
30 | Temperature range shows the average daily max. and min. | 300
20 | | 200
| Average monthly rainfall in mm |
0 | | 0
J F M A M J J A S O N D

Algiers
°C Altitude 59 m mm
40 | 400
30 | 300
20 | 200
10 | 100
0 | 0
J F M A M J J A S O N D

Timbuktu
°C Altitude 263 m mm
50 | 500
40 | 400
30 | 300
20 | 200
10 | 100
0 | 0
J F M A M J J A S O N D

Conakry
°C Altitude 7 m mm
| 1300
| 1200
| 1100
| 1000
| 900
| 800
| 700
| 600
40 | 500
30 | 400
20 | 300
10 | 200
0 | 100
| 0
J F M A M J J A S O N D

Nairobi
°C Altitude 1820 m mm
40 | 400
30 | 300
20 | 200
10 | 100
0 | 0
J F M A M J J A S O N D

Walvis Bay
°C Altitude 7 m mm
40 | 400
30 | 300
20 | 200
10 | 100
0 | 0
J F M A M J J A S O N D

WWW
**Met Office Forecast**
www.metoffice.gov.uk
**World Meteorological Organization**
www.wmo.int
**BBC Weather**
www.bbc.co.uk/weather

Algiers
Tropic of Cancer
Timbuktu
Conakry
Equator
Nairobi

**Annual rainfall**
mm
3000
2000
1000
500
250
0

• Location of places on climate graphs

Walvis Bay
Tropic of Capricorn

Scale 1 : 77 000 000

Tropic of Cancer
Equator

**Climate regions**

Wet subtropical, coolest month above 0 °C, warmest month above 22 °C

Mediterranean, rainy with mild wet winter, dry summer

Semi-arid, dry climate

Desert climate

Rainy tropical climate with no winter, coolest month above 18 °C

Rainy tropical climate, constantly wet throughout the year

Tropic of Capricorn

Scale 1 : 77 000 000

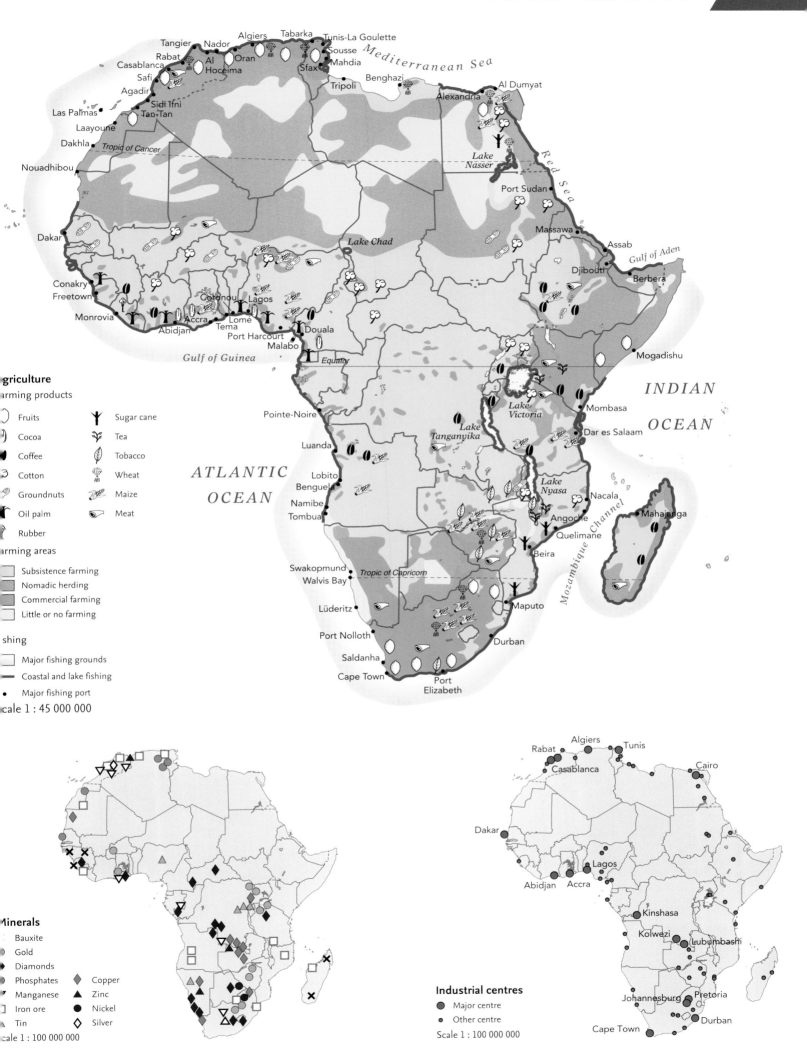

Tangier
Algiers
Tabarka
Tunis-La Goulette
Nador
Rabat
Al
Hoceima
Oran
Sousse
Mahdia
Casablanca
Sfax
Safi
Benghazi
Agadir
Tripoli
Sidi Ifni
Al Dumyat
Tan-Tan
Alexandria
Las Palmas
Laayoune
Dakhla
*Tropic of Cancer*
*Mediterranean Sea*
*Lake Nasser*
*Red Sea*
Nouadhibou
Port Sudan
Massawa
Dakar
Assab
*Lake Chad*
*Gulf of Aden*
Djibouti
Berbera
Conakry
Freetown
Cotonou
Lagos
Monrovia
Lomé
Abidjan
Accra
Tema
Port Harcourt
Douala
Malabo
*Gulf of Guinea*
*Equator*
Mogadishu
*INDIAN OCEAN*
Pointe-Noire
*Lake Victoria*
Mombasa
Luanda
*Lake Tanganyika*
Dar es Salaam
*ATLANTIC OCEAN*
Lobito
Benguela
Namibe
*Lake Nyasa*
Nacala
Tombua
Angoche
Quelimane
Mahajanga
*Mozambique Channel*
Beira
Swakopmund
*Tropic of Capricorn*
Walvis Bay
Maputo
Lüderitz
Durban
Port Nolloth
Saldanha
Cape Town
Port Elizabeth

**Agriculture**

**Farming products**

| | | | |
|---|---|---|---|
| Fruits | | Sugar cane | |
| Cocoa | | Tea | |
| Coffee | | Tobacco | |
| Cotton | | Wheat | |
| Groundnuts | | Maize | |
| Oil palm | | Meat | |
| Rubber | | | |

**Farming areas**

- Subsistence farming
- Nomadic herding
- Commercial farming
- Little or no farming

**Fishing**

- Major fishing grounds
- Coastal and lake fishing
- Major fishing port

Scale 1 : 45 000 000

**Minerals**

- Bauxite
- Gold
- Diamonds
- Phosphates
- Manganese
- Iron ore
- Tin

- Copper
- Zinc
- Nickel
- Silver

Scale 1 : 100 000 000

**Industrial centres**

- Major centre
- Other centre

Scale 1 : 100 000 000

Algiers
Rabat
Tunis
Casablanca
Cairo
Dakar
Lagos
Abidjan
Accra
Kinshasa
Kolwezi
Lubumbashi
Johannesburg
Pretoria
Cape Town
Durban

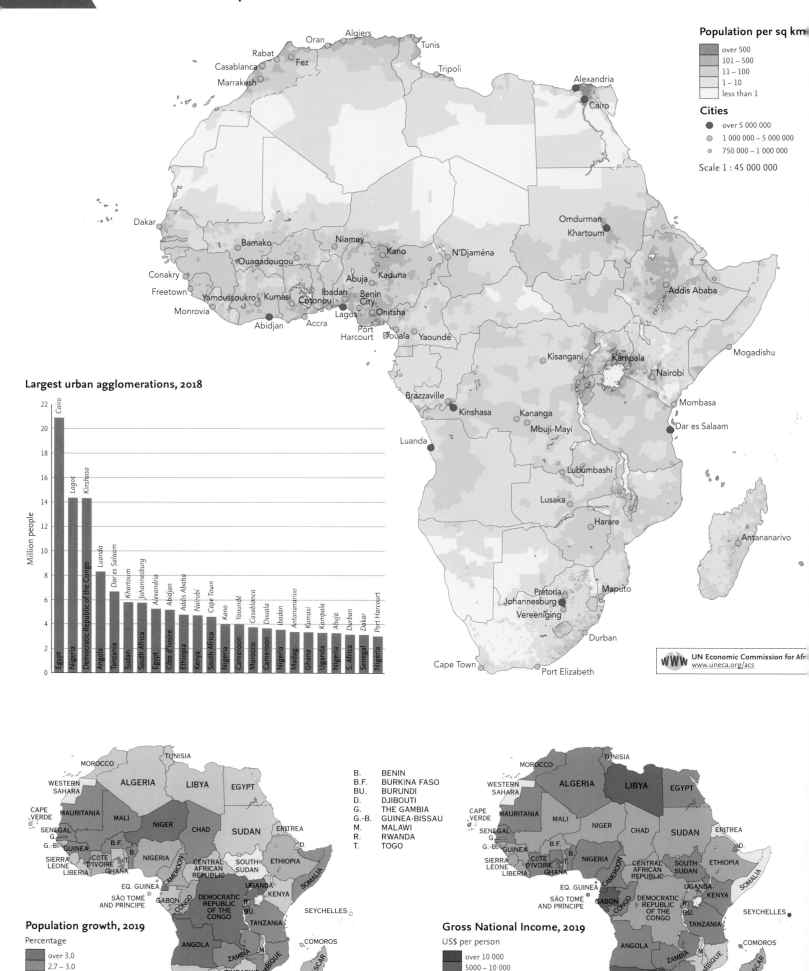

Population per sq km
- over 500
- 101 – 500
- 11 – 100
- 1 – 10
- less than 1

Cities
- over 5 000 000
- 1 000 000 – 5 000 000
- 750 000 – 1 000 000

Scale 1 : 45 000 000

Oran
Algiers
Rabat
Casablanca
Fez
Marrakesh
Tunis
Tripoli
Alexandria
Cairo
Dakar
Bamako
Niamey
Kano
N'Djaména
Omdurman
Khartoum
Ouagadougou
Conakry
Abuja
Kaduna
Freetown
Yamoussoukro
Kumasi
Ibadan
Cotonou
Benin City
Addis Ababa
Monrovia
Onitsha
Abidjan
Accra
Lagos
Port Harcourt
Douala
Yaoundé
Kisangani
Kampala
Mogadishu
Nairobi
Brazzaville
Mombasa
Kinshasa
Kananga
Dar es Salaam
Luanda
Mbuji-Mayi
Lubumbashi
Lusaka
Harare
Antananarivo
Pretoria
Johannesburg
Vereeniging
Maputo
Durban
Cape Town
Port Elizabeth

www **UN Economic Commission for Afr**
www.uneca.org/acs

## Largest urban agglomerations, 2018

Million people

Cairo — Egypt
Lagos — Nigeria
Kinshasa — Democratic Republic of the Congo
Luanda — Angola
Dar es Salaam — Tanzania
Khartoum — Sudan
Johannesburg — South Africa
Alexandria — Egypt
Abidjan — Côte d'Ivoire
Addis Ababa — Ethiopia
Nairobi — Kenya
Cape Town — South Africa
Kano — Nigeria
Yaoundé — Cameroon
Casablanca — Morocco
Douala — Cameroon
Ibadan — Nigeria
Antananarivo — Madag.
Kumasi — Ghana
Kampala — Uganda
Abuja — Nigeria
Durban — S. Africa
Dakar — Senegal
Port Harcourt — Nigeria

## Population growth, 2019

Percentage
- over 3.0
- 2.7 – 3.0
- 2.5 – 2.7
- 1.0 – 2.5
- less than 1.0
- no data

Scale 1 : 100 000 000

MOROCCO
TUNISIA
WESTERN SAHARA
ALGERIA
LIBYA
EGYPT
CAPE VERDE
MAURITANIA
MALI
NIGER
CHAD
SUDAN
ERITREA
SENEGAL
G.
G.-B.
GUINEA
B.F.
NIGERIA
CENTRAL AFRICAN REPUBLIC
SOUTH SUDAN
ETHIOPIA
SIERRA LEONE
CÔTE D'IVOIRE
GHANA
CAMEROON
SOMALIA
LIBERIA
EQ. GUINEA
UGANDA
KENYA
SÃO TOMÉ AND PRÍNCIPE
GABON
CONGO
DEMOCRATIC REPUBLIC OF THE CONGO
BU.
TANZANIA
SEYCHELLES
ANGOLA
ZAMBIA
M
MOZAMBIQUE
COMOROS
ZIMBABWE
MADAGASCAR
MAURITIUS
NAMIBIA
BOTSWANA
ESWATINI (SWAZILAND)
SOUTH AFRICA
LESOTHO

B.      BENIN
B.F.    BURKINA FASO
BU.     BURUNDI
D.      DJIBOUTI
G.      THE GAMBIA
G.-B.   GUINEA-BISSAU
M.      MALAWI
R.      RWANDA
T.      TOGO

## Gross National Income, 2019

US$ per person
- over 10 000
- 5000 – 10 000
- 1000 – 5000
- 500 – 1000
- less than 500
- no data

Scale 1 : 100 000 000

MOROCCO
TUNISIA
WESTERN SAHARA
ALGERIA
LIBYA
EGYPT
CAPE VERDE
MAURITANIA
MALI
NIGER
CHAD
SUDAN
ERITREA
SENEGAL
G.-B.
GUINEA
B.F.
NIGERIA
CENTRAL AFRICAN REPUBLIC
SOUTH SUDAN
ETHIOPIA
SIERRA LEONE
CÔTE D'IVOIRE
GHANA
CAMEROON
SOMALIA
LIBERIA
EQ. GUINEA
UGANDA
KENYA
SÃO TOMÉ AND PRÍNCIPE
GABON
CONGO
DEMOCRATIC REPUBLIC OF THE CONGO
BU.
R.
TANZANIA
SEYCHELLES
ANGOLA
ZAMBIA
MOZAMBIQUE
COMOROS
ZIMBABWE
MADAGASCAR
MAURITIUS
NAMIBIA
BOTSWANA
ESWATINI (SWAZILAND)
SOUTH AFRICA
LESOTHO

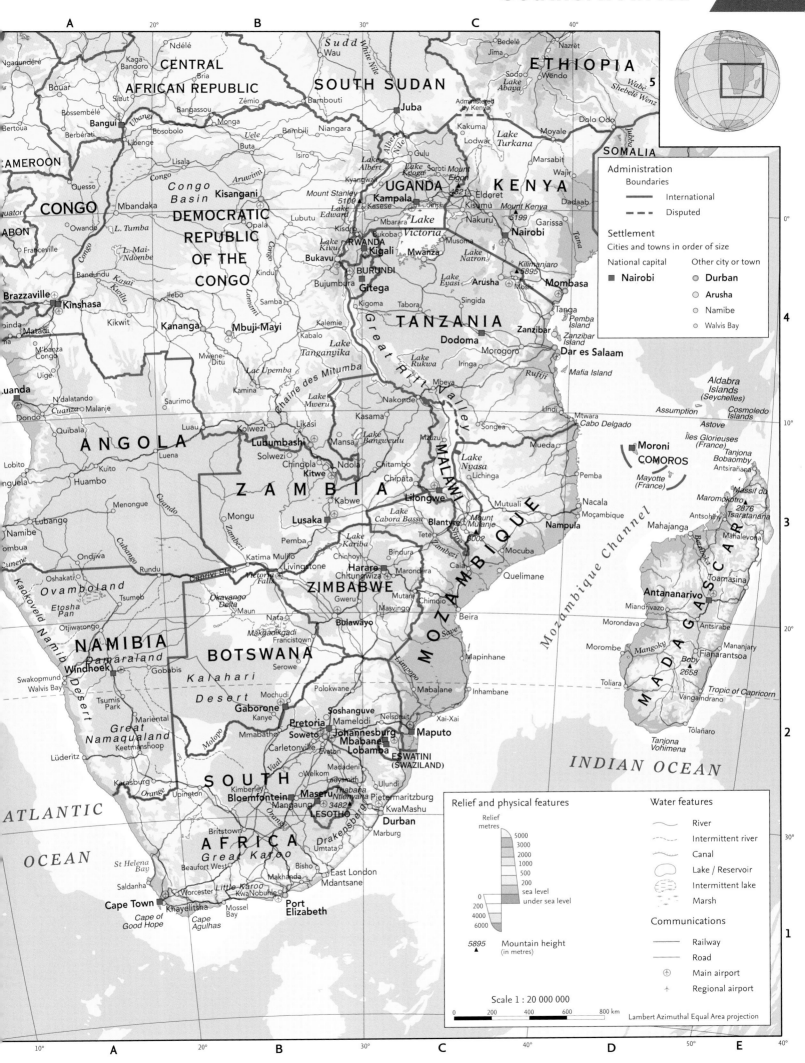

Ndélé
CENTRAL
AFRICAN REPUBLIC
Sudd
Wau
SOUTH SUDAN
White Nile
ETHIOPIA
Bedele
Jima
Nazrēt
5
Ngaundéré
Kaga
Bandoro
Sibut
Bangassou
Zémio
Bambouti
Juba
Administered by Kenya
Kakuma
Lodwar
Lake Turkana
Sodo
Lake Abaya
Wendo
Dolo Odo
Wabē Shebelē Wenz
Bouar
Bossembélé
Bangui
Bsobolo
Monga
Niangara
Gulu
Moyale
SOMALIA
Bertoua
Berbérati
Ubangi
Libenge
Uele
Bambili
Isiro
Juba
Dadaab
Jubba
CAMEROON
Ouesso
Lisala
Aruwimi
Buta
Lake Albert
Kyangwali
Mount Elgon
4321
Soroti
Eldoret
Marsabit
Wajir
Owando
Mbandaka
Congo
Congo Basin
Kisangani
Mount Stanley
5109
Lake Edward
Kasese
Kampala
UGANDA
Jinja
Kisumu
Nakuru
Mount Kenya
5199
Garissa
Nairobi
KENYA
GABON
Franceville
L. Tumba
DEMOCRATIC REPUBLIC OF THE CONGO
Opala
Lubutu
Lake Kivu
Bukavu
RWANDA
Kigali
Mbarara
Bukoba
Lake Victoria
Mwanza
Musoma
Lake Natron
Kilimanjaro
5895
Mombasa
CONGO
L. Mai-Ndombe
Kindu
BURUNDI
Bujumbura
Gitega
Kigoma
Lake Eyasi
Arusha
Moshi
Tanga
Brazzaville
Kinshasa
Bandundu
Ilebo
Kasai
Kwilu
Lomami
Samba
Kalemie
Kigoma
Tabora
Singida
Pemba Island
M'banza Congo
Matadi
Kikwit
Kananga
Mbuji-Mayi
Lac Upemba
Lake Tanganyika
Kabalo
TANZANIA
Dodoma
Morogoro
Dar es Salaam
Zanzibar
Zanzibar Island
4
Luanda
N'dalatando
Cuanza
Malanje
Mwene-Ditu
Kamina
Great Rift Valley
Lake Rukwa
Iringa
Rufiji
Mafia Island
Dondo
Uige
Chaine des Mitumba
Saurimo
Lake Mweru
Kasama
Mbeya
Nakonde
Lindi
Mtwara
Cabo Delgado
Assumption
Aldabra Islands (Seychelles)
Cosmoledo Islands
Luanda
Quibala
Cuanza
Luau
Kolwezi
Likasi
Lake Bangweulu
Mansa
Mzuzu
Songea
Mueda
Astove
Íles Glorieuses (France)
ANGOLA
Lobito
Benguela
Kuito
Huambo
Lubumbashi
Solwezi
Chingola
Kitwe
Ndola
Chitambo
Chipata
MALAWI
Lake Nyasa
Lichinga
Pemba
Moroni
COMOROS
Tanjona Bobaomby
Antsiranana
Namibe
Menongue
ZAMBIA
Kabwe
Lilongwe
Blantyre
Mount Mulanje
3002
Nacala
Moçambique
Mayotte (France)
Maromokotro
2876
Tsaratanana
Massif du Tsaratanana
Lombua
Lubango
Cuando
Mongu
Lusaka
Lake Cabora Bassa
Tete
MOZAMBIQUE
Mocuba
Mahajanga
Antsohihy
Mahalevona
Namibe
Ondjiva
Cubango
Katima Mulilo
Lake Kariba
Chinhoyi
Bindura
Caia
Quelimane
Mozambique Channel
MADAGASCAR
Cunene
Oshakati
Rundu
Caprivi Strip
Victoria Falls
Livingstone
Harare
Chitungwiza
Marondera
Beira
Mahanga
Antananarivo
Toamasina
Kaokoveld
Etosha Pan
Tsumeb
Okavango Delta
Maun
Gweru
ZIMBABWE
Masvingo
Mutare
Chimoio
Save
Miandrivazo
Morondava
Antsirabe
Ovamboland
Damaraland
Otjiwarongo
Nata
Makgadikgadi
Bulawayo
Mapinhane
Morombe
Mangoky
Fianarantsoa
Mananjary
NAMIBIA
Windhoek
Gobabis
Kalahari Desert
Francistown
Serowe
Limpopo
Mabalane
Inhambane
Boby 2658
Toliara
Vangaindrano
Tropic of Capricorn
Swakopmund
Walvis Bay
Namib Desert
Tsumis Park
BOTSWANA
Gaborone
Mochudi
Kanye
Polokwane
Xai-Xai
Maputo
INDIAN OCEAN
Tanjona Vohimena
Great Namaqualand
Mariental
Molopo
Mmabatho
Soshanguve
Mamelodi
Nelspruit
Xai-Xai
Maputo
Lüderitz
Keetmanshoop
Pretoria
Soweto
Johannesburg
Mbabane
ESWATINI (SWAZILAND)
Karasburg
Orange
Upington
Vaal
Carletonville
Evaton
Lobamba
Madadeni
Welkom
Ladysmith
Ulundi
Pietermaritzburg
KwaMashu
Kimberley
Bloemfontein
Mangaung
Maseru
LESOTHO
Thabana Ntlenyana 3482
Durban
Marburg
Saldanha
St Helena Bay
Britstown
SOUTH AFRICA
Great Karoo
Umtata
Bisho
East London
Mdantsane
ATLANTIC OCEAN
Beaufort West
Little Karoo
Makhanda
Cape Town
Khayelitsha
Cape of Good Hope
Mossel Bay
Cape Agulhas
Worcester
KwaNobuhle
Port Elizabeth
30°

**Administration**

Boundaries

——— International

- - - - Disputed

**Settlement**

Cities and towns in order of size

National capital | Other city or town
■ Nairobi | ● Durban
| ◉ Arusha
| ○ Namibe
| ∘ Walvis Bay

**Relief and physical features**

Relief metres
5000
3000
2000
1000
500
200
sea level
0
200 under sea level
4000
6000

5895 ▲ Mountain height (in metres)

Scale 1 : 20 000 000

0   200   400   600   800 km

Lambert Azimuthal Equal Area projection

**Water features**

〰 River

〜 Intermittent river

~ Canal

◯ Lake / Reservoir

⬭ Intermittent lake

▨ Marsh

**Communications**

——— Railway

——— Road

⊕ Main airport

✈ Regional airport

# Northern Africa

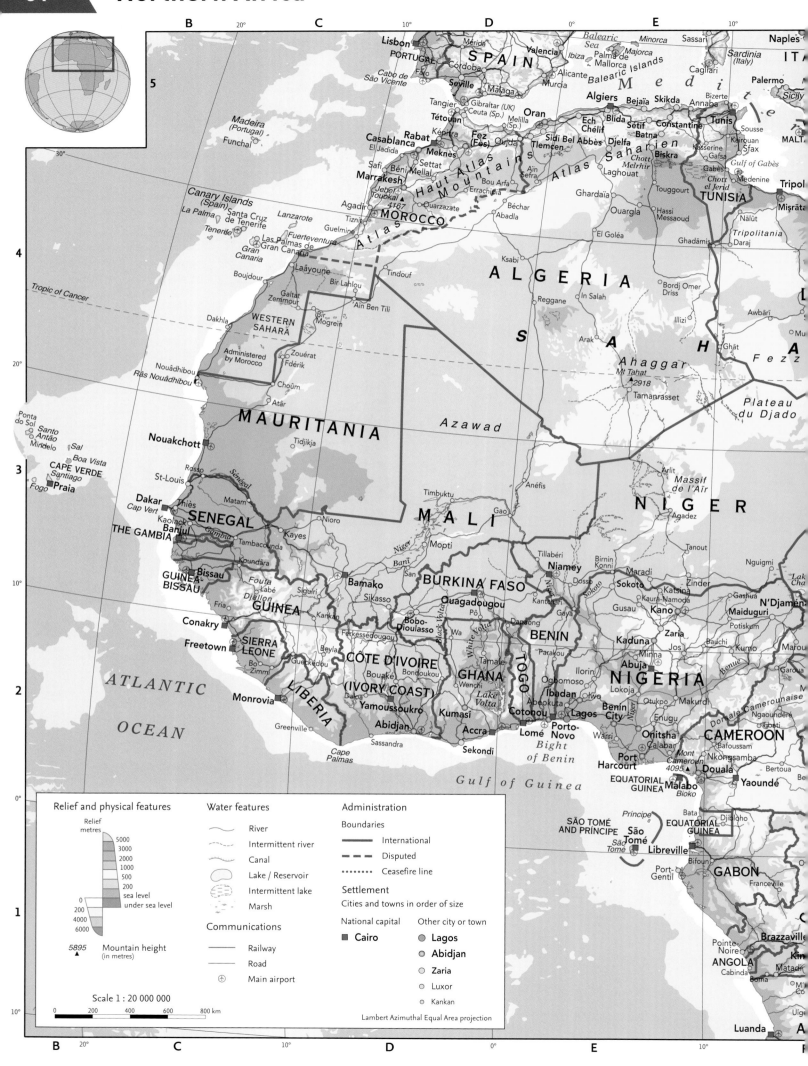

**Relief and physical features**

Relief metres
- 5000
- 3000
- 2000
- 1000
- 500
- 200
- 0 sea level
- under sea level
- 200
- 4000
- 6000

▲ 5895 Mountain height (in metres)

**Communications**
- Railway
- Road
- ⊕ Main airport

**Water features**
- River
- Intermittent river
- Canal
- Lake / Reservoir
- Intermittent lake
- Marsh

**Administration**

Boundaries
- International
- Disputed
- Ceasefire line

**Settlement**

Cities and towns in order of size

National capital
- ■ Cairo

Other city or town
- ● Lagos
- ● Abidjan
- ○ Zaria
- ○ Luxor
- ○ Kankan

Scale 1 : 20 000 000

0   200   400   600   800 km

Lambert Azimuthal Equal Area projection

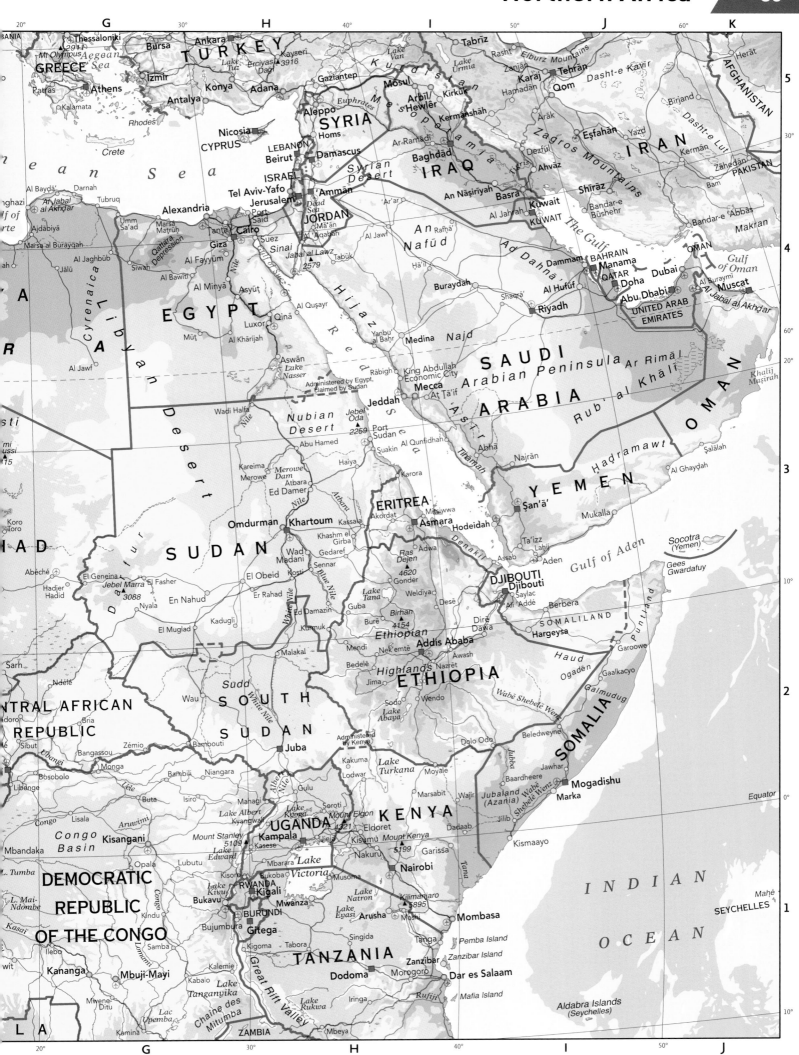

# Asia Relief

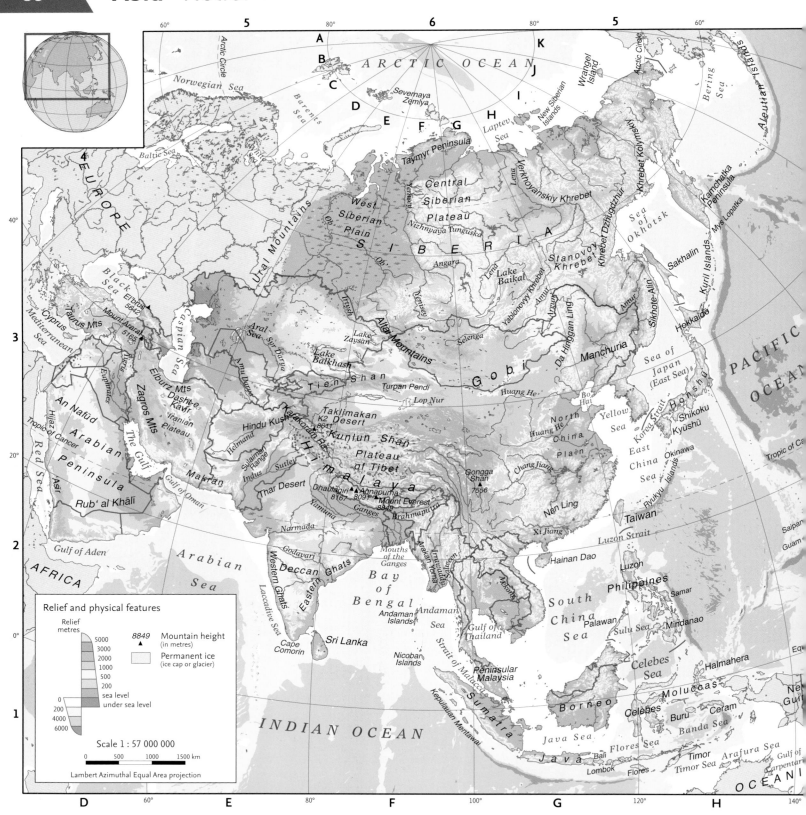

ARCTIC OCEAN

Norwegian Sea

EUROPE

Baltic Sea

Barents Sea

Severnaya Zemlya

Taymyr Peninsula

West Siberian Plain

Central Siberian Plateau

S I B E R I A

Nizhnyaya Tunguska

Laptev Sea

New Siberian Islands

Wrangel Island

Bering Sea

Aleutian Islands

Arctic Circle

Ural Mountains

Ob

Irtysh

Yenisey

Angara

Lena

Verkhoyanskiy Khrebet

Khrebet Kolymskiy

Kamchatka Peninsula

Mys Lopatka

Black Sea

Elbrus 5642

Mount Ararat 5165

Caspian Sea

Aral Sea

Syr Darya

Lake Zaysan

Altai Mountains

Lake Baikal

Selenga

Yenisey

Stanovoy Khrebet

Yablonovyy Khrebet

Amur

Khrebet Dzhugdzhur

Argun

Da Hinggan Ling

Manchuria

Amur

Sikhote-Alin'

Sea of Okhotsk

Sakhalin

Kuril Islands

Hokkaido

Mediterranean Sea

Cyprus

Taurus Mts

Tigris

Euphrates

Elburz Mts

Dasht-e Kavir

Iranian Plateau

Zagros Mts

The Gulf

Amu Darya

Lake Balkhash

Tien Shan

Turpan Pendi

Lop Nur

Taklimakan Desert

K2 8611

Kunlun Shan

Plateau of Tibet

Gobi

Huang He

Huang He

Bo Hai

North China Plain

Yellow Sea

Chang Jiang

Korea Strait

Honshu

Kyushu

Shikoku

Sea of Japan (East Sea)

Bo Hai

East China Sea

Okinawa

Ryukyu Islands

PACIFIC OCEAN

Tropic of Cancer

An Nafūd

Arabian Peninsula

Hijaz

Asir

Red Sea

Rub' al Khālī

Hindu Kush

Karakoram Ra.

Helmand

Sulaiman Range

Indus

Makran

Gulf of Oman

Thar Desert

Sutlej

Himalaya

Dhaulagiri 8167

Annapurna 8091

Mount Everest 8849

Yamuna

Ganges

Brahmaputra

Gongga Shan 7556

Nan Ling

Xi Jiang

Taiwan

Luzon Strait

Gulf of Aden

AFRICA

Arabian Sea

Narmada

Godavari

Deccan

Western Ghats

Eastern Ghats

Bay of Bengal

Mouths of the Ganges

Arakan Yoma

Irrawaddy

Salween

Mekong

Hainan Dao

Luzon

South China Sea

Philippines

Samar

Palawan

Sulu Sea

Mindanao

Saipan

Guam

Tropic of Cancer

Laccadive Sea

Cape Comorin

Sri Lanka

Andaman Islands

Andaman Sea

Gulf of Thailand

Nicobar Islands

Strait of Malacca

Peninsular Malaysia

Kepulauan Mentawai

Sumatra

Borneo

Celebes

Celebes Sea

Molucca

Buru

Ceram

Halmahera

New Guinea

INDIAN OCEAN

Java

Bali

Lombok

Java Sea

Flores Sea

Flores

Timor

Timor Sea

Banda Sea

Arafura Sea

Gulf of Carpentaria

OCEANIA

### Relief and physical features

Relief metres

5000
3000
2000
1000
500
200
sea level
0
under sea level
200
4000
6000

8849 ▲ Mountain height (in metres)

Permanent ice (ice cap or glacier)

Scale 1 : 57 000 000

0    500    1000    1500 km

Lambert Azimuthal Equal Area projection

## Cross-section

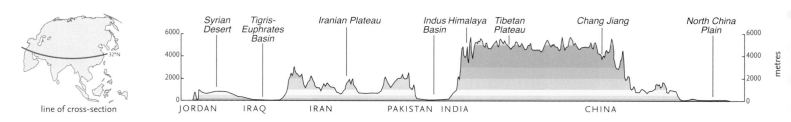

line of cross-section

Syrian Desert

Tigris-Euphrates Basin

Iranian Plateau

Indus Himalaya Basin

Tibetan Plateau

Chang Jiang

North China Plain

6000
4000
2000
0

metres

6000
4000
2000
0

JORDAN    IRAQ    IRAN    PAKISTAN    INDIA    CHINA

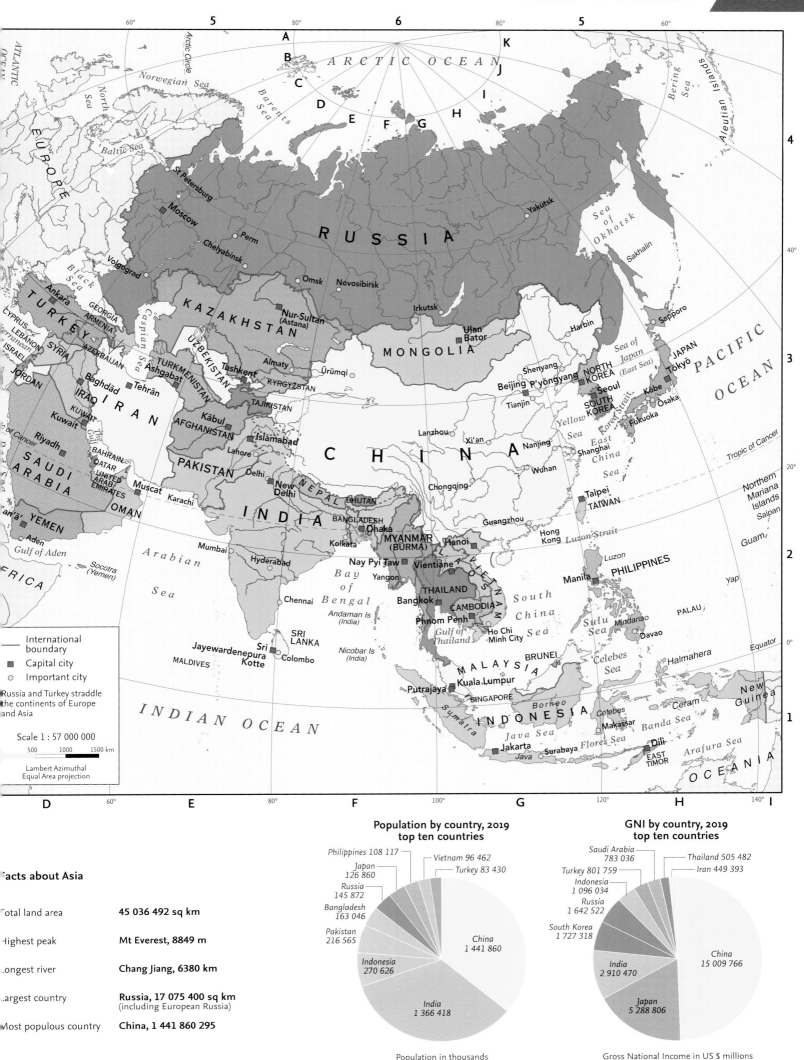

Facts about Asia

| | |
|---|---|
| Total land area | 45 036 492 sq km |
| Highest peak | Mt Everest, 8849 m |
| Longest river | Chang Jiang, 6380 km |
| Largest country | Russia, 17 075 400 sq km (including European Russia) |
| Most populous country | China, 1 441 860 295 |

International boundary
Capital city
Important city
Russia and Turkey straddle the continents of Europe and Asia

Scale 1 : 57 000 000
500  1000  1500 km
Lambert Azimuthal Equal Area projection

**Population by country, 2019 top ten countries**

Philippines 108 117
Japan 126 860
Russia 145 872
Bangladesh 163 046
Pakistan 216 565
Indonesia 270 626
India 1 366 418
Vietnam 96 462
Turkey 83 430
China 1 441 860

Population in thousands

**GNI by country, 2019 top ten countries**

Saudi Arabia 783 036
Turkey 801 759
Indonesia 1 096 034
Russia 1 642 522
South Korea 1 727 318
India 2 910 470
Japan 5 288 806
Thailand 505 482
Iran 449 393
China 15 009 766

Gross National Income in US $ millions

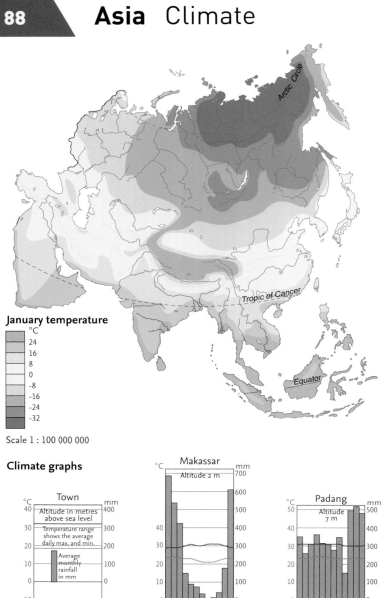

**January temperature**

°C
24
16
8
0
-8
-16
-24
-32

Scale 1 : 100 000 000

**July temperature**

°C
32
24
16
8

Scale 1 : 100 000 000

**Climate graphs**

**Town**

°C                                              mm
40    Altitude in metres                       400
      above sea level
30    Temperature range                        300
      shows the average
20    daily max. and min.                       200
10         Average                              100
           monthly
 0         rainfall                               0
           in mm
-10
   J FMAM J J A SOND

**Makassar**

°C                              mm
                               700
    Altitude 2 m
50                             600
                               500
40
                               400
30
                               300
20
                               200
10                             100

 0                               0
   J FMAM J J A SOND

**Padang**

°C                         mm
50                         500
    Altitude
    7 m
40                         400

30                         300

20                         200

10                         100

 0                           0
   J FMAM J J A SOND

**Riyadh**

°C                         mm
50                         500
    Altitude 590 m
40                         400

30                         300

20                         200

10                         100

 0                           0
   J FMAM J J A SOND

**Shanghai**

°C                         mm
50                         500
    Altitude 7 m
40                         400

30                         300

20                         200

10                         100

 0                           0
   J FMAM J J A SOND

**Tomsk**

°C                         mm
30                         300
    Altitude 122 m
20                         200

10                         100

 0                           0

-10

-20

-30
   J FMAM J J A SOND

**Annual rainfall**

mm
3000
2000
1000
500
250
0

• Location of
  places on
  climate graphs

Scale 1 : 100 000 000

WWW   Met Office Forecast
      www.metoffice.gov.uk
      World Meteorological Organization
      www.wmo.int
      BBC Weather
      www.bbc.co.uk/weather

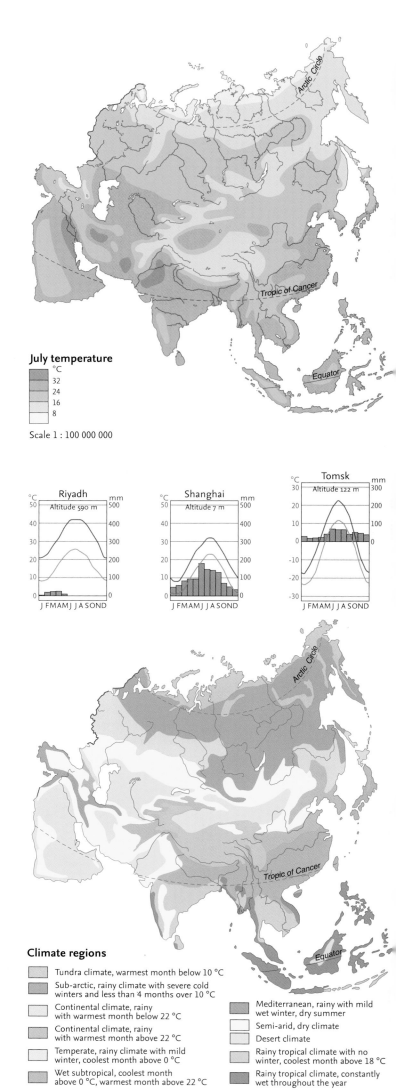

**Climate regions**

Tundra climate, warmest month below 10 °C

Sub-arctic, rainy climate with severe cold
winters and less than 4 months over 10 °C

Continental climate, rainy
with warmest month below 22 °C

Continental climate, rainy
with warmest month above 22 °C

Temperate, rainy climate with mild
winter, coolest month above 0 °C

Wet subtropical, coolest month
above 0 °C, warmest month above 22 °C

Mediterranean, rainy with mild
wet winter, dry summer

Semi-arid, dry climate

Desert climate

Rainy tropical climate with no
winter, coolest month above 18 °C

Rainy tropical climate, constantly
wet throughout the year

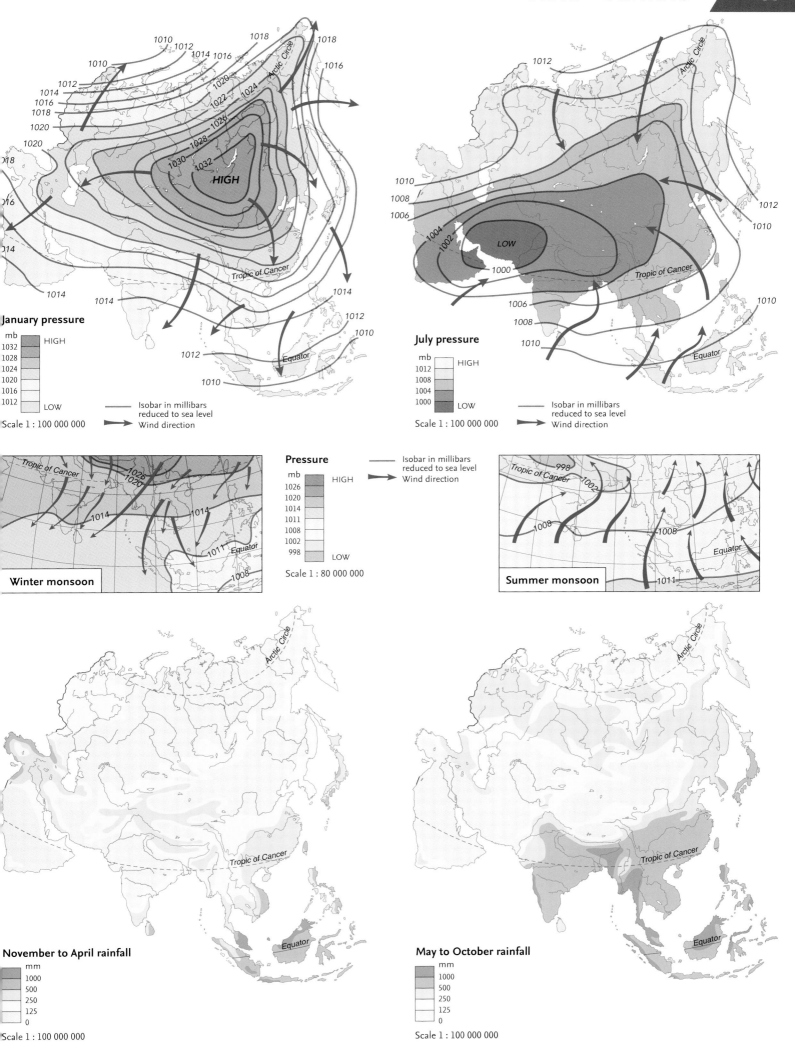

**January pressure**

mb
1032 HIGH
1028
1024
1020
1016
1012 LOW

—— Isobar in millibars
reduced to sea level
➤ Wind direction

Scale 1 : 100 000 000

**July pressure**

mb
1012 HIGH
1008
1004
1000 LOW

—— Isobar in millibars
reduced to sea level
➤ Wind direction

Scale 1 : 100 000 000

**Winter monsoon**

**Pressure**

mb
1026 HIGH
1020
1014
1011
1008
1002
998 LOW

—— Isobar in millibars
reduced to sea level
➤ Wind direction

Scale 1 : 80 000 000

**Summer monsoon**

**November to April rainfall**

mm
1000
500
250
125
0

Scale 1 : 100 000 000

**May to October rainfall**

mm
1000
500
250
125
0

Scale 1 : 100 000 000

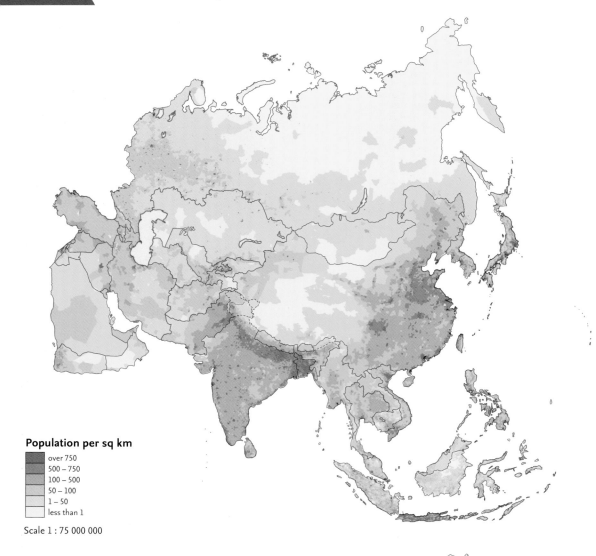

## Population per sq km

| | |
|---|---|
| ███ | over 750 |
| ███ | 500 – 750 |
| ███ | 100 – 500 |
| ███ | 50 – 100 |
| ░░░ | 1 – 50 |
| ░░░ | less than 1 |

Scale 1 : 75 000 000

**WWW** UN Economic and Social Commission
for Asia and the Pacific
www.unescap.org

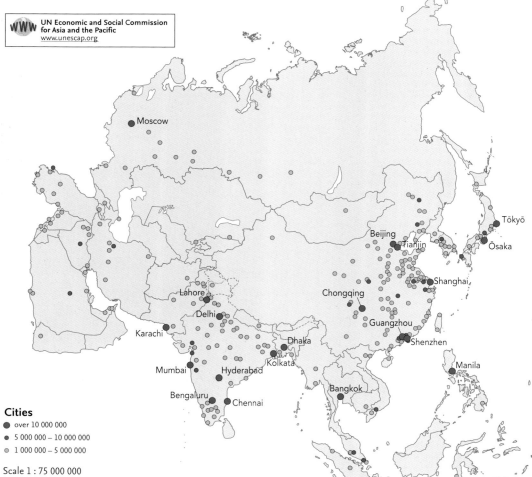

### Cities

● over 10 000 000
● 5 000 000 – 10 000 000
○ 1 000 000 – 5 000 000

Scale 1 : 75 000 000

### Top 10 densely populated countries, 20⋮

| Country | Population per sq km |
|---|---|
| Singapore | 9083 |
| Bahrain | 2375 |
| Maldives | 1781 |
| Bangladesh | 1132 |
| Taiwan | 657 |
| Lebanon | 655 |
| South Korea | 515 |
| India | 431 |
| Israel | 385 |
| Philippines | 360 |

### Population pyramids, 2020

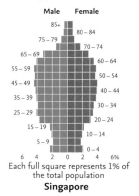

Each full square represents 1% of
the total population

**Singapore**

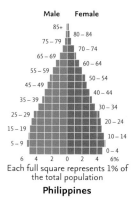

Each full square represents 1% of
the total population

**Philippines**

### Population growth, 1950 – 2050

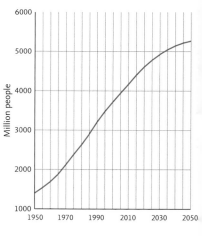

### Top 5 largest urban agglomerations, 20⋮

| Urban agglomeration | Population |
|---|---|
| **Tōkyō** Japan | 37 393 129 |
| **Delhi** India | 30 290 936 |
| **Shanghai** China | 27 058 479 |
| **Dhaka** Bangladesh | 21 005 860 |
| **Beijing** China | 20 462 610 |

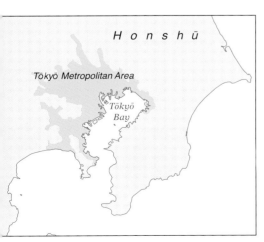

*Tōkyō Metropolitan Area*

*H o n s h ū*

*Tōkyō Bay*

Tōkyō, the capital of Japan, has been the world's most populous metropolitan area since 1970.

This false-colour Landsat 7 image shows this vast conurbation, situated on the eastern shore of the Japanese island of Honshū. Tōkyō Bay dominates the centre of this scene. The greater Tōkyō area fans out in a crescent shape around the western, northern, and eastern shores of Tōkyō Bay. Pressure on the land has led to major land reclamation projects in the bay – obvious from the angular shape of the coastline. Tōkyō International airport is built entirely on reclaimed land.

Urban
Cropland
Cropland and woodland
Grassland and grazing
Grassland and woodland
Temperate forest
Tropical forest
Coniferous forest
Scrubland or desert
Swamp and marsh
Tundra

Scale 1 : 50 000 000

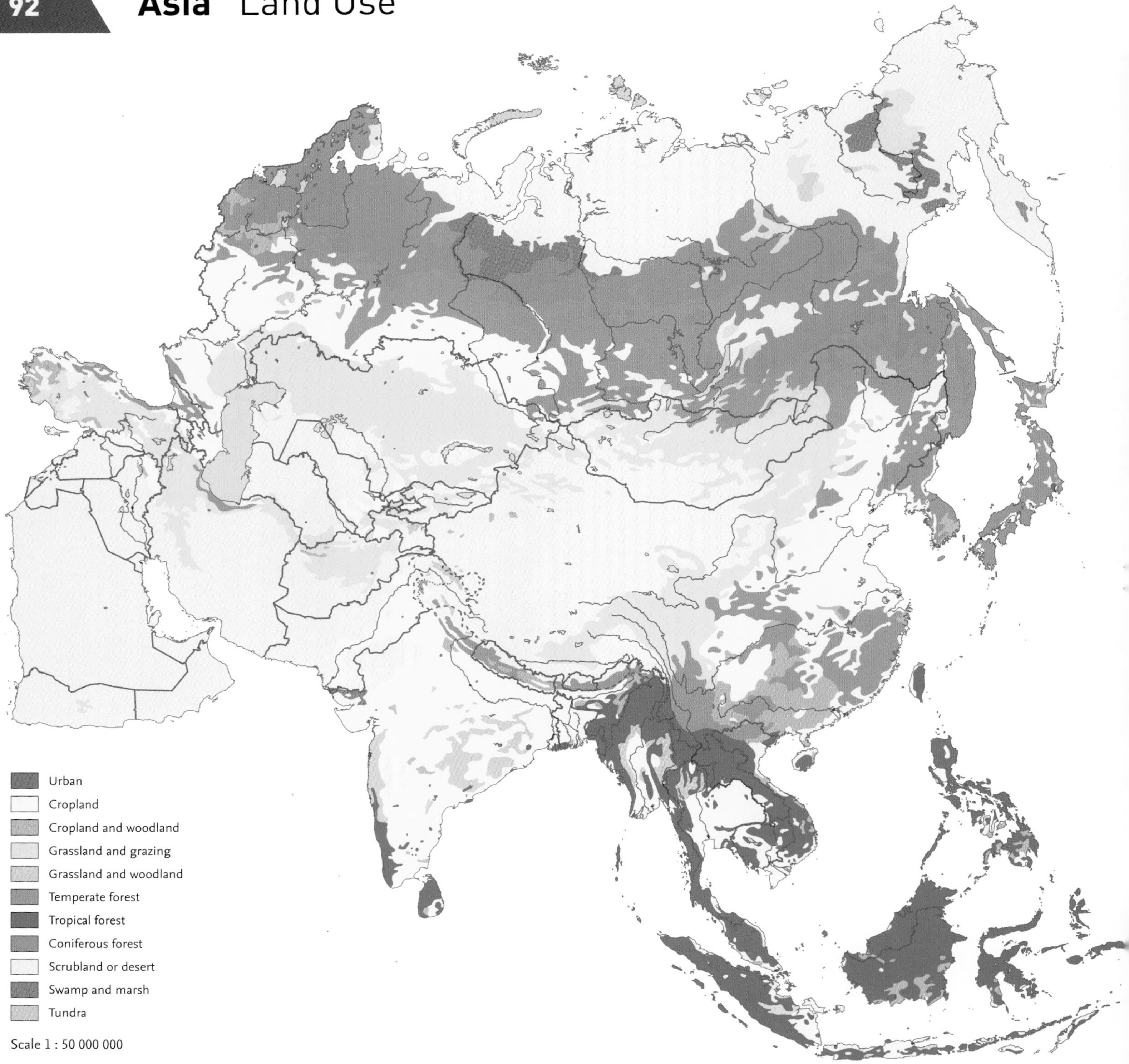

**Land use by region, 2018**

Arable land
Permanent crops
Forest
Other

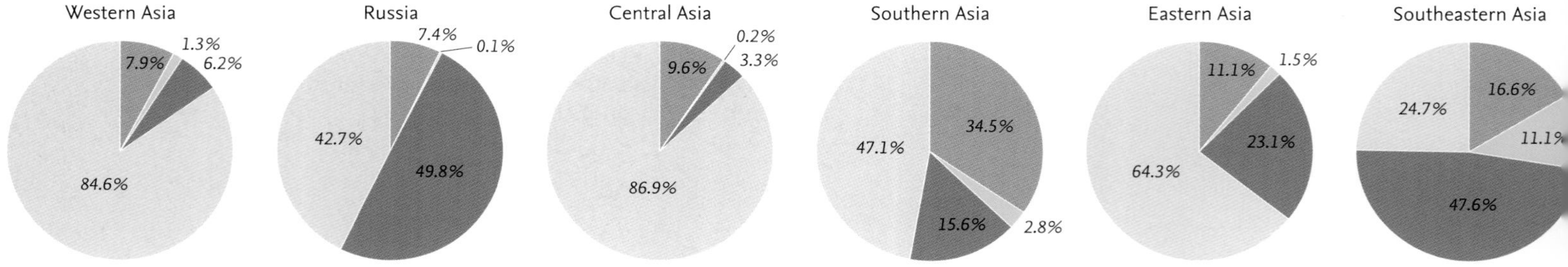

Russia
Central
Western
Eastern
Southern
Southeastern

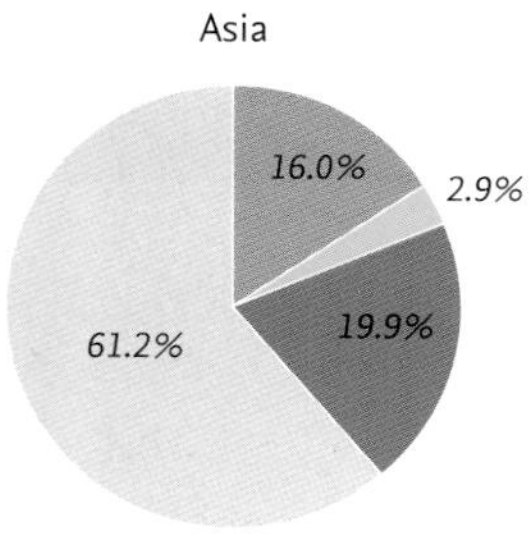

**Asia**

16.0%   2.9%
61.2%   19.9%

**Western Asia**
1.3%
7.9%   6.2%
84.6%

**Russia**
7.4%   0.1%
42.7%
49.8%

**Central Asia**
0.2%
9.6%   3.3%
86.9%

**Southern Asia**
34.5%
47.1%
15.6%   2.8%

**Eastern Asia**
11.1%   1.5%
64.3%
23.1%

**Southeastern Asia**
16.6%
24.7%   11.1%
47.6%

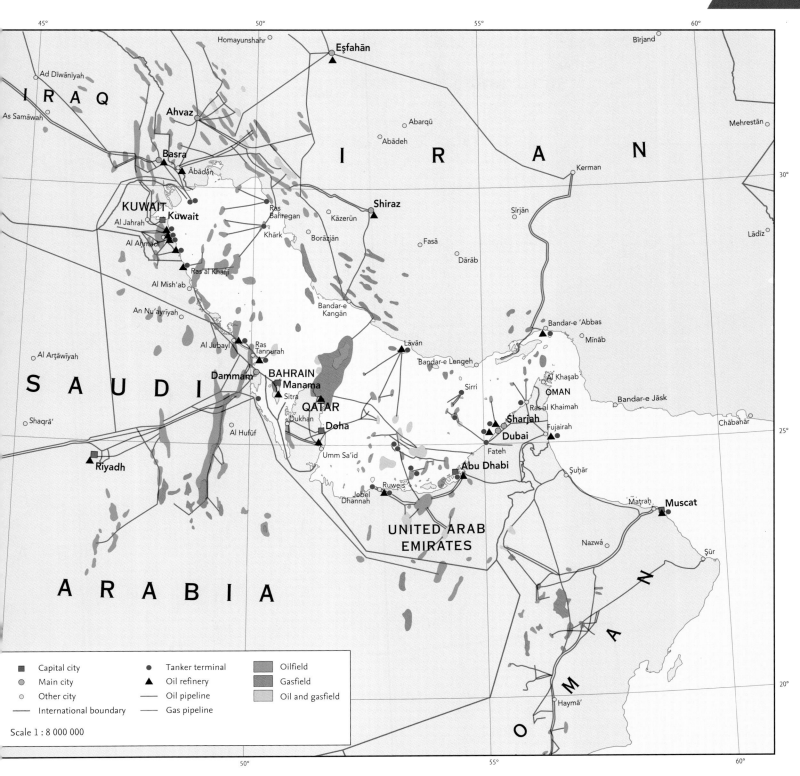

**and gas production**

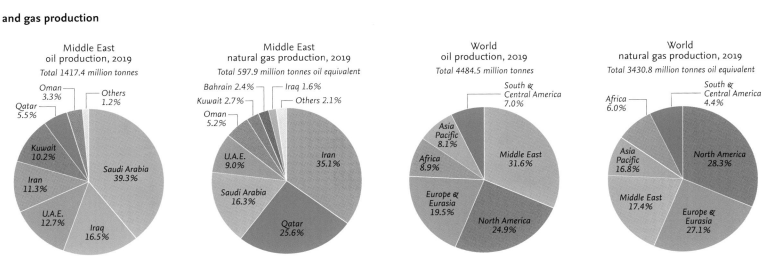

Middle East
oil production, 2019
*Total 1417.4 million tonnes*

- Oman 3.3%
- Others 1.2%
- Qatar 5.5%
- Kuwait 10.2%
- Iran 11.3%
- U.A.E. 12.7%
- Iraq 16.5%
- Saudi Arabia 39.3%

Middle East
natural gas production, 2019
*Total 597.9 million tonnes oil equivalent*

- Bahrain 2.4%
- Iraq 1.6%
- Kuwait 2.7%
- Others 2.1%
- Oman 5.2%
- U.A.E. 9.0%
- Saudi Arabia 16.3%
- Qatar 25.6%
- Iran 35.1%

World
oil production, 2019
*Total 4484.5 million tonnes*

- South & Central America 7.0%
- Asia Pacific 8.1%
- Africa 8.9%
- Europe & Eurasia 19.5%
- Middle East 31.6%
- North America 24.9%

World
natural gas production, 2019
*Total 3430.8 million tonnes oil equivalent*

- Africa 6.0%
- South & Central America 4.4%
- Asia Pacific 16.8%
- Middle East 17.4%
- North America 28.3%
- Europe & Eurasia 27.1%

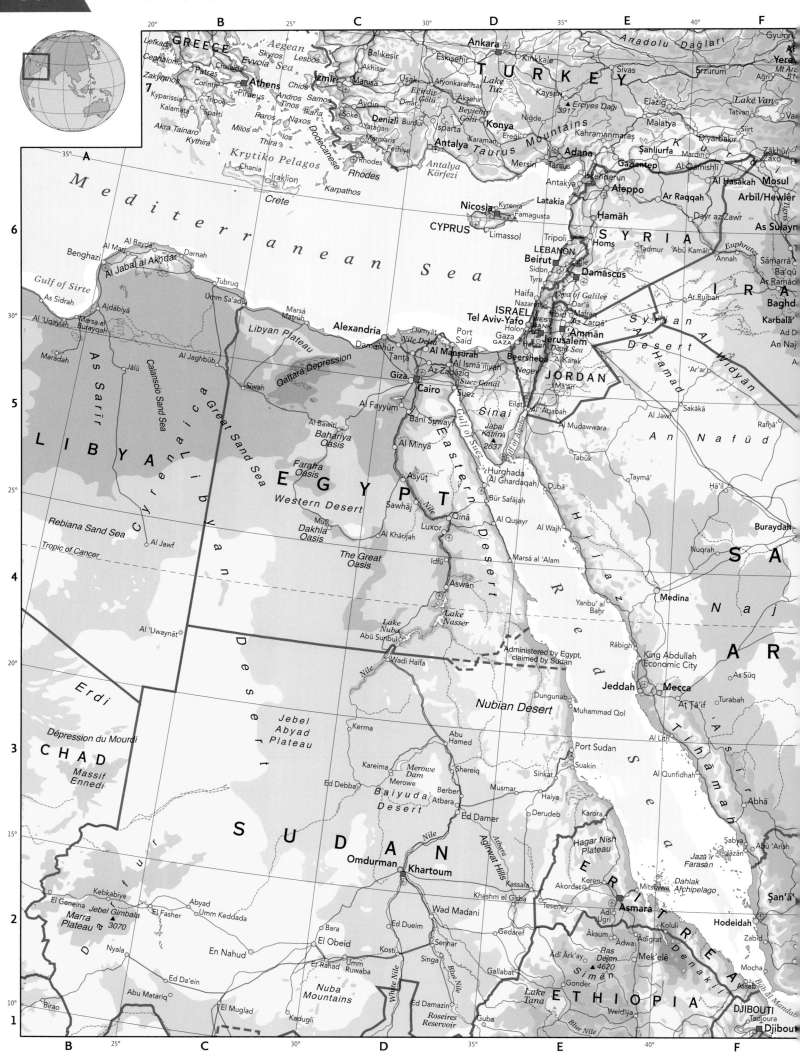

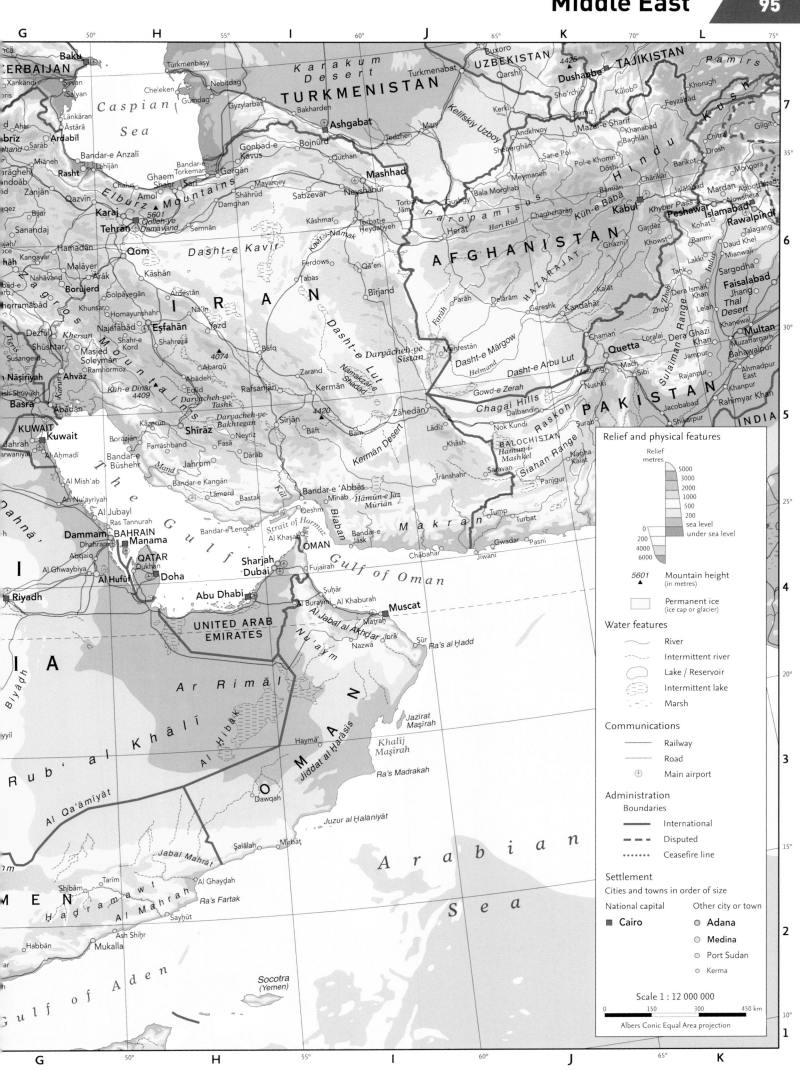

**G** 50° **H** 55° **I** 60° **J** 65° **K** 70° **L** 75°

ERBAIJAN
Baku

*Caspian*
*Sea*

Türkmenbaşy
Cheleken
Nebitdag
Gyzylarbat

*Karakum*
*Desert*
Buxoro
Qarshi

**UZBEKISTAN**
4425
Dushanbe **TAJIKISTAN**
*Pamirs*

Xankändi
Şirvan
Salyan
Gumdag
Bakharden
Turkmenabat
Kerki
Sho'rchi
Külob
Khorugh

Ahar
Ardabīl
Bandar-e Anzalī
Gonbad-e Kavus
Bojnūrd
Tedzhen
Mary
Sar-e Pol
Andkhvoy
Sheberghän
Mazar-e Sharif
Khanabad
Feyzäbäd
Gilgit

abriz
Sarāb
Ashgabat
Quchan
Meymaneh
Pol-e Khomri
Baghlän
Bämiän
Chitral
Drosh

Rasht
Lahījān
Ghaem
Torkeman
Gorgān
Mashhad
Neyshābūr
Bala Morghab
Gushgy
Chaghcharan
Kūh-e Bābā
Chärikär
Jaläläbäd
Mardan
Abbottabad
Mongora

Zanjān
Chalus
Amol
Sari
Mayamey
Sabzevar
Torbat-e Jäm
Herat
*Paropamisus*
Kabul
Khyber Pass
Peshawar
Islamabad
Rawalpindi

Qazvīn
Karaj
5601
Qolleh-ye
Damāvand
Semnān
Damghan
Shāhrūd
Torbat-e Heydariyeh
Kāshmar
Hari Rūd
Gardēz
Khowst
Banmi

Bījār
Tehrān
**I    R    A    N**
Ferdows
Qā'en
Ghazni
Lakki
Mianwali

hah
Hamadān
Qom
*Dasht-e Kavir*
Tabas
Birjand
Farāh
Delārām
**A F G H A N I S T A N**
Gereshk
Kandahär
Chaman
Kälät
Zhob
Dera Ismail Khan
Thal
Desert
Faisalabad
Jhang

Kangavar
Malāyer
Arāk
Kāshān
Golpāyegān
Nā'īn
Yazd
*HAZARAJAT*
Dasht-e Mārgow
*Dasht-e Arbu Lut*
Mastung
Zhob
Loralai
Khanewal
Multan

ad-e
Borūjerd
Khunsār
Homayunshahr
Najafābād
Esfahān
4074
Abarqū
Helmand
Gowd-e Zerah
Quetta
Mach
Sibi
Jampur
Muzaffargarh
Bahawalpur

horramābād
Dezful
Shahr-e Kord
Shahrezā
Bāfq
Mehrestan
*Chagai Hills*
Dalbandin
BALOCHISTAN
Nushki
Dera Ghazi Khan
Ahmadpur East

Tigris
Shūshtar
Masjed Soleymān
Ramhormoz
Ardestān
Zarand
Kermān
Zāhedān
Nok Kundi
Khāsh
*Hamun-i-Mashkel*
Nagha
Jacobabad
Khanpur

Nāşirīyah
Ahvāz
Kūh-e Dīnar
4409
Rafsanjān
4420
Bāft
Bam
Lādīz
*Raskoh Range*
Surab
Shikarpur
Rahimyar Khan

Basra
Ābādān
*Daryācheh-ye Tashk*
Sīrjān
*Kermān Desert*
Irānshahr
Saravan
Panjgur
*Siahan Range*
Kalat
INDIA

sh Shuyūkh
Najafābād
*Daryācheh-ye Bakhtegān*
Neyriz
Fasā
Dārāb
Bandar-e 'Abbās
Mināb
*Hāmūn-e Jaz Mūrīān*
Turbat
Tump
Turbat

**KUWAIT**
Kuwait
Kāzerūn
Shīrāz
Borāzjān
Farrāshband
Jahrom
*Kūl*
Bastak
Qeshm
Bandar-e Jāsk
*Makran*
Gwadar
Pasni

Jahrah
Al Ahmadī
arwaniyah
Bandar-e Būshehr
Bandar-e Kangān
Lāmerd
Bandar-e Lengeh
*Strait of Hormuz*
Al Khaşab
*Biaban*
Chābahār
Jiwani

Ān Nu'ayrīyah
*The  Gulf*
OMAN
Sharjah
Dubai
Fujairah

Al Jubayl
Ras Tannurah
Şuhār
Al Khaburah
Muscat

Dammam
**BAHRAIN**
Manama
QATAR
Dukhān
Doha
Al Buraymi
Al Jabal al Akhḍar
Maţraḥ

Abqaiq
Al Hufūf
Abu Dhabi
**UNITED ARAB EMIRATES**
Ibrī
Nazwā
Şūr

Riyadh
Al Ghwaybiya
Nu'aym
Ra's al Ḥadd

**S A U D I   A R A B I A**
*Ar  Rimāl*
Al Hibāk
Ibrā

*Biyādh*
**O  M  A  N**
Jazīrat Maşīrah

*Rub'  al  Khālī*
Haymā'
*Khalīj Maşīrah*

Al Qa'āmīyāt
Ra's Madrakah

yyil
*Jiddat al Ḥarāsīs*
Dawqah

**Relief and physical features**

Relief
metres
5000
3000
2000
1000
500
200
0    sea level
200    under sea level
4000
6000

5601 ▲ Mountain height (in metres)

Permanent ice (ice cap or glacier)

**Water features**
~~~ River
---- Intermittent river
◯ Lake / Reservoir
Intermittent lake
Marsh

**Communications**
—— Railway
— Road
⊕ Main airport

**Administration**
Boundaries
—— International
---- Disputed
···· Ceasefire line

**Settlement**
Cities and towns in order of size
National capital       Other city or town
■ Cairo                ◉ Adana
                       ◉ Medina
                       ◯ Port Sudan
                       ◦ Kerma

Scale 1 : 12 000 000
0      150      300      450 km
Albers Conic Equal Area projection

Şalālah
Mirbaţ

Jabal Mahrāt
*Juzur al Ḥalānīyāt*

MEN
Habbān
Mukalla
Shibām
Tarim
Al Ghaydah
Ra's al Hadd

*Ḥaḍramawt*
*Al Mahrah*
Ra's Fartak

Ash Shiḥr
Sayhūt

*Arabian*
*Sea*

m
Gulf of Aden
*Socotra*
*(Yemen)*

**G** 50° **H** 55° **I** 60° **J** 65° **K**

# Pakistan, India, Bangladesh and Myanmar

**Relief and physical features**

Relief
metres

5000
3000
2000
1000
500
200
sea level
0
under sea level
200
4000
6000

8849 ▲ Mountain height (in metres)

Permanent ice (ice cap or glacier)

**Water features**

River
Intermittent river
Canal
Lake / Reservoir
Intermittent lake
Marsh

**Communications**

Railway
Road
⊕ Main airport

**Administration**

Boundaries

International
Disputed
Internal
Ceasefire line

**Settlement**

Cities and towns in order of size

National capital
■ Dhaka

Other city or town
● Mumbai
● Jaipur
○ Ranchi
○ Jammu
○ Ghazni

Scale 1 : 15 000 000

0      150      300      450 km

Lambert Azimuthal Equal Area projection

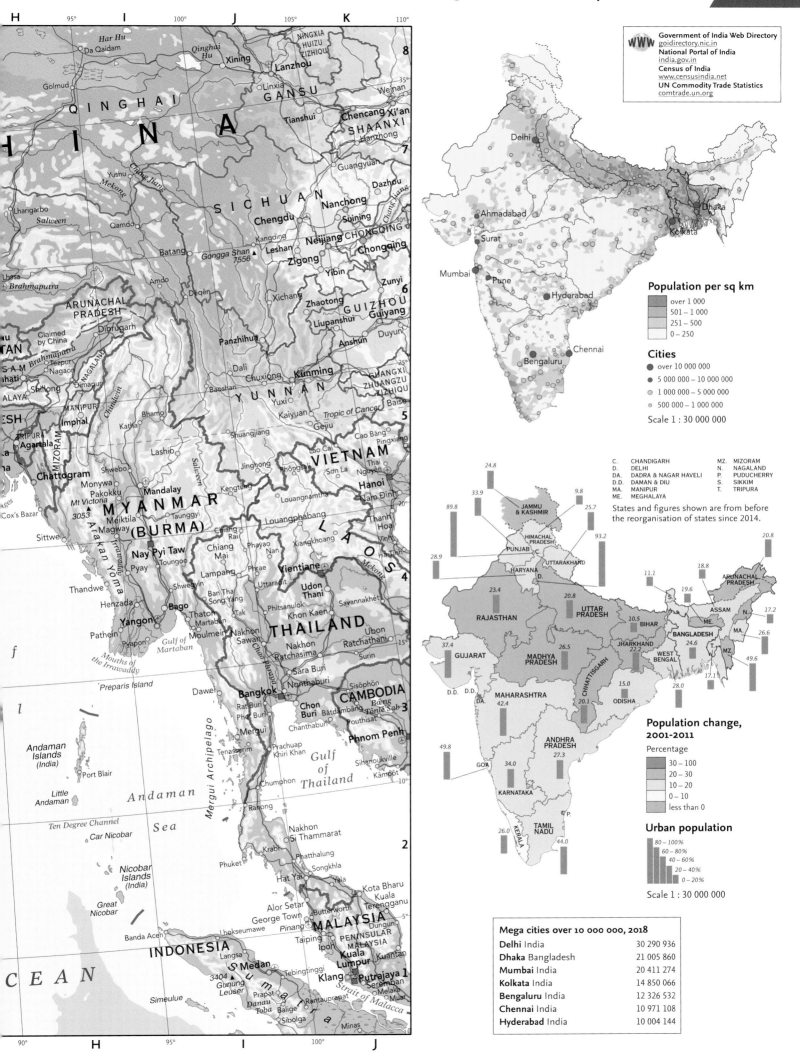

H 95° I 100° J 105° K 110°

Har Hu
Da Qaidam
Qinghai Hu
Xining
Lanzhou
8
Golmud
QINGHAI
Linxia
GANSU
Weinan
Tianshui
35°
CHINA
Chencang Xi'an
SHAANXI
Hanzhong
7
Guangyuan
SICHUAN
Nanchong
Dazhou
Yushu
Chengdu
Suining
Chang Jiang
Mekong
CHONGQING
Lharigarbo
Kangding
Neijiang
Chongqing
Yibin
Lhasa
Leshan
Gongga Shan 7556
Zigong
Zunyi
Brahmaputra
Batang
Amdo
Dêqên
Xichang
Zhaotong
GUIZHOU
6
Panzhihua
Guiyang
ARUNACHAL PRADESH
Dibrugarh
Liupanshui
Duyun
Anshun
Claimed by China
30°
Tezpur
Nagaon
Dali
Chuxiong
Kunming
GUANGXI ZHUANGZU ZIZHIQU
Brahmaputra
NAGALAND
Baoshan
Yuxi
Shillong
Dimapur
Yunnan
25°
MANIPUR
Bhamo
Kaiyuan
Gejiu
Tropic of Cancer
Baise
MEGHALAYA
Imphal
Katha
Shuangjiang
Lao Cai
Cao Bang
Pingxiang
Agartala
MIZORAM
Lashio
Jinghong
Phôngsali
Thai Nguyen
VIETNAM
Chattogram
Shwebo
Monywa
Mandalay
Kengtung
Louangnamtha
Son La
Hanoi
Pakokku
Taunggyi
Chiang Rai
Nam Dinh
Mt Victoria 3053
Meiktila
Magway
MYANMAR (BURMA)
Chiang Mai
Phayao
Nan
Xiangkhoang
LAOS
Thanh Hoa
20°
Cox's Bazar
Arakan Yoma
Nay Pyi Taw
Pyay
Toungoo
Lampang
Phrae
Vientiane
Udon Thani
Mekong
Ha Tinh
Vinh
Sittwe
Thandwe
Irrawaddy
Uttaradit
Phitsanulok
Khon Kaen
Savannakhét
Henzada
Shwegyin
Ban Thai Song Yang
Tak
Nakhon Sawan
THAILAND
Ubon Ratchathani
15°
Bago
Thaton
Martaban
Nakhon Ratchasima
Yangon
Moulmein
Sara Buri
Surin
Pathein
Pyapon
Gulf of Martaban
Chao Phraya
Nonthaburi
Sisóphón
CAMBODIA
Mouths of the Irrawaddy
Dawei
Bangkok
Rat Buri
Chon Buri
Bätdâmbâng
Bœng Tônlé Sab
Phet Buri
Pouthisat
Preparis Island
Merqui
Chanthaburi
Phnom Penh
Andaman Islands (India)
Tenasserim
Prachuap Khiri Khan
Gulf of Thailand
Sihanoukville
10°
Port Blair
Chumphon
Kâmpôt
Little Andaman
Ranong
Nakhon Si Thammarat
Ten Degree Channel
Car Nicobar
Andaman Sea
Krabi
Phatthalung
Phuket
Songkhla
2
Nicobar Islands (India)
Hat Yai
Yala
Kota Bharu
Kuala Terengganu
Great Nicobar
Alor Setar
Butterworth
Dungun
5°
George Town
Pinang
MALAYSIA
Banda Aceh
Taiping
Ipoh
PENINSULAR MALAYSIA
Kuantan
Lhokseumawe
Langsa
Kuala Lumpur
INDONESIA
Tebingtinggi
Medan
Klang
Putrajaya
1
3404 Gunung Leuser
Prapat
Seremban
Melaka
Simeulue
Danau Toba
Balige
Strait of Malacca
Muar
Sibolga
Minas

H 90° 95° I 100° J

WWW Government of India Web Directory
goidirectory.nic.in
National Portal of India
india.gov.in
Census of India
www.censusindia.net
UN Commodity Trade Statistics
comtrade.un.org

Delhi
Dhaka
Ahmadabad
Surat
Kolkata
Mumbai
Pune
Hyderabad
Chennai
Bengaluru

## Population per sq km
over 1 000
501 – 1 000
251 – 500
0 – 250

## Cities
over 10 000 000
5 000 000 – 10 000 000
1 000 000 – 5 000 000
500 000 – 1 000 000

Scale 1 : 30 000 000

C.      CHANDIGARH          MZ.   MIZORAM
D.      DELHI               N.    NAGALAND
DA.    DADRA & NAGAR HAVELI  P.    PUDUCHERRY
D.D.   DAMAN & DIU          S.    SIKKIM
MA.    MANIPUR             T.    TRIPURA
ME.    MEGHALAYA

States and figures shown are from before
the reorganisation of states since 2014.

24.8
33.9        9.8
89.8    JAMMU & KASHMIR    25.7
28.9    PUNJAB    HIMACHAL PRADESH    93.2    20.8
HARYANA    UTTARAKHAND    11.1    18.8    ARUNACHAL PRADESH
D.    19.6    S    ASSAM
23.4    UTTAR PRADESH    17.2
RAJASTHAN    20.8    10.5    ME.    N.    26.6
BIHAR    BANGLADESH    MA.
37.4    26.5    JHARKHAND    24.6    T.    49.6
GUJARAT    MADHYA PRADESH    22.2    WEST BENGAL    MZ.
D.D. D.D.    CHHATTISGARH    17.1
DA.    15.0    28.0
MAHARASHTRA    20.1    ODISHA
42.4    ANDHRA PRADESH
49.8    27.3
GOA    34.0
KARNATAKA
TAMIL NADU
26.0    KERALA    44.0

## Population change, 2001-2011
Percentage
30 – 100
20 – 30
10 – 20
0 – 10
less than 0

## Urban population
80 – 100%
60 – 80%
40 – 60%
20 – 40%
0 – 20%

Scale 1 : 30 000 000

## Mega cities over 10 000 000, 2018
| | | |
|---|---|---|
| Delhi India | | 30 290 936 |
| Dhaka Bangladesh | | 21 005 860 |
| Mumbai India | | 20 411 274 |
| Kolkata India | | 14 850 066 |
| Bengaluru India | | 12 326 532 |
| Chennai India | | 10 971 108 |
| Hyderabad India | | 10 004 144 |

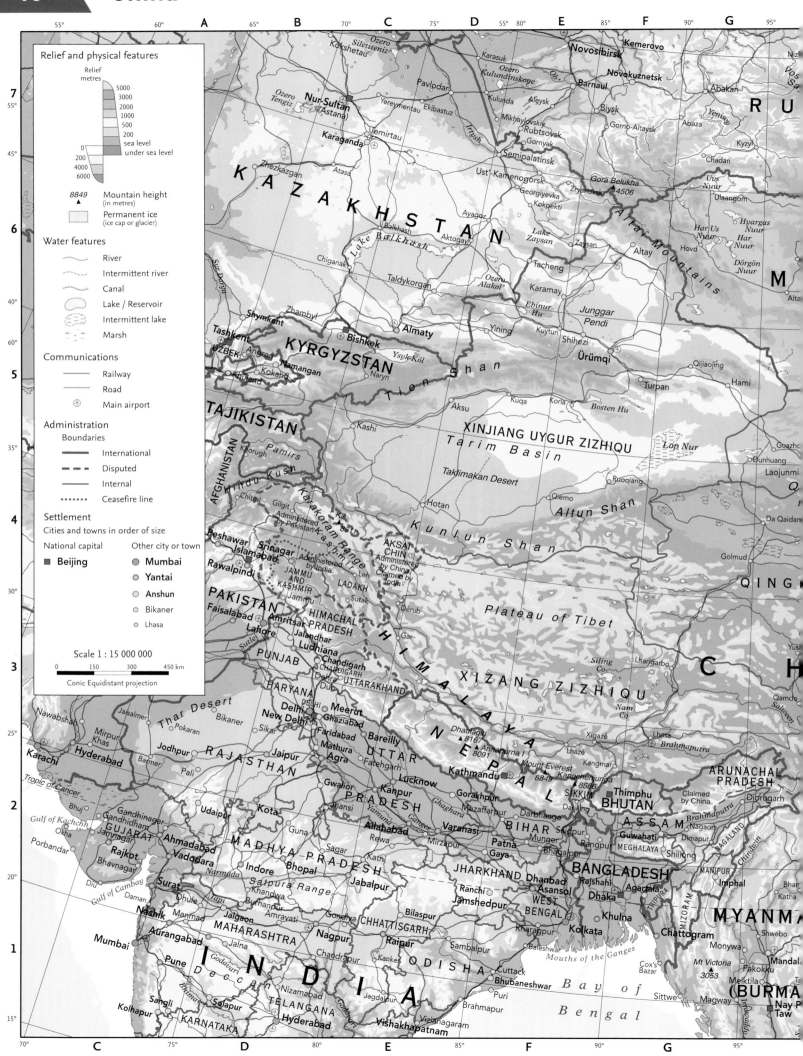

**Relief and physical features**

Relief
metres
5000
3000
2000
1000
500
200
0 sea level
under sea level
200
4000
6000

*8849* ▲ Mountain height (in metres)

Permanent ice (ice cap or glacier)

**Water features**

River
Intermittent river
Canal
Lake / Reservoir
Intermittent lake
Marsh

**Communications**

Railway
Road
⊕ Main airport

**Administration**

Boundaries
International
Disputed
Internal
Ceasefire line

**Settlement**

Cities and towns in order of size

National capital | Other city or town
■ **Beijing** | ● **Mumbai**
| ● **Yantai**
| ● Anshun
| ◦ Bikaner
| ◦ Lhasa

Scale 1 : 15 000 000

0    150    300    450 km

Conic Equidistant projection

RUSSIA

KAZAKHSTAN

Kemerovo
Novosibirsk
Novokuznetsk
Abakan
Barnaul
Biysk
Gorno-Altaysk
Abaza
Kyzyl
Chadan
Gora Belukha ▲4506
Altay
Uvs Nuur
Ulaangom
Hyargas Nuur
Har Us Nuur
Dörgön Nuur
Har Nuur

Novosibirsk
Ob'
Karasuk
Ozero Kulundinskoye
Kulunda
Mikhaylovskiy
Rubtsovsk
Gornyak
Semipalatinsk
Ust'-Kamenogorsk
Zyryanovsk
Zaysan
Lake Zaysan
Altai Mountains

MONGOLIA

Altay

Nur-Sultan (Astana)
Kokshetau
Ozero Siletiteniz
Pavlodar
Ekibastuz
Yereymentau
Temirtau
Karaganda
Atasu
Zhezkazgan
Balkhash
Aktogay
Chiganak
Lake Balkhash

Georgiyevka
Kokpekti
Ayagoz
Tacheng

Ebinur Hu
Junggar Pendi
Karamay
Kuytun
Shihezi
Ürümqi
Qijiaojing
Yining
Turpan
Hami

Taldykorgan
Shymkent
Zhambyl
Almaty

Tashkent
UZBEK.
Angren
Andijon
Namangan
Kokand
Khujand
Bishkek
KYRGYZSTAN
Naryn
Ysyk-Köl
Tien Shan
Aksu
Kuqa
Korla
Bosten Hu

TAJIKISTAN
Kashi
Pamirs
Khorugh
Kashi

XINJIANG UYGUR ZIZHIQU
Tarim Basin
Taklimakan Desert
Lop Nur
Ruoqiang
Qiemo
Hotan
Altun Shan
Da Qaidam
Golmud
Laojunmi
Dunhuang
Guazho

AFGHANISTAN
Hindu Kush
Chitral
Gilgit
Karakoram Range
K2 8611
Administered by Pakistan
Kashmir
Peshawar
Islamabad
Srinagar
Rawalpindi
Administered by India
JAMMU AND KASHMIR
Leh
Jammu
LADAKH
Sutak

AKSAI CHIN
Administered by China
Claimed by India
Dêrub
Gar

Kunlun Shan
QINGHAI
QING

Plateau of Tibet
XIZANG ZIZHIQU
Siling Co
Lharigarbo
C
H
Nam Co
Lhasa
Xigazê
Lhazê
Qamdo
Salwe
Brahmaputra

PAKISTAN
Faisalabad
Lahore
Amritsar
Jalandhar
Ludhiana
Chandigarh
CHANDIGARH
UTTARAKHAND
PUNJAB
Sutlej
HIMACHAL PRADESH
HIMALAYA
NEPAL
Dhaulagiri ▲8167
Annapurna I ▲8091
Mount Everest 8849
Kathmandu
Kangchenjunga 8586
SIKKIM
Darjiling
Thimphu
BHUTAN
Kangmar
Dibrugarh
ARUNACHAL PRADESH
Claimed by China
ASSAM
Brahmaputra
Dimapur
Nagaon
NAGALAND

HARYANA
Delhi
New Delhi
Meerut
Ghaziabad
Faridabad
Mathura
Agra
Fatehgarh
Bareilly
UTTAR PRADESH
Lucknow
Kanpur
Gorakhpur
Muzaffarpur
Darbhanga
BIHAR
Patna
Munger
Bhagalpur
Saidpur
Rangpur
Rajshahi
Guwahati
MEGHALAYA
Shillong
MANIPUR
Imphal

Nawabshah
Jaisalmer
Bikaner
Pokaran
Sikar
Jaipur
RAJASTHAN
Jodhpur
Ajmer
Thar Desert
Mirpur Khas
Karachi
Hyderabad
Barmer
Pali
Udaipur
Kota
Gwalior
Jhansi
Guna
Sagar
MADHYA PRADESH
Bhopal
Indore
Narmada
Satpura Range
Khandwa
Jabalpur
Allahabad
Rewa
Mirzapur
Varanasi
Kathi
Gaya
JHARKHAND
Dhanbad
Asansol
Ranchi
Jamshedpur
WEST BENGAL
Dhaka
Agartala
TRIPURA
BANGLADESH
Khulna
Kolkata
MIZORAM
Chattogram
Chindwin

Tropic of Cancer
Gulf of Kachchh
Okha
Jamnagar
Porbandar
Diu
Bhuj
Gandhinagar
Gandhidham
GUJARAT
Rajkot
Bhavnagar
Vadodara
Ahmadabad
Surat
Dhule
Daman
Tapi
Jalgaon
Manmad
Gulf of Cambay
Nashik
Aurangabad
Jalna
MAHARASHTRA
Amravati
Nagpur
Gondiya
Burhanpur
Deccan
INDIA
Godavari
Pune
Bhima
Solapur
Sangli
Kolhapur
KARNATAKA
Nizamabad
TELANGANA
Hyderabad
Cuddapah

Raipur
CHHATTISGARH
Bilaspur
Kanker
Chandrapur
Jagdalpur
Sambalpur
ODISHA
Bhubaneshwar
Cuttack
Puri
Brahmapur
Baleshwar
Kharagpur
Mouths of the Ganges
Cox's Bazar
Sittwe
Bay of Bengal

Vishakhapatnam
Vizianagaram

MYANMAR (BURMA)
Mt Victoria ▲3053
Monywa
Shwebo
Mandal
Meiktila
Magway
Pakokku
Nay P
Taw
Irrawaddy

55°  60°  65°  70°  75°  80°  85°  90°  95°

70°  75°  80°  85°  90°  95°

A  B  C  D  E  F  G

7  6  5  4  3  2  1

GOLIA

NEI MONGOL ZIZHIQU (INNER MONGOLIA)

Gobi

Yablonovyy Khrebet

Da Hinggan Ling

MANCHURIA

HEILONGJIANG

JILIN

LIAONING

NORTH KOREA

SOUTH KOREA

Sea of Japan (East Sea)

Honshū

JAPAN

Kyūshū

Shikoku

HEBEI

SHANXI

SHANDONG

Bo Hai

Korea Bay

Yellow Sea

Huang He

NINGXIA HUIZU ZIZHIQU

Qinghai Hu

Huang He

SHAANXI

HENAN

ANHUI

JIANGSU

East China Sea

Ryukyu Islands

Okinawa

HUBEI

CHONGQING

ZHEJIANG

Chang Jiang

Poyang Hu

Dongting Hu

HUNAN

JIANGXI

FUJIAN

Nan Ling

GUIZHOU

TAIWAN

China claims Taiwan as its 23rd province

PACIFIC OCEAN

YUNNAN

GUANGXI ZHUANGZU ZIZHIQU

GUANGDONG

Xi Jiang

Hong Kong

HONG KONG

Macao (Aomen)

Taiwan Strait

Luzon Strait

Batan Islands

Babuyan Islands

VIETNAM

LAOS

Gulf of Tongking

Leizhou Bandao

HAINAN

PHILIPPINES

Luzon

*Cities and place names:*

Zima, Kachug, Lake Baikal, Irkutsk, Slyudyanka, Angarsk, Ulan-Ude, Kyakhta, Khorinsk, Chita, Sretensk, Karymskoye, Karymskoye, Borzya, Svobodnyy, Blagoveshchensk, Komsomol'sk-na-Amure, Ti'ban, Khabarovsk

Sibirskoye, Slyudyanka, Bulgan, Darhan, Bayan-Uul, Choybalsan, Manzhouli, Hulun Nur, Hulun Buir, Buyr Nuur, Nenjiang, Bekan, Amur, Birobidzhan, Yichun, Hegang, Jiamusi, Jixi

Tsetserleg, Arvayheer, Mandalgovi, Saynshand, Baruun Urt, Qiqihar, Daqing, Ulanhot, Baicheng, Taonan, Songyuan, Harbin, Fuyu, Mudanjiang, Lake Khanka, Ussuriysk, Vladivostok, Nakhodka

Ulan Bator, Xilinhot, Tongliao, Siping, Liaoyuan, Changchun, Jilin, Tonghua, Yanji, Ch'ŏngjin, Kimch'aek

Hohhot, Jining, Zhangjiakou, Chifeng, Chengde, Jinzhou, Shenyang, Fuxin, Fushun, Benxi, Anshan, Yingkou, Dandong, Hamhŭng, Wŏnsan

Baotou, Datong, Beijing, Tangshan, Tianjin, Lianshan, Qinhuangdao, Dalian, P'yŏngyang, Namp'o, Haeju, Kaesŏng, Chuncheon, Seoul, Incheon, Koyang, Oki-shotō, Tottori

Wuhai, Shizuishan, Yinchuan, Baoding, Shijiazhuang, Dezhou, Dongying, Yantai, Weihai, Shandong Bandao, Daejeon, Masan, Busan, Hiroshima, Okayama, Kobe, Matsuyama, Kōchi

Wuwei, Taiyuan, Yangquan, Xingtai, Jinan, Zibo, Weifang, Qingdao, Rizhao, Jeonju, Gwangju, Cheju-do, Sasebo, Kita-Kyūshū, Fukuoka, Kumamoto, Nagasaki, Miyazaki, Kagoshima

Lanzhou, Linxia, Changzhi, Handan, Anyang, Jining, Xintai, Heze, Zaozhuang, Lianyungang, Yancheng, Korea Strait, Tsushima, Daegu

Xining, Linfen, Jiaozuo, Kaifeng, Xinxiang, Huaibei, Suzhou, Suqian, Zhangshu, Jiangsu, Nantong

Tianshui, Chencang, Weinan, Luoyang, Zhengzhou, Shangqiu, Fuyang, Bengbu, Huainan, Yangzhou, Changzhou, Suzhou, Shanghai

Guangyuan, Xi'an, Pingdingshan, Nanyang, Xinyang, Hefei, Lu'an, Nanjing, Wuxi, Jiaxing

Dazhou, Hanzhong, Zaoyang, Xiangyang, Suizhou, Tongling, Wuhu, Huzhou, Hangzhou, Cixi, Ningbo

Chengdu, Nanchong, Wanzhou, Yichang, Jingmen, Jingzhou, Wuhan, Huangshi, Jiujiang, Jingdezhen, Jinhua, Shaoxing, Taizhou

Kangding, Neijiang, Suining, Ershi, Chongqing, Yueyang, Nanchang, Quzhou, Wenzhou

Gongga Shan 7556, Leshan, Zigong, Yibin, Zunyi, Changde, Yiyang, Changsha, Zhuzhou, Xiangtan, Ji'an, Nanping, Matsu Tao, Fuzhou, Keelung

Xichang, Zhaotong, Panzhihua, Liupanshui, Anshun, Duyun, Guiyang, Shaoyang, Hengyang, Yongzhou, Chenzhou, Pingxiang, Ganzhou, Sanming, Putian, Taichung, Hsinchu, Taipei

Dali, Chuxiong, Kunming, Yuxi, Guilin, Hechi, Liuzhou, Shaoguan, Meizhou, Xiamen, Quanzhou, Zhangping, Jinjiang, Tainan, Jiayi, Kaohsiung, Taitung

Jinghong, Kaiyuan, Gejiu, Baise, Wuzhou, Guangzhou, Foshan, Huizhou, Shenzhen, Lufeng, Jieyang, Shantou, Puning

Lao Cai, Nanning, Yulin, Jiangmen, Zhongshan, Hong Kong

Cao Bang, Pingxiang, Qinzhou, Beihai, Zhanjiang

Hanoi, Hai Phong, Nam Định, Thai Binh, Thanh Hoa, Dongfang, Haikou, Qionghai, Laoag, San Fernando, Aparri, Tuguegarao, Ilagan

Louangnamtha, Phongsali, Son La, Thai Nguyen, Louangphabang, Vinh

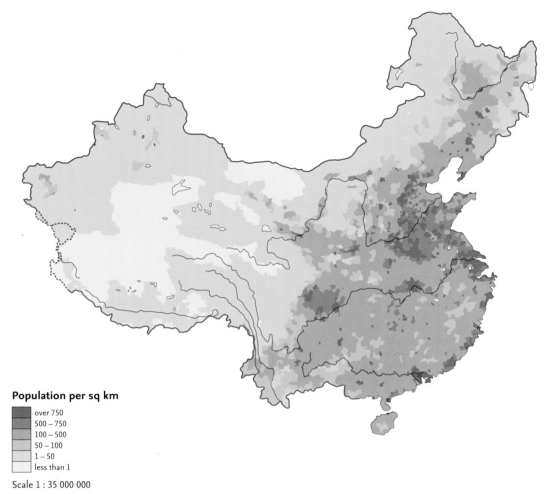

## Population per sq km

- ▮ over 750
- ▮ 500 – 750
- ▮ 100 – 500
- ▮ 50 – 100
- ▮ 1 – 50
- ▯ less than 1

Scale 1 : 35 000 000

National Bureau of Statistics of China
www.stats.gov.cn/english

### Top 10 densely populated provinces

| Province | Population per sq km |
|---|---|
| Macao | 22 247 |
| Hong Kong | 6800 |
| Shanghai | 3814 |
| Beijing | 1323 |
| Tianjin | 1307 |
| Jiangsu | 783 |
| Shandong | 637 |
| Guangdong | 621 |
| Henan | 572 |
| Zhejiang | 556 |

### Population growth rates

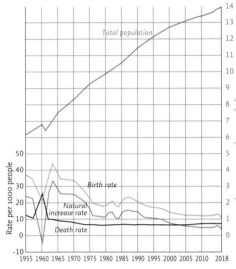

### Population movement

- ▮ Major origins of migrants, 2000
- → Main direction of movement of migrants
- → Other direction of movement of migrants

Scale 1 : 70 000 000

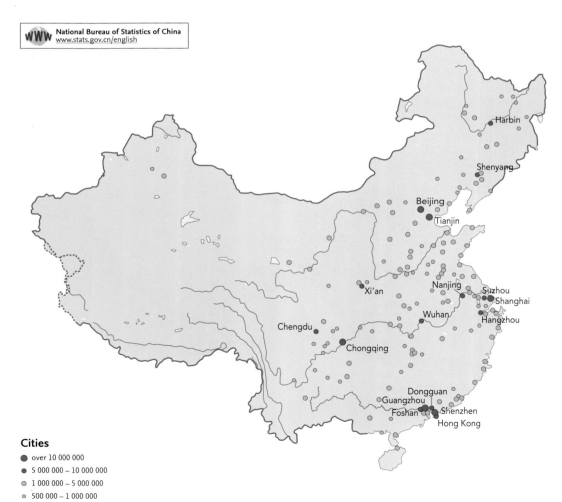

## Cities

- ● over 10 000 000
- ● 5 000 000 – 10 000 000
- ○ 1 000 000 – 5 000 000
- ○ 500 000 – 1 000 000

Scale 1 : 35 000 000

### Top 10 largest urban agglomerations, 2018

| Urban agglomeration | Population |
|---|---|
| Shanghai | 27 058 479 |
| Beijing | 20 462 610 |
| Chongqing | 15 872 179 |
| Tianjin | 13 589 078 |
| Guangzhou | 13 301 532 |
| Shenzhen | 12 356 820 |
| Chengdu | 9 135 768 |
| Nanjing | 8 847 372 |
| Wuhan | 8 364 978 |
| Xi'an | 8 000 965 |

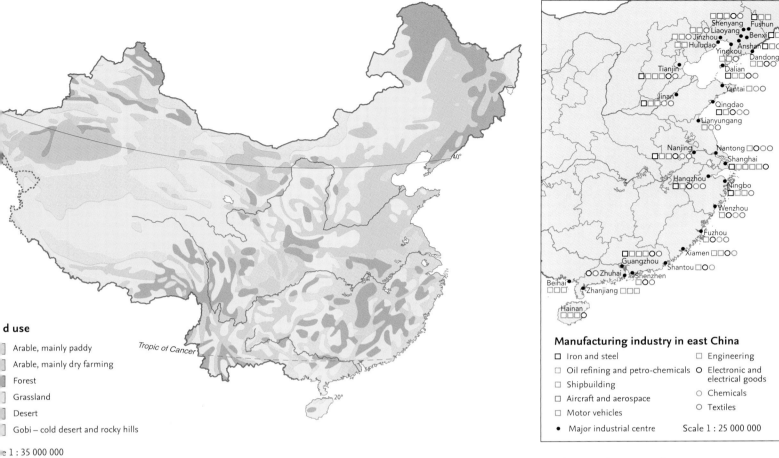

**d use**

- Arable, mainly paddy
- Arable, mainly dry farming
- Forest
- Grassland
- Desert
- Gobi – cold desert and rocky hills

Tropic of Cancer

e 1 : 35 000 000

**Manufacturing industry in east China**

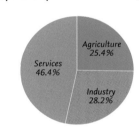

| | |
|---|---|
| □ Iron and steel | □ Engineering |
| □ Oil refining and petro-chemicals | O Electronic and electrical goods |
| □ Shipbuilding | |
| □ Aircraft and aerospace | O Chemicals |
| □ Motor vehicles | O Textiles |
| ● Major industrial centre | Scale 1 : 25 000 000 |

**Employment by economic sector, 2019**

Services 46.4%
Agriculture 25.4%
Industry 28.2%

**in trading partners, 2018**

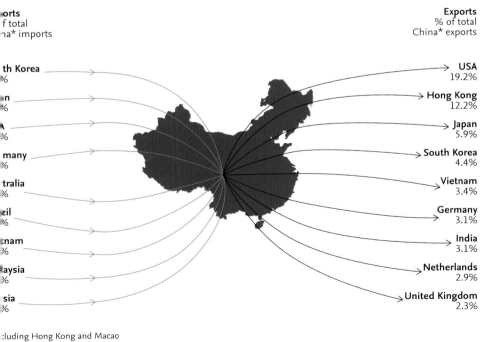

**orts**
f total
na* imports

th Korea
n
A
many
tralia
zil
nam
aysia
sia

**Exports**
% of total
China* exports

USA 19.2%
Hong Kong 12.2%
Japan 5.9%
South Korea 4.4%
Vietnam 3.4%
Germany 3.1%
India 3.1%
Netherlands 2.9%
United Kingdom 2.3%

:luding Hong Kong and Macao

**Trade**

Imports, 2018

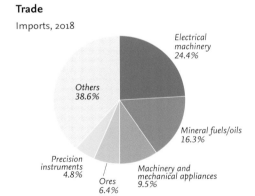

Electrical machinery 24.4%
Others 38.6%
Mineral fuels/oils 16.3%
Precision instruments 4.8%
Ores 6.4%
Machinery and mechanical appliances 9.5%

Exports, 2018

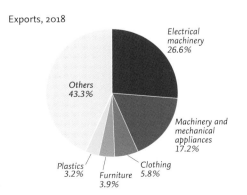

Electrical machinery 26.6%
Others 43.3%
Machinery and mechanical appliances 17.2%
Plastics 3.2%
Furniture 3.9%
Clothing 5.8%

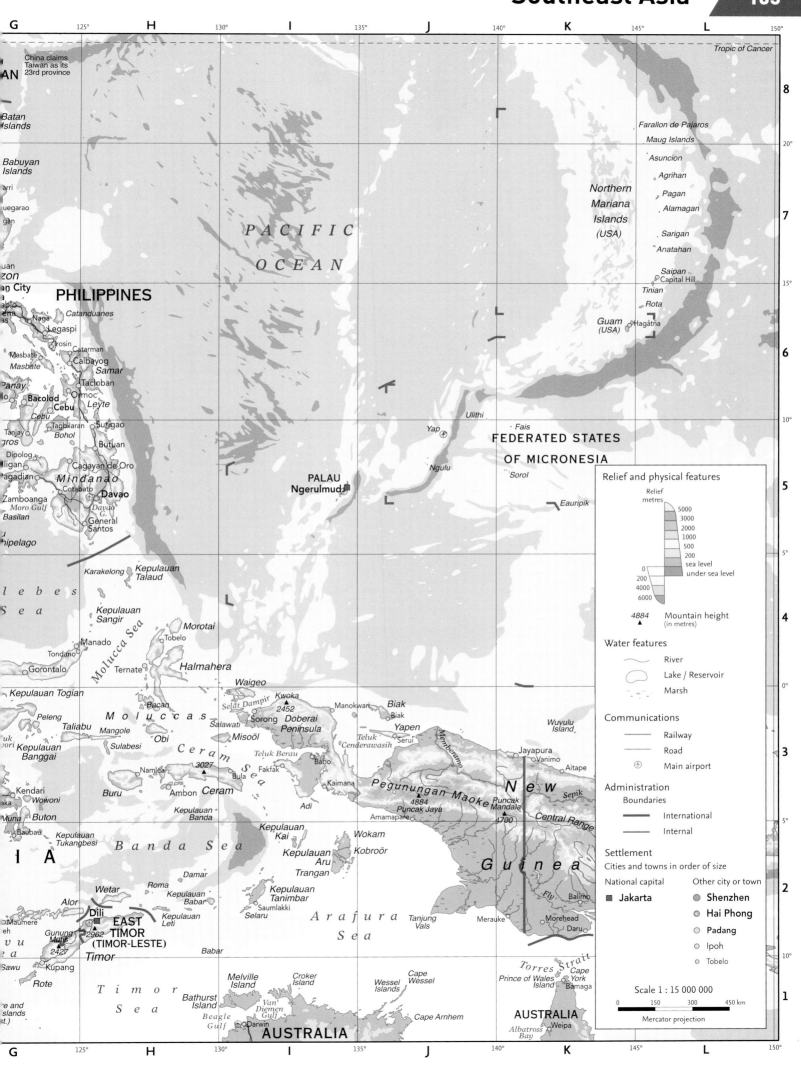

G 125° H 130° I 135° J 140° K 145° L 150°

Tropic of Cancer

China claims
Taiwan as its
23rd province

Batan
Islands

Babuyan
Islands

arri

uegarao

gan

zon

n City

PHILIPPINES

Naga
Legaspi
Irosin
Catarman
Calbayog
Samar
Catanduanes

Masbate
Masbate
Panay
Bacolod
Cebu
Cebu
Ormoc
Leyte
Tacloban

Tanjay
gros
Tagbilaran
Bohol
Surigao
Butuan

Dipolog
iligan
agadian
Cagayan de Oro
Cotabato
Davao
Zamboanga
Basilan
Davao
G.
Moro Gulf
General
Santos
hipelago

PACIFIC

OCEAN

Northern
Mariana
Islands
(USA)

Farallon de Pajaros

Maug Islands

Asuncion

Agrihan

Pagan

Alamagan

Sarigan

Anatahan

Saipan
Capital Hill

Tinian

Rota

Guam
(USA)
Hagåtña

Ulithi

Yap
Yap

Ngulu

Fais

FEDERATED STATES
OF MICRONESIA

PALAU
Ngerulmud

Sorol

Eauripik

Karakelong
Kepulauan
Talaud

lebes
Sea

Kepulauan
Sangir

Morotai

Manado
Tondano
Tobelo
Ternate
Gorontalo
Halmahera

Waigeo

Kepulauan Togian

Moluccas
Peleng
Taliabu
Kepulauan
Banggai
Mangole
Obi
Sulabesi
Bacan
Selat Dampir
Kwoka
2452
Sorong
Salawati
Misoöl
Doberai
Peninsula
Manokwari

Biak
Biak
Yapen
Serui
Teluk
Cenderawasih

Wuvulu
Island

New

Jayapura
Vanimo
Aitape

Kendari
Wowoni
Namlea
3027
Buru
Ceram Sea
Teluk Berau
Bula
Fakfak
Babo
Kaimana
Adi
Pegunungan Maoke
4884
Puncak Jaya
Amamapare
Puncak
Mandala
4700
Central Range
Sepik

Guinea

Membramo

Muna
Buton
Baubau
Ambon
Ceram
Kepulauan
Banda

IA

Kepulauan
Tukangbesi
Banda Sea
Kepulauan
Kai
Wokam
Kepulauan
Aru
Kobroör
Trangan

Damar
Roma
Kepulauan
Babar
Kepulauan
Tanimbar
Saumlakki
Selaru
Arafura
Sea
Tanjung
Vals
Merauke
Morehead
Daru

Flu
Balimo

Alor
Wetar
Dili
EAST
TIMOR
(TIMOR-LESTE)
Gunung
Mutis
2962
eh
2427
Timor
Babar
Kepulauan
Leti

Maumere
vu
a
Kupang
Rote

Timor
Sea

Melville
Island
Croker
Island
Wessel
Islands
Cape
Wessel

Torres Strait
Cape
York
Bamaga
Prince of Wales
Island

re and
slands
st.)

Sawu

Bathurst
Island
Beagle
Gulf
Van
Diemen
Gulf
Darwin
Cape Arnhem

AUSTRALIA

AUSTRALIA
Albatross
Bay
Weipa

## Relief and physical features

Relief
metres

5000
3000
2000
1000
500
200
0 sea level
under sea level
200
4000
6000

4884 ▲ Mountain height
(in metres)

## Water features

~ River

Lake / Reservoir

Marsh

## Communications

Railway

Road

⊕ Main airport

## Administration

Boundaries

International

Internal

## Settlement

Cities and towns in order of size

National capital Other city or town

■ Jakarta ⬤ Shenzhen

◉ Hai Phong

◎ Padang

○ Ipoh

○ Tobelo

Scale 1 : 15 000 000

0 150 300 450 km

Mercator projection

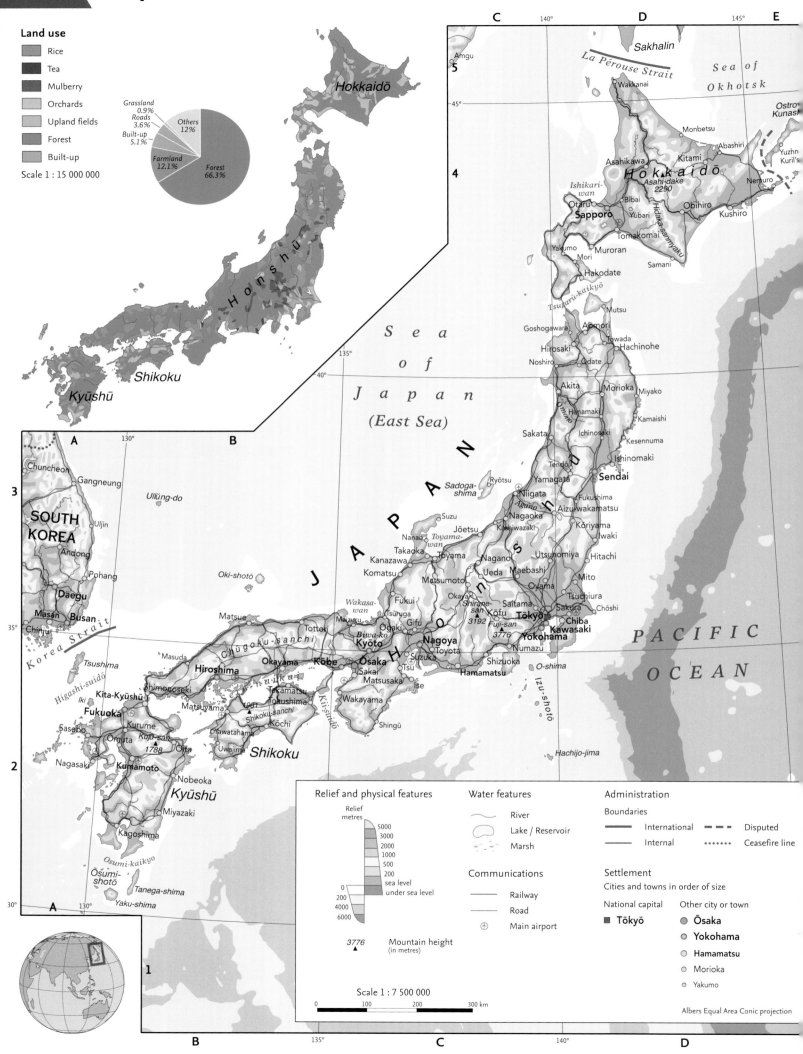

## Land use

- Rice
- Tea
- Mulberry
- Orchards
- Upland fields
- Forest
- Built-up

Scale 1 : 15 000 000

Grassland 0.9%
Roads 3.6%
Built-up 5.1%
Others 12%
Farmland 12.1%
Forest 66.3%

Hokkaidō

Honshū

Shikoku

Kyūshū

Sakhalin
La Pérouse Strait
Sea of Okhotsk
Ostrov Kunashir
Amgu
Wakkanai
Yuzhno-Kuril'sk
Monbetsu
Abashiri
Asahikawa
Kitami
Hokkaidō
Nemuro
Ishikari-wan
Asahi-dake 2290
Kushiro
Otaru
Bibai
Yūbari
Obihiro
Sapporo
Hidaka-sanmyaku
Yakumo
Tomakomai
Samani
Mori
Muroran
Hakodate
Tsugaru-kaikyō
Mutsu
Goshogawara
Aomori
Sea of Japan (East Sea)
Hirosaki
Towada
Hachinohe
Noshiro
Ōdate
Akita
Ōmono
Morioka
Miyako
Sadoga-shima
Hanamaki
Ryōtsu
Sakata
Ichinoseki
Kamaishi
Tendō
Kesennuma
Suzu
Yamagata
Ishinomaki
Niigata
Sendai
Nagaoka
Fukushima
Nanao
Toyama-wan
Aizuwakamatsu
Kōriyama
Jōetsu
Kashiwazaki
Iwaki
Agano
Takaoka
Toyama
Nagano
Utsunomiya
Hitachi
Kanazawa
Ueda
Maebashi
Komatsu
Matsumoto
Mito
Okaya
Oyama
Fukui
Tsuchiura
Shirane-san 3192
Kōfu
Tsuruga
Gifu
Saitama
Chōshi
Ōgaki
Fuji-san 3776
Tōkyō
Maizuru
Biwa-ko
Nagoya
Chiba
Matsue
Tottori
Kyōto
Suzuka
Yokohama
Kawasaki
Toyota
Wakasa-wan
Chūgoku-sanchi
Ōsaka
Tsu
Numazu
Masuda
Okayama
Kōbe
Shizuoka
O-shima
Hiroshima
Sakai
Hamamatsu
Matsusaka
Izu-shotō
Shimonoseki
Takamatsu
Ise
Kita-Kyūshū
Matsuyama
Tokushima
Shikoku-sanchi
Fukuoka
1981
Kōchi
Wakayama
Iki
Kurume
Ōwatahama
Shingū
Tsushima
Ōita
Uwajima
Shikoku
Higashi-suidō
Sasebo
Ōmuta
Kuju-san 1788
Nagasaki
Kumamoto
Nobeoka
Miyazaki
Kyūshū
Kagoshima
Ōsumi-kaikyō
Ōsumi-shotō
Tanega-shima
Yaku-shima
Hachijo-jima
PACIFIC OCEAN

SOUTH KOREA
Chuncheon
Gangneung
Uljin
Ullŭng-do
Andong
Pohang
Daegu
Masan
Busan
Chinju
Korea Strait
Oki-shotō

J A P A N   A L P S
H O N S H Ū

### Relief and physical features

Relief metres
5000
3000
2000
1000
500
200
sea level
0
under sea level
200
4000
6000

### Water features

- River
- Lake / Reservoir
- Marsh

### Communications

- Railway
- Road
- ⊕ Main airport

3776 ▲ Mountain height (in metres)

### Administration

Boundaries
- International
- Internal
- Disputed
- Ceasefire line

### Settlement

Cities and towns in order of size

National capital
- ■ Tōkyō

Other city or town
- Ōsaka
- Yokohama
- Hamamatsu
- Morioka
- Yakumo

Scale 1 : 7 500 000

0   100   200   300 km

Albers Equal Area Conic projection

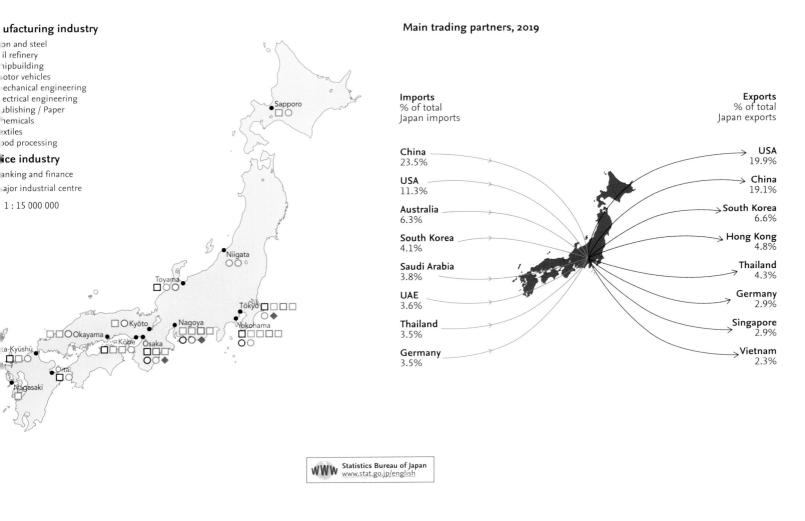

### ufacturing industry

- on and steel
- l refinery
- hipbuilding
- otor vehicles
- echanical engineering
- ectrical engineering
- ublishing / Paper
- hemicals
- xtiles
- od processing

### ice industry

- anking and finance
- ajor industrial centre

1 : 15 000 000

Sapporo

Niigata
Toyama
Tōkyō
Kyōto
Nagoya
Yokohama
Okayama
Kōbe
Osaka
a-Kyūshū
Ōita
Nagasaki

### Main trading partners, 2019

**Imports**
% of total
Japan imports

China 23.5%
USA 11.3%
Australia 6.3%
South Korea 4.1%
Saudi Arabia 3.8%
UAE 3.6%
Thailand 3.5%
Germany 3.5%

**Exports**
% of total
Japan exports

USA 19.9%
China 19.1%
South Korea 6.6%
Hong Kong 4.8%
Thailand 4.3%
Germany 2.9%
Singapore 2.9%
Vietnam 2.3%

**www** **Statistics Bureau of Japan**
www.stat.go.jp/english

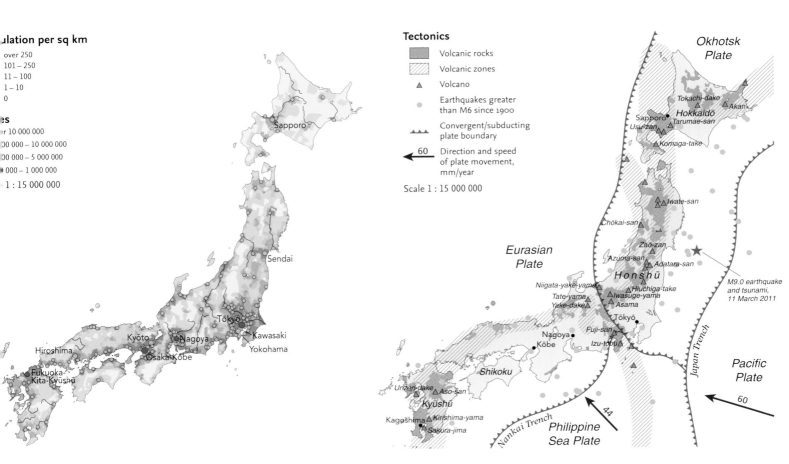

### ulation per sq km

- over 250
- 101 – 250
- 11 – 100
- 1 – 10
- 0

### es

- r 10 000 000
- 00 000 – 10 000 000
- 00 000 – 5 000 000
- 000 – 1 000 000

1 : 15 000 000

Sapporo
Sendai
Tōkyō
Kawasaki
Yokohama
Kyōto
Nagoya
Hiroshima
Osaka Kōbe
Fukuoka-
Kita-Kyūshū

### Tectonics

- Volcanic rocks
- Volcanic zones
- ▲ Volcano
- Earthquakes greater than M6 since 1900
- Convergent/subducting plate boundary
- ← 60 Direction and speed of plate movement, mm/year

Scale 1 : 15 000 000

Okhotsk Plate
Tokachi-dake
Akan
Sapporo
Hokkaidō Tarumae-san
Usu-zan
Komaga-take
Iwate-san
Chōkai-san
Zaō-zan
Eurasian Plate
Azuma-san
Adatara-san
Honshū
M9.0 earthquake and tsunami, 11 March 2011
Niigata-yake-yama
Huchiga-take
Tate-yama
Iwasuge-yama
Yake-dake
Asama
Tōkyō
Nagoya
Fuji-san
Kōbe
Izu-tobu
Japan Trench
Shikoku
Pacific Plate
Unzen-dake
Aso-san
60
Kyūshū
Kirishima-yama
Kagoshima
Sakura-jima
Nankai Trench
44
Philippine Sea Plate

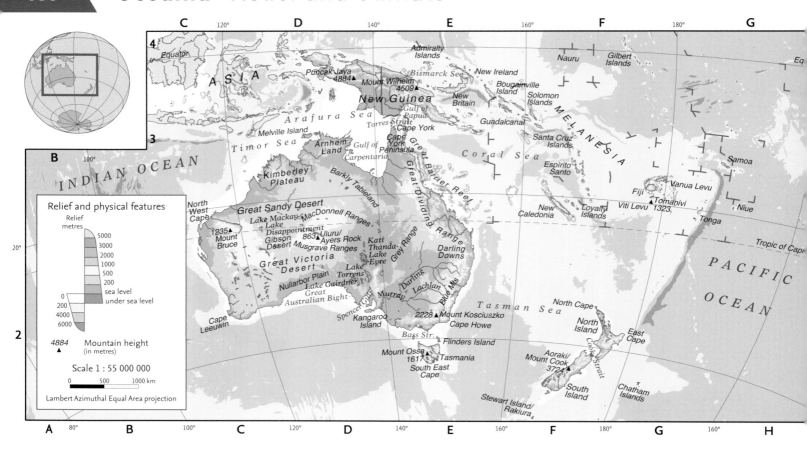

**Relief and physical features**

Relief metres

5000
3000
2000
1000
500
200
0 sea level
under sea level
200
4000
6000

4884 ▲ Mountain height (in metres)

Scale 1 : 55 000 000

0 500 1000 km

Lambert Azimuthal Equal Area projection

**Cross-section**

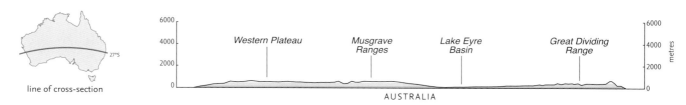

line of cross-section

AUSTRALIA

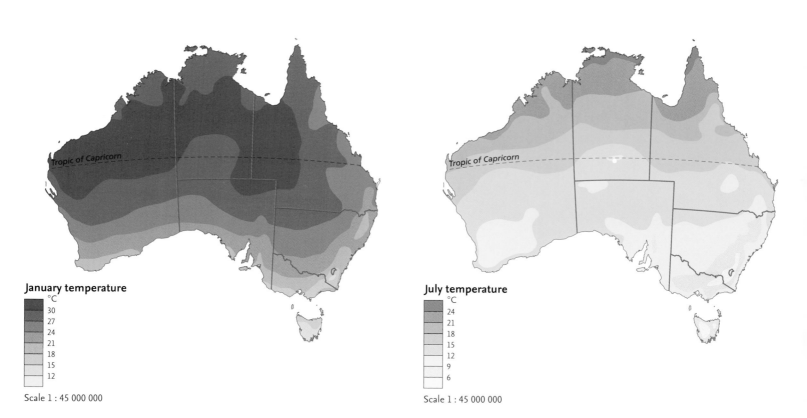

**January temperature**
°C
30
27
24
21
18
15
12

Scale 1 : 45 000 000

**July temperature**
°C
24
21
18
15
12
9
6

Scale 1 : 45 000 000

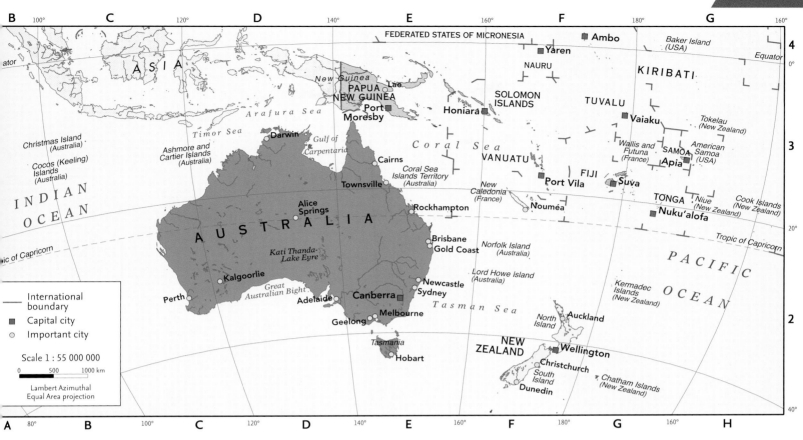

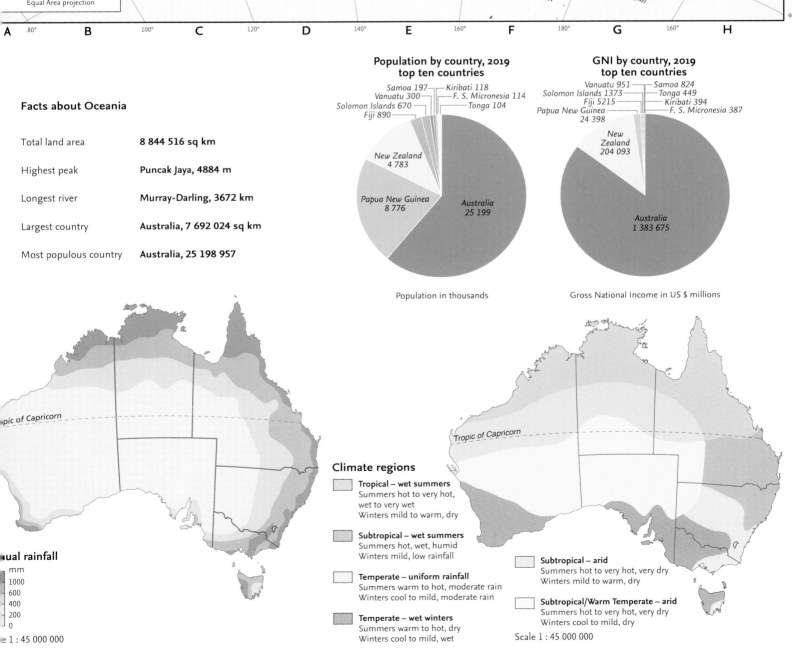

## Facts about Oceania

| | |
|---|---|
| Total land area | **8 844 516 sq km** |
| Highest peak | **Puncak Jaya, 4884 m** |
| Longest river | **Murray-Darling, 3672 km** |
| Largest country | **Australia, 7 692 024 sq km** |
| Most populous country | **Australia, 25 198 957** |

### Population by country, 2019
top ten countries

Samoa 197 — Kiribati 118
Vanuatu 300 — F. S. Micronesia 114
Solomon Islands 670 — Tonga 104
Fiji 890

New Zealand 4 783

Papua New Guinea 8 776

Australia 25 199

Population in thousands

### GNI by country, 2019
top ten countries

Vanuatu 951 — Samoa 824
Solomon Islands 1373 — Tonga 449
Fiji 5215 — Kiribati 394
Papua New Guinea 24 398 — F. S. Micronesia 387

New Zealand 204 093

Australia 1 383 675

Gross National Income in US $ millions

## Climate regions

**Tropical – wet summers**
Summers hot to very hot,
wet to very wet
Winters mild to warm, dry

**Subtropical – wet summers**
Summers hot, wet, humid
Winters mild, low rainfall

**Temperate – uniform rainfall**
Summers warm to hot, moderate rain
Winters cool to mild, moderate rain

**Temperate – wet winters**
Summers warm to hot, dry
Winters cool to mild, wet

**Subtropical – arid**
Summers hot to very hot, very dry
Winters mild to warm, dry

**Subtropical/Warm Temperate – arid**
Summers hot to very hot, very dry
Winters cool to mild, dry

Scale 1 : 45 000 000

Annual rainfall

mm
1000
600
400
200
0

Scale 1 : 45 000 000

# Australia and New Zealand

**Relief and physical features**

Relief metres

5000
3000
2000
1000
500
200
sea level
0
200
4000
6000
under sea level

▲ 4884  Mountain height (in metres)

**Water features**

～ River
～ Intermittent river
Lake / Reservoir
Intermittent lake
Marsh
Coral reef

**Communications**

Railway
Road
⊕ Main airport

**Administration**

Boundaries
International
Internal

**Settlement**
Cities and towns in order of size

National capital
■ Canberra

Other city or town
◉ Sydney
◎ Gold Coast
◦ Newcastle
· Darwin

Scale 1 : 20 000 000

0   200   400   600   800 km

Lambert Azimuthal Equal Area projection

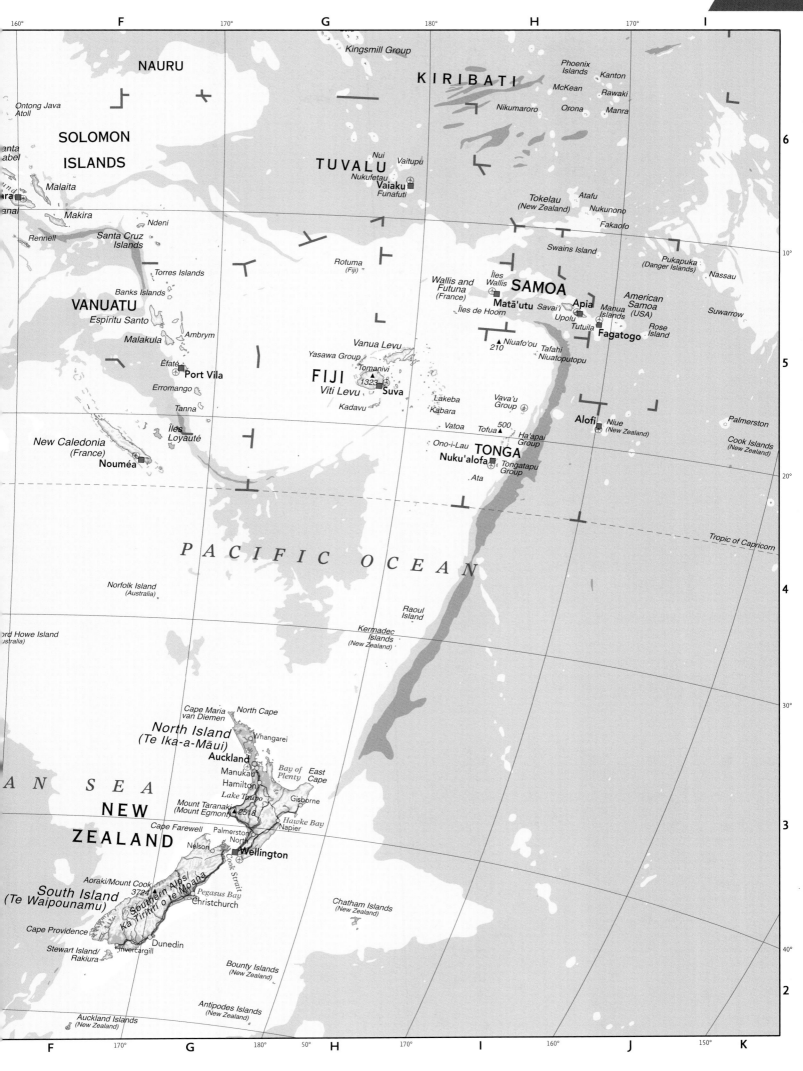

NAURU

SOLOMON
ISLANDS

Ontong Java
Atoll

Santa
abel

an

Malaita

Makira

Ndeni

Rennell

Santa Cruz
Islands

Torres Islands

VANUATU

Banks Islands

Espíritu Santo

Malakula

Ambrym

Éfaté

Port Vila

Erromango

Tanna

Îles
Loyauté

New Caledonia
(France)

Nouméa

KINGSMILL Group

KIRIBATI

Phoenix
Islands

Kanton

McKean

Rawaki

Nikumaroro

Orona

Manra

TUVALU

Nui

Vaitupu

Nukufetau

Vaiaku

Funafuti

Tokelau
(New Zealand)

Atafu

Nukunono

Fakaofo

Swains Island

Pukapuka
(Danger Islands)

Nassau

Rotuma
(Fiji)

Wallis and
Futuna
(France)

Îles
Wallis

SAMOA

American
Samoa
(USA)

Suwarrow

Matā'utu

Savai'i

Apia

Manua
Islands

Îles de Hoorn

Upolu

Tutuila

Rose
Island

Vanua Levu

Yasawa Group

Tomanivi
1323

210

Niuafo'ou

Tafahi

Niuatoputopu

Fagatogo

FIJI

Suva

Viti Levu

Kadavu

Lakeba

Kabara

Vava'u
Group

Vatoa

Tofua
500

Ha'apai
Group

Alofi

Niue
(New Zealand)

Palmerston

Ono-i-Lau

TONGA

Cook Islands
(New Zealand)

Nuku'alofa

Tongatapu
Group

Ata

PACIFIC OCEAN

Tropic of Capricorn

Norfolk Island
(Australia)

ord Howe Island
Australia)

Raoul
Island

Kermadec
Islands
(New Zealand)

Cape Maria
van Diemen

North Cape

AN SEA

North Island
(Te Ika-a-Māui)

Whangarei

Auckland

Manukau

Bay of
Plenty

East
Cape

Hamilton

Lake Taupo

Gisborne

NEW

Mount Taranaki
(Mount Egmont)

2518

Hawke Bay

ZEALAND

Cape Farewell

Palmerston
North

Napier

Nelson

Wellington

Aoraki/Mount Cook
3724

Cook Strait

South Island
(Te Waipounamu)

Southern Alps
Kā Tiritiri o te Moana

Pegasus Bay

Christchurch

Chatham Islands
(New Zealand)

Cape Providence

Dunedin

Stewart Island/
Rakiura

Invercargill

Bounty Islands
(New Zealand)

Auckland Islands
(New Zealand)

Antipodes Islands
(New Zealand)

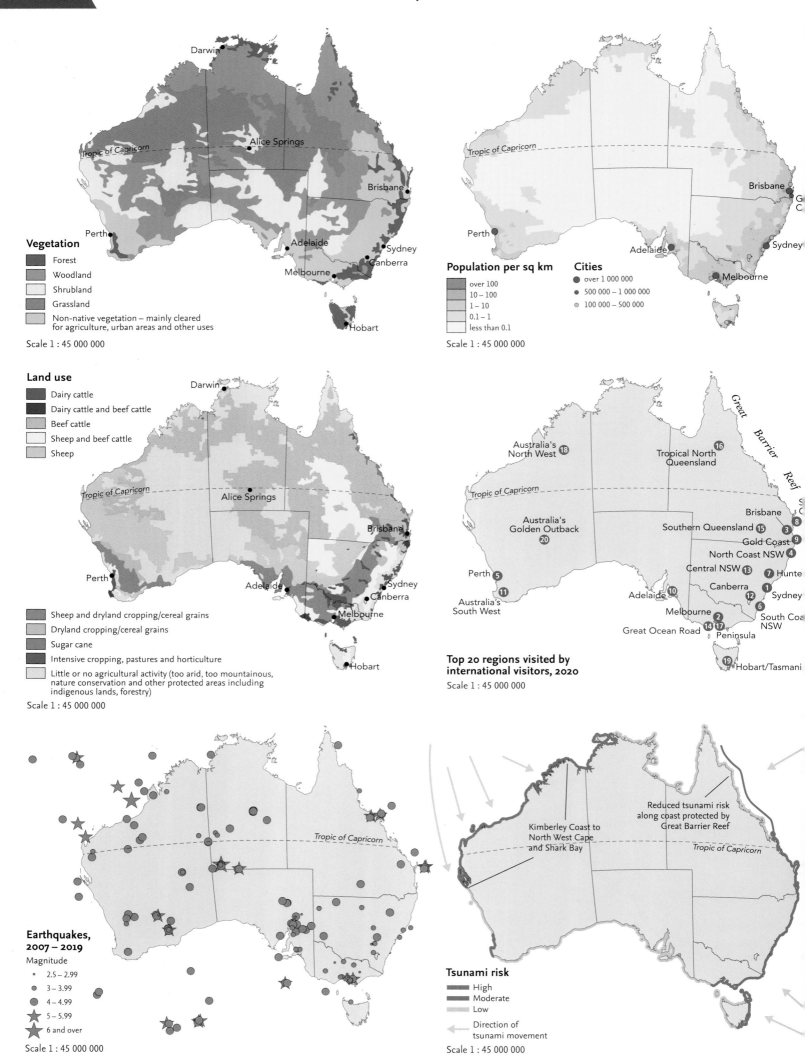

**Vegetation**
- Forest
- Woodland
- Shrubland
- Grassland
- Non-native vegetation – mainly cleared for agriculture, urban areas and other uses

Scale 1 : 45 000 000

Darwin
Alice Springs
Tropic of Capricorn
Brisbane
Perth
Adelaide
Sydney
Canberra
Melbourne
Hobart

**Population per sq km**
- over 100
- 10 – 100
- 1 – 10
- 0.1 – 1
- less than 0.1

**Cities**
- over 1 000 000
- 500 000 – 1 000 000
- 100 000 – 500 000

Scale 1 : 45 000 000

Tropic of Capricorn
Brisbane
G C
Perth
Adelaide
Sydney
Melbourne

**Land use**
- Dairy cattle
- Dairy cattle and beef cattle
- Beef cattle
- Sheep and beef cattle
- Sheep

Darwin
Tropic of Capricorn
Alice Springs
Brisbane
Perth
Adelaide
Sydney
Canberra
Melbourne
Hobart

- Sheep and dryland cropping/cereal grains
- Dryland cropping/cereal grains
- Sugar cane
- Intensive cropping, pastures and horticulture
- Little or no agricultural activity (too arid, too mountainous, nature conservation and other protected areas including indigenous lands, forestry)

Scale 1 : 45 000 000

Great Barrier Reef S
Australia's North West ⑱
Tropical North Queensland ⑯
Tropic of Capricorn
Australia's Golden Outback ⑳
Brisbane
Southern Queensland ⑮
⑧
③
⑨
Gold Coast ④
North Coast NSW
Central NSW ⑬
⑦ Hunte
Perth ⑤
Canberra
① Sydney
⑫
Adelaide ⑩
⑥
Australia's South West
⑪
South Coa
Melbourne
② NSW
Great Ocean Road ⑭ ⑰
Peninsula
⑲ Hobart/Tasmani

**Top 20 regions visited by international visitors, 2020**

Scale 1 : 45 000 000

**Earthquakes, 2007 – 2019**

Magnitude
- 2.5 – 2.99
- 3 – 3.99
- 4 – 4.99
- 5 – 5.99
- 6 and over

Tropic of Capricorn

Scale 1 : 45 000 000

Kimberley Coast to North West Cape and Shark Bay
Reduced tsunami risk along coast protected by Great Barrier Reef
Tropic of Capricorn

**Tsunami risk**
- High
- Moderate
- Low
- Direction of tsunami movement

Scale 1 : 45 000 000

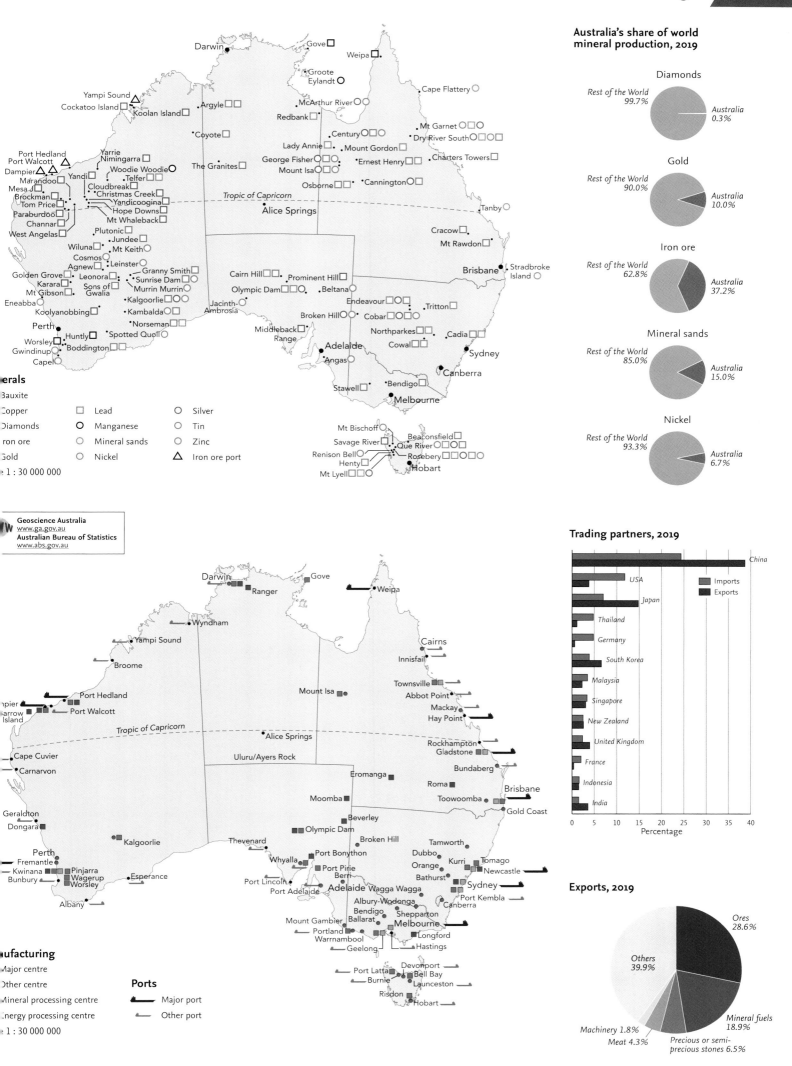

**Australia's share of world mineral production, 2019**

Diamonds — Rest of the World 99.7%, Australia 0.3%
Gold — Rest of the World 90.0%, Australia 10.0%
Iron ore — Rest of the World 62.8%, Australia 37.2%
Mineral sands — Rest of the World 85.0%, Australia 15.0%
Nickel — Rest of the World 93.3%, Australia 6.7%

**Minerals**

Bauxite · Copper · Diamonds · Iron ore · Gold · Lead · Manganese · Mineral sands · Nickel · Silver · Tin · Zinc · Iron ore port

Scale 1 : 30 000 000

Geoscience Australia
www.ga.gov.au
Australian Bureau of Statistics
www.abs.gov.au

**Trading partners, 2019** — Imports, Exports — China, USA, Japan, Thailand, Germany, South Korea, Malaysia, Singapore, New Zealand, United Kingdom, France, Indonesia, India — Percentage

**Manufacturing**

Major centre · Other centre · Mineral processing centre · Energy processing centre

**Ports** — Major port · Other port

Scale 1 : 30 000 000

**Exports, 2019** — Ores 28.6%, Others 39.9%, Mineral fuels 18.9%, Precious or semi-precious stones 6.5%, Meat 4.3%, Machinery 1.8%

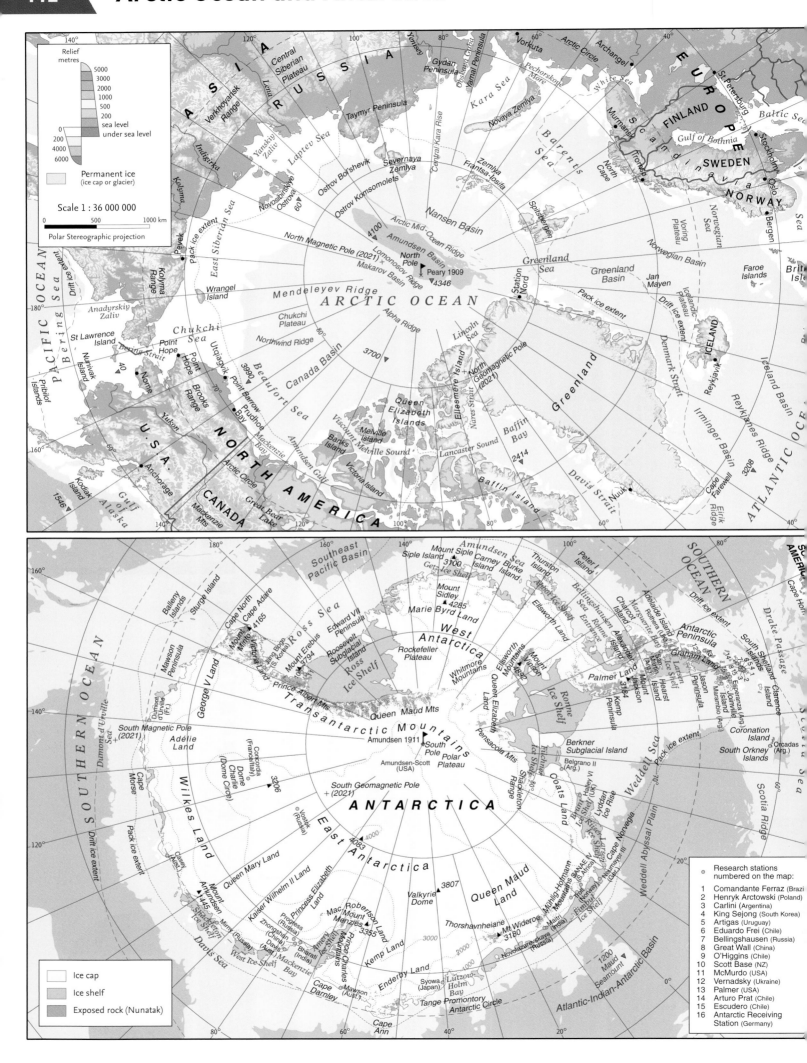

## United Nations factfile

**Established:**
October 1945

**Headquarters:**
New York, USA

**Purpose:**
- maintain international peace and security.
- develop friendly relations among nations.
- help to solve international, economic, social cultural and humanitarian problems.
- help promote respect for human rights.
- be a centre for harmonizing the actions of nations in attaining these ends.

**Structure:**
The 6 principal organs of the UN are:
General Assembly
Security Council
Economic and Social Council
Trusteeship Council (suspended since 1994)
International Court of Justice
Secretariat

**Members:**
There are 193 members.
Taiwan, Vatican City and Kosovo are the only non-member countries.

## Headquarters of UN agencies

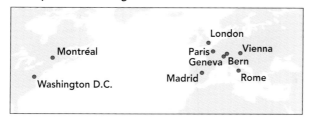

| City | Organization |
|---|---|
| **Rome,** Italy | Food and Agricultural Organization |
| **Washington D.C.,** USA | The World Bank |
| **Montréal,** Canada | International Civil Aviation Organization |
| **Rome,** Italy | International Fund for Agricultural Development |
| **Geneva,** Switzerland | International Labour Organization |
| **London,** UK | International Maritime Organization |
| **Washington D.C.,** USA | International Monetary Fund |
| **Geneva,** Switzerland | International Telecommunication Union |
| **Paris,** France | UNESCO |
| **Vienna,** Austria | UN Industrial Development Organization |
| **Bern,** Switzerland | Universal Postal Union |
| **Geneva,** Switzerland | WHO |
| **Geneva,** Switzerland | World Intellectual Property Organization |
| **Geneva,** Switzerland | World Meteorological Organization |
| **Madrid,** Spain | World Tourism Organization |

## Structure of United Nations

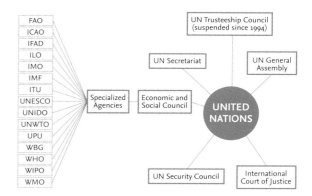

**United Nations**
www.un.org
**Commonwealth**
www.thecommonwealth.org

- Commonwealth of Nations
- NATO – North Atlantic Treaty Organization
- Pacific Islands Forum
- Arab League
- ASEAN – Association of Southeast Asian Nations

- Colombo Plan
- ALADI (LAIA) – Latin American Integration Association
- CARICOM – Caribbean Community
- African Union

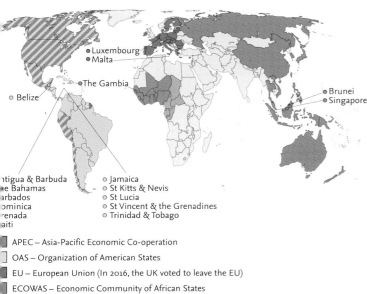

- APEC – Asia-Pacific Economic Co-operation
- OAS – Organization of American States
- EU – European Union (In 2016, the UK voted to leave the EU)
- ECOWAS – Economic Community of African States
- CEMAC – Economic and Monetary Community of Central Africa

- OECD – Organisation for Economic Co-operation and Development
- SADC – Southern African Development Community
- OPEC – Organization of Petroleum Exporting Countries

Scale 1 : 130 000 000

Countries shaded grey on all maps are not members of the organizations listed

# **World** Political

**Settlement**
■ National capital

Scale 1 : 80 000 000

0   800   1600   2400 km

GREENLAND
(Denmark)

RUSSIA     U.S.A.

Arctic Circle

C A N A D A

Ottawa

UNITED
STATES
OF AMERICA

Washington D.C.

Tropic of Cancer

Hawai'ian
Islands
(USA)

Havana
Nassau     THE BAHAMAS

MEXICO

Mexico City     CUBA
Kingston     DOMINICAN REP.     San Juan
Belmopan     HAITI     PUERTO RICO (USA)
BELIZE     JAMAICA
GUATEMALA     HONDURAS
Guatemala City     Tegucigalpa
EL SALVADOR     NICARAGUA
Managua     Caracas     TRINIDAD & TOBAGO
COSTA RICA     Panama City     Port of Spain
San José     PANAMA     VENEZUELA
                Georgetown     Paramaribo
                Bogotá     GUYANA     Cayenne
                COLOMBIA     SURINAME     FRENCH GUIANA
Quito
Galapagos Is (Ec)     ECUADOR

GREENLAND
Nuuk (Godthåb)     Reykjavík     ICELAND

Rab
MORC
Laâyoune
WESTERN SAHARA
MAURITANI
Nouakchott
CAPE VERDE     SENEGAL
Dakar     B
THE GAMBIA     Bissau
GUINEA-BISSAU     Ouag
Conakry     GUINEA
Freetown     Ya
SIERRA LEONE
Monrovia
LIBERIA

PACIFIC

OCEAN

KIRIBATI

Equator

Marquesas Is (Fr)

French
Polynesia

American Samoa
Apia
SAMOA

Cook Islands (NZ)

Society Is (Fr)

Tuamotu Archipelago

Tahiti

PERU

Lima

BRAZIL

ATLANTI

OCEAN

Nuku'alofa
TONGA

Tropic of Capricorn

Pitcairn Island (UK)

Easter I. (Chile)

La Paz
BOLIVIA
Sucre

Brasília

PARAGUAY

Asunción

CHILE

Valparaíso
Santiago

ARGENTINA

Buenos Aires     Montevideo
URUGUAY

Falkland Islands (UK)

South Georgia and South Sandwich Islands (UK)

SO

A     B     1     C     D     E

ICELAND
Reykjavík

NORWAY     SWEDEN     FINLAND
                Helsinki
Oslo
Stockholm     Tallinn
                ESTONIA
            Riga     LATVIA     RUSSIA
DENMARK     LITHUANIA     Moscow
Copenhagen     Vilnius
UNITED     RUSSIA     Minsk
KINGDOM     Amsterdam     Berlin     Warsaw     BELARUS
Dublin     The Hague     NETH.     POLAND     Kiev
IRELAND     Brussels     GERMANY     UKRAINE
London     BELGIUM     Prague
            LUX.     CZECHIA     SLOVAKIA
Paris     Vienna     Bratislava     MOLDOVA
            L     AUSTRIA     HUNGARY     Chișinău
FRANCE     Bern     SW.     Budapest     ROMANIA
            SL     Ljubljana     Zagreb     Belgrade     Bucharest
ANDORRA     CROATIA     B.H.     SERBIA     BULGARIA
MONACO     S.M.     Sarajevo     Podgorica     M.     Sofia
                ITALY     V.C.     K.     Pristina     Skopje
PORTUGAL     Madrid     Rome     M.     N.M.
Lisbon     SPAIN     Tirana     ALBANIA     TURKEY
                GREECE
                Athens
MALTA

**Europe**

B.H.     BOSNIA AND HERZEGOVINA
K.       KOSOVO
L.       LIECHTENSTEIN
LUX.     LUXEMBOURG
M.       MONTENEGRO
NETH.    NETHERLANDS
N.M.     NORTH MACEDONIA
S.M.     SAN MARINO
SW.      SWITZERLAND
V.C.     VATICAN CITY

International boundaries in
the sea shown on this map
indicate ownership of islands
and island groups only. They
do not infer the alignment of
legal maritime boundaries.

Not all countries are named
on the map.

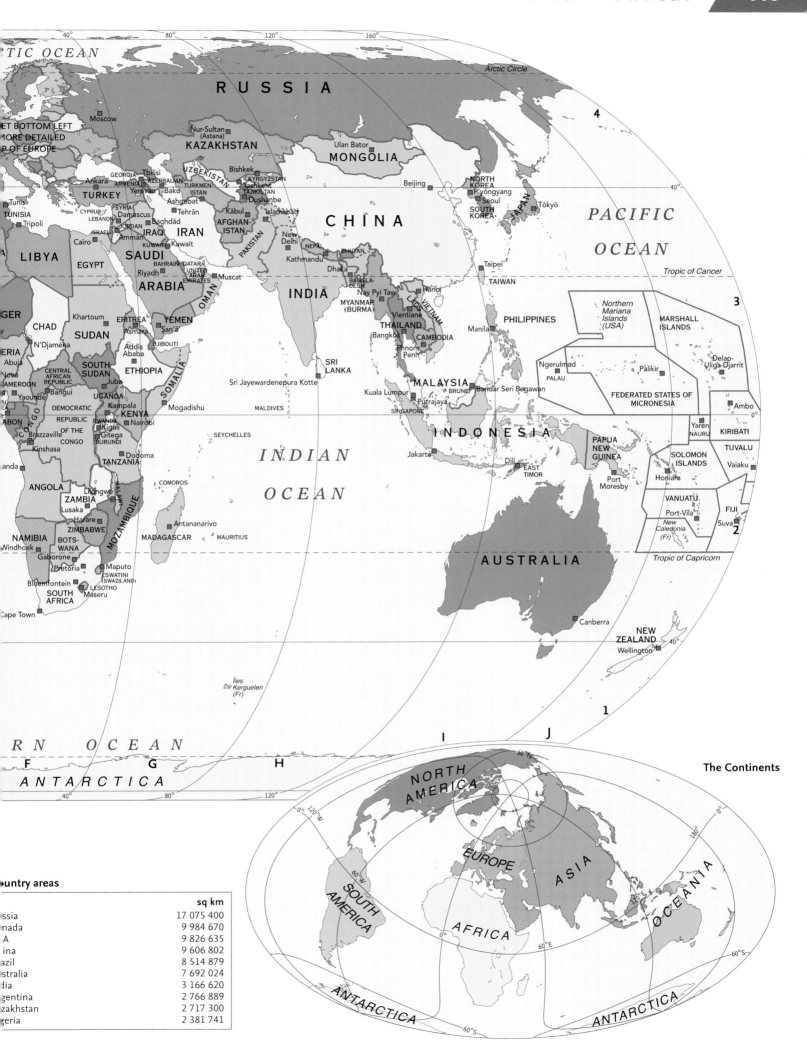

TIC OCEAN

RUSSIA

Arctic Circle

Moscow

ET BOTTOM LEFT
MORE DETAILED
P OF EUROPE

Nur-Sultan
(Astana)

KAZAKHSTAN

Ulan Bator

MONGOLIA

Bishkek

4

GEORGIA  Tbilisi
Ankara  ARMENIA  AZERBAIJAN
TURKEY  Yerevan  Baku
CYPRUS  SYRIA  Damascus
LEBANON  JORDAN  Baghdad
ISRAEL  Amman  IRAQ
Tunis
TUNISIA
Tripoli

UZBEKISTAN
Tashkent  KYRGYZSTAN
TURKMEN-  TAJIKISTAN
ISTAN  Dushanbe
Ashgabat  Kabul
Tehran  AFGHAN-
ISTAN  Islamabad
New
Delhi

Beijing

NORTH
KOREA
P'yŏngyang
SOUTH
KOREA  Seoul

JAPAN  Tōkyō

40°

PACIFIC

OCEAN

LIBYA  EGYPT
Cairo

SAUDI
Riyadh
ARABIA

KUWAIT  Kuwait
BAHRAIN  QATAR
UNITED
ARAB
EMIRATES  Muscat

IRAN

PAKISTAN

CHINA

NEPAL
Kathmandu  BHUTAN

Dhaka

INDIA

BANGLA-
DESH

Nay Pyi Taw

Taipei

TAIWAN

Tropic of Cancer

3

OMAN

YEMEN
San'ā

Hanoi

LAOS  VIETNAM

MYANMAR
(BURMA)

Vientiane

PHILIPPINES
Manila

Northern
Mariana
Islands
(USA)

MARSHALL
ISLANDS

GER
CHAD
N'Djaména

ERIA
Abuja

Novo
AMEROON
Yaounde

ABON

Brazzaville

Kinshasa

anda

ERITREA
Khartoum  Asmara
SUDAN  DJIBOUTI
Addis
Ababa
SOUTH
SUDAN  Juba  ETHIOPIA
CENTRAL
AFRICAN
REPUBLIC
Bangui  UGANDA  Kampala
DEMOCRATIC  KENYA
REPUBLIC  Kigali  Nairobi
OF THE  RWANDA
CONGO  Gitega  BURUNDI
Dodoma
TANZANIA

SRI
LANKA

Sri Jayewardenepura Kotte

Mogadishu

MALDIVES

SEYCHELLES

THAILAND
Bangkok  CAMBODIA
Phnom
Penh

MALAYSIA
Kuala Lumpur  BRUNEI  Bandar Seri Begawan
Putrajaya
SINGAPORE

INDONESIA

Ngerulmud  Palikir
PALAU

FEDERATED STATES OF
MICRONESIA

Ambo

Yaren
NAURU  KIRIBATI

Delap-
Uliga-Djarrit

INDIAN

OCEAN

COMOROS

Antananarivo

MADAGASCAR  MAURITIUS

Jakarta

Dili
EAST
TIMOR

PAPUA
NEW
GUINEA

Port
Moresby

Honiara

SOLOMON
ISLANDS

TUVALU

Vaiaku

ANGOLA
ZAMBIA  Lilongwe
Lusaka  MALAWI
Harare
ZIMBABWE
NAMIBIA  BOTS-
WANA
Windhoek  Gaborone
Pretoria
Bloemfontein  Maputo
ESWATINI
(SWAZILAND)
LESOTHO
SOUTH  Maseru
AFRICA
Cape Town

MOZAMBIQUE

AUSTRALIA

VANUATU

Port-Vila
New
Caledonia
(Fr)

FIJI

Suva

2

Tropic of Capricorn

Canberra

NEW
ZEALAND

40°

Wellington

Îles
Kerguelen
(Fr)

1

I  J

RN  OCEAN

F  G  H

ANTARCTICA

40°  80°  120°

NORTH
AMERICA

EUROPE

ASIA

SOUTH
AMERICA

AFRICA

OCEANIA

ANTARCTICA

ANTARCTICA

60°N
0°  120°W
60°W
60°E
0°
180°
60°S
60°S

untry areas

| | sq km |
|---|---|
| ssia | 17 075 400 |
| nada | 9 984 670 |
| A | 9 826 635 |
| ina | 9 606 802 |
| azil | 8 514 879 |
| stralia | 7 692 024 |
| dia | 3 166 620 |
| gentina | 2 766 889 |
| zakhstan | 2 717 300 |
| geria | 2 381 741 |

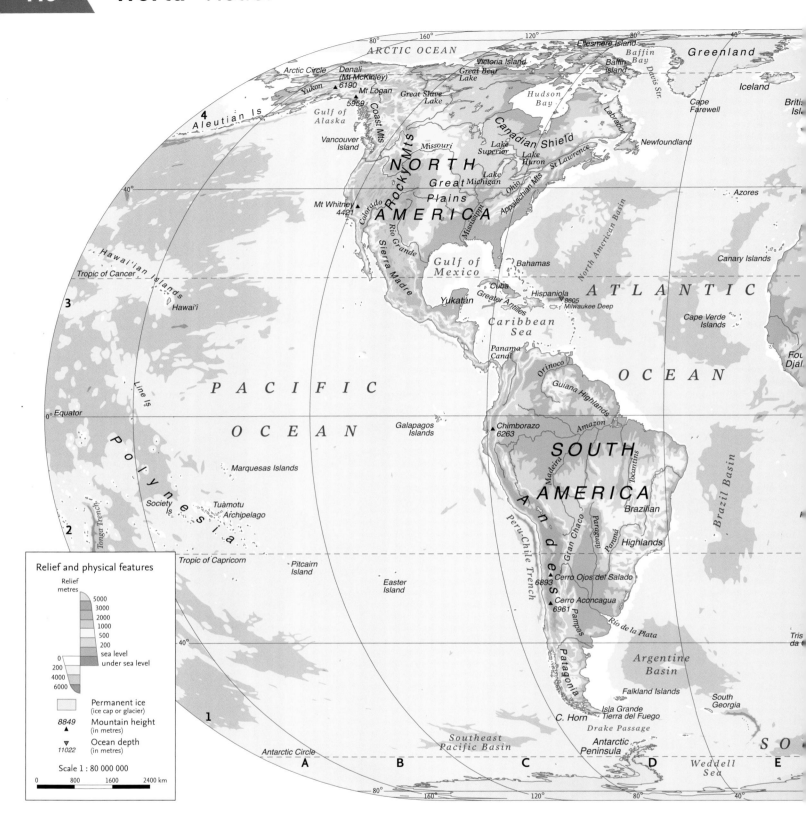

## Mountain heights

| | metres |
|---|---|
| Mt Everest (China/Nepal) | 8849 |
| K2 (China/Pakistan) | 8611 |
| Kangchenjunga (India/Nepal) | 8586 |
| Dhaulagiri I (Nepal) | 8167 |
| Annapurna I (Nepal) | 8091 |
| Cerro Aconcagua (Argentina) | 6961 |
| Cerro Ojos del Salado (Arg./Chile) | 6893 |
| Chimborazo (Ecuador) | 6310 |
| Denali (Mt McKinley) (USA) | 6190 |
| Mt Logan (Canada) | 5959 |

## Island areas

| | sq km |
|---|---|
| Greenland | 2 175 600 |
| New Guinea | 808 510 |
| Borneo | 745 561 |
| Madagascar | 587 040 |
| Baffin Island | 507 451 |
| Sumatra | 473 606 |
| Honshū | 227 414 |
| Great Britain | 218 476 |
| Victoria Island | 217 291 |
| Ellesmere Island | 196 236 |

## Continents

| | sq k |
|---|---|
| Asia | 45 036 4 |
| Africa | 30 343 5 |
| North America | 24 680 3 |
| South America | 17 815 4 |
| Antarctica | 12 093 0 |
| Europe | 9 908 5 |
| Oceania | 8 844 5 |

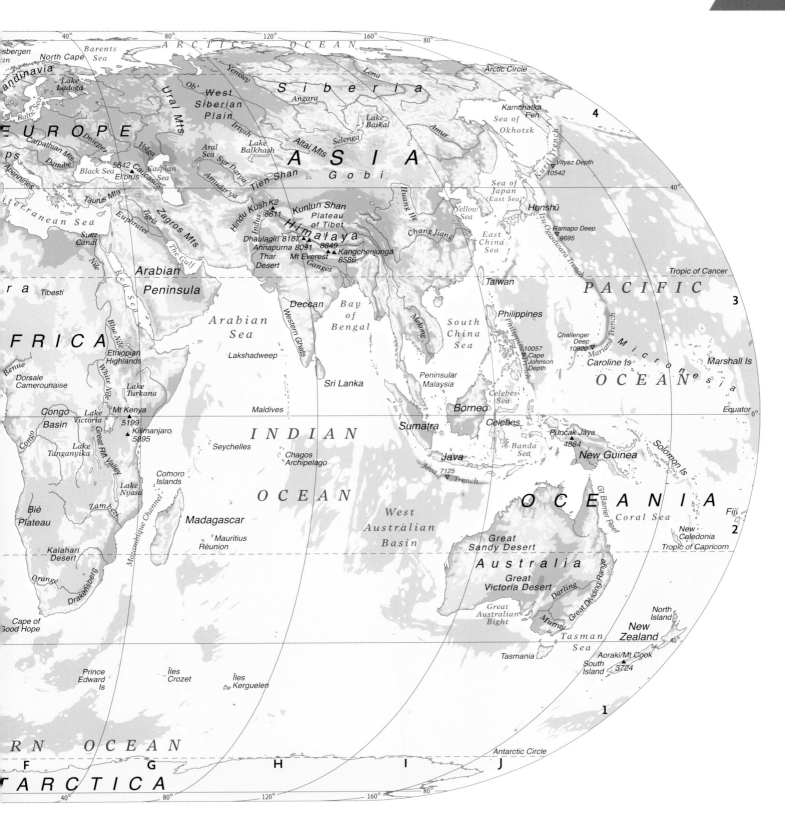

**Oceans**

| | sq km |
|---|---|
| ...cific Ocean | 166 241 000 |
| ...antic Ocean | 86 557 000 |
| ...dian Ocean | 73 427 000 |
| ...ctic Ocean | 9 485 000 |

**Lake areas**

| | sq km |
|---|---|
| Caspian Sea | 371 000 |
| Lake Superior | 82 100 |
| Lake Victoria | 68 870 |
| Lake Huron | 59 600 |
| Lake Michigan | 57 800 |
| Lake Tanganyika | 32 600 |
| Great Bear Lake | 31 328 |
| Lake Baikal | 30 500 |
| Lake Nyasa | 29 500 |

**River lengths**

| | km |
|---|---|
| Nile (Africa) | 6695 |
| Amazon (S. America) | 6516 |
| Chang Jiang (Asia) | 6380 |
| Mississippi-Missouri (N. America) | 5969 |
| Ob'-Irtysh (Asia) | 5568 |
| Yenisey-Angara-Selenga (Asia) | 5550 |
| Huang He (Asia) | 5464 |
| Congo (Africa) | 4667 |
| Río de la Plata-Paraná (S. America) | 4500 |
| Irtysh (Asia) | 4440 |

Eckert IV projection

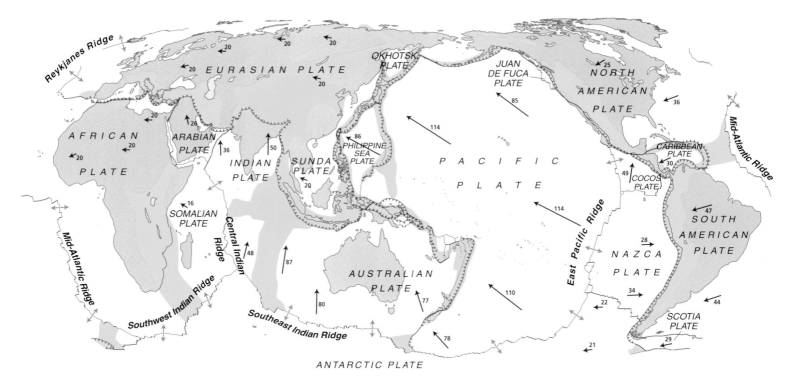

## Tectonic plates

⌃⌃⌃⌃⌃ Convergent plate boundary – where plates collide and one plate is pulled down (subducted) into the mantle and destroyed, or plates thicken and fracture in complex patterns

Scale 1 : 170 000 000

Divergent plate boundary – where plates move away from each other and new crust is created as magma reaches the surface

Transform plate boundary – where plates are dragged horizontally past each other, creating great friction and many faults

Diffuse boundary zone – broad zone in which plate movement and change to the Earth's surface occur over a wide region, often in complex patterns with many micro-plates

←⁴⁴ General direction of plate movement and approximate speed, mm/year

←→ Movement at divergent plate boundaries

## Continental drift

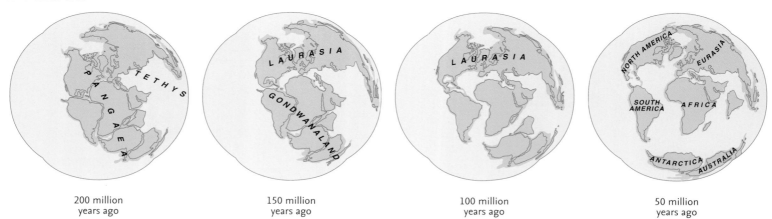

| 200 million years ago | 150 million years ago | 100 million years ago | 50 million years ago |

## Major earthquakes since 1982

| Year | Location | Magnitude | Deaths | Year | Location | Magnitude | Deaths | Year | Location | Magnitude | Deaths |
|------|----------|-----------|--------|------|----------|-----------|--------|------|----------|-----------|--------|
| 1982 | Dhamar, Yemen | 6.0 | 3000 | 1992 | Flores, Indonesia | 7.5 | 2500 | 2001 | Gujarat, India | 6.9 | 20 085 |
| 1983 | Eastern Turkey | 7.1 | 1500 | 1992 | Erzincan, Turkey | 6.8 | 500 | 2002 | Hindu Kush, Afghanistan | 6.0 | 1000 |
| 1985 | Santiago, Chile | 7.8 | 177 | 1992 | Cairo, Egypt | 5.9 | 550 | 2003 | Boumerdes, Algeria | 5.8 | 2266 |
| 1985 | Michoacán, Mexico | 8.1 | 20 000 | 1993 | Northern Japan | 7.8 | 185 | 2003 | Bam, Iran | 6.6 | 26 271 |
| 1986 | El Salvador | 7.5 | 1000 | 1993 | Maharashtra, India | 6.4 | 9748 | 2004 | Sumatra, Indonesia | 9.0 | 283 106 |
| 1987 | Ecuador | 7.0 | 2000 | 1994 | Kuril Islands, Russia | 8.3 | 10 | 2005 | Sumatra, Indonesia | 8.7 | 1313 |
| 1988 | Yunnan, China | 7.6 | 1000 | 1995 | Kōbe, Japan | 7.2 | 5502 | 2005 | Muzzafarabad, Pakistan | 7.6 | 80 361 |
| 1988 | Spitak, Armenia | 6.9 | 25 000 | 1995 | Sakhalin, Russia | 7.6 | 2500 | 2008 | Sichuan Province, China | 8.0 | 87 476 |
| 1988 | Nepal / India | 6.9 | 1000 | 1996 | Yunnan, China | 7.0 | 251 | 2010 | Léogâne, Haiti | 7.0 | 222 570 |
| 1990 | Manjil, Iran | 7.7 | 50 000 | 1998 | Papua New Guinea | 7.0 | 2183 | 2011 | Tōhoku, Japan | 9.0 | 14 500 |
| 1990 | Luzon, Philippines | 7.7 | 1600 | 1999 | İzmit, Turkey | 7.4 | 17 118 | 2015 | Gorkha, Nepal | 7.8 | 8831 |
| 1991 | Uttar Pradesh, India | 6.1 | 1600 | 1999 | Chi-Chi, Taiwan | 7.7 | 2400 | 2018 | Sulawesi, Indonesia | 6.4 | 4300 |

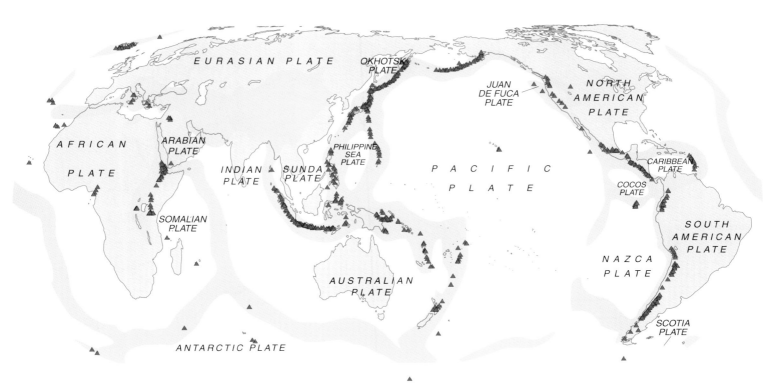

## Volcanoes

Earthquake and volcano zone ▲ Major volcanoes

Scale 1 : 170 000 000

### Major volcanic eruptions since 1980

| Year | Location | Year | Location |
|------|----------|------|----------|
| 1980 | Mount St Helens, USA | 1993 | Mayon, Philippines |
| 1982 | El Chichónal, Mexico | 1993 | Volcán Galeras, Colombia |
| 1982 | Gunung Galunggung, Indonesia | 1994 | Volcán Llaima, Chile |
| 1983 | Kilauea, Hawaii | 1994 | Rabaul, Papua New Guinea |
| 1983 | Ō-yama, Japan | 1997 | Soufrière Hills, Montserrat |
| 1985 | Nevado del Ruiz, Colombia | 2000 | Hekla, Iceland |
| 1986 | Lake Nyos, Cameroon | 2001 | Mount Etna, Italy |
| 1991 | Hekla, Iceland | 2002 | Nyiragongo, Dem. Rep. of the Congo |
| 1991 | Mount Pinatubo, Philippines | 2010 | Eyjafjallajökull, Iceland |
| 1991 | Unzen-dake, Japan | 2018 | Anak Krakatoa, Indonesia |

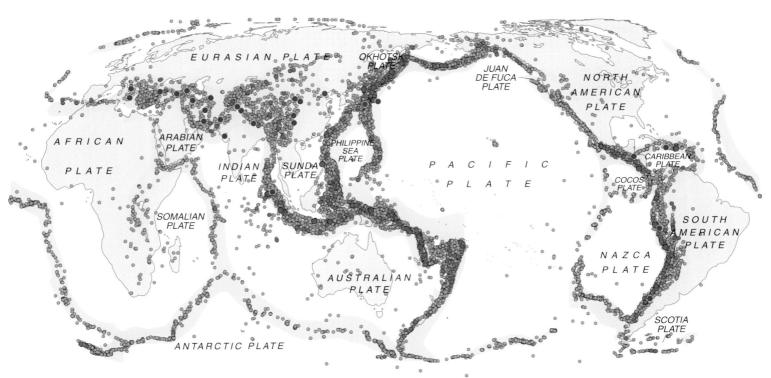

## Earthquakes and tsunamis

Earthquake and volcano zone

● Major tsunamis since 1990

Major earthquakes since 1900
● 'Deadliest' earthquakes
● Greater than 7.5 on the moment magnitude scale
· 5.5–7.5 on the moment magnitude scale

Scale 1 : 170 000 000

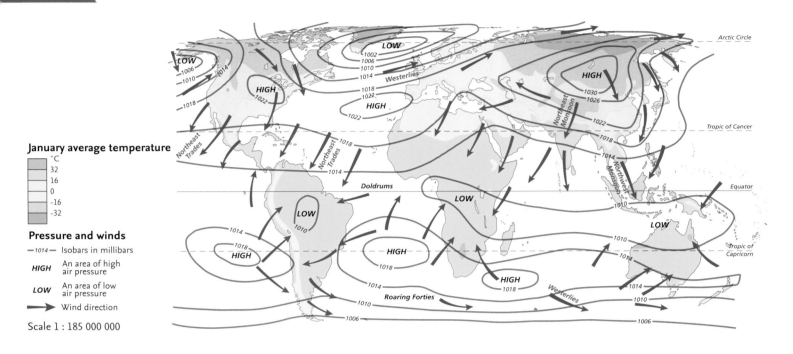

### January average temperature

°C
32
16
0
-16
-32

**Pressure and winds**

─1014─ Isobars in millibars

HIGH An area of high air pressure

LOW An area of low air pressure

→ Wind direction

Scale 1 : 185 000 000

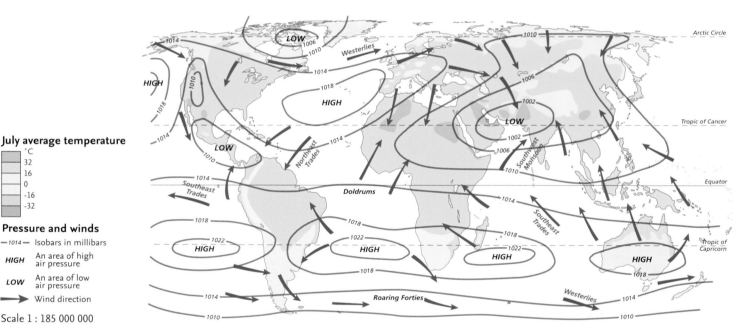

### July average temperature

°C
32
16
0
-16
-32

**Pressure and winds**

─1014─ Isobars in millibars

HIGH An area of high air pressure

LOW An area of low air pressure

→ Wind direction

Scale 1 : 185 000 000

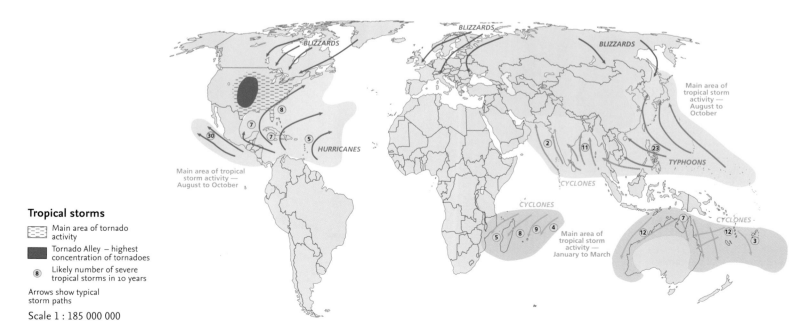

### Tropical storms

Main area of tornado activity

Tornado Alley – highest concentration of tornadoes

⑧ Likely number of severe tropical storms in 10 years

Arrows show typical storm paths

Scale 1 : 185 000 000

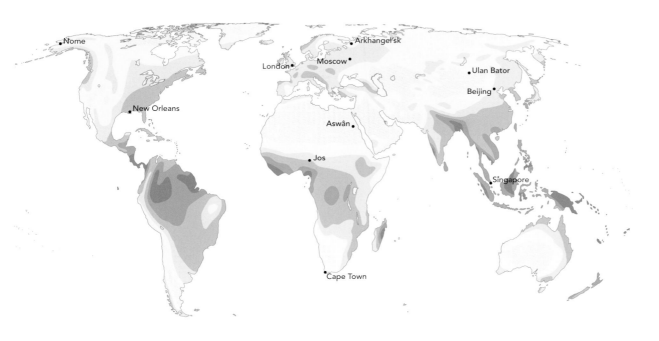

### Average annual rainfall

| | mm |
|---|---|
| | 3000 |
| | 2000 |
| | 1000 |
| | 500 |
| | 250 |
| | 0 |

Scale 1 : 185 000 000

## Climate graphs

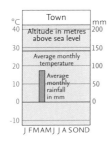

Town
Altitude in metres above sea level
Average monthly temperature
Average monthly rainfall in mm

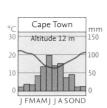

Cape Town — Altitude 12 m

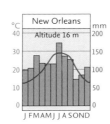

New Orleans — Altitude 16 m

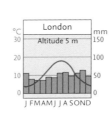

London — Altitude 5 m

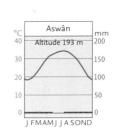

Aswân — Altitude 193 m

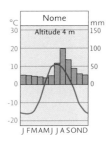

Nome — Altitude 4 m

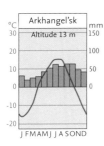

Arkhangel'sk — Altitude 13 m

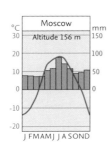

Moscow — Altitude 156 m

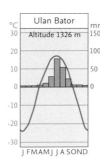

Ulan Bator — Altitude 1326 m

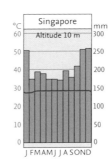

Singapore — Altitude 10 m

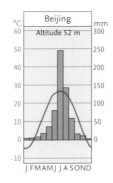

Beijing — Altitude 52 m

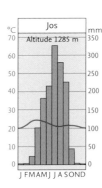

Jos — Altitude 1285 m

## Major tropical storms since 2003

| Year | Name | Location | Deaths |
|---|---|---|---|
| 2003 | Maemi | South Korea | 130 |
| 2004 | Ivan | Southern USA | 52 |
| 2005 | Katrina | Southern USA | 1836 |
| 2006 | Bilis | China | 820 |
| 2007 | Sidr | Bangladesh | 4234 |
| 2008 | Nargis | Myanmar | 138 366 |
| 2009 | Parma | Philippines | 501 |
| 2010 | Agatha | Guatemala | 174 |
| 2011 | Washi | Philippines | 1439 |
| 2012 | Sandy | Eastern USA | 148 |
| 2013 | Haiyan | Philippines | 7986 |
| 2014 | Hudhud | Eastern India/Nepal | 109 |
| 2016 | Matthew | Caribbean | 546 |
| 2017 | Maria | Caribbean | 3059 |
| 2019 | Idai | Southeast Africa | >1300 |

## World weather extremes

| | | |
|---|---|---|
| Hottest place | 34.4 °C (annual mean) | Dalol, Ethiopia |
| Driest place | 0.1 mm (annual mean) | Atacama Desert, Chile |
| Most sunshine | 90% (4000 hours) (annual mean) | Yuma, Arizona, USA |
| Least sunshine | Nil for 182 days each year | South Pole |
| Coldest place | -56.6 °C (annual mean) | Plateau Station, Antarctica |
| Wettest place | 11 873 mm (annual mean) | Meghalaya, India |
| Most rainy days | Up to 350 per year | Mount Waialeale, Hawaii, USA |
| Greatest snowfall | 31 102 mm (19.2.1971 – 18.2.1972) | Mount Rainier, Washington, USA |
| Windiest place | 322 km per hour in gales | Commonwealth Bay, Antarctica |

World Meteorological Organization
www.wmo.int
Met Office
www.metoffice.gov.uk/weather

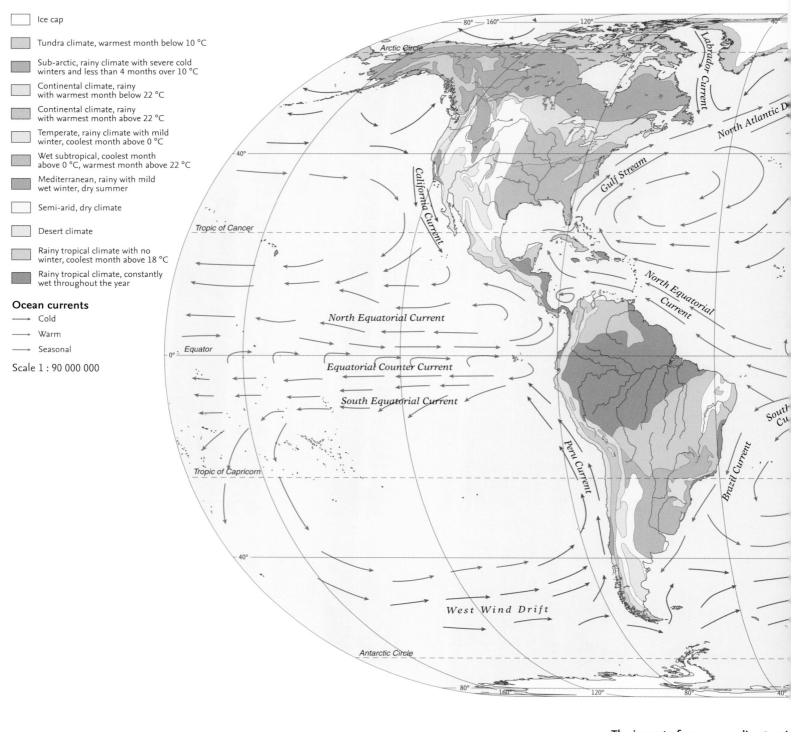

| | |
|---|---|
| | Ice cap |
| | Tundra climate, warmest month below 10 °C |
| | Sub-arctic, rainy climate with severe cold winters and less than 4 months over 10 °C |
| | Continental climate, rainy with warmest month below 22 °C |
| | Continental climate, rainy with warmest month above 22 °C |
| | Temperate, rainy climate with mild winter, coolest month above 0 °C |
| | Wet subtropical, coolest month above 0 °C, warmest month above 22 °C |
| | Mediterranean, rainy with mild wet winter, dry summer |
| | Semi-arid, dry climate |
| | Desert climate |
| | Rainy tropical climate with no winter, coolest month above 18 °C |
| | Rainy tropical climate, constantly wet throughout the year |

**Ocean currents**

→ Cold

→ Warm

→ Seasonal

Scale 1 : 90 000 000

**The impact of oceans on climate: ai**

**Normal circulation**

The oceans have a significant impact on climate. Under normal conditions, easterly winds push warm surface water across the Pacific Ocean to Australia, forming a large area of warmer water to the northeast. This brings rain to northern and eastern Australia.

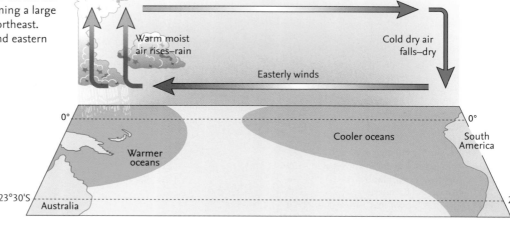

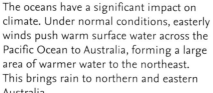

World Meteorological Organization
www.wmo.int
Met Office
www.metoffice.gov.uk
United Nations Environment Programme
www.unep.org
World Conservation Monitoring Centre
www.unep-wcmc.org
World Resources Institute
www.wri.org

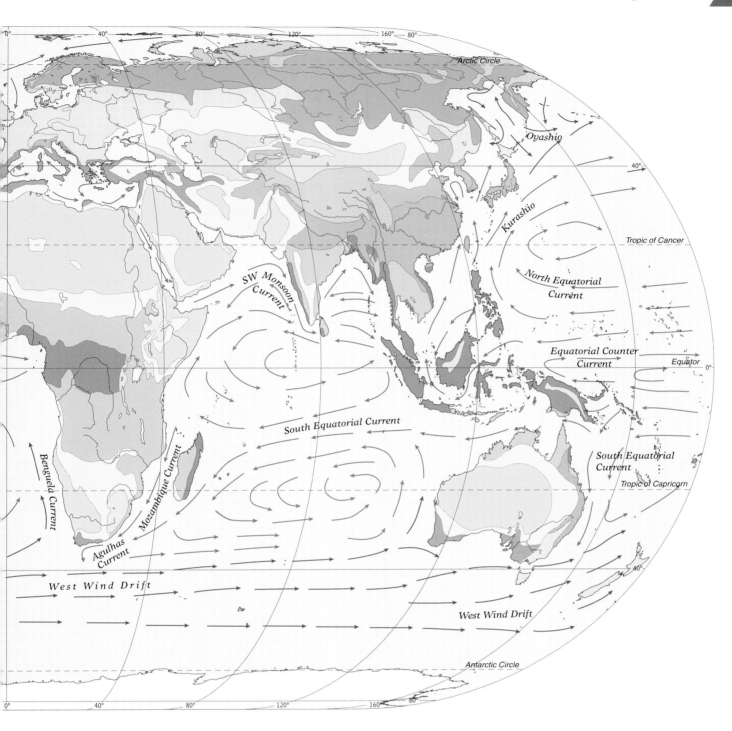

Oyashio

Kurashio

SW Monsoon Current

North Equatorial Current

Equatorial Counter Current

South Equatorial Current

South Equatorial Current

Benguela Current

Mozambique Current

Agulhas Current

West Wind Drift

West Wind Drift

Arctic Circle

Tropic of Cancer

Equator

Tropic of Capricorn

Antarctic Circle

**circulation in the Pacific Ocean**

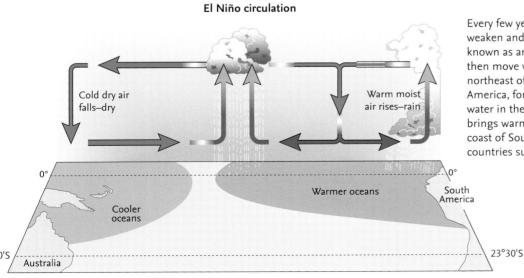

**El Niño circulation**

Cold dry air falls–dry

Warm moist air rises–rain

Cooler oceans

Warmer oceans

South America

Australia

0°

23°30'S

Every few years, these easterly winds weaken and reverse, which causes what is known as an El Niño event. The winds then move warm water from the northeast of Australia towards South America, forming a large area of warmer water in the eastern Pacific Ocean. This brings warmer conditions and rain to the coast of South America, and drought to countries such as Australia and Indonesia.

# **World** Climate Statistics

52.25N 4.05W

| Aberystwyth | Jan | Feb | Mar | Apr | May | Jun | Jul | Aug | Sep | Oct | Nov | Dec |
|---|---|---|---|---|---|---|---|---|---|---|---|---|
| Temperature - max. (°C) | 7 | 7 | 9 | 11 | 15 | 17 | 18 | 18 | 16 | 13 | 10 | 8 |
| Temperature - min. (°C) | 2 | 2 | 3 | 5 | 7 | 10 | 12 | 12 | 11 | 8 | 5 | 4 |
| Rainfall - (mm) | 97 | 72 | 60 | 56 | 65 | 76 | 99 | 93 | 108 | 118 | 111 | 96 |

16.55N 99.52W

| Acapulco | Jan | Feb | Mar | Apr | May | Jun | Jul | Aug | Sep | Oct | Nov | Dec |
|---|---|---|---|---|---|---|---|---|---|---|---|---|
| Temperature - max. (°C) | 31 | 31 | 31 | 32 | 32 | 33 | 32 | 33 | 32 | 32 | 32 | 31 |
| Temperature - min. (°C) | 22 | 22 | 22 | 23 | 25 | 25 | 25 | 25 | 24 | 24 | 23 | 22 |
| Rainfall - (mm) | 6 | 1 | 0 | 1 | 36 | 281 | 256 | 252 | 349 | 159 | 28 | 8 |

36.46N 3.04E

| Algiers | Jan | Feb | Mar | Apr | May | Jun | Jul | Aug | Sep | Oct | Nov | Dec |
|---|---|---|---|---|---|---|---|---|---|---|---|---|
| Temperature - max. (°C) | 15 | 16 | 17 | 20 | 23 | 26 | 28 | 29 | 27 | 23 | 19 | 16 |
| Temperature - min. (°C) | 9 | 9 | 11 | 13 | 15 | 18 | 21 | 22 | 21 | 17 | 13 | 11 |
| Rainfall - (mm) | 112 | 84 | 74 | 41 | 46 | 15 | 0 | 5 | 41 | 79 | 130 | 137 |

36.52S 174.46E

| Auckland | Jan | Feb | Mar | Apr | May | Jun | Jul | Aug | Sep | Oct | Nov | Dec |
|---|---|---|---|---|---|---|---|---|---|---|---|---|
| Temperature - max. (°C) | 23 | 24 | 22 | 20 | 17 | 15 | 15 | 15 | 16 | 18 | 20 | 22 |
| Temperature - min. (°C) | 15 | 16 | 15 | 12 | 10 | 8 | 7 | 8 | 9 | 11 | 12 | 14 |
| Rainfall - (mm) | 75 | 65 | 94 | 105 | 103 | 139 | 146 | 121 | 116 | 91 | 93 | 91 |

1.26S 48.29W

| Belém | Jan | Feb | Mar | Apr | May | Jun | Jul | Aug | Sep | Oct | Nov | Dec |
|---|---|---|---|---|---|---|---|---|---|---|---|---|
| Temperature - max. (°C) | 31 | 30 | 31 | 31 | 31 | 31 | 31 | 31 | 32 | 32 | 32 | 32 |
| Temperature - min. (°C) | 22 | 22 | 23 | 23 | 23 | 22 | 22 | 22 | 22 | 22 | 22 | 22 |
| Rainfall - (mm) | 318 | 358 | 358 | 320 | 259 | 170 | 150 | 112 | 89 | 84 | 66 | 155 |

54.36N 5.55W

| Belfast | Jan | Feb | Mar | Apr | May | Jun | Jul | Aug | Sep | Oct | Nov | Dec |
|---|---|---|---|---|---|---|---|---|---|---|---|---|
| Temperature - max. (°C) | 6 | 7 | 9 | 12 | 15 | 18 | 18 | 18 | 16 | 13 | 9 | 7 |
| Temperature - min. (°C) | 2 | 2 | 3 | 4 | 6 | 9 | 11 | 11 | 9 | 7 | 4 | 3 |
| Rainfall - (mm) | 80 | 52 | 50 | 48 | 52 | 68 | 94 | 77 | 80 | 83 | 72 | 90 |

52.29N 1.53W

| Birmingham | Jan | Feb | Mar | Apr | May | Jun | Jul | Aug | Sep | Oct | Nov | Dec |
|---|---|---|---|---|---|---|---|---|---|---|---|---|
| Temperature - max. (°C) | 5 | 6 | 9 | 12 | 16 | 19 | 20 | 20 | 17 | 13 | 9 | 6 |
| Temperature - min. (°C) | 2 | 2 | 3 | 5 | 7 | 10 | 12 | 12 | 10 | 7 | 5 | 3 |
| Rainfall - (mm) | 74 | 54 | 50 | 53 | 64 | 50 | 69 | 69 | 61 | 69 | 84 | 67 |

53.49N 3.03W

| Blackpool | Jan | Feb | Mar | Apr | May | Jun | Jul | Aug | Sep | Oct | Nov | Dec |
|---|---|---|---|---|---|---|---|---|---|---|---|---|
| Temperature - max. (°C) | 7 | 7 | 9 | 11 | 15 | 17 | 19 | 19 | 17 | 14 | 10 | 7 |
| Temperature - min. (°C) | 1 | 1 | 2 | 4 | 7 | 10 | 12 | 12 | 10 | 8 | 4 | 2 |
| Rainfall - (mm) | 78 | 54 | 64 | 51 | 53 | 59 | 61 | 78 | 86 | 93 | 89 | 87 |

30.07S 145.54E

| Bourke | Jan | Feb | Mar | Apr | May | Jun | Jul | Aug | Sep | Oct | Nov | Dec |
|---|---|---|---|---|---|---|---|---|---|---|---|---|
| Temperature - max. (°C) | 37 | 36 | 33 | 28 | 23 | 18 | 18 | 21 | 25 | 29 | 34 | 36 |
| Temperature - min. (°C) | 21 | 21 | 18 | 13 | 8 | 6 | 4 | 6 | 9 | 13 | 17 | 19 |
| Rainfall - (mm) | 36 | 38 | 28 | 28 | 25 | 28 | 23 | 20 | 20 | 23 | 31 | 36 |

44.26N 26.06E

| Bucharest | Jan | Feb | Mar | Apr | May | Jun | Jul | Aug | Sep | Oct | Nov | Dec |
|---|---|---|---|---|---|---|---|---|---|---|---|---|
| Temperature - max. (°C) | 1 | 4 | 10 | 18 | 23 | 27 | 30 | 30 | 25 | 18 | 10 | 4 |
| Temperature - min. (°C) | -7 | -5 | -1 | 5 | 10 | 14 | 16 | 15 | 11 | 6 | 2 | -3 |
| Rainfall - (mm) | 29 | 26 | 28 | 59 | 77 | 121 | 53 | 45 | 45 | 29 | 36 | 27 |

32.48N 79.58W

| Charleston | Jan | Feb | Mar | Apr | May | Jun | Jul | Aug | Sep | Oct | Nov | Dec |
|---|---|---|---|---|---|---|---|---|---|---|---|---|
| Temperature - max. (°C) | 14 | 15 | 19 | 23 | 27 | 30 | 31 | 31 | 28 | 24 | 19 | 15 |
| Temperature - min. (°C) | 6 | 7 | 10 | 14 | 19 | 23 | 24 | 24 | 22 | 16 | 11 | 7 |
| Rainfall - (mm) | 74 | 84 | 86 | 71 | 81 | 119 | 185 | 168 | 130 | 81 | 58 | 71 |

51.47N

| Clacton-on-Sea | Jan | Feb | Mar | Apr | May | Jun | Jul | Aug | Sep | Oct | Nov |
|---|---|---|---|---|---|---|---|---|---|---|---|
| Temperature - max. (°C) | 6 | 6 | 9 | 11 | 15 | 18 | 20 | 20 | 18 | 15 | 10 |
| Temperature - min. (°C) | 2 | 2 | 3 | 5 | 8 | 11 | 13 | 14 | 12 | 9 | 5 |
| Rainfall - (mm) | 49 | 31 | 43 | 40 | 40 | 45 | 43 | 43 | 48 | 48 | 55 |

9.31N 13

| Conakry | Jan | Feb | Mar | Apr | May | Jun | Jul | Aug | Sep | Oct | Nov |
|---|---|---|---|---|---|---|---|---|---|---|---|
| Temperature - max. (°C) | 31 | 31 | 32 | 32 | 32 | 30 | 28 | 28 | 29 | 31 | 31 |
| Temperature - min. (°C) | 22 | 23 | 23 | 24 | 23 | 22 | 22 | 23 | 23 | 23 | 24 |
| Rainfall - (mm) | 3 | 3 | 10 | 23 | 158 | 559 | 1298 | 1054 | 683 | 371 | 122 |

12.27S 13

| Darwin | Jan | Feb | Mar | Apr | May | Jun | Jul | Aug | Sep | Oct | Nov |
|---|---|---|---|---|---|---|---|---|---|---|---|
| Temperature - max. (°C) | 32 | 32 | 33 | 33 | 33 | 31 | 31 | 32 | 33 | 34 | 34 |
| Temperature - min. (°C) | 25 | 25 | 25 | 24 | 23 | 21 | 19 | 21 | 23 | 25 | 26 |
| Rainfall - (mm) | 386 | 312 | 254 | 97 | 15 | 3 | 0 | 3 | 13 | 51 | 119 |

42.19N 83

| Detroit | Jan | Feb | Mar | Apr | May | Jun | Jul | Aug | Sep | Oct | Nov |
|---|---|---|---|---|---|---|---|---|---|---|---|
| Temperature - max. (°C) | -1 | 0 | 6 | 13 | 19 | 25 | 28 | 27 | 23 | 16 | 8 |
| Temperature - min. (°C) | -7 | -8 | -3 | 3 | 9 | 14 | 17 | 17 | 13 | 7 | 1 |
| Rainfall - (mm) | 53 | 53 | 64 | 64 | 84 | 91 | 84 | 69 | 71 | 61 | 61 |

53.20N 6

| Dublin | Jan | Feb | Mar | Apr | May | Jun | Jul | Aug | Sep | Oct | Nov |
|---|---|---|---|---|---|---|---|---|---|---|---|
| Temperature - max. (°C) | 8 | 8 | 10 | 13 | 15 | 18 | 20 | 19 | 17 | 14 | 10 |
| Temperature - min. (°C) | 1 | 2 | 3 | 4 | 6 | 9 | 11 | 11 | 9 | 6 | 4 |
| Rainfall - (mm) | 67 | 55 | 51 | 45 | 60 | 57 | 70 | 74 | 72 | 70 | 67 |

55.04N

| Dumfries | Jan | Feb | Mar | Apr | May | Jun | Jul | Aug | Sep | Oct | Nov |
|---|---|---|---|---|---|---|---|---|---|---|---|
| Temperature - max. (°C) | 6 | 6 | 8 | 11 | 14 | 17 | 19 | 18 | 16 | 13 | 9 |
| Temperature - min. (°C) | 1 | 1 | 2 | 3 | 6 | 9 | 11 | 10 | 9 | 6 | 3 |
| Rainfall - (mm) | 110 | 76 | 81 | 53 | 72 | 63 | 71 | 93 | 104 | 117 | 100 |

29.51S 3

| Durban | Jan | Feb | Mar | Apr | May | Jun | Jul | Aug | Sep | Oct | Nov |
|---|---|---|---|---|---|---|---|---|---|---|---|
| Temperature – max. (°C) | 28 | 28 | 28 | 26 | 24 | 23 | 23 | 23 | 23 | 24 | 25 |
| Temperature – min. (°C) | 21 | 21 | 20 | 17 | 14 | 11 | 10 | 12 | 15 | 16 | 18 |
| Rainfall (mm) | 119 | 126 | 132 | 84 | 56 | 34 | 35 | 49 | 73 | 110 | 118 |

55.57N 3

| Edinburgh | Jan | Feb | Mar | Apr | May | Jun | Jul | Aug | Sep | Oct | Nov |
|---|---|---|---|---|---|---|---|---|---|---|---|
| Temperature - max. (°C) | 6 | 7 | 9 | 11 | 14 | 17 | 18 | 18 | 16 | 13 | 9 |
| Temperature - min. (°C) | 1 | 1 | 2 | 4 | 6 | 9 | 11 | 11 | 9 | 7 | 3 |
| Rainfall - (mm) | 54 | 40 | 47 | 39 | 49 | 50 | 59 | 63 | 66 | 63 | 56 |

55.52N 4

| Glasgow | Jan | Feb | Mar | Apr | May | Jun | Jul | Aug | Sep | Oct | Nov |
|---|---|---|---|---|---|---|---|---|---|---|---|
| Temperature - max. (°C) | 6 | 7 | 9 | 12 | 15 | 18 | 19 | 19 | 16 | 13 | 9 |
| Temperature - min. (°C) | 0 | 0 | 2 | 3 | 6 | 9 | 10 | 10 | 9 | 6 | 2 |
| Rainfall - (mm) | 96 | 63 | 65 | 50 | 62 | 58 | 68 | 83 | 95 | 98 | 105 |

60.10N 2

| Helsinki | Jan | Feb | Mar | Apr | May | Jun | Jul | Aug | Sep | Oct | Nov |
|---|---|---|---|---|---|---|---|---|---|---|---|
| Temperature - max. (°C) | -3 | -4 | 0 | 6 | 14 | 19 | 22 | 20 | 15 | 8 | 3 |
| Temperature - min. (°C) | -9 | -10 | -7 | -1 | 4 | 9 | 13 | 12 | 8 | 3 | -1 |
| Rainfall - (mm) | 56 | 42 | 36 | 44 | 41 | 51 | 51 | 68 | 71 | 73 | 68 |

6.22S 39

| Iguatu | Jan | Feb | Mar | Apr | May | Jun | Jul | Aug | Sep | Oct | Nov |
|---|---|---|---|---|---|---|---|---|---|---|---|
| Temperature - max. (°C) | 34 | 33 | 32 | 31 | 31 | 31 | 32 | 32 | 35 | 36 | 36 |
| Temperature - min. (°C) | 23 | 23 | 23 | 23 | 22 | 22 | 21 | 21 | 22 | 23 | 23 |
| Rainfall - (mm) | 89 | 173 | 185 | 160 | 61 | 61 | 36 | 5 | 18 | 18 | 10 |

**60.09N 1.09W**

| rwick | Jan | Feb | Mar | Apr | May | Jun | Jul | Aug | Sep | Oct | Nov | Dec |
|---|---|---|---|---|---|---|---|---|---|---|---|---|
| Temperature - max. (°C) | 5 | 5 | 6 | 8 | 10 | 13 | 14 | 14 | 13 | 10 | 7 | 6 |
| Temperature - min. (°C) | 1 | 1 | 2 | 3 | 5 | 7 | 9 | 9 | 8 | 6 | 3 | 2 |
| Rainfall - (mm) | 127 | 93 | 93 | 72 | 64 | 64 | 67 | 78 | 113 | 119 | 140 | 147 |

**51.30N 0.07W**

| ndon | Jan | Feb | Mar | Apr | May | Jun | Jul | Aug | Sep | Oct | Nov | Dec |
|---|---|---|---|---|---|---|---|---|---|---|---|---|
| Temperature - max. (°C) | 8 | 8 | 11 | 13 | 17 | 20 | 23 | 23 | 19 | 15 | 11 | 9 |
| Temperature - min. (°C) | 2 | 2 | 4 | 5 | 8 | 11 | 14 | 13 | 11 | 8 | 5 | 3 |
| Rainfall - (mm) | 52 | 34 | 42 | 45 | 47 | 53 | 38 | 47 | 57 | 62 | 52 | 54 |

**5.06S 119.27E**

| akassar | Jan | Feb | Mar | Apr | May | Jun | Jul | Aug | Sep | Oct | Nov | Dec |
|---|---|---|---|---|---|---|---|---|---|---|---|---|
| Temperature - max. (°C) | 29 | 29 | 29 | 30 | 31 | 30 | 30 | 31 | 31 | 31 | 30 | 29 |
| Temperature - min. (°C) | 23 | 24 | 23 | 23 | 23 | 22 | 21 | 21 | 21 | 22 | 23 | 23 |
| Rainfall - (mm) | 686 | 536 | 424 | 150 | 89 | 74 | 36 | 10 | 15 | 43 | 178 | 610 |

**53.29N 2.15W**

| anchester | Jan | Feb | Mar | Apr | May | Jun | Jul | Aug | Sep | Oct | Nov | Dec |
|---|---|---|---|---|---|---|---|---|---|---|---|---|
| Temperature - max. (°C) | 6 | 7 | 9 | 12 | 15 | 18 | 20 | 20 | 17 | 14 | 9 | 7 |
| Temperature - min. (°C) | 1 | 1 | 3 | 4 | 7 | 10 | 12 | 12 | 10 | 8 | 4 | 2 |
| Rainfall - (mm) | 69 | 50 | 61 | 51 | 61 | 67 | 65 | 79 | 74 | 77 | 78 | 78 |

**48.08N 11.35E**

| unich | Jan | Feb | Mar | Apr | May | Jun | Jul | Aug | Sep | Oct | Nov | Dec |
|---|---|---|---|---|---|---|---|---|---|---|---|---|
| Temperature - max. (°C) | 1 | 3 | 9 | 14 | 18 | 21 | 23 | 23 | 20 | 13 | 7 | 2 |
| Temperature - min. (°C) | -5 | -5 | -1 | 3 | 7 | 11 | 13 | 12 | 9 | 4 | 0 | -4 |
| Rainfall - (mm) | 59 | 53 | 48 | 62 | 109 | 125 | 139 | 107 | 85 | 66 | 57 | 47 |

**1.17S 36.48E**

| airobi | Jan | Feb | Mar | Apr | May | Jun | Jul | Aug | Sep | Oct | Nov | Dec |
|---|---|---|---|---|---|---|---|---|---|---|---|---|
| Temperature - max. (°C) | 25 | 26 | 25 | 24 | 22 | 21 | 21 | 21 | 24 | 24 | 23 | 23 |
| Temperature - min. (°C) | 12 | 13 | 14 | 14 | 13 | 12 | 11 | 11 | 11 | 13 | 13 | 13 |
| Rainfall - (mm) | 38 | 64 | 125 | 211 | 158 | 46 | 15 | 23 | 31 | 53 | 109 | 86 |

**56.25N 5.28W**

| ban | Jan | Feb | Mar | Apr | May | Jun | Jul | Aug | Sep | Oct | Nov | Dec |
|---|---|---|---|---|---|---|---|---|---|---|---|---|
| Temperature - max. (°C) | 6 | 7 | 9 | 11 | 14 | 16 | 17 | 17 | 15 | 12 | 9 | 7 |
| Temperature - min. (°C) | 2 | 1 | 3 | 4 | 7 | 9 | 11 | 11 | 9 | 7 | 4 | 3 |
| Rainfall - (mm) | 146 | 109 | 83 | 90 | 72 | 87 | 120 | 116 | 141 | 169 | 146 | 172 |

**0.58S 100.23E**

| dang | Jan | Feb | Mar | Apr | May | Jun | Jul | Aug | Sep | Oct | Nov | Dec |
|---|---|---|---|---|---|---|---|---|---|---|---|---|
| Temperature - max. (°C) | 31 | 31 | 31 | 31 | 31 | 31 | 31 | 31 | 30 | 30 | 30 | 30 |
| Temperature - min. (°C) | 23 | 23 | 23 | 24 | 24 | 23 | 23 | 23 | 23 | 23 | 23 | 23 |
| Rainfall - (mm) | 351 | 259 | 307 | 363 | 315 | 307 | 277 | 348 | 152 | 495 | 518 | 480 |

**31.56S 115.47E**

| rth | Jan | Feb | Mar | Apr | May | Jun | Jul | Aug | Sep | Oct | Nov | Dec |
|---|---|---|---|---|---|---|---|---|---|---|---|---|
| Temperature - max. (°C) | 29 | 29 | 27 | 24 | 21 | 18 | 17 | 18 | 19 | 21 | 24 | 27 |
| Temperature - min. (°C) | 17 | 17 | 16 | 14 | 12 | 10 | 9 | 9 | 10 | 12 | 14 | 16 |
| Rainfall - (mm) | 8 | 10 | 20 | 43 | 130 | 180 | 170 | 145 | 86 | 56 | 20 | 13 |

**50.22N 4.08W**

| ymouth | Jan | Feb | Mar | Apr | May | Jun | Jul | Aug | Sep | Oct | Nov | Dec |
|---|---|---|---|---|---|---|---|---|---|---|---|---|
| Temperature - max. (°C) | 8 | 8 | 10 | 12 | 15 | 18 | 19 | 19 | 18 | 15 | 11 | 9 |
| Temperature - min. (°C) | 4 | 4 | 5 | 6 | 8 | 11 | 13 | 13 | 12 | 9 | 7 | 5 |
| Rainfall - (mm) | 99 | 74 | 69 | 53 | 63 | 53 | 70 | 77 | 78 | 91 | 113 | 110 |

**53.09S 70.57W**

| unta Arenas | Jan | Feb | Mar | Apr | May | Jun | Jul | Aug | Sep | Oct | Nov | Dec |
|---|---|---|---|---|---|---|---|---|---|---|---|---|
| Temperature - max. (°C) | 14 | 14 | 12 | 10 | 7 | 5 | 4 | 6 | 8 | 11 | 12 | 14 |
| Temperature - min. (°C) | 7 | 7 | 5 | 4 | 2 | 1 | -1 | 1 | 2 | 3 | 4 | 6 |
| Rainfall - (mm) | 38 | 23 | 33 | 36 | 33 | 41 | 28 | 31 | 23 | 28 | 18 | 36 |

**0.14S 78.30W**

| Quito | Jan | Feb | Mar | Apr | May | Jun | Jul | Aug | Sep | Oct | Nov | Dec |
|---|---|---|---|---|---|---|---|---|---|---|---|---|
| Temperature - max. (°C) | 22 | 22 | 22 | 21 | 21 | 22 | 22 | 23 | 23 | 22 | 22 | 22 |
| Temperature - min. (°C) | 8 | 8 | 8 | 8 | 8 | 7 | 7 | 7 | 7 | 8 | 7 | 8 |
| Rainfall - (mm) | 99 | 112 | 142 | 175 | 137 | 43 | 20 | 31 | 69 | 112 | 97 | 79 |

**24.43N 46.41E**

| Riyadh | Jan | Feb | Mar | Apr | May | Jun | Jul | Aug | Sep | Oct | Nov | Dec |
|---|---|---|---|---|---|---|---|---|---|---|---|---|
| Temperature - max. (°C) | 21 | 23 | 28 | 32 | 38 | 42 | 42 | 42 | 39 | 34 | 29 | 21 |
| Temperature - min. (°C) | 8 | 9 | 13 | 18 | 22 | 25 | 26 | 24 | 22 | 16 | 13 | 9 |
| Rainfall - (mm) | 3 | 20 | 23 | 25 | 10 | 0 | 0 | 0 | 0 | 0 | 0 | 0 |

**33.28S 70.39W**

| Santiago | Jan | Feb | Mar | Apr | May | Jun | Jul | Aug | Sep | Oct | Nov | Dec |
|---|---|---|---|---|---|---|---|---|---|---|---|---|
| Temperature - max. (°C) | 29 | 29 | 27 | 23 | 18 | 14 | 15 | 17 | 19 | 22 | 26 | 28 |
| Temperature - min. (°C) | 12 | 11 | 9 | 7 | 5 | 3 | 3 | 4 | 6 | 7 | 9 | 11 |
| Rainfall - (mm) | 3 | 3 | 5 | 13 | 64 | 84 | 76 | 56 | 31 | 15 | 8 | 5 |

**52.08N 106.39W**

| Saskatoon | Jan | Feb | Mar | Apr | May | Jun | Jul | Aug | Sep | Oct | Nov | Dec |
|---|---|---|---|---|---|---|---|---|---|---|---|---|
| Temperature - max. (°C) | -13 | -11 | -3 | 9 | 18 | 22 | 25 | 24 | 17 | 11 | -1 | -9 |
| Temperature - min. (°C) | -24 | -22 | -14 | -3 | 3 | 9 | 11 | 9 | 3 | -3 | -11 | -19 |
| Rainfall - (mm) | 23 | 13 | 18 | 18 | 36 | 66 | 61 | 48 | 38 | 23 | 13 | 15 |

**37.24N 5.58W**

| Seville | Jan | Feb | Mar | Apr | May | Jun | Jul | Aug | Sep | Oct | Nov | Dec |
|---|---|---|---|---|---|---|---|---|---|---|---|---|
| Temperature - max. (°C) | 15 | 17 | 20 | 24 | 27 | 32 | 36 | 36 | 32 | 26 | 20 | 16 |
| Temperature - min. (°C) | 6 | 7 | 9 | 11 | 13 | 17 | 20 | 20 | 18 | 14 | 10 | 7 |
| Rainfall - (mm) | 66 | 61 | 90 | 57 | 41 | 8 | 1 | 5 | 19 | 70 | 67 | 79 |

**31.15N 121.29E**

| Shanghai | Jan | Feb | Mar | Apr | May | Jun | Jul | Aug | Sep | Oct | Nov | Dec |
|---|---|---|---|---|---|---|---|---|---|---|---|---|
| Temperature - max. (°C) | 8 | 8 | 13 | 19 | 25 | 28 | 32 | 32 | 28 | 23 | 17 | 12 |
| Temperature - min. (°C) | 1 | 1 | 4 | 10 | 15 | 19 | 23 | 23 | 19 | 14 | 7 | 2 |
| Rainfall - (mm) | 48 | 58 | 84 | 94 | 94 | 180 | 147 | 142 | 130 | 71 | 51 | 36 |

**16.46N 2.59W**

| Timbuktu | Jan | Feb | Mar | Apr | May | Jun | Jul | Aug | Sep | Oct | Nov | Dec |
|---|---|---|---|---|---|---|---|---|---|---|---|---|
| Temperature - max. (°C) | 27 | 31 | 34 | 38 | 41 | 40 | 37 | 35 | 37 | 37 | 33 | 28 |
| Temperature - min. (°C) | 14 | 17 | 21 | 24 | 27 | 29 | 27 | 27 | 26 | 24 | 19 | 15 |
| Rainfall - (mm) | 0 | 0 | 0 | 0 | 4 | 19 | 62 | 79 | 33 | 3 | 0 | 0 |

**56.30N 85.01E**

| Tomsk | Jan | Feb | Mar | Apr | May | Jun | Jul | Aug | Sep | Oct | Nov | Dec |
|---|---|---|---|---|---|---|---|---|---|---|---|---|
| Temperature - max. (°C) | -18 | -13 | -6 | 3 | 12 | 19 | 23 | 20 | 14 | 3 | -9 | -16 |
| Temperature - min. (°C) | -24 | -22 | -17 | -7 | 3 | 9 | 12 | 10 | 4 | -3 | -14 | -22 |
| Rainfall - (mm) | 28 | 18 | 20 | 23 | 41 | 69 | 66 | 66 | 41 | 51 | 46 | 38 |

**49.16N 123.08W**

| Vancouver | Jan | Feb | Mar | Apr | May | Jun | Jul | Aug | Sep | Oct | Nov | Dec |
|---|---|---|---|---|---|---|---|---|---|---|---|---|
| Temperature - max. (°C) | 5 | 7 | 10 | 14 | 18 | 21 | 23 | 23 | 18 | 14 | 9 | 6 |
| Temperature - min. (°C) | 0 | 1 | 3 | 4 | 8 | 11 | 12 | 12 | 9 | 7 | 4 | 2 |
| Rainfall - (mm) | 218 | 147 | 127 | 84 | 71 | 64 | 31 | 43 | 91 | 147 | 211 | 224 |

**22.58S 14.30E**

| Walvis Bay | Jan | Feb | Mar | Apr | May | Jun | Jul | Aug | Sep | Oct | Nov | Dec |
|---|---|---|---|---|---|---|---|---|---|---|---|---|
| Temperature - max. (°C) | 23 | 23 | 23 | 24 | 23 | 23 | 21 | 20 | 19 | 19 | 22 | 22 |
| Temperature - min. (°C) | 15 | 16 | 15 | 13 | 11 | 9 | 8 | 8 | 9 | 11 | 12 | 14 |
| Rainfall - (mm) | 0 | 5 | 8 | 3 | 3 | 0 | 0 | 3 | 0 | 0 | 0 | 0 |

**53.58N 1.05W**

| York | Jan | Feb | Mar | Apr | May | Jun | Jul | Aug | Sep | Oct | Nov | Dec |
|---|---|---|---|---|---|---|---|---|---|---|---|---|
| Temperature - max. (°C) | 6 | 7 | 10 | 13 | 16 | 19 | 21 | 21 | 18 | 14 | 10 | 7 |
| Temperature - min. (°C) | 2 | 2 | 3 | 5 | 7 | 10 | 12 | 12 | 11 | 8 | 5 | 4 |
| Rainfall - (mm) | 59 | 46 | 37 | 41 | 50 | 50 | 62 | 68 | 55 | 56 | 65 | 50 |

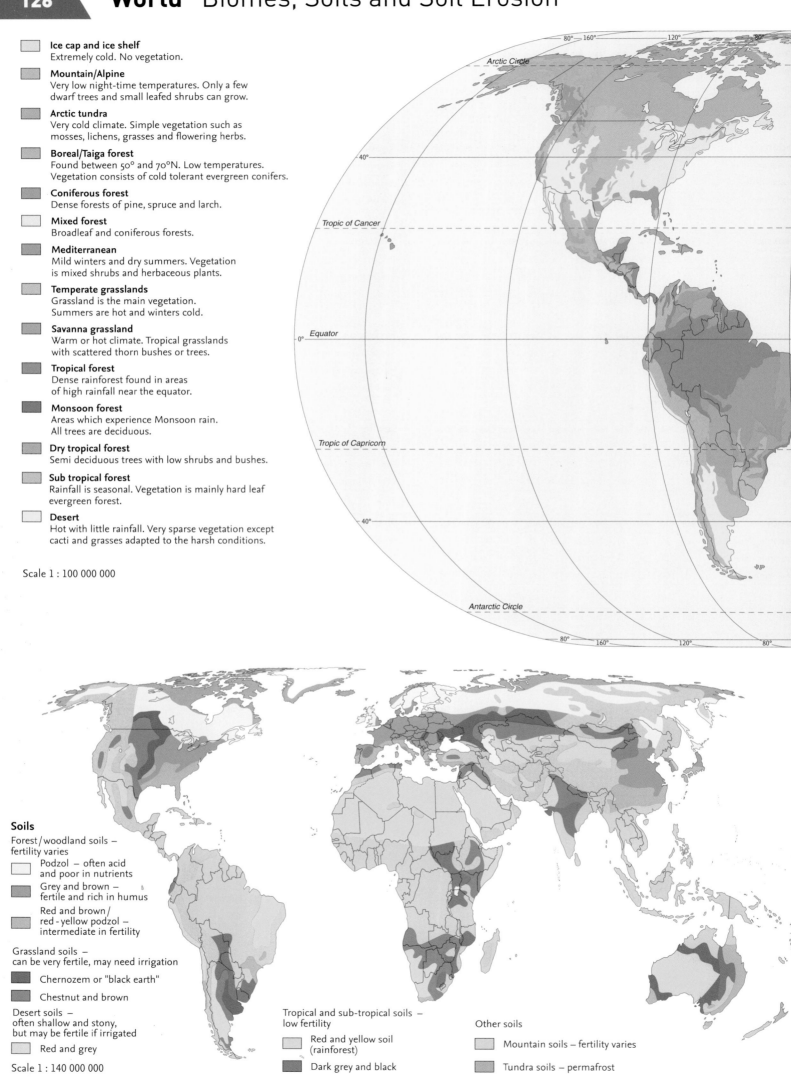

**Ice cap and ice shelf**
Extremely cold. No vegetation.

**Mountain/Alpine**
Very low night-time temperatures. Only a few dwarf trees and small leafed shrubs can grow.

**Arctic tundra**
Very cold climate. Simple vegetation such as mosses, lichens, grasses and flowering herbs.

**Boreal/Taiga forest**
Found between 50° and 70°N. Low temperatures. Vegetation consists of cold tolerant evergreen conifers.

**Coniferous forest**
Dense forests of pine, spruce and larch.

**Mixed forest**
Broadleaf and coniferous forests.

**Mediterranean**
Mild winters and dry summers. Vegetation is mixed shrubs and herbaceous plants.

**Temperate grasslands**
Grassland is the main vegetation. Summers are hot and winters cold.

**Savanna grassland**
Warm or hot climate. Tropical grasslands with scattered thorn bushes or trees.

**Tropical forest**
Dense rainforest found in areas of high rainfall near the equator.

**Monsoon forest**
Areas which experience Monsoon rain. All trees are deciduous.

**Dry tropical forest**
Semi deciduous trees with low shrubs and bushes.

**Sub tropical forest**
Rainfall is seasonal. Vegetation is mainly hard leaf evergreen forest.

**Desert**
Hot with little rainfall. Very sparse vegetation except cacti and grasses adapted to the harsh conditions.

Scale 1 : 100 000 000

**Soils**

Forest/woodland soils – fertility varies

Podzol – often acid and poor in nutrients

Grey and brown – fertile and rich in humus

Red and brown / red-yellow podzol – intermediate in fertility

Grassland soils – can be very fertile, may need irrigation

Chernozem or "black earth"

Chestnut and brown

Desert soils – often shallow and stony, but may be fertile if irrigated

Red and grey

Scale 1 : 140 000 000

Tropical and sub-tropical soils – low fertility

Red and yellow soil (rainforest)

Dark grey and black

Other soils

Mountain soils – fertility varies

Tundra soils – permafrost

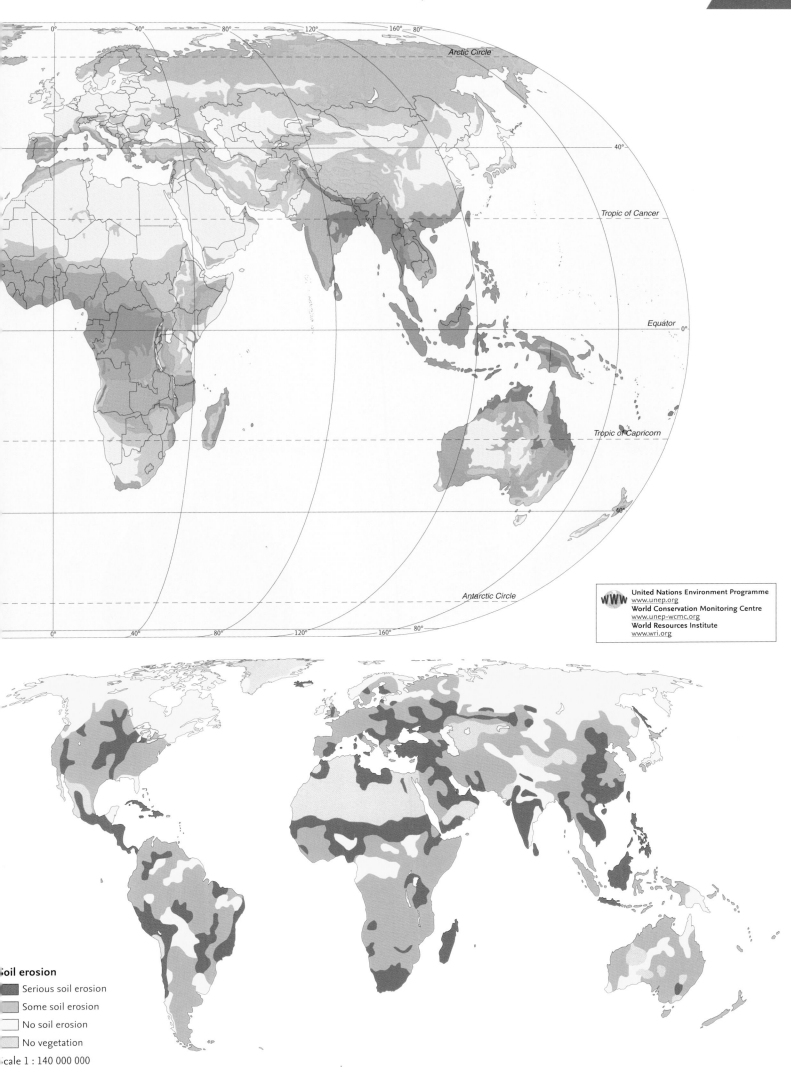

Arctic Circle

40°

Tropic of Cancer

Equator · 0°

Tropic of Capricorn

40°

Antarctic Circle

WWW **United Nations Environment Programme**
www.unep.org
**World Conservation Monitoring Centre**
www.unep-wcmc.org
**World Resources Institute**
www.wri.org

**Soil erosion**

Serious soil erosion

Some soil erosion

No soil erosion

No vegetation

Scale 1 : 140 000 000

# **World** Agriculture

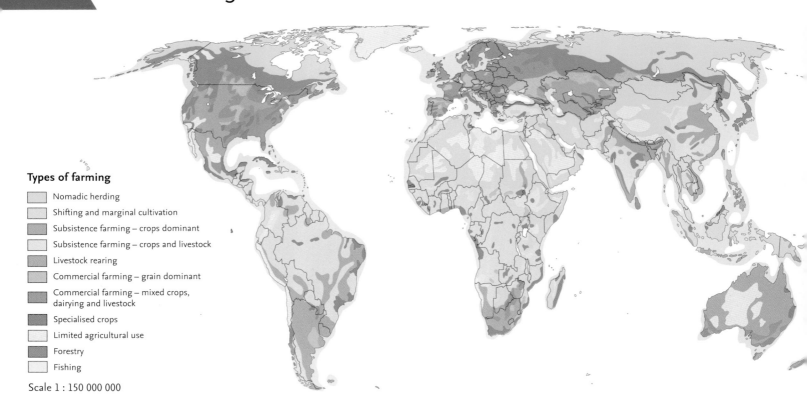

## Types of farming

- Nomadic herding
- Shifting and marginal cultivation
- Subsistence farming – crops dominant
- Subsistence farming – crops and livestock
- Livestock rearing
- Commercial farming – grain dominant
- Commercial farming – mixed crops, dairying and livestock
- Specialised crops
- Limited agricultural use
- Forestry
- Fishing

Scale 1 : 150 000 000

## World cereal production, 2018

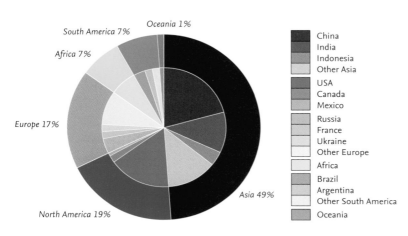

Oceania 1%
South America 7%
Africa 7%
Europe 17%
North America 19%
Asia 49%

China
India
Indonesia
Other Asia
USA
Canada
Mexico
Russia
France
Ukraine
Other Europe
Africa
Brazil
Argentina
Other South America
Oceania

## World meat production, 2018

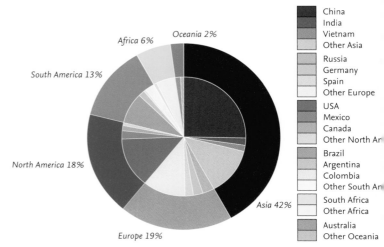

Africa 6%
Oceania 2%
South America 13%
North America 18%
Europe 19%
Asia 42%

China
India
Vietnam
Other Asia
Russia
Germany
Spain
Other Europe
USA
Mexico
Canada
Other North America
Brazil
Argentina
Colombia
Other South America
South Africa
Other Africa
Australia
Other Oceania

## Projected population growth, 2013 – 2050

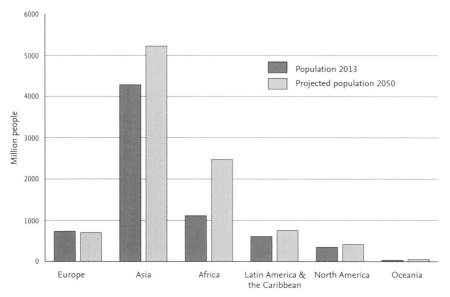

Population 2013
Projected population 2050

Europe · Asia · Africa · Latin America & the Caribbean · North America · Oceania

Million people

## Closing the food gap

Required increase in crop production to feed 9.7 billion people in 2050.

**119%**

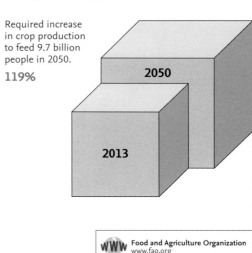

2050
2013

**Food and Agriculture Organization**
www.fao.org

## EDCs and LEDCs

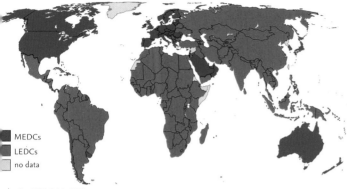

MEDCs
LEDCs
no data

ale 1 : 300 000 000

ternational organizations generally agree that countries can be categorized into re economically developed countries (MEDCs) and less economically developed untries (LEDCs). The group of MEDCs includes the following countries/regions: nada; USA; Panama; Chile; Uruguay; Europe as far east as the Baltic states, land, Slovakia, Romania and Croatia; Greece; Cyprus; Israel; Saudi Arabia, wait; Bahrain; Qatar; UAE; Oman; Seychelles; South Korea; Japan; Brunei; ngapore; Australia; New Zealand; several small Pacific and Caribbean islands.

## Level of development

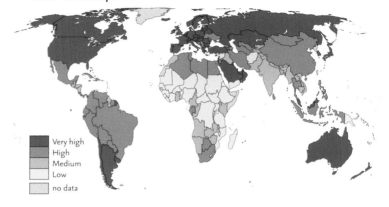

Very high
High
Medium
Low
no data

This map categorizes countries by their stage of development: Very high; High; Medium; Low. Indicators, such as life expectancy as an index of population health and longevity, education as measured by adult literacy and school enrolment, and standards of living based on the GDP per capita, are used to measure the level of development. The development of regions, cities or villages can also be assessed using these indicators.

## w development

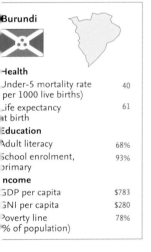

**Burundi**

**Health**
| | |
|---|---|
| Under-5 mortality rate (per 1000 live births) | 40 |
| Life expectancy at birth | 61 |

**Education**
| | |
|---|---|
| Adult literacy | 68% |
| School enrolment, primary | 93% |

**Income**
| | |
|---|---|
| GDP per capita | $783 |
| GNI per capita | $280 |
| Poverty line (% of population) | 78% |

## Medium development

**India**

**Health**
| | |
|---|---|
| Under-5 mortality rate (per 1000 live births) | 28 |
| Life expectancy at birth | 69 |

**Education**
| | |
|---|---|
| Adult literacy | 74% |
| School enrolment, primary | 90% |

**Income**
| | |
|---|---|
| GDP per capita | $7034 |
| GNI per capita | $2130 |
| Poverty line (% of population) | 21% |

## High development

**Brazil**

**Health**
| | |
|---|---|
| Under-5 mortality rate (per 1000 live births) | 12 |
| Life expectancy at birth | 76 |

**Education**
| | |
|---|---|
| Adult literacy | 93% |
| School enrolment, primary | 96% |

**Income**
| | |
|---|---|
| GDP per capita | $15 259 |
| GNI per capita | $9130 |
| Poverty line (% of population) | 4% |

## Very high development

**Australia**

**Health**
| | |
|---|---|
| Under-5 mortality rate (per 1000 live births) | 3 |
| Life expectancy at birth | 83 |

**Education**
| | |
|---|---|
| Adult literacy | >95% |
| School enrolment, primary | 96 |

**Income**
| | |
|---|---|
| GDP per capita | $53 320 |
| GNI per capita | $54 190 |
| Poverty line (% of population) | 0.5% |

## DP per capita, 1990 – 2019

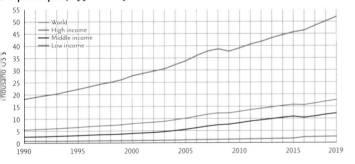

## GNI per capita, 1990 – 2019

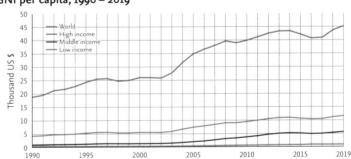

## imary school enrolment, 1990 – 2018

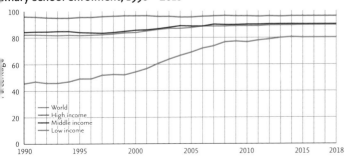

## Life expectancy, 1990 – 2018

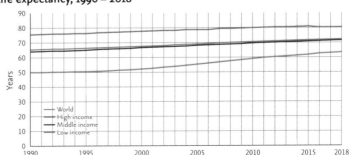

## Population comparisons

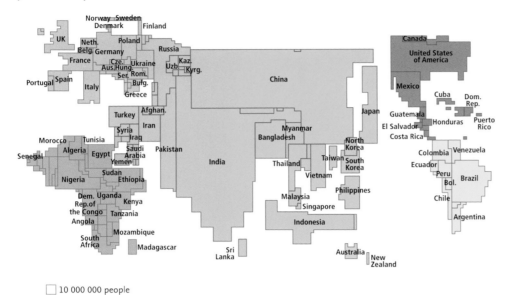

☐ 10 000 000 people

## Population structure, 1950 – 2090

Each full square represents 1% of the total population

### World

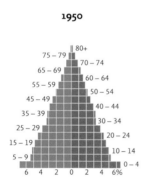
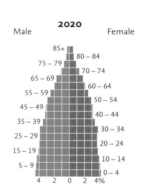
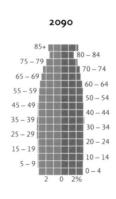

### More developed regions

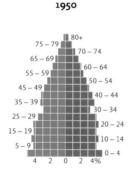
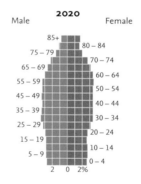
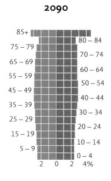

### Least developed regions

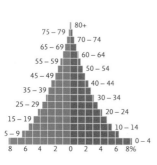
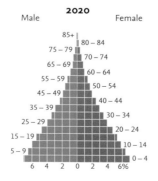
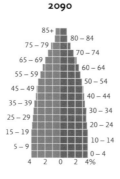

## Largest countries by population, 2019

| Country and continent | Population |
|---|---|
| **China** Asia | 1 441 860 29 |
| **India** Asia | 1 366 417 75 |
| **United States of America** N America | 329 064 91 |
| **Indonesia** Asia | 270 625 56 |
| **Pakistan** Asia | 216 565 31 |
| **Brazil** S America | 211 049 51 |
| **Nigeria** Africa | 200 963 60 |
| **Bangladesh** Asia | 163 046 17 |
| **Russia** Asia/Europe | 145 872 26 |
| **Mexico** N America | 127 575 52 |
| **Japan** Asia | 126 860 29 |
| **Ethiopia** Africa | 112 078 72 |
| **Philippines** Asia | 108 116 62 |
| **Egypt** Africa | 100 388 07 |
| **Vietnam** Asia | 96 462 10 |
| **Dem. Rep. of the Congo** Africa | 86 790 56 |
| **Germany** Europe | 83 517 04 |
| **Turkey** Asia | 83 429 60 |
| **Iran** Asia | 82 913 89 |
| **Thailand** Asia | 69 625 58 |

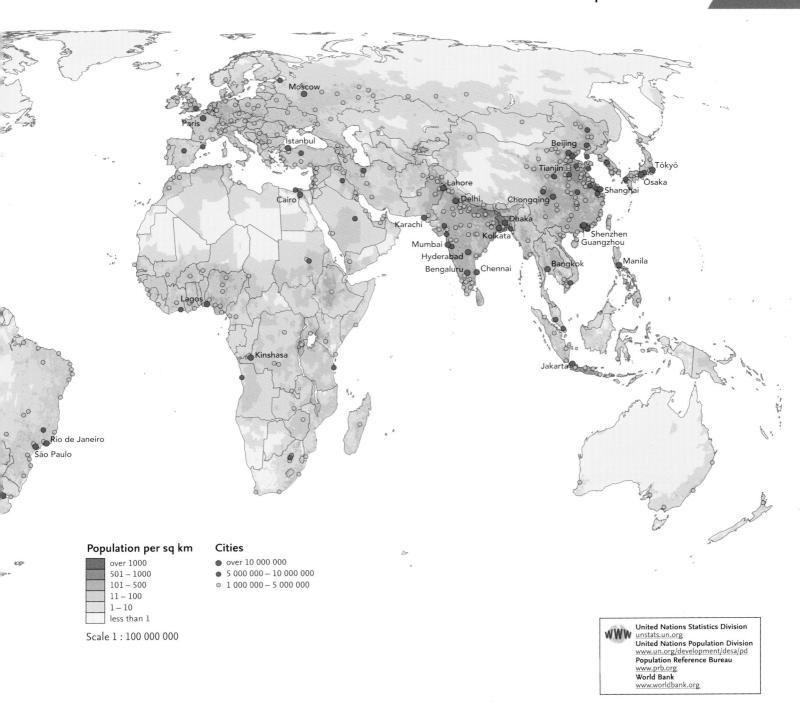

**Population per sq km**

| | |
|---|---|
| | over 1000 |
| | 501 – 1000 |
| | 101 – 500 |
| | 11 – 100 |
| | 1 – 10 |
| | less than 1 |

Scale 1 : 100 000 000

**Cities**
- over 10 000 000
- 5 000 000 – 10 000 000
- 1 000 000 – 5 000 000

**ld population growth, 1750 – 2050**

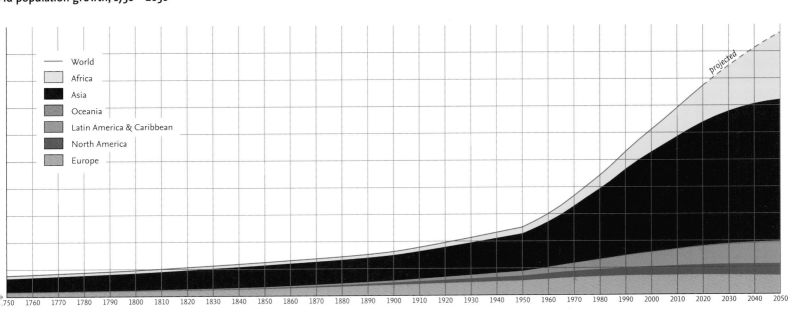

World
Africa
Asia
Oceania
Latin America & Caribbean
North America
Europe

*projected*

1750 1760 1770 1780 1790 1800 1810 1820 1830 1840 1850 1860 1870 1880 1890 1900 1910 1920 1930 1940 1950 1960 1970 1980 1990 2000 2010 2020 2030 2040 2050

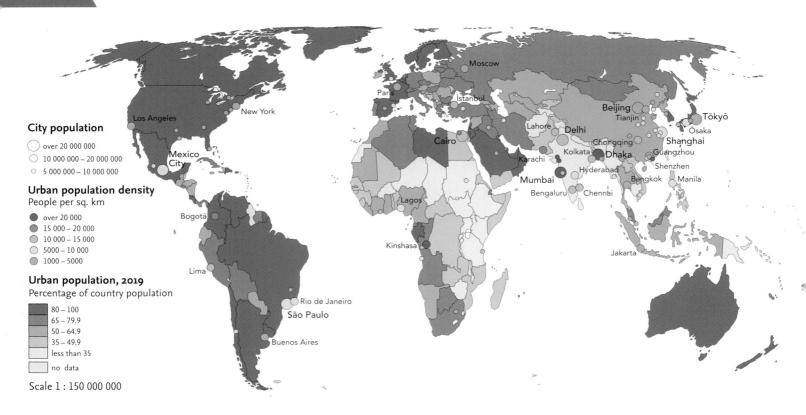

**City population**

○ over 20 000 000
○ 10 000 000 – 20 000 000
○ 5 000 000 – 10 000 000

**Urban population density**
People per sq. km

● over 20 000
● 15 000 – 20 000
● 10 000 – 15 000
● 5000 – 10 000
● 1000 – 5000

**Urban population, 2019**
Percentage of country population

- 80 – 100
- 65 – 79.9
- 50 – 64.9
- 35 – 49.9
- less than 35
- no data

Scale 1 : 150 000 000

## Largest urban agglomerations, 2018

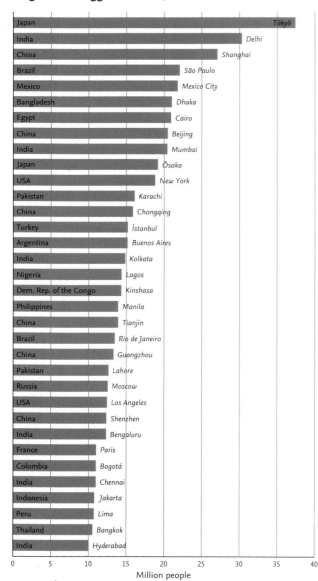

| Country | City |
|---|---|
| Japan | Tōkyō |
| India | Delhi |
| China | Shanghai |
| Brazil | São Paulo |
| Mexico | Mexico City |
| Bangladesh | Dhaka |
| Egypt | Cairo |
| China | Beijing |
| India | Mumbai |
| Japan | Ōsaka |
| USA | New York |
| Pakistan | Karachi |
| China | Chongqing |
| Turkey | İstanbul |
| Argentina | Buenos Aires |
| India | Kolkata |
| Nigeria | Lagos |
| Dem. Rep. of the Congo | Kinshasa |
| Philippines | Manila |
| China | Tianjin |
| Brazil | Rio de Janeiro |
| China | Guangzhou |
| Pakistan | Lahore |
| Russia | Moscow |
| USA | Los Angeles |
| China | Shenzhen |
| India | Bengaluru |
| France | Paris |
| Colombia | Bogotá |
| India | Chennai |
| Indonesia | Jakarta |
| Peru | Lima |
| Thailand | Bangkok |
| India | Hyderabad |

0   5   10   15   20   25   30   35   40
Million people

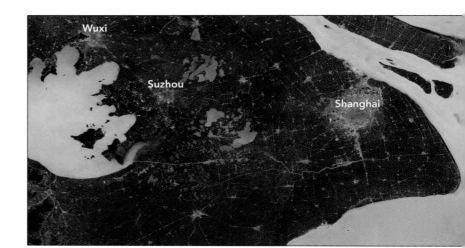

## Shanghai urban growth

The images above show the city of Shanghai, located on the east coast of China. The top image is from the mid 1980s when Shanghai was a compact industrial city of about 12 million inhabitants. Since then it has grown rapidly to become one of the largest urban areas in the world with a population of over 27 million people.

The lower image is from 2017 and shows that Shanghai has merged with Suzhou and Wuxi to the west, creating one continuous metropolitan area.

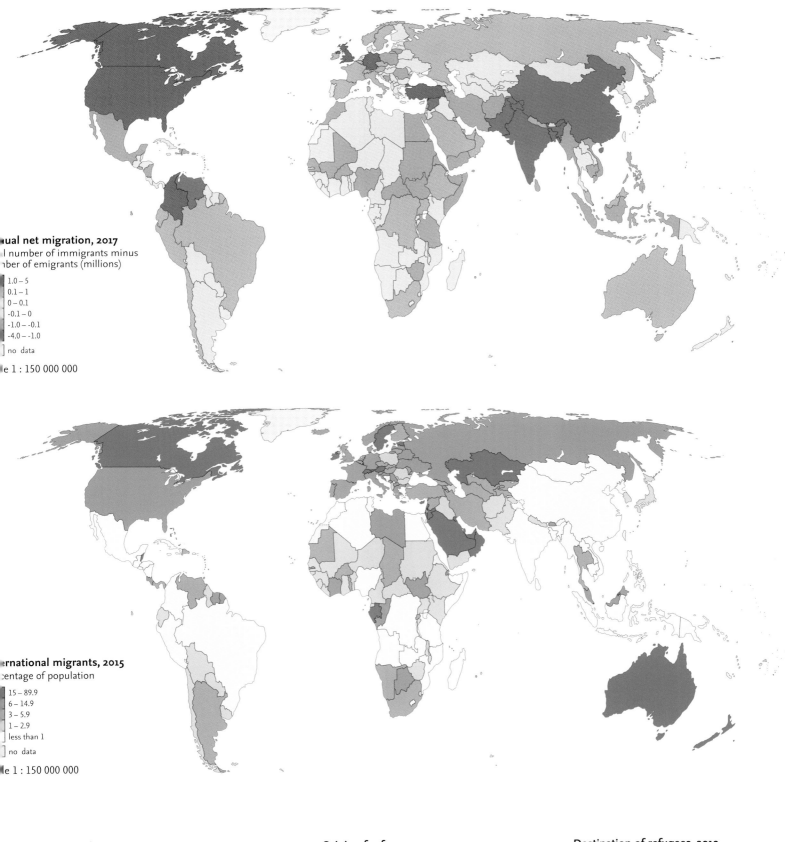

Annual net migration, 2017

Total number of immigrants minus
number of emigrants (millions)

- 1.0 – 5
- 0.1 – 1
- 0 – 0.1
- -0.1 – 0
- -1.0 – -0.1
- -4.0 – -1.0
- no data

Scale 1 : 150 000 000

International migrants, 2015

Percentage of population

- 15 – 89.9
- 6 – 14.9
- 3 – 5.9
- 1 – 2.9
- less than 1
- no data

Scale 1 : 150 000 000

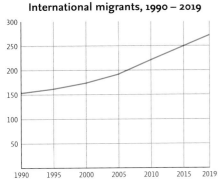

**International migrants, 1990 – 2019**

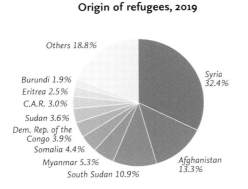

**Origin of refugees, 2019**

Others 18.8%
Burundi 1.9%
Eritrea 2.5%
C.A.R. 3.0%
Sudan 3.6%
Dem. Rep. of the Congo 3.9%
Somalia 4.4%
Myanmar 5.3%
South Sudan 10.9%
Afghanistan 13.3%
Syria 32.4%

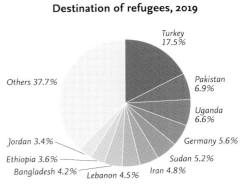

**Destination of refugees, 2019**

Turkey 17.5%
Pakistan 6.9%
Uganda 6.6%
Germany 5.6%
Sudan 5.2%
Iran 4.8%
Lebanon 4.5%
Bangladesh 4.2%
Ethiopia 3.6%
Jordan 3.4%
Others 37.7%

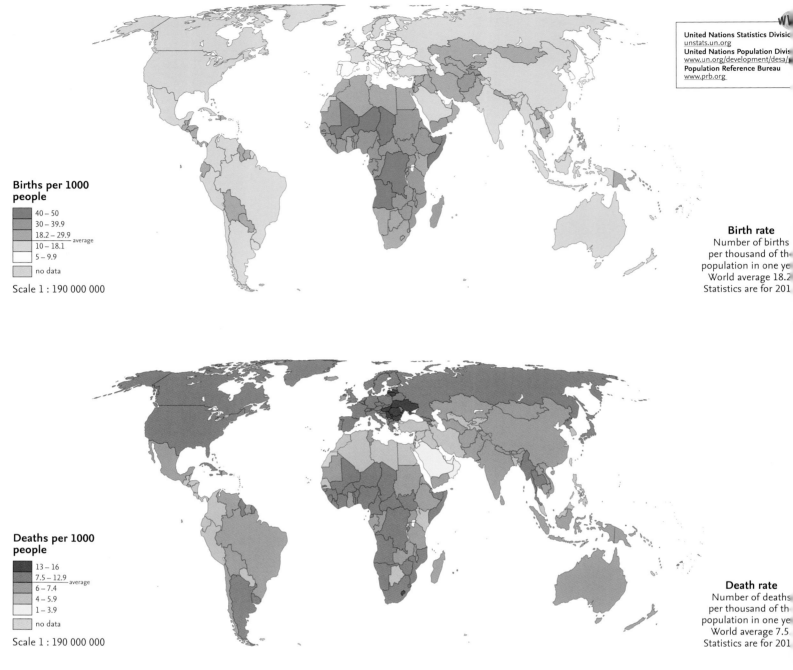

W
United Nations Statistics Divisio
unstats.un.org
United Nations Population Divis
www.un.org/development/desa/
Population Reference Bureau
www.prb.org

**Births per 1000 people**

- 40 – 50
- 30 – 39.9
- 18.2 – 29.9 average
- 10 – 18.1
- 5 – 9.9
- no data

Scale 1 : 190 000 000

**Birth rate**
Number of births
per thousand of the
population in one ye
World average 18.2
Statistics are for 201

**Deaths per 1000 people**

- 13 – 16
- 7.5 – 12.9 average
- 6 – 7.4
- 4 – 5.9
- 1 – 3.9
- no data

Scale 1 : 190 000 000

**Death rate**
Number of deaths
per thousand of th
population in one ye
World average 7.5
Statistics are for 201

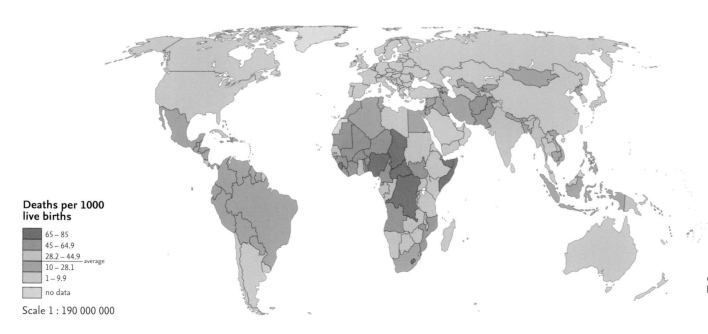

**Deaths per 1000 live births**

- 65 – 85
- 45 – 64.9
- 28.2 – 44.9 average
- 10 – 28.1
- 1 – 9.9
- no data

Scale 1 : 190 000 000

**Infant mortality ra**
Number of infants
dying before reachir
one year of age, per 1
live births in a given y
World average 28.2
Statistics are for 201

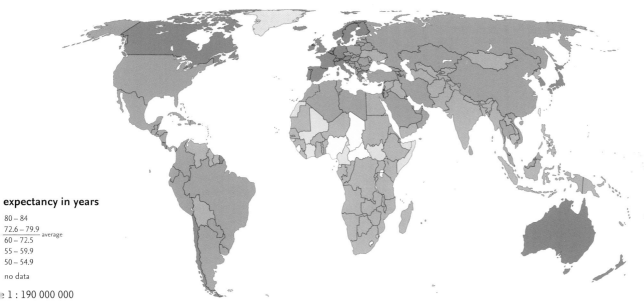

**www**

UNESCO
www.unesco.org
**World Health Organization**
www.who.int
**World Bank**
www.worldbank.org

## expectancy in years

- 80 – 84
- 72.6 – 79.9 — average
- 60 – 72.5
- 55 – 59.9
- 50 – 54.9
- no data

e 1 : 190 000 000

### Life expectancy
Average age a newborn infant would live to if patterns of mortality prevailing for all people at the time of its birth were to stay the same throughout its life. World average 72.6. Statistics are for 2018.

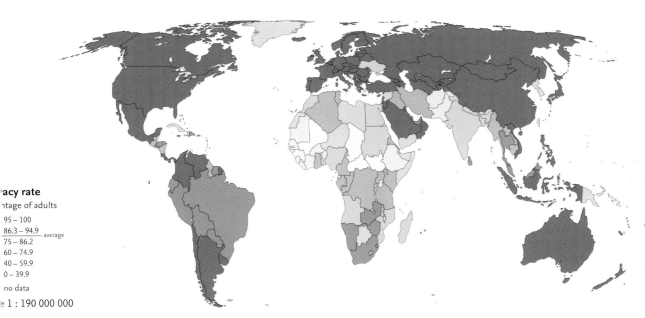

## acy rate

ntage of adults

- 95 – 100
- 86.3 – 94.9 — average
- 75 – 86.2
- 60 – 74.9
- 40 – 59.9
- 0 – 39.9
- no data

e 1 : 190 000 000

### Literacy
Percentage of the population over 15 years old which is literate. The definition of 'literate' may vary greatly. World average 86.3%. Statistics are for 2014 – 2018.

## tors per 000 people

- 400 – 850
- 250 – 399
- 157 – 249 — average
- 100 – 156
- 50 – 99
- 10 – 49
- 1 – 9
- no data

e 1 : 190 000 000

### Doctors
Number of physicians per thousand of the population. World average 157. Statistics are for 2014 – 2018.

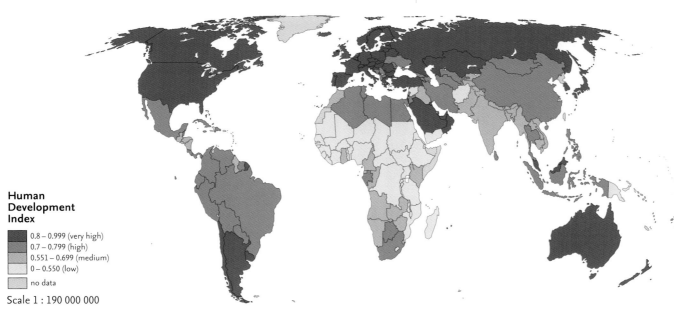

**Human Development Index**

- 0.8 – 0.999 (very high)
- 0.7 – 0.799 (high)
- 0.551 – 0.699 (medium)
- 0 – 0.550 (low)
- no data

Scale 1 : 190 000 000

**World Bank**
www.worldbank.org
**United Nations Development Program**
www.undp.org
**Sustainable Development Goals**
sdgs.un.org/goals

**HDI**
Measures the achievements of a coun based on indicators o life expectancy, knowled and standard of living World average 0.717. Statistics are for 2019

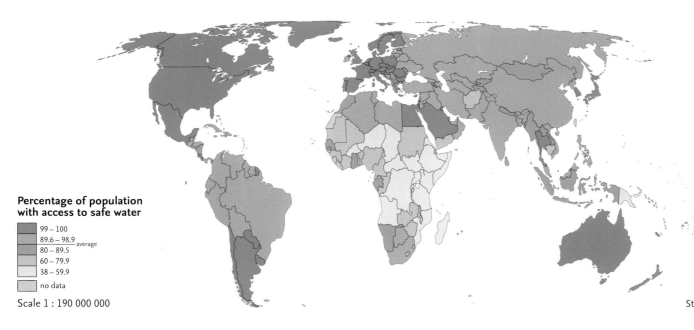

**Percentage of population with access to safe water**

- 99 – 100
- 89.6 – 98.9 average
- 80 – 89.5
- 60 – 79.9
- 38 – 59.9
- no data

Scale 1 : 190 000 000

**Access to safe water**
Percentage of the population with reasonable access to an adequate amount of water from an improved source. World average 89.6% Statistics are for 2015 – 2

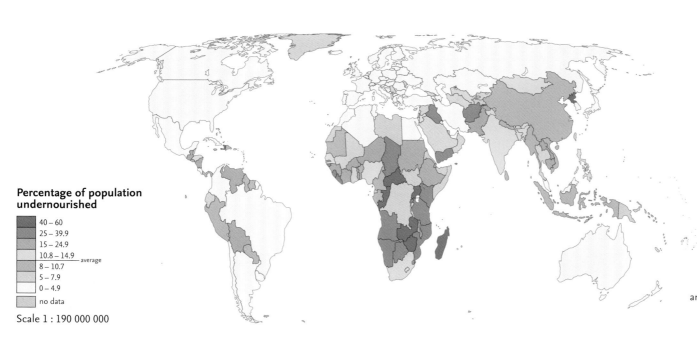

**Percentage of population undernourished**

- 40 – 60
- 25 – 39.9
- 15 – 24.9
- 10.8 – 14.9 average
- 8 – 10.7
- 5 – 7.9
- 0 – 4.9
- no data

Scale 1 : 190 000 000

**Nutrition**
Percentage of the population undernourished in developing countries and countries in transiti World average 10.8% Statistics are for 2017

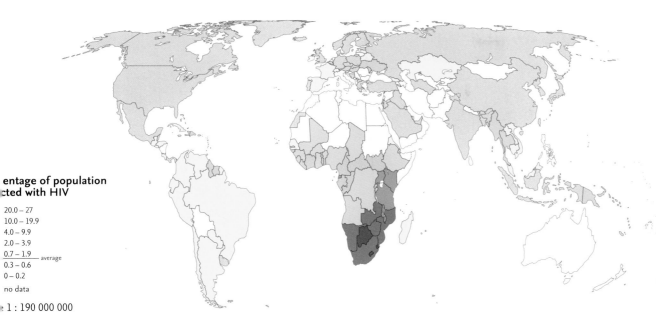

**entage of population
cted with HIV**

20.0 – 27
10.0 – 19.9
4.0 – 9.9
2.0 – 3.9
0.7 – 1.9 ——— average
0.3 – 0.6
0 – 0.2
no data

1 : 190 000 000

**Prevalence of HIV**
Percentage of the
population aged 15–49
who are infected with HIV.
World average 0.7%.
Statistics are for 2019.

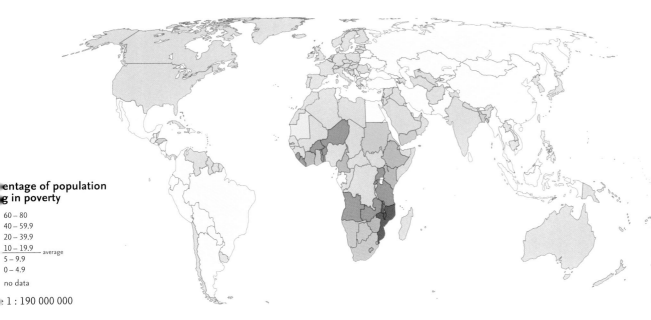

**entage of population
g in poverty**

60 – 80
40 – 59.9
20 – 39.9
10 – 19.9 ——— average
5 – 9.9
0 – 4.9
no data

1 : 190 000 000

**Poverty in
developing countries**
Percentage of the population
of developing countries living
on less than US$ 1.90 a day.
World average 10%.
Statistics are for 2014 – 2018.

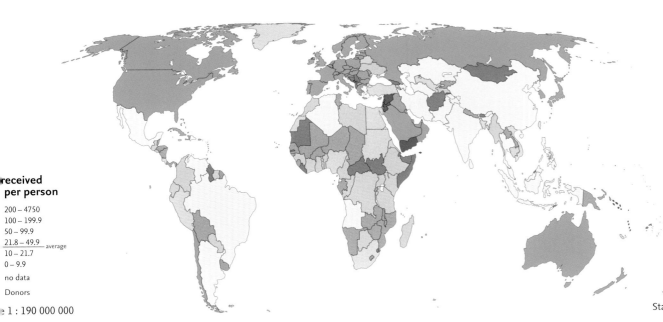

**received
per person**

200 – 4750
100 – 199.9
50 – 99.9
21.8 – 49.9 ——— average
10 – 21.7
0 – 9.9
no data
Donors

1 : 190 000 000

**Aid received**
Official development
assistance received
in US$ per person.
World average US$ 21.8.
Statistics are for 2017 – 2018.

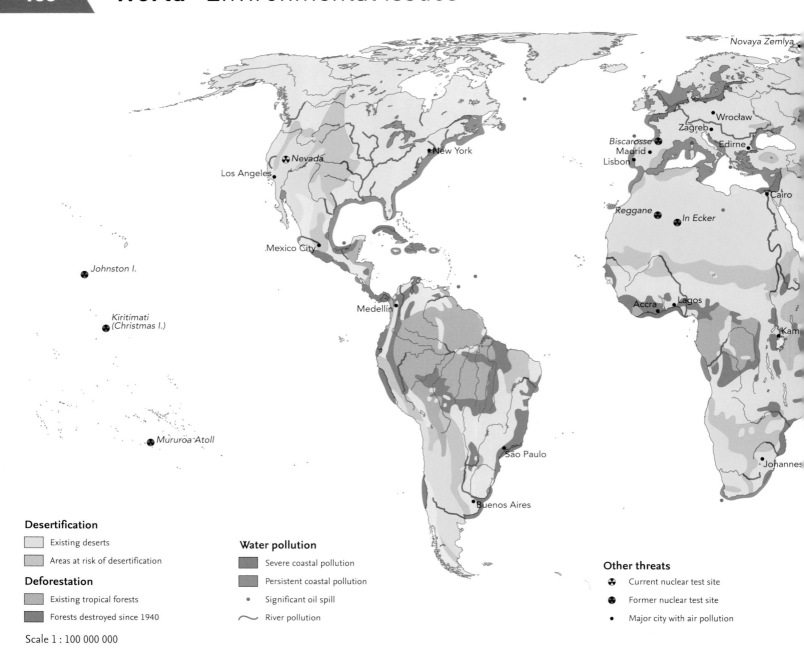

## Desertification

Existing deserts

Areas at risk of desertification

## Deforestation

Existing tropical forests

Forests destroyed since 1940

Scale 1 : 100 000 000

### Water pollution

Severe coastal pollution

Persistent coastal pollution

• Significant oil spill

~ River pollution

### Other threats

☢ Current nuclear test site

☢ Former nuclear test site

• Major city with air pollution

*Map labels:* Novaya Zemlya, Nevada, New York, Los Angeles, Mexico City, Johnston I., Kiritimati (Christmas I.), Medellín, Mururoa Atoll, São Paulo, Buenos Aires, Biscarosse, Madrid, Lisbon, Zagreb, Wrocław, Edirne, Cairo, Reggane, In Ecker, Accra, Lagos, Kam, Johannes

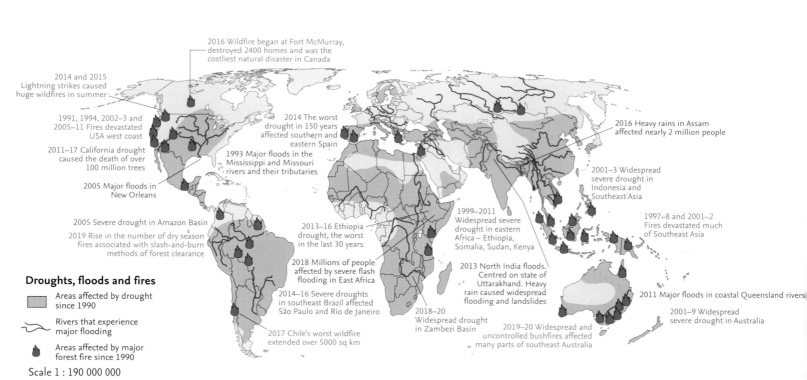

2016 Wildfire began at Fort McMurray, destroyed 2400 homes and was the costliest natural disaster in Canada

2014 and 2015 Lightning strikes caused huge wildfires in summer

1991, 1994, 2002–3 and 2005–11 Fires devastated USA west coast

2011–17 California drought caused the death of over 100 million trees

2005 Major floods in New Orleans

2005 Severe drought in Amazon Basin

2019 Rise in the number of dry season fires associated with slash-and-burn methods of forest clearance

2014 The worst drought in 150 years affected southern and eastern Spain

1993 Major floods in the Mississippi and Missouri rivers and their tributaries

2016 Heavy rains in Assam affected nearly 2 million people

2001–3 Widespread severe drought in Indonesia and Southeast Asia

1997–8 and 2001–2 Fires devastated much of Southeast Asia

2013–16 Ethiopia drought, the worst in the last 30 years

1999–2011 Widespread severe drought in eastern Africa – Ethiopia, Somalia, Sudan, Kenya

2018 Millions of people affected by severe flash flooding in East Africa

2013 North India floods. Centred on state of Uttarakhand. Heavy rain caused widespread flooding and landslides

2011 Major floods in coastal Queensland rivers

2014–16 Severe droughts in southeast Brazil affected São Paulo and Rio de Janeiro

2018–20 Widespread drought in Zambezi Basin

2001–9 Widespread severe drought in Australia

2017 Chile's worst wildfire extended over 5000 sq km

2019–20 Widespread and uncontrolled bushfires affected many parts of southeast Australia

### Droughts, floods and fires

Areas affected by drought since 1990

~ Rivers that experience major flooding

Areas affected by major forest fire since 1990

Scale 1 : 190 000 000

### Number of threatened species, 2020

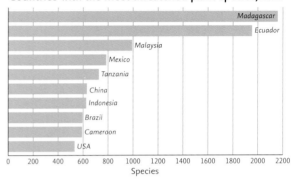

### Countries with the most threatened plant species, 2020

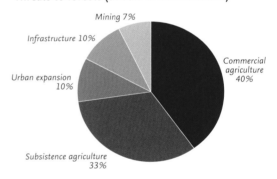

### Threats to forests (drivers of deforestation)

Mining 7%
Infrastructure 10%
Urban expansion 10%
Commercial agriculture 40%
Subsistence agriculture 33%

WWW    United Nations Environment Programme
www.unep.org
World Conservation Monitoring Centre
www.unep-wcmc.org
World Resources Institute
www.wri.org
UNESCO World Heritage Sites
whc.unesco.org

### Forest area change, 2011 – 2016

| World | -229 470 sq km |
|---|---|
| Africa | -195 951 sq km |
| Asia | 54 334 sq km |
| Europe | 17 902 sq km |
| North America | -1405 sq km |
| South America | -133 333 sq km |
| Oceania | 28 985 sq km |

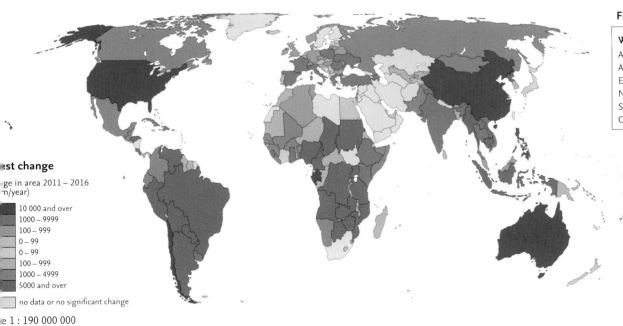

st change

ge in area 2011 – 2016
m/year)

10 000 and over
1000 – 9999
100 – 999
0 – 99
0 – 99
100 – 999
1000 – 4999
5000 and over

no data or no significant change

e 1 : 190 000 000

## Global warming, 1910 – 2019

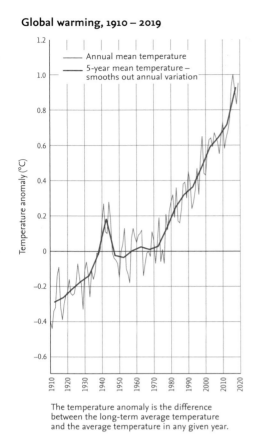

The temperature anomaly is the difference between the long-term average temperature and the average temperature in any given year.

www

World Meteorological Organization
www.wmo.int
**Met Office**
www.metoffice.gov.uk/weather
**Intergovernmental Panel on Climate Change**
www.ipcc.ch

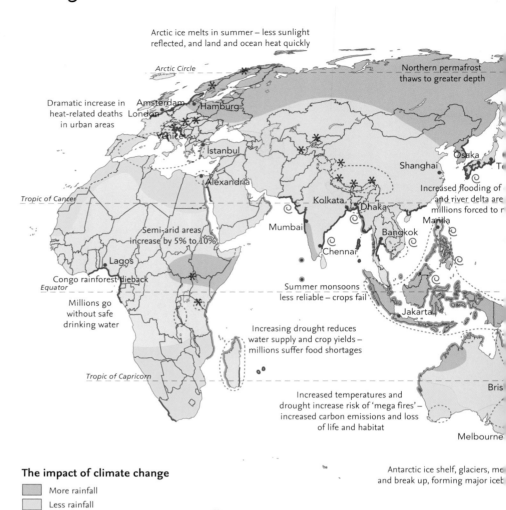

Arctic ice melts in summer – less sunlight reflected, and land and ocean heat quickly

Northern permafrost thaws to greater depth

Dramatic increase in heat-related deaths in urban areas

Increased flooding of and river delta are millions forced to r

Semi-arid areas increase by 5% to 10%

Congo rainforest dieback

Millions go without safe drinking water

Summer monsoons less reliable – crops fail

Increasing drought reduces water supply and crop yields – millions suffer food shortages

Increased temperatures and drought increase risk of 'mega fires' – increased carbon emissions and loss of life and habitat

Antarctic ice shelf, glaciers, me and break up, forming major iceb

### The impact of climate change

- More rainfall
- Less rainfall
- ✳ Melting glaciers, ice and snow
- ℮ Increasing frequency and intensity of tropical windstorms
- Climate change eco-hotspots
- Coral reefs at risk
- Coastal areas at risk of sea-level rise

Scale 1 : 125 000 0

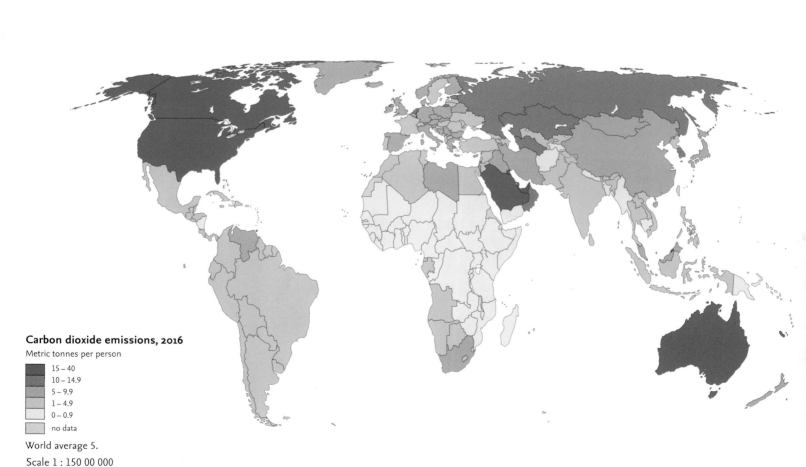

## Carbon dioxide emissions, 2016

Metric tonnes per person

- 15 – 40
- 10 – 14.9
- 5 – 9.9
- 1 – 4.9
- 0 – 0.9
- no data

World average 5.

Scale 1 : 150 00 000

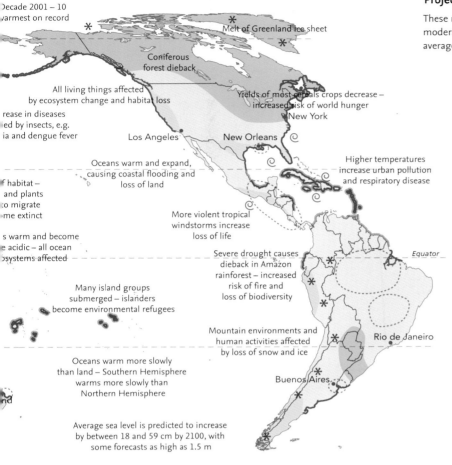

Decade 2001 – 10
warmest on record

Melt of Greenland ice sheet

Coniferous
forest dieback

All living things affected
by ecosystem change and habitat loss

Yields of most cereals crops decrease –
increased risk of world hunger
New York

rease in diseases
ed by insects, e.g.
ia and dengue fever

Los Angeles

New Orleans

f habitat –
and plants
o migrate
me extinct

Oceans warm and expand,
causing coastal flooding and
loss of land

Higher temperatures
increase urban pollution
and respiratory disease

s warm and become
e acidic – all ocean
osystems affected

More violent tropical
windstorms increase
loss of life

Severe drought causes
dieback in Amazon
rainforest – increased
risk of fire and
loss of biodiversity

Equator

Many island groups
submerged – islanders
become environmental refugees

Mountain environments and
human activities affected
by loss of snow and ice

Rio de Janeiro

Oceans warm more slowly
than land – Southern Hemisphere
warms more slowly than
Northern Hemisphere

Buenos Aires

Average sea level is predicted to increase
by between 18 and 59 cm by 2100, with
some forecasts as high as 1.5 m

## Projected annual mean temperature change

These maps show projected change in annual mean surface air temperature given
moderate growth in CO2 emissions, for three time periods, compared with the
average temperature for 1980 – 99.

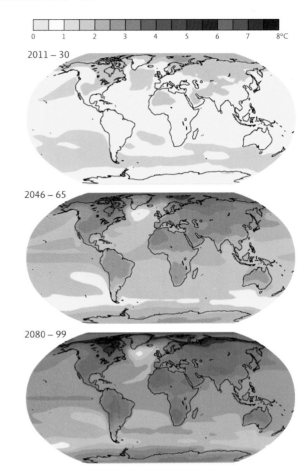

0  1  2  3  4  5  6  7  8°C

2011 – 30

2046 – 65

2080 – 99

mate change
lnerability index, 2020

Extreme (0 – 2.5)
High (2.5 – 5)
Medium (5 – 7.5)
Low (7.5 – 10)
No data

Verisk Maplecroft

ale 1 : 205 000 000

e climate change vulnerability index ranks how likely a country is to be harmed by
anging patterns in climate, natural hazards and ecosystems caused by climate change,
d how well prepared it is to combat the impacts of climate change. Denmark, with its
h levels of development, is the country best equipped to deal with climate change.
e highest risk country, Central African Republic, is vulnerable to climate extremes and
anging weather patterns. Its population is highly sensitive to climate change given high
verty levels, limited healthcare, political violence, and pressure on natural resources.

## Highest vulnerability

| 1 | Central African Republic | 5 | Sierra Leone | 8 | Yemen |
| 2 | Haiti | 6 | Liberia | 9 | Eritrea |
| 3 | Dem. Rep. of the Congo | 7 | South Sudan | 10 | Rwanda |
| 4 | Burundi | | | | |

Of the 39 countries most at risk, 33 are in Africa.

**Fuel production, 2019**

Percentage of world production

| >25% | 11 – 25% | 1 – 10% | |
|---|---|---|---|
| | | | Gas |
| | | | Oil |
| | | | Coal |

Scale 1 : 190 000 000

International Energy A
www.iea.org
BP Statistical Review o
World Energy
www.bp.com

**Energy production**

Million tonnes
oil equivalent

| | |
|---|---|
| | 1000 – 3000 |
| | 100 – 999.9 |
| | 10 – 99.9 |
| | 1 – 9.9 |
| | 0 – 0.9 |
| | no data |

Scale 1 : 190 000 000

**Energy product**
Expressed as the nu
of tonnes oil equiv
produced in one y
Statistics are for 2

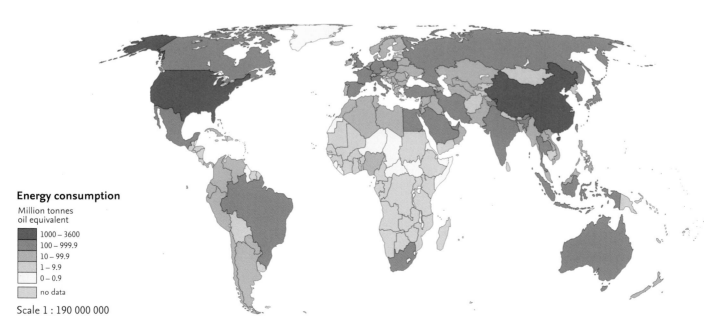

**Energy consumption**

Million tonnes
oil equivalent

| | |
|---|---|
| | 1000 – 3600 |
| | 100 – 999.9 |
| | 10 – 99.9 |
| | 1 – 9.9 |
| | 0 – 0.9 |
| | no data |

Scale 1 : 190 000 000

**Energy consump**
Expressed as the nu
of tonnes oil equiva
used in one yea
Statistics are for 2

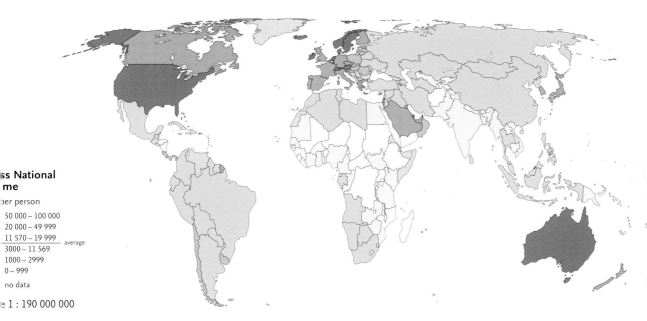

**GNI**
Gross National Income
is the value of production
of goods and services of
each country measured
in US$ per person in one year.
World average US$ 11 570.
Statistics are for 2015 – 2019.

ss National
me

per person

| | 50 000 – 100 000 |
|---|---|
| | 20 000 – 49 999 |
| | 11 570 – 19 999 | average |
| | 3000 – 11 569 |
| | 1000 – 2999 |
| | 0 – 999 |
| | no data |

e 1 : 190 000 000

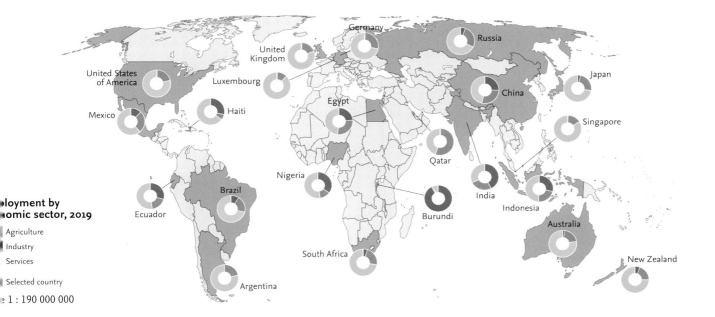

loyment by
omic sector, 2019

Agriculture

Industry

Services

Selected country

e 1 : 190 000 000

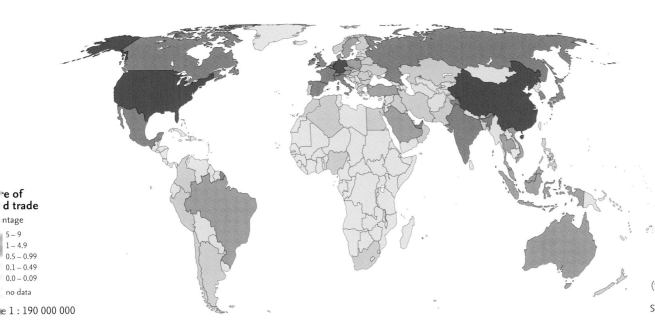

**Trade**
Percentage of world trade
(total of imports and exports
divided by world total).
Statistics are for 2015 – 2019.

re of
d trade

ntage

| | 5 – 9 |
|---|---|
| | 1 – 4.9 |
| | 0.5 – 0.99 |
| | 0.1 – 0.49 |
| | 0.0 – 0.09 |
| | no data |

e 1 : 190 000 000

The Ecological Footprint measures the area of biologically productive land and water required to produce the resources an individual or a population consumes and to absorb the waste it generates. A country's Ecological Footprint is usually expressed in global hectares (gha) per person – the average area of land required to support each of that country's inhabitants.

Since 1961, when the data from which the Ecological Footprint is calculated first became available, there has been a marked increase in the contribution made by the carbon footprint – that is, the amount of forest land needed to absorb emissions of carbon dioxide ($CO_2$). Most $CO_2$ emissions come from the burning of fossil fuels.

Ecological Footprint is often compared with biocapacity, or the ability of the land to supply resources and absorb waste. A country's biocapacity, which can also be expressed in global hectares per person, is its total amount of biologically productive land divided by its population.

The demands of humanity, as measured by the Ecological Footprint, first exceeded the Earth's biocapacity in the 1970s. Since then, we have been using up biological resources faster than the Earth can regenerate them. Rapid steps could end this so-called 'overshoot' by the middle of the 21st century, lessen the risk of ecological collapse and create a biocapacity reserve.

## World Ecological Footprint, 1961 – 2016

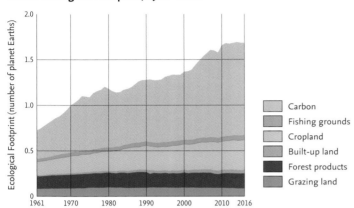

## Return to sustainability

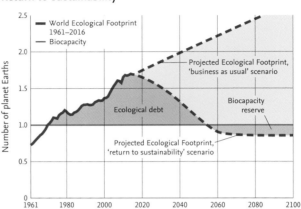

## Ecological Footprint per country, per person, 2016

World average Ecological Footprint: 2.75 global hectares per person
World average biocapacity: 1.63 global hectares per person

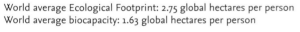

## Biocapacity by country, 2016

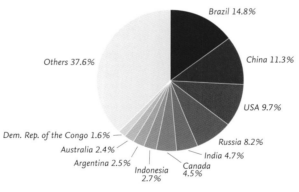

Brazil 14.8%
China 11.3%
USA 9.7%
Russia 8.2%
India 4.7%
Canada 4.5%
Indonesia 2.7%
Argentina 2.5%
Australia 2.4%
Dem. Rep. of the Congo 1.6%
Others 37.6%

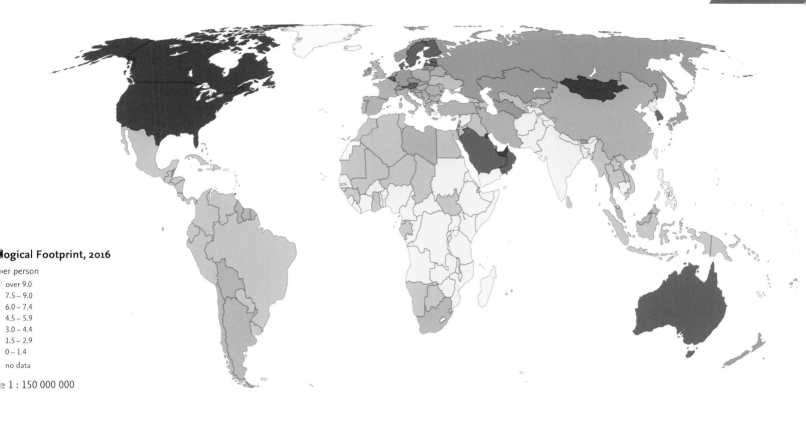

### logical Footprint, 2016

er person
- over 9.0
- 7.5 – 9.0
- 6.0 – 7.4
- 4.5 – 5.9
- 3.0 – 4.4
- 1.5 – 2.9
- 0 – 1.4
- no data

e 1 : 150 000 000

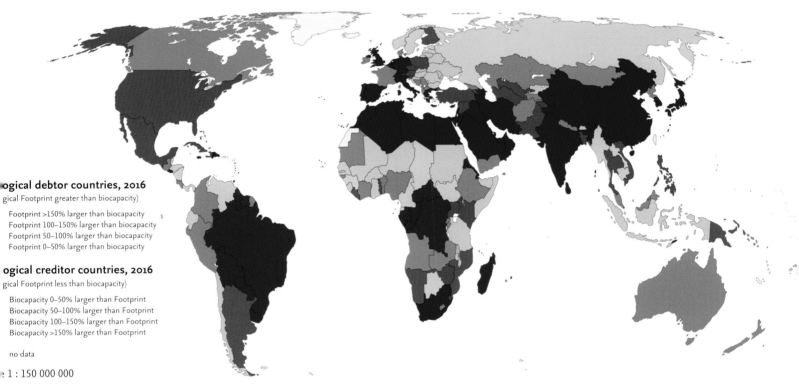

### ogical debtor countries, 2016
(gical Footprint greater than biocapacity)

- Footprint >150% larger than biocapacity
- Footprint 100–150% larger than biocapacity
- Footprint 50–100% larger than biocapacity
- Footprint 0–50% larger than biocapacity

### ogical creditor countries, 2016
(gical Footprint less than biocapacity)

- Biocapacity 0–50% larger than Footprint
- Biocapacity 50–100% larger than Footprint
- Biocapacity 100–150% larger than Footprint
- Biocapacity >150% larger than Footprint

no data

e 1 : 150 000 000

**Global Footprint Network**
www.footprintnetwork.org
**Footprint calculator**
http://footprint.wwf.org.uk

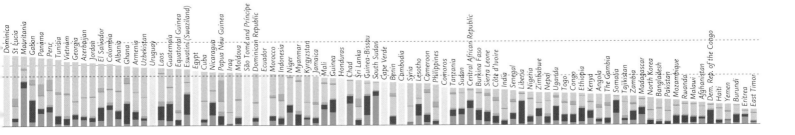

# **World** Tourism

World Tourism Organization
unwto.org
UNESCO World Heritage Sites
whc.unesco.org

## World's top tourist destinations, 2019

| Tourist arrivals (million) | |
|---|---|
| France | 89.4 |
| Spain | 83.7 |
| United States of America | 79.3 |
| China | 65.7 |
| Italy | 64.5 |
| Turkey | 51.2 |
| Mexico | 45.0 |
| Thailand | 39.8 |
| Germany | 39.6 |
| United Kingdom | 39.4 |

| Market share | % |
|---|---|
| France | 6.1 |
| Spain | 5.7 |
| United States of America | 5.4 |
| China | 4.5 |
| Italy | 4.4 |
| Turkey | 3.5 |
| Mexico | 3.1 |
| Thailand | 2.7 |
| Germany | 2.7 |
| United Kingdom | 2.7 |

PACIFIC OCEAN

### Tourist locations

- ■ Safari / Wilderness / Trekking area
- ■ Beach / Leisure resort
- ■ City resort
- ■ Cultural / Historical resort

Scale 1 : 90 000 000

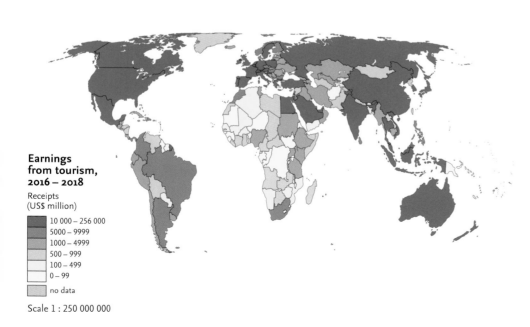

## Earnings from tourism, 2016 – 2018

Receipts (US$ million)

- 10 000 – 256 000
- 5000 – 9999
- 1000 – 4999
- 500 – 999
- 100 – 499
- 0 – 99
- no data

Scale 1 : 250 000 000

## International tourism receipts, 2000 – 2019 (US$ billion)

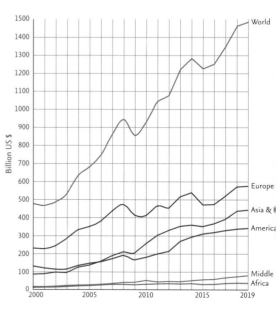

World
Europe
Asia &
America
Middle
Africa

ARCTIC OCEAN

SEE PAGE 37
EUROPE TOURISM

PACIFIC
OCEAN

*Fès*
*Marrakesh*
*Cyprus*
*Aleppo*
*Cairo/Pyramids*
*Petra*
*Red Sea*
*Luxor*
*Abu Dhabi*
*Mecca*
*Timbuktu*
*Lake Baikal*
*Beijing*
*Great Wall*
*Kyōto*
*Tōkyō*
*Xi'an*
*Shanghai*
*Delhi*
*Lhasa*
*Jaipur*
*Agra/ Mt Everest*
*Taj Mahal*
*Hong Kong*
*Sundarbans*
*Chiang Mai*
*Goa*
*Angkor*
*Bangkok*
*Koh Sumai*
*Sri Lanka*
*Phuket*
*Maldives*
*Singapore*
*Mt Kinabalu*

ATLANTIC
OCEAN

*East African National Parks*
*Mombasa*
*Seychelles*
*Comoros*

INDIAN
OCEAN

*Komodo National Park*
*Bali*

*Lake Kariba*
*Victoria Falls*
*Chobe National Park*
*Hwange National Park*
*Fossil Hominid Sites*
*Kruger National Park*
*Mauritius*
*Reunion*

*Great Barrier Reef Marine Park*
*Fiji*

*Uluru*
*Gold Coast*
*Durban*
*Cape Town*
*South African National Parks*

*Blue Mountains*
*Sydney*
*Melbourne*
*North Island*
*Auckland*
*South Island*

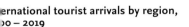

**ernational tourist arrivals by region,**
**00 – 2019**

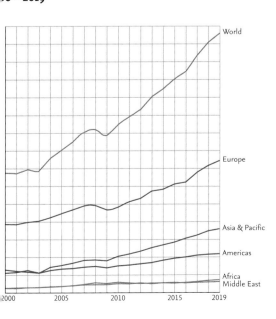

World
Europe
Asia & Pacific
Americas
Africa
Middle East

2000    2005    2010    2015    2019

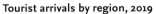

**Tourist arrivals by region, 2019**

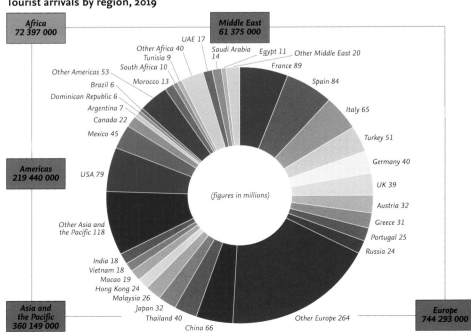

**Africa 72 397 000**

**Middle East 61 375 000**

UAE 17
Other Africa 40
Tunisia 9
Saudi Arabia 14
Egypt 11
Other Middle East 20
South Africa 10
France 89
Other Americas 53
Morocco 13
Spain 84
Brazil 6
Dominican Republic 6
Italy 65
Argentina 7
Turkey 51
Canada 22
Germany 40
Mexico 45
UK 39

**Americas 219 440 000**

USA 79
(figures in millions)
Austria 32
Greece 31
Portugal 25

**Other Asia and the Pacific 118**

Russia 24

India 18
Vietnam 18
Macao 19
Hong Kong 24
Malaysia 26
Japan 32
Thailand 40
China 66
Other Europe 264

**Asia and the Pacific 360 149 000**

**Europe 744 293 000**

# World Communications

## Telephone lines

Fixed telephone subscriptions per 100 people

- 50 – 80
- 30 – 49.9
- 10 – 29.9
- 0 – 9.9
- no data

World average 12.8.
Statistics are for 2015 – 2019.

Scale 1 : 190 000 000

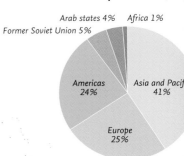

### Fixed telephone lines, 20...

- Arab states 4%
- Africa 1%
- Former Soviet Union 5%
- Americas 24%
- Asia and Pacif... 41%
- Europe 25%

World : 930 000 000

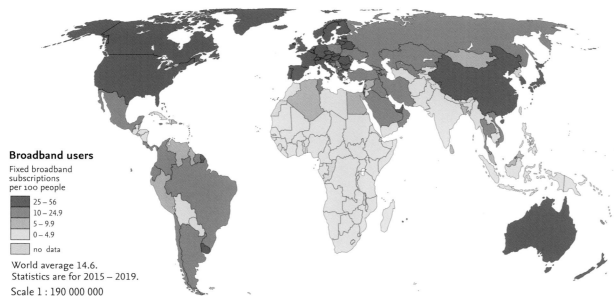

## Broadband users

Fixed broadband subscriptions per 100 people

- 25 – 56
- 10 – 24.9
- 5 – 9.9
- 0 – 4.9
- no data

World average 14.6.
Statistics are for 2015 – 2019.

Scale 1 : 190 000 000

### Broadband users, 2019

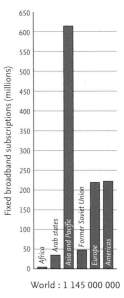

Fixed broadband subscriptions (millions)

(categories: Africa, Arab states, Asia and Pacific, Former Soviet Union, Europe, Americas)

World : 1 145 000 000

### Mobile phone subscriptions

- Former Soviet Union 4%
- Arab states 5%
- Europe 10%
- Africa 10%
- Americas 13%
- Asia and Pacific 58%

World : 8 300 000 000

## Mobile phone subscriptions, 2018

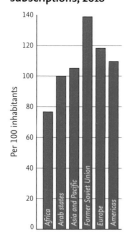

Per 100 inhabitants

(categories: Africa, Arab states, Asia and Pacific, Former Soviet Union, Europe, Americas)

## Growth in mobile phone subscriptions, 2010 – 2019

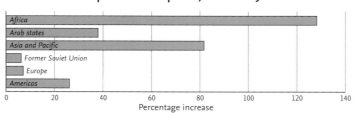

- Africa
- Arab states
- Asia and Pacific
- Former Soviet Union
- Europe
- Americas

Percentage increase

## Mobile phone subscriptions

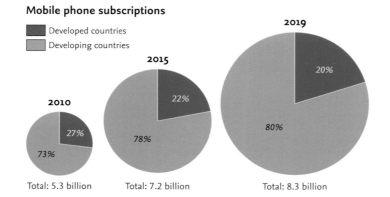

- Developed countries
- Developing countries

2010: 27% / 73% — Total: 5.3 billion
2015: 22% / 78% — Total: 7.2 billion
2019: 20% / 80% — Total: 8.3 billion

## World communication equipm... 2010 – 2019

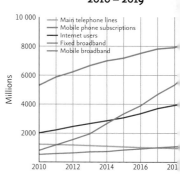

- Main telephone lines
- Mobile phone subscriptions
- Internet users
- Fixed broadband
- Mobile broadband

Millions

2010 2012 2014 2016 201...

WWW International Telecommunication Union
www.itu.int
TeleGeography
www.telegeography.com

## op 20 busiest airports, 2017

| Airport | Passengers carried |
| --- | --- |
| Atlanta | 103 902 992 |
| Beijing | 95 786 442 |
| Dubai | 88 242 099 |
| Tōkyō Haneda | 85 408 975 |
| Los Angeles | 84 557 968 |
| Chicago | 79 828 183 |
| London Heathrow | 78 014 598 |
| Hong Kong | 72 664 075 |
| Shanghai | 70 001 237 |
| Paris | 69 471 442 |
| Amsterdam | 68 515 425 |
| Dallas/Fort Worth | 67 092 194 |
| Guangzhou | 65 887 473 |
| Frankfurt | 64 500 386 |
| İstanbul | 64 119 374 |
| New Delhi | 63 451 503 |
| Jakarta | 63 015 620 |
| Singapore | 62 220 000 |
| Incheon | 62 157 834 |
| Denver | 61 379 396 |

### Air passengers carried in millions

- 100 – 900
- 25 – 99.9
- 10 – 24.9
- 1 – 9.9
- 0 – 0.9
- no data
- Main airport
- Other airport
- Main air route

Scale 1 : 140 000 000

### Passengers carried
Air passengers carried include both domestic and international aircraft passengers.
Statistics are for 2014 – 2018.

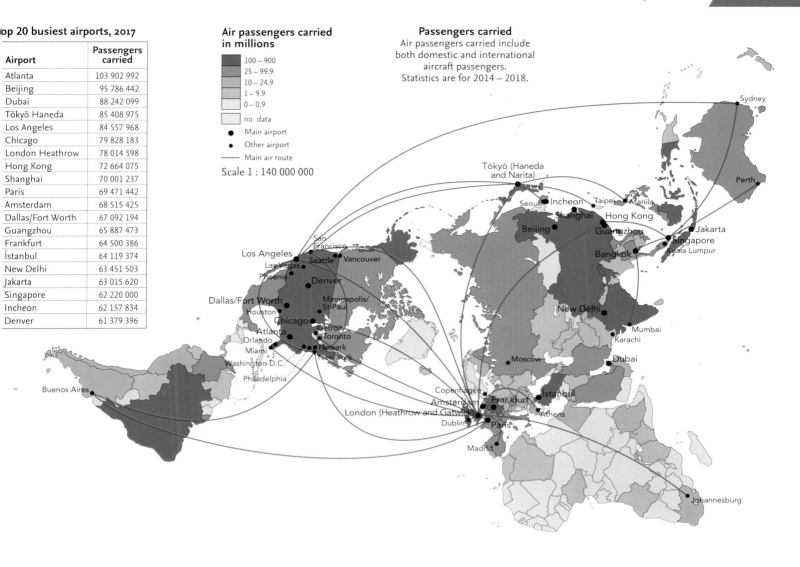

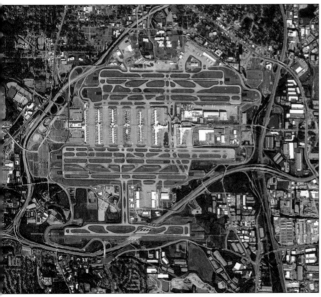

sfield-Jackson Atlanta International Airport is the busiest in the
d, with over 100 million passengers passing through each year.
e courtesy of the Earth Science and Remote Sensing Unit,
A Johnson Space Center.

Airports Council International (ACI)
www.aci.aero
NASA Johnson Space Center
http://eol.jsc.nasa.gov

### Journey times by air
- Main city
- Air route
- 7.50 Journey time (in hours and minutes)

Scale 1 : 220 000 000

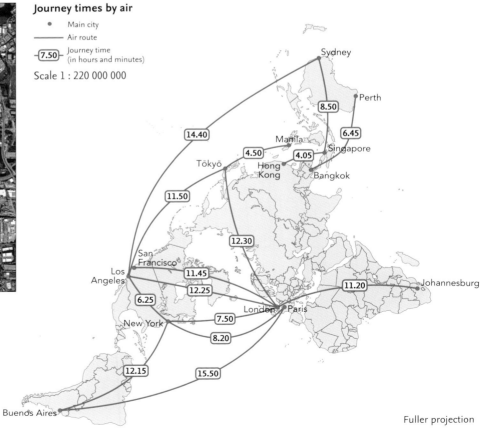

Fuller projection

| Flag | Country | Capital city | Population total 2019 | Density persons per sq km 2019 | Birth rate per 1000 population 2018 | Death rate per 1000 population 2018 | Life expectancy in years 2018 | Population change % 2019 | Urban population % 2019 |
|---|---|---|---|---|---|---|---|---|---|
| | Afghanistan | Kābul | 38 041 757 | 58 | 32 | 6 | 64 | 2.3 | 26 |
| | Albania | Tirana | 2 880 913 | 100 | 12 | 8 | 78 | -0.4 | 61 |
| | Algeria | Algiers | 43 053 054 | 18 | 24 | 5 | 77 | 1.9 | 73 |
| | Andorra | Andorra la Vella | 77 146 | 165 | 7 | 4 | .. | 0.2 | 88 |
| | Angola | Luanda | 31 825 299 | 25 | 41 | 8 | 61 | 3.2 | 66 |
| | Antigua and Barbuda | St John's | 97 115 | 219 | 15 | 6 | 77 | 0.9 | 25 |
| | Argentina | Buenos Aires | 44 780 675 | 16 | 17 | 8 | 77 | 1.0 | 92 |
| | Armenia | Yerevan | 2 957 728 | 99 | 14 | 10 | 75 | 0.2 | 63 |
| | Australia | Canberra | 25 198 957 | 3 | 13 | 6 | 83 | 1.5 | 86 |
| | Austria | Vienna | 8 955 108 | 106 | 10 | 10 | 82 | 0.4 | 59 |
| | Azerbaijan | Baku | 10 047 719 | 116 | 14 | 6 | 73 | 0.8 | 56 |
| | Bahamas, The | Nassau | 389 486 | 27 | 14 | 7 | 74 | 1.0 | 83 |
| | Bahrain | Manama | 1 641 164 | 2 375 | 14 | 2 | 77 | 4.5 | 89 |
| | Bangladesh | Dhaka | 163 046 173 | 1 132 | 18 | 6 | 72 | 1.0 | 37 |
| | Barbados | Bridgetown | 287 021 | 667 | 11 | 9 | 79 | 0.1 | 31 |
| | Belarus | Minsk | 9 452 409 | 45 | 10 | 13 | 74 | -0.2 | 79 |
| | Belgium | Brussels | 11 539 326 | 378 | 10 | 11 | 82 | 0.5 | 98 |
| | Belize | Belmopan | 390 351 | 16 | 21 | 5 | 74 | 1.9 | 46 |
| | Benin | Porto-Novo | 11 801 151 | 104 | 36 | 9 | 61 | 2.7 | 48 |
| | Bhutan | Thimphu | 763 094 | 16 | 17 | 6 | 71 | 1.2 | 42 |
| | Bolivia | La Paz/Sucre | 11 513 102 | 10 | 22 | 7 | 71 | 1.4 | 70 |
| | Bosnia and Herzegovina | Sarajevo | 3 300 998 | 64 | 8 | 11 | 77 | -0.7 | 49 |
| | Botswana | Gaborone | 2 303 703 | 3 | 25 | 6 | 69 | 2.2 | 70 |
| | Brazil | Brasília | 211 049 519 | 24 | 14 | 6 | 76 | 0.8 | 87 |
| | Brunei | Bandar Seri Begawan | 433 296 | 75 | 15 | 4 | 76 | 1.0 | 78 |
| | Bulgaria | Sofia | 7 000 117 | 63 | 9 | 15 | 75 | -0.7 | 75 |
| | Burkina Faso | Ouagadougou | 20 321 383 | 74 | 38 | 8 | 61 | 2.8 | 30 |
| | Burundi | Gitega | 11 530 577 | 414 | 39 | 8 | 61 | 3.1 | 13 |
| | Cambodia | Phnom Penh | 16 486 542 | 91 | 22 | 6 | 70 | 1.5 | 24 |
| | Cameroon | Yaoundé | 25 876 387 | 54 | 35 | 9 | 59 | 2.6 | 57 |
| | Canada | Ottawa | 37 411 038 | 3 | 10 | 8 | 82 | 1.4 | 81 |
| | Cape Verde | Praia | 549 936 | 136 | 19 | 6 | 73 | 1.1 | 66 |
| | Central African Republic | Bangui | 4 745 179 | 7 | 35 | 12 | 53 | 1.7 | 42 |
| | Chad | N'Djaména | 15 946 882 | 12 | 42 | 12 | 54 | 3.0 | 23 |
| | Chile | Santiago/Valparaíso | 18 952 035 | 25 | 12 | 6 | 80 | 1.2 | 88 |
| | China | Beijing | 1 441 860 295 | 150 | 11 | 7 | 77 | 0.4 | 60 |
| | Colombia | Bogotá | 50 339 443 | 44 | 15 | 6 | 77 | 1.4 | 81 |
| | Comoros | Moroni | 850 891 | 456 | 32 | 7 | 64 | 2.2 | 29 |
| | Congo | Brazzaville | 5 380 504 | 15 | 33 | 7 | 64 | 2.6 | 67 |
| | Congo, Dem. Rep. of the | Kinshasa | 86 790 568 | 37 | 41 | 9 | 60 | 3.2 | 45 |
| | Costa Rica | San José | 5 047 561 | 98 | 14 | 5 | 80 | 1.0 | 80 |
| | Côte d'Ivoire | Yamoussoukro | 25 716 554 | 79 | 36 | 10 | 57 | 2.6 | 51 |
| | Croatia | Zagreb | 4 130 299 | 73 | 9 | 13 | 78 | -0.5 | 57 |
| | Cuba | Havana | 11 333 484 | 102 | 10 | 9 | 79 | 0.0 | 77 |
| | Cyprus | Nicosia | 1 198 574 | 129 | 10 | 7 | 81 | 0.8 | 67 |
| | Czechia | Prague | 10 689 213 | 135 | 11 | 11 | 79 | 0.4 | 74 |
| | Denmark | Copenhagen | 5 771 877 | 133 | 11 | 10 | 81 | 0.4 | 88 |
| | Djibouti | Djibouti | 973 557 | 41 | 21 | 7 | 67 | 1.5 | 78 |
| | Dominica | Roseau | 71 808 | 95 | .. | .. | .. | 0.3 | 71 |

| Land | | Education and Health | | | Development | | | Communications | | Country | Time Zones |
|---|---|---|---|---|---|---|---|---|---|---|---|
| Area sq km | Forest thousand sq km 2016 | Adult literacy % 2018 | Doctors per 100 000 population 2018 | Nutrition population undernourished % 2017 | Energy consumption million tonnes oil equivalent 2017 | GNI per capita US$ 2019 | HDI index 2018 | Mobile phones subs per 100 population 2019 | Broadband users subs per 100 population 2019 | | + or - GMT |
| 652 225 | 14 | 43.0 | 28 | 29.8 | 3.7 | 540 | 0.496 | 59.4 | 0.1 | Afghanistan | +4½ |
| 28 748 | 8 | 98.1 | 122 | 6.2 | 2.8 | 5 240 | 0.791 | 91.3 | 15.1 | Albania | +1 |
| 2 381 741 | 20 | 81.4 | 172 | 3.9 | 60.5 | 3 970 | 0.759 | 109.4 | 8.3 | Algeria | +1 |
| 465 | <1 | >95 | 333 | .. | .. | .. | 0.857 | 114.0 | 47.1 | Andorra | +1 |
| 1 246 700 | 577 | 66.0 | 21 | 25.0 | 9.2 | 3 050 | 0.574 | 46.6 | 0.4 | Angola | +1 |
| 442 | <1 | 99.0 | 296 | .. | 0.3 | 16 660 | 0.776 | 192.8 | 9.4 | Antigua and Barbuda | -4 |
| 2 766 889 | 268 | 99.0 | 399 | 4.6 | 97.8 | 11 200 | 0.830 | 130.9 | 19.6 | Argentina | -3 |
| 29 800 | 3 | 99.7 | 440 | 4.3 | 3.8 | 4 680 | 0.760 | 122.3 | 13.0 | Armenia | +4 |
| 7 692 024 | 1 251 | >95 | 368 | <5 | 153.1 | 54 910 | 0.938 | 110.6 | 34.5 | Australia | +8 to +10½ |
| 83 855 | 39 | >95 | 517 | <5 | 37.7 | 51 300 | 0.914 | 119.8 | 28.1 | Austria | +1 |
| 86 600 | 12 | 99.8 | 345 | <5 | 15.0 | 4 480 | 0.754 | 107.0 | 19.3 | Azerbaijan | +4 |
| 13 939 | 5 | .. | 201 | .. | 1.1 | 31 780 | 0.805 | 109.3 | 21.1 | Bahamas, The | -5 |
| 691 | <1 | 97.5 | 93 | .. | 18.1 | 22 110 | 0.838 | 115.8 | 12.5 | Bahrain | +3 |
| 143 998 | 14 | 73.9 | 58 | 14.7 | 36.6 | 1 940 | 0.614 | 101.5 | 5.0 | Bangladesh | +6 |
| 430 | <1 | 99.6 | 248 | 3.9 | 0.6 | 17 380 | 0.813 | 108.6 | 37.2 | Barbados | -4 |
| 207 600 | 87 | 99.8 | 519 | <5 | 24.3 | 6 280 | 0.817 | 122.9 | 33.9 | Belarus | +2 |
| 30 520 | 7 | >95 | 307 | <5 | 67.0 | 47 350 | 0.919 | 99.7 | 39.8 | Belgium | +1 |
| 22 965 | 14 | .. | 112 | 7.5 | 0.3 | 4 450 | 0.720 | 65.3 | 7.6 | Belize | -6 |
| 112 620 | 43 | 42.4 | 8 | 10.1 | 2.4 | 1 250 | 0.520 | 87.7 | 0.2 | Benin | +1 |
| 46 620 | 28 | 66.6 | 42 | .. | 1.5 | 2 970 | 0.617 | 95.6 | 1.2 | Bhutan | +6 |
| 1 098 581 | 545 | 92.5 | 159 | 17.1 | 8.7 | 3 530 | 0.703 | 100.8 | 4.4 | Bolivia | -4 |
| 51 130 | 22 | .. | 216 | <5 | 6.2 | 6 150 | 0.769 | 111.9 | 22.6 | Bosnia and Herzegovina | +1 |
| 581 370 | 107 | .. | 53 | 26.4 | 2.4 | 7 660 | 0.728 | 173.8 | 2.0 | Botswana | +2 |
| 8 514 879 | 4 926 | 93.2 | 216 | <5 | 317.6 | 9 130 | 0.761 | 98.8 | 15.4 | Brazil | -2 to -5 |
| 5 765 | 4 | 97.2 | 161 | 3.2 | 4.5 | 32 230 | 0.845 | 128.6 | 12.5 | Brunei | +8 |
| 110 994 | 38 | >95 | 403 | 3.6 | 19.5 | 9 410 | 0.816 | 116.2 | 27.6 | Bulgaria | +2 |
| 274 200 | 53 | 41.2 | 8 | 20.0 | 1.2 | 790 | 0.434 | 100.2 | 0.1 | Burkina Faso | 0 |
| 27 835 | 3 | 68.4 | 10 | .. | 0.1 | 280 | 0.423 | 57.6 | 0.0 | Burundi | +2 |
| 181 035 | 93 | 80.5 | 19 | 16.4 | 4.2 | 1 480 | 0.581 | 129.9 | 1.1 | Cambodia | +7 |
| 475 442 | 186 | 77.1 | 9 | 9.9 | 3.8 | 1 500 | 0.563 | 81.8 | 0.8 | Cameroon | +1 |
| 9 984 670 | 3 470 | >95 | 261 | <5 | 381.9 | 46 370 | 0.922 | 92.5 | 39.8 | Canada | -3½ to -8 |
| 4 033 | <1 | 86.8 | 78 | 12.6 | 0.3 | 3 630 | 0.651 | 108.3 | 3.2 | Cape Verde | -1 |
| 622 436 | 222 | 37.4 | 7 | 59.6 | 0.2 | 520 | 0.381 | 32.3 | 0.0 | Central African Republic | +1 |
| 1 284 000 | 47 | 22.3 | 4 | 37.5 | 0.1 | 700 | 0.401 | 48.1 | 0.0 | Chad | +1 |
| 756 945 | 180 | 96.4 | 259 | 2.7 | 38.1 | 15 010 | 0.847 | 132.2 | 18.1 | Chile | -3, -4 & -6 |
| 9 606 802 | 2 099 | 96.8 | 198 | 8.6 | 3 516.4 | 10 410 | 0.758 | 120.4 | 31.3 | China | +8 |
| 1 141 748 | 585 | 95.1 | 218 | 4.8 | 42.1 | 6 510 | 0.761 | 131.7 | 13.8 | Colombia | -5 |
| 1 862 | <1 | 58.8 | 27 | .. | 0.1 | 1 420 | 0.538 | 67.6 | 0.1 | Comoros | +3 |
| 342 000 | 223 | 80.3 | 16 | 40.3 | 2.4 | 1 750 | 0.609 | 95.3 | .. | Congo | +1 |
| 2 345 410 | 1 523 | 77.0 | 7 | .. | 3.3 | 520 | 0.459 | 42.8 | 0.0 | Congo, Dem. Rep. of the | +1 & +2 |
| 51 100 | 28 | 97.9 | 289 | 4.8 | 5.4 | 11 700 | 0.794 | 161.9 | 17.9 | Costa Rica | -6 |
| 322 463 | 104 | 47.2 | 23 | 19.0 | 4.5 | 2 290 | 0.516 | 145.3 | 0.8 | Côte d'Ivoire | 0 |
| 56 538 | 19 | >95 | 300 | <5 | 8.8 | 14 910 | 0.837 | 106.6 | 28.0 | Croatia | +1 |
| 110 860 | 33 | .. | 842 | <5 | 10.1 | 7 480 | 0.778 | 53.0 | 1.6 | Cuba | -5 |
| 9 251 | 2 | >95 | 195 | 5.6 | 3.0 | 27 710 | 0.873 | 143.8 | 37.8 | Cyprus | +2 |
| 78 864 | 27 | >95 | 412 | <5 | 44.9 | 22 000 | 0.891 | 123.5 | 33.5 | Czechia | +1 |
| 43 075 | 6 | >95 | 401 | <5 | 18.6 | 63 240 | 0.930 | 125.5 | 44.0 | Denmark | +1 |
| 23 200 | <1 | .. | 22 | 18.9 | 0.3 | 3 540 | 0.495 | 41.2 | 2.7 | Djibouti | +3 |
| 750 | <1 | .. | 112 | 6.2 | 0.1 | 8 090 | 0.724 | 105.8 | 16.1 | Dominica | -4 |

.. data available

| Flag | Country | Capital city | Population total 2019 | Density persons per sq km 2019 | Birth rate per 1000 population 2018 | Death rate per 1000 population 2018 | Life expectancy in years 2018 | Population change % 2019 | Urban population % 2019 |
|---|---|---|---|---|---|---|---|---|---|
| | Dominican Republic | Santo Domingo | 10 738 957 | 221 | 20 | 6 | 74 | 1.1 | 82 |
| | East Timor | Dili | 1 293 120 | 86 | 29 | 6 | 69 | 2.0 | 31 |
| | Ecuador | Quito | 17 373 657 | 63 | 20 | 5 | 77 | 1.7 | 64 |
| | Egypt | Cairo | 100 388 076 | 100 | 26 | 6 | 72 | 2.0 | 43 |
| | El Salvador | San Salvador | 6 453 550 | 306 | 18 | 7 | 73 | 0.5 | 73 |
| | Equatorial Guinea | Malabo | 1 355 982 | 48 | 33 | 9 | 58 | 3.5 | 73 |
| | Eritrea | Asmara | 3 497 117 | 29 | 30 | 7 | 66 | 1.3 | 41 |
| | Estonia | Tallinn | 1 325 649 | 29 | 11 | 12 | 78 | 0.4 | 69 |
| | Eswatini (Swaziland) | Lobamba/Mbabane | 1 148 133 | 66 | 26 | 9 | 59 | 1.1 | 24 |
| | Ethiopia | Addis Ababa | 112 078 727 | 98 | 32 | 7 | 66 | 2.6 | 21 |
| | Fiji | Suva | 889 955 | 48 | 21 | 8 | 67 | 0.7 | 57 |
| | Finland | Helsinki | 5 532 159 | 16 | 9 | 10 | 82 | 0.1 | 85 |
| | France | Paris | 65 129 731 | 119 | 11 | 9 | 83 | 0.1 | 81 |
| | Gabon | Libreville | 2 172 578 | 8 | 32 | 7 | 66 | 2.5 | 90 |
| | Gambia, The | Banjul | 2 347 696 | 207 | 39 | 8 | 62 | 2.9 | 62 |
| | Georgia | Tbilisi | 3 996 762 | 57 | 13 | 13 | 74 | -0.2 | 59 |
| | Germany | Berlin | 83 517 046 | 233 | 10 | 12 | 81 | 0.3 | 77 |
| | Ghana | Accra | 30 417 858 | 127 | 29 | 7 | 64 | 2.2 | 57 |
| | Greece | Athens | 10 473 452 | 79 | 8 | 11 | 82 | -0.2 | 79 |
| | Grenada | St George's | 112 002 | 296 | 16 | 10 | 72 | 0.5 | 36 |
| | Guatemala | Guatemala City | 17 581 476 | 161 | 25 | 5 | 74 | 1.6 | 51 |
| | Guinea | Conakry | 12 771 246 | 51 | 36 | 8 | 61 | 2.8 | 37 |
| | Guinea-Bissau | Bissau | 1 920 917 | 53 | 35 | 10 | 58 | 2.5 | 44 |
| | Guyana | Georgetown | 782 775 | 3 | 20 | 7 | 70 | 0.5 | 27 |
| | Haiti | Port–au–Prince | 11 263 079 | 405 | 24 | 9 | 64 | 1.3 | 56 |
| | Honduras | Tegucigalpa | 9 746 115 | 86 | 22 | 4 | 75 | 1.6 | 58 |
| | Hungary | Budapest | 9 684 680 | 104 | 10 | 13 | 76 | -0.1 | 72 |
| | Iceland | Reykjavík | 339 037 | 3 | 12 | 6 | 83 | 2.4 | 94 |
| | India | New Delhi | 1 366 417 756 | 431 | 18 | 7 | 69 | 1.0 | 34 |
| | Indonesia | Jakarta | 270 625 567 | 140 | 18 | 6 | 72 | 1.1 | 56 |
| | Iran | Tehrān | 82 913 893 | 50 | 19 | 5 | 76 | 1.4 | 75 |
| | Iraq | Baghdād | 39 309 789 | 89 | 29 | 5 | 70 | 2.3 | 71 |
| | Ireland | Dublin | 4 882 498 | 69 | 13 | 6 | 82 | 1.5 | 63 |
| | Israel | Jerusalem [disputed] | 8 519 373 | 385 | 21 | 5 | 83 | 1.9 | 93 |
| | Italy | Rome | 60 550 092 | 200 | 7 | 11 | 83 | -0.2 | 71 |
| | Jamaica | Kingston | 2 948 277 | 268 | 16 | 8 | 74 | 0.5 | 56 |
| | Japan | Tōkyō | 126 860 299 | 335 | 7 | 11 | 84 | -0.2 | 92 |
| | Jordan | 'Ammān | 10 101 697 | 113 | 22 | 4 | 74 | 1.5 | 91 |
| | Kazakhstan | Nur-Sultan (Astana) | 18 551 428 | 6 | 22 | 7 | 73 | 1.3 | 58 |
| | Kenya | Nairobi | 52 573 967 | 90 | 29 | 5 | 66 | 2.3 | 28 |
| | Kiribati | Ambo | 117 608 | 164 | 28 | 6 | 68 | 1.5 | 55 |
| | Kosovo | Pristina | 1 798 506 | 164 | 16 | 7 | 72 | -0.2 | .. |
| | Kuwait | Kuwait | 4 207 077 | 236 | 14 | 3 | 75 | 1.7 | 100 |
| | Kyrgyzstan | Bishkek | 6 415 851 | 32 | 27 | 5 | 71 | 2.1 | 37 |
| | Laos | Vientiane | 7 169 456 | 30 | 24 | 6 | 68 | 1.5 | 36 |
| | Latvia | Rīga | 1 906 740 | 29 | 10 | 15 | 75 | -0.8 | 68 |
| | Lebanon | Beirut | 6 855 709 | 655 | 18 | 4 | 79 | 0.1 | 89 |
| | Lesotho | Maseru | 2 125 267 | 70 | 27 | 14 | 54 | 0.8 | 29 |
| | Liberia | Monrovia | 4 937 374 | 44 | 33 | 8 | 64 | 2.4 | 52 |

| Area sq km | Forest thousand sq km 2016 | Adult literacy % 2018 | Doctors per 100 000 population 2018 | Nutrition population under-nourished % 2017 | Energy consumption million tonnes oil equivalent 2017 | GNI per capita US$ 2019 | HDI index 2018 | Mobile phones subs per 100 population 2019 | Broadband users subs per 100 population 2019 | Country | Time Zones + or - GMT |
|---|---|---|---|---|---|---|---|---|---|---|---|
| 48 442 | 20 | 93.8 | 156 | 9.5 | 8.6 | 8 090 | 0.745 | 83.3 | 8.3 | Dominican Republic | -4 |
| 14 874 | 7 | 68.1 | 72 | 24.9 | 0.2 | 1 890 | 0.626 | 110.2 | 0.1 | East Timor | +9 |
| 272 045 | 125 | 92.8 | 204 | 7.9 | 18.0 | 6 080 | 0.758 | 91.3 | 12.0 | Ecuador | -5 |
| 001 450 | <1 | 71.2 | 45 | 4.5 | 101.3 | 2 690 | 0.700 | 95.0 | 7.6 | Egypt | +2 |
| 21 041 | 3 | 89.0 | 157 | 9.0 | 3.3 | 4 000 | 0.667 | 146.9 | 7.7 | El Salvador | -6 |
| 28 051 | 16 | .. | 40 | .. | 1.5 | 6 460 | 0.588 | 45.2 | 0.1 | Equatorial Guinea | +1 |
| 17 400 | 15 | 76.6 | 6 | .. | 0.3 | .. | 0.434 | 20.4 | 0.0 | Eritrea | +3 |
| 45 200 | 22 | >95 | 448 | 2.9 | 2.3 | 23 220 | 0.882 | 147.2 | 33.9 | Estonia | +2 |
| 17 364 | 6 | 88.4 | 33 | 20.6 | 0.5 | 3 590 | 0.608 | 93.5 | 0.7 | Eswatini (Swaziland) | +2 |
| 33 880 | 125 | 51.8 | 8 | 20.6 | 8.1 | 850 | 0.470 | 37.2 | 0.1 | Ethiopia | +3 |
| 18 330 | 10 | 99.1 | 86 | 3.7 | 1.0 | 5 860 | 0.724 | 117.8 | 1.5 | Fiji | +12 |
| 38 145 | 222 | >95 | 381 | <5 | 30.5 | 49 580 | 0.925 | 129.2 | 32.5 | Finland | +2 |
| 43 965 | 171 | >95 | 327 | <5 | 260.3 | 42 400 | 0.891 | 110.6 | 45.7 | France | +1 |
| 67 667 | 232 | 84.7 | 68 | 10.5 | 1.7 | 7 210 | 0.702 | 138.3 | 1.4 | Gabon | +1 |
| 11 295 | 5 | 50.8 | 10 | 10.2 | 0.2 | 740 | 0.466 | 139.5 | 0.2 | Gambia, The | 0 |
| 69 700 | 28 | 99.4 | 712 | 7.9 | 6.2 | 4 740 | 0.786 | 134.7 | 23.6 | Georgia | +4 |
| 57 022 | 114 | >95 | 425 | <5 | 353.4 | 48 520 | 0.939 | 128.4 | 42.0 | Germany | +1 |
| 38 537 | 94 | 79.0 | 14 | 5.5 | 6.9 | 2 220 | 0.596 | 134.3 | 0.2 | Ghana | 0 |
| 31 957 | 41 | 97.9 | 548 | <5 | 29.4 | 20 320 | 0.872 | 113.5 | 39.3 | Greece | +2 |
| 378 | <1 | 98.6 | 141 | .. | 0.1 | 9 980 | 0.763 | 104.2 | 22.8 | Grenada | -4 |
| 08 890 | 35 | 81.3 | 35 | 15.2 | 8.0 | 4 610 | 0.651 | 118.7 | 3.1 | Guatemala | -6 |
| 45 857 | 63 | 32.0 | 8 | 16.5 | 1.2 | 950 | 0.466 | 100.8 | 0.0 | Guinea | 0 |
| 36 125 | 20 | 45.6 | 13 | 28.0 | 0.1 | 820 | 0.461 | 82.8 | 0.1 | Guinea-Bissau | 0 |
| 14 969 | 165 | 85.6 | 80 | 8.1 | 0.8 | 5 180 | 0.670 | 83.0 | 8.4 | Guyana | -4 |
| 27 750 | <1 | 61.7 | 23 | 49.3 | 1.2 | 790 | 0.503 | 57.5 | 0.3 | Haiti | -5 |
| 12 088 | 45 | 87.2 | 31 | 12.9 | 4.3 | 2 390 | 0.623 | 72.7 | 4.0 | Honduras | -6 |
| 93 030 | 21 | 99.1 | 341 | <5 | 26.3 | 16 140 | 0.845 | 106.1 | 32.9 | Hungary | +1 |
| 02 820 | <1 | >95 | 408 | <5 | 5.6 | 72 850 | 0.938 | 122.0 | 40.8 | Iceland | 0 |
| 66 620 | 709 | 74.4 | 86 | 14.5 | 768.6 | 2 130 | 0.647 | 84.3 | 1.5 | India | +5½ |
| 19 445 | 903 | 95.7 | 43 | 8.3 | 180.5 | 4 050 | 0.707 | 127.5 | 3.5 | Indonesia | +7 to +9 |
| 48 000 | 107 | 85.5 | 158 | 4.9 | 292.8 | 5 420 | 0.797 | 142.4 | 10.4 | Iran | +3½ |
| 38 317 | 8 | 85.6 | 71 | 29.0 | 47.1 | 5 740 | 0.689 | 95.0 | 11.7 | Iraq | +3 |
| 70 282 | 8 | >95 | 331 | <5 | 16.1 | 62 210 | 0.942 | 105.4 | 29.9 | Ireland | 0 |
| 22 072 | 2 | .. | 462 | <5 | 26.4 | 43 290 | 0.906 | 126.8 | 29.1 | Israel | +2 |
| 01 245 | 94 | 99.2 | 398 | <5 | 171.3 | 34 460 | 0.883 | 133.1 | 28.7 | Italy | +1 |
| 10 991 | 3 | 88.1 | 131 | 8.0 | 3.2 | 5 250 | 0.726 | 102.6 | 10.8 | Jamaica | -5 |
| 77 727 | 250 | >95 | 241 | <5 | 494.7 | 41 690 | 0.915 | 141.4 | 32.6 | Japan | +9 |
| 89 206 | <1 | 98.2 | 232 | 12.2 | 10.9 | 4 300 | 0.723 | 77.0 | 4.7 | Jordan | +2 |
| 17 300 | 33 | 99.8 | 398 | <5 | 92.0 | 8 810 | 0.817 | 138.6 | 13.2 | Kazakhstan | +5 & +6 |
| 82 646 | 44 | 81.5 | 16 | 29.4 | 8.2 | 1 750 | 0.579 | 103.8 | 0.9 | Kenya | +3 |
| 717 | <1 | .. | 20 | 2.7 | 0.0 | 3 350 | 0.623 | 46.5 | 0.1 | Kiribati | +12 to +14 |
| 10 908 | .. | .. | .. | .. | 2.2 | 4 640 | .. | .. | .. | Kosovo | +1 |
| 17 818 | <1 | 96.1 | 265 | 2.8 | 40.1 | 34 290 | 0.808 | 174.2 | 2.0 | Kuwait | +3 |
| 98 500 | 6 | 99.6 | 221 | 7.1 | 6.0 | 1 240 | 0.674 | 134.4 | 4.2 | Kyrgyzstan | +6 |
| 36 800 | 190 | 84.7 | 37 | 16.5 | 10.2 | 2 570 | 0.604 | 60.8 | 1.1 | Laos | +7 |
| 64 589 | 34 | >95 | 319 | <5 | 4.4 | 17 730 | 0.854 | 108.7 | 26.7 | Latvia | +2 |
| 10 452 | 1 | 95.1 | 210 | 11.0 | 9.5 | 7 600 | 0.730 | 61.8 | 6.1 | Lebanon | +2 |
| 30 355 | <1 | 76.6 | 7 | 13.1 | 0.4 | 1 360 | 0.518 | 113.8 | 0.3 | Lesotho | +2 |
| 11 369 | 41 | 48.3 | 4 | 37.2 | 0.4 | 580 | 0.465 | 56.6 | 0.2 | Liberia | 0 |

ata available

| Flag | Country | Capital city | Population total 2019 | Density persons per sq km 2019 | Birth rate per 1000 population 2018 | Death rate per 1000 population 2018 | Life expectancy in years 2018 | Population change % 2019 | Urba popula % 201ç |
|------|---------|--------------|------------------------|--------------------------------|--------------------------------------|--------------------------------------|-------------------------------|--------------------------|---------------------|
| | Libya | Tripoli | 6 777 453 | 3 | 19 | 5 | 73 | 1.5 | 80 |
| | Liechtenstein | Vaduz | 38 020 | 237 | 10 | 7 | 83 | 0.3 | 14 |
| | Lithuania | Vilnius | 2 759 631 | 42 | 10 | 14 | 76 | -0.5 | 68 |
| | Luxembourg | Luxembourg | 615 730 | 238 | 10 | 7 | 82 | 2.0 | 91 |
| | Madagascar | Antananarivo | 26 969 306 | 45 | 33 | 6 | 67 | 2.7 | 38 |
| | Malawi | Lilongwe | 18 628 749 | 157 | 34 | 7 | 64 | 2.6 | 17 |
| | Malaysia | Kuala Lumpur/Putrajaya | 31 949 789 | 95 | 17 | 5 | 76 | 1.3 | 77 |
| | Maldives | Male | 530 957 | 1 781 | 14 | 3 | 79 | 2.9 | 40 |
| | Mali | Bamako | 19 658 023 | 15 | 42 | 10 | 59 | 3.0 | 43 |
| | Malta | Valletta | 440 377 | 1 393 | 9 | 8 | 82 | 3.7 | 95 |
| | Marshall Islands | Delap-Uliga-Djarrit | 58 791 | 324 | .. | .. | .. | 0.7 | 77 |
| | Mauritania | Nouakchott | 4 525 698 | 4 | 34 | 7 | 65 | 2.7 | 55 |
| | Mauritius | Port Louis | 1 269 670 | 622 | 10 | 9 | 74 | 0.0 | 41 |
| | Mexico | Mexico City | 127 575 529 | 64 | 18 | 6 | 75 | 1.1 | 80 |
| | Micronesia, Fed. States of | Palikir | 113 811 | 162 | 23 | 7 | 68 | 1.0 | 23 |
| | Moldova | Chişinău | 4 043 258 | 119 | 10 | 12 | 72 | -1.8 | 43 |
| | Monaco | Monaco-Ville | 38 967 | 19 483 | 6 | 7 | .. | 0.7 | 100 |
| | Mongolia | Ulan Bator | 3 225 166 | 2 | 24 | 6 | 70 | 1.7 | 69 |
| | Montenegro | Podgorica | 627 988 | 45 | 12 | 11 | 77 | 0.0 | 67 |
| | Morocco | Rabat | 36 471 766 | 81 | 19 | 5 | 76 | 1.2 | 63 |
| | Mozambique | Maputo | 30 366 043 | 37 | 38 | 9 | 60 | 2.9 | 37 |
| | Myanmar (Burma) | Nay Pyi Taw | 54 045 422 | 79 | 18 | 8 | 67 | 0.6 | 31 |
| | Namibia | Windhoek | 2 494 524 | 3 | 29 | 8 | 63 | 1.9 | 51 |
| | Nauru | Yaren | 10 764 | 512 | .. | .. | .. | -1.0 | 100 |
| | Nepal | Kathmandu | 28 608 715 | 194 | 20 | 6 | 70 | 1.8 | 20 |
| | Netherlands | Amsterdam/The Hague | 17 097 123 | 411 | 10 | 9 | 82 | 0.6 | 92 |
| | New Zealand | Wellington | 4 783 062 | 17 | 12 | 7 | 82 | 1.6 | 87 |
| | Nicaragua | Managua | 6 545 503 | 50 | 21 | 5 | 74 | 1.2 | 59 |
| | Niger | Niamey | 23 310 719 | 18 | 46 | 8 | 62 | 3.8 | 17 |
| | Nigeria | Abuja | 200 963 603 | 217 | 38 | 12 | 54 | 2.6 | 51 |
| | North Korea | P'yŏngyang | 25 666 158 | 212 | 14 | 9 | 72 | 0.5 | 62 |
| | North Macedonia | Skopje | 2 083 458 | 81 | 11 | 10 | 76 | 0.0 | 58 |
| | Norway | Oslo | 5 376 480 | 16 | 10 | 8 | 83 | 0.7 | 83 |
| | Oman | Muscat | 4 974 992 | 16 | 19 | 2 | 78 | 3.0 | 85 |
| | Pakistan | Islamabad | 216 565 317 | 245 | 28 | 7 | 67 | 2.0 | 37 |
| | Palau | Ngerulmud | 18 001 | 36 | 14 | 8 | .. | 0.6 | 80 |
| | Panama | Panama City | 4 246 440 | 55 | 19 | 5 | 78 | 1.7 | 68 |
| | Papua New Guinea | Port Moresby | 8 776 119 | 18 | 27 | 7 | 64 | 2.0 | 13 |
| | Paraguay | Asunción | 7 044 639 | 17 | 21 | 6 | 74 | 1.3 | 62 |
| | Peru | Lima | 32 510 462 | 25 | 18 | 6 | 77 | 1.6 | 78 |
| | Philippines | Manila | 108 116 622 | 360 | 21 | 6 | 71 | 1.4 | 47 |
| | Poland | Warsaw | 37 887 771 | 121 | 10 | 11 | 78 | 0.0 | 60 |
| | Portugal | Lisbon | 10 226 178 | 114 | 9 | 11 | 81 | -0.1 | 66 |
| | Qatar | Doha | 2 832 071 | 247 | 10 | 1 | 80 | 1.8 | 99 |
| | Romania | Bucharest | 19 364 558 | 81 | 10 | 14 | 75 | -0.6 | 54 |
| | Russia | Moscow | 145 872 260 | 8 | 12 | 12 | 73 | -0.1 | 75 |
| | Rwanda | Kigali | 12 626 938 | 479 | 32 | 5 | 69 | 2.6 | 17 |
| | St Kitts and Nevis | Basseterre | 52 834 | 202 | .. | .. | .. | 0.7 | 31 |
| | St Lucia | Castries | 182 795 | 296 | 12 | 7 | 76 | 0.5 | 19 |

| Land | | Education and Health | | | Development | | | Communications | | Country | Time Zones |
|---|---|---|---|---|---|---|---|---|---|---|---|
| Area sq km | Forest thousand sq km 2016 | Adult literacy % 2018 | Doctors per 100 000 population 2018 | Nutrition population under-nourished % 2017 | Energy consumption million tonnes oil equivalent 2017 | GNI per capita US$ 2019 | HDI index 2018 | Mobile phones subs per 100 population 2019 | Broadband users subs per 100 population 2019 | | + or - GMT |
| 759 540 | 2 | .. | 209 | .. | 14.4 | 7 640 | 0.708 | 91.5 | 4.8 | Libya | +1 |
| 160 | <1 | >95 | .. | .. | .. | .. | 0.917 | 127.1 | 45.4 | Liechtenstein | +1 |
| 65 200 | 22 | >95 | 635 | <5 | 7.2 | 18 990 | 0.869 | 168.8 | 28.7 | Lithuania | +2 |
| 2 586 | <1 | >95 | 301 | <5 | 4.6 | 73 910 | 0.909 | 135.8 | 37.4 | Luxembourg | +1 |
| 587 041 | 125 | 74.8 | 18 | 44.4 | 1.4 | 520 | 0.521 | 40.6 | 0.1 | Madagascar | +3 |
| 118 484 | 31 | 62.1 | 4 | 17.5 | 0.8 | 380 | 0.485 | 47.8 | 0.1 | Malawi | +2 |
| 332 965 | 222 | 94.8 | 154 | <5 | 88.3 | 11 200 | 0.804 | 139.6 | 9.3 | Malaysia | +8 |
| 298 | <1 | 97.7 | 456 | 10.3 | 0.6 | 9 650 | 0.719 | 155.9 | 9.9 | Maldives | +5 |
| 240 140 | 46 | 35.5 | 13 | 6.3 | 1.5 | 880 | 0.427 | 115.1 | 0.6 | Mali | 0 |
| 316 | <1 | 94.5 | 286 | <5 | 3.2 | 27 290 | 0.885 | 144.1 | 45.2 | Malta | +1 |
| 181 | <1 | .. | 42 | .. | .. | 4 860 | 0.698 | 27.6 | 1.7 | Marshall Islands | +12 |
| 030 700 | 2 | 53.5 | 19 | 10.4 | 1.0 | 1 660 | 0.527 | 104.1 | 0.2 | Mauritania | 0 |
| 2 040 | <1 | 91.3 | 253 | 6.5 | 2.3 | 12 740 | 0.796 | 151.4 | 21.6 | Mauritius | +4 |
| 972 545 | 659 | 95.4 | 238 | 3.6 | 199.5 | 9 430 | 0.767 | 95.1 | 15.0 | Mexico | -5 to -8 |
| 701 | <1 | .. | 18 | .. | 0.0 | 3 400 | 0.614 | 20.7 | 3.4 | Micronesia, F. S. of | +10 & +11 |
| 33 700 | 4 | 99.4 | 321 | .. | 3.3 | 3 930 | 0.711 | 89.4 | 16.6 | Moldova | +2 |
| 2 | .. | .. | 751 | .. | .. | .. | .. | 86.7 | 52.5 | Monaco | +1 |
| 565 000 | 125 | 98.4 | 286 | 13.4 | 5.8 | 3 780 | 0.735 | 137.0 | 9.8 | Mongolia | +7 & +8 |
| 13 812 | 8 | 98.8 | 276 | <5 | 1.1 | 9 010 | 0.816 | 183.3 | 28.5 | Montenegro | +1 |
| 446 550 | 56 | 73.8 | 73 | 3.4 | 21.1 | 3 190 | 0.676 | 128.0 | 4.8 | Morocco | +1 |
| 799 380 | 377 | 60.7 | 8 | 27.9 | 7.3 | 480 | 0.446 | 47.7 | 0.2 | Mozambique | +2 |
| 676 577 | 285 | 75.5 | 68 | 10.6 | 13.1 | 1 390 | 0.584 | 113.8 | 0.2 | Myanmar (Burma) | +6½ |
| 824 292 | 68 | 91.5 | 42 | 27.3 | 2.0 | 5 060 | 0.645 | 113.2 | 2.5 | Namibia | +2 |
| 21 | <1 | .. | 135 | .. | 0.0 | 14 230 | .. | 94.6 | .. | Nauru | +12 |
| 147 181 | 36 | 67.9 | 75 | 8.7 | 4.1 | 1 090 | 0.579 | 139.4 | 2.8 | Nepal | +5¾ |
| 41 526 | 4 | >95 | 361 | <5 | 98.2 | 53 200 | 0.934 | 127.3 | 43.6 | Netherlands | +1 |
| 270 534 | 102 | >95 | 359 | <5 | 23.2 | 42 670 | 0.921 | 134.9 | 34.7 | New Zealand | +12 & +12¾ |
| 130 000 | 31 | 82.6 | 98 | 17.0 | 2.5 | 1 910 | 0.651 | 88.4 | 3.3 | Nicaragua | -6 |
| 267 000 | 11 | .. | 4 | 16.5 | 0.9 | 560 | 0.377 | 40.6 | 0.0 | Niger | +1 |
| 923 768 | 66 | 62.0 | 38 | 13.4 | 38.8 | 2 030 | 0.534 | 88.2 | 0.0 | Nigeria | +1 |
| 120 538 | 49 | .. | 368 | 47.8 | 7.9 | .. | .. | 15.0 | .. | North Korea | +9 |
| 25 713 | 10 | 97.8 | 287 | 3.2 | 2.5 | 5 910 | 0.759 | 98.7 | 21.3 | North Macedonia | +1 |
| 323 878 | 121 | >95 | 292 | <5 | 48.0 | 82 500 | 0.954 | 107.2 | 41.3 | Norway | +1 |
| 309 500 | <1 | 95.7 | 200 | 6.8 | 28.7 | 15 330 | 0.834 | 138.2 | 10.2 | Oman | +4 |
| 881 888 | 14 | 59.1 | 98 | 20.3 | 85.0 | 1 530 | 0.560 | 76.4 | 0.8 | Pakistan | +5 |
| 497 | <1 | 96.6 | 142 | .. | .. | 17 280 | 0.814 | .. | 6.9 | Palau | +9 |
| 77 082 | 46 | 95.4 | 157 | 10.0 | 11.1 | 14 950 | 0.795 | 131.8 | 13.5 | Panama | -5 |
| 462 840 | 336 | .. | 7 | .. | 2.4 | 2 780 | 0.543 | 47.6 | 0.2 | Papua New Guinea | +10 & +11 |
| 406 752 | 150 | 94.0 | 135 | 10.7 | 13.1 | 5 510 | 0.724 | 107.0 | 4.6 | Paraguay | -4 |
| 285 216 | 738 | 94.4 | 130 | 9.7 | 28.2 | 6 740 | 0.759 | 131.8 | 7.9 | Peru | -5 |
| 300 000 | 83 | 98.2 | 60 | 13.3 | 46.2 | 3 850 | 0.712 | 154.8 | 3.9 | Philippines | +8 |
| 312 683 | 95 | >95 | 238 | <5 | 110.1 | 15 200 | 0.872 | 138.0 | 20.6 | Poland | +1 |
| 88 940 | 32 | 96.1 | 512 | <5 | 26.9 | 23 080 | 0.850 | 116.5 | 38.8 | Portugal | 0 |
| 11 437 | <1 | 93.5 | 249 | .. | 54.5 | 63 410 | 0.848 | 138.3 | 10.1 | Qatar | +3 |
| 237 500 | 69 | 98.8 | 298 | <5 | 35.5 | 12 630 | 0.816 | 117.1 | 27.3 | Romania | +2 |
| 075 400 | 8 149 | 99.7 | 401 | <5 | 828.0 | 11 260 | 0.824 | 164.4 | 22.6 | Russia | +2 to +12 |
| 26 338 | 5 | 73.2 | 13 | 36.8 | 0.4 | 820 | 0.536 | 76.5 | 0.1 | Rwanda | +2 |
| 261 | <1 | .. | 268 | .. | 0.1 | 19 030 | 0.777 | 147.7 | 55.8 | St Kitts and Nevis | -4 |
| 616 | <1 | .. | 64 | .. | 0.2 | 11 020 | 0.745 | 101.7 | 17.7 | St Lucia | -4 |

data available

| Flag | Key Information | | Population | | | | | | Urba popula |
|---|---|---|---|---|---|---|---|---|---|
| | Country | Capital city | Population total 2019 | Density persons per sq km 2019 | Birth rate per 1000 population 2018 | Death rate per 1000 population 2018 | Life expectancy in years 2018 | Population change % 2019 | % 2019 |
| | St Vincent and the Grenadines | Kingstown | 110 593 | 284 | 14 | 9 | 72 | 0.3 | 53 |
| | Samoa | Apia | 197 093 | 69 | 24 | 5 | 73 | 0.5 | 18 |
| | San Marino | San Marino | 33 864 | 555 | 7 | 7 | .. | 0.2 | 97 |
| | São Tomé and Príncipe | São Tomé | 215 048 | 223 | 32 | 5 | 70 | 1.9 | 74 |
| | Saudi Arabia | Riyadh | 34 268 529 | 15 | 18 | 3 | 75 | 1.7 | 84 |
| | Senegal | Dakar | 16 296 362 | 82 | 35 | 6 | 68 | 2.8 | 48 |
| | Serbia | Belgrade | 6 973 722 | 90 | 9 | 15 | 76 | -0.5 | 56 |
| | Seychelles | Victoria | 97 741 | 214 | 17 | 9 | 73 | 0.9 | 57 |
| | Sierra Leone | Freetown | 7 813 207 | 108 | 33 | 12 | 54 | 2.1 | 42 |
| | Singapore | Singapore | 5 804 343 | 9 083 | 9 | 5 | 83 | 1.1 | 100 |
| | Slovakia | Bratislava | 5 457 012 | 111 | 11 | 10 | 77 | 0.1 | 54 |
| | Slovenia | Ljubljana | 2 078 654 | 102 | 9 | 10 | 81 | 0.7 | 55 |
| | Solomon Islands | Honiara | 669 821 | 23 | 32 | 4 | 73 | 2.6 | 24 |
| | Somalia | Mogadishu | 15 442 906 | 24 | 42 | 11 | 57 | 2.9 | 46 |
| | South Africa | Bloemfontein/Cape Town/Pretoria | 58 558 267 | 48 | 21 | 9 | 64 | 1.3 | 67 |
| | South Korea | Seoul | 51 225 321 | 515 | 6 | 6 | 83 | 0.2 | 81 |
| | South Sudan | Juba | 11 062 114 | 17 | 35 | 10 | 58 | 0.8 | 20 |
| | Spain | Madrid | 44 437 855 | 88 | 8 | 9 | 83 | 0.6 | 81 |
| | Sri Lanka | Sri Jayewardenepura Kotte | 21 323 734 | 325 | 16 | 7 | 77 | 0.6 | 19 |
| | Sudan | Khartoum | 42 813 237 | 22 | 32 | 7 | 65 | 2.4 | 35 |
| | Suriname | Paramaribo | 581 363 | 3 | 19 | 7 | 72 | 0.9 | 66 |
| | Sweden | Stockholm | 10 036 391 | 22 | 11 | 9 | 83 | 1.1 | 88 |
| | Switzerland | Bern | 8 591 361 | 208 | 10 | 8 | 84 | 0.7 | 74 |
| | Syria | Damascus | 17 070 132 | 92 | 24 | 5 | 72 | 1.0 | 55 |
| | Taiwan | Taipei | 23 773 881 | 657 | .. | .. | .. | .. | .. |
| | Tajikistan | Dushanbe | 9 321 023 | 65 | 31 | 5 | 71 | 2.4 | 27 |
| | Tanzania | Dodoma | 58 005 461 | 61 | 37 | 6 | 65 | 3.0 | 35 |
| | Thailand | Bangkok | 69 625 581 | 135 | 10 | 8 | 77 | 0.3 | 51 |
| | Togo | Lomé | 8 082 359 | 142 | 33 | 8 | 61 | 2.4 | 42 |
| | Tonga | Nuku'alofa | 104 497 | 139 | 24 | 7 | 71 | 1.3 | 23 |
| | Trinidad and Tobago | Port of Spain | 1 394 969 | 271 | 13 | 8 | 73 | 0.4 | 53 |
| | Tunisia | Tunis | 11 694 721 | 71 | 18 | 6 | 76 | 1.1 | 69 |
| | Turkey | Ankara | 83 429 607 | 107 | 16 | 5 | 77 | 1.3 | 76 |
| | Turkmenistan | Ashgabat | 5 942 094 | 12 | 24 | 7 | 68 | 1.6 | 52 |
| | Tuvalu | Vaiaku | 11 655 | 466 | .. | .. | .. | 1.2 | 63 |
| | Uganda | Kampala | 44 269 587 | 183 | 38 | 7 | 63 | 3.6 | 24 |
| | Ukraine | Kiev | 43 993 643 | 72 | 9 | 15 | 72 | -0.5 | 69 |
| | United Arab Emirates | Abu Dhabi | 9 770 526 | 125 | 10 | 1 | 78 | 1.4 | 87 |
| | United Kingdom | London | 66 796 800 | 277 | 11 | 9 | 81 | 0.6 | 84 |
| | United States of America | Washington D.C. | 329 064 917 | 33 | 12 | 9 | 79 | 0.5 | 82 |
| | Uruguay | Montevideo | 3 461 731 | 19 | 14 | 9 | 78 | 0.4 | 95 |
| | Uzbekistan | Tashkent | 32 981 715 | 73 | 23 | 5 | 72 | 1.9 | 50 |
| | Vanuatu | Port Vila | 299 882 | 24 | 30 | 5 | 70 | 2.4 | 25 |
| | Vatican City | Vatican City | 815 | 1 630 | .. | .. | .. | .. | .. |
| | Venezuela | Caracas | 28 515 829 | 31 | 18 | 7 | 72 | -1.2 | 88 |
| | Vietnam | Hanoi | 96 462 108 | 292 | 17 | 6 | 75 | 1.0 | 37 |
| | Yemen | Şan'ā' | 29 161 922 | 55 | 30 | 6 | 66 | 2.3 | 37 |
| | Zambia | Lusaka | 17 861 034 | 23 | 36 | 6 | 64 | 2.9 | 44 |
| | Zimbabwe | Harare | 14 645 473 | 37 | 31 | 8 | 61 | 1.4 | 32 |

| Land | | Education and Health | | | Development | | | Communications | | Country | Time Zones |
|---|---|---|---|---|---|---|---|---|---|---|---|
| Area sq km | Forest thousand sq km 2016 | Adult literacy % 2018 | Doctors per 100 000 population 2018 | Nutrition population under-nourished % 2017 | Energy consumption million tonnes oil equivalent 2017 | GNI per capita US$ 2019 | HDI index 2018 | Mobile phones subs per 100 population 2019 | Broadband users subs per 100 population 2019 | | + or - GMT |
| 389 | <1 | .. | 66 | 5.7 | 0.1 | 7 460 | 0.728 | 92.9 | 19.5 | St Vincent and the Grenadines | -4 |
| 2 831 | 2 | 99.1 | 34 | 2.7 | 0.1 | 4 180 | 0.707 | 63.6 | 0.9 | Samoa | +13 |
| 61 | <1 | >95 | 611 | .. | .. | .. | .. | 114.4 | 32.7 | San Marino | +1 |
| 964 | <1 | 92.8 | 5 | 7.0 | 0.1 | 1 960 | 0.609 | 77.1 | 0.8 | São Tomé and Príncipe | 0 |
| 200 000 | 10 | 95.3 | 261 | 7.1 | 277.3 | 22 850 | 0.857 | 120.5 | 19.9 | Saudi Arabia | +3 |
| 196 720 | 82 | 51.9 | 7 | 11.3 | 3.3 | 1 450 | 0.514 | 109.7 | 0.9 | Senegal | 0 |
| 77 453 | 27 | 98.8 | 311 | 5.7 | 16.2 | 7 020 | 0.799 | 96.4 | 18.5 | Serbia | +1 |
| 455 | <1 | 95.9 | 212 | .. | 0.4 | 16 870 | 0.801 | 198.2 | 27.6 | Seychelles | +4 |
| 71 740 | 31 | 43.2 | 3 | 25.6 | 0.4 | 500 | 0.438 | 86.1 | .. | Sierra Leone | 0 |
| 639 | <1 | 97.3 | 229 | .. | 91.5 | 59 590 | 0.935 | 156.4 | 25.8 | Singapore | +8 |
| 49 035 | 19 | >95 | 342 | 3.4 | 18.6 | 19 320 | 0.857 | 135.6 | 29.1 | Slovakia | +1 |
| 20 251 | 12 | 99.7 | 309 | <5 | 7.3 | 25 750 | 0.902 | 120.8 | 30.2 | Slovenia | +1 |
| 28 370 | 22 | .. | 19 | 8.9 | 0.1 | 2 050 | 0.557 | 71.4 | 0.2 | Solomon Islands | +11 |
| 637 657 | 63 | .. | 2 | .. | 0.3 | .. | .. | 51.0 | 0.7 | Somalia | +3 |
| 219 090 | 92 | 87.0 | 91 | 6.2 | 143.4 | 6 040 | 0.705 | 165.6 | 2.1 | South Africa | +2 |
| 99 274 | 62 | .. | 236 | <5 | 311.7 | 33 720 | 0.906 | 134.5 | 42.8 | South Korea | +9 |
| 644 329 | 72 | 34.5 | .. | .. | 0.4 | 1 090 | 0.413 | 33.5 | 0.0 | South Sudan | +3 |
| 504 782 | 185 | 98.4 | 387 | <5 | 144.6 | 30 390 | 0.893 | 118.3 | 33.4 | Spain | +1 |
| 65 610 | 21 | 91.7 | 100 | 9.0 | 9.7 | 4 020 | 0.780 | 142.7 | 7.3 | Sri Lanka | +5½ |
| 861 484 | 190 | 60.7 | 26 | 20.1 | 9.3 | 590 | 0.508 | 77.1 | 0.1 | Sudan | +2 |
| 163 820 | 153 | 94.4 | 121 | 8.5 | 1.0 | 5 540 | 0.724 | 140.0 | 13.8 | Suriname | -3 |
| 449 964 | 281 | >95 | 398 | <5 | 55.9 | 55 840 | 0.937 | 126.3 | 39.8 | Sweden | +1 |
| 41 293 | 13 | >95 | 430 | <5 | 29.6 | 85 500 | 0.946 | 127.2 | 45.2 | Switzerland | +1 |
| 184 026 | 5 | .. | 129 | .. | 9.9 | .. | 0.549 | 113.6 | 8.7 | Syria | +2 |
| 36 179 | .. | .. | .. | .. | 117.8 | .. | .. | .. | .. | Taiwan | +8 |
| 143 100 | 4 | 99.8 | 210 | .. | 5.7 | 1 030 | 0.656 | 111.5 | 0.1 | Tajikistan | +5 |
| 945 087 | 457 | 77.9 | 1 | 30.7 | 7.3 | 1 080 | 0.528 | 82.2 | 1.8 | Tanzania | +3 |
| 513 115 | 164 | 93.8 | 81 | 7.8 | 137.6 | 7 260 | 0.765 | 186.2 | 14.5 | Thailand | +7 |
| 56 785 | 2 | 63.8 | 8 | 16.1 | 1.0 | 690 | 0.513 | 77.2 | 0.4 | Togo | 0 |
| 748 | <1 | 99.4 | 54 | .. | 0.1 | 4 300 | 0.717 | 59.4 | 3.5 | Tonga | +13 |
| 5 130 | 2 | .. | 417 | 5.5 | 22.8 | 16 890 | 0.799 | 155.1 | 24.7 | Trinidad and Tobago | -4 |
| 164 150 | 11 | 79.0 | 130 | 4.3 | 10.3 | 3 360 | 0.739 | 126.3 | 10.2 | Tunisia | +1 |
| 779 452 | 118 | 96.2 | 185 | <5 | 162.0 | 9 610 | 0.807 | 96.8 | 17.1 | Turkey | +3 |
| 488 100 | 41 | 99.7 | 222 | 5.4 | 43.8 | 6 740 | 0.710 | 162.9 | 0.1 | Turkmenistan | +5 |
| 25 | <1 | .. | 92 | .. | 0.0 | 5 620 | .. | 70.4 | 4.0 | Tuvalu | +12 |
| 241 038 | 19 | 76.5 | 17 | 41.0 | 2.5 | 780 | 0.528 | 57.3 | 0.2 | Uganda | +3 |
| 603 700 | 97 | .. | 299 | 3.5 | 91.2 | 3 370 | 0.750 | 130.6 | 16.2 | Ukraine | +2 & +4 (Crimea) |
| 77 700 | 3 | 93.2 | 253 | 2.6 | 117.7 | 43 470 | 0.866 | 200.6 | 31.2 | United Arab Emirates | +4 |
| 243 609 | 32 | >95 | 281 | <5 | 209.0 | 42 370 | 0.920 | 118.4 | 39.6 | United Kingdom | 0 |
| 826 635 | 3 104 | >95 | 261 | <5 | 2 461.5 | 65 760 | 0.920 | 129.0 | 34.7 | United States | -5 to -10 |
| 176 215 | 19 | 98.7 | 508 | <5 | 5.5 | 16 230 | 0.808 | 138.1 | 29.3 | Uruguay | -3 |
| 447 400 | 32 | >95 | 237 | 6.3 | 45.2 | 1 800 | 0.710 | 101.2 | 13.9 | Uzbekistan | +5 |
| 12 190 | 4 | 87.5 | 17 | 7.2 | 0.1 | 3 170 | 0.597 | 88.4 | 1.6 | Vanuatu | +11 |
| 0.5 | .. | .. | .. | .. | .. | .. | .. | .. | .. | Vatican City | +1 |
| 912 050 | 465 | 97.1 | .. | 21.2 | 62.9 | .. | 0.726 | 58.1 | 9.0 | Venezuela | -4 |
| 329 565 | 149 | 95.0 | 83 | 9.3 | 81.8 | 2 540 | 0.693 | 141.2 | 15.4 | Vietnam | +7 |
| 527 968 | 5 | .. | 53 | 38.9 | 3.5 | 940 | 0.463 | 53.7 | 1.4 | Yemen | +3 |
| 752 614 | 485 | 86.8 | 119 | 46.7 | 4.5 | 1 450 | 0.591 | 96.4 | 0.5 | Zambia | +2 |
| 390 759 | 137 | 88.7 | 21 | 51.3 | 4.1 | 1 390 | 0.563 | 90.1 | 1.4 | Zimbabwe | +2 |

data available

Pages 158–163 show a variety of demographic and economic indicators by the world's seven regional groupings (defined by the World Bank), as shown on the right.

The colours on the maps below show the average figures for each region. The highest and lowest countries for most indicators are also named.

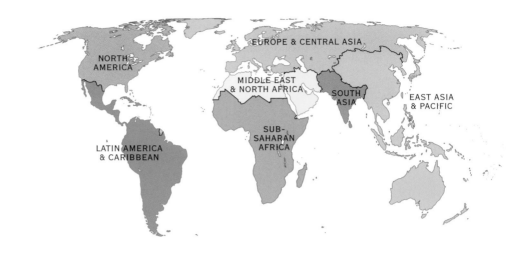

Scale 1 : 250 000 000

## Birth rate

Number of births per 1000 people

- 25 – 35.2
- 20 – 24.9
- 15 – 19.9
- 10 – 14.9
- no data

World average 18.2
Statistics are for 2018

Scale 1 : 250 000 000

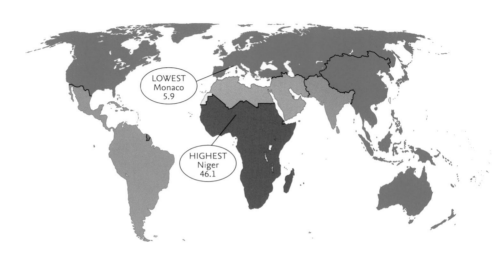

## Death rate

Number of deaths per 1000 people

- 10 – 10.1
- 8 – 9.9
- 7 – 7.9
- 4 – 6.9
- no data

World average 7.5
Statistics are for 2018

Scale 1 : 250 000 000

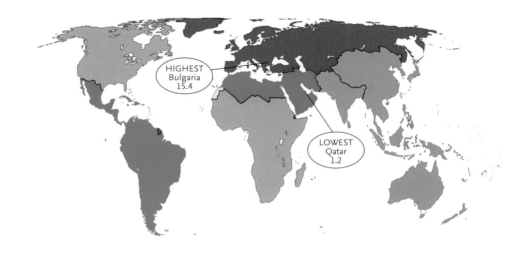

## Infant mortality rate

Number of infants dying before reaching one year of age, per 1000 live births

- 20 – 51.7
- 15 – 19.9
- 10 – 14.9
- 5 – 9.9
- no data

World average 28.2
Statistics are for 2019

Scale 1 : 250 000 000

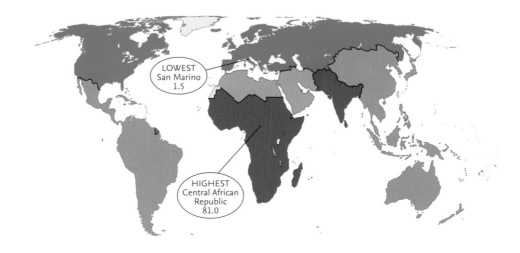

## Life expectancy

Years

- 75 – 78.9
- 70 – 74.9
- 65 – 69.9
- 60 – 64.9
- no data

World average 72.6
Statistics are for 2018

Scale 1 : 250 000 000

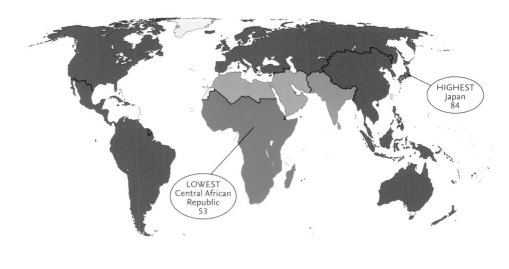

HIGHEST
Japan
84

LOWEST
Central African
Republic
53

## Population growth

Annual average growth, percentage

- 2.2 – 2.7
- 1.5 – 2.1
- 0.8 – 1.4
- 0.3 – 0.7
- no data

World average 1.1
Statistics are for 2019

Scale 1 : 250 000 000

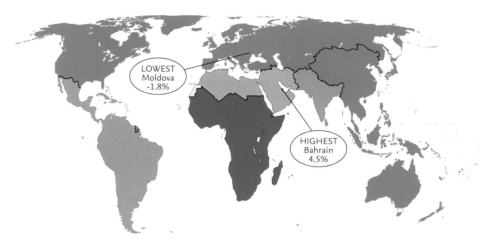

LOWEST
Moldova
-1.8%

HIGHEST
Bahrain
4.5%

## Migration

Annual net migration, millions

- 0 – 7.9
- -2 – 0
- -4 – -2
- -6.3 – -4
- no data

Statistics are for 2017

Scale 1 : 250 000 000

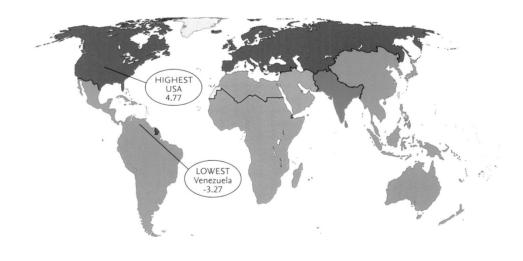

HIGHEST
USA
4.77

LOWEST
Venezuela
-3.27

## Urbanization

Urban population, percentage

- 75 – 90
- 60 – 74.9
- 45 – 59.9
- 30 – 44.9
- no data

World average 55.7
Statistics are for 2019

Scale 1 : 250 000 000

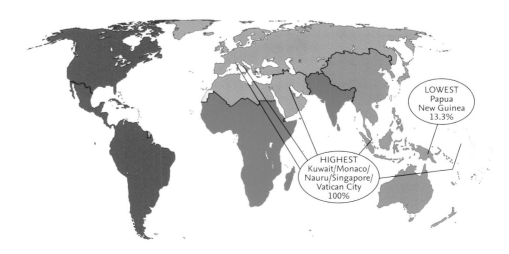

LOWEST
Papua
New Guinea
13.3%

HIGHEST
Kuwait/Monaco/
Nauru/Singapore/
Vatican City
100%

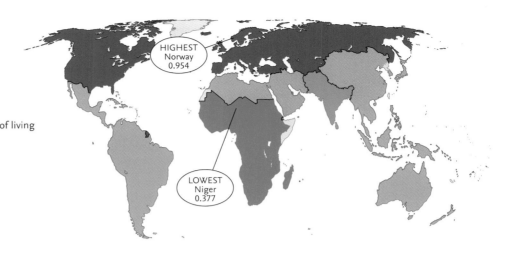

## Human Development Index
HDI is based on life expectancy, knowledge and standard of living

- 0.800 – 0.999 (very high)
- 0.700 – 0.799 (high)
- 0.551 – 0.699 (medium)
- 0 – 0.550 (low)
- no data

World average 0.731
Statistics are for 2018

Scale 1 : 250 000 000

HIGHEST
Norway
0.954

LOWEST
Niger
0.377

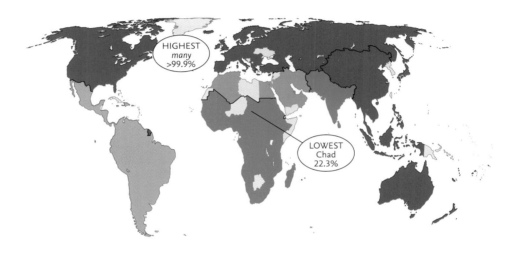

## Literacy rate
Percentage of adults

- 95 – 99.9
- 90 – 94.9
- 75 – 89.9
- 60 – 74.9
- no data

World average 86.3
Statistics are for 2018

Scale 1 : 250 000 000

HIGHEST
*many*
>99.9%

LOWEST
Chad
22.3%

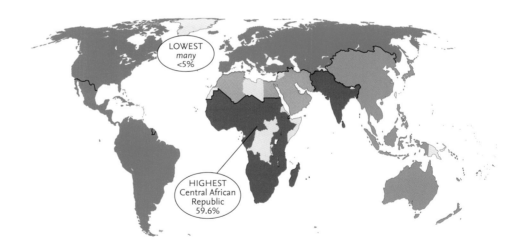

## Nutrition
Percentage of population undernourished

- 10 – 22
- 9 – 9.9
- 8 – 8.9
- 2.5 – 7.9
- no data

World average 10.8
Statistics are for 2017

Scale 1 : 250 000 000

LOWEST
*many*
<5%

HIGHEST
Central African
Republic
59.6%

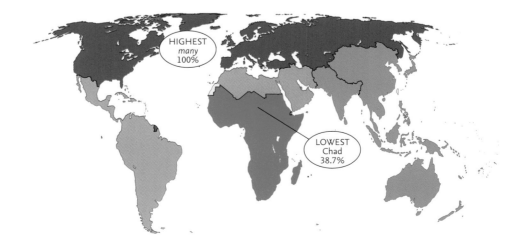

## Access to safe water
Percentage of population with access
to water from an improved source

- 98 – 100
- 94 – 97.9
- 90 – 93.9
- 60 – 89.9
- no data

World average 89.6
Statistics are for 2017

Scale 1 : 250 000 000

HIGHEST
*many*
100%

LOWEST
Chad
38.7%

## Doctors
Number of physicians per 100 000 people

- 300 – 399
- 200 – 299
- 100 – 199
- 0 – 99
- no data

World average 157
Statistics are for 2017

Scale 1 : 250 000 000

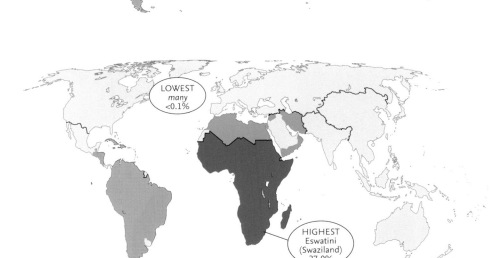

HIGHEST
Cuba
842

LOWEST
Tanzania
1

## HIV
Percentage of population aged 15–49 infected with HIV

- 0.6 – 4
- 0.4 – 0.5
- 0.1 – 0.3
- no data

World average 0.7
Statistics are for 2019

Scale 1 : 250 000 000

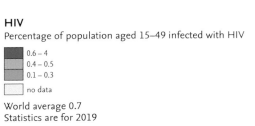

LOWEST
*many*
<0.1%

HIGHEST
Eswatini
(Swaziland)
27.0%

## Poverty
Percentage of population living on less than US$ 1.90 a day

- 20 – 42.3
- 10 – 19.9
- 5 – 9.9
- 1 – 4.9
- no data

World average 10.0
Statistics are for 2013 – 2018

Scale 1 : 250 000 000

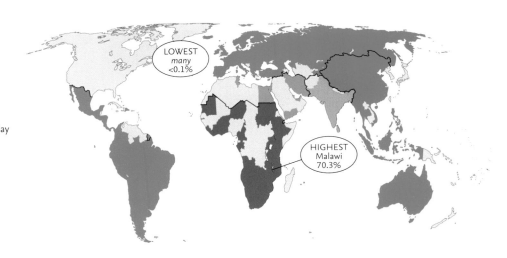

LOWEST
*many*
<0.1%

HIGHEST
Malawi
70.3%

## Aid
Official development assistance received, US$ per person

- 20 – 71.4
- 10 – 19.9
- 5 – 9.9
- 0 – 4.9
- no data
- Donors

World average 21.8
Statistics are for 2018

Scale 1 : 250 000 000

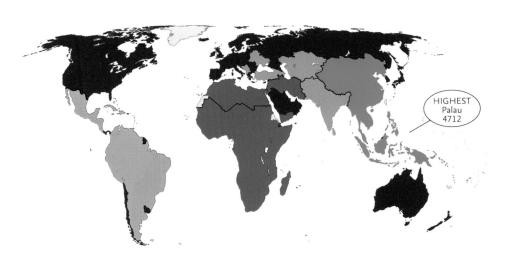

HIGHEST
Palau
4712

**Regional Indicators**

## Gross National Income

GNI is the value of production of goods
and services of each country, US$ per person

- 25 000 – 64 000
- 10 000 – 24 999
- 5000 – 9999
- 1000 – 4999
- no data

World average 11 570
Statistics are for 2019

Scale 1 : 250 000 000

HIGHEST
Switzerland
85 500

LOWEST
Burundi
280

## Trade

Percentage of world trade

- 30.1 – 40
- 10.1 – 30
- 5.1 – 10
- 1 – 5
- no data

Statistics are for 2019

Scale 1 : 250 000 000

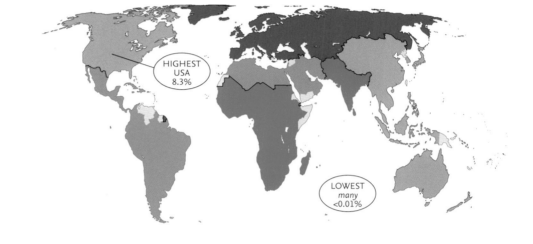

HIGHEST
USA
8.3%

LOWEST
many
<0.01%

## Energy production

Million tonnes oil equivalent

- 3000 – 4100
- 2000 – 2999
- 750 – 1999
- 0 – 749
- no data

Statistics are for 2017

Scale 1 : 250 000 000

HIGHEST
China
2825.0

LOWEST
many
0

## Energy consumption

Million tonnes oil equivalent

- 3000 – 5300
- 2000 – 2999
- 1000 – 1999
- 0 – 999
- no data

Statistics are for 2017

Scale 1 : 250 000 000

LOWEST
Kiribati
0.02

HIGHEST
China
3516.4

## Carbon dioxide emissions

Metric tonnes per person

- 10 – 15.5
- 5 – 9.9
- 0 – 4.9
- no data

World average 5.0
Statistics are for 2016

Scale 1 : 250 000 000

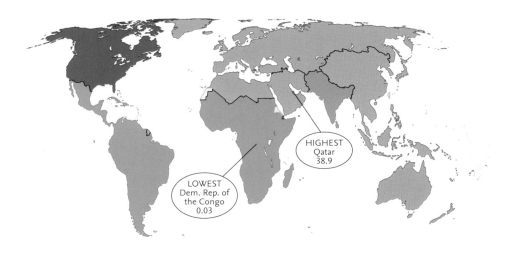

## Mobile phones

Subscriptions per 100 people

- 115 – 125
- 105 – 114.9
- 95 – 104.9
- 80 – 94.9
- no data

World average 106.5
Statistics are for 2018

Scale 1 : 250 000 000

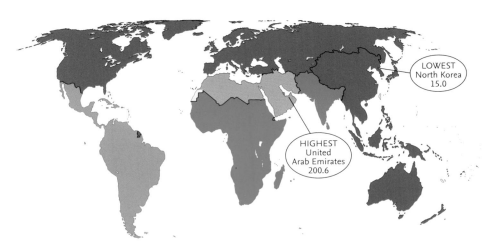

## Air passengers

Millions carried

- 1000 – 1400
- 500 – 999
- 100 – 499
- 0 – 99
- no data

World average 423
Statistics are for 2018

Scale 1 : 250 000 000

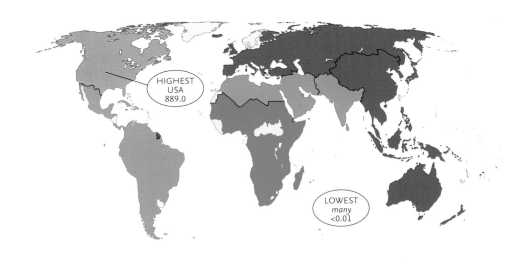

## Tourism

Earnings from international tourism, US$ billion

- 500 – 655
- 300 – 499
- 100 – 299
- 0 – 99
- no data

Statistics are for 2018

Scale 1 : 250 000 000

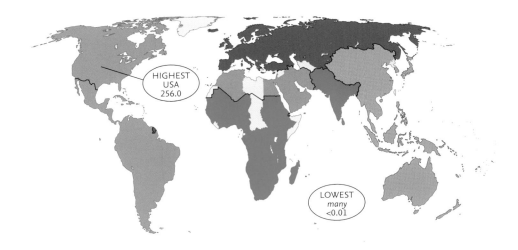

## Using the Dictionary

Geographical terms in the dictionary are arranged alphabetically.

**Bold** words in an entry identify key terms which are explained in greater detail within separate entries of their own.

Important terms which do not have separate entries are shown in *italic* and are explained in the entry in which they occur.

# A

**abrasion**  The wearing away of the landscape by rivers, **glaciers**, the sea or wind, caused by the load of debris that they carry. *See also* **corrasion**.

**abrasion platform**  *See* **wave-cut platform**.

**accuracy**  A measure of the degree of correctness.

**acid rain**  Rain that contains a high concentration of pollutants, notably sulphur and nitrogen oxides. These pollutants are produced from factories, power stations burning **fossil fuels**, and car exhausts. Once in the **atmosphere**, the sulphur and nitrogen oxides combine with moisture to give sulphuric and nitric acids which fall as corrosive rain.

**administrative region**  An area in which organizations carry out administrative functions; for example, the regions of local health authorities and water companies, and commercial sales regions.

**adult literacy rate**  A percentage measure which shows the proportion of an adult population able to read. It is one of the measures used to assess the level of development of a country.

**aerial photograph**  A photograph taken from above the ground. There are two types of aerial photograph – a vertical photograph (or 'bird's-eye view') and an oblique photograph where the camera is held at an angle. Aerial photographs are often taken from aircraft and provide useful information for map-making and surveys. *Compare* **satellite image**.

**afforestation**  The conversion of open land to forest; especially, in Britain, the planting of coniferous trees in upland areas for commercial gain. *Compare* **deforestation**.

**agglomerate**  A mass of coarse rock fragments or blocks of lava produced during a volcanic eruption.

**agribusiness**  Modern **intensive farming** which uses machinery and artificial fertilizers to increase **yield** and output.
Thus agriculture resembles an industrial process in which the general running and managing of the farm could parallel that of large-scale industry.

**agriculture**  Human management of the **environment** to produce food. The numerous forms of agriculture fall into three groups:

commercial agriculture, subsistence agriculture and **peasant agriculture**. *See also* **agribusiness**.

**aid**  The provision of finance, personnel and equipment for furthering economic development and improving standards of living in the **Third World**. Most aid is organized by international institutions (e.g. the United Nations), by charities (e.g. Oxfam) (*see* **non-governmental organizations** (NGOs) or by national governments. Aid to a country from the international institutions is called *multilateral aid*. Aid from one country to another is called *bilateral aid*.

**air mass**  A large body of air with generally the same temperature and moisture conditions throughout. Warm or cold and moist air masses usually develop over large bodies of water (**oceans**). Hot or cold and dry air masses develop over large land areas (**continents**).

**alluvial fan**  A cone of **sediment** deposited at an abrupt change of slope; for example, where a post-glacial stream meets the flat floor of a **U-shaped valley**. Alluvial fans are also common in arid regions where streams flowing off **escarpments** may periodically carry large loads of sediment during **flash floods**.

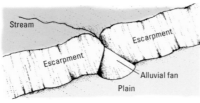
*alluvial fan*

**alluvium**  Material deposited by a river in its middle and lower course. Alluvium comprises **silt**, sand and coarser debris eroded from the river's upper course and transported downstream. Alluvium is deposited in a graded sequence: coarsest first (heaviest) and finest last (lightest). Regular floods in the lower course create extensive layers of alluvium which can build up to a considerable depth on the **flood plain**.

**alp**  A gentle slope above the steep sides of a glaciated valley, often used for summer grazing. *See also* **transhumance**.

*alp*

**analysis**  The examination of the constituent parts of a complex entity.

**anemometer**  An instrument for measuring the velocity of the wind. An anemometer should be fixed on a post at least 5 m above ground level. The wind blows the cups around and the speed is read off the dial in km/hr (or knots).

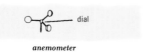
*anemometer*

**annotation**  Labels in the form of text or graphics that can be individually selected, positioned or stored in a database.

**antarctic circle**  Imaginary line that encircles the South Pole at **latitude** 66° 32'S.

**anthracite**  A hard form of **coal** with a high carbon content and few impurities.

**anticline**  An arch in folded **strata**; the opposite of **syncline**. *See* **fold**.

**anticyclone**  An area of high atmospheric pressure with light winds, clear skies and settled **weather**. In summer, anticyclones are associated with warm and sunny conditions; in winter, they bring frost and fog as well as sunshine.

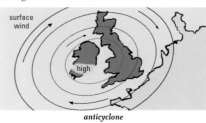
*anticyclone*

**API (application programming interface)**  A set of interfaces, methods, procedures and tools used to build or customise a software program.

**aquifer**  *See* **artesian basin**.

**arable farming**  The production of cereal and root crops – as opposed to the keeping of livestock.

**arc**  A coverage feature class representing lines and polygon boundaries.

**archipelago**  A group or chain of islands.

**arctic circle**  Imaginary line that encircles the North Pole at **latitude** 66° 32'N.

**arête**  A knife-edged ridge separating two **corries** in a glaciated upland. The arête is formed by the progressive enlargement of corries by **weathering** and **erosion**. *See also* **pyramidal peak**.

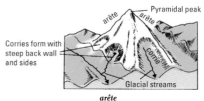
*arête*

**artesian basin**  This consists of a shallow **syncline** with a layer of **permeable rock**, e.g. chalk, sandwiched between two impermeable layers, e.g. clay. Where the permeable rock is exposed at the surface, rainwater will enter the rock and the rock will become saturated. This is known as an *aquifer*. Boreholes can be sunk into the structure to tap the water in the aquifer.

**asymmetrical fold**  Folded **strata** where the two limbs are at different angles to the horizontal.

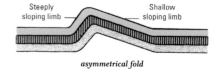
*asymmetrical fold*

**atlas**  A collection of maps.

**atmosphere**  The air which surrounds the Earth, and consists of three layers:
the *troposphere* (6 to 10km from the Earth's surface), the *stratosphere* (50km from the Earth's surface), and the *mesosphere* and *ionosphere*, an ionised region of rarefied gases (1000km from the Earth's surface). The atmosphere comprises oxygen (21%), nitrogen (78%), carbon dioxide, argon, helium and other gases in minute quantities.

**attrition**  The process by which a river's load is

eroded through particles, such as pebbles and boulders, striking each other.

# B

**backwash** The return movement of seawater off the beach after a wave has broken. *See also* **longshore drift** and **swash**.

**bar graph** A graph on which the values of a certain variable are shown by the length of shaded columns, which are numbered in sequence. *Compare* **histogram**.

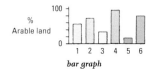
*bar graph*

**barchan** A type of crescent-shaped sand dune formed in desert regions where the wind direction is very constant. Wind blowing round the edges of the dune causes the crescent shape, while the dune may advance in a downwind direction as particles are blown over the crest.

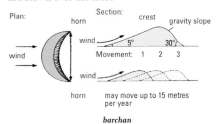
*barchan*

**barograph** An aneroid **barometer** connected to an arm and inked pen which records pressure changes continuously on a rotating drum. The drum usually takes a week to make one rotation.

**barometer** An instrument for measuring atmospheric pressure. There are two types, the *mercury barometer* and the *aneroid barometer*. The mercury barometer consists of a glass tube containing mercury which fluctuates in height as pressure varies. The aneroid barometer is a small metal box from which some of the air has been removed. The box expands and contracts as the air pressure changes. A series of levers joined to a pointer shows pressure on a dial.

**barrage** A type of dam built across a wide stretch of water, e.g. an estuary, for the purposes of water management. Such a dam may be intended to provide water supply, to harness wave energy or to control flooding, etc. There is a large barrage across Cardiff Bay in South Wales.

**basalt** A dark, fine-grained extrusive **igneous rock** formed when **magma** emerges onto the Earth's surface and cools rapidly. A succession of basalt **lava flows** may lead to the formation of a **lava plateau**.

**base flow** The water flowing in a stream which is fed only by **groundwater**. During dry periods it is only the base flow which passes through the stream channel.

**base map** Map on which thematic information can be placed.

**batholith** A large body of igneous material intruded into the Earth's **crust**. As the batholith slowly cools, large-grained **rocks** such as **granite** are formed.

Batholiths may eventually be exposed at the Earth's surface by the removal of overlying rocks through **weathering** and **erosion**.

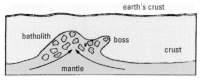
*batholith*

**bay** An indentation in the coastline with a **headland** on either side. Its formation is due to the more rapid **erosion** of softer rocks.

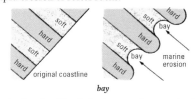
*bay*

**beach** A strip of land sloping gently towards the sea, usually recognized as the area lying between high and low tide marks.

*beach*

**bearing** A compass reading between 0 and 360 degrees, indicating direction of one location from another.

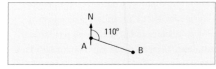
*bearing* *The bearing from A to B is 110°.*

**Beaufort wind scale** An international scale of wind velocities, ranging from 0 (calm) to 12 (hurricane).

**bedrock** The solid rock which usually lies beneath the soil.

**bergschrund** A large **crevasse** located at the rear of a **corrie** icefield in a glaciated region, formed by the weight of the ice in the corrie dragging away from the rear wall as the **glacier** moves downslope.

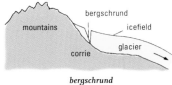
*bergschrund*

**biodiversity** The existence of a wide variety of plant and animal species in their natural environment.

**biogas** The production of methane and carbon dioxide, which can be obtained from plant or crop waste. Biogas is an example of a renewable source of energy (*see* **renewable resources, nonrenewable resources**).

**biomass** The total number of living organisms, both plant and animal, in a given area.

**biome** A complex community of plants and animals in a specific physical and climatic region. *See* **climate**.

**biosphere** The part of the Earth which contains living organisms. The biosphere contains a variety of **habitats**, from the highest mountains to the deepest oceans.

**birth rate** The number of live births per 1000 people in a population per year.

**bituminous coal** Sometimes called house coal – a medium-quality **coal** with some impurities; the typical domestic coal. It is also the major fuel source for **thermal power stations**.

**block mountain** *or* **horst** A section of the Earth's **crust** uplifted by faulting. Mt Ruwenzori in the East African Rift System is an example of a block mountain.

**blowhole** A crevice, **joint** or **fault** in coastal rocks, enlarged by marine **erosion**. A blowhole often leads from the rear of a cave (formed by wave action at the foot of a **cliff**) up to the cliff top. As waves break in the cave they erode the roof at the point of weakness and eventually a hole is formed. Air and sometimes spray are forced up the blowhole to erupt at the surface.

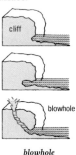
*blowhole*

**bluff** *See* **river cliff**.

**boreal forest** *See* **taiga**.

**boulder clay** *or* **till** The unsorted mass of debris dragged along by a **glacier** as *ground moraine* and dumped as the glacier melts. Boulder clay may be several metres thick and may comprise any combination of finely ground 'rock flour', sand, pebbles or boulders.

**breakwater** *or* **groyne** A wall built at right angles to a beach in order to prevent sand loss due to **longshore drift**.

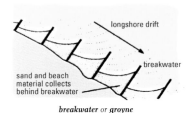
*breakwater or groyne*

**breccia** Rock fragments cemented together by a matrix of finer material; the fragments are angular and unsorted. An example of this is volcanic breccia, which is made up of coarse angular fragments of **lava** and **crust** rocks welded by finer material such as ash and **tuff**.

**buffers** Memory devices for temporarily storing data.

**bush fallowing** *or* **shifting cultivation** A system of **agriculture** in which there are no permanent fields. For example in the **tropical rainforest**, remote societies cultivate forest clearings for one year and then move on. The system functions successfully when forest **regeneration** occurs over a sufficiently long period to allow the soil to regain its fertility.

**bushfire** An uncontrolled fire in forests and grasslands.

**business park** An out-of-town site accommodating offices, high-technology companies and light industry. *Compare* **science park**.

**butte** An outlier of a **mesa** in arid regions.

# C

**cache** A small high-speed memory that improves computer performance.

**caldera** A large crater formed by the collapse of the summit cone of a **volcano** during an eruption. The caldera may contain subsidiary cones built up by subsequent eruptions, or a crater lake if the volcano is extinct or dormant.

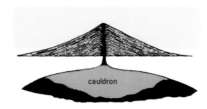
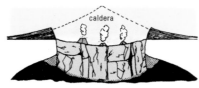

*caldera*

**canal** An artificial waterway, usually connecting existing **rivers**, **lakes** or **oceans**, constructed for navigation and transportation.

**canyon** A deep and steep-sided river valley occurring where rapid vertical **corrasion** takes place in arid regions. In such an **environment** the rate of **weathering** of the valley sides is slow. If the **rocks** of the region are relatively soft then the canyon profile becomes even more pronounced. The Grand Canyon of the Colorado River in the USA is the classic example.

*canyon*

**capital city** Seat of government of a country or political unit.

**cartogram** A map showing statistical data in diagrammatic form.

**cartography** The technique of drawing maps or charts.

**catchment** 1. In **physical geography**, an alternative term to **river basin**.

2. In **human geography**, an area around a town or city – hence 'labour catchment' means the area from which an urban workforce is drawn.

**cavern** In **limestone** country, a large underground cave formed by the dissolving of limestone by subterranean streams.

*See also* **stalactite**, **stalagmite**.

**cay** A small low **island** or bank composed of sand and coral fragments. Commonly found in the Caribbean Sea.

**CBD (Central Business District)** This is the central zone of a town or city, and is characterized by high accessibility, high land values and limited space. The visible result of these factors is a concentration of high-rise buildings at the city centre. The CBD is dominated by retail and business functions, both of which require maximum accessibility.

**CFCs (Chlorofluorocarbons)** Chemicals used in the manufacture of some aerosols, the cooling systems of refrigerators and fast-food cartons. These chemicals are harmful to the **ozone** layer.

**chalk** A soft, whitish **sedimentary rock** formed by the accumulation of small fragments of skeletal matter from marine organisms; the rock may be almost pure calcium carbonate. Due to the **permeable** and soluble nature of the rock, there is little surface **drainage** in chalk landscapes.

**channel** *See* **strait**.

**chernozem** A deep, rich soil of the plains of southern Russia. The upper **horizons** are rich in lime and other plant nutrients; in the dry **climate** the predominant movement of **soil** moisture is upwards (*contrast* with **leaching**), and lime and other chemical nutrients therefore accumulate in the upper part of the **soil profile**.

**choropleth** A symbol or marked area on a map which denotes the distribution of some property.

**choropleth map** *See* **shading map**.

**cirrus** High, wispy or strand-like, thin **cloud** associated with the advance of a **depression**.

**clay** A soil composed of very small particles of **sediment**, less than 0.002 mm in diameter. Due to the dense packing of these minute particles, clay is almost totally impermeable, i.e. it does not allow water to drain through. Clay soils very rapidly waterlog in wet weather.

**cliff** A steep rockface between land and sea, the profile of which is determined largely by the nature of the coastal rocks. For example, resistant rocks such as **granite** (e.g. at Land's End, England) will produce steep and rugged cliffs.

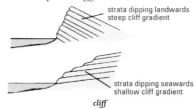

*cliff*

**climate** The average atmospheric conditions prevailing in a region, as distinct from its **weather**. A statement of climate is concerned with long-term trends. Thus the climate of, for example, the Amazon Basin is described as hot and wet all the year round; that of the Mediterranean Region as having hot dry summers and mild wet winters. *See* **extreme climate**, **maritime climate**.

**clint** A block of **limestone**, especially when part of a **limestone pavement**, where the surface is composed of clints and **grykes**.

**cloud** A mass of small water drops or ice crystals formed by the **condensation** of water vapour in the **atmosphere**, usually at a considerable height above the Earth's surface. There are three main types of cloud: **cumulus**, **stratus** and **cirrus**, each of which has many variations.

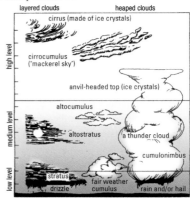

*cloud*

**CMYK** A colour model that combines cyan, magenta, yellow and black to create a range of colours in printing.

**coal** A **sedimentary rock** composed of decayed and compressed vegetative matter. Coal is usually classified according to a scale of hardness and purity ranging from **anthracite** (the hardest), through **bituminous coal** and **lignite** to **peat**.

**cold front** *See* **depression**.

**commercial agriculture** A system of **agriculture** in which food and materials are produced specifically for sale in the market, in contrast to **subsistence agriculture**. Commercial agriculture tends to be capital intensive. *See also* **agribusiness**.

**Common Agricultural Policy (CAP)**
The policy of the European Union to support and subsidize certain crops and methods of animal husbandry.

**common land** Land which is not in the ownership of an individual or institution, but which is historically available to any member of the local community.

**communications** The contacts and linkages in an **environment**. For example, roads and railways are communications, as are telephone systems, newspapers, and radio and television.

**commuter zone** An area on or near to the outskirts of an urban area. Commuters are among the most affluent and mobile members of the urban community and can afford the greatest physical separation of home and work.

**concordant coastline** A coastline that is parallel to mountain ranges immediately inland. A rise in sea level or a sinking of the land cause the valleys to be flooded by the sea and the mountains to become a line of islands. *Compare* **discordant coastline**.

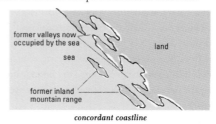

*concordant coastline*

**condensation** The process by which cooling vapour turns into a liquid. **Clouds**, for example, are formed by the condensation of water vapour in the **atmosphere**.

coniferous forest A forest of **evergreen** trees such as pine, spruce and fir. Natural coniferous forests occur considerably further north than forests of broad-leaved **deciduous** species, as coniferous trees are able to withstand harsher climatic conditions. The **taiga** areas of the northern hemisphere consist of coniferous forests.

conservation The preservation and management of the natural **environment**. In its strictest form, conservation may mean total protection of endangered species and habitats, as in nature reserves. In some cases, conservation of the man-made environment, e.g. ancient buildings, is undertaken.

continent One of the earth's large land masses. The world's continents are generally defined as Asia, Africa, North America, South America, Europe, Oceania and Antarctica.

continental climate The climate at the centre of large landmasses, typified by a large annual range in temperature, with precipitation most likely in the summer.

continental drift The theory that the Earth's continents move gradually over a layer of semi-molten rock underneath the Earth's **crust**. It is thought that the present-day continents once formed the supercontinent, **Pangaea**, which existed approximately 200 million years ago. *See also* **Gondwanaland**, **Laurasia** and **plate tectonics**.

continental shelf The seabed bordering the continents, which is covered by shallow water – usually of less than 200 metres. Along some coastlines the continental shelf is so narrow it is almost absent.

contour A line drawn on a map to join all places at the same height above sea level.

conurbation A continuous built-up urban area formed by the merging of several formerly separate towns or cities. Twentieth-century **urban sprawl** has led to the merging of towns.

coombe *See* **dry valley**.

cooperative A system whereby individuals pool their **resources** in order to optimize individual gains.

coordinates A set of numbers that defines the location of a point with reference to a system of axes.

core 1. In **physical geography**, the core is the innermost zone of the Earth. It is probably solid at the centre, and composed of iron and nickel.
2. In **human geography**, a central place or central region, usually the centre of economic and political activity in a region or nation.

corrasion The abrasive action of an agent of **erosion** (rivers, ice, the sea) caused by its load. For example the pebbles and boulders carried along by a river wear away the channel bed and the river bank. *Compare* with **hydraulic action**.

corrie, cirque *or* cwm A bowl-shaped hollow on a mountainside in a glaciated region; the area where a valley **glacier** originates. In glacial times the corrie contained an icefield, which in cross section appears as in diagram *a* above. The shape of the corrie is determined by the rotational erosive force of ice as the glacier moves downslope (diagram *b*).

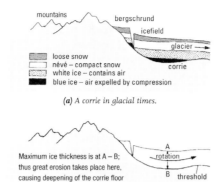

mountains
bergschrund
icefield
glacier
corrie

◼ loose snow
◻ névé – compact snow
▨ white ice – contains air
◼ blue ice – air expelled by compression

*(a)* A corrie in glacial times.

Maximum ice thickness is at A – B; thus great erosion takes place here, causing deepening of the corrie floor below the level of the threshold

A
rotation
B
threshold

*(b)* Erosion of a corrie.

corrosion **Erosion** by solution action, such as the dissolving of **limestone** by running water.

crag Rocky outcrop on a valley side formed, for example, when a **truncated spur** exists in a glaciated valley.

crag and tail A feature of lowland **glaciation**, where a resistant rock outcrop withstands **erosion** by a **glacier** and remains as a feature after the **Ice Age**. Rocks of volcanic or metamorphic origin are likely to produce such a feature. As the ice advances over the crag, material will be eroded from the face and sides and will be deposited as a mass of boulder clay and debris on the leeward side, thus producing a 'tail'.

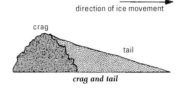

direction of ice movement →
crag
tail

*crag and tail*

crevasse A crack or fissure in a **glacier** resulting from the stressing and fracturing of ice at a change in **gradient** or valley shape.

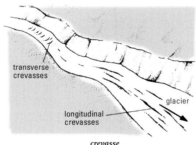

transverse crevasses
glacier
longitudinal crevasses

*crevasse*

cross section A drawing of a vertical section of a line of ground, deduced from a map. It depicts the **topography** of a system of **contours**.

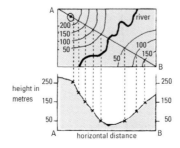

A
river
200
150
100
50
50
100
150
B
height in metres
250
150
50
250
150
50
A
horizontal distance
B

*cross section* Map and corresponding cross section.

crust The outermost layer of the Earth, representing only 0.1% of the Earth's total volume. It comprises continental crust and oceanic crust, which differ from each other in age as well as in physical and chemical characteristics. The crust, together with the uppermost layer of the **mantle**, is also known as the *lithosphere*.

culvert An artificial drainage channel for transporting water quickly from place to place.

cumulonimbus A heavy, dark **cloud** of great vertical height. It is the typical thunderstorm cloud, producing heavy showers of rain, snow or hail. Such clouds form where intense solar radiation causes vigorous convection.

cumulus A large **cloud** (smaller than a **cumulonimbus**) with a 'cauliflower' head and almost horizontal base. It is indicative of fair or, at worst, showery **weather** in generally sunny conditions.

cut-off *See* **oxbow lake**.

cyclone *See* **hurricane**.

# D

dairying A **pastoral farming** system in which dairy cows produce milk that is used by itself or used to produce dairy products such as cheese, butter, cream and yoghurt.

dam A barrier built across a stream, river or **estuary** to create a body of water.

data A series of observations, measurements or facts which can be operated on by a computer programme.

data capture Any process for converting information into a form that can be handled by a computer.

database A large store of information. A GIS database includes data about spatial locations and shapes of geographical features.

datum A single piece of information.

death rate The number of deaths per 1000 people in a population per year.

deciduous woodland Trees which are generally of broad-leaved rather than **coniferous** habit, and which shed their leaves during the cold season.

deflation The removal of loose sand by wind **erosion** in desert regions. It often exposes a bare rock surface beneath.

deforestation The practice of clearing trees. Much deforestation is a result of development pressures, e.g. trees are cut down to provide land for agriculture and industry. *Compare* **afforestation**.

delta A fan-shaped mass consisting of the deposited load of a river where it enters the sea. A delta only forms where the river deposits material at a faster rate than can be removed by coastal currents. While deltas may take almost any shape and size, three types are generally recognized, as shown in the diagram overleaf.

DEM (Digital elevation model) Representation of the relief of a topographic surface.

denudation The wearing away of the Earth's surface by the processes of **weathering** and **erosion**.

depopulation A long-term decrease in the population of any given area, frequently caused by economic migration to other areas.

deposition The laying down of **sediments** resulting from **denudation**.

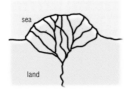
Arcuate delta,
e.g. Nile.
Note bifurcation of
river into
distributaries in delta

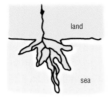
Bird's foot delta,
e.g. Mississippi

Estuarine delta,
e.g. Amazon

*delta*

**depression** An area of low atmospheric pressure occurring where warm and cold air masses come into contact. The passage of a depression is marked by thickening cloud, rain, a period of dull and drizzly weather and then clearing skies with showers. A depression develops as in the diagrams below.

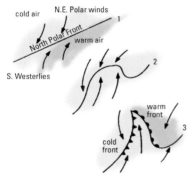

*(a) The development of a depression.*

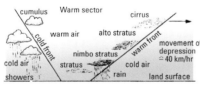

*(b) The passage of a depression.*

**desert** An area where all forms of **precipitation** are so low that very little, if anything, can grow.

Deserts can be broadly divided into three types, depending upon average temperatures:
(a) *hot deserts:* occur in tropical latitudes in regions of high pressure where air is sinking and therefore making rainfall unlikely. See **cloud**.
(b) *temperate deserts:* occur in mid-latitudes in areas of high pressure. They are far inland, so moisture-bearing winds rarely deposit rainfall in these areas.
(c) *cold deserts:* occur in the northern latitudes, again in areas of high pressure. Very low temperatures throughout the year mean the air is unable to hold much moisture.

**desertification** The encroachment of **desert** conditions into areas which were once productive. Desertification can be due partly to climatic change, i.e. a move towards a drier climate in

some parts of the world (possibly due to **global warming**), though human activity has also played a part through bad farming practices. The problem is particularly acute along the southern margins of the Sahara desert in the Sahel region between Mali and Mauritania in the west, and Ethiopia and Somalia in the east.

**developing countries** A collective term for those nations in Africa, Asia and Latin America which are undergoing the complex processes of modernization, **industrialization** and **urbanization**. *See also* **Third World**.

**dew point** The temperature at which the **atmosphere**, being cooled, becomes saturated with water vapour. This vapour is then deposited as drops of dew.

**digitising** Translating into a digital format for computer processing.

**dip slope** The gentler of the two slopes on either side of an escarpment crest; the dip slope inclines in the direction of the dipping **strata**; the steep slope in front of the crest is the **scarp slope**.

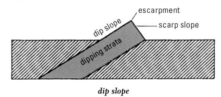

*dip slope*

**discharge** The volume of run-off in the channels of a **river basin**.

**discordant coastline** A coastline that is at right angles to the mountains and valleys immediately inland. A rise in sea level or a sinking of the land will cause the valleys to be flooded. A flooded river valley is known as a **ria**, whilst a flooded glaciated valley is known as a **fjord**. *Compare* **concordant coastline**.

*discordant coastline*

**distributary** An outlet stream which drains from a larger river or stream. Often found in a **delta** area. *Compare* **tributary**.

**doldrums** An equatorial belt of low atmospheric pressure where the **trade winds** converge. Winds are light and variable but the strong upward movement of air caused by this convergence produces frequent thunderstorms and heavy rains.

**domain name** That part of an internet address which identifies a group of computers by country or institution.

**dormitory settlement** A village located beyond the edge of a city but inhabited by residents who work in that city (*see* **commuter zone**).

**drainage** The removal of water from the land surface by processes such as streamflow and infiltration.

**drainage basin** *See* **river basin**.

**drift** Material transported and deposited by glacial action on the Earth's surface. *See also* **boulder clay**.

**drought** A prolonged period where rainfall falls below the requirement for a region.

**dry valley** *or* **coombe** A feature of **limestone** and **chalk** country, where valleys have been eroded in dry landscapes.

**dune** A mound or ridge of drifted sand, occurring on the sea coast and in deserts.

**dyke** 1. An artificial **drainage** channel.
2. An artificial bank built to protect low-lying land from flooding.
3. A vertical or semi-vertical igneous intrusion occurring where a stream of **magma** has extended through a line of weakness in the surrounding **rock**. *See* **igneous rock**.

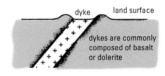

*dyke* Cross section of eroded dyke, showing how metamorphic margins, harder than dyke or surrounding rocks, resist erosion.

# E

**earthquake** A movement or tremor of the Earth's crust. Earthquakes are associated with plate boundaries (*see* **plate tectonics**) and especially with subduction zones, where one plate plunges beneath another. Here the crust is subjected to tremendous stress. The rocks are forced to bend, and eventually the stress is so great that the rocks 'snap' along a **fault** line.

**eastings** The first element of a **grid reference**. *See* **northings**.

**ecology** The study of living things, their interrelationships and their relationships with the **environment**.

**ecosystem** A natural system comprising living organisms and their **environment**. The concept can be applied at the global scale or in the context of a smaller defined environment. The principle of the ecosystem is constant: all elements are intricately linked by flows of energy and nutrients.

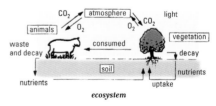

*ecosystem*

**El Niño** The occasional development of warm ocean surface waters along the coast of Ecuador and Peru. Where this warming occurs the tropical Pacific trade winds weaken and the usual up-welling of cold, deep ocean water is reduced. El Niño normally occurs late in the calendar year and lasts for a few weeks to a few months and can have a dramatic impact on weather patterns throughout the world.

**emigration** The movement of population out of a given area or country.

**employment structure** The distribution of the workforce between the **primary**, **secondary**, **tertiary**

and **quaternary sectors** of the economy. Primary employment is in **agriculture**, mining, forestry and fishing; secondary in manufacturing; tertiary in the retail, service and administration category; quaternary in information and expertise.

**environment** Physical surroundings: **soil**, vegetation, wildlife and the **atmosphere**.

**equator** The great circle of the Earth with a **latitude** of 0°, lying equidistant from the poles.

**erosion** The wearing away of the Earth's surface by running water (rivers and streams), moving ice (**glaciers**), the sea and the wind. These are called the *agents* of erosion.

**erratic** A boulder of a certain rock type resting on a surface of different geology. For example, blocks of **granite** resting on a surface of carboniferous **limestone** (e.g. deposited by a **glacier**).

**escarpment** A ridge of high ground as, for example, the **chalk** escarpments of southern England (the Downs and the Chilterns).

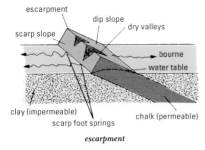

*escarpment*

**esker** A low, winding ridge of pebbles and finer **sediment** on a glaciated lowland.

**estuary** The broad mouth of a river where it enters the sea. An estuary forms where opposite conditions to those favourable for **delta** formation exist: deep water offshore, strong marine currents and a smaller **sediment** load.

**ethnic group** A group of people with a common identity such as culture, religion or skin colour.

**evaporation** The process whereby a substance changes from a liquid to a vapour. Heat from the sun evaporates water from seas, lakes, rivers, etc., and this process produces water vapour in the **atmosphere**.

**evergreen** A vegetation type in which leaves are continuously present. *Compare* **deciduous woodland**.

**exfoliation** A form of **weathering** whereby the outer layers of a **rock** or boulder shear off due to the alternate expansion and contraction produced by diurnal heating and cooling. Such a process is especially active in **desert** regions.

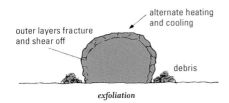

*exfoliation*

**exports** Goods and services sold to a foreign country (*compare* **imports**).

**extensive farming** A system of **agriculture** in which relatively small amounts of capital or labour investment are applied to relatively large areas of land. For example, sheep ranching is an extensive form of farming, and yields per unit area are low.

**external processes** Landscape-forming processes such as **weather** and **erosion**, in contrast to internal processes.

**extreme climate** A climate that is characterized by large ranges of temperature and sometimes of rainfall. *Compare* **temperate climate**, **maritime climate**.

# F

**fault** A fracture in the Earth's crust on either side of which the **rocks** have been relatively displaced. Faulting occurs in response to stress in the Earth's crust; the release of this stress in fault movement is experienced as an **earthquake**. *See also* **rift valley**.

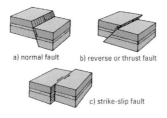

*fault* The main types.

**feature class** A collection of features with the same properties, attributes and spatial reference.

**fell** Upland rough grazing in a **hill farming** system, for example in the English Lake District.

**fjord** A deep, generally straight inlet of the sea along a glaciated coast. A fjord is a glaciated valley which has been submerged either by a post-glacial rise in sea level or a subsidence of the land.

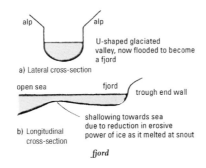

*fjord*

**flash flood** A sudden increase in river **discharge** and overland flow due to a violent rainstorm in the upper **river basin**.

**flood plain** The broad, flat valley floor of the lower course of a river, levelled by annual flooding and by the lateral and downstream movement of **meanders**.

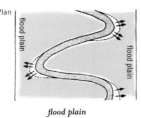

*flood plain*

**flow line** A diagram showing volumes of movement, e.g. of people, goods or information between places. The width of the flow line is proportional to the amount of movement, for example in portraying commuter flows into an urban centre from surrounding towns and villages.

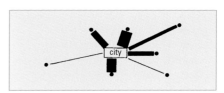

*Flow line* Commuter flows into a city.

**fodder crop** A crop grown for animal feed.

**fold** A bending or buckling of once horizontal rock **strata**. Many folds are the result of rocks being crumpled at plate boundaries (*see* **plate tectonics**), though **earthquakes** can also cause rocks to fold, as can igneous **intrusions**.

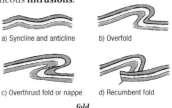

*fold*

**fold mountains** Mountains which have been formed by large-scale and complex folding. Studies of typical fold mountains (the Himalaya, Andes, Alps and Rockies) indicate that folding has taken place deep inside the Earth's **crust** and upper **mantle** as well as in the upper layers of the crust.

**fossil fuel** Any naturally occurring carbon or hydrocarbon fuel, notably coal, oil, peat and natural gas. These fuels have been formed by decomposed prehistoric organisms.

**free trade** The movement of goods and services between countries without any restrictions (such as quotas, tariffs or taxation) being imposed.

**freeze-thaw** A type of physical **weathering** whereby **rocks** are denuded by the freezing of water in cracks and crevices on the rock face. Water expands on freezing, and this process causes stress and fracture along any line of weakness in the rock. **Nivation** debris accumulates at the bottom of a rock face as **scree**.

**front** A boundary between two air masses. *See also* **depression**.

# G

**gazetteer** A list of place names with their geographical coordinates.

**GDP** *See* **Gross Domestic Product**.

**geosyncline** A basin (a large **syncline**) in which thick marine sediments have accumulated.

**geothermal energy** A method of producing power from heat contained in the lower layers of the Earth's **crust**. New Zealand and Iceland both use superheated water or steam from geysers and volcanic **springs** to heat buildings and for hothouse cultivation and also to drive steam turbines to generate electricity. Geothermal energy is an example of a renewable resource of energy (*see* **renewable resources**, **nonrenewable resources**).

**glaciation** A period of cold **climate** during which time **ice sheets** and **glaciers** are the dominant forces of **denudation**.

**glacier** A body of ice occupying a valley and originating in a **corrie** or icefield. A glacier moves at a rate of several metres per day, the precise

speed depending upon climatic and **topographic** conditions in the area in question.

**global warming** *or* **greenhouse effect** The warming of the Earth's atmosphere caused by an excess of carbon dioxide,which acts like a blanket, preventing the natural escape of heat. This situation has been developing over the last 150 years because of (a) the burning of **fossil fuels**, which releases vast amounts of carbon dioxide into the **atmosphere**, and (b) **deforestation**, which results in fewer trees being available to take up carbon dioxide (*see* **photosynthesis**).

**globalization** The process that enables financial markets and companies to operate internationally (as a result of deregulation and improved communications). **Transnational corporations** now locate their manufacturing in places that best serve their global market at the lowest cost.

**GNI (gross national income)** *formerly* **GNP (gross national product)** The total value of the goods and services produced annually by a nation, plus net property income from abroad.

**Gondwanaland** The southern-hemisphere super-continent, consisting of the present South America, Africa, India, Australasia and Antarctica, which split from **Pangaea** *c.*200 million years ago. Gondwanaland is part of the theory of **continental drift**. *See also* **plate tectonics**.

**GPS (global positioning system)** A system of earth-orbiting satellites, transmitting signals continuously towards earth, which enable the position of a receiving device on the earth's surface to be accurately estimated from the difference in arrival of the signals.

**gradient** 1. The measure of steepness of a line or slope. In mapwork, the average gradient between two points can be calculated as:

$$\frac{\text{difference in altitude}}{\text{distance apart}}$$

2. The measure of change in a property such as density. In **human geography** gradients are found in, for example, **population density**, land values and **settlement** ranking.

**granite** An **igneous rock** having large crystals due to slow cooling at depth in the Earth's **crust**.

**green belt** An area of land, usually around the outskirts of a town or city on which building and other developments are restricted by legislation.

**greenfield site** A development site for industry, retailing or housing that has previously been used only for agriculture or recreation. Such sites are frequently in the **green belt**.

**greenhouse effect** *See* **global warming**.

**Greenwich Meridian** *See* **prime meridian**.

**grid reference** A method for specifying position on a map. *See* **eastings** and **northings**.

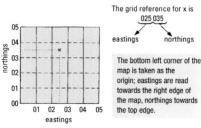

*grid reference*

**Gross Domestic Product (GDP)** The total value of all goods and services produced domestically by a nation during a year. It is equivalent to **Gross National Income (GNI)** minus investment incomes from foreign nations.

**groundwater** Water held in the bedrock of a region, having percolated through the **soil** from the surface. Such water is an important **resource** in areas where **surface run-off** is limited or absent.

**groyne** *See* **breakwater**.

**gryke** An enlarged joint between blocks of **limestone** (**clints**), especially in a **limestone pavement**.

**gulf** A large coastal indentation, similar to a **bay** but larger in extent. Commonly formed as a result of rising sea levels.

# H

**habitat** A preferred location for particular species of plants and animals to live and reproduce.

**hanging valley** A tributary valley entering a main valley at a much higher level because of deepening of the main valley, especially by glacial erosion.

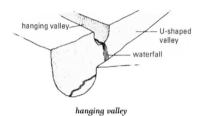

*hanging valley*

**HDI (human development index)** A measurement of a country's achievements in three areas: longevity, knowledge and standard of living. Longevity is measured by life expectancy at birth; knowledge is measured by a combination of the adult literacy rate and the combined gross primary, secondary and tertiary school enrolment ratio; standard of living is measured by **GNI** per capita.

**headland** A promontory of resistant **rock** along the coastline. *See* **bay**.

**hemisphere** Any half of a globe or sphere. The earth has traditionally been divided into hemispheres by the **equator** (northern and southern hemispheres) and by the **prime meridian** and **International Date Line** (eastern and western hemispheres).

**hill farming** A system of **agriculture** where sheep (and to a lesser extent cattle) are grazed on upland rough pasture.

**hill shading** Shadows drawn on a map to create a 3-dimensional effect and a sense of visual relief.

**histogram** A graph for showing values of classed data as the areas of bars.

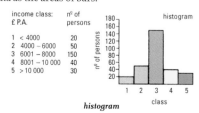

*histogram*

**horizon** The distinct layers found in the **soil profile**. Usually three horizons are identified – A, B and C, as in the diagram.

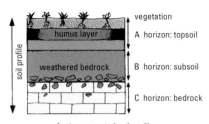

*horizon A typical soil profile.*

**horst** *See* **block mountain**.

**horticulture** The growing of plants and flowers for commercial sale. It is now an international trade, for example, orchids are grown in Southeast Asia for sale in Europe.

**human geography** The study of people and their activities in terms of patterns and processes of population, **settlement**, economic activity and **communications**. *Compare* **physical geography**.

**hunter/gatherer economy** A pre-agricultural phase of development in which people survive by hunting and gathering the animal and plant **resources** of the natural **environment**. No cultivation or herding is involved.

**hurricane, cyclone** *or* **typhoon** A wind of force 12 on the **Beaufort wind scale**, i.e. one having a velocity of more than 118 km per hour. Hurricanes can cause great damage by wind as well as from the storm waves and floods that accompany them.

**hydraulic action** The erosive force of water alone, as distinct from **corrasion**. A river or the sea will erode partially by the sheer force of moving water and this is termed 'hydraulic action'.

**hydroelectric power** The generation of electricity by turbines driven by flowing water. Hydroelectricity is most efficiently generated in rugged **topography** where a head of water can most easily be created, or on a large river where a dam can create similar conditions. Whatever the location, the principle remains the same – that water descending via conduits from an upper storage area passes through turbines and thus creates electricity.

**hydrological cycle** The cycling of water through sea, land and **atmosphere**.

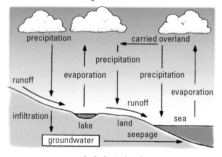

*hydrological cycle*

**hydrosphere** All the water on Earth, including that present in the **atmosphere** as well as in oceans, seas, **ice sheets**, etc.

**hygrometer** An instrument for measuring the relative humidity of the **atmosphere**. It comprises two thermometers, one of which is kept moist by a wick inserted in a water reservoir. Evaporation from the wick reduces the temperature of the 'wet bulb' thermometer, and the difference between the dry and the wet bulb temperatures is used to calculate relative humidity from standard tables.

# I

**Ice Age** A period of **glaciation** in which a cooling of **climate** leads to the development of **ice sheets, ice caps** and valley **glaciers**.

**ice cap** A covering of permanent ice over a relatively small land mass, e.g. Iceland.

**ice sheet** A covering of permanent ice over a substantial continental area such as Antarctica.

**iceberg** A large mass of ice which has broken off an **ice sheet** or **glacier** and left floating in the sea.

**ID (Identifier)** A unique value given to a particular object.

**igneous rock** A **rock** which originated as **magma** (molten rock) at depth in or below the Earth's **crust**. Igneous rocks are generally classified according to crystal size, colour and mineral composition. *See also* **plutonic rock**.

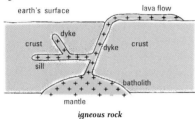
*igneous rock*

**immigration** The movement of people into a country or region from other countries or regions.

**impermeable rock** A rock that is non-porous and therefore incapable of taking in water or of allowing it to pass through between the grains. *Compare* **impervious rock**. *See also* **permeable rock**.

**impervious rock** A non-porous rock with no cracks or fissures through which water might pass.

**imports** Goods or services bought into one country from another (*compare* **exports**).

**industrialization** The development of industry on an extensive scale.

**infiltration** The gradual movement of water into the ground.

**infrastructure** The basic structure of an organization or system. The infrastructure of a city includes, for example, its roads and railways, schools, factories, power and water supplies.

**inner city** The ring of buildings around the **Central Business District (CBD)** of a town or city.

**intensive farming** A system of **agriculture** where relatively large amounts of capital and/or labour are invested on relatively small areas of land.

**interglacial** A warm period between two periods of **glaciation** and cold **climate**. The present interglacial began about 10,000 years ago.

**interlocking spurs** Obstacles of hard **rock** round which a river twists and turns in a V-shaped valley. **Erosion** is pronounced on the concave banks, and this ultimately causes the development of spurs which alternate on either side of the river and interlock as shown in the diagram.

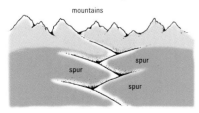
*interlocking spurs A V-shaped valley with interlocking spurs.*

**International Date Line** An imaginary line which approximately follows 180° **longitude**. The area of the world just east of the line is one day ahead of the area just west of the line.

**international trade** The exchange of goods and services between countries.

**intrusion** A body of **igneous rock** injected into the Earth's **crust** from the **mantle** below. *See* **dyke, sill, batholith**.

**ionosphere** *See* **atmosphere**.

**irrigation** A system of artificial watering of the land in order to grow crops. Irrigation is particularly important in areas of low or unreliable rainfall.

**island** A mass of land, smaller than a continent, which is completely surrounded by water.

**isobar** A line joining points of equal atmospheric pressure, as on the meteorological map below.

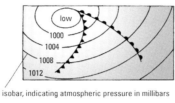
*isobar, indicating atmospheric pressure in millibars*
*isobar*

**isohyet** A line on a meteorological map joining places of equal rainfall.

**isotherm** A line on a meteorological map joining places of equal temperature.

# J

**joint** A vertical or semi-vertical fissure in a **sedimentary rock**, contrasted with roughly horizontal bedding planes. In **igneous rocks** jointing may occur as a result of contraction on cooling from the molten state. Joints should be distinguished from **faults** in that they are on a much smaller scale and there is no relative displacement of the rocks on either side of the joint. Joints, being lines of weakness are exploited by **weathering**.

# K

**kame** A short ridge of sand and gravel deposited from the water of a melted glacier.

**karst topography** An area of **limestone** scenery where **drainage** is predominantly subterranean.

**kettle hole** A small depression or hollow in a glacial outwash plain, formed when a block of ice embedded in the outwash deposits eventually melts, causing the **sediment** above to subside.

# L

**laccolith** An igneous **intrusion**, domed and often of considerable dimensions, caused where a body of viscous **magma** has been intruded into the **strata** of the Earth's **crust**. These strata are buckled upwards over the laccolith.

*laccolith*

**lagoon** 1. An area of sheltered coastal water behind a bay bar or **tombolo**.
2. The calm water behind a coral reef.

*lagoon*

**lahar** A landslide of volcanic debris mixed with water down the sides of a volcano, caused either by heavy rain or the heat of the volcano melting snow and ice.

**lake** A body of water completely surrounded by land.

**land tenure** A system of land ownership or allocation.

**land use** The function of an area of land. For example, the land use in rural areas could be farming or forestry, whereas urban land use could be housing or industry.

**landform** Any natural feature of the Earth's surface, such as mountains or valleys.

**laterite** A hard (literally 'brick-like') soil in tropical regions caused by the baking of the upper **horizons** by exposure to the sun.

**latitude** Distance north or south of the equator, as measured by degrees of the angle at the Earth's centre:

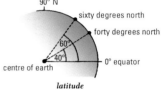
*latitude*

**Laurasia** The northern hemisphere supercontinent, consisting of the present North America, Europe and Asia (excluding India), which split from **Pangaea** c. 200 million years ago. Laurasia is part of the theory of **continental drift**. *See also* **plate tectonics**.

**lava** **Magma** extruded onto the Earth's surface via some form of volcanic eruption. Lava varies in viscosity (*see* **viscous lava**), colour and chemical composition. Acidic lavas tend to be viscous and flow slowly; basic lavas tend to be nonviscous and flow quickly. Commonly, **lava flows** comprise basaltic material, as for example in the process of sea-floor spreading (*see* **plate tectonics**).

**lava flow** A stream of **lava** issuing from some form of volcanic eruption. *See also* **viscous lava**.

**lava plateau** A relatively flat upland composed of layer upon layer of approximately horizontally bedded lavas. An example of this is the Deccan Plateau of India.

**leaching** The process by which soluble substances such as mineral salts are washed out of the upper soil layer into the lower layer by rain water.

**levée** The bank of a river, raised above the general level of the **flood plain** by **sediment** deposition during flooding. When the river bursts its banks, relatively coarse sediment is deposited first, and recurrent flooding builds up the river's banks accordingly. *See* diagram overleaf.

**lignite** A soft form of **coal**, harder than **peat** but softer than **bituminous coal**.

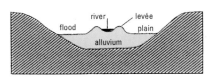

*levée*

**limestone** Calcium-rich **sedimentary rock** formed by the accumulation of the skeletal matter of marine organisms.

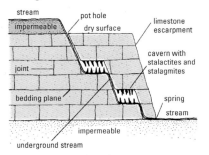

*limestone*

**limestone pavement** An exposed **limestone** surface on which the joints have been enlarged by the action of rainwater dissolving the limestone to form weak carbonic acid. These enlarged joints, or **grykes**, separate roughly rectangular blocks of limestone called **clints**.

*limestone pavement*

**location** The position of population, settlement and economic activity in an area or areas. Location is a basic theme in **human geography**.

**loess** A very fine **silt** deposit, often of considerable thickness, transported by the wind prior to **deposition**. When irrigated, loess can be very fertile and, consequently, high **yields** can be obtained from crops grown on loess deposits.

**longitude** A measure of distance on the Earth's surface east or west of the Greenwich Meridian, an imaginary line running from pole to pole through Greenwich in London. Longitude, like **latitude**, is measured in degrees of an angle taken from the centre of the Earth.

The precise location of a place can be given by a **grid reference** comprising longitude and latitude. *See also* **map projection**, **prime meridian**.

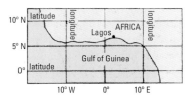

**longitude** *A grid showing the location of Lagos, Nigeria.*

**longshore drift** The net movement of material along a beach due to the oblique approach of waves to the shore. Beach deposits move in a zig-zag fashion, as shown in the diagram. Longshore drift is especially active on long, straight coastlines.

As waves approach, sand is carried up the beach by the **swash**, and retreats back down the beach with the **backwash**. Thus a single representative grain of sand will migrate in the pattern A, B, C, D, E, F in the diagram.

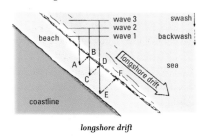

*longshore drift*

# M

**magma** Molten rock originating in the Earth's **mantle**; it is the source of all **igneous rocks**.

**malnutrition** The condition of being poorly nourished, as contrasted with **undernutrition**, which is lack of a sufficient quantity of food. The diet of a malnourished person may be high in starchy foods but is invariably low in protein and essential minerals and vitamins.

**mantle** The largest of the concentric zones of the Earth's structure, overlying the **core** and surrounded in turn by the **crust**.

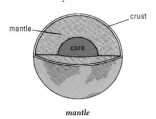

*mantle*

**manufacturing industry** The making of articles using physical labour or machinery, especially on a large scale. *See* **secondary sector**.

**map** Diagrammatic representation of an area – for example part of the earth's surface.

**map projection** A method by which the curved surface of the Earth is shown on a flat surface map. As it is not possible to show all the Earth's features accurately on a flat surface, some projections aim to show direction accurately at the expense of area, some the shape of the land and oceans, while others show correct area at the expense of accurate shape.

One of the projections most commonly used is the *Mercator projection*, devised in 1569, in which all lines of **latitude** are the same length as the equator. This results in increased distortion of area, moving from the equator towards the poles. This projection is suitable for navigation charts.

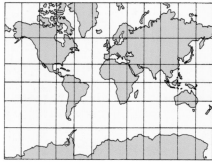

**map projection** *Mercator projection.*

The *Mollweide projection* shows the land masses the correct size in relation to each other but there is distortion of shape. As the Mollweide projection has no area distortion it is useful for showing distributions such as population distribution.

The only true representation of the Earth's surface is a globe.

**map projection** *Mollweide projection.*

**marble** A whitish, crystalline **metamorphic rock** produced when **limestone** is subjected to great heat or pressure (or both) during Earth movements.

**maritime climate** A **temperate climate** that is affected by the closeness of the sea, giving a small annual range of temperatures – a coolish summer and a mild winter – and rainfall throughout the year. Britain has a maritime climate. *Compare* **extreme climate.**

**market gardening** An intensive type of **agriculture** traditionally located on the margins of urban areas to supply fresh produce on a daily basis to the city population. Typical market-garden produce includes salad crops, such as tomatoes, lettuce, cucumber, etc., cut flowers, fruit and some green vegetables.

**mask** A method of hiding features on a map to improve legibility.

**maximum and minimum thermometer**
An instrument for recording the highest and lowest temperatures over a 24-hour period.

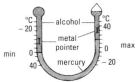

**maximum and minimum thermometer**

**meander** A large bend, especially in the middle or lower stages of a river's course. *See* **flood plain**. A meander is the result of lateral **corrasion**, which becomes dominant over vertical corrasion as the **gradient** of the river's course decreases. The characteristic features of a meander are summarized in the diagrams below. *See also* **oxbow lake.**

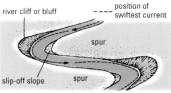

**meander** *A river meander.*

**meander** *Fully formed meanders.*

**mesa** A flat-topped, isolated hill in arid regions.

A mesa has a protective cap of hard **rock** underlain by softer, more readily eroded **sedimentary rock**. A **butte** is a relatively small outlier of a mesa.

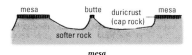

*mesa*

**mesosphere** *See* **atmosphere**.

**metadata** All Information used to describe content, quality, condition, origin and other characteristics of data.

**metamorphic rock** A **rock** which has been changed by intensive heat or pressure. Metamorphism implies an increase in hardness and resistance to **erosion**. Shale, for example, may be metamorphosed by pressure into **slate**; **sandstone** by heat into **quartzite**, **limestone** into **marble**. Metamorphism of pre-existing rocks is associated with the processes of **folding**, **faulting** and **vulcanicity**.

**migration** A permanent or semipermanent change of residence.

**monoculture** The growing of a single crop.

**monsoon** The term strictly means 'seasonal wind' and is used generally to describe a situation where there is a reversal of wind direction from one season to another. This is especially the case in South and Southeast Asia, where two monsoon winds occur, both related to the extreme pressure gradients created by the large land mass of the Asian continent.

**moraine** A collective term for debris deposited on or by **glaciers** and ice bodies in general. Several types of moraine are recognized: *lateral* moraine forms along the edges of a valley glacier where debris eroded from the valley sides, or weathered from the slopes above the glacier, collects; *medial* moraine forms where two lateral moraines meet at a glacier junction; *englacial* moraine is material which is trapped within the body of the glacier; and *ground* moraine is material eroded from the floor of the valley and used by the glacier as an abrasive tool. A *terminal* moraine is material bulldozed by the glacier during its advance and deposited at its maximum down-valley extent. *Recessional* moraines may be deposited at standstills during a period of general glacial retreat.

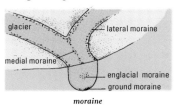

*moraine*

**mortlake** *See* **oxbow lake**.

**mountain** A natural upward projection of the Earth's surface, higher and steeper than a hill, and often having a rocky summit.

# N

**national park** An area of scenic countryside protected by law from uncontrolled development. A national park has two main functions:
(a) to conserve the natural beauty of the landscape;
(b) to enable the public to visit and enjoy the countryside for leisure and recreation.

**natural hazard** A natural event which, in extreme cases, can lead to loss of life and destruction of property. Some natural hazards result from geological events, such as **earthquakes** and the eruption of **volcanoes**, whilst others are due to weather events such as **hurricanes**, floods and droughts.

**natural increase** The increase in population due to the difference between **birth rate** and **death rate**.

**neap tides** *See* **tides**.

**névé** Compact snow. In a **corrie** icefield, for example, four layers are recognized: blue and white ice at the bottom of the ice mass; névé overlying the ice and powder snow on the surface.

**new town** A new urban location created
(a) to provide overspill accommodation for a large city or **conurbation**;
(b) to provide a new focus for industrial development.

**newly industrialized country (NIC)**
A **developing country** which is becoming industrialized, for example Malaysia and Thailand. Some NICs have successfully used large-scale development to move into the industrialized world. Usually the capital for such developments comes from outside the country.

**nivation** The process of **weathering** by snow and ice, particularly through **freeze-thaw** action. Particularly active in cold **climates** and high altitudes – for example on exposed slopes above a **glacier**.

**node** A point representing the beginning or ending point of an edge or arc.

**nomadic pastoralism** A system of **agriculture** in dry grassland regions. People and stock (cattle, sheep, goats) are continually moving in search of pasture and water. The pastoralists subsist on meat, milk and other animal products.

**non-governmental organizations (NGOs)** Independent organizations, such as charities (Oxfam, Water Aid) which provide aid and expertise to economically developing countries.

**nonrenewable resources** Resources of which there is a fixed supply, which will eventually be exhausted. Examples of these are metal ores and **fossil fuels**. *Compare* **renewable resources**.

**North and South** A way of dividing the industrialized nations, found predominantly in the North from those less developed nations in the South. The gap which exists between the rich 'North' and the poor 'South' is called the *development gap*.

**northings** The second element of a **grid reference**. *See* **eastings**.

**nuclear power station** An electricity-generating plant using nuclear fuel as an alternative to the conventional **fossil fuels** of coal, oil and gas.

**nuée ardente** A very hot and fast-moving cloud of gas, ash and rock that flows close to the ground after a violent ejection from a volcano. It is very destructive.

**nunatak** A mountain peak projecting above the general level of the ice near the edge of an **ice sheet**.

**nutrient cycle** The cycling of nutrients through the **environment**.

# O

**ocean** A large area of sea. The world's oceans are the Pacific, Atlantic, Indian and Arctic. The Southern Ocean is made up of the areas of the Pacific, Atlantic and Indian Oceans south of latitude 60°S.

**ocean current** A movement of the surface water of an ocean.

**opencast mining** A type of mining where the mineral is extracted by direct excavation rather than by shaft or drift methods.

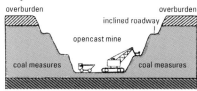

*opencast mining*

**organic farming** A system of farming that avoids the use of any artificial fertilizers or chemical pesticides, using only organic fertilizers and pesticides derived directly from animal or vegetable matter. Yields from organic farming are lower, but the products are sold at a premium price.

**overfold** *See* **fold**.

**oxbow lake, mortlake** *or* **cut-off**
A crescent-shaped lake originating in a **meander** that was abandoned when **erosion** breached the neck between bends, allowing the stream to flow straight on, bypassing the meander. The ends of the meander rapidly silt up and it becomes separated from the river.

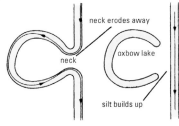

*oxbow lake*

**ozone** A form of oxygen found in a layer in the **stratosphere**, where it protects the Earth's surface from ultraviolet rays.

# P

**Pangaea** The supercontinent or universal land mass in which all continents were joined together approximately 200 million years ago. *See* **continental drift**.

**passage** *See* **strait**.

**pastoral farming** A system of farming in which the raising of livestock is the dominant element. *See also* **nomadic pastoralism**.

**peasant agriculture** The growing of crops or raising of animals, partly for subsistence needs and partly for market sale. Peasant agriculture is thus an intermediate stage between subsistence and commercial farming.

**peat** Partially decayed and compressed vegetative

matter accumulating in areas of high rainfall and/ or poor **drainage**.

**peneplain** A region that has been eroded until it is almost level. The more resistant rocks will stand above the general level of the land.

**per capita income** The **GNI** (gross national income) of a country divided by the size of its population. It gives the average income per head of the population if the national income were shared out equally. Per capita income comparisons are used as one indicator of levels of economic development.

**periglacial features** A periglacial landscape is one which has not been glaciated *per se*, but which has been affected by the severe **climate** prevailing around the ice margin.

**permafrost** The permanently frozen subsoil that is a feature of areas of **tundra**.

**permeable rock** Rock through which water can pass via a network of pores between the grains. *Compare* **pervious rock**. *See also* **impermeable rock**.

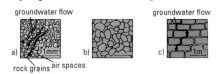

*permeable rock* (**a**) *Permeable rock*, (**b**) *impermeable rock*, (**c**) *pervious rock*.

**pervious rock** Rock which, even if non-porous, can allow water to pass through via interconnected joints, bedding planes and fissures. An example is **limestone**. *Compare* **permeable rock**. *See also* **impervious rock**.

**photosynthesis** The process by which green plants make carbohydrates from carbon dioxide and water, and give off oxygen. Photosynthesis balances **respiration**.

**physical feature** *See* **topography**.

**physical geography** The study of our **environment**, comprising such elements as geomorphology, hydrology, pedology, meteorology, climatology and biogeography.

**pie chart** A circular graph for displaying values as proportions:

The journey to work: mode of transport. (Sample of urban population)

| Mode | No. | % | Sector° (% x 3.6) |
|---|---|---|---|
| Foot | 25 | 3.2 | 11.5 |
| Cycle | 10 | 1.3 | 4.7 |
| Bus | 86 | 11.1 | 40.0 |
| Train | 123 | 15.9 | 57.2 |
| Car | 530 | 68.5 | 246.6 |
| Total | 774 | 100 | 360 |
|  |  | per cent | degrees |

*pie chart*

**plain** A level or almost level area of land.

**plantation agriculture** A system of **agriculture** located in a tropical or semi-tropical **environment**, producing commodities for export to Europe, North America and other industrialized regions. Coffee, tea, bananas, rubber and sisal are examples of plantation crops.

**plateau** An upland area with a fairly flat surface and steep slopes. Rivers often dissect plateau surfaces.

**plate tectonics** The theory that the Earth's **crust** is divided into seven large, rigid plates, and several smaller ones, which are moving relative to each other over the upper layers of the Earth's **mantle**. *See* **continental drift**. **Earthquakes** and volcanic activity occur at the boundaries between the plates.

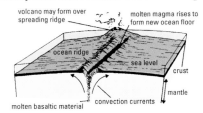

*a) Constructive plate boundary*

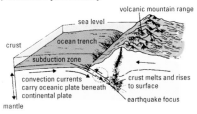

*b) Destructive plate boundary*

*plate tectonics*

**plucking** A process of glacial **erosion** whereby, during the passage of a valley **glacier** or other ice body, ice forming in cracks and fissures drags out material from a **rock** face. This is particularly the case with the backwall of a **corrie**.

**plug** The solidified material which seals the vent of a **volcano** after an eruption.

**plutonic rock** **Igneous rock** formed at depth in the Earth's **crust**; its crystals are large due to the slow rate of cooling. **Granite**, such as is found in **batholiths** and other deep-seated intrusions, is a common example.

**podzol** The characteristic **soil** of the **taiga** coniferous forests of Canada and northern Russia. Podzols are leached, greyish soils: iron and lime especially are leached out of the upper horizons, to be deposited as *hardpan* in the B **horizon**.

**pollution** Environmental damage caused by improper management of **resources**, or by careless human activity.

**polygons** Closed shapes defined by a connected sequences of coordinate pairs, where the first and last coordinate pair are the same.

**polyline** A series of connected segments which form a path to define a shape.

**population change** The increase of a population, the components of which are summarized in the following diagram.

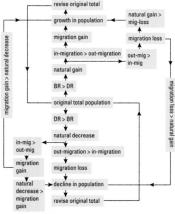

BR= birth rate    DR= death rate

*population change*

**population density** The number of people per unit area. Population densities are usually expressed per square kilometre.

**population distribution** The pattern of population location at a given **scale**.

**population explosion** On a global **scale**, the dramatic increase in population during the 20th century. The graph below shows world **population growth**.

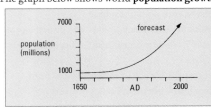

*population explosion*

**population growth** An increase in the population of a given region. This may be the result of natural increase (more births than deaths) or of in-migration, or both.

**population pyramid** A type of **bar graph** used to show population structure, i.e. the age and sex composition of the population for a given region or nation.

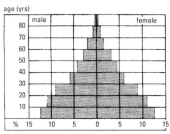

*a) population pyramid* Pyramid for India, showing high birth rates and death rates.

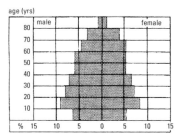

*b) population pyramid* Pyramid for England and Wales, showing low birth and death rates.

**pothole** 1. A deep hole in limestone, caused by the enlargement of a **joint** through the dissolving effect of rainwater.

2. A hollow scoured in a river bed by the swirling of pebbles and small boulders in eddies.

**precipitation** Water deposited on the Earth's surface in the form of e.g. rain, snow, sleet, hail and dew.

**prevailing wind** The dominant wind direction of a region. Prevailing winds are named by the direction from which they blow.

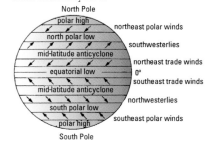

**primary keys** A set of properties in a database that uniquely identifies each record.

**primary sector** That sector of the national economy which deals with the production of primary materials: **agriculture**, mining, forestry and fishing. Primary products such as these have had no processing or manufacturing involvement. The total economy comprises the primary sector, the **secondary sector**, the **tertiary sector** and the **quaternary sector**.

**primary source** *See* **secondary source**.

**prime meridian** *or* **Greenwich Meridian** The line of 0° longitude passing through Greenwich in London.

**pumped storage** Water pumped back up to the storage lake of a **hydroelectric power** station, using surplus 'off-peak' electricity.

**pyramidal peak** A pointed mountain summit resulting from the headward extension of **corries** and **arêtes**. Under glacial conditions a given summit may develop corries on all sides, especially those facing north and east. As these erode into the summit, a formerly rounded profile may be changed into a pointed, steep-sided peak.

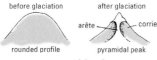

***pyramidal peak***

**pyroclasts** Rocky debris emitted during a volcanic eruption, usually following a previous emission of gases and prior to the outpouring of **lava** – although many eruptions do not reach the final lava stage.

# Q

**quality of life** The level of wellbeing of a community and of the area in which the community lives.

**quartz** One of the commonest minerals found in the Earth's **crust**, and a form of silica (silicon+oxide). Most **sandstones** are composed predominantly of quartz.

**quartzite** A very hard and resistant **rock** formed by the metamorphism of **sandstone**.

**quaternary sector** That sector of the economy providing information and expertise. This includes the microchip and microelectronics industries. Highly developed economies are seeing an increasing number of their workforce employed in this sector. *Compare* **primary sector**, **secondary sector**, **tertiary sector**.

**query** A request to select features or records from a database.

# R

**rain gauge** An instrument used to measure rainfall. Rain passes through a funnel into the jar below and

***rain gauge***

is then transferred to a measuring cylinder. The reading is in millimetres and indicates the depth of rain which has fallen over an area. *See* diagram.

**raised beach** *See* **wave-cut platform**.

**range** A long series or chain of mountains.

**rapids** An area of broken, turbulent water in a river channel, caused by a stratum of resistant **rock** that dips downstream. The softer rock immediately upstream and downstream erodes more quickly, leaving the resistant rock sticking up, obstructing the flow of the water. *Compare* **waterfall**.

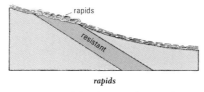

***rapids***

**raster** A pattern of closely spaced rows of dots that form an image.

**raw materials** The **resources** supplied to industries for subsequent manufacturing processes.

**reef** A ridge of rock, sand or coral whose top lies close to the sea's surface.

**regeneration** Renewed growth of, for example, forest after felling. Forest regeneration is crucial to the long-term stability of many **resource** systems, from **bush fallowing** to commercial forestry.

**region** An area of land which has marked boundaries or unifying internal characteristics. Geographers may identify regions according to physical, climatic, political, economic or other factors.

**rejuvenation** Renewed vertical **corrasion** by rivers in their middle and lower courses, caused by a fall in sea level, or a rise in the level of land relative to the sea.

**relative humidity** The relationship between the actual amount of water vapour in the air and the amount of vapour the air could hold at a particular temperature. This is usually expressed as a percentage. Relative humidity gives a measure of dampness in the **atmosphere**, and this can be determined by a **hygrometer**.

**relief** The differences in height between any parts of the Earth's surface. Hence a relief map will aim to show differences in the height of land by, for example, **contour** lines or by a colour key.

**remote sensing** The gathering of information by the use of electronic or other sensing devices in satellites.

**renewable resources** Resources that can be used repeatedly, given appropriate management and conservation. *Compare* **non-renewable resources**.

**representative fraction** The fraction of real size to which objects are reduced on a map; for example, on a 1:50 000 map, any object is shown at 1/50 000 of its real size.

**reserves** Resources which are available for future use.

**reservoir** A natural or artificial lake used for collecting or storing water, especially for water supply or **irrigation**.

**resolution** The smallest allowable separation between two coordinate values in a feature class.

**resource** Any aspect of the human and physical **environments** which people find useful in satisfying their needs.

**respiration** The release of energy from food in the cells of all living organisms (plants as well as animals). The process normally requires oxygen and releases carbon dioxide. It is balanced by **photosynthesis**.

**revolution** The passage of the Earth around the sun; one revolution is completed in 365.25 days. Due to the tilt of the Earth's axis ($23\frac{1}{2}°$ from the vertical), revolution results in the sequence of seasons experienced on the Earth's surface.

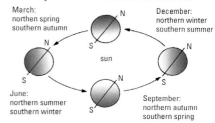

***revolution*** *The seasons of the year.*

**ria** A submerged river valley, caused by a rise in sea level or a subsidence of the land relative to the sea.

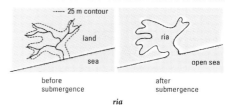

***ria***

**ribbon lake** A long, relatively narrow lake, usually occupying the floor of a U-shaped glaciated valley. A ribbon lake may be caused by the *overdeepening* of a section of the valley floor by glacial **abrasion**.

**Richter scale** A scale of **earthquake** measurement that describes the magnitude of an earthquake according to the amount of energy released, as recorded by **seismographs**.

**rift valley** A section of the Earth's **crust** which has been downfaulted. The **faults** bordering the rift valley are approximately parallel. There are two main theories related to the origin of rift valleys. The first states that tensional forces within the Earth's crust have caused a block of land to sink between parallel faults. The second theory states that compression within the Earth's crust has caused faulting in which two side blocks have risen up towards each other over a central block.

The most complex rift valley system in the world is that ranging from Syria in the Middle East to the river Zambezi in East Africa.

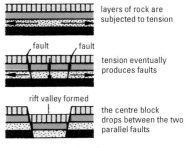

***rift valley***

**river** A large natural stream of fresh water flowing along a definite course, usually into the sea.

**river basin** The area drained by a river and its tributaries, sometimes referred to as a **catchment** area.

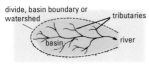

*river basin*

**river cliff** *or* **bluff** The outer bank of a **meander**. The cliff is kept steep by undercutting since river **erosion** is concentrated on the outer bank. *See* **meander** and **river's course**.

**river's course** The route taken by a river from its source to the sea. There are three major sections: the upper course, middle course and lower course.

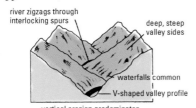

*river's course* Upper course.

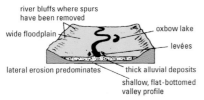

*river's course* Lower course.

**river terrace** A platform of land beside a river. This is produced when a river is **rejuvenated** in its middle or lower courses. The river cuts down into its **flood plain**, which then stands above the new general level of the river as paired terraces.

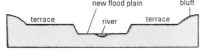

*river terrace* Paired river terraces above a flood plain.

**roche moutonnée** An outcrop of resistant **rock** sculpted by the passage of a **glacier**.

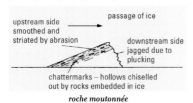

*roche moutonnée*

**rock** The solid material of the Earth's **crust**. *See* **igneous rock**, **sedimentary rock**, **metamorphic rock**.

**rotation** The movement of the Earth about its own axis. One rotation is completed in 24 hours. Due to the tilt of the Earth's axis, the length of day and night varies at different points on the Earth's surface. Days become longer with increasing latitude north; shorter with increasing latitude south. The situation is reversed during the northern midwinter (= the southern midsummer). *See* diagram.

**rural depopulation** The loss of population from the countryside as people move away from rural areas towards cities and **conurbations**.

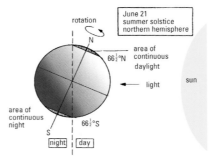

*rotation* The tilt of the Earth at the northern summer and southern winter solstice.

**rural–urban migration** The movement of people from rural to urban areas. *See* **migration** and **rural depopulation**.

# S

**saltpan** A shallow basin, usually in a desert region, containing salt which has been deposited from an evaporated salt lake.

**sandstone** A common **sedimentary rock** deposited by either wind or water. Sandstones vary in texture from fine- to coarse- grained, but are invariably composed of grains of **quartz**, cemented by such substances as calcium carbonate or silica.

**satellite image** An image giving information about an area of the Earth or another planet, obtained from a satellite. Instruments on an Earth-orbiting satellite, such as Landsat, continually scan the Earth and sense the brightness of reflected light. When the information is sent back to Earth, computers turn it into *false-colour images* in which built-up areas appear in one colour (perhaps blue), vegetation in another (often red), bare ground in a third, and water in a fourth colour, making it easy to see their distribution and to monitor any changes. *Compare* **aerial photograph**.

**savanna** The grassland regions of Africa which lie between the **tropical rainforest** and the hot **deserts**. In South America, the *Llanos* and *Campos* regions are representative of the savanna type.

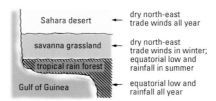

*savanna* The position of the savanna in West Africa.

**scale** The size ratio represented by a map; for example, on a map of scale 1:25 000, the real landscape is portrayed at 1/25 000 of its actual size.

**scarp slope** The steeper of the two slopes which comprise an **escarpment** of inclined **strata**. *Compare* **dip slope**.

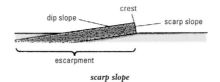

*scarp slope*

**science park** A site accommodating several companies involved in scientific work or research.

Science parks are linked to universities and tend to be located on **greenfield** and/or landscaped sites. *Compare* **business park**.

**scree** *or* **talus** The accumulated **weathering** debris below a **crag** or other exposed rock face. Larger boulders will accumulate at the base of the scree, carried there by greater momentum.

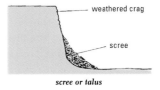

*scree or talus*

**sea level** The average height of the surface of the oceans and seas.

**secondary sector** The sector of the economy which comprises manufacturing and processing industries, in contrast with the **primary sector** which produces **raw materials**, the **tertiary sector** which provides **services**, and the **quaternary sector** which provides information.

**secondary source** A supply of information or data that has been researched or collected by an individual or group of people and made available for others to use; census data is an example of this. A *primary source* of data or information is one collected at first hand by the researcher who needs it; for example, a traffic count in an area, undertaken by a student for his or her own project.

**sediment** The material resulting from the **weathering** and **erosion** of the landscape, which has been deposited by water, ice or wind. It may be reconsolidated to form **sedimentary rock**.

**sedimentary rock** A rock which has been formed by the consolidation of **sediment** derived from pre-existing rocks. **Sandstone** is a common example of a rock formed in this way. **Chalk** and **limestone** are other types of sedimentary rock, derived from organic and chemical precipitations.

**seif dune** A linear sand dune, the ridge of sand lying parallel to the prevailing wind direction. The eddying movement of the wind keeps the sides of the dune steep.

*seif dunes*

**seismograph** An instrument which measures and records the seismic waves which travel through the Earth during an **earthquake**.

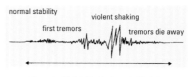

*seismograph* A typical seismograph trace.

**seismology** The study of **earthquakes**.

**serac** A pinnacle of ice formed by the tumbling and shearing of a **glacier** at an ice fall, i.e. the broken ice associated with a change in **gradient** of the valley floor.

**service industry** The people and organizations that provide a service to the public.

**settlement** Any location chosen by people as a permanent or semi-permanent dwelling place.

**shading map** *or* **choropleth map** A map in which shading of varying intensity is used. For example, the pattern of **population densities** in a region.

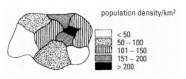
*shading map*

**shanty town** An area of unplanned, random, urban development often around the edge of a city. The shanty town is a major element of the structure of many **Third World** cities such as São Paulo, Mexico City, Nairobi, Kolkata and Lagos. The shanty town is characterized by high-density/low-quality dwellings, often constructed from the simplest materials such as scrap wood, corrugated iron and plastic sheeting – and by the lack of standard services such as sewerage and water supply, power supplies and refuse collection.

**shape files** A storage format for storing the location, shape and attributes of geographic features.

**shifting cultivation** *See* **bush fallowing**.

**shoreface terrace** A bank of **sediment** accumulating at the change of slope which marks the limit of a marine **wave-cut platform**.

Material removed from the retreating cliff base is transported by the undertow off the wave-cut platform to be deposited in deeper water offshore.

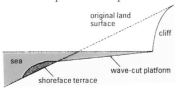
*shoreface terrace*

**silage** Any **fodder crop** harvested whilst still green. The crop is kept succulent by partial fermentation in a *silo*. It is used as animal feed during the winter.

**sill 1.** An igneous intrusion of roughly horizontal disposition. *See* **igneous rock**.
**2.** (Also called **threshold**) the lip of a **corrie**.

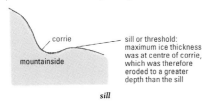
*sill*

**silt** Fine **sediment**, the component particles of which have a mean diameter of between 0.002 mm and 0.02 mm.

**sinkhole** *See* **pothole**.

**slash and burn** *See* **tropical rainforest**.

**slate** Metamorphosed shale or **clay**. Slate is a dense, fine-grained **rock** distinguished by the characteristic of *perfect cleavage*, i.e. it can be split along a perfectly smooth plane.

**slip** The amount of vertical displacement of **strata** at a **fault**.

**smog** A mixture of smoke and fog associated with urban and industrial areas, that creates an unhealthy **atmosphere**.

**snow line** The altitude above which permanent snow exists, and below which any snow that falls will not persist during the summer months.

**socioeconomic group** A group defined by particular social and economic characteristics, such as educational qualifications, type of job, and earnings.

**soil** The loose material which forms the uppermost layer of the Earth's surface, composed of the *inorganic fraction*, i.e. material derived from the **weathering** of bedrock, and the *organic fraction* – that is material derived from the decay of vegetable matter.

**soil erosion** The accelerated breakdown and removal of soil due to poor management. Soil erosion is particularly a problem in harsh **environments**.

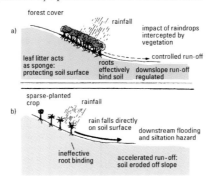
*soil erosion a) Stable environment, b) unstable environment.*

**soil profile** The sequence of layers or **horizons** usually seen in an exposed soil section.

**solar power** Heat radiation from the sun converted into electricity or used directly to provide heating. Solar power is an example of a renewable source of energy (*see* **renewable resources**).

**solifluction** A process whereby thawed surface soil creeps downslope over a permanently frozen **subsoil (permafrost)**.

**spatial distribution** The pattern of locations of, for example, population or **settlement** in a region.

**spit** A low, narrow bank of sand and shingle built out into an **estuary** by the process of **longshore drift**.

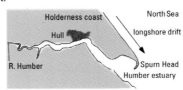
*spit Spurn Head, a coastal spit.*

**spring** The emergence of an underground stream at the surface, often occurring where **impermeable rock** underlies **permeable rock** or **pervious rock** or **strata**.

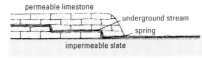
*spring Rainwater enters through the fissures of the limestone and the stream springs out where the limestone meets slate.*

**spring tides** *See* **tides**.

**squatter settlement** An area of peripheral urban settlement in which the residents occupy land to which they have no legal title. *See* **shanty town**.

**stack** A coastal feature resulting from the collapse

of a natural arch. The stack remains after less resistant **strata** have been worn away by **weathering** and marine **erosion**.

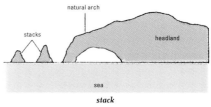
*stack*

**stalactite** A column of calcium carbonate hanging from the roof of a **limestone** cavern. As water passes through the limestone it dissolves a certain proportion, which is then precipitated by **evaporation** of water droplets dripping from the cavern roof. The drops splashing on the floor of a cavern further evaporate to precipitate more calcium carbonate as a **stalagmite**.

**stalagmite** A column of calcium carbonate growing upwards from a cavern floor. *Compare* **stalactite**. Stalactites and stalagmites may meet, forming a column or pillar.

**staple diet** The basic foodstuff which comprises the daily meals of a given people.

**stereoplotter** An instrument used for projecting an aerial photograph and converting locations of objects on the image to x-, y-, and z-coordinates. It plots these coordinates as a map.

**Stevenson's screen** A shelter used in weather stations, in which thermometers and other instruments may be hung.

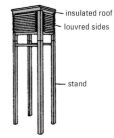
*Stevenson's screen*

**strait, channel** *or* **passage** A narrow body of water, between two land masses, which links two larger bodies of water.

**strata** Layers of **rock** superimposed one upon the other.

**stratosphere** The layer of the **atmosphere** which lies immediately above the troposphere and below the mesosphere and ionosphere. Within the stratosphere, temperature increases with altitutude.

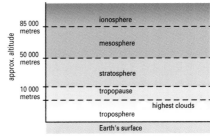
*stratosphere*

**stratus** Layer-cloud of uniform grey appearance, often associated with the warm sector of a **depression**. Stratus is a type of low **cloud** which may hang as mist over mountain tops.

**striations** The grooves and scratches left on bare **rock** surfaces by the passage of a **glacier**.

**strip cropping** A method of **soil** conservation whereby different crops are planted in a series of strips, often following **contours** around a hillside. The purpose of such a sequence of cultivation is to arrest the downslope movement of soil. *See* **soil erosion.**

**subduction zone** *See* **plate tectonics.**

**subsistence agriculture** A system of **agriculture** in which farmers produce exclusively for their own consumption, in contrast to **commercial agriculture** where farmers produce purely for sale at the market.

**subsoil** *See* **soil profile.**

**suburbs** The outer, and largest, parts of a town or city.

**surface run-off** That proportion of rainfall received at the Earth's surface which runs off either as channel flow or overland flow. It is distinguished from the rest of the rainfall, which either percolates into the soil or evaporates back into the **atmosphere.**

**sustainable development** The ability of a country to maintain a level of economic development, thus enabling the majority of the population to have a reasonable standard of living.

**swallow hole** *See* **pothole.**

**swash** The rush of water up the beach as a wave breaks. *See also* **backwash** and **longshore drift.**

**syncline** A trough in folded **strata**; the opposite of **anticline.** *See* **fold.**

# T

**taiga** The extensive **coniferous forests** of Siberia and Canada, lying immediately south of the arctic **tundra.**

**talus** *See* **scree.**

**tarn** The postglacial lake which often occupies a **corrie.**

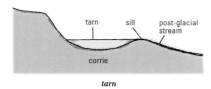

*tarn*

**temperate climate** A climate typical of mid-latitudes. Such a climate is intermediate between the extremes of hot (tropical) and cold (polar) climates. *Compare* **extreme climate.** *See also* **maritime climate.**

**terminal moraine** *See* **moraine.**

**terracing** A means of **soil** conservation and land utilization whereby steep hillsides are engineered into a series of flat ledges which can be used for **agriculture**, held in places by stone banks to prevent **soil erosion.**

*terracing*

**tertiary sector** That sector of the economy which provides **services** such as transport, finance and

retailing, as opposed to the **primary sector** which provides **raw materials**, the **secondary sector** which processes and manufactures products, and the **quaternary sector** which provides information and expertise.

**thermal power station** An electricity-generating plant which burns **coal**, oil or natural gas to produce steam to drive turbines.

**Third World** A collective term for the poor nations of Africa, Asia and Latin America, as opposed to the 'first world' of capitalist, developed nations and the 'second world' of formerly communist, developed nations. The terminology is far from satisfactory as there are great social and political variations within the 'Third World'. Indeed, there are some countries where such extreme poverty prevails that these could be regarded as a fourth group. Alternative terminology includes '**developing countries**', 'economically developing countries' and 'less economically developed countries' (LEDC). **Newly industrialized countries** are those showing greatest economic development.

**threshold** *See* **sill** (sense 2).

**tidal range** The mean difference in water level between high and low tides at a given location. *See* **tides.**

**tides** The alternate rise and fall of the surface of the sea, approximately twice a day, caused by the gravitational pull of the moon and, to a lesser extent, of the sun.

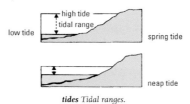

*tides* Tidal ranges.

**till** *See* **boulder clay.**

**tombolo** A **spit** which extends to join an island to the mainland.

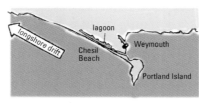

*tombolo* Chesil Beach, England.

**topography** The composition of the visible landscape, comprising both physical features and those made by people.

**topsoil** The uppermost layer of **soil**, more rich in organic matter than the underlying **subsoil**. *See* **horizon, soil profile.**

**tornado** A violent storm with winds circling around a small area of extremely low pressure. Characterized by a dark funnel-shaped cloud. Winds associated with tornadoes can reach speeds of over 480 km/h (300 mph).

**trade winds** Winds which blow from the subtropical belts of high pressure towards the equatorial belt of low pressure. In the northern hemisphere, the winds blow from the northeast and in the southern hemisphere from the southeast.

**transhumance** The practice whereby herds of farm

animals are moved between regions of different climates. Pastoral farmers (*see* **pastoral farming**) take their herds from valley pastures in the winter to mountain pastures in the summer. *See also* **alp.**

**transnational corporation (TNC)** A company that has branches in many countries of the world, and often controls the production of the primary product and the sale of the finished article.

**tributary** A stream or river which feeds into a larger one. *Compare* **distributary.**

**tropical rainforest** The dense forest cover of the equatorial regions, reaching its greatest extent in the Amazon Basin of South America, the Congo Basin of Africa, and in parts of Southeast Asia and Indonesia. There has been much concern in recent years about the rate at which the world's rainforests are being cut down and burnt. The burning of large tracts of rainforest is thought to be contributing to **global warming**. Many governments and **conservation** bodies are now examining ways of protecting the remaining rainforests, which are unique **ecosystems** containing millions of plant and animal species.

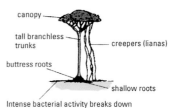

Intense bacterial activity breaks down fallen leaves, etc., to return nutrients to soil surface for immediate uptake by roots. Soils themselves are infertile: the nutrient cycle is concentrated in the vegetation and top few inches of soil.

*a forest giant in the tropical rainforest*

**tropics** The region of the Earth lying between the *tropics of Cancer* ($23\frac{1}{2}$°N) and *Capricorn* ($23\frac{1}{2}$°S). *See* **latitude.**

**troposphere** *See* **atmosphere.**

**trough** An area of low pressure, not sufficiently well-defined to be regarded as a **depression.**

**truncated spur** A spur of land that previously projected into a valley and has been completely or partially cut off by a moving **glacier.**

**tsunami** A very large, and often destructive, sea wave produced by a submarine **earthquake**. Tsunamis tend to occur along the coasts of Japan and parts of the Pacific Ocean, and can be the cause of large numbers of deaths.

**tuff** Volcanic ash or dust which has been consolidated into **rock.**

**tundra** The barren, often bare-rock plains of the far north of North America and Eurasia where subarctic conditions prevail and where, as a result, vegetation is restricted to low-growing, hardy shrubs and mosses and lichens.

**typhoon** *See* **hurricane.**

# U

**undernutrition** A lack of a sufficient quantity of food, as distinct from **malnutrition** which is a consequence of an unbalanced diet.

**urban decay** The process of deterioration in the **infrastructure** of parts of the city. It is the result of

long-term shifts in patterns of economic activity, residential **location** and **infrastructure**.

**urban sprawl** The growth in extent of an urban area in response to improvements in transport and rising incomes, both of which allow a greater physical separation of home and work.

**urbanization** The process by which a national population becomes predominantly urban through a **migration** of people from the countryside to cities, and a shift from agricultural to industrial employment.

**U-shaped valley** A glaciated valley, characteristically straight in plan and U-shaped in **cross section**. *See* diagram. *Compare* **V-shaped valley**.

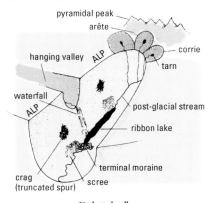

**U-shaped valley**

# V

**valley** A long depression in the Earth's surface, usually containing a river, formed by **erosion** or by movements in the Earth's **crust**.

**vector** A quantity that has both magnitude and direction.

**vegetation** The plant life of a particular region.

**viscous lava** **Lava** that resists the tendency to flow. It is sticky, flows slowly and congeals rapidly. *Non-viscous* lava is very fluid, flows quickly and congeals slowly.

**volcanic rock** A category of **igneous rock** which comprises those rocks formed from **magma** which has reached the Earth's surface. **Basalt** is an example of a volcanic rock.

**volcano** A fissure in the Earth's **crust** through which **magma** reaches the Earth's surface. There are four main types of volcano:
(a) *Acid lava cone* – a very steep-sided cone composed entirely of acidic, **viscous lava** which flows slowly and congeals very quickly.
(b) *Composite volcano* – a single cone comprising alternate layers of ash (or other **pyroclasts**) and lava.

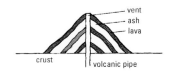

**volcano** Composite volcano.

(c) *Fissure volcano* – a volcano that erupts along a linear fracture in the crust, rather than from a single cone.
(d) *Shield volcano* – a volcano composed of very basic, non-viscous lava which flows quickly and

congeals slowly, producing a very gently sloping cone.

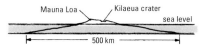

**volcano** Shield volcano.

**V-shaped valley** A narrow, steep-sided valley made by the rapid erosion of rock by streams and rivers. It is V-shaped in cross-section. *Compare* **U-shaped valley**.

**vulcanicity** A collective term for those processes which involve the intrusion of **magma** into the **crust**, or the extrusion of such molten material onto the Earth's surface.

# W

**wadi** A dry watercourse in an arid region; occasional rainstorms in the desert may cause a temporary stream to appear in a wadi.

**warm front** *See* **depression**.

**waterfall** An irregularity in the long profile of a **river's course**, usually located in the upper course. *Compare* **rapids**.

**waterfall**

**watershed** The boundary, often a ridge of high ground, between two **river basins**.

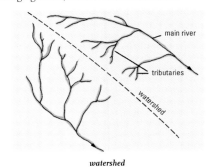

**watershed**

**water table** The level below which the ground is permanently saturated. The water table is thus the upper level of the **groundwater**. In areas where **permeable rock** predominates, the water table may be at some considerable depth.

**wave-cut platform** *or* **abrasion platform** A gently sloping surface eroded by the sea along a coastline.

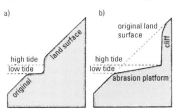

**wave-cut platform** a) Early in formation, b) later in formation.

**weather** The day-to-day conditions of e.g. rainfall, temperature and pressure, as experienced at a particular location.

**weather chart** A map or chart of an area giving

details of **weather** experienced at a particular time of day. Weather charts are sometimes called *synoptic charts*, as they give a synopsis of the weather at a particular time.

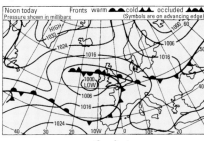

**weather chart**

**weather station** A place where all elements of the weather are measured and recorded. Each station will have a **Stevenson's screen** and a variety of instruments such as a **maximum and minimum thermometer**, a **hygrometer**, a **rain gauge**, a **wind vane** and an **anemometer**.

**weathering** The breakdown of rocks *in situ*; contrasted with **erosion** in that no large-scale transport of the denuded material is involved.

**wet and dry bulb thermometer** *See* **hygrometer**.

**wind vane** An instrument used to indicate wind direction. It consists of a rotating arm which always points in the direction from which the wind blows.

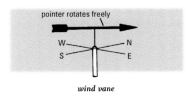

**wind vane**

# Y

**yardang** Long, roughly parallel ridges of **rock** in arid and semi-arid regions. The ridges are undercut by wind **erosion** and the corridors between them are swept clear of sand by the wind. The ridges are oriented in the direction of the prevailing wind.

**yield** The productivity of land as measured by the weight or volume of produce per unit area.

# Z

**zeugen** *Pedestal rocks* in arid regions; wind **erosion** is concentrated near the ground, where **corrasion** by wind-borne sand is most active. This leads to undercutting and the pedestal profile emerges.

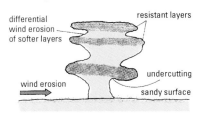

**zeugen**

## How to use the Index

All the names on the maps in this atlas, except some of those on the special topic maps, are included in the index.

The names are arranged in **alphabetical order.** Where the name has more than one word the separate words are considered as one to decide the position of the name in the index:

Thetford
The Trossachs
The Wash
The Weald
Thiers
Thiès

Where there is more than one place with the same name, the country name is used to decide the order:

London Canada
London England

If both places are in the same country, the county or state name is also used:

Avon *r.* Brist. England
Avon *r.* Dor. England

Each entry in the index starts with the name of the place or feature, followed by the name of the country or region in which it is located. This is followed by the number of the most appropriate page on which the name appears, usually the largest scale map. Next comes the alphanumeric reference followed by the latitude and longitude.

Names of physical features such as rivers, capes, mountains etc are followed by a description. The descriptions are usually shortened to one or two letters – these abbreviations are keyed below. Town names are followed by a description only when the name may be confused with that of a physical feature:

**Big Trout Lake** *town*

To help to distinguish the different parts of each entry, different styles of type are used:

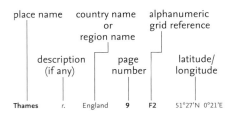

| | | |
|---|---|---|
| place name | country name or region name | alphanumeric grid reference |
| description (if any) | page number | latitude/ longitude |
| **Thames** | *r.* England **9** F2 | 51°27'N 0°21'E |

To use the **alphanumeric grid reference** to find a feature on the map, first find the correct page and then look at the letters and numbers printed outside the frame along the top, bottom and sides of the map.

When you have found the correct letter and number follow the grid boxes up and along until you find the correct grid box in which the feature appears. You must then search the grid box until you find the name of the feature.

The **latitude and longitude reference** gives a more exact description of the position of the feature.

Page 1 of the atlas describes lines of latitude and lines of longitude, and explains how they are numbered and divided into degrees and minutes. Each name in the index has a different latitude and longitude reference, so the feature can be located accurately. The lines of latitude and lines of longitude shown on each map are numbered in degrees. These numbers are printed in black along the top, bottom and sides of the map frame.

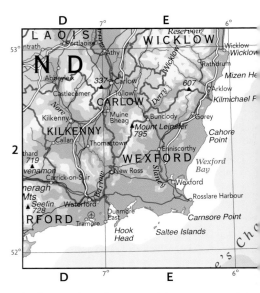

The drawing above shows part of the map on page 18 and the lines of latitude and lines of longitude.

The index entry for Wexford is given as follows:

**Wexford** Ireland **18** E2 ...................... 52°20'N 6°28'W

To locate Wexford, first find latitude 52°N and estimate 20 minutes north from 52 degrees to find 52°20'N, then find longitude 6°W and estimate 28 minutes west from 6 degrees to find 6°28'W. The symbol for the town of Wexford is where latitude 52°20'N and longitude 6°28'W meet.

On maps at a smaller scale than the map of Ireland, it is not possible to show every line of latitude and longitude. Only every 5 or 10 degrees of latitude and longitude may be shown. On these maps you must estimate the degrees and minutes to find the exact location of a feature.

## Abbreviations

| | | | | | |
|---|---|---|---|---|---|
| A. and B. | Argyll and Bute | *i.* | island | Oreg. | Oregon |
| Afgh. | Afghanistan | Ill. | Illinois | Orkn. | Orkney |
| Ala. | Alabama | I. o. W. | Isle of Wight | Oxon. | Oxfordshire |
| Ang. | Angus | *is* | islands | Pacific Oc. | Pacific Ocean |
| *b.* | bay | *l.* | lake | P. and K. | Perth and Kinross |
| Baja Calif. | Baja California | La. | Louisiana | P'boro. | Peterborough |
| Bangl. | Bangladesh | Lancs. | Lancashire | Pem. | Pembrokeshire |
| Bos. and Herz. | Bosnia and Herzegovina | Leics. | Leicestershire | *pen.* | peninsula |
| Brist. | Bristol | Lincs. | Lincolnshire | Phil. | Philippines |
| *c.* | cape | Lux. | Luxembourg | P.N.G. | Papua New Guinea |
| Cambs. | Cambridgeshire | Man. | Manitoba | *pt* | point |
| C.A.R. | Central African Republic | Mass. | Massachusetts | *r.* | river |
| Colo. | Colorado | Me. | Maine | *r. mouth* | river mouth |
| Corn. | Cornwall | Mich. | Michigan | *resr* | reservoir |
| Cumb. | Cumbria | Minn. | Minnesota | S. Africa | South Africa |
| *d.* | internal division e.g. county, state | Miss. | Mississippi | S. America | South America |
| Del. | Delaware | Mo. | Missouri | S. Atlantic Oc. | South Atlantic Ocean |
| Dem. Rep. Congo | Democratic Republic of the Congo | Mor. | Moray | S. C. | South Carolina |
| | | *mt.* | mountain | S. China Sea | South China Sea |
| Derbys. | Derbyshire | *mts* | mountains | Shetl. | Shetland |
| *des.* | desert | N. Africa | North Africa | S. Korea | South Korea |
| Dev. | Devon | Na h-E. S. | Na h-Eileanan Siar | Som. | Somerset |
| Dom. Rep. | Dominican Republic | N. America | North America | S. Pacific Oc. | South Pacific Ocean |
| Don. | Donegal | N. Atlantic Oc. | North Atlantic Ocean | *str.* | strait |
| Dor. | Dorset | *nature res.* | nature reserve | Suff. | Suffolk |
| Dur. | Durham | N. C. | North Carolina | Switz. | Switzerland |
| Equat. Guinea | Equatorial Guinea | Neth. | Netherlands | T. and W. | Tyne and Wear |
| Ess. | Essex | Neth. Antilles | Netherlands Antilles | Tel. Wre. | Telford and Wrekin |
| *est.* | estuary | Nev. | Nevada | Tex. | Texas |
| E. Sussex | East Sussex | New. | Newport | Tipp. | Tipperary |
| E. Yorks. | East Riding of Yorkshire | Nfld. and Lab. | Newfoundland and Labrador | U.A.E. | United Arab Emirates |
| *f.* | physical feature, e.g. valley, plain, geographic area | N. Korea | North Korea | U.K. | United Kingdom |
| | | N. M. | New Mexico | U.S.A. | United States of America |
| Falk. | Falkirk | N. Mariana Is | Northern Marianas Islands | Va. | Virginia |
| *g.* | gulf | Norf. | Norfolk | *vol.* | volcano |
| Ga. | Georgia | Northum. | Northumberland | Vt. | Vermont |
| Glos. | Gloucestershire | Notts. | Nottinghamshire | Water. | Waterford |
| Hants. | Hampshire | N. Pacific Oc. | North Pacific Ocean | Warwicks. | Warwickshire |
| High. | Highland | N. Y. | New York | Wick. | Wicklow |
| *hd* | headland | Oc. | Ocean | W. Va. | West Virginia |
| | | Oh. | Ohio | Wyo. | Wyoming |

France 9 H2.................................................51°00'N 2°07'E
nraa Denmark 43 B1......................................55°02'N 9°25'E
en Germany 46 B4........................................50°46'N 6°05'E
org Denmark 43 B2.......................................57°03'N 9°55'E
Germany 46 D3.........................................48°50'N 10°06'E
Belgium 42 D3...........................................50°56'N 4°03'E
us Denmark 43 B2........................................56°09'N 10°12'E
än Iran 95 G6.............................................30°20'N 48°15'E
eh Iran 95 H6.............................................31°08'N 52°36'E
la Algeria 84 D5..........................................31°00'N 2°43'W
an Russia 55 K3..........................................53°42'N 91°25'E
qū Iran 95 H6.............................................31°06'N 53°17'E
hiri Japan 104 D4........................................44°01'N 144°15'E
a, Lake Ethiopia 85 H2...................................6°19'N 37°53'E
a Russia 98 G8............................................52°40'N 90°06'E
ville France 44 D7........................................50°06'N 1°50'E
yfeale Ireland 18 E2......................................52°23'N 9°18'E
y Head Scotland 15 F2...................................54°46'N 3°58'W
yleix Ireland 18 D2.......................................52°55'N 7°21'W
ttabad Pakistan 95 L6....................................34°13'N 73°17'E
hé Chad 85 G3............................................13°50'N 20°49'E
kuta Nigeria 84 E2........................................7°07'N 3°18'E
aeron Wales 10 C4.......................................52°15'N 4°15'W
chirder Scotland 17 G2...................................57°34'N 2°38'W
dare Wales 10 D3.........................................51°43'N 3°27'W
daron Wales 10 C4........................................52°48'N 4°43'W
deen Scotland 17 G2......................................57°09'N 2°06'W
deen d. Scotland 20 D5...................................57°10'N 2°11'W
deen s. Russia 62 G6......................................45°28'N 98°31'W
deenshire d. Scotland 20 D5..............................57°21'N 2°32'W
feldy Scotland 17 F1.......................................56°37'N 3°52'W
ford England 13 F2.......................................53°50'N 1°21'W
foyle Scotland 14 E4......................................56°11'N 4°23'W
gavenny Wales 10 D3.....................................51°49'N 3°01'W
gele Wales 10 D5..........................................53°17'N 3°35'W
our Scotland 17 F2.......................................57°29'N 3°13'W
porth Wales 10 C4........................................52°08'N 4°33'W
soch Wales 10 C4.........................................52°50'N 4°30'W
sillery Wales 10 D3........................................51°44'N 3°08'W
ystwyth Wales 10 C4.....................................52°25'N 4°05'W
Saudi Arabia 94 F3.......................................18°14'N 42°27'E
an Côte d'Ivoire 84 D2...................................5°21'N 4°02'W
ne U.S.A. 62 G3...........................................32°26'N 99°45'W
gdon England 8 D2.......................................51°40'N 1°17'W
gton Scotland 15 F3......................................55°30'N 3°41'W
i, Lake Canada 63 J6.....................................48°55'N 80°01'W
azia d. Georgia 53 E2.....................................43°15'N 40°45'E
ne Scotland 17 G2........................................57°05'N 2°47'W
Saudi Arabia 95 G5.......................................25°56'N 49°42'E
Arīsh Saudi Arabia 94 F3................................16°59'N 42°45'E
Dhabi U.A.E. 95 H4......................................24°28'N 54°20'E
Hamed Sudan 85 H3.....................................19°30'N 33°24'E
Nigeria 84 E2............................................9°06'N 7°19'E
Kamäl Syria 94 F6.......................................34°26'N 40°56'E
Nujaym Libya 49 G3....................................30°28'N 15°27'E
Sunbul Egypt 94 D4......................................22°26'N 31°39'E
Sudan 94 C2.............................................13°46'N 26°26'E
iiza Spain 45 A5..........................................42°13'N 8°16'W
oneta Mexico 66 C5......................................22°30'N 105°25'W
lco Mexico 66 E4.........................................16°55'N 99°52'W
gua Venezuela 72 C7.....................................9°33'N 69°11'W
Ghana 84 D2.............................................5°35'N 0°14'W
ngton England 13 E2.....................................53°45'N 2°22'W
oös r. Greece 50 D4.......................................38°20'N 21°06'E
Island Ireland 18 A3......................................53°56'N 10°00'W
sk Russia 55 N3...........................................56°17'N 90°34'E
alaig mt. Scotland 16 D2.................................57°11'N 5°09'W
ns Island Bahamas 67 J5.................................22°18'N 74°08'W
England 9 G3.............................................52°38'N 1°33'E
cagua, Cerro mt. Argentina 73 B3.....................32°38'S 70°01'W
ruña Spain 45 A5.........................................43°22'N 8°23'W
r. Spain 45 C4.............................................41°33'N 4°51'W
's Peak China 96 F2......................................6°49'N 80°28'E
a Turkey 51 K3............................................36°59'N 35°19'E
azarı Turkey 51 L5........................................40°47'N 30°23'E
ahnä' des. Saudi Arabia 95 G5..........................20°40'N 46°52'E
bury England 8 D3........................................52°01'N 1°19'W
r'īyah Saudi Arabia 95 G4................................24°45'N 46°34'E
Ababa Ethiopia 85 H2....................................9°01'N 38°45'E
wänīyah Iraq 94 F6......................................31°59'N 44°59'E
ide Australia 108 C3.....................................34°56'S 138°40'E
Yemen 94 F2.............................................12°49'N 44°59'E
, Gulf of Somalia/Yemen 85 I3..........................11°44'N 45°16'E
Indonesia 103 I3.........................................4°15'S 133°27'E
rk'ay Ethiopia 94 E2.....................................13°24'N 38°03'E
at Ethiopia 94 E2.........................................14°16'N 39°29'E
gri Eritrea 94 E2..........................................14°52'N 38°48'E
man Turkey 51 M3........................................36°46'N 38°17'E
ralty Islands P.N.G. 108 D6..............................1°44'S 146°17'E
r r. France 44 E3..........................................43°32'N 1°33'E
tic Sea Europe 48 F5......................................44°19'N 13°24'E
Ethiopia 85 H3...........................................14°09'N 38°52'E
ck le Street England 13 F2...............................53°34'N 1°12'W
a r. Russia 55 O4........................................66°42'N 136°32'E
an Sea Croatia/Turkey 50 F4.............................39°00'N 24°51'E
anistan Asia 95 K6.......................................33°53'N 65°52'E
78
akarahisar Turkey 51 I4..................................38°46'N 30°33'E
ez Niger 84 E3.............................................16°57'N 7°59'E
r Morocco 84 D5.........................................30°27'N 9°37'W
o r. Japan 104 C3.........................................37°58'N 139°02'E
ala Ind 97 H5.............................................23°50'N 91°16'E
France 44 E3.............................................43°18'N 3°28'E
France 44 D4.............................................44°12'N 0°38'E
Dimitrios Greece 50 E3...................................37°49'N 23°51'E
Efstratios i. Greece 50 F4.................................39°30'N 25°01'E
Konstantinos Greece 50 E4..............................38°45'N 22°51'E
Nikolaos Greece 50 F2...................................35°12'N 25°43'E
at Hills Sudan 94 E3......................................16°26'N 35°03'E
India 96 E6...............................................27°09'N 78°02'E
ento Italy 48 F4..........................................37°18'N 13°35'E
an i. N. Mariana Is 103 L7...............................18°46'N 145°42'E
dulce Panama 67 H2....................................8°12'N 80°33'W
scalientes Mexico 66 D5..................................21°51'N 102°21'W
scalientes d. Mexico 66 D5...............................21°57'N 102°11'W
ar de Campoo Spain 45 C5..............................42°47'N 4°10'W
as Spain 45 E2............................................37°25'N 1°35'W
nas, Cape S. Africa 83 B1.................................34°50'S 20°03'E
gar f. Algeria 84 E4.......................................23°10'N 4°23'E
Iran 95 G7...............................................38°27'N 47°02'E
ad Germany 46 E5........................................50°57'N 7°01'E
adabad India 96 E5......................................23°03'N 72°37'E
dpur East Pakistan 96 D6...............................29°10'N 71°22'E

Ahvāz Iran 95 G6.........................................31°15'N 48°40'E
Aigialousa Cyprus 51 K2.................................35°31'N 34°11'E
Aigina i. Greece 50 E3....................................37°41'N 23°31'E
Ailsa Craig i. Scotland 14 D3.............................55°15'N 5°06'W
Aïn Beïda Algeria 48 E4...................................35°47'N 7°25'E
'Aïn Ben Tili Mauritania 84 D4...........................25°58'N 9°31'W
Aïn Sefra Algeria 84 D5...................................32°42'N 0°35'W
Aïr, Massif de l' mts Niger 84 E3.........................18°46'N 8°15'E
Airdrie Canada 60 G3.....................................51°17'N 114°01'W
Airdrie Scotland 15 F3....................................55°52'N 3°58'W
Aisne r. France 44 E6......................................49°26'N 2°51'E
Aitape P.N.G. 103 K3.....................................3°09'S 142°22'E
Aix-en-Provence France 44 F3............................43°32'N 5°27'E
Aizkraukle Latvia 47 K7...................................56°36'N 25°15'E
Aizu-wakamatsu Japan 104 C3..........................37°29'N 139°56'E
Ajaccio France 44 H2.....................................41°55'N 8°44'E
Ajdābiyā Libya 85 G5.....................................30°45'N 20°13'E
Akbulak Russia 53 F3.....................................50°59'N 55°36'E
Akçakale Turkey 51 M3...................................36°43'N 38°57'E
Akdağmadeni Turkey 51 K4..............................39°39'N 35°54'E
Akhalkalaki Georgia 53 E2................................41°25'N 43°29'E
Akhḍar, Al Jabal al mts Libya 49 H3.....................31°46'N 20°46'E
Akhḍar, Al Jabal al mts Oman 95 I4.....................23°22'N 57°00'E
Akhisar Turkey 51 G4.....................................38°55'N 27°50'E
Akhtubinsk Russia 53 E2.................................48°20'N 46°05'E
Akimiski Island Canada 61 J3.............................53°08'N 81°17'W
Akita Japan 104 D3.......................................39°43'N 140°07'E
Akkajaure l. Sweden 43 D4...............................67°41'N 17°29'E
Aknoul Morocco 45 D1...................................34°38'N 3°51'W
Akordat Eritrea 85 H3....................................15°31'N 37°54'E
Akpatok Island Canada 61 L4............................60°24'N 67°45'W
Akranes Iceland 43 X2....................................64°19'N 22°05'W
Akron U.S.A. 63 J5........................................41°07'N 81°33'W
Aksai Chin Asia 96 E8.....................................35°08'N 79°11'E
Aksaray Turkey 51 K4.....................................38°23'N 34°02'E
Aksarka Russia 52 G4.....................................66°31'N 67°51'E
Akşehir Turkey 51 I4......................................38°21'N 31°24'E
Aksu China 98 E6..........................................41°06'N 80°21'E
Āksum Ethiopia 94 E2....................................14°07'N 38°46'E
Aktau Kazakhstan 53 F2..................................43°39'N 51°12'E
Aktobe Kazakhstan 53 F3.................................50°13'N 57°10'E
Aktogay Kazakhstan 54 I2................................47°06'N 79°42'E
Alabama d. U.S.A. 63 I3..................................32°41'N 86°42'W
Alabama r. U.S.A. 63 I3...................................31°09'N 87°57'W
Alagoinhas Brazil 72 F5...................................12°07'S 38°17'W
Al Aḥmadī Kuwait 95 G5.................................29°04'N 48°02'E
Alakol', Ozero l. Kazakhstan 98 E7......................46°03'N 81°30'E
Alakurtti Russia 43 G4....................................66°58'N 30°20'E
Alamagan i. N. Mariana Is 103 L7.......................17°35'N 145°52'E
Åland Islands Finland 43 D3..............................60°28'N 19°53'E
Alanya Turkey 51 J3.......................................36°33'N 32°00'E
Alappuzha India 96 E2....................................9°30'N 76°21'E
Al 'Aqabah Jordan 94 E5.................................29°31'N 35°01'E
Al Arṭāwīyah Saudi Arabia 95 G5........................26°30'N 45°21'E
Alaşehir Turkey 51 H4....................................38°21'N 28°30'E
Alaska d. U.S.A. 60 D4....................................63°41'N 143°45'W
Alaska, Gulf of U.S.A. 60 D3.............................58°10'N 147°57'W
Alaska Peninsula U.S.A. 60 C3............................55°18'N 162°25'W
Alaska Range mts U.S.A. 60 D4..........................63°19'N 148°01'W
Alausí Ecuador 72 B6.....................................2°10'S 78°52'W
Alavus Finland 43 E3......................................62°35'N 23°37'E
Alaw, Llyn resr Wales 10 C5..............................53°21'N 4°25'W
Albacete Spain 45 E3......................................39°00'N 1°50'W
Alba Iulia Romania 50 E8.................................46°05'N 23°36'E
Albania Europe 50 C5.....................................41°56'N 19°34'E
Albany Australia 108 A3..................................34°58'S 117°54'E
Albany r. Canada 61 J3....................................52°08'N 81°59'W
Albany U.S.A. 63 L5.......................................42°40'N 73°46'W
Albatross Bay Australia 103 K1...........................12°41'S 141°44'E
Al Bawītī Egypt 85 G4.....................................28°21'N 28°50'E
Al Baydā' Libya 85 G5.....................................32°44'N 21°44'E
Alberche r. Spain 45 C3...................................39°58'N 4°46'W
Albert France 42 B2.......................................49°59'N 2°39'E
Albert, Lake Dem. Rep. Congo/Uganda 83 C5
.............................................................1°43'N 30°52'E
Alberta d. Canada 60 G3..................................52°45'N 113°59'W
Albert Lea U.S.A. 63 H5...................................43°39'N 93°22'W
Albert Nile r. South Sudan/Uganda 85 H2...............3°36'N 32°02'E
Albi France 44 E3..........................................43°56'N 2°08'E
Al Biyāḍh f. Saudi Arabia 95 G4..........................20°57'N 46°14'E
Alborán, Isla de i. Spain 45 D1...........................35°57'N 3°02'W
Alboran Sea Europe 45 C1................................36°00'N 4°00'W
Albuquerque U.S.A. 62 E4...............................35°07'N 106°38'W
Al Buraymī Oman 95 I4...................................24°14'N 55°46'E
Albury Australia 108 D3...................................36°03'S 146°54'E
Alcalá de Henares Spain 45 D4...........................40°29'N 3°21'W
Alcalá la Real Spain 45 D2................................37°28'N 3°55'W
Alcañiz Spain 45 E4.......................................41°03'N 0°07'W
Alcázar de San Juan Spain 45 D3........................39°23'N 3°11'W
Alcester England 8 D3.....................................52°13'N 1°52'W
Alcoy/Alcoi Spain 45 E3..................................38°42'N 0°27'W
Alcúdia Spain 45 G3.......................................39°52'N 3°08'E
Aldabra Islands Seychelles 85 I1..........................9°16'S 46°30'E
Aldan Russia 55 N3.......................................58°36'N 125°25'E
Aldan r. Russia 55 N4.....................................63°32'N 128°46'E
Aldbrough England 13 G2................................53°50'N 0°07'W
Aldeburgh England 9 G3..................................52°09'N 1°36'E
Alderley Edge England 13 E2.............................53°18'N 2°14'W
Alderney i. Channel Is 11 Z9..............................49°42'N 2°15'W
Aldershot England 8 E2...................................51°15'N 0°45'W
Aldingham England 12 D3................................54°08'N 3°06'W
Aldridge England 8 D3....................................52°36'N 1°55'W
Aleksandrovsk-Sakhalinskiy Russia 55 P3...............51°08'N 142°21'E
Aleksin Russia 47 Q6......................................54°31'N 37°05'E
Alençon France 44 D6.....................................48°26'N 0°06'E
Aleppo Syria 94 E7........................................36°12'N 37°09'E
Alès France 44 F4..........................................44°08'N 4°05'E
Alessandria Italy 46 C1...................................44°55'N 8°38'E
Ålesund Norway 43 A4....................................62°28'N 6°12'E
Aleutian Islands U.S.A. 60 A3............................53°03'N 176°15'W
Aleutian Range mts U.S.A. 60 C3........................56°10'N 159°17'W
Alexander Archipelago is U.S.A. 60 E3..................57°59'N 137°33'W
Alexandra, Cape S. Atlantic Oc. 73 F1..................54°05'S 37°56'W
Alexandria Egypt 85 G5..................................31°13'N 29°58'E
Alexandria Romania 50 E8................................43°58'N 25°20'E
Alexandria Scotland 14 E3................................55°59'N 4°35'W
Alexandria La. U.S.A. 63 H3..............................31°17'N 92°28'W
Alexandria Va. U.S.A. 63 K4..............................38°48'N 77°05'W
Alexandroupoli Greece 50 F5.............................40°51'N 25°53'E
Aleysk Russia 98 E8.......................................52°30'N 82°51'E
Al Fayyūm Egypt 85 H4..................................29°18'N 30°51'E
Alford England 13 H2.....................................53°16'N 0°11'E
Alfreton England 13 F2....................................53°06'N 1°23'W
Algarve f. Portugal 45 A2..................................37°16'N 8°07'W
Algeciras Spain 45 C2.....................................36°07'N 5°27'W
Algeria Africa 84 E4.......................................30°15'N 3°31'E

Al Ghaydah Yemen 95 H3................................16°14'N 52°13'E
Al Ghurdaqah Egypt 49 J2...............................27°12'N 33°48'E
Al Ghwaybiyah Saudi Arabia 95 G5.....................25°14'N 49°43'E
Algiers Algeria 84 E5......................................36°46'N 3°04'E
Algorta Spain 45 D5.......................................43°21'N 2°59'W
Al Ḥasakah Syria 94 F7...................................36°30'N 40°44'E
Al Ḥibāk des. Saudi Arabia 95 H3........................19°30'N 52°27'E
Al Hoceïma Morocco 48 C4..............................35°15'N 3°56'W
Al Hufūf Saudi Arabia 95 G5.............................25°22'N 49°35'E
Aliağa Turkey 50 G4.......................................38°47'N 26°58'E
'Ali 'Addé Djibouti 85 I3..................................11°08'N 42°53'E
Aliakmonas r. Greece 50 E5...............................40°28'N 22°38'E
Âli Bayramlı Azerbaijan 95 G7............................39°56'N 48°56'E
Alicante Spain 45 E3......................................38°21'N 0°28'W
Alice Springs town Australia 108 C4......................23°42'S 133°52'E
Alingsås Sweden 43 C2...................................57°56'N 12°33'E
Al Ismā'īlīyah Egypt 49 J3.................................30°35'N 32°17'E
Al Jaghbūb Libya 85 G4..................................29°43'N 24°31'E
Al Jahrah Kuwait 95 G5...................................29°20'N 47°41'E
Al Jawf Libya 85 G4.......................................24°14'N 23°24'E
Al Jawf Saudi Arabia 94 E5................................29°47'N 39°55'E
Al Jawsh Libya 48 F3......................................32°01'N 11°42'E
Al Jubayl Saudi Arabia 95 G5.............................27°02'N 49°38'E
Aljustrel Portugal 45 A2...................................37°53'N 8°10'W
Al Karak Jordan 94 E6.....................................31°10'N 35°42'E
Al Khābūrah Oman 95 I4.................................23°58'N 57°06'E
Al Khārijah Egypt 85 H4..................................25°24'N 30°33'E
Al Khaṣab Oman 95 I5.....................................26°11'N 56°14'E
Al Khums Libya 48 F3.....................................32°35'N 14°22'E
Alkmaar Neth. 42 D5......................................52°38'N 4°45'E
Al Kūt Iraq 95 G6..........................................32°31'N 45°47'E
Allahabad India 96 F6.....................................25°25'N 81°52'E
Allakh-Yun' Russia 55 O4.................................61°05'N 138°03'E
Allegheny r. U.S.A. 63 K5..................................40°27'N 79°59'W
Allegheny Mountains U.S.A. 63 J4......................36°46'N 82°22'W
Allen, Lough l. Ireland 18 C4.............................54°09'N 8°03'W
Allendale Town England 13 E3...........................54°54'N 2°15'W
Allentown U.S.A. 63 K5...................................40°37'N 75°30'W
Aller r. Germany 46 C5....................................52°57'N 9°11'E
Al Lith Saudi Arabia 94 F4................................20°10'N 40°16'E
Alloa Scotland 15 F4......................................56°07'N 3°47'W
Almansa Spain 45 E3......................................38°52'N 1°05'W
Al Manṣūrah Egypt 49 J3................................31°02'N 31°23'E
Almanzor mt. Spain 45 C4...............................40°15'N 5°18'W
Al Marj Libya 49 H3.......................................32°29'N 20°50'E
Almaty Kazakhstan 54 I2.................................43°16'N 77°01'E
Almelo Neth. 42 F5........................................52°21'N 6°40'E
Almendra, Embalse de resr Spain 45 B4...............41°17'N 6°14'W
Almería Spain 45 D2.......................................36°50'N 2°27'W
Al'met'yevsk Russia 53 F3................................54°51'N 52°23'E
Almina, Punta pt Spain 45 C1............................35°54'N 5°16'W
Al Minyā Egypt 85 H4.....................................28°05'N 30°45'E
Almodôvar Portugal 45 A2...............................37°31'N 8°04'W
Almond r. Scotland 15 F4.................................56°25'N 3°28'W
Al Mudawwara Jordan 94 E5............................29°19'N 36°02'E
Almuñécar Spain 45 D2..................................36°44'N 3°41'W
Alnwick England 13 F4....................................55°25'N 1°42'W
Alofi Niue 109 I5...........................................19°03'S 169°54'W
Alor i. Indonesia 103 G2..................................8°17'S 124°45'E
Alor Setar Malaysia 102 C5...............................6°08'N 100°22'E
Alpena U.S.A. 63 J6.......................................45°03'N 83°27'W
Alpine U.S.A. 62 F3.......................................30°18'N 103°35'W
Alps mts Europe 48 F6....................................46°00'N 7°30'E
Al Qa'āmīyāt f. Saudi Arabia 95 G3.....................17°59'N 47°47'E
Al Qaddāhīyah Libya 48 G3.............................31°22'N 15°12'E
Al Qāmishlī Syria 94 F7...................................37°03'N 41°13'E
Al Qaryatayn Syria 51 L2.................................34°13'N 37°14'E
Al Qunfidhah Saudi Arabia 94 F3........................19°09'N 41°04'E
Al Quṣayr Egypt 85 H4...................................26°07'N 34°13'E
Alsager England 13 E2....................................53°06'N 2°18'W
Alston England 13 E3......................................54°49'N 2°26'W
Altaelva r. Norway 43 E5..................................69°57'N 23°20'E
Altai Mountains Asia 98 F7...............................48°00'N 90°00'E
Altamira Brazil 72 D6......................................3°14'S 52°14'W
Altay China 98 F7..........................................47°48'N 88°10'E
Altay Mongolia 98 F7.....................................46°18'N 96°15'E
Altiplano f. Bolivia 72 C5..................................16°24'S 69°39'W
Altiplano Mexicano mts N. America 56 E3
.............................................................24°00'N 105°00'W
Alton England 8 E2........................................51°09'N 0°58'W
Altoona U.S.A. 63 K5.....................................40°30'N 78°24'W
Altötting Germany 46 E3.................................48°14'N 12°41'E
Altrincham England 13 E2................................53°23'N 2°21'W
Altun Shan mts China 98 F5..............................37°45'N 86°38'E
Alturas U.S.A. 62 B5......................................41°30'N 120°31'W
Al 'Uqaylah Libya 49 G3..................................30°13'N 19°12'E
Al 'Uwaynāt Libya 94 B4.................................21°46'N 24°51'E
Älvdalen Sweden 43 C3..................................61°13'N 14°04'E
Alveley England 8 C3......................................52°27'N 2°21'W
Älvsbyn Sweden 43 E4...................................65°40'N 21°00'E
Al Wajh Saudi Arabia 94 E5..............................26°17'N 36°25'E
Alwen Reservoir Wales 10 D5.............................53°05'N 3°35'W
Al Widyān f. Iraq/Saudi Arabia 94 F6....................32°00'N 40°22'E
Alyth Scotland 17 F1......................................56°38'N 3°14'W
Alytus Lithuania 47 K8....................................54°23'N 24°03'E
Amadeus, Lake Australia 108 C4.........................24°50'S 131°09'E
Amadjuak Lake Canada 61 K4...........................64°57'N 71°09'W
Amadora Portugal 45 A3..................................38°46'N 9°14'W
Åmål Sweden 43 C2.......................................59°03'N 12°44'E
Amamapare Indonesia 103 J3............................4°53'S 136°58'E
Amapá Brazil 72 D7.......................................2°02'N 50°50'W
Amarillo U.S.A. 62 F4.....................................35°15'N 101°50'W
Amasya Turkey 51 K5.....................................40°39'N 35°50'E
Amazon r. S. America 72 D7..............................0°01'N 50°37'W
Amazon, Mouths of the Brazil 72 E7....................0°41'N 49°28'W
Ambarchik Russia 55 R4..................................69°35'N 162°13'E
Ambergate England 13 F2................................53°04'N 1°29'W
Ambergris Cay i. Belize 66 G4............................18°00'N 87°52'W
Amble England 13 F4.....................................55°20'N 1°35'W
Ambleside England 12 E3.................................54°26'N 2°58'W
Ambo Kiribati 107 ......................................1°21'N 172°57'E
Ambon Indonesia 103 H3.................................3°43'S 128°11'E
Ambrym i. Vanuatu 109 F5...............................16°12'S 168°13'E
Ameland i. Neth. 42 E6...................................53°28'N 5°48'E
American Samoa is S. Pacific Oc. 109 I5.................12°00'S 170°00'W
Amersfoort Neth. 42 E5...................................52°09'N 5°23'E
Amersham England 9 E2.................................51°41'N 0°36'W
Amesbury England 8 D2..................................51°10'N 1°47'W
Amfissa Greece 50 E4......................................38°32'N 22°22'E
Amgun' r. Russia 55 O3...................................52°01'N 139°38'E
Amiens France 44 E6......................................49°54'N 2°18'E
Amlwch Wales 10 C5.....................................53°25'N 4°21'W
'Ammān Jordan 94 E6....................................31°57'N 35°56'E
Ammanford Wales 10 D3.................................51°48'N 3°59'W
Amol Iran 95 H7...........................................36°27'N 52°20'E
Amorgos i. Greece 50 F3..................................36°49'N 25°54'E
Amos Canada 61 K2......................................48°34'N 78°08'W

Ampthill England 9 E3....................................52°02'N 0°30'W
Amravati India 96 E5......................................20°56'N 77°51'E
Amritsar India 96 D7......................................31°34'N 74°56'E
Amstelveen Neth. 42 D5.................................52°19'N 4°52'E
Amsterdam Neth. 42 D5..................................52°23'N 4°54'E
Amstetten Austria 46 F3..................................48°08'N 14°52'E
Amu Darya r. Asia 54 H2.................................43°50'N 59°00'E
Amund Ringnes Island Canada 61 I5....................78°17'N 96°35'W
Amundsen Gulf Canada 60 F5............................70°25'N 121°26'W
Amuntai Indonesia 102 F3...............................2°25'S 115°13'E
Amur r. Russia 55 P3......................................53°17'N 140°37'E
Anabar r. Russia 55 M5...................................73°13'N 113°31'E
Anadolu Dağları mts Turkey 51 L5.......................40°59'N 36°11'E
Anadyr' Russia 55 S4......................................64°44'N 177°20'E
Anadyrskiy Zaliv b. Russia 55 T4.........................63°56'N 177°42'W
Anambas, Kepulauan is Indonesia 102 D4..............3°17'N 105°55'E
Anamur Turkey 51 J3.....................................36°06'N 32°50'E
Anapa Russia 51 L7.......................................44°54'N 37°20'E
Anápolis Brazil 72 E5......................................16°20'S 48°55'W
Anatahan i. N. Mariana Is 103 L7........................16°21'N 145°42'E
Anatolia f. Turkey 51 J4...................................38°58'N 33°19'E
Anchorage U.S.A. 60 D4..................................61°12'N 149°52'W
Ancona Italy 46 F5.........................................43°37'N 13°31'E
Åndalsnes Norway 43 A3.................................62°34'N 7°42'E
Andalusia f. Spain 45 C2..................................37°35'N 4°10'W
Andaman Islands India 97 H3............................12°46'N 93°17'E
Andaman Sea Indian Oc. 97 I3..........................11°33'N 95°19'E
Anderlecht Belgium 42 D3...............................50°49'N 4°18'E
Andermatt Switz. 46 C2..................................46°38'N 8°36'E
Anderson r. Canada 60 F4................................69°41'N 128°56'W
Anderson U.S.A. 60 D4...................................64°22'N 149°12'W
Andes mts S. America 73 B6..............................9°10'S 77°03'W
Andfjorden str. Norway 43 D5............................68°53'N 16°04'E
Andhra Pradesh d. India 96 E4...........................16°03'N 79°11'E
Andkhvoy Afgh. 95 K7....................................36°59'N 65°08'E
Andong S. Korea 104 A3..................................36°33'N 128°43'E
Andorra Europe 45 F5.....................................42°32'N 1°35'E
Andorra la Vella Andorra 45 F5...........................42°31'N 1°32'E
Andover England 8 D2...................................51°12'N 1°29'W
Andøya i. Norway 43 C5..................................69°11'N 15°48'E
Andreas Isle of Man 12 C3...............................54°22'N 4°27'W
Andria Italy 49 G5.........................................41°14'N 16°18'E
Andros i. Bahamas 67 I5..................................24°25'N 78°09'W
Andros i. Greece 50 F3....................................37°53'N 24°57'E
Andújar Spain 45 C3......................................38°02'N 4°03'W
Anéfis Mali 84 E3..........................................18°02'N 0°32'E
Anegada i. Virgin Is (U.K.) 67 L4.........................18°44'N 64°19'W
Aneto mt. Spain 45 F5.....................................42°38'N 0°39'E
Angara r. Russia 55 K3....................................58°05'N 92°59'E
Angarsk Russia 99 I8......................................52°24'N 103°45'E
Ånge Sweden 43 C3.......................................62°32'N 15°40'E
Ángel de la Guarda, Isla i. Mexico 66 B6
.............................................................29°25'N 113°24'W
Ängelholm Sweden 43 C2................................56°15'N 12°52'E
Angers France 44 C5......................................47°28'N 0°33'W
Anglesey i. Wales 10 C5..................................53°18'N 4°23'W
Angola Africa 83 A3.......................................11°40'S 17°34'E
Angola Basin f. Atlantic Oc. 117 F2......................15°00'S 0°00'E
Angoulême France 44 D4.................................45°39'N 0°10'E
Angren Uzbekistan 98 C6................................41°02'N 70°07'E
Anguilla i. Central America 67 L4.........................18°14'N 63°02'W
Angus d. Scotland 20 D5..................................56°43'N 2°55'W
Anhui d. China 99 L4......................................32°10'N 117°07'E
Ankara Turkey 51 J4.......................................39°56'N 32°50'E
Anlaby England 13 G2....................................53°45'N 0°26'W
Annaba Algeria 84 E5.....................................36°54'N 7°46'E
An Nabk Syria 51 L2......................................34°01'N 36°44'E
An Nafūd des. Saudi Arabia 94 F5.......................28°28'N 41°17'E
'Annah Iraq 94 F6.........................................34°25'N 41°56'E
An Najaf Iraq 94 F6........................................31°59'N 44°20'E
Annalee r. Ireland 18 D4..................................54°02'N 7°23'W
Annalong Northern Ireland 14 D2.......................54°06'N 5°54'W
Annan Scotland 15 F2....................................54°59'N 3°15'W
Annan r. Scotland 15 F2..................................54°59'N 3°16'W
Annapolis U.S.A. 63 K4...................................38°58'N 76°30'W
Annapurna mt. Nepal 96 F6..............................28°34'N 83°49'E
Ann Arbor U.S.A. 63 J5...................................42°17'N 83°45'W
An Nāşirīyah Iraq 95 G6..................................31°01'N 46°14'E
An Nawfalīyah Libya 49 G3..............................30°51'N 17°52'E
Annecy France 44 G4.....................................45°54'N 6°08'E
Anniston U.S.A. 63 I3.....................................33°39'N 85°43'W
An Nu'ayrīyah Saudi Arabia 95 G5......................27°29'N 48°26'E
An Nuşayrīyah, Jabal mts Syria 51 L2...................35°15'N 36°05'E
Ansbach Germany 46 D3.................................49°18'N 10°36'E
Anshan China 99 M6.....................................41°06'N 123°02'E
Anshun China 99 J3.......................................26°15'N 105°57'E
Anstruther Scotland 15 G4...............................56°13'N 2°42'W
Antakya Turkey 51 L3.....................................36°11'N 36°07'E
Antalya Turkey 51 I3......................................36°53'N 30°41'E
Antalya Körfezi g. Turkey 51 I3...........................36°40'N 30°58'E
Antananarivo Madagascar 83 D3........................18°54'S 47°33'E
Antarctica 112
Antarctic Peninsula f. Antarctica 116 D1...............65°00'S 64°00'W
An Teallach mt. Scotland 16 D2..........................57°48'N 5°16'W
Antequera Spain 45 C2...................................37°02'N 4°33'W
Antibes France 44 G3.....................................43°35'N 7°07'E
Anticosti, Île d' i. Canada 61 L2...........................49°27'N 62°59'W
Antigua i. Antigua 67 L4..................................17°02'N 61°43'W
Antigua and Barbuda Central America 67 L4
.............................................................17°20'N 61°20'W
Antikythira i. Greece 50 E2................................35°52'N 23°20'E
Antipodes Islands New Zealand 109 G2................49°39'S 178°44'E
Antofagasta Chile 73 B4..................................23°37'S 70°22'W
Antrim Northern Ireland 14 C2...........................54°43'N 6°12'W
Antrim f. Northern Ireland 18 E4.........................54°59'N 6°22'W
Antrim and Newtownabbey d. Northern Irealnd 21 B4
.............................................................54°43'N 6°16'W
Antrim Hills Northern Ireland 14 C3.....................55°05'N 6°16'W
Antsirabe Madagascar 83 D3............................19°53'S 47°03'E
Antsirañana Madagascar 83 D3..........................12°19'S 49°17'E
Antsohihy Madagascar 83 D3............................14°53'S 47°59'E
Antwerp Belgium 42 D4..................................51°12'N 4°26'E
Antwerpen d. Belgium 42 D4.............................51°17'N 4°46'E
Anyang China 99 K5......................................36°04'N 114°22'E
Anzhero-Sudzhensk Russia 54 J3.......................56°06'N 86°02'E
Aomori Japan 104 D4.....................................40°49'N 140°45'E
Aoraki/Mount Cook mt. New Zealand 109 G2
.............................................................43°37'S 170°08'E
Apalachee Bay U.S.A. 63 J2..............................29°59'N 84°06'W
Aparri Phil. 103 G7........................................18°21'N 121°40'E
Apatity Russia 43 H4......................................67°34'N 33°23'E
Apeldoorn Neth. 42 E5...................................52°12'N 5°58'E
Apennines mts Italy 48 F5................................44°37'N 9°47'E
Apia Samoa 109 H5.......................................13°50'S 171°44'W
Apostolos Andreas, Cape Cyprus 51 K2...............35°41'N 34°35'E
Appalachian Mountains U.S.A. 63 J4....................36°08'N 83°01'W
Appleby-in-Westmorland England 13 E3...............54°35'N 2°29'W

Appledore England 11 C3 .............51°03'N 4°12'W
Aqaba, Gulf of Asia 94 D5 ..........29°19'N 34°54'E
Arabian Peninsula Asia 85 I4 .........24°00'N 45°00'E
Arabian Sea Indian Oc. 86 E2 .......18°08'N 66°38'E
Aracaju Brazil 72 F5 ..................10°52'S 37°03'W
Araçatuba Brazil 73 D4 ...............21°12'S 50°22'W
Aracena, Sierra de hills Spain 45 B2 ...37°51'N 7°07'W
Arad Romania 50 D8 ..................46°11'N 21°21'E
Arafura Sea Australia/Indonesia 108 C6 ..9°04'S 132°58'E
Aragon f. Spain 45 E4 .................41°20'N 0°50'W
Aragón r. Spain 45 E4 .................42°13'N 1°45'W
Araguaia r. Brazil 72 E6 ..............5°24'S 48°41'W
Araguaína Brazil 72 E6 ...............7°20'S 48°12'W
Arak Algeria 84 E4 ...................25°18'N 3°39'E
Ārāk Iran 95 G6 .....................34°05'N 49°42'E
Arakan Yoma mts Myanmar 97 H5 ....20°18'N 94°07'E
Aral Sea Kazakhstan/Uzbekistan 54 H2 ..45°07'N 60°05'E
Aral'sk Kazakhstan 54 H2 ............46°46'N 61°43'E
Aranda de Duero Spain 45 D4 ........41°41'N 3°40'W
Aran Island Ireland 18 C4 ............54°59'N 8°35'W
Aran Islands Ireland 18 B3 ............53°07'N 9°44'W
Aranjuez Spain 45 D4 .................40°02'N 3°36'W
Arapgir Turkey 51 M4 .................39°02'N 38°29'E
Arapis, Akra pt Greece 50 F5 .........40°27'N 24°00'E
'Ar'ar Saudi Arabia 94 F6 .............30°58'N 40°58'E
Araraquara Brazil 73 E4 ..............21°47'S 48°06'W
Ararat, Mount Turkey 53 E1 ...........39°45'N 44°15'E
Arbīl/Hewlêr Iraq 94 F7 ...............36°11'N 44°01'E
Arboga Sweden 43 C2 ................59°23'N 15°51'E
Arbroath Scotland 15 G4 ..............56°34'N 2°35'W
Arbu Lut, Dasht-e des. Afgh. 95 J5 ...29°57'N 63°56'E
Arcachon France 44 C4 ...............44°40'N 1°10'W
Arctic Bay town Canada 61 J5 .........72°55'N 85°10'W
Arctic Ocean 112
Arctic Red r. Canada 60 E4 ...........67°27'N 133°44'W
Ardabīl Iran 95 G7 ...................38°14'N 48°15'E
Ardas r. Greece 50 G5 ................41°40'N 26°30'E
Ardèche r. France 44 F4 ..............44°16'N 4°39'E
Ardennes f. Belgium 42 D2 ...........49°56'N 4°52'E
Ardestān Iran 95 H6 ..................33°20'N 52°21'E
Ardglass Northern Ireland 14 D2 ......54°15'N 5°36'W
Ardila r. Portugal 45 B3 ..............38°10'N 7°28'W
Ardnamurchan, Point of Scotland 16 C1 ..56°43'N 6°13'W
Ardrishaig Scotland 14 D4 ............56°01'N 5°27'W
Ardrossan Scotland 14 E3 ............55°39'N 4°49'W
Ards and North Down d. Northern Ireland 21 C4
....................54°28'N 5°37'W
Ards Peninsula Northern Ireland 14 D2 ..54°30'N 5°25'W
Ardvasar Scotland 16 D2 .............57°03'N 5°54'W
Arena, Point U.S.A. 62 B4 ............38°57'N 123°44'W
Arendal Norway 43 B2 ...............58°27'N 8°46'E
Arenig Fawr hill Wales 10 D4 .........52°55'N 3°45'W
Arequipa Peru 72 B5 .................16°23'S 71°32'W
Arganda Spain 45 D4 ................40°18'N 3°25'W
Argentan France 44 C6 ...............48°45'N 0°01'W
Argentina S. America 73 C3 ..........35°00'S 68°00'W
Argentino, Lago l. Argentina 73 B1 ...50°20'S 72°51'W
Argenton-sur-Creuse France 44 D5 ....46°36'N 1°31'E
Argeş r. Romania 50 G7 ..............44°13'N 26°37'E
Argun' r. China/Russia 99 M8 .........53°18'N 121°20'E
Argyle, Lake Australia 108 B5 ........16°37'S 128°41'E
Argyll f. Scotland 14 D4 ..............56°08'N 5°19'W
Argyll and Bute d. Scotland 20 C4 ....55°46'N 5°25'W
Arica Chile 72 B5 ...................18°29'S 70°20'W
Arienas, Loch l. Scotland 14 D4 ......56°35'N 5°46'W
Arinos r. Brazil 72 D5 ................10°25'S 58°13'W
Ariquemes Brazil 72 C5 ..............9°59'S 63°05'W
Arisaig Scotland 16 D1 ...............56°55'N 5°50'W
Arisaig, Sound of str. Scotland 16 D1 ..56°50'N 5°57'W
Arizona d. U.S.A. 62 D3 ..............34°11'N 111°37'W
Arkadelphia U.S.A. 63 H3 ...........34°09'N 93°03'W
Arkaig, Loch l. Scotland 16 D1 .......56°58'N 5°13'W
Arkansas d. U.S.A. 63 H4 ............35°49'N 92°00'W
Arkansas r. U.S.A. 63 H3 ............33°49'N 91°08'W
Arkansas City U.S.A. 62 G4 ..........37°04'N 97°03'W
Arkhangel'sk Russia 52 E4 ...........64°33'N 40°33'E
Arklow Ireland 18 E2 .................52°48'N 6°10'W
Arkona, Kap c. Germany 46 E6 .......54°41'N 13°27'E
Arles France 44 F3 ...................43°41'N 4°38'E
Arlit Niger 84 E3 ....................18°42'N 7°21'E
Arlon Belgium 42 E2 .................49°41'N 5°49'E
Armagh Northern Ireland 14 C2 .......54°20'N 6°39'W
Armagh f. Northern Ireland 14 ........54°18'N 6°39'W
Armagh City, Banbridge and Craigavon d. Northern Ireland
....................21 B4 54°19'N 6°39'W
Armant Egypt 49 J2 ..................25°37'N 32°32'E
Armavir Russia 53 E2 ................45°01'N 41°06'E
Armenia Asia 53 E2 ..................40°26'N 44°30'E
Armenia Colombia 72 B7 .............4°30'N 75°39'W
Armidale Australia 108 E3 ............30°32'S 151°41'E
Armyans'k Ukraine 51 J8 .............46°07'N 33°41'E
Arnhem Neth. 42 E4 .................51°59'N 5°55'E
Arnhem, Cape Australia 108 C5 .......12°19'S 136°58'E
Arnhem Land f. Australia 108 C5 ......13°26'S 133°07'E
Arnsberg Germany 46 C4 ............51°23'N 8°04'E
Ar Ramādī Iraq 94 F6 ................33°23'N 43°16'E
Arran i. Scotland 14 D3 ..............55°35'N 5°20'W
Ar Raqqah Syria 94 E7 ...............35°57'N 39°01'E
Arras France 44 E7 ..................50°17'N 2°46'E
Arrecife Canary Islands 45 Z2 ........28°57'N 13°33'W
Arriaga Mexico 66 F4 ................16°16'N 93°52'W
Arrieta Canary Islands 45 Z2 .........29°08'N 13°28'W
Ar Rimāl f. Saudi Arabia 95 H4 .......21°43'N 52°53'E
Arrochar Scotland 14 E4 .............56°12'N 4°44'W
Ar Ruṭbah Iraq 94 F6 ................33°01'N 40°11'E
Arta Greece 50 D4 ...................39°10'N 20°59'E
Artesia U.S.A. 62 F3 .................32°52'N 104°25'W
Artois f. France 42 A3 ...............50°40'N 1°55'E
Artois, Collines de l' hills France 9 G1 ..50°40'N 1°55'E
Artsyz Ukraine 51 H7 ................45°59'N 29°27'E
Aru, Kepulauan is Indonesia 103 I2 ..6°09'S 134°05'E
Aruba i. Central America 67 K3 ......12°30'N 69°56'W
Arunachal Pradesh d. India 97 H6 .....27°28'N 92°48'E
Arundel England 11 E1 ...............50°51'N 0°33'W
Arusha Tanzania 83 C4 ...............3°22'S 36°37'E
Aruwimi r. Dem. Rep. Congo 83 B5 ....1°13'N 23°36'E
Arvayheer Mongolia 99 I7 ............46°08'N 102°47'E
Arviat Canada 61 I4 ..................61°12'N 94°09'W
Arvidsjaur Sweden 43 D4 .............65°35'N 19°12'E
Arvika Sweden 43 C2 ................59°39'N 12°37'E
Arzamas Russia 52 E3 ...............55°23'N 43°49'E
Asad, Buḩayrat al resr Syria 51 M3 ...36°05'N 38°03'E
Asahi-dake vol. Japan 104 D4 ........43°41'N 142°54'E
Asahikawa Japan 104 D4 .............43°46'N 142°23'E
Asansol India 96 G5 .................23°41'N 87°01'E
Ascension Island Atlantic Oc. 78 B2 ..8°00'S 14°00'W

Åsele Sweden 43 D4 .................64°10'N 17°22'E
Asenovgrad Bulgaria 50 F6 ...........42°00'N 24°52'E
Asfordby England 8 E3 ...............52°46'N 0°57'W
Ashbourne England 13 F2 ............53°01'N 1°44'W
Ashbourne Ireland 18 E3 .............53°31'N 6°23'W
Ashburton watercourse Australia 108 A4 ..21°43'S 114°54'E
Ashburton England 11 D2 ............50°31'N 3°45'W
Ashby de la Zouch England 8 D3 ......52°45'N 1°28'W
Ashford England 9 F2 ................51°09'N 0°53'E
Ashgabat Turkmenistan 54 G1 ........37°53'N 58°21'E
Ashington England 13 F4 .............55°11'N 1°34'W
Ashland U.S.A. 63 H6 ...............46°35'N 90°53'W
Ashmore and Cartier Islands Australia 108 B5
....................12°38'S 122°40'E
Ash Shiḩr Yemen 95 G2 ..............14°49'N 49°45'E
Ashton-under-Lyne England 13 E2 .....53°30'N 2°06'W
Asia 86
Asipovichy Belarus 47 M5 ............53°18'N 28°38'E
'Asīr f. Saudi Arabia 94 F4 ..........20°53'N 40°14'E
Askern England 13 F2 ...............53°37'N 1°09'W
Askim Norway 43 B2 ................59°35'N 11°10'E
Asmara Eritrea 85 H3 ................15°20'N 38°56'E
Åsnen l. Sweden 43 C2 ..............56°37'N 14°50'E
Aspang-Markt Austria 46 G2 ..........47°33'N 16°05'E
Aspatria England 12 D3 ..............54°46'N 3°20'W
Aspen U.S.A. 62 E4 ..................39°11'N 106°49'W
Assab Eritrea 85 I3 ..................12°59'N 42°43'E
Assam d. India 97 H6 ................26°14'N 91°22'E
As Samāwah Iraq 94 G6 ..............31°15'N 45°19'E
As Sarīr f. Libya 49 H2 ..............27°02'N 21°36'E
Assen Neth. 42 F6 ...................53°00'N 6°33'E
As Sidrah Libya 49 G3 ...............30°38'N 18°18'E
Assilah Morocco 45 B1 ...............35°28'N 6°02'W
Assiniboine, Mount Canada 60 G3 ....50°57'N 115°34'W
As Sulaymānīyah/Slêmanî Iraq 95 G7 ..35°32'N 45°27'E
Assumption i. Seychelles 83 D4 ......9°30'S 47°20'E
As Sūq Saudi Arabia 94 F4 ..........21°57'N 41°59'E
Assynt, Loch l. Scotland 16 D3 .......58°11'N 5°05'W
Astana Kazakhstan 54 I3 .............51°09'N 71°27'E
Āstārā Iran 95 G7 ...................38°27'N 48°52'E
Asti Italy 46 C1 .....................44°54'N 8°13'E
Astorga Spain 45 B5 .................42°28'N 6°03'W
Astoria U.S.A. 62 B6 .................46°08'N 123°46'W
Astove i. Seychelles 83 D4 ...........10°05'S 47°40'E
Astrakhan' Russia 53 E2 .............46°20'N 48°03'E
Asunción i. N. Mariana Is 103 L7 .....19°40'N 145°25'E
Asunción Paraguay 73 D4 ............25°16'S 57°39'W
Aswān Egypt 85 H4 ..................24°02'N 32°56'E
Asyūţ Egypt 85 H4 ..................27°07'N 31°08'E
Atacama Desert Chile 73 C4 ..........26°13'S 69°39'W
Atafu i. Tokelau 109 H6 ..............8°33'S 172°30'W
Atâr Mauritania 84 C4 ...............20°32'N 13°03'W
Atasu Kazakhstan 54 I2 ..............48°42'N 71°37'E
Atatürk Barajı resr Turkey 51 M3 .....37°28'N 38°26'E
Atbara Sudan 85 H3 .................17°43'N 33°55'E
Atbara r. Sudan 85 H3 ...............17°40'N 33°58'E
Ath Belgium 42 C3 ..................50°38'N 3°47'E
Athabasca r. Canada 60 G3 ..........58°28'N 111°09'W
Athabasca, Lake Canada 60 H3 .......59°17'N 109°24'W
Athboy Ireland 18 E3 ................53°37'N 6°55'W
Athenry Ireland 18 C3 ...............53°18'N 8°45'W
Athens Greece 50 E3 ................37°59'N 23°43'E
Atherstone England 8 D3 ............52°35'N 1°33'W
Athlone Ireland 18 D3 ...............53°25'N 7°57'W
Atholl, Forest of Scotland 17 E1 ......56°51'N 4°10'W
Athos mt. Greece 50 F5 ..............40°10'N 24°19'E
Athy Ireland 18 E2 ..................52°59'N 6°59'W
Ati Chad 85 F3 .....................13°14'N 18°20'E
Atikokan Canada 63 H6 ..............48°45'N 91°37'W
Atlanta U.S.A. 63 I4 .................33°46'N 84°22'W
Atlantic City U.S.A. 63 L4 ...........39°21'N 74°26'W
Atlantic Ocean 116 D3
Atlas Mountains Africa 84 D5 .........30°13'N 7°41'W
Atlas Saharien mts Algeria 84 E5 .....32°41'N 0°20'E
Aṭ Ṭā'if Saudi Arabia 94 F4 ..........21°15'N 40°20'E
Attleborough England 9 G3 ..........52°31'N 1°01'E
Atyrau Kazakhstan 53 F2 .............47°08'N 51°56'E
Aube r. France 44 E6 ................48°34'N 3°43'E
Auchterarder Scotland 15 F4 .........56°18'N 3°42'W
Auchtermuchty Scotland 15 F4 .......56°18'N 3°14'W
Auckland New Zealand 109 G3 .......36°52'S 174°46'E
Auckland Islands New Zealand 109 F1 ..50°43'S 166°12'E
Auderville France 11 Z9 ..............49°43'N 1°55'W
Audlem England 8 C3 ...............52°59'N 2°31'W
Audruicq France 9 H1 ...............50°52'N 2°05'E
Augher Northern Ireland 14 B2 .......54°25'N 7°08'W
Aughton England 13 F2 ..............53°22'N 1°19'W
Augsburg Germany 46 D3 ...........48°22'N 10°52'E
Augusta Ga. U.S.A. 63 J3 ............33°28'N 82°02'W
Augusta Me. U.S.A. 63 M5 ...........44°19'N 69°46'W
Aulnoye-Aymeries France 42 C3 ......50°12'N 3°51'E
Aurangabad India 96 E4 ..............19°53'N 75°24'E
Aurich Germany 42 G6 ...............53°28'N 7°30'E
Aurora U.S.A. 62 F4 .................39°43'N 104°53'W
Auskerry i. Scotland 17 G4 ..........59°02'N 2°33'W
Austin U.S.A. 62 G3 .................30°16'N 97°42'W
Australia Oceania 108 B4 ............27°17'S 129°18'E
Australian Capital Territory d. Australia 108 D3
....................35°27'S 148°52'E
Austria Europe 46 E2 ................47°12'N 13°26'E
Authie r. France 9 G1 ...............50°22'N 1°37'E
Auvergne, Monts d' mts France 44 E4 ..45°45'N 2°59'E
Auxerre France 44 E5 ...............47°48'N 3°35'E
Avallon France 44 E5 ...............47°30'N 3°54'E
Avanos Turkey 51 K4 ................38°43'N 34°51'E
Aveiro Portugal 45 A4 ...............40°39'N 8°38'W
Avesta Sweden 43 D3 ...............60°09'N 16°10'E
Aveyron r. France 44 D4 .............44°05'N 1°16'E
Aviemore Scotland 17 F2 ............57°12'N 3°49'W
Avignon France 44 F3 ...............43°57'N 4°49'E
Ávila Spain 45 C4 ...................40°40'N 4°41'W
Avilés Spain 45 C5 ..................43°33'N 5°54'W
Avon r. Brist. England 8 C2 ..........51°29'N 2°40'W
Avon r. Dor. England 8 D1 ...........50°44'N 1°46'W
Avon r. Glos. England 8 C3 ..........52°00'N 2°08'W
Avon r. Scotland 17 F2 ..............57°25'N 3°22'W
Avonmore r. Ireland 10 A4 ...........52°48'N 6°08'W
Avonmouth England 8 C2 ............51°30'N 2°42'W
Åwash Ethiopia 85 I2 ................8°59'N 40°10'E
Awbārī Libya 84 F4 .................26°34'N 12°46'E
Awbārī, Idhān des. Libya 48 F2 ......27°23'N 10°25'E
Awe, Loch l. Scotland 14 D4 .........56°16'N 5°14'W
Axe r. England 11 D2 ...............50°43'N 3°04'W
Axel Heiberg Island Canada 61 I5 ....79°47'N 91°17'W
Axminster England 8 C1 .............50°47'N 2°59'W
Ayacucho Peru 72 B5 ...............13°10'S 74°13'W
Ayagoz Kazakhstan 54 J2 ............47°56'N 80°23'E

Ayan Russia 55 O3 ..................56°26'N 138°12'E
Aydarko'l ko'li l. Uzbekistan 54 H2 ...41°02'N 66°33'E
Aydın Turkey 51 G3 .................37°50'N 27°49'E
Aylesbury England 8 E2 .............51°49'N 0°48'W
Aylsham England 9 G2 ..............51°14'N 1°12'E
Aylsham England 9 G3 ..............52°48'N 1°15'E
Ayr r. Scotland 14 E3 ...............55°28'N 4°38'W
Ayr Scotland 14 E3 .................55°28'N 4°38'W
Ayr, Point of Wales 10 D5 ..........53°21'N 3°18'W
Ayre, Point of Isle of Man 12 C3 ....54°25'N 4°22'W
Ayvalık Turkey 50 G4 ...............39°17'N 26°41'E
Azawad f. Mali 84 D4 ...............20°20'N 3°00'W
Azerbaijan Asia 53 E2 ..............40°23'N 48°09'E
Azopol'ye Russia 52 E4 .............65°18'N 45°11'E
Azores i. Portugal 116 E3 ...........37°45'N 25°40'W
Azov, Sea of Russia/Ukraine 53 D2 ..46°03'N 36°47'E
Azrou Morocco 48 B3 ...............33°26'N 5°11'W
Azuero, Península de pen. Panama 67 H2 ..7°39'N 80°41'W
Azul, Cordillera mts Peru 72 B6 .....8°31'S 75°56'W
Az Zaqāzīq Egypt 49 J3 .............30°35'N 31°30'E
Az Zarqā' Jordan 94 E6 .............32°04'N 36°05'E

# B

Baardheere Somalia 85 I2 ...........2°19'N 42°18'E
Bābā, Kūh-e mts Afgh. 95 K6 ........34°48'N 68°27'E
Babadag Romania 51 H7 ............44°54'N 28°42'E
Babaeski Turkey 50 G5 ..............41°26'N 27°06'E
Bāb al Mandab str. Africa/Asia 94 F2 ..12°21'N 43°26'E
Babar i. Indonesia 103 H2 ...........7°57'S 129°51'E
Babbacombe Bay England 11 D2 .....50°31'N 3°28'W
Babia Góra mt. Poland 46 H3 ........49°35'N 19°32'E
Babo Indonesia 103 I3 ..............2°35'S 133°21'E
Babruysk Belarus 47 M5 .............53°09'N 29°14'E
Bab-Termas hill Morocco 45 D1 ......34°29'N 3°53'W
Babuyan Islands Phil. 103 G7 ........19°13'N 121°59'E
Bacabal Brazil 72 E6 ................4°16'S 44°47'W
Bacan i. Indonesia 103 H3 ..........0°44'S 127°35'E
Bacău Romania 47 L2 ...............46°34'N 26°55'E
Back r. Canada 61 I4 ................66°32'N 95°51'W
Backwater Reservoir Scotland 17 F1 ..56°44'N 3°13'W
Bacolod Phil. 103 G6 ...............10°37'N 122°57'E
Bac Liêu Vietnam 102 D5 ...........9°15'N 105°45'E
Banda Sea Indonesia 103 I2 .........5°40'S 130°00'E
Bandırma Turkey 51 G5 ..............40°21'N 27°58'E
Bandon Ireland 18 C1 ...............51°45'N 8°44'W
Bandon r. Ireland 18 C1 .............51°45'N 8°42'W
Bandundu Dem. Rep. Congo 83 A4 ...3°17'S 17°22'E
Bandung Indonesia 102 D2 ..........6°56'S 107°37'E
Banff Canada 60 G3 ................51°11'N 115°33'W
Banff Scotland 17 G2 ...............57°40'N 2°31'W
Bangassou C.A.R. 85 G2 .............4°44'N 22°49'E
Banggai, Kepulauan is Indonesia 103 G3 ..1°59'S 123°24'E
Bangka i. Indonesia 102 C3 .........2°07'S 106°07'E
Bangkok Thailand 102 C6 ...........13°44'N 100°30'E
Bangladesh Asia 97 H5 .............23°47'N 89°43'E
Bangor Northern Ireland 14 D2 ......54°39'N 5°40'W
Bangor U.S.A. 63 M5 ...............44°48'N 68°46'W
Bangor Wales 10 C5 ...............53°14'N 4°08'W
Bangui C.A.R. 85 F2 ................4°20'N 18°37'E
Bangweulu, Lake Zambia 83 B3 ......11°13'S 29°47'E
Bani r. Mali 84 D3 ..................14°30'N 4°12'W
Banī Mazār Egypt 49 J2 .............28°29'N 30°48'E
Banī Suwayf Egypt 49 J2 ............29°05'N 31°05'E
Banī Walīd Libya 48 F3 ..............31°47'N 14°01'E
Bāniyās Syria 51 K2 .................35°11'N 35°57'E
Banja Luka Bos. and Herz. 50 B7 ....44°46'N 17°10'E
Banjarmasin Indonesia 102 E3 .......3°23'S 114°36'E
Banjul Gambia 84 C3 ...............13°27'N 16°35'W
Banks Island Canada 60 F5 ..........73°06'N 121°23'W
Banks Islands Vanuatu 109 F5 .......13°55'S 167°32'E
Banmi Pakistan 95 L6 ...............33°00'N 70°38'E
Bann r. Ireland 10 A4 ...............52°33'N 6°41'W
Bann r. Northern Ireland 14 C3 ......55°09'N 6°47'W
Ban Tha Song Yang Thailand 102 B7 ..17°34'N 97°55'E
Bantry Ireland 18 B1 ................51°41'N 9°27'W
Bantry Bay Ireland 18 B1 ...........51°34'N 9°48'W
Baoding China 99 L5 ...............38°46'N 115°29'E
Baoshan China 99 H3 ...............25°07'N 99°09'E
Baotou China 99 K6 ................40°31'N 110°00'E
Ba'qūbah Iraq 94 F6 ................33°42'N 44°37'E
Bar Montenegro 50 C6 .............42°05'N 19°06'E
Bara Sudan 94 D2 ..................13°40'N 30°24'E
Baracoa Cuba 67 J5 ................20°21'N 74°30'W
Baranavichy Belarus 47 L5 ..........53°08'N 26°00'E
Baranīs Egypt 49 K1 ................23°53'N 35°29'E
Barbacena Brazil 73 E4 .............21°13'S 43°44'W
Barbados Central America 67 M3 ....13°09'N 59°36'W
Barbuda i. Antigua 67 L4 ............17°39'N 61°48'W
Barcaldine Australia 108 D4 .........23°32'S 145°18'E
Barcelona Spain 45 G4 .............41°25'N 2°11'E
Barcelona Venezuela 72 C8 .........10°06'N 64°43'W
Bárðarbunga mt. Iceland 43 Y2 ......64°38'N 17°32'W
Bardney England 13 G2 .............53°13'N 0°19'W
Bardsey Island Wales 10 C4 .........52°45'N 4°48'W
Bardsey Sound str. Wales 10 C4 .....52°47'N 4°46'W
Bareilly India 96 E6 ................28°22'N 79°26'E
Barentsburg Arctic Oc. 54 ...........77°49'N 14°18'E
Barents Sea Arctic Oc. 54 F5 ........75°18'N 42°40'E
Barham England 9 G2 ..............51°12'N 1°10'E
Bari Italy 49 G5 ...................41°07'N 16°53'E
Barinas Venezuela 72 B7 ...........8°34'N 70°12'W
Barisan, Pegunungan mts Indonesia 102 C3
....................1°12'S 100°28'E
Barkly Tableland f. Australia 108 C5 ..18°06'S 135°29'E
Bârlad Romania 50 G8 ..............46°13'N 27°41'E
Barlee, Lake Australia 108 A4 .......28°58'S 119°26'E
Barmer India 96 D6 ................25°44'N 71°23'E
Barmouth Wales 10 C4 .............52°43'N 4°03'W
Barmouth Bay Wales 10 C4 .........52°43'N 4°05'W
Barnard Castle England 13 F3 .......54°33'N 1°55'W
Barnaul Russia 54 J3 ...............53°22'N 83°45'E
Barnet England 9 E2 ...............51°39'N 0°12'W
Barnoldswick England 13 E2 ........53°55'N 2°11'W
Barnsley England 13 F2 .............53°33'N 1°29'W
Barnstaple England 11 C3 ..........51°05'N 4°03'W
Barnstaple or Bideford Bay England 11 C3
....................51°05'N 4°25'W
Barquisimeto Venezuela 72 C8 ......10°03'N 69°18'W
Barra i. Scotland 16 B1 .............56°59'N 7°27'W
Barra, Sound of str. Scotland 16 B2 ..57°04'N 7°20'W
Barranquilla Colombia 72 B8 ........10°59'N 74°47'W
Barretos Brazil 73 E4 ...............20°35'S 48°35'W
Barrhead Scotland 14 E3 ............55°48'N 4°23'W
Barrow r. Ireland 18 E2 .............52°23'N 6°58'W
Barrow, Point U.S.A. 60 C5 .........71°23'N 156°29'W

ow-in-Furness England 12 D3..................54°07'N 3°13'W
ow Island Australia 108 A4..........20°49'S 115°22'E
y Wales 11 D3..........................51°24'N 3°17'W
tow U.S.A. 62 C3....................34°54'N 117°01'W
n Turkey 51 J5...........................41°38'N 32°21'E
on-upon-Humber England 13 G2.....53°41'N 0°27'W
oszyce Poland 46 I6................54°15'N 20°49'E
un-Urt Mongolia 99 K7.........46°31'N 113°22'E
saw Belarus 47 M6.....................54°14'N 28°31'E
hurch England 8 C3.................52°47'N 2°51'W
Switz. 46 B2.............................47°33'N 7°35'E
an i. Phil. 103 G5.......................6°32'N 121°52'E
don England 9 F2......................51°35'N 0°29'E
ngstoke England 8 D2................51°16'N 1°06'W
Iraq 95 H6..............................30°29'N 47°48'E
enthwaite Lake England 12 D3.....54°40'N 3°14'W
e-Terre Guadeloupe 67 L4..........16°01'N 61°44'W
Rock i. Guadel 15 G4...............56°05'N 2°38'W
Strait Australia 108 D3............39°43'S 146°11'E
ak Iran 95 H5.............................27°12'N 54°25'E
a France 44 H3........................42°42'N 9°27'E
ogne Belgium 42 E3.................50°00'N 5°43'E
Equat. Guinea 84 E2.................1°50'N 9°48'E
baňó, Golfo de b. Cuba 67 H5.....22°16'N 82°38'W
n Indonesia 102 C4...............1°09'N 104°01'E
ng China 99 H4........................30°01'N 99°08'E
ng Indonesia 97 I6.................6°57'S 109°43'E
ngas Phil. 103 G6..................13°46'N 121°01'E
Islands Phil. 103 G8..............20°46'N 122°05'E
mbâng Cambodia 102 C6..........13°06'N 103°14'E
England 8 C2............................51°23'N 2°22'W
and North East Somerset d. England 21 D2
..................................................51°21'N 2°28'W
gate Scotland 15 F3.................55°54'N 3°39'W
urst Australia 108 D3............33°25'S 149°34'E
urst Canada 61 L2..................47°36'N 65°39'W
urst Island Australia 108 C5........11°29'S 130°11'E
urst Island Canada 61 I5.........75°49'N 98°59'W
y England 13 F2.......................53°43'N 1°38'W
Algeria 84 E5..........................35°32'N 6°13'E
n Rouge U.S.A. 63 H3...........30°27'N 91°11'W
caloa Sri Lanka 96 F2...............7°42'N 81°39'E
e England 9 F1...........................50°55'N 0°29'E
Pulau-pulau is Indonesia 102 B3.....0°14'S 98°16'E
mi Georgia 53 E2..................41°39'N 41°38'E
au Indonesia 103 G2..............5°29'S 122°37'E
hi Nigeria 84 E3.....................10°19'N 9°50'E
u Brazil 73 E4...........................22°20'S 49°05'W
ka Latvia 47 K7......................56°25'N 24°13'E
en Germany 46 F4.................51°11'N 14°26'E
n i. Indonesia 102 E2................5°48'S 112°34'E
ino Cuba 67 I5.......................20°22'N 76°38'W
hongor Mongolia 99 I7.........46°09'N 100°41'E
n-Uul Mongolia 99 K7.........48°55'N 112°44'E
rt Turkey 51 N5......................40°15'N 40°14'E
City Mich. U.S.A. 63 J5...........43°35'N 83°53'W
City Tex. U.S.A. 63 G2............28°59'N 96°02'W
aratskaya Guba Russia 52 G4.....69°29'N 66°01'E
ak Russia 53 F3.......................52°31'N 58°15'E
ne France 44 C3......................43°29'N 1°29'W
uth Germany 46 F5.................43°26'N 11°36'E
al Kabīr, Wādī watercourse Libya 48 G3
..................................................31°11'N 15°53'E
Spain 45 D2.............................37°30'N 2°46'W
dyuzyu, Gora mt. Azerbaijan 53 E2......41°12'N 47°52'E
ny Head England 9 F1..............50°44'N 0°15'E
onsfield England 8 E2.............51°36'N 0°39'W
e Gulf Australia 103 H1.........12°04'S 129°55'E
inster England 8 C1.................50°49'N 2°45'W
lmore Canada 63 I6...............49°36'N 87°58'W
ka Cabo c. Dom. Rep. 67 J4.......17°38'N 71°23'W
, Isla i. Dom. Rep. 67 J4.........17°36'N 71°30'W
ort Sea Canada/U.S.A. 60 F5.....73°19'N 129°52'W
ort West S. Africa 83 B1...........32°20'S 22°36'E
y Scotland 17 E2.....................57°29'N 4°28'W
y r. Scotland 17 E2..................57°29'N 4°27'W
y Firth est. Scotland 17 E2........57°29'N 4°23'W
maris Wales 10 C5..................53°16'N 4°05'W
mont U.S.A. 63 H3................30°05'N 94°09'W
mont France 11 Z9.................49°40'N 1°50'W
ne France 44 F5.......................47°01'N 4°50'E
vais France 44 E6...................49°26'N 2°05'E
er r. Canada 60 H3.................55°22'N 107°45'W
er Creek town Canada 60 D4.....62°23'N 140°49'W
gs England 9 G3......................52°28'N 1°34'E
reá Spain 45 B5.......................42°51'N 7°09'W
Algeria 84 D5..........................31°36'N 2°13'W
ngham England 13 G2..............53°24'N 0°49'W
ey U.S.A. 63 J4........................37°47'N 81°11'W
e England 13 F3.........................54°17'N 1°35'W
ē Ethiopia 85 H2.......................8°28'N 36°21'E
ord England 9 E3.....................52°08'N 0°28'W
ord d. England 21 E3..............52°10'N 0°28'W
ngton England 13 F4..............55°08'N 1°36'W
orth England 8 D3.................52°29'N 1°28'W
heba Israel 49 J3.....................31°15'N 34°48'E
lle Lough l. Northern Ireland 14 C2....54°47'N 6°27'W
n China 99 N7.........................48°11'N 126°31'E
i China 99 J2...........................21°27'N 109°08'E
g China 99 L5.........................39°52'N 116°27'E
an Oir hill Scotland 14 D3.........55°54'N 5°59'W
Dearg mt. High. Scotland 16 E2.....57°47'N 4°56'W
Dearg mt. P. and K. Scotland 17 F1.....56°53'N 3°53'W
Heasgarnich mt. Scotland 14 E4.....56°31'N 4°35'W
Mozambique 83 C3.................19°50'S 34°52'E
Lebanon 49 K3.......................33°52'N 35°30'E
Scotland 14 E3........................55°45'N 4°38'W
Romania 47 J2.........................46°40'N 22°23'E
ortugal 45 B3.........................38°01'N 7°52'W
Algeria 84 E5..........................36°44'N 5°03'E
Spain 45 C4.............................40°24'N 5°46'W
csaba Hungary 46 I2................46°41'N 21°05'E
Pakistan 96 C6.......................26°12'N 66°21'E
us Europe 47 L5......................54°01'N 28°39'E
átów Poland 46 H4..................51°22'N 19°22'E
er Islands Canada 61 K3..........56°10'N 78°47'W
ey Russia 53 F3......................54°05'N 54°08'E
weyne Somalia 85 I2................4°44'N 45°13'E
l Brazil 72 E6..........................1°26'S 48°29'W
st City England 8 E2................52°23'N 1°29'W
st Northern Ireland 14 D2.........54°36'N 5°55'W
st d. Northern Ireland 21 C4.......54°35'N 5°55'W
st Lough inlet Northern Ireland 14 D2
..................................................54°40'N 5°52'W

Belford England 13 F4................55°36'N 1°50'W
Belgium Europe 42 D3...............50°55'N 4°14'E
Belgorod Russia 53 D3.............50°35'N 36°37'E
Belgrade Serbia 50 D7...............44°48'N 20°29'E
Belitung i. Indonesia 102 D3.......2°47'S 108°14'E
Belize town Belize 66 G4............17°31'N 88°14'W
Belize Central America 66 G4.......17°10'N 88°18'W
Bellac France 44 D5..................46°08'N 1°03'E
Belle-Île i. France 44 B5.............47°19'N 3°15'W
Belle Isle, Strait of Canada 61 M3......51°16'N 56°57'W
Bellingham England 13 E4..........55°09'N 2°15'W
Bellingham U.S.A. 62 B6............48°45'N 122°28'W
Bellinzona Switz. 46 C2.............46°12'N 9°01'E
Belluno Italy 46 E6...................46°08'N 12°13'E
Belmopan Belize 66 G4.............17°14'N 88°46'W
Belmullet Ireland 18 B4.............54°14'N 9°59'W
Belo Horizonte Brazil 73 E5.......19°55'S 43°56'W
Beloretsk Russia 53 F3..............53°55'N 58°24'E
Beloye, Ozero Russia 52 D4........60°10'N 38°00'E
Belozersk Russia 52 D3.............60°02'N 37°47'E
Belper England 13 F2................53°02'N 1°29'W
Belukha, Gora mt. Kazakhstan/Russia 54 J2
..................................................49°50'N 86°41'E
Belush'ye Russia 52 E4.............66°55'N 47°36'E
Belyy Russia 47 O6..................55°50'N 32°57'E
Bembridge England 8 D1...........50°41'N 1°05'W
Bemidji U.S.A. 63 H6................47°27'N 94°52'W
Ben Alder mt. Scotland 17 E1......56°49'N 4°28'W
Benavente Spain 45 C5..............42°00'N 5°40'W
Benbane Head Northern Ireland 14 C3......55°15'N 6°30'W
Benbecula i. Scotland 16 B2........57°27'N 7°23'W
Ben Cleuch hill Scotland 15 F4......56°11'N 3°46'W
Ben Cruachan mt. Scotland 14 D4.....56°25'N 5°08'W
Bend U.S.A. 62 B5....................44°04'N 121°17'W
Bender Moldova 49 I6...............46°49'N 29°29'E
Bendigo Australia 108 D3..........36°46'S 144°18'E
Benešov Czechia 46 F3..............49°47'N 14°42'E
Bengal, Bay of sea Indian Oc. 96 G4......17°51'N 88°40'E
Bengaluru India 96 E3...............12°57'N 77°34'E
Bengbu China 99 L4.................32°54'N 117°23'E
Benghazi Libya 85 G5................32°06'N 20°04'E
Bengkulu Indonesia 102 C3.........3°45'S 102°18'E
Benguela Angola 83 A3.............12°36'S 13°21'E
Ben Hope hill Scotland 17 E3.......58°25'N 4°36'W
Beni r. Bolivia 72 C5................11°01'S 66°07'W
Benidorm Spain 45 E3..............38°32'N 0°08'W
Béni Mellal Morocco 84 D5.........32°17'N 6°25'W
Benin Africa 84 E3....................8°26'N 2°11'E
Benin, Bight of g. Africa 84 E2......5°17'N 3°27'E
Benin City Nigeria 84 E2.............6°19'N 5°36'E
Beni-Saf Algeria 48 C4..............35°20'N 1°21'W
Benjamim Constant Brazil 72 C6......4°23'S 69°58'W
Ben Klibreck hill Scotland 17 E3......58°15'N 4°24'W
Ben Lawers mt. Scotland 14 E4......56°33'N 4°13'W
Ben Lomond hill Scotland 14 E4......56°11'N 4°38'W
Ben Loyal hill Scotland 17 E3........58°24'N 4°27'W
Ben Lui mt. Scotland 14 E4.........56°24'N 4°49'W
Ben Macdui mt. Scotland 17 F2......57°05'N 3°40'W
Ben More hill Scotland 14 C4........56°25'N 6°00'W
Ben More mt. Scotland 14 E4........56°23'N 4°32'W
Ben More Assynt hill Scotland 16 E3......58°08'N 4°51'W
Ben Nevis mt. Scotland 16 D1......56°48'N 5°00'W
Bentley England 13 F2...............53°33'N 1°09'W
Benue r. Nigeria 84 E2................7°49'N 6°48'E
Ben Vorlich hill Scotland 14 E4......56°21'N 4°13'W
Ben Wyvis mt. Scotland 17 E2......57°41'N 4°35'W
Benxi China 99 M6...................41°16'N 123°45'E
Beoraid, Loch l. Scotland 16 D1......56°54'N 5°36'W
Berat Albania 50 C5..................40°42'N 19°58'E
Berau, Teluk b. Indonesia 103 I3......2°28'S 132°36'E
Berber Sudan 94 D3..................18°00'N 34°02'E
Berbera Somalia 85 I3................10°24'N 45°02'E
Berbérati C.A.R. 84 F2...............4°14'N 15°47'E
Berck France 9 G1....................50°25'N 1°35'E
Berdyans'k Ukraine 49 K6...........46°46'N 36°48'E
Berdychiv Ukraine 47 M3...........49°53'N 28°36'E
Berens River town Canada 60 I3......52°21'N 97°01'W
Berezivka Ukraine 47 N2............47°12'N 30°55'E
Berezniki Russia 52 F3...............59°25'N 56°48'E
Berezovo Russia 52 G4..............63°54'N 65°07'E
Bergama Turkey 50 G4...............39°07'N 27°11'E
Bergamo Italy 46 C1.................45°42'N 9°41'E
Bergen Norway 43 A4................60°23'N 5°22'E
Bergerac France 44 D4..............44°51'N 0°29'E
Bergisch Gladbach Germany 46 B4......50°58'N 7°08'E
Bering Sea N. Pacific Oc. 56 B5......60°00'N 170°00'E
Bering Strait Russia/U.S.A. 55 U4......66°18'N 168°40'W
Berkel r. Neth. 42 F5................52°08'N 6°11'E
Berkeley England 8 C2..............51°41'N 2°27'W
Berkshire Downs hills England 8 D2......51°30'N 1°20'W
Berlin Germany 46 E5...............52°31'N 13°23'E
Bermuda i. N. Atlantic Oc. 67 L7......32°24'N 64°56'W
Bern Switz. 46 B2.....................46°57'N 7°27'E
Berneray i. Na h-E. S. Scotland 16 B1......56°47'N 7°38'W
Berneray i. Na h-E. S. Scotland 16 B2......57°44'N 7°18'W
Berry Head England 11 D2.........50°24'N 3°29'W
Bertoua Cameroon 84 F2............4°35'N 13°41'E
Berwick-upon-Tweed England 13 E4......55°46'N 2°00'W
Besançon France 44 G5.............47°15'N 6°01'E
Bessbrook Northern Ireland 14 C2......54°12'N 6°23'W
Betanzos Spain 45 A5...............43°17'N 8°12'W
Beth, Oued r. Morocco 45 B1......34°25'N 6°26'W
Bethesda Wales 10 C5..............53°11'N 4°03'W
Béthune France 42 B3...............50°31'N 2°38'E
Betsiboka r. Madagascar 83 D3......15°58'S 46°27'E
Bettystown Ireland 10 A5...........53°42'N 6°15'W
Betws-y-coed Wales 10 D5.........53°05'N 3°48'W
Beult r. England 9 F2................51°13'N 0°25'E
Beverley England 13 G2.............53°51'N 0°26'W
Bewdley England 8 C3..............52°23'N 2°19'W
Bewl Water resr England 9 F2......51°04'N 0°23'E
Bexhill England 9 F1.................50°50'N 0°29'E
Beykoz Turkey 51 H5................41°07'N 29°05'E
Beyla Guinea 84 D2..................8°41'N 8°41'W
Beyneu Kazakhstan 53 F2...........45°18'N 55°11'E
Beypazarı Turkey 51 I5..............40°10'N 31°56'E
Beyşehir Turkey 51 I3...............37°42'N 31°43'E
Beyşehir Gölü l. Turkey 51 I3......37°42'N 31°33'E
Bhagalpur India 96 G5...............25°15'N 86°56'E
Bhamo Myanmar 97 I5..............24°18'N 97°17'E
Bhavnagar India 96 D5..............21°46'N 72°14'E
Bhima r. India 96 E4.................16°26'N 77°23'E
Bhopal India 96 E5...................23°15'N 77°23'E
Bhubaneshwar India 96 G5.........20°13'N 85°53'E
Bhuj India 96 C5.....................23°11'N 69°44'E
Bhutan Asia 97 H6...................27°38'N 90°33'E

Biak Indonesia 103 J3................1°12'S 136°05'E
Biak i. Indonesia 103 J3..............0°59'S 135°59'E
Biała Podlaska Poland 47 J5........52°02'N 23°07'E
Białystok Poland 47 J5..............53°08'N 23°10'E
Biarritz France 44 C3................43°29'N 1°33'W
Bibai Japan 104 D4..................43°18'N 141°52'E
Biberach an der Riß Germany 46 C3......48°06'N 9°47'E
Bicester England 8 D2...............51°54'N 1°09'W
Bidar India 96 E4.....................17°54'N 77°34'E
Biddulph England 13 E2.............53°07'N 2°10'W
Bidean nam Bian mt. Scotland 16 D1......56°39'N 5°02'W
Bideford England 11 C3.............51°01'N 4°12'W
Biel/Bienne Switz. 46 B2............47°09'N 7°15'E
Bielefeld Germany 46 C5...........52°01'N 8°32'E
Biella Italy 46 C1.....................45°34'N 8°04'E
Bielsko-Biała Poland 46 H3........49°49'N 19°03'E
Bié Plateau f. Angola 78 C2........13°00'S 17°00'E
Bifoun Gabon 84 F1..................0°15'S 10°25'E
Biga Turkey 50 G5...................40°13'N 27°13'E
Bigbury Bay England 11 D2........50°15'N 3°54'W
Biggar Scotland 15 F3...............55°37'N 3°31'W
Biggleswade England 9 E3.........52°05'N 0°16'W
Bighorn r. U.S.A. 62 E6..............46°10'N 107°30'W
Bighorn Mountains U.S.A. 62 E5......44°06'N 106°55'W
Big Spring U.S.A. 62 F3.............32°16'N 101°24'W
Big Trout Lake town Canada 61 J3......53°49'N 89°50'W
Bihać Bos. and Herz. 50 A7........44°49'N 15°53'E
Bihar d. India 96 G5.................24°13'N 85°37'E
Bihor, Vârful mt. Romania 47 J2......46°27'N 22°44'E
Bijär Iran 95 G6......................35°51'N 47°37'E
Bijeljina Bos. and Herz. 50 C7......44°46'N 19°14'E
Bijelo Polje Montenegro 50 C6......43°02'N 19°45'E
Bikaner India 96 D6..................28°00'N 73°23'E
Bilaspur India 98 E2.................22°05'N 82°09'E
Bila Tserkva Ukraine 47 N3........49°48'N 30°07'E
Bilbao Spain 45 D5...................43°15'N 2°54'W
Bilecik Turkey 51 H5.................40°09'N 29°57'E
Bilhorod-Dnistrovs'kyy Ukraine 49 J6......46°11'N 30°20'E
Billericay England 9 F2..............51°38'N 0°25'E
Billingham England 13 F3...........54°37'N 1°17'W
Billinghay England 13 G2...........53°05'N 0°17'W
Billings U.S.A. 62 E6.................45°48'N 108°27'W
Billingshurst England 9 E2.........51°01'N 0°27'W
Bill of Portland hd England 8 C1......50°30'N 2°30'W
Bilopillya Ukraine 47 P4.............51°09'N 34°20'E
Biloxi U.S.A. 63 I3....................30°24'N 88°57'W
Bilston Scotland 15 F3..............55°52'N 3°11'W
Bilton England 13 G2................53°47'N 0°15'W
Bimini Islands Bahamas 67 I6......25°46'N 79°14'W
Bindura Zimbabwe 83 C3...........17°18'S 31°19'E
Bingham England 8 E3..............52°57'N 0°57'W
Binghamton U.S.A. 63 K5..........42°06'N 75°55'W
Bingley England 13 F2...............53°51'N 1°50'W
Bintulu Malaysia 102 E4.............3°12'N 113°03'E
Bioko i. Equat. Guinea 84 E2........3°16'N 8°31'E
Birak Libya 48 F4....................27°33'N 14°16'E
Birao C.A.R. 94 B2...................10°15'N 22°48'E
Birecik Turkey 51 L3.................37°01'N 37°59'E
Birhan mt. Ethiopia 85 H3...........10°43'N 37°52'E
Birjand Iran 95 I6.....................32°53'N 59°08'E
Birkenhead England 12 D2..........53°23'N 3°01'W
Birmingham England 8 D3..........52°29'N 1°53'W
Birmingham U.S.A. 63 I3............33°32'N 86°47'W
Bīr Mogreïn Mauritania 84 C4......25°14'N 11°34'W
Birnin Konni Niger 84 E3............13°48'N 5°14'E
Birobidzhan Russia 99 O7...........48°45'N 132°52'E
Birr Ireland 18 D3....................53°06'N 7°55'W
Birsay Scotland 17 F4...............59°08'N 3°18'W
Birstall England 8 D3................52°41'N 1°07'W
Biržai Lithuania 47 K7...............56°12'N 24°45'E
Biscay, Bay of sea France/Spain 45 C5......45°40'N 5°07'W
Bischofshofen Austria 46 E2........47°25'N 13°13'E
Bishkek Kyrgyzstan 98 C6..........42°54'N 74°32'E
Bisho S. Africa 83 B1................32°51'S 27°24'E
Bishop Auckland England 13 F3......54°40'N 1°41'W
Bishops Lydeard England 11 D3......51°04'N 3°11'W
Bishop's Stortford England 9 F2......51°52'N 0°10'E
Bishop's Waltham England 8 D1......50°57'N 1°13'W
Biskra Algeria 84 E5.................34°49'N 5°44'E
Bismarck U.S.A. 62 F6...............46°50'N 100°46'W
Bismarck Sea P.N.G. 108 D6........4°01'S 149°01'E
Bissau Guinea,ÀèBissau 84 C3......11°53'N 15°38'W
Bistra r. Serbia 50 D6................42°09'N 20°59'E
Bistriţa Romania 47 K2..............47°09'N 24°30'E
Bistriţa r. Romania 47 L2............46°30'N 26°58'E
Bitburg Germany 42 F2..............49°58'N 6°32'E
Bitola North Macedonia 50 D5......41°01'N 21°20'E
Bitterroot Range mts U.S.A. 62 D6......47°16'N 115°41'W
Biwa-ko l. Japan 104 C3.............35°09'N 135°59'E
Biysk Russia 54 J3...................52°31'N 85°17'E
Bizerte Tunisia 48 E4................37°16'N 9°52'E
Bjørnøya i. Arctic Oc. 54 C5........74°24'N 19°07'E
Blackburn England 13 E2...........53°45'N 2°29'W
Blackburn with Darwen d. England 21 D3......53°41'N 2°27'W
Black Combe hill England 12 D3......54°15'N 3°20'W
Blackfield England 8 D1.............50°49'N 1°22'W
Black Forest mts Germany 46 C2......47°56'N 8°08'E
Black Head England 11 B2..........50°00'N 5°07'W
Black Hill England 13 F2.............53°32'N 1°53'W
Black Isle pen. Scotland 17 E2......57°35'N 4°19'W
Blackpool England 12 D2...........53°49'N 3°03'W
Blackpool d. England 21 D3.........53°49'N 3°01'W
Black Sea Asia/Europe 51 M6......42°31'N 38°22'E
Blacksod Bay Ireland 18 A4........54°03'N 10°03'W
Black Volta r. Africa 84 D2.........8°29'N 0°51'W
Blackwater r. England 9 F2.........51°44'N 0°41'E
Blackwater r. Meath Ireland 18 E3......53°39'N 6°41'W
Blackwater r. Water. Ireland 18 D2......52°08'N 7°51'W
Blackwater r. Northern Ireland 14 C2......54°31'N 6°34'W
Blackwood Wales 10 D3.............51°40'N 3°12'W
Blaenau Ffestiniog Wales 10 D4......52°59'N 3°57'W
Blaenau Gwent d. Wales 21 D2......51°46'N 3°12'W
Blaenavon Wales 10 D3..............51°47'N 3°06'W
Blagdon England 8 C2...............51°20'N 2°43'W
Blagoevgrad Bulgaria 50 E6.........42°01'N 23°06'E
Blagoveshchensk Russia 55 N3......50°17'N 127°29'E
Blair Atholl Scotland 17 F1..........56°46'N 3°51'W
Blairgowrie Scotland 15 F4.........56°35'N 3°21'W
Blanc, Mont mt. France/Italy 44 G4......45°50'N 6°51'E
Blanca, Bahía b. Argentina 73 C3......39°08'S 61°47'W
Blanche, Lake Australia 108 C4......29°15'S 139°42'E
Blanc Nez, Cap c. France 9 G1......50°56'N 1°44'E
Blanco, Cape U.S.A. 62 B5.........42°51'N 124°34'W
Blandford Forum England 8 C1......50°51'N 2°10'W
Blanquilla, Isla i. Venezuela 67 L3......11°51'N 64°35'W

Blantyre Malawi 83 C3...............15°47'S 35°02'E
Blarney Ireland 18 C1................51°56'N 8°34'W
Bletchley England 8 E2.............51°59'N 0°45'W
Blida Algeria 84 E5...................36°33'N 2°55'E
Bloemfontein S. Africa 83 B2......29°07'S 26°13'E
Blois France 44 D5...................47°35'N 1°20'E
Bloody Foreland pt Ireland 18 C5......55°10'N 8°18'W
Bloomington U.S.A. 63 I5...........39°29'N 88°59'W
Blue Mountains U.S.A. 62 C6......45°27'N 118°38'W
Blue Nile r. Sudan 85 H3............15°38'N 32°30'E
Blue Stack hill Ireland 14 A2........54°45'N 8°05'W
Blue Stack Mountains hills Ireland 18 C4......54°42'N 8°14'W
Blyth Northum. England 13 F4......55°08'N 1°30'W
Blyth Notts. England 13 F2.........53°22'N 1°04'W
Blytheville U.S.A. 63 I4..............35°56'N 89°52'W
Bo Sierra Leone 84 C2..............7°55'N 11°45'W
Boa Vista Brazil 72 C7...............2°51'N 60°43'W
Boa Vista i. Cape Verde 84 B3......16°05'N 22°40'W
Bobaomby, Tanjona c. Madagascar 83 D3......11°57'S 49°15'E
Bobo-Dioulasso Burkina Faso 84 D3......11°11'N 4°18'W
Bóbr r. Poland 46 F4.................52°03'N 15°04'E
Boby mt. Madagascar 83 D2........22°13'S 46°54'E
Bocholt Germany 46 B4.............51°50'N 6°36'E
Boddam Scotland 17 H2............57°28'N 1°47'W
Bodélé f. Chad 85 F3................16°12'N 16°17'E
Boden Sweden 43 E4................65°49'N 21°41'E
Bodenham England 8 C3............52°09'N 2°41'W
Bodmin England 11 C2..............50°28'N 4°43'W
Bodmin Moor f. England 11 C2......50°34'N 4°36'W
Bodø Norway 43 C4.................67°17'N 14°23'E
Bodrum Turkey 50 G3...............37°02'N 27°25'E
Boğazlıyan Turkey 51 K4............39°11'N 35°15'E
Boggeragh Mountains hills Ireland 18 B2......52°01'N 9°01'E
Bogie r. Scotland 17 G2.............57°27'N 2°46'W
Bognor Regis England 8 E1.........50°47'N 0°40'W
Bogor Indonesia 102 D2.............6°35'S 106°45'E
Bogotá Colombia 72 B7..............4°35'N 74°04'W
Bo Hai g. China 99 L5...............38°32'N 119°14'E
Bohain-en-Vermandois France 42 C2......49°59'N 3°28'E
Bohemian Forest mts Germany 46 E3......49°42'N 12°27'E
Bohol i. Phil. 103 G5.................9°55'N 124°16'E
Boise U.S.A. 62 C5...................43°38'N 116°11'W
Bojnürd Iran 95 I7....................37°27'N 57°19'E
Bolhrad Ukraine 49 I6...............45°41'N 28°37'E
Bolívar, Pico mt. Venezuela 67 J2......8°33'N 70°59'W
Bolivia S. America 72 C5............16°23'S 64°00'W
Bollnäs Sweden 43 D3...............61°21'N 16°24'E
Bolmen l. Sweden 43 C2............56°52'N 13°43'E
Bologna Italy 46 D1.................44°29'N 11°22'E
Bol'shevik, Ostrov i. Russia 55 L5......78°39'N 102°16'E
Bol'shezemel'skaya Tundra f. Russia 52 F4
..................................................67°00'N 58°00'E
Bol'shoy Aluy r. Russia 55 Q4......66°29'N 159°26'E
Bol'shoy Lyakhovskiy, Ostrov i. Russia 55 P5
..................................................73°26'N 142°14'E
Bolsover England 13 F2.............53°14'N 1°17'W
Bolt Head England 11 D2...........50°12'N 3°47'W
Bolton England 13 E2................53°35'N 2°26'W
Bolu Turkey 51 I5.....................40°44'N 31°36'E
Bolus Head Ireland 18 A1...........51°47'N 10°20'W
Bolzano Italy 46 D2..................46°29'N 11°21'E
Boma Dem. Rep. Congo 83 A4......5°48'S 13°03'E
Bømlo i. Norway 43 A2.............59°45'N 5°13'E
Bon, Cap c. Tunisia 48 F4...........37°04'N 11°04'E
Bonaire i. Neth. Antilles 67 K3......12°02'N 68°12'W
Bonar Bridge Scotland 17 E2......57°54'N 4°21'W
Bonavista Canada 61 M2...........48°33'N 52°43'W
Bondoukou Côte d'Ivoire 84 D2......8°03'N 2°48'W
Bo'ness Scotland 15 F4.............56°01'N 3°36'W
Bonifacio France 44 H2.............41°23'N 9°10'E
Bonifacio, Strait of France/Italy 44 H2......41°15'N 8°45'E
Bonn Germany 46 B4................50°44'N 7°04'E
Bonnyrigg Scotland 15 F3..........55°52'N 3°06'W
Bontosunggu Indonesia 102 F2......5°41'S 119°43'E
Boothia, Gulf of Canada 61 J4......68°48'N 86°41'W
Boothia Peninsula Canada 61 I5......70°40'N 94°39'W
Bootle England 12 D2...............53°27'N 2°59'W
Bor Turkey 51 K3....................37°54'N 34°33'E
Borås Sweden 43 C2.................57°44'N 12°57'E
Borāzjān Iran 95 H5.................29°16'N 51°12'E
Bordeaux France 44 C4.............44°51'N 0°34'W
Borden Island Canada 60 G5........78°31'N 111°01'W
Borden Peninsula Canada 61 J5......72°45'N 82°32'W
Bordj Messaouda Algeria 48 E3......30°10'N 9°25'E
Bordj Omer Driss Algeria 84 E4......28°11'N 6°47'E
Boreray i. Scotland 16 B2...........57°42'N 7°16'W
Borgarnes Iceland 43 X2............64°32'N 21°55'W
Borisoglebsk Russia 53 E3..........51°23'N 42°05'E
Borken Germany 42 F4..............51°50'N 6°51'E
Borkum i. Germany 42 F4...........53°37'N 6°44'E
Borlänge Sweden 43 C3.............60°29'N 15°26'E
Borneo i. Asia 102 E4...............0°08'N 113°25'E
Bornholm i. Denmark 43 C1........55°09'N 14°38'E
Bornova Turkey 50 G4...............38°27'N 27°11'E
Borodyanka Ukraine 47 M4.........50°39'N 29°56'E
Boroughbridge England 13 F3......54°06'N 1°24'W
Borovichi Russia 52 D3..............58°23'N 33°55'E
Borovskoy Kazakhstan 52 G3......53°47'N 64°12'E
Borūjerd Iran 95 G6..................33°53'N 48°43'E
Boryspil' Ukraine 47 N4.............50°21'N 30°58'E
Borzna Ukraine 47 O4...............51°15'N 32°26'E
Borzya Russia 55 M3................50°11'N 116°31'E
Bosanska Dubica Bos. and Herz. 50 B7......45°11'N 16°48'E
Bosna r. Bos. and Herz. 50 C7......45°04'N 18°29'E
Bosnia and Herzegovina Europe 50 B7......44°23'N 17°40'E
Bosobolo Dem. Rep. Congo 83 A4......4°10'N 19°52'E
Bosporus str. Turkey 51 H5.........41°20'N 29°06'E
Bossembélé C.A.R. 85 F2...........5°15'N 17°38'E
Bosten Hu l. China 98 F6............41°53'N 87°24'E
Boston England 9 E3.................52°58'N 0°01'W
Boston U.S.A. 63 L5..................42°23'N 71°06'W
Boston Spa England 13 F2..........53°54'N 1°20'W
Botevgrad Bulgaria 50 E6...........42°54'N 23°47'E
Bothnia, Gulf of Finland/Sweden 43 D3......61°09'N 19°15'E
Botoşani Romania 47 L2.............47°45'N 26°39'E
Botswana Africa 83 B2..............24°56'S 22°47'E
Bottesford England 13 G2..........53°33'N 0°38'W
Bouaké Côte d'Ivoire 84 D2........7°42'N 5°03'W
Bouar C.A.R. 84 F2...................5°56'N 15°35'E
Bou Arfa Morocco 84 D5............32°34'N 1°56'W
Bougainville Island P.N.G. 108 E6......6°04'S 154°53'E
Bouillon Belgium 42 E2.............49°48'N 5°04'E
Boujdour Western Sahara 84 C4......26°08'N 14°28'W
Boulder U.S.A. 62 E5................40°02'N 105°16'W
Boulogne-Billancourt France 44 E6......48°50'N 2°15'E
Boulogne-sur-Mer France 44 D7......50°43'N 1°37'E
Bounty Islands New Zealand 109 G2......47°40'S 179°02'E

Bourg-en-Bresse France 44 F5 ............46°12'N 5°14'E
Bourges France 44 E5 ............47°05'N 2°24'E
Bourke Australia 108 D3 ............30°07'S 145°54'E
Bourne England 9 E3 ............52°46'N 0°23'W
Bournemouth England 8 D1 ............50°43'N 1°53'W
Bournemouth, Christchurch and Poole d. England 21 E2 ............50°45'N 1°50'W
Bou Saâda Algeria 48 D4 ............35°13'N 4°11'E
Bow r. Canada 62 D6 ............49°58'N 111°41'W
Bowes England 13 E3 ............54°31'N 2°00'W
Bowland, Forest of England 12 E2 ............53°59'N 2°33'W
Boxtel Neth. 42 E4 ............51°35'N 5°20'E
Boyabat Turkey 51 K5 ............41°28'N 34°46'E
Boyle Ireland 18 C3 ............53°58'N 8°18'W
Boyne r. Ireland 18 E3 ............53°43'N 6°15'W
Bozeman U.S.A. 62 D6 ............45°42'N 111°02'W
Bozüyük Turkey 51 I4 ............39°55'N 30°01'E
Braan r. Scotland 15 F4 ............56°34'N 3°36'W
Brabant Wallon d. Belgium 42 D3 ............50°39'N 4°35'E
Brač i. Croatia 50 B6 ............43°17'N 16°31'E
Bracadale, Loch b. Scotland 16 C2 ............57°21'N 6°33'W
Bräcke Sweden 43 C3 ............62°46'N 15°26'E
Brackley England 8 D3 ............52°02'N 1°08'W
Bracknell England 8 E2 ............51°25'N 0°45'W
Bracknell Forest d. England 21 E2 ............51°24'N 0°45'W
Brad Romania 50 E8 ............46°07'N 22°48'E
Bradford England 13 F2 ............53°48'N 1°45'W
Bradford-on-Avon England 8 C2 ............51°21'N 2°15'W
Braemar Scotland 17 F2 ............57°00'N 3°24'W
Braga Portugal 45 A4 ............41°33'N 8°26'W
Bragança Brazil 72 E6 ............1°00'S 46°49'W
Bragança Portugal 45 B4 ............41°49'N 6°45'W
Brahmapur India 96 F4 ............19°21'N 84°52'E
Brahmaputra r. China/India 98 G2 ............23°36'N 90°31'E
Brăila Romania 51 G7 ............45°17'N 27°58'E
Braintree England 9 F2 ............51°53'N 0°33'E
Brämön i. Sweden 43 D3 ............62°13'N 17°45'E
Brampton England 12 E3 ............54°57'N 2°44'W
Branco r. Brazil 72 C7 ............1°18'S 61°52'W
Brandenburg an der Havel Germany 46 E5 ............52°25'N 12°34'E
Brandesburton England 13 G2 ............53°55'N 0°18'W
Brandon Canada 60 I2 ............49°51'N 99°57'W
Brandon England 9 F3 ............52°27'N 0°37'E
Brandon Head Ireland 18 A2 ............52°17'N 10°13'W
Brandon Mountain hill Ireland 18 A2 ............52°14'N 10°15'W
Bransgore England 8 D1 ............50°47'N 1°44'W
Brasília Brazil 72 E5 ............15°49'S 47°57'W
Brașov Romania 50 F7 ............45°40'N 25°36'E
Bratislava Slovakia 46 G3 ............48°09'N 17°06'E
Bratsk Russia 55 L3 ............56°16'N 101°41'E
Braunau am Inn Austria 46 E3 ............48°16'N 13°02'E
Braunschweig Germany 46 D5 ............52°17'N 10°32'E
Braunton England 11 C3 ............51°06'N 4°10'W
Brawley U.S.A. 62 C3 ............32°58'N 115°32'W
Bray Ireland 18 E3 ............53°12'N 6°07'W
Bray Head Ireland 18 A1 ............51°52'N 10°25'W
Brazil S. America 73 D6 ............29°58'S 54°33'W
Brazil Basin f. Atlantic Oc. 116 E2 ............15°00'S 30°00'W
Brazilian Highlands mts Brazil 72 E5 ............17°00'S 48°00'W
Brazos r. U.S.A. 62 G2 ............28°52'N 95°25'W
Brazzaville Congo 84 F1 ............4°17'S 15°11'E
Breamish r. England 13 E4 ............55°41'N 2°13'W
Brechin Scotland 17 G1 ............56°44'N 2°39'W
Breckland f. England 9 F3 ............52°26'N 0°39'E
Brecon Wales 10 D3 ............51°57'N 3°24'W
Brecon Beacons f. Wales 10 D3 ............51°53'N 3°26'W
Breda Neth. 42 D4 ............51°35'N 4°46'E
Breiðafjörður b. Iceland 43 W2 ............65°03'N 24°07'W
Breiðdalsvík Iceland 43 Z2 ............64°48'N 14°02'W
Bremen Germany 46 C5 ............53°05'N 8°51'E
Bremerhaven Germany 46 C5 ............53°33'N 8°35'E
Brenner Pass Austria/Italy 46 D2 ............46°59'N 11°32'E
Brentwood England 9 F2 ............51°37'N 0°19'E
Brescia Italy 46 D1 ............45°32'N 10°13'E
Bressanone Italy 46 D2 ............46°43'N 11°40'E
Bressay i. Scotland 17 H5 ............60°16'N 1°18'W
Bressuire France 44 C5 ............46°50'N 0°30'W
Brest Belarus 47 J5 ............52°05'N 23°40'E
Brest France 44 A6 ............48°24'N 4°29'W
Bretton Wales 10 D5 ............53°10'N 2°58'W
Bria C.A.R. 85 G2 ............6°32'N 21°59'E
Briançon France 44 G4 ............44°54'N 6°38'E
Brianne, Llyn resr Wales 10 D4 ............52°08'N 3°45'W
Bride r. Ireland 18 D2 ............52°04'N 7°52'W
Bridgend Wales 11 D3 ............51°30'N 3°35'W
Bridgend d. Wales 21 D2 ............51°34'N 3°33'W
Bridgeport U.S.A. 63 L5 ............41°12'N 73°12'W
Bridgetown Barbados 67 M3 ............13°05'N 59°36'W
Bridgnorth England 8 C3 ............52°32'N 2°25'W
Bridgwater England 11 D3 ............51°08'N 3°00'W
Bridgwater Bay England 11 D3 ............51°16'N 3°19'W
Bridlington England 13 G3 ............54°05'N 0°12'W
Bridlington Bay England 13 G3 ............54°03'N 0°07'W
Bridport England 8 C1 ............50°44'N 2°45'W
Brig Switz. 46 B2 ............46°19'N 7°59'E
Brigg England 13 G2 ............53°33'N 0°29'W
Brighstone England 8 D1 ............50°39'N 1°23'W
Brightlingsea England 9 G2 ............51°49'N 1°01'E
Brighton England 9 E1 ............50°49'N 0°08'W
Brighton and Hove d. England 21 E2 ............50°51'N 0°08'W
Brindisi Italy 49 G5 ............40°38'N 17°56'E
Brisbane Australia 108 E4 ............27°33'S 153°03'E
Bristol England 8 C2 ............51°27'N 2°35'W
Bristol d. England 21 D2 ............51°27'N 2°35'W
Bristol U.S.A. 63 J4 ............36°36'N 82°10'W
Bristol Bay U.S.A. 60 B3 ............57°22'N 161°29'W
Bristol Channel est. England 8 B2 ............51°20'N 4°16'W
British Columbia d. Canada 60 F3 ............51°49'N 121°48'W
British Empire Range mts Canada 61 J6 ............82°22'N 80°08'W
British Isles Europe 116 E4 ............54°00'N 5°00'W
Briton Ferry Wales 10 D3 ............51°38'N 3°49'W
Britstown S. Africa 83 B1 ............30°35'S 23°30'E
Brittany f. France 44 B6 ............48°10'N 3°22'W
Brittas Bay Ireland 10 A4 ............52°52'N 6°03'E
Brive-la-Gaillarde France 44 D4 ............45°10'N 1°32'E
Brixham England 11 D2 ............50°24'N 3°30'W
Brno Czechia 46 G3 ............49°11'N 16°37'E
Broad r. U.S.A. 63 J3 ............34°00'N 81°04'W
Broadback r. Canada 63 K7 ............51°21'N 78°50'W
Broad Bay Scotland 16 C3 ............58°16'N 6°15'W
Broad Law hill Scotland 15 F3 ............55°30'N 3°21'W
Broadstairs England 9 G2 ............51°22'N 1°26'E
Broadway England 8 D3 ............52°02'N 1°51'W
Broadwey England 8 C1 ............50°39'N 2°28'W
Broadwindsor England 8 C1 ............50°49'N 2°48'W
Brockenhurst England 8 D1 ............50°49'N 1°34'W

Brock Island Canada 60 G5 ............77°53'N 114°21'W
Brodeur Peninsula Canada 61 J5 ............71°50'N 88°32'W
Brodick Scotland 14 D3 ............55°35'N 5°09'W
Brody Ukraine 47 K4 ............50°05'N 25°09'E
Broken Hill town Australia 108 D3 ............31°55'S 141°27'E
Bromley England 9 F2 ............51°24'N 0°01'E
Bromsgrove England 8 C3 ............52°20'N 2°04'W
Bromyard England 8 C3 ............52°11'N 2°30'W
Brønderslev Denmark 43 B2 ............57°17'N 9°58'E
Brønnøysund Norway 43 C4 ............65°28'N 12°12'E
Brooke England 9 G3 ............52°33'N 1°23'E
Brooke's Point town Phil. 102 F5 ............8°50'N 117°51'E
Brookings U.S.A. 62 G5 ............44°19'N 96°44'W
Brooks Canada 62 D7 ............50°35'N 111°54'W
Brooks Range mts U.S.A. 60 D4 ............69°18'N 144°41'W
Broom, Loch inlet Scotland 16 D2 ............57°56'N 5°19'W
Broome Australia 108 B5 ............17°57'S 122°14'E
Brora Scotland 17 F3 ............58°01'N 3°51'W
Brora r. Scotland 17 F3 ............58°01'N 3°50'W
Brosna r. Ireland 18 D3 ............53°13'N 7°57'W
Brotton England 13 G3 ............54°34'N 0°56'W
Brough Cumb. England 13 E3 ............54°32'N 2°19'W
Brough E. Yorks. England 13 G2 ............53°44'N 0°34'W
Brough Head Scotland 17 F4 ............59°08'N 3°21'W
Brough Ness pt Scotland 17 G3 ............58°44'N 2°58'W
Broughshane Northern Ireland 14 C3 ............54°54'N 6°12'W
Brownhills England 8 D3 ............52°39'N 1°56'W
Broxburn Scotland 15 F3 ............55°56'N 3°28'W
Bruay-la-Buissière France 42 B3 ............50°29'N 2°33'E
Brue r. England 8 C2 ............51°13'N 2°59'W
Brugge Belgium 42 C4 ............51°12'N 3°15'E
Brunei Asia 102 E4 ............5°06'N 114°18'E
Brunflo Sweden 43 C3 ............63°05'N 14°51'E
Brunswick U.S.A. 63 J3 ............31°09'N 81°30'W
Brussels Belgium 42 D3 ............50°50'N 4°21'E
Bruton England 8 C2 ............51°07'N 2°27'W
Bryansk Russia 53 D3 ............53°15'N 34°23'E
Bryher i. England 11 A1 ............49°57'N 6°22'W
Brynamman Wales 10 D3 ............51°49'N 3°52'W
Brynmawr Wales 10 D3 ............51°48'N 3°10'W
Buca Turkey 50 G4 ............38°22'N 27°11'E
Bucaramanga Colombia 72 B7 ............7°05'N 73°09'W
Bucharest Romania 50 G7 ............44°26'N 26°06'E
Buckhaven Scotland 15 F4 ............56°11'N 3°02'W
Buckie Scotland 17 G2 ............57°41'N 2°58'W
Buckingham England 8 E2 ............51°59'N 0°59'W
Buckinghamshire d. England 21 E2 ............51°47'N 0°56'W
Buckley Wales 10 D5 ............53°10'N 3°05'W
Budapest Hungary 46 H2 ............47°30'N 19°04'E
Buddon Ness pt Scotland 15 G4 ............56°28'N 2°43'W
Bude England 11 C2 ............50°50'N 4°32'W
Bude Bay England 11 C2 ............50°50'N 4°38'W
Budennovsk Russia 53 E2 ............44°45'N 44°06'E
Buenaventura Colombia 72 B7 ............3°52'N 77°00'W
Buenos Aires Argentina 73 D3 ............34°36'S 58°24'W
Buenos Aires, Lago l. Argentina/Chile 73 B2 ............46°31'S 72°13'W
Buffalo N.Y. U.S.A. 63 K5 ............42°53'N 78°52'W
Buffalo Wyo. U.S.A. 62 E5 ............44°20'N 106°41'W
Bug r. Poland 47 J5 ............51°30'N 23°39'E
Buguruslan Russia 53 F3 ............53°35'N 52°23'E
Builth Wells Wales 10 D4 ............52°09'N 3°24'W
Bujumbura Burundi 85 G1 ............3°24'S 29°22'E
Bukavu Dem. Rep. Congo 83 B4 ............2°30'S 28°49'E
Bukittinggi Indonesia 102 C3 ............0°15'S 100°20'E
Bukoba Tanzania 83 C4 ............1°18'S 31°48'E
Bula Indonesia 103 I3 ............3°06'S 130°28'E
Bulawayo Zimbabwe 83 B2 ............20°09'S 28°36'E
Bulgan Mongolia 99 I7 ............48°48'N 103°28'E
Bulgaria Europe 50 F6 ............42°51'N 25°15'E
Bulun Russia 55 N5 ............70°59'N 127°10'E
Bunbury Australia 108 A3 ............33°20'S 115°36'E
Bunclody Ireland 18 E2 ............52°39'N 6°39'W
Buncrana Ireland 18 D5 ............55°09'N 7°27'W
Bundaberg Australia 108 E4 ............24°52'S 152°22'E
Bundoran Ireland 18 C4 ............54°28'N 8°18'W
Bungay England 9 G3 ............52°27'N 1°27'E
Buôn Ma Thuột Vietnam 102 D6 ............12°38'N 108°05'E
Buraydah Saudi Arabia 94 F5 ............26°20'N 43°57'E
Burbage England 8 D2 ............51°21'N 1°40'W
Burdur Turkey 51 I3 ............37°43'N 30°17'E
Bure r. England 9 G3 ............52°37'N 1°43'E
Burë Ethiopia 85 H3 ............10°50'N 36°57'E
Burford England 8 D2 ............51°48'N 1°38'W
Burgas Bulgaria 50 G6 ............42°30'N 27°28'E
Burgess Hill town England 9 E1 ............50°57'N 0°08'W
Burghausen Germany 46 E3 ............48°10'N 12°50'E
Burghead Scotland 17 F2 ............57°42'N 3°29'W
Burgh le Marsh England 13 H2 ............53°10'N 0°14'E
Burgos Spain 45 D5 ............42°21'N 3°41'W
Burhanpur India 96 E5 ............21°18'N 76°14'E
Burkina Faso Africa 84 D3 ............11°39'N 1°18'W
Burlington Colo. U.S.A. 62 F4 ............39°19'N 102°17'W
Burlington Iowa U.S.A. 63 H5 ............40°49'N 91°06'W
Burlington Vt. U.S.A. 63 L5 ............44°28'N 73°13'W
Burma Asia 97 I5 ............22°37'N 95°02'E
Burnham England 8 E2 ............51°32'N 0°39'W
Burnham Market England 9 F3 ............52°57'N 0°44'E
Burnham-on-Crouch England 9 F2 ............51°38'N 0°49'E
Burnham-on-Sea England 8 C2 ............51°14'N 2°59'W
Burnie Australia 108 D2 ............41°03'S 145°57'E
Burniston England 13 G3 ............54°19'N 0°27'W
Burnley England 13 E2 ............53°47'N 2°15'W
Burns U.S.A. 62 C5 ............43°36'N 119°01'W
Burns Lake town Canada 60 F3 ............54°15'N 125°46'W
Burntisland Scotland 15 F4 ............56°04'N 3°14'W
Burntwood Green England 8 D3 ............52°41'N 1°54'W
Burra i. Scotland 17 H5 ............60°05'N 1°22'W
Burray i. Scotland 17 G3 ............58°51'N 2°53'W
Burro, Serranías del mts Mexico 66 D6 ............29°02'N 102°00'W
Burrow Head Scotland 14 E2 ............54°41'N 4°23'W
Burry Inlet Wales 10 C3 ............51°38'N 4°18'W
Burry Port Wales 10 C3 ............51°41'N 4°16'W
Bursa Turkey 51 H5 ............40°14'N 29°03'E
Bûr Safâjah Egypt 49 J2 ............26°45'N 33°55'E
Burscough Bridge England 12 E2 ............53°36'N 2°51'W
Burton-in-Kendal England 12 E3 ............54°11'N 2°43'W
Burton Latimer England 8 E3 ............52°22'N 0°41'W
Burton upon Trent England 8 D3 ............52°48'N 1°39'W
Buru i. Indonesia 103 H3 ............3°24'S 126°35'E
Burundi Africa 85 H1 ............3°06'S 30°03'E
Burwash Landing Canada 60 E4 ............61°21'N 138°58'W
Burwell England 9 F3 ............52°16'N 0°20'E
Burwick Scotland 17 G3 ............58°45'N 2°58'W
Bury England 13 E2 ............53°36'N 2°18'W
Bury St Edmunds England 9 F3 ............52°15'N 0°44'E
Busan S. Korea 99 N5 ............35°09'N 129°03'E

Bush r. Northern Ireland 14 C3 ............55°13'N 6°31'W
Bushmills Northern Ireland 14 C3 ............55°12'N 6°31'W
Buta Dem. Rep. Congo 83 B5 ............2°49'N 24°45'E
Bute i. Scotland 14 D3 ............55°49'N 5°06'W
Bute, Sound of str. Scotland 14 D3 ............55°44'N 5°19'W
Buton i. Indonesia 103 G3 ............4°57'S 123°00'E
Butte U.S.A. 62 D6 ............46°01'N 112°32'W
Butterworth Malaysia 102 C5 ............5°22'N 100°22'E
Buttevant Ireland 18 C2 ............52°14'N 8°40'W
Butt of Lewis hd Scotland 16 C3 ............58°32'N 6°17'W
Butuan Phil. 103 H5 ............8°56'N 125°32'E
Buxoro Uzbekistan 54 H1 ............39°46'N 64°25'E
Buxton England 13 F2 ............53°16'N 1°55'W
Buy Russia 52 E3 ............58°29'N 41°32'E
Buyr Nuur l. Mongolia 99 L7 ............47°47'N 117°53'E
Büyük Ağrı Dağı mt. Turkey 94 F7 ............39°44'N 44°15'E
Büyükmenderes r. Turkey 51 G3 ............38°28'N 27°11'E
Buzău Romania 50 G7 ............45°09'N 26°48'E
Buzuluk Russia 53 F3 ............52°45'N 52°09'E
Byarezina r. Belarus 47 K5 ............53°48'N 25°58'E
Byaroza Belarus 47 K5 ............52°32'N 24°59'E
Bydgoszcz Poland 46 H5 ............53°08'N 18°02'E
Byfield England 8 D3 ............52°11'N 1°14'W
Bylot Island Canada 61 K5 ............73°07'N 79°01'W
Byrranga, Gory mts Russia 55 K5 ............74°25'N 99°53'E
Bytom Poland 46 H4 ............50°21'N 18°55'E

## C

Cabanatuan Phil. 103 G7 ............15°31'N 120°58'E
Caban Coch Reservoir Wales 10 D4 ............52°15'N 3°35'W
Cabimas Venezuela 72 B8 ............10°23'N 71°26'W
Cabinda Angola 84 F1 ............5°33'S 12°15'E
Cabo Frio Brazil 73 E4 ............22°51'S 42°02'W
Cabonga, Réservoir Canada 63 K6 ............47°21'N 76°32'W
Cabora Bassa, Lake resr Mozambique 83 C3 ............15°46'S 31°11'E
Caborca Mexico 66 B7 ............30°44'N 112°09'W
Cabot Strait Canada 61 L2 ............47°39'N 60°16'W
Cabrera, Sierra de la mts Spain 45 B5 ............42°13'N 6°51'W
Cabriel r. Spain 45 E3 ............39°16'N 1°04'W
Cáceres Brazil 72 D5 ............16°05'S 57°41'W
Cáceres Spain 45 B3 ............39°29'N 6°21'W
Cachimbo, Serra do hills Brazil 72 D6 ............9°18'S 54°11'W
Cachoeiro de Itapemirim Brazil 73 E4 ............20°51'S 41°08'W
Cadillac U.S.A. 63 I5 ............44°14'N 85°23'W
Cádiz Spain 45 B2 ............36°32'N 6°17'W
Cádiz, Golfo de g. Spain 45 B2 ............36°44'N 7°14'W
Caen France 44 C6 ............49°11'N 0°21'W
Caerleon Wales 10 E3 ............51°37'N 2°57'W
Caernarfon Wales 10 C5 ............53°08'N 4°16'W
Caernarfon Bay Wales 10 C5 ............53°06'N 4°34'W
Caerphilly Wales 10 D3 ............51°35'N 3°13'W
Caerphilly d. Wales 21 D2 ............51°38'N 3°11'W
Caerwent Wales 10 E3 ............51°37'N 2°46'W
Cagayan de Oro Phil. 103 G5 ............8°29'N 124°39'E
Cagliari Italy 48 E4 ............39°13'N 9°08'E
Caha Mountains hills Ireland 18 B1 ............51°41'N 9°44'W
Cahirciveen Ireland 18 A1 ............51°57'N 10°13'W
Cahore Point Ireland 18 E2 ............52°33'N 6°11'W
Cahors France 44 D4 ............44°28'N 1°26'E
Cahul Moldova 51 H7 ............45°54'N 28°12'E
Caia Mozambique 83 C3 ............17°50'S 35°19'E
Caiabis, Serra dos hills Brazil 72 D5 ............12°46'S 56°21'W
Caicos Islands Turks and Caicos Is 67 J5 ............21°45'N 71°53'W
Caimodorro mt. Spain 45 E4 ............40°32'N 1°40'W
Cairn Gorm mt. Scotland 17 F2 ............57°07'N 3°39'W
Cairngorm Mountains Scotland 17 F2 ............57°08'N 3°45'W
Cairnryan Scotland 14 D2 ............54°59'N 5°02'W
Cairns Australia 108 D5 ............16°54'S 145°45'E
Cairn Toul mt. Scotland 17 F2 ............57°03'N 3°43'W
Cairo Egypt 85 H5 ............30°01'N 31°15'E
Caister-on-Sea England 9 G3 ............52°39'N 1°44'E
Caistor England 13 G2 ............53°30'N 0°19'W
Caithness f. Scotland 17 F3 ............58°24'N 3°22'W
Cajamarca Peru 72 B6 ............7°11'S 78°31'W
Calabar Nigeria 84 E2 ............4°59'N 8°19'E
Calafat Romania 50 E6 ............43°59'N 22°57'E
Calais France 44 D7 ............50°57'N 1°51'E
Calais U.S.A. 63 M6 ............45°10'N 67°18'W
Calama Chile 73 C4 ............22°29'S 68°56'W
Calamian Group is Phil. 102 F6 ............11°59'N 119°29'E
Calamocha Spain 45 E4 ............40°56'N 1°17'W
Calanscio Sand Sea des. Libya 49 H3 ............30°11'N 22°22'E
Calapan Phil. 103 G6 ............13°24'N 121°11'E
Călărași Romania 50 G7 ............44°12'N 27°19'E
Calatayud Spain 45 E4 ............41°22'N 1°37'W
Calbayog Phil. 103 G6 ............12°05'N 124°37'E
Caldas da Rainha Portugal 45 A3 ............39°24'N 9°08'W
Caldey Island Wales 10 C3 ............51°38'N 4°40'W
Calf of Man i. Isle of Man 12 C3 ............54°04'N 4°50'W
Calgary Canada 62 D7 ............51°02'N 114°04'W
Cali Colombia 72 B7 ............3°26'N 76°28'W
Caliente U.S.A. 62 D4 ............37°37'N 114°31'W
California d. U.S.A. 62 B5 ............41°35'N 122°50'W
California, Gulf of Mexico 66 B7 ............30°51'N 113°58'W
Callan Ireland 18 D2 ............52°32'N 7°24'W
Callander Scotland 14 E4 ............56°15'N 4°13'W
Callanish Scotland 16 C3 ............58°12'N 6°45'W
Callao Peru 72 B5 ............12°04'S 77°08'W
Callington England 11 C2 ............50°30'N 4°19'W
Calne England 8 C2 ............51°26'N 2°00'W
Caltanissetta Italy 48 F4 ............37°30'N 14°03'E
Calvi France 44 H3 ............42°34'N 8°45'E
Cam r. England 9 F3 ............52°34'N 0°21'E
Camagüey Cuba 67 I5 ............21°23'N 77°54'W
Camagüey, Archipiélago de is Cuba 67 I5 ............22°44'N 78°34'W
Ca Mau, Mui c. Vietnam 102 C5 ............8°35'N 104°45'E
Camberley England 8 E2 ............51°20'N 0°44'W
Cambodia Asia 102 D6 ............13°05'N 105°10'E
Camborne England 11 B2 ............50°13'N 5°18'W
Cambrai France 42 C3 ............50°10'N 3°14'E
Cambrian Mountains Wales 10 D4 ............52°33'N 3°40'W
Cambridge England 9 F3 ............52°12'N 0°08'E
Cambridge Bay town Canada 60 H4 ............69°02'N 105°14'W
Cambridgeshire d. England 21 E3 ............52°25'N 0°02'E
Camelford England 11 C2 ............50°37'N 4°41'W
Cameroon Africa 84 F2 ............5°45'N 12°41'E
Cameroun, Mont vol. Cameroon 84 E2 ............4°09'N 9°12'E
Cametá Brazil 72 E6 ............2°13'S 49°30'W
Campbell River town Canada 60 F3 ............50°01'N 125°14'W
Campbeltown Scotland 14 D3 ............55°25'N 5°36'W
Campeche Mexico 66 F4 ............19°51'N 90°30'W
Campeche d. Mexico 66 F4 ............18°53'N 90°28'W

Campeche, Bahía de g. Mexico 66 F4 ............19°30'N 93
Campina Grande Brazil 72 F6 ............7°14'S 35°
Campinas Brazil 73 E4 ............22°55'S 47°
Campo Grande Brazil 73 D4 ............20°24'S 54°
Campos Brazil 73 E4 ............21°45'S 41°
Câmpulung Moldovenesc Romania 47 K2 ............47°32'N 25°
Camrose Wales 10 B3 ............51°50'N 5°
Çan Turkey 50 G5 ............40°02'N 27°
Canada N. America 60 F4 ............46°44'N 81°
Canadian r. U.S.A. 62 G4 ............35°11'N 95°
Canadian Shield f. N. America 56 F4 ............50°00'N 80°
Çanakkale Turkey 50 G5 ............40°08'N 26°
Canarreos, Archipiélago de los is Cuba 67 H5 ............21°44'N 82°
Canary Islands N. Atlantic Oc. 45 X2 ............30°08'N 18°
Canaveral, Cape U.S.A. 63 J2 ............28°26'N 80°
Canberra Australia 108 D3 ............35°19'S 149°
Cancún Mexico 66 G5 ............21°10'N 86°
Caniapiscau r. Canada 61 L3 ............57°39'N 69°
Caniapiscau, Lac l. Canada 61 K3 ............54°21'N 70°
Canisp hill Scotland 16 D3 ............58°07'N 5°
Çankaya Turkey 51 J4 ............39°53'N 32°
Çankırı Turkey 51 J5 ............40°36'N 33°
Canna i. Scotland 16 C2 ............57°04'N 6°
Cannes France 44 G3 ............43°33'N 7°
Cannock England 8 C3 ............52°41'N 2°
Canora Canada 62 F7 ............51°39'N 102°
Cantabrian Mountains Spain 45 C5 ............43°07'N 4°
Canterbury England 9 G2 ............51°17'N 1°
Cân Thơ Vietnam 102 D6 ............10°01'N 105°
Canvey Island England 9 F2 ............51°31'N 0°
Cao Bằng Vietnam 102 D8 ............22°41'N 106°
Capbreton France 44 C3 ............43°39'N 1°
Cape Breton Island Canada 61 L2 ............46°45'N 60°
Capel St Mary England 9 G3 ............52°00'N 1°
Cape Town S. Africa 83 A1 ............33°57'S 18°
Cape Verde N. Atlantic Oc. 84 B3 ............15°47'N 24°
Cape York Peninsula Australia 108 D5 ............12°33'S 142°
Cap-Haïtien Haiti 67 J4 ............19°46'N 72°
Capital Hill town N. Mariana Is 103 L7 ............15°12'N 145°
Capraia, Isola di i. Italy 48 E5 ............43°04'N 9°
Capricorn Channel Australia 108 E4 ............22°20'S 151°
Caprivi Strip f. Namibia 83 B3 ............18°11'S 21°
Caquetá r. Colombia 72 C6 ............1°27'S 69°
Caracal Romania 50 F7 ............44°07'N 24°
Caracas Venezuela 72 C8 ............10°28'N 66°
Caransebeș Romania 50 E7 ............45°25'N 22°
Caratasca, Laguna de lagoon Honduras 67 H4 ............15°20'N 83°
Caratinga Brazil 73 E5 ............19°45'S 42°
Caravaca de la Cruz Spain 45 E3 ............38°07'N 1°
Carbonara, Capo c. Italy 48 E4 ............39°06'N 9°
Carcassonne France 44 E3 ............43°13'N 2°
Cardiff Wales 11 D3 ............51°29'N 3°
Cardiff d. Wales 21 D2 ............51°30'N 3°
Cardigan Wales 10 C4 ............52°05'N 4°
Cardigan Bay Wales 10 C4 ............52°33'N 4°
Carei Romania 47 J2 ............47°41'N 22°
Carey, Lake Australia 108 B4 ............28°57'S 122°
Caribbean Sea N. Atlantic Oc. 67 H4 ............19°03'N 83°
Caribou Mountains Canada 60 G3 ............59°02'N 115°
Carletonville S. Africa 83 B2 ............26°21'S 27°
Carlingford Lough inlet Ireland/U.K. 18 E4 ............54°05'N 6°
Carlisle England 12 E3 ............54°54'N 2°
Carlow Ireland 18 E2 ............52°50'N 6°
Carlow d. Ireland 18 E2 ............52°47'N 6°
Carluke Scotland 15 F3 ............55°44'N 3°
Carmacks Canada 60 E4 ............62°05'N 136°
Carmarthen Wales 10 C3 ............51°51'N 4°
Carmarthen Bay Wales 10 C3 ............51°38'N 4°
Carmarthenshire d. Wales 21 C2 ............51°57'N 4°
Carmel Head Wales 10 C5 ............53°24'N 4°
Carmen, Isla i. Mexico 66 B6 ............25°59'N 111°
Carnac France 44 B5 ............47°35'N 3°
Carn Dearg hill Scotland 17 E2 ............57°06'N 4°
Carndonagh Ireland 14 B3 ............55°15'N 7°
Carnedd Llywelyn mt. Wales 10 D5 ............53°10'N 3°
Carnedd y Filiast hill Wales 10 D4 ............52°59'N 3°
Carnegie, Lake Australia 108 B4 ............26°10'S 122°
Carn Eighe mt. Scotland 16 D2 ............57°17'N 5°
Carnforth England 12 E3 ............54°08'N 2°
Carnic Alps mts Italy 46 E2 ............46°40'N 12°
Car Nicobar i. India 97 H2 ............9°10'N 92°
Carnlough Northern Ireland 14 D2 ............54°59'N 5°
Carn Mòr hill Scotland 17 F2 ............57°15'N 3°
Carnot, Cape Australia 108 C3 ............34°55'S 135°
Carnoustie Scotland 15 G4 ............56°30'N 2°
Carnsore Point Ireland 18 E2 ............52°10'N 6°
Caroline Islands N. Pacific Oc. 117 I3 ............6°35'N 144°
Carpathian Mountains Europe 47 J3 ............48°45'N 23°
Carpentaria, Gulf of Australia 108 C5 ............14°06'S 139°
Carpentras France 44 F4 ............44°04'N 5°
Carra, Lough l. Ireland 18 B3 ............53°44'N 9°
Carranza, Cabo c. Chile 73 B3 ............35°36'S 72
Carrantuohill mt. Ireland 18 B1 ............51°59'N 9°
Carrara Italy 46 D1 ............44°04'N 10°
Carrickfergus Northern Ireland 14 D2 ............54°43'N 5°
Carrickmacross Ireland 18 E3 ............53°59'N 6°
Carrick-on-Shannon Ireland 18 C3 ............53°56'N 8°
Carrick-on-Suir Ireland 18 D2 ............52°21'N 7°
Carron r. Falk. Scotland 15 F4 ............56°02'N 3°
Carron r. High. Scotland 16 E2 ............57°53'N 4°
Carrowmore Lake Ireland 18 B4 ............54°11'N 9°
Carson City U.S.A. 62 C4 ............39°10'N 119°
Carsphairn Scotland 14 E3 ............55°13'N 4°
Cartagena Colombia 72 B8 ............10°..'N 75°
Cartagena Spain 45 E2 ............37°36'N 0°
Carteret France 11 Z9 ............49°23'N 1°
Carteret, Cap de c. France 11 Z9 ............49°22'N 1°
Carterton England 8 D2 ............51°46'N 1°
Cartmel England 12 E3 ............54°12'N 2°
Caruaru Brazil 72 F6 ............8°13'S 35°
Carvin France 42 B3 ............50°29'N 2°
Casablanca Morocco 84 D5 ............33°35'N 7°
Casa Grande U.S.A. 62 D3 ............32°53'N 111°
Cascade Range mts Canada/U.S.A. 60 F2 ............41°49'N 122°
Cascavel Brazil 73 D4 ............24°55'S 53°
Cashel Ireland 18 D2 ............52°31'N 7°
Casper U.S.A. 62 E5 ............42°52'N 106°
Caspian Lowland f. Kazakhstan/Russia 53 E2 ............44°15'N 45°
Caspian Sea l. Asia/Europe 53 F2 ............42°00'N 51°
Cassiar Mountains Canada 60 E3 ............59°40'N 130°
Cassley r. Scotland 16 E2 ............57°58'N 4°
Castanhal Brazil 72 E6 ............1°18'S 47°

ello de la Plana Spain 45 E3 .......... 39°59'N 0°02'W
ebar Ireland 18 B3 .......... 53°51'N 9°17'W
ebay Scotland 15 F2 .......... 56°57'N 7°29'W
eblayney Ireland 18 E4 .......... 54°07'N 6°43'W
e Cary England 8 C2 .......... 51°05'N 2°31'W
ecomer Ireland 18 D2 .......... 52°48'N 7°13'W
econnell Ireland 18 C2 .......... 52°43'N 8°30'W
ederg Northern Ireland 14 B2 .......... 54°42'N 7°35'W
e Donington England 8 D3 .......... 52°50'N 1°20'W
e Douglas Scotland 15 F2 .......... 54°56'N 3°56'W
eford England 13 F2 .......... 53°43'N 1°21'W
eisland Ireland 18 B2 .......... 52°14'N 9°27'W
etown Isle of Man 12 C3 .......... 54°05'N 4°39'W
es France 44 E3 .......... 43°36'N 2°14'E
ries St Lucia 67 L3 .......... 14°00'N 60°59'W
o Verde Portugal 45 A2 .......... 37°42'N 8°05'W
onia f. Spain 45 E4 .......... 41°50'N 1°30'E
marca Argentina 73 C4 .......... 28°26'S 65°45'W
nduanes i. Phil. 103 G6 .......... 13°46'N 124°14'E
nia Italy 48 G4 .......... 37°30'N 15°05'E
nzaro Italy 49 G4 .......... 38°55'N 16°36'E
rman Phil. 103 G6 .......... 12°29'N 124°38'E
ham England 9 E2 .......... 51°17'N 0°05'W
sland Bahamas 67 I5 .......... 24°28'N 75°30'W
che, Cabo c. Mexico 66 G5 .......... 21°37'N 87°06'W
rick England 13 F3 .......... 54°23'N 1°38'W
a r. Colombia 67 J2 .......... 8°54'N 74°29'W
aia Brazil 72 F6 .......... 3°42'S 38°42'W
asus mts Asia/Europe 53 E2 .......... 43°53'N 40°00'E
ry France 42 C2 .......... 48°49'N 2°15'E
bra Coast and Glens d. Northern Ireland 20 B4 .......... 54°58'N 6°28'W
n Ireland 18 D3 .......... 53°59'N 7°22'W
d. Ireland 18 D3 .......... 53°57'N 7°15'W
ton England 9 G3 .......... 52°46'N 1°10'E
s Brazil 72 E6 .......... 4°54'S 43°19'W
s do Sul Brazil 73 D4 .......... 29°13'S 51°11'W
nne French Guiana 72 D7 .......... 4°53'N 52°21'W
rac Cayman Is. 67 I4 .......... 19°43'N 79°48'W
an Islands Central America 67 H4 .......... 19°31'N 81°15'W
Phil. 103 G6 .......... 10°17'N 123°55'E
i. Phil. 103 G6 .......... 10°26'N 123°53'E
r. U.S.A. 63 J5 .......... 43°40'N 84°23'W
City U.S.A. 62 D4 .......... 37°41'N 113°04'W
Rapids town U.S.A. 63 H5 .......... 41°59'N 91°40'W
os, Isla i. Mexico 66 A6 .......... 28°11'N 115°20'W
d Hungary 46 H2 .......... 47°10'N 19°48'E
es i. Indonesia 102 G3 .......... 2°01'S 120°29'E
es Sea Indonesia/Phil. 102 G4 .......... 3°03'N 121°10'E
Slovenia 46 F2 .......... 46°14'N 15°15'E
Germany 46 D5 .......... 52°38'N 10°05'E
Sea Ireland/U.K. 11 A2 .......... 50°54'N 6°33'W
, Llyn l. Wales 10 D4 .......... 52°57'N 3°43'W
erawasih, Teluk b. Indonesia 103 J3 .......... 2°05'S 135°33'E
al, Cordillera mts Colombia 72 B7 .......... 1°38'N 76°51'W
al, Cordillera mts Peru 72 B6 .......... 10°02'S 76°25'W
al African Republic Africa 85 G2 .......... 6°25'N 20°12'E
al Bedfordshire d. England 21 E3 .......... 51°59'N 0°30'W
al Range mts P.N.G. 103 K3 .......... 4°57'S 142°36'E
al Russian Upland Russia 53 D3 .......... 53°00'N 38°00'E
al Siberian Plateau f. Russia 55 M4 .......... 67°03'N 110°35'E
alonia i. Greece 50 D4 .......... 38°14'N 20°21'E
i. Indonesia 103 H3 .......... 3°03'S 129°24'E
n Sea Indonesia 103 I3 .......... 2°33'S 130°11'E
digion d. Wales 21 D3 .......... 52°19'N 3°58'W
avodă Romania 51 H7 .......... 44°21'N 28°02'E
Ivo, Isla i. Mexico 66 C5 .......... 24°10'N 109°48'W
de Pasco Peru 72 B5 .......... 10°42'S 76°14'W
Spain 45 B5 .......... 43°41'N 7°26'W
Budějovice Czechia 46 F3 .......... 48°59'N 14°29'E
je Montenegro 50 C6 .......... 42°23'N 18°55'E
N. Africa 84 B4 .......... 35°35'N 5°20'W
nnes mts France 44 E3 .......... 43°50'N 3°17'E
an Turkey 51 K3 .......... 37°01'N 35°47'E
an r. Turkey 51 K3 .......... 36°42'N 35°37'E
ahār Iran 95 J5 .......... 25°18'N 60°38'E
Africa 85 F3 .......... 15°07'N 18°13'E
, Lake Africa 84 F3 .......... 13°27'N 14°24'E
an Russia 98 G8 .......... 51°18'N 91°31'E
ron U.S.A. 62 F5 .......... 42°50'N 102°57'W
ai Hills Afgh./Pakistan 96 B6 .......... 29°17'N 63°23'E
ncharān Afgh. 95 K6 .......... 34°28'N 65°03'E
os Archipelago is Indian Oc. 117 G2 .......... 6°00'S 72°00'E
England 8 D1 .......... 50°36'N 1°19'W
ida Greece 50 E4 .......... 38°27'N 23°08'E
enger Deep f. N. Pacific Oc. 117 I3 .......... 11°17'N 142°30'E
ans-en-Champagne France 44 F6 .......... 48°58'N 4°22'E
n-sur-Saône France 44 F5 .......... 46°48'N 4°51'E
Iran 95 H7 .......... 36°37'N 51°26'E
nan Pakistan 96 C7 .......... 30°55'N 66°28'E
béry France 44 F4 .......... 45°34'N 5°55'E
onix-Mont-Blanc France 44 G4 .......... 45°55'N 6°52'E
paign U.S.A. 63 I5 .......... 40°06'N 88°17'W
aplain, Lake Canada/U.S.A. 63 L5 .......... 44°23'N 73°22'W
dalar r. U.S.A. 60 D4 .......... 66°36'N 145°51'W
digarh India 96 E7 .......... 30°42'N 76°48'E
digarh India 98 D4 .......... 30°43'N 76°52'E
drapur India 96 E4 .......... 19°57'N 79°21'E
gchun China 99 N6 .......... 43°53'N 125°20'E
g China 99 K3 .......... 29°03'N 111°42'E
g Jiang r. China 99 M4 .......... 31°24'N 121°48'E
gsha China 99 K3 .......... 28°10'N 112°59'E
gzhi China 99 K5 .......... 36°06'N 113°09'E
gzhou China 99 L4 .......... 31°47'N 119°59'E
ia France 50 E4 .......... 35°30'N 24°02'E
uèn Morocco 48 B4
ala, Laguna de l. Mexico 66 D5 .......... 20°15'N 103°04'W
ayevo Kazakhstan 73 F3 .......... 50°12'N 51°08'E
el-en-le-Frith England 13 F2 .......... 53°20'N 1°54'W
eltown England 13 F2 .......... 53°20'N 1°54'W
eau Canada 61 J2 .......... 47°51'N 83°24'W
kär India 95 K7 .......... 35°02'N 69°15'E
kayuvom Russia 52 F4 .......... 65°49'N 54°51'E
bury England 8 D2 .......... 51°52'N 1°29'W
eroi Belgium 42 D3 .......... 50°25'N 4°27'E
es, Cape U.S.A. 63 K4 .......... 37°10'N 75°58'W
eston S. C. U.S.A. 63 K3 .......... 32°48'N 79°58'W
eston W. Va. U.S.A. 63 J4 .......... 38°21'N 81°39'W
estown Ireland 18 B3 .......... 53°58'N 9°47'W
eville-Mézières France 44 F6 .......... 49°46'N 4°44'E

Charlotte U.S.A. 63 J4 .......... 35°14'N 80°50'W
Charlottesville U.S.A. 63 K4 .......... 38°02'N 78°30'W
Charlottetown Canada 61 L2 .......... 46°16'N 63°09'W
Chartres France 44 D6 .......... 48°27'N 1°30'E
Chassiron, Pointe de pt France 44 C5 .......... 46°03'N 1°24'W
Châteaubriant France 44 C5 .......... 47°43'N 1°22'W
Châteaudun France 44 D6 .......... 48°04'N 1°20'E
Châteauroux France 44 D5 .......... 46°48'N 1°41'E
Château-Thierry France 44 E6 .......... 49°03'N 3°25'E
Châtellerault France 44 D5 .......... 46°49'N 0°33'E
Chatham England 9 F2 .......... 51°23'N 0°31'E
Chatham Islands New Zealand 109 H2 .......... 43°24'S 176°11'W
Chattahoochee r. U.S.A. 63 J3 .......... 30°55'N 84°58'W
Chattanooga U.S.A. 63 I4 .......... 35°02'N 85°21'W
Chatteris England 9 F3 .......... 52°27'N 0°03'E
Chattogram Bangl. 97 H5 .......... 22°20'N 91°49'E
Chaumont France 44 F6 .......... 48°07'N 5°08'E
Cheadle England 8 D3 .......... 52°59'N 1°59'W
Cheboksary Russia 52 E3 .......... 56°09'N 47°13'E
Cheboygan U.S.A. 63 J6 .......... 45°39'N 84°28'W
Cheddar England 8 C2 .......... 51°17'N 2°47'W
Cheju-do i. S. Korea 99 N4 .......... 33°34'N 126°43'E
Chekhov Russia 47 Q6 .......... 55°09'N 37°28'E
Cheleken Turkmenistan 95 H7 .......... 39°25'N 53°01'E
Chełm Poland 47 J4 .......... 51°08'N 23°29'E
Chelmer r. England 9 F2 .......... 51°45'N 0°40'E
Chelmsford England 9 F2 .......... 51°44'N 0°29'E
Cheltenham England 8 C2 .......... 51°54'N 2°04'W
Chelyabinsk Russia 52 G3 .......... 55°11'N 61°24'E
Chemnitz Germany 46 E4 .......... 50°50'N 12°56'E
Chencang China 99 J4 .......... 34°21'N 107°09'E
Chengde China 99 L6 .......... 40°52'N 117°58'E
Chengdu China 99 I4 .......... 30°43'N 104°04'E
Chennai India 96 F3 .......... 13°06'N 80°16'E
Chenzhou China 99 K3 .......... 25°44'N 113°00'E
Chepstow Wales 10 D5 .......... 51°38'N 2°40'W
Cher r. France 44 D5 .......... 47°20'N 0°29'E
Cherbourg-Octeville France 44 C6 .......... 49°38'N 1°37'W
Cherepovets Russia 52 D3 .......... 59°08'N 37°55'E
Chergui, Chott ech l. Algeria 48 D3 .......... 34°03'N 0°16'W
Cherkasy Ukraine 47 O3 .......... 49°26'N 32°05'E
Cherkessk Russia 53 E2 .......... 44°13'N 42°03'E
Chernihiv Ukraine 47 N4 .......... 51°29'N 31°19'E
Chernivtsi Ukraine 47 K3 .......... 48°19'N 25°56'E
Chernyakhovsk Russia 47 I6 .......... 54°38'N 21°49'E
Chernyshevskiy Russia 55 M4 .......... 62°56'N 112°36'E
Chervonohrad Ukraine 47 K4 .......... 50°23'N 24°14'E
Cherwell r. England 8 D2 .......... 51°44'N 1°15'W
Chesapeake Bay U.S.A. 63 K4 .......... 38°05'N 76°14'W
Chesham England 9 E2 .......... 51°43'N 0°37'W
Cheshire East d. England 21 D3 .......... 53°09'N 2°18'W
Cheshire West and Chester d. England 21 D3 .......... 53°11'N 2°46'W
Cheshskaya Guba b. Russia 52 E4 .......... 67°20'N 46°30'E
Cheshunt England 9 F2 .......... 51°42'N 0°02'W
Chesil Beach f. England 8 C1 .......... 50°38'N 2°36'W
Chester England 12 E2 .......... 53°12'N 2°54'W
Chesterfield England 13 F2 .......... 53°14'N 1°25'W
Chester-le-Street England 13 F3 .......... 54°52'N 1°34'W
Chetumal Mexico 66 G4 .......... 18°30'N 88°18'W
Cheviot Hills England 13 E4 .......... 55°12'N 2°39'W
Chew Magna England 8 C2 .......... 51°21'N 2°37'W
Chew Valley Lake resr England 8 C2 .......... 51°20'N 2°38'W
Cheyenne U.S.A. 62 F5 .......... 41°09'N 104°49'W
Cheyenne r. U.S.A. 62 F5 .......... 44°44'N 101°09'W
Chhattisgarh d. India 96 F5 .......... 21°29'N 81°46'E
Chiang Mai Thailand 102 B7 .......... 18°47'N 98°59'E
Chiang Rai Thailand 102 B7 .......... 19°55'N 99°53'E
Chiapas d. Mexico 66 F4 .......... 16°23'N 92°17'W
Chiba Japan 104 D3 .......... 35°37'N 140°07'E
Chibougamau Canada 61 K2 .......... 49°55'N 74°22'W
Chicago U.S.A. 63 I5 .......... 41°55'N 87°38'W
Chichester England 8 E1 .......... 50°50'N 0°46'W
Chiclayo Peru 72 B6 .......... 6°44'S 79°51'W
Chicoutimi Canada 61 K2 .......... 48°26'N 71°03'W
Chidley, Cape Canada 61 L4 .......... 60°26'N 64°20'W
Chiemsee l. Germany 46 E2 .......... 47°52'N 12°28'E
Chifeng China 99 L6 .......... 42°11'N 119°02'E
Chiganak Kazakhstan 54 I2 .......... 45°10'N 73°57'E
Chihuahua Mexico 66 C6 .......... 28°38'N 106°07'W
Chihuahua d. Mexico 66 C6 .......... 29°10'N 106°11'W
Chile S. America 73 B3 .......... 34°06'S 71°23'W
Chilham England 9 F2 .......... 51°15'N 0°58'E
Chillán Chile 73 B3 .......... 36°37'S 72°07'W
Chiloé, Isla de i. Chile 73 B2 .......... 42°26'S 74°29'W
Chilpancingo Mexico 66 E4 .......... 17°33'N 99°30'W
Chiltern Hills England 8 E2 .......... 51°39'N 0°50'W
Chimborazo mt. Ecuador 72 B6 .......... 1°27'S 78°50'W
Chimbote Peru 72 B6 .......... 9°03'S 78°35'W
Chimboy Uzbekistan 53 F2 .......... 42°56'N 59°47'E
Chimoio Mozambique 83 C3 .......... 19°07'S 33°28'E
China Asia 98 H3 .......... 38°59'N 78°40'E
Chindwin r. Myanmar 97 I5 .......... 21°27'N 95°15'E
Chingola Zambia 83 B3 .......... 12°33'S 27°54'E
Chinhoyi Zimbabwe 83 C3 .......... 17°21'S 30°11'E
Chinju S. Korea 104 A3 .......... 35°10'N 128°05'E
Chioggia Italy 46 E1 .......... 45°12'N 12°16'E
Chios Greece 50 G4 .......... 38°22'N 26°08'E
Chios i. Greece 50 F4 .......... 38°24'N 25°58'E
Chipata Zambia 83 C3 .......... 13°37'S 32°38'E
Chippenham England 8 C2 .......... 51°27'N 2°07'W
Chipping Campden England 8 D3 .......... 52°03'N 1°47'W
Chipping Norton England 8 D2 .......... 51°57'N 1°32'W
Chipping Ongar England 9 F2 .......... 51°42'N 0°15'E
Chipping Sodbury England 8 C2 .......... 51°32'N 2°23'W
Chiriquí, Golfo de b. Panama 67 H2 .......... 8°02'N 82°04'W
Chirk Wales 10 D4 .......... 52°56'N 3°03'W
Chirnside Scotland 15 G3 .......... 55°48'N 2°12'W
Chirripo mt. Costa Rica 67 H2 .......... 9°30'N 83°30'W
Chisasibi Canada 61 K3 .......... 53°49'N 78°59'W
Chişinău Moldova 49 I6 .......... 47°02'N 28°50'E
Chistopol' Russia 52 F3 .......... 55°21'N 50°36'E
Chita Russia 55 M3 .......... 51°54'N 113°27'E
Chitambo Zambia 83 C3 .......... 12°54'S 30°37'E
Chitradurga India 96 E3 .......... 14°14'N 76°22'E
Chittoor India 96 E3 .......... 13°12'N 79°05'E
Chitungwiza Zimbabwe 83 C3 .......... 18°01'S 31°04'E
Chojnice Poland 46 G5 .......... 53°42'N 17°34'E
Cholet France 44 C5 .......... 47°04'N 0°53'W
Chomutov Czechia 46 E4 .......... 50°28'N 13°24'E
Chon Buri Thailand 102 C6 .......... 13°22'N 101°02'E
Ch'ŏngjin N. Korea 99 N6 .......... 41°46'N 129°45'E
Chongqing China 99 J3 .......... 29°34'N 106°32'E
Chongqing d. China 99 J4 .......... 30°04'N 107°39'E

Chonos, Archipiélago de los is Chile 73 B2 .......... 44°59'S 75°31'W
Chorley England 12 E2 .......... 53°39'N 2°38'W
Chornobyl' Ukraine 47 N4 .......... 51°16'N 30°14'E
Chornomors'ke Ukraine 51 J7 .......... 45°30'N 32°43'E
Chortkiv Ukraine 47 K3 .......... 49°01'N 25°47'E
Chōshi Japan 104 D3 .......... 35°44'N 140°49'E
Choûm Mauritania 84 C4 .......... 21°20'N 12°59'W
Choybalsan Mongolia 99 K7 .......... 47°57'N 114°34'E
Christchurch England 8 D1 .......... 50°44'N 1°47'W
Christchurch New Zealand 109 G2 .......... 43°31'S 172°37'E
Christmas Island Indian Oc. 102 D1 .......... 10°30'S 105°44'E
Chūgoku-sanchi mts Japan 104 B2 .......... 34°45'N 132°19'E
Chukchi Sea Russia/U.S.A. 55 T4 .......... 69°12'N 171°31'W
Chukotskiy Poluostrov pen. Russia 55 T4 .......... 65°58'N 175°16'W
Chulmleigh England 11 D2 .......... 50°55'N 3°52'W
Chumphon Thailand 102 B6 .......... 10°31'N 99°13'E
Chuncheon S. Korea 99 N5 .......... 37°52'N 127°46'E
Chunya r. Russia 55 K4 .......... 61°36'N 96°31'E
Chur Switz. 46 C2 .......... 46°51'N 9°32'E
Churchill Canada 61 I3 .......... 58°44'N 94°05'W
Churchill r. Man. Canada 61 I3 .......... 58°11'N 94°23'W
Churchill r. Nfld. and Lab. Canada 61 L3 .......... 53°16'N 60°14'W
Churchill, Cape Canada 61 I3 .......... 58°45'N 93°16'W
Church Stretton England 8 C3 .......... 52°32'N 2°48'W
Chusovoy Russia 52 F3 .......... 58°18'N 57°48'E
Chuxiong China 99 I3 .......... 25°02'N 101°32'E
Ciechanów Poland 46 I5 .......... 52°53'N 20°38'E
Ciego de Ávila Cuba 67 I5 .......... 21°51'N 78°45'W
Cienfuegos Cuba 67 H5 .......... 22°10'N 80°25'W
Cigüela r. Spain 45 D3 .......... 39°08'N 3°43'W
Cihanbeyli Turkey 51 J4 .......... 38°40'N 32°56'E
Cilacap Indonesia 102 D2 .......... 7°41'S 109°00'E
Cimone, Monte mt. Italy 46 D1 .......... 44°11'N 10°42'E
Cinca r. Spain 45 F4 .......... 41°26'N 0°21'E
Cincinnati U.S.A. 63 J4 .......... 39°06'N 84°32'W
Cinderford England 8 C2 .......... 51°49'N 2°30'W
Ciney Belgium 42 E3 .......... 50°18'N 5°06'E
Cinto, Monte mt. France 44 H3 .......... 42°23'N 8°56'E
Cirebon Indonesia 102 D2 .......... 6°45'S 108°34'E
Cirencester England 8 D2 .......... 51°43'N 1°58'W
City of Edinburgh d. Scotland 20 D4 .......... 55°56'N 3°17'W
City of Kingston upon Hull d. England 21 E3 .......... 53°46'N 0°19'W
Ciudad Bolívar Venezuela 72 C7 .......... 8°01'N 63°35'W
Ciudad del Carmen Mexico 66 F4 .......... 18°39'N 91°51'W
Ciudad Delicias Mexico 66 C6 .......... 28°10'N 105°30'W
Ciudad de Valles Mexico 66 E5 .......... 21°59'N 99°00'W
Ciudad Guayana Venezuela 72 C7 .......... 8°22'N 62°37'W
Ciudad Ixtepec Mexico 66 E4 .......... 16°35'N 95°06'W
Ciudad Juárez Mexico 66 C7 .......... 31°44'N 106°28'W
Ciudad Madero Mexico 66 E5 .......... 22°19'N 97°51'W
Ciudad Obregón Mexico 66 C6 .......... 27°28'N 109°57'W
Ciudad Real Spain 45 D3 .......... 38°59'N 3°54'W
Ciudad Rodrigo Spain 45 B4 .......... 40°36'N 6°31'W
Ciudad Victoria Mexico 66 E5 .......... 23°45'N 99°08'W
Ciutadella de Menorca Spain 45 G4 .......... 40°00'N 3°52'E
Civitavecchia Italy 48 F5 .......... 42°05'N 11°48'E
Çivril Turkey 51 H4 .......... 38°18'N 29°43'E
Cixi China 99 M4 .......... 30°10'N 121°14'E
Clackmannanshire d. Scotland 20 D5 .......... 56°09'N 3°45'W
Clacton-on-Sea England 9 G2 .......... 51°47'N 1°09'E
Claonaig Scotland 14 D3 .......... 55°45'N 5°24'W
Clara Ireland 18 D3 .......... 53°20'N 7°37'W
Clare d. Ireland 18 C2 .......... 52°53'N 8°50'W
Clare r. Ireland 18 B3 .......... 53°19'N 9°03'W
Clare Island Ireland 18 A3 .......... 53°49'N 10°01'W
Claremorris Ireland 18 C3 .......... 53°43'N 8°59'W
Clarksville U.S.A. 63 I4 .......... 36°32'N 87°20'W
Clay Cross England 13 F2 .......... 53°10'N 1°25'W
Claydon England 9 G3 .......... 52°06'N 1°07'E
Clay Head Isle of Man 12 C3 .......... 54°12'N 4°23'W
Clayton U.S.A. 62 F4 .......... 36°28'N 103°12'W
Clear, Cape Ireland 18 B1 .......... 51°25'N 9°31'W
Clear Island Ireland 18 B1 .......... 51°26'N 9°28'W
Cleator Moor England 12 D3 .......... 54°31'N 3°31'W
Cleethorpes England 13 G2 .......... 53°33'N 0°02'W
Cleobury Mortimer England 8 C3 .......... 52°23'N 2°29'W
Clermont-Ferrand France 44 E4 .......... 45°46'N 3°05'E
Clevedon England 8 C2 .......... 51°26'N 2°51'W
Cleveland U.S.A. 63 J5 .......... 41°30'N 81°41'W
Cleveland Hills England 13 F3 .......... 54°22'N 1°13'W
Cleveleys England 12 D2 .......... 53°53'N 3°02'W
Clew Bay Ireland 18 B3 .......... 53°48'N 9°47'W
Cliffe England 9 F2 .......... 51°28'N 0°30'E
Clinton U.S.A. 62 G4 .......... 35°32'N 98°58'W
Clipperton, Île N. Pacific Oc. 56 E2 .......... 10°21'N 109°19'W
Clisham hill Scotland 16 C2 .......... 57°58'N 6°49'W
Clitheroe England 12 E2 .......... 53°52'N 2°23'W
Clogher Head Ireland 18 E3 .......... 53°48'N 6°13'W
Clonakilty Ireland 18 C1 .......... 51°37'N 8°53'W
Clones Ireland 18 D4 .......... 54°10'N 7°13'W
Clonmel Ireland 18 D2 .......... 52°21'N 7°43'W
Cloud Peak U.S.A. 62 E5 .......... 44°24'N 107°01'W
Clovis U.S.A. 62 F3 .......... 34°27'N 103°12'W
Cluanie, Loch l. Scotland 16 D2 .......... 57°09'N 5°07'W
Cluj-Napoca Romania 47 J2 .......... 46°46'N 23°36'E
Clun England 8 B3 .......... 52°25'N 3°02'W
Clydach Wales 10 D3 .......... 51°42'N 3°54'W
Clyde r. Scotland 15 E3 .......... 55°55'N 4°29'W
Clyde, Firth of est. Scotland 14 E3 .......... 55°25'N 4°59'W
Clydebank Scotland 14 E3 .......... 55°54'N 4°24'W
Clyde River town Canada 61 L5 .......... 70°23'N 68°31'W
Coahuila d. Mexico 66 D6 .......... 27°30'N 102°08'W
Coalville England 8 D3 .......... 52°43'N 1°22'W
Coastal Plain f. U.S.A. 63 H3 .......... 30°25'N 94°23'W
Coast Mountains Canada 60 E3 .......... 52°40'N 127°48'W
Coast Ranges mts U.S.A. 62 B5 .......... 40°40'N 123°39'W
Coatbridge Scotland 15 E3 .......... 55°52'N 4°01'W
Coats Island Canada 61 J4 .......... 62°41'N 82°53'W
Coatzacoalcos Mexico 66 F4 .......... 18°08'N 94°26'W
Cobar Australia 108 D3 .......... 31°31'S 145°48'E
Cobh Ireland 18 C1 .......... 51°51'N 8°18'W
Cochabamba Bolivia 72 C5 .......... 17°25'S 66°11'W
Cochrane Canada 63 J6 .......... 49°04'N 81°03'W
Cockburnspath Scotland 15 G3 .......... 55°56'N 2°22'W
Cockermouth England 12 D3 .......... 54°40'N 3°22'W
Coco r. Honduras/Nicaragua 67 H3 .......... 14°58'N 83°15'W
Coco, Isla del i. N. Pacific Oc. 68 B4 .......... 5°32'N 87°04'W
Cocos Islands Indian Oc. 102 B1 .......... 11°56'S 96°56'E
Cocuy, Sierra Nevada del mt. Colombia 67 J2 .......... 6°28'N 72°19'W
Cod, Cape U.S.A. 63 L5 .......... 41°58'N 70°01'W
Coddington England 13 G2 .......... 53°05'N 0°45'W
Codó Brazil 72 E6 .......... 4°28'S 43°50'W
Codsall England 8 C2 .......... 52°38'N 2°11'W

Coeur d'Alene U.S.A. 62 C6 .......... 47°41'N 116°47'W
Coffs Harbour Australia 108 E3 .......... 30°19'S 153°06'E
Coggeshall England 9 F2 .......... 51°52'N 0°42'E
Coiba, Isla de i. Panama 67 H2 .......... 7°27'N 81°51'W
Coigeach, Rubha pt Scotland 16 D3 .......... 58°06'N 5°28'W
Coimbatore India 96 E3 .......... 10°59'N 76°57'E
Coimbra Portugal 45 A4 .......... 40°13'N 8°25'W
Colchester England 9 F2 .......... 51°53'N 0°54'E
Coldstream Scotland 15 G3 .......... 55°39'N 2°15'W
Coleford England 8 C2 .......... 51°48'N 2°37'W
Coleraine Northern Ireland 14 C3 .......... 55°08'N 6°40'W
Colima Mexico 66 D4 .......... 19°14'N 103°45'W
Colima d. Mexico 66 D4 .......... 19°03'N 103°59'W
Colima, Nevado de vol. Mexico 66 D4 .......... 19°33'N 103°37'W
Coll i. Scotland 16 C1 .......... 56°36'N 6°36'W
Collier Bay Australia 108 B5 .......... 16°15'S 124°15'E
Colmar France 44 G6 .......... 48°05'N 7°21'E
Colne England 12 E2 .......... 53°51'N 2°11'W
Colne r. England 9 F2 .......... 51°51'N 0°57'E
Cologne Germany 46 B4 .......... 50°56'N 6°57'E
Colombia S. America 72 B7 .......... 3°45'N 72°22'W
Colombo Sri Lanka 96 E2 .......... 6°56'N 79°50'E
Colón Panama 67 I2 .......... 9°22'N 79°55'W
Colonsay i. Scotland 14 C4 .......... 56°05'N 6°15'W
Colorado r. Argentina 73 C3 .......... 39°42'S 62°07'W
Colorado r. Mexico/U.S.A. 62 C3 .......... 31°56'N 115°01'W
Colorado d. U.S.A. 62 E4 .......... 39°02'N 105°31'W
Colorado r. U.S.A. 62 G2 .......... 28°40'N 96°01'W
Colorado Plateau f. U.S.A. 62 E4 .......... 37°27'N 109°54'W
Colorado Springs town U.S.A. 62 F4 .......... 38°52'N 104°47'W
Coltishall England 9 G3 .......... 52°44'N 1°22'E
Columbia U.S.A. 63 J3 .......... 33°59'N 81°01'W
Columbia r. U.S.A. 62 B6 .......... 46°11'N 123°23'W
Columbia, Mount Canada 60 G3 .......... 52°08'N 117°25'W
Columbus Ga. U.S.A. 63 J3 .......... 32°32'N 84°59'W
Columbus Miss. U.S.A. 63 I3 .......... 33°33'N 88°25'W
Columbus Oh. U.S.A. 63 J4 .......... 39°58'N 83°00'W
Colville r. U.S.A. 60 C5 .......... 70°20'N 150°32'W
Colwyn Bay town Wales 10 D5 .......... 53°18'N 3°43'W
Comacchio Italy 46 E1 .......... 44°41'N 12°11'E
Combe Martin England 11 C3 .......... 51°12'N 4°01'W
Comber Northern Ireland 14 D2 .......... 54°33'N 5°44'W
Comeragh Mountains Ireland 18 D2 .......... 52°18'N 7°39'W
Como Italy 46 C1 .......... 45°48'N 9°05'E
Como, Lake Italy 46 C1 .......... 45°57'N 9°11'E
Comodoro Rivadavia Argentina 73 C2 .......... 45°56'S 67°30'W
Comorin, Cape India 86 E2 .......... 8°04'N 77°35'E
Comoros Africa 83 D3 .......... 11°50'S 44°17'E
Comrat Moldova 51 H8 .......... 46°18'N 28°40'E
Comrie Scotland 15 F4 .......... 56°23'N 3°59'W
Conakry Guinea 84 C2 .......... 9°31'N 13°42'W
Concarneau France 44 B5 .......... 47°53'N 3°55'W
Concepción Chile 73 B3 .......... 36°50'S 73°04'W
Conception, Point U.S.A. 62 B3 .......... 34°27'N 120°26'W
Conchos r. Mexico 66 D6 .......... 29°35'N 104°29'W
Concord U.S.A. 63 L5 .......... 43°12'N 71°33'W
Concordia Argentina 73 D3 .......... 31°23'S 57°59'W
Congleton England 13 E2 .......... 53°10'N 2°13'W
Congo Africa 84 F1 .......... 2°24'S 15°10'E
Congo r. Congo/Dem. Rep. Congo 83 A4 .......... 6°05'S 12°26'E
Congo, Democratic Republic of the Africa 83 B4 .......... 3°43'S 22°17'E
Congo Basin f. Africa 85 G2 .......... 1°00'S 20°00'E
Coningsby England 13 G2 .......... 53°06'N 0°10'W
Coniston England 12 D3 .......... 54°22'N 3°05'W
Coniston Water l. England 12 D3 .......... 54°19'N 3°04'W
Conn, Lough l. Ireland 18 B4 .......... 54°01'N 9°16'W
Connah's Quay Wales 10 D5 .......... 53°13'N 3°04'W
Connecticut d. U.S.A. 63 L5 .......... 41°41'N 72°36'W
Connecticut r. U.S.A. 63 L5 .......... 41°16'N 72°22'W
Connemara f. Ireland 18 B3 .......... 53°28'N 9°52'W
Conon Bridge Scotland 17 E2 .......... 57°34'N 4°26'W
Consett England 13 F3 .......... 54°51'N 1°50'W
Con Son i. Vietnam 102 D5 .......... 8°42'N 106°40'E
Constance, Lake Germany/Switz. 46 C2 .......... 47°40'N 9°17'E
Constanța Romania 51 H7 .......... 44°11'N 28°37'E
Constantine Algeria 84 E5 .......... 36°23'N 6°38'E
Conwy Wales 10 D5 .......... 53°17'N 3°50'W
Conwy r. Wales 10 D5 .......... 53°10'N 3°37'W
Conwy r. Wales 10 D5 .......... 53°14'N 3°48'W
Conwy Bay Wales 10 C5 .......... 53°16'N 4°02'W
Cook Islands S. Pacific Oc. 109 I5 .......... 20°05'S 160°06'W
Cookstown Northern Ireland 14 C2 .......... 54°39'N 6°45'W
Cook Strait New Zealand 109 G2 .......... 40°32'S 174°01'E
Cooktown Australia 108 D5 .......... 15°28'S 145°17'E
Coolangatta Australia 108 E4 .......... 28°10'S 153°31'E
Cooper Creek watercourse Australia 108 C4 .......... 28°29'S 137°43'E
Coos Bay town U.S.A. 62 B5 .......... 43°21'N 124°12'W
Copenhagen Denmark 43 C1 .......... 55°40'N 12°34'E
Copiapó Chile 73 B4 .......... 27°18'S 70°23'W
Copinsay i. Scotland 17 G3 .......... 58°54'N 2°40'W
Corabia Romania 50 F6 .......... 43°47'N 24°29'E
Coral Harbour Canada 61 J4 .......... 64°12'N 83°19'W
Coral Sea S. Pacific Oc. 108 E5 .......... 13°25'S 151°06'E
Coral Sea Islands Territory Australia 108 E5 .......... 15°01'S 150°43'E
Corbie France 42 B2 .......... 49°55'N 2°31'E
Corbridge England 13 E3 .......... 54°58'N 2°01'W
Corby England 8 E3 .......... 52°29'N 0°41'W
Córdoba Argentina 73 C3 .......... 31°24'S 64°11'W
Córdoba Mexico 66 E4 .......... 18°55'N 96°53'W
Córdoba Spain 45 C2 .......... 37°53'N 4°46'W
Córdoba, Sierras de mts Argentina 73 C3 .......... 32°55'S 64°22'W
Corfe Castle England 8 C1 .......... 50°38'N 2°03'W
Corfu i. Greece 50 C4 .......... 39°36'N 19°47'E
Corinth Greece 50 E3 .......... 37°56'N 22°55'E
Corixa Grande r. Bolivia/Brazil 72 D5 .......... 17°30'S 57°56'W
Cork Ireland 18 C1 .......... 51°54'N 8°28'W
Cork d. Ireland 18 C2 .......... 52°01'N 8°39'W
Cork City d. Ireland 18 C2 .......... 51°54'N 8°28'W
Çorlu Turkey 51 G5 .......... 41°09'N 27°48'E
Corner Brook Canada 61 M2 .......... 48°54'N 57°47'W
Cornwall d. England 21 C2 .......... 50°32'N 4°33'W
Cornwall, Cape England 11 B2 .......... 50°08'N 5°47'W
Cornwallis Island Canada 61 I5 .......... 75°08'N 94°56'W
Coro Venezuela 72 C8 .......... 11°23'N 69°40'W
Coronado, Bahía de b. Costa Rica 67 H2 .......... 8°55'N 83°48'W
Coronation Gulf Canada 60 G4 .......... 68°08'N 112°32'W
Corpus Christi U.S.A. 62 G2 .......... 27°44'N 97°27'W
Corral de Cantos mt. Spain 45 C3 .......... 39°34'N 4°27'W
Corrib, Lough l. Ireland 18 B3 .......... 53°27'N 9°19'W
Corrientes Argentina 73 D4 .......... 27°27'S 58°46'W
Corrientes, Cabo c. Mexico 66 C5 .......... 20°26'N 105°42'W
Corse, Cap c. France 44 H3 .......... 43°00'N 9°22'E
Corserine hill Scotland 14 E3 .......... 55°09'N 4°21'W
Corsham England 8 C2 .......... 51°26'N 2°11'W

Corsica i. France 44 H3 ..............................42°20'N 8°29'E
Corte France 44 H3..................................42°18'N 9°09'E
Cortegana Spain 45 B2............................37°55'N 6°49'W
Cortina d'Ampezzo Italy 46 E2........46°32'N 12°09'E
Corton England 9 G3................................52°31'N 1°45'E
Çorum Turkey 51 K5...............................40°33'N 34°57'E
Corumbá Brazil 72 D5.............................19°00'S 57°37'W
Corwen Wales 10 D4...............................52°59'N 3°22'W
Cosenza Italy 49 G4.................................39°18'N 16°15'E
Cosmoledo Islands Seychelles 83 D4.......9°30'S 49°00'E
Cosne-Cours-sur-Loire France 44 E5......47°25'N 2°56'E
Costa Blanca f. Spain 45 E3...................38°03'N 0°20'W
Costa Brava f. Spain 45 G4.....................41°28'N 3°05'E
Costa del Sol f. Spain 45 C2...................36°25'N 5°06'W
Costa de Mosquitos f. Nicaragua 67 H3....12°08'N 83°52'W
Costa Rica Central America 67 H3.......10°08'N 84°19'W
Cotabato Phil. 103 G5..............................7°13'N 124°14'E
Côte d'Azur f. France 44 G3....................43°33'N 7°13'E
Côte d'Ivoire Africa 84 D2........................7°35'N 4°22'W
Cothi r. Wales 10 C3................................51°52'N 4°10'W
Cotonou Benin 84 E2...............................6°21'N 2°27'E
Cotopaxi, Volcán vol. Ecuador 72 B6.....0°39'S 78°26'W
Cotswold Hills England 8 C2..................51°36'N 2°15'W
Cottbus Germany 46 F4...........................51°45'N 14°21'E
Cottenham England 9 F3..........................52°17'N 0°08'E
Cottesmore England 8 E3.......................52°43'N 0°40'W
Coulogne France 42 A3...........................50°55'N 1°53'E
Coupar Angus Scotland 15 F4................56°33'N 3°16'W
Courland Lagoon b. Lithuania/Russia 43 E1
............................................................55°16'N 21°06'E
Coutances France 44 C6..........................49°03'N 1°27'W
Coventry England 8 D3...........................52°24'N 1°31'W
Covilhã Portugal 45 B4............................40°17'N 7°29'W
Cowan, Lake Australia 108 B3................31°45'S 121°59'E
Cowbridge Wales 11 D3..........................51°28'N 3°27'W
Cowdenbeath Scotland 15 F4.................56°07'N 3°20'W
Cowes England 8 D1...............................50°46'N 1°18'W
Cowfold England 9 E1.............................50°59'N 0°16'W
Cow Green Reservoir England 13 E3.......54°40'N 2°20'W
Cox's Bazar Bangl. 97 H5.......................21°27'N 91°59'E
Coyhaique Chile 73 B2............................45°36'S 72°05'W
Cozumel, Isla de i. Mexico 66 G5...........20°22'N 86°55'W
Craig U.S.A. 62 E5...................................40°31'N 107°32'W
Craigavon Northern Ireland 14 C2.........54°26'N 6°21'W
Craig Goch Reservoir Wales 10 D4........52°19'N 3°37'W
Craignure Scotland 14 D4.......................56°28'N 5°43'W
Crail Scotland 15 G4................................56°16'N 2°38'W
Craiova Romania 50 E7............................44°19'N 23°48'E
Cramlington England 13 F4.....................55°05'N 1°35'W
Cranbrook Canada 60 G2........................49°32'N 115°45'W
Cranleigh England 9 E2...........................51°08'N 0°29'W
Crawley England 9 E2..............................51°07'N 0°11'W
Creag Meagaidh mt. Scotland 17 E1......56°57'N 4°36'W
Credenhill England 8 C3..........................52°05'N 2°48'W
Crediton England 11 D2...........................50°48'N 3°39'W
Cree Lake Canada 60 H3.........................57°31'N 106°29'W
Cremona Italy 46 D1................................45°08'N 10°01'E
Cres i. Croatia 50 A7................................44°51'N 14°28'E
Crescent City U.S.A. 62 B5.....................41°47'N 124°09'W
Creston U.S.A. 63 H5...............................41°03'N 94°22'W
Creswell England 13 F2...........................53°16'N 1°13'W
Crete i. Greece 50 F2...............................35°28'N 24°41'E
Creuse r. France 44 D5............................47°00'N 0°34'E
Crewe England 13 E2..............................53°06'N 2°26'W
Crewkerne England 8 C1.........................50°53'N 2°48'W
Crianlarich Scotland 14 E4......................56°24'N 4°37'W
Criccieth Wales 10 C4.............................52°55'N 4°14'W
Criciúma Brazil 73 E4..............................28°45'S 49°25'W
Crickhowell Wales 10 D3........................51°51'N 3°08'W
Crieff Scotland 15 F4...............................56°23'N 3°50'W
Criffel hill Scotland 15 F2.......................54°57'N 3°38'W
Crimea pen. Ukraine 49 J6......................45°20'N 34°05'E
Crimond Scotland 17 H2.........................57°36'N 1°55'W
Croatia Europe 50 B7...............................45°02'N 15°14'E
Croisilles France 9 H1..............................50°12'N 2°53'E
Croker Island Australia 103 I1.................11°04'S 132°38'E
Cromarty Scotland 17 E2........................57°41'N 4°02'W
Cromarty Firth est. Scotland 17 E2........57°38'N 4°19'W
Cromdale, Hills of Scotland 17 F2..........57°19'N 3°31'W
Cromer England 9 G3..............................52°56'N 1°18'E
Cronamuck Mountain hill Ireland 14 B2....54°54'N 7°51'W
Crook England 13 F3................................54°43'N 1°45'W
Crooked Island Bahamas 67 J5..............22°48'N 74°14'W
Crooked Island Passage str. Bahamas 67 J5
............................................................22°29'N 74°55'W
Croom Ireland 18 C2...............................52°31'N 8°43'W
Crosby England 12 D2.............................53°29'N 3°02'W
Cross Fell hill England 13 E3...................54°42'N 2°29'W
Crossgar Northern Ireland 14 D2.............54°24'N 5°45'W
Crossmaglen Northern Ireland 14 C2.....54°04'N 6°36'W
Crotone Italy 49 G4.................................39°05'N 17°08'E
Crouch r. England 9 F2............................51°38'N 0°36'E
Crowborough England 9 F2.....................51°04'N 0°10'E
Crowland England 9 E3...........................52°41'N 0°10'W
Crowle England 13 G2.............................53°37'N 0°50'W
Crowthorne England 8 E2........................51°22'N 0°48'W
Croyde England 11 C3.............................51°08'N 4°13'W
Croydon England 9 E2.............................51°23'N 0°06'W
Crozet Islands Indian Oc. 117 G1...........47°00'S 52°00'E
Cruden Bay town Scotland 17 H2...........57°25'N 1°51'W
Crumlin Northern Ireland 14 C2..............54°38'N 6°13'W
Cruz, Cabo c. Cuba 67 I4.........................19°51'N 77°43'W
Cruzeiro do Sul Brazil 72 B6...................7°41'S 72°40'W
Cuando r. Angola/Zambia 83 B3............17°39'S 23°24'E
Cuanza r. Angola 83 A4...........................9°21'S 13°08'E
Cuauhtémoc Mexico 66 C6.....................28°24'N 106°53'W
Cuba Central America 67 H5...................21°18'N 80°06'W
Cubango r. Angola/Namibia 83 B3..........18°01'S 21°26'E
Cuckfield England 9 E2............................51°00'N 0°09'W
Cúcuta Colombia 72 B7...........................7°53'N 72°31'W
Cuddalore India 96 E3.............................11°42'N 79°43'E
Cuenca Ecuador 72 B6............................2°53'S 79°00'W
Cuenca Spain 45 D4................................40°04'N 2°08'W
Cuenca, Serranía de mts Spain 45 D4...40°00'N 2°00'W
Cuernavaca Mexico 66 E4.......................18°56'N 99°11'W
Cuiabá Brazil 72 D5.................................15°33'S 56°04'W
Cuilcagh hill Ireland/U.K. 14 B2..............54°12'N 7°49'W
Cuillin Sound str. Scotland 16 C2...........57°08'N 6°21'W
Culiacán Mexico 66 C5............................24°47'N 107°27'W
Cullen Scotland 17 G2.............................57°41'N 2°49'W
Cullera Spain 45 E3.................................39°10'N 0°13'E
Cullompton England 11 D2......................50°51'N 3°23'W
Cullybackey Northern Ireland 14 C2......54°53'N 6°21'W
Cul Mòr hill Scotland 16 D3....................58°03'N 5°07'W
Culzean Bay Scotland 14 E3...................55°21'N 4°49'W
Cumaná Venezuela 72 C8........................10°24'N 64°09'W

Cumberland r. U.S.A. 63 I4......................36°30'N 87°49'W
Cumberland Sound str. Canada 61 L4......64°08'N 63°14'W
Cumbernauld Scotland 15 F3.................55°57'N 3°59'W
Cumbria d. England 21 D4......................54°42'N 3°17'W
Cumnock Scotland 14 E3........................55°27'N 4°16'W
Cunene r. Angola 83 A3...........................17°15'S 11°46'E
Cuneo Italy 48 E5.....................................44°24'N 7°33'E
Cupar Scotland 15 F4...............................56°19'N 3°01'W
Cupica, Golfo de b. Colombia 67 I2.........6°25'N 77°46'W
Curaçao i. Neth. Antilles 67 K3...............12°12'N 69°04'W
Curitiba Brazil 73 E4................................25°28'S 49°17'W
Cusco Peru 72 B5....................................13°31'S 71°59'W
Cushendall Northern Ireland 14 C3.........55°05'N 6°04'W
Cuttack India 96 G6.................................20°27'N 85°55'E
Cuxhaven Germany 46 C5.......................53°52'N 8°42'E
Cuyo Islands Phil. 103 G6.......................11°11'N 121°01'E
Cyclades is Greece 50 F3........................37°14'N 24°37'E
Cyprus Asia 51 J2....................................35°38'N 33°17'E
Cyrenaica f. Libya 49 H2..........................26°00'N 22°24'E
Czechia Europe 46 F3..............................49°38'N 15°37'E
Częstochowa Poland 46 H4.....................50°48'N 19°07'E

D

Dąbrowa Górnicza Poland 46 H4............50°21'N 19°15'E
Dachau Germany 46 D3...........................48°15'N 11°27'E
Dadaab Kenya 85 I3.................................0°07'N 40°19'E
Daegu S. Korea 99 N5.............................35°52'N 128°35'E
Daejeon S. Korea 99 N5..........................36°22'N 127°28'E
Dagupan Phil. 102 G7..............................16°04'N 120°21'E
Da Hinggan Ling mts China 99 L6...........43°33'N 117°52'E
Dahlak Archipelago is Eritrea 94 F3.......15°58'N 40°04'E
Dahm, Ramlat des. Saudi Arabia/Yemen 94 G3
............................................................17°09'N 45°00'E
Dailly Scotland 14 E3...............................55°17'N 4°43'W
Dakar Senegal 84 C3...............................14°43'N 17°28'W
Dakhla Western Sahara 84 C4................23°42'N 15°56'W
Dakhla Oasis Egypt 94 C5.......................25°25'N 28°53'E
Dakol'ka r. Belarus 47 M5........................52°08'N 28°52'E
Dalaman Turkey 51 H3.............................36°47'N 28°48'E
Đa Lat Vietnam 102 D6............................11°56'N 108°26'E
Dalbandin Pakistan 95 J5........................28°56'N 64°30'E
Dalbeattie Scotland 15 F2.......................54°56'N 3°49'W
Dali China 99 H3......................................25°33'N 100°13'E
Dalian China 99 M5.................................38°51'N 121°37'E
Dalkeith Scotland 15 F3..........................55°54'N 3°04'W
Dallas U.S.A. 62 G3.................................32°46'N 96°48'W
Dalmally Scotland 14 E4.........................56°24'N 4°58'W
Dalmatia f. Bos. and Herz./Croatia 50 A7....44°01'N 15°30'E
Dalmellington Scotland 14 E3.................55°19'N 4°24'W
Dalry Scotland 14 E3................................55°43'N 4°43'W
Dalrymple Scotland 14 E3.......................55°24'N 4°35'W
Dalrymple, Mount Australia 108 D4........20°59'S 148°37'E
Dalton U.S.A. 63 I3...................................34°49'N 84°56'W
Dalton-in-Furness England 12 D3...........54°09'N 3°11'W
Daly r. Australia 108 C5...........................13°31'S 130°28'E
Daman India 96 D5..................................20°24'N 72°58'E
Damanhûr Egypt 49 J3............................31°02'N 30°28'E
Damar i. Indonesia 103 H2......................7°08'S 128°32'E
Damaraland f. Namibia 83 A2.................21°58'S 16°55'E
Damascus Syria 94 E6.............................33°30'N 36°20'E
Damāvand, Qolleh-ye mt. Iran 95 H7.....35°58'N 52°07'E
Damghan Iran 95 H7................................36°09'N 54°19'E
Dammam Saudi Arabia 95 H5.................26°24'N 50°10'E
Dampier Australia 108 A4.......................20°41'S 116°47'E
Dampir, Selat str. Indonesia 103 I3........0°40'S 130°43'E
Đa Nang Vietnam 102 D7........................16°01'N 108°12'E
Dandong China 99 M6.............................40°06'N 124°22'E
Dane r. England 13 E2.............................53°15'N 2°31'W
Danube r. Bulgaria/Croatia/Serbia 49 I6....45°26'N 29°38'E
Danube Delta Romania/Ukraine 51 H7...45°11'N 29°13'E
Danville U.S.A. 63 K4...............................36°35'N 79°24'W
Dapaong Togo 84 E3...............................10°53'N 0°15'E
Da Qaidam China 98 H5..........................37°49'N 95°18'E
Daqing China 99 N7.................................46°28'N 125°01'E
Dar'ā Syria 94 E6.....................................32°38'N 36°07'E
Dārāb Iran 95 H5......................................28°45'N 54°32'E
Darabani Romania 47 L3..........................48°11'N 26°36'E
Daraj r. Belarus 47 M5.............................52°04'N 28°04'E
Darbhanga India 96 G6...........................26°10'N 85°57'E
Dardanelles str. Turkey 50 G5.................40°12'N 26°25'E
Dar es Salaam Tanzania 83 C4...............6°48'S 39°16'E
Darhan Mongolia 99 J7............................49°23'N 105°49'E
Darién, Golfo del g. Colombia 72 B7.......8°56'N 77°01'W
Darjiling India 96 G6................................27°02'N 88°19'E
Darling r. Australia 108 D3.......................34°05'S 141°56'E
Darling Downs hills Australia 108 D4......27°58'S 149°54'E
Darlington England 13 F3.........................54°31'N 1°33'W
Darlington d. England 21 E4....................54°33'N 1°34'W
Darmstadt Germany 44 H6......................49°52'N 8°38'E
Darnah Libya 85 G5.................................32°42'N 22°40'E
Dart r. England 11 D2..............................50°25'N 3°39'W
Dartford England 9 F2.............................51°27'N 0°13'E
Dartmoor hills England 11 C2.................50°36'N 4°01'W
Dartmouth Canada 63 N5........................44°41'N 63°34'W
Dartmouth England 11 D2.......................50°21'N 3°35'W
Darton England 13 F2..............................53°35'N 1°31'W
Daru P.N.G. 103 K2..................................9°03'S 143°12'E
Darwen England 13 E2.............................53°42'N 2°28'W
Darwin Australia 108 C5...........................12°27'S 130°51'E
Datong China 99 K6.................................40°03'N 113°20'E
Daud Khel Pakistan 95 L6.......................32°51'N 71°37'E
Daugava r. Latvia 43 F1...........................57°03'N 24°04'E
Daugavpils Latvia 43 F1...........................55°53'N 26°31'E
Dauphin Canada 60 H3............................51°09'N 100°02'W
Dauphiné f. France 44 F4.........................45°22'N 5°07'E
Davangere India 96 E3............................14°27'N 75°51'E
Davao Phil. 103 H5...................................7°05'N 125°34'E
Davao Gulf Phil. 103 H5...........................6°22'N 125°49'E
Davenport U.S.A. 63 H5...........................41°32'N 90°33'W
Daventry England 8 D3............................52°15'N 1°10'W
David Panama 67 H2...............................8°27'N 82°25'W
Davis Strait Canada/Greenland 61 M4....63°48'N 56°19'W
Davos Switz. 46 C2...................................46°48'N 9°49'E
Dawei Myanmar 97 I3..............................14°06'N 98°13'E
Dawlish England 11 D2.............................50°35'N 3°28'W
Dawqah Oman 95 H3...............................18°37'N 54°04'E
Dawson Canada 60 E4.............................64°04'N 139°24'W
Dawson Creek town Canada 60 F3.........55°46'N 120°17'W
Daxian China 99 K7..................................31°05'N 107°29'E
Dayr az Zawr Syria 94 F7.........................35°19'N 40°06'E
Dayton U.S.A. 63 J4.................................39°45'N 84°11'W
Daytona Beach town U.S.A. 63 J2...........29°08'N 81°05'W

Dazhou China 99 J4.................................31°12'N 107°28'E
Dead Sea l. Asia 94 E6............................31°08'N 35°27'E
Deal England 9 G2...................................51°13'N 1°24'E
Dean, Forest of England 8 C2.................51°48'N 2°32'W
Dearne r. England 13 F2..........................53°29'N 1°14'W
Death Valley f. U.S.A. 62 C4....................36°34'N 117°01'W
Debak Malaysia 102 E4............................1°31'N 111°29'E
Debar North Macedonia 50 D5................41°31'N 20°31'E
Debenham England 9 G3........................52°14'N 1°11'E
Debrecen Hungary 47 J2.........................47°32'N 21°37'E
Debre Zeyit Ethiopia 83 C5.....................8°45'N 38°57'E
Debre India 96 E4...................................18°40'N 77°05'E
Deccan f. India 96 E4...............................18°40'N 77°05'E
Děčín Czechia 46 F4.................................50°47'N 14°13'E
Dee r. Scotland 17 G2..............................57°09'N 2°05'W
Dee est. Wales 10 D5..............................53°18'N 3°09'W
Dee r. Wales 10 D5..................................53°13'N 3°01'W
Deele r. Ireland 14 B2..............................54°51'N 7°28'W
De Grey r. Australia 108 A4.....................20°19'S 119°14'E
Dehra Dun India 96 E7.............................30°20'N 78°05'E
Dej Romania 47 J2...................................47°09'N 23°53'E
Delano Peak U.S.A. 62 D4.......................38°23'N 112°21'W
Delārām Afgh. 95 J6................................32°11'N 63°28'E
Delaware d. U.S.A. 63 K4.........................38°58'N 75°28'W
Delft Neth. 42 D5......................................52°01'N 4°21'E
Delfzijl Neth. 42 F6..................................53°20'N 6°55'E
Delgado, Cabo c. Mozambique 83 D3....10°41'S 40°36'E
Delhi India 96 E6......................................28°38'N 77°17'E
Delhi d. India 96 E6..................................28°38'N 77°08'E
Delice r. Turkey 51 K5..............................40°31'N 34°13'E
Del Rio U.S.A. 62 F2.................................29°21'N 100°54'W
Demanda, Sierra de la mts Spain 45 D5....42°13'N 3°27'W
Deming U.S.A. 62 E3...............................32°16'N 107°45'W
Demirci Turkey 51 H4..............................39°02'N 28°39'E
Demirkazık Tepe mt. Turkey 51 K3.........37°48'N 35°09'E
Dempo, Gunung vol. Indonesia 102 C3....4°02'S 103°06'E
Denakil f. Africa 85 I3...............................14°27'N 40°44'E
Denali U.S.A. 60 C4..................................63°05'N 150°20'W
Denbigh Wales 10 D5...............................53°11'N 3°25'W
Denbighshire d. Wales 21 D3..................53°06'N 3°20'W
Den Burg Neth. 42 D6..............................53°03'N 4°49'E
Dendermonde Belgium 42 D4..................51°01'N 4°07'E
Den Helder Neth. 42 D5...........................52°58'N 4°46'E
Denizli Turkey 51 H3................................37°45'N 29°05'E
Denmark Europe 43 B2............................56°13'N 10°09'E
Denmark Strait Greenland/Iceland 61 P4....66°13'N 28°09'W
Denny Scotland 15 F4..............................56°01'N 3°54'W
Denpasar Indonesia 102 F2.....................8°41'S 115°10'E
Denton U.S.A. 62 G3...............................33°15'N 97°08'W
D'Entrecasteaux Islands P.N.G. 108 E6....9°38'S 151°02'E
Denver U.S.A. 62 E4.................................39°45'N 105°02'W
Dêqên China 99 H3..................................28°26'N 98°50'E
Dera Ghazi Khan Pakistan 96 D7............30°05'N 70°44'E
Dera Ismail Khan Pakistan 96 D7............31°51'N 70°56'E
Derbent Russia 53 E2...............................42°04'N 48°17'E
Derby Australia 108 B5.............................17°19'S 123°38'E
Derby England 8 D3.................................52°55'N 1°28'W
Derby d. England 21 E3............................52°55'N 1°28'W
Derbyshire d. England 21 E3....................53°11'N 1°36'W
Dereham England 9 F3............................52°41'N 0°56'E
Derg r. Ireland/U.K. 18 D4........................54°44'N 7°26'W
Derg, Lough l. Don. Ireland 18 D4...........54°37'N 7°51'W
Derg, Lough l. Tipp. Ireland 18 C2...........52°54'N 8°28'W
Derry Ireland 18 E2..................................52°41'N 6°40'W
Derry Northern Ireland 14 C2..................54°59'N 7°20'W
Derry and Strabane d. Northern Ireland 20 B4
............................................................54°56'N 7°10'W
Derryveagh Mountains Ireland 18 C4.....54°56'N 8°14'W
Dersingham England 9 F3.......................52°51'N 0°31'E
Dêrub China 98 D4...................................33°25'N 79°46'E
Derudeb Sudan 94 E3..............................17°38'N 36°05'E
Derwent r. England 13 F2.........................53°45'N 0°58'W
Derwent Reservoir Derbys. England 13 F2....53°25'N 1°44'W
Derwent Reservoir Dur. England 13 F3....54°52'N 1°58'W
Derwent Water l. England 12 D3.............54°34'N 3°09'W
Desaguadero r. Argentina 73 C3.............34°03'S 66°43'W
Desē Ethiopia 85 H3................................11°07'N 39°38'E
Des Moines U.S.A. 63 H5........................41°36'N 93°37'W
Des Moines r. U.S.A. 63 H5.....................40°23'N 91°28'W
Desna r. Russia 47 P5..............................50°32'N 30°33'E
Desna r. Russia/Ukraine 47 N4...............50°32'N 30°33'E
Dessau-Roßlau Germany 46 E4..............51°50'N 12°15'E
Desventuradas, Islas is Chile 68 B2........26°54'S 80°00'W
Detroit U.S.A. 63 J5.................................42°19'N 83°04'W
Deva Romania 50 E7................................45°54'N 22°55'E
Deveron r. Scotland 17 G2.......................57°40'N 2°31'W
Deventer Neth. 42 F5...............................52°15'N 6°10'E
Devil's Bit Mountain hill Ireland 18 D2....52°49'N 7°55'W
Devil's Bridge Wales 10 D4......................52°23'N 3°51'W
Devil's Lake town U.S.A. 62 G6................48°02'N 98°46'W
Devizes England 8 D2..............................51°21'N 1°59'W
Devon d. England 21 D2...........................50°50'N 3°51'W
Devon r. England 13 G2...........................53°04'N 0°50'W
Devon r. Scotland 15 F4...........................56°07'N 3°51'W
Devon Island Canada 61 I5.....................75°00'N 91°06'W
Devonport Australia 108 D2.....................41°11'S 146°20'E
Devrez r. Turkey 51 K4.............................41°27'N 35°01'E
Dewsbury England 13 F2.........................53°41'N 1°38'W
Dezfūl Iran 95 G6......................................32°22'N 48°24'E
Dezhou China 99 L5.................................37°25'N 116°19'E
Dhahran Saudi Arabia 95 H5..................26°19'N 50°07'E
Dhaka Bangl. 97 H5.................................23°43'N 90°24'E
Dhamār Yemen 94 F2..............................14°34'N 44°26'E
Dhanbad India 96 G5...............................23°47'N 86°25'E
Dharwad India 96 E4................................15°27'N 75°04'E
Dhaulagiri mt. Nepal 96 F6.....................28°40'N 83°28'E
Dhule India 96 E5.....................................20°53'N 74°52'E
Diablo, Picacho del mt. Mexico 66 A7....30°57'N 115°24'W
Diamantina watercourse Australia 108 C4....26°30'S 139°22'E
Diamantina, Chapada f. Brazil 72 E5......14°21'S 43°09'W
Dibrugarh India 97 H6..............................27°27'N 94°55'E
Dickinson U.S.A. 62 F6............................46°53'N 102°48'W
Didcot England 8 D2................................51°36'N 1°15'W
Dieppe France 44 D6...............................49°55'N 1°05'E
Diest Belgium 42 E3.................................50°59'N 5°03'E
Digne-les-Bains France 44 G4.................44°06'N 6°15'E
Dijon France 44 F5...................................47°20'N 5°03'E
Diksmuide Belgium 42 B4........................51°02'N 2°52'E
Dili East Timor 103 H2.............................8°35'S 125°36'E
Dillon U.S.A. 62 D6..................................45°13'N 112°37'W
Dimapur India 97 H6................................25°54'N 93°47'E
Dimitrovgrad Bulgaria 50 F6....................42°03'N 25°35'E
Dimitrovgrad Russia 53 E3.......................54°13'N 49°35'E
Dinan France 44 B6.................................48°27'N 2°03'W
Dinant Belgium 42 D3..............................50°16'N 4°56'E
Dinar Turkey 51 I4....................................38°04'N 30°10'E

Dīnār, Kūh-e mt. Iran 95 H6....................30°49'N 51°30'E
Dinard France 44 B6................................48°38'N 2°03'W
Dinaric Alps mts Bos. and Herz./Croatia 50 B7
............................................................44°13'N 16°30'E
Dindigul India 96 E3.................................10°22'N 77°58'E
Dingle Ireland 18 A2.................................52°08'N 10°16'W
Dingle Bay Ireland 18 A2.........................52°00'N 10°15'W
Dingwall Scotland 17 E2..........................57°36'N 4°26'W
Dipolog Phil. 103 G5................................8°39'N 123°20'E
Dir Pakistan 95 L7....................................35°12'N 71°53'E
Dirë Dawa Ethiopia 85 I2.........................9°34'N 41°50'E
Dirranbandi Australia 108 D4..................28°35'S 148°14'E
Disappointment, Cape S. Atlantic Oc. 73 F1
............................................................54°51'S 36°06'W
Disappointment, Lake Australia 108 B4....23°05'S 122°40'E
Disko I. Greenland 61 M4.........................69°44'N 53°00'W
Diss England 9 G3...................................52°23'N 1°07'E
Distington England 12 D3.........................54°36'N 3°32'W
Distrito Federal d. Mexico 66 E4.............19°15'N 99°09'W
Diu India 96 D5........................................20°40'N 71°00'E
Divnoye Russia 49 L6..............................45°55'N 43°21'E
Divriği Turkey 51 M4................................39°22'N 38°07'E
Dixon Entrance str. Canada/U.S.A. 60 E3
............................................................54°18'N 133°00'W
Diyarbakır Turkey 49 L4...........................37°55'N 40°16'E
Djado, Plateau du f. Niger 84 F4.............21°30'N 12°00'E
Djelfa Algeria 84 E5.................................34°38'N 3°14'E
Djibloho Equat. Guinea 84 F2..................1°35'N 10°38'E
Djibouti Africa 85 I3.................................11°34'N 42°40'E
Djibouti town Djibouti 85 I3.....................11°32'N 43°04'E
Djouce Mountain hill Ireland 10 A5.........53°08'N 6°13'W
Dnieper r. Belarus 47 N4..........................51°16'N 30°36'E
Dnieper r. Ukraine 47 O2.........................46°30'N 32°25'E
Dniester r. Moldova 47 N2.......................46°25'N 30°00'E
Dniester r. Ukraine 47 M3........................48°06'N 28°00'E
Dnipro Ukraine 47 P3..............................48°30'N 35°04'E
Dniprodzerzhyns'k Ukraine 47 P3..........48°30'N 34°40'E
Dniprorudne Ukraine 47 P2......................47°23'N 34°59'E
Doba Chad 85 F2......................................8°40'N 16°50'E
Doberai Peninsula Indonesia 103 I3.......1°19'S 132°56'E
Doboj Bos. and Herz. 50 C7.....................44°45'N 18°06'E
Dobrich Bulgaria 51 G6............................43°33'N 27°50'E
Dochart r. Scotland 14 E4.........................56°28'N 4°19'W
Docking England 9 F3..............................52°54'N 0°38'E
Dodecanese is Greece 50 G2..................36°57'N 27°15'E
Dodge City U.S.A. 62 F4..........................37°46'N 100°01'W
Dodman Point England 11 C2..................50°13'N 4°48'W
Dodoma Tanzania 83 C4..........................6°10'S 35°46'E
Doetinchem Neth. 42 F4..........................51°58'N 6°17'E
Doha Qatar 95 H5.....................................25°17'N 51°32'E
Dokkum Neth. 42 E6.................................53°19'N 5°59'E
Dolbenmaen Wales 10 C4.......................52°58'N 4°18'W
Dole France 44 F5.....................................47°06'N 5°29'E
Dolgellau Wales 10 D4.............................52°45'N 3°53'W
Dolomites mts Italy 46 D1........................46°42'N 11°38'E
Dolo Odo Ethiopia 85 I2...........................4°09'N 42°04'E
Dolyna Ukraine 47 J3...............................48°58'N 23°59'E
Dolyns'ka Ukraine 47 O3.........................48°07'N 32°46'E
Dominica Central America 67 L4..............15°18'N 61°20'W
Dominican Republic Central America 67 J4
............................................................18°57'N 70°19'W
Don r. Russia 54 F2..................................47°06'N 39°17'E
Don r. Scotland 17 G2..............................57°10'N 2°05'W
Donaghadee Northern Ireland 14 D2......54°38'N 5°32'W
Don Benito Spain 45 C3...........................38°58'N 5°52'W
Doncaster England 13 F2.........................53°31'N 1°07'W
Dondo Angola 83 A4................................9°41'S 14°26'E
Donegal Ireland 18 C4.............................54°39'N 8°06'W
Donegal d. Ireland 18 C4.........................54°56'N 8°00'W
Donegal Bay Ireland 18 C4......................54°31'N 8°16'W
Donegal Point Ireland 18 B2...................52°43'N 9°39'W
Donets'k Ukraine 49 K6............................47°59'N 37°49'E
Dongara Australia 108 A4........................29°17'S 114°56'E
Dongfang China 99 J1..............................19°03'N 108°39'E
Đông Hơi Vietnam 102 D7.......................17°26'N 106°37'E
Dongting Hu l. China 99 K3......................29°20'N 112°40'E
Dongying China 99 L5..............................37°25'N 118°30'E
Donostia Spain 45 D5...............................43°19'N 1°59'W
Doon r. Scotland 14 E3............................55°26'N 4°42'W
Doon, Loch l. Scotland 14 E3..................55°15'N 4°23'W
Dorchester England 8 C1.........................50°43'N 2°27'W
Dordogne r. France 44 C4........................45°00'N 0°32'W
Dordrecht Neth. 42 D4.............................51°48'N 4°40'E
Dörgön Nuur l. Mongolia 98 G7..............47°33'N 93°33'E
Dorking England 9 E2...............................51°14'N 0°20'W
Dornbirn Austria 46 C2.............................47°26'N 9°45'E
Dornoch Scotland 17 E2...........................57°53'N 4°02'W
Dornoch Firth est. Scotland 17 E2...........57°51'N 4°04'W
Dorsale Camerounaise f. Cameroon/Nigeria 84 F2
............................................................5°59'N 10°45'E
Dorset d. England 21 D2...........................50°53'N 2°27'W
Dortmund Germany 46 B4........................51°30'N 7°28'E
Dos Bahías, Cabo c. Argentina 73 C2.....44°56'S 65°32'W
Dōshī Afgh. 95 K7....................................35°38'N 68°40'E
Dosso Niger 84 E3...................................13°03'N 3°12'E
Dothan U.S.A. 63 I3.................................31°14'N 85°24'W
Douai France 44 E7..................................50°22'N 3°05'E
Douala Cameroon 84 E2..........................4°03'N 9°43'E
Douglas Isle of Man 12 C3.......................54°09'N 4°29'W
Douglas Scotland 15 F3...........................55°33'N 3°51'W
Douglas U.S.A. 62 E3...............................31°20'N 109°33'W
Doullens France 42 B3.............................50°09'N 2°20'E
Doune Scotland 15 E4..............................56°11'N 4°04'W
Dounreay Scotland 17 F3.........................58°35'N 3°44'W
Dourados Brazil 73 D4.............................22°13'S 54°49'W
Douro r. Portugal 45 A4............................41°09'N 8°39'W
Dove r. Derbys. England 8 D4.................52°50'N 1°35'W
Dove r. Suff. England 9 G3......................52°21'N 1°11'E
Dover England 9 G2.................................51°08'N 1°19'E
Dover U.S.A. 63 K4..................................39°09'N 75°31'W
Dover, Strait of France/U.K. 9 G1............50°53'N 1°30'E
Down d. Northern Ireland 18 F4...............54°20'N 5°56'W
Downham Market England 9 F3...............52°36'N 0°22'E
Downpatrick Northern Ireland 14 D2.......54°19'N 5°42'W
Downpatrick Head Ireland 18 B4............54°19'N 9°20'W
Downton England 8 D1............................50°59'N 1°44'W
Drâa, Hammada du f. Algeria 48 B2.......28°29'N 8°10'W
Drachten Neth. 42 F6...............................53°06'N 6°06'E
Draguignan France 44 G3........................43°32'N 6°28'E
Drahichyn Belarus 47 K5..........................52°11'N 25°10'E
Drakensberg mts Lesotho/S. Africa 83 B2....29°59'S 28°06'E
Drama Greece 50 F5................................41°09'N 24°09'E
Drammen Norway 43 B2..........................59°45'N 10°12'E
Draperstown Northern Ireland 14 C2.......54°48'N 6°47'W
Drau r. Austria 46 E2................................46°38'N 14°08'E
Drava r. Europe 50 C7..............................45°33'N 18°55'E
Drenthe d. Neth. 42 F5.............................52°53'N 6°40'E

den Germany 46 E4 .................................51°03'N 13°45'E
x France 44 D6 .....................................48°44'N 1°23'E
eld England 13 G2 ...............................54°00'N 0°27'W
r, Bos. and Herz./Serbia 50 C7..........44°55'N 19°22'E
eta-Turnu Severin Romania 50 E7....44°37'N 22°40'E
heda England 18 E3 ...........................53°43'N 6°21'W
obych Ukraine 47 J3 ..........................49°22'N 23°32'E
wich Spa England 8 C3 .....................52°16'N 2°09'W
nore Northern Ireland 14 C2 ............54°25'N 6°08'W
field England 13 F2 ............................53°18'N 1°28'W
h Pakistan 95 L7 .................................35°33'N 71°50'E
nheller Canada 60 G3 .........................51°27'N 112°42'W
more Scotland 14 E2 ...........................54°41'N 4°54'W
kininkai Lithuania 47 K5 .....................53°59'N 24°01'E
r. Belarus 47 N5 ..................................53°03'N 30°03'E
rn Fawr hill Wales 10 D4 ...................52°13'N 3°40'W
hen Scotland 14 E4 ..............................56°04'N 4°27'W
te, Pico mt. Dom. Rep. 67 J4 ...........19°03'N 70°59'W
i Saudi Arabia 94 E5............................27°20'N 35°45'E
i U.A.E. 95 I5 ........................................24°15'N 55°17'E
wnt Lake Canada 60 H4 .....................63°05'N 101°38'W
o Australia 108 D3 ..............................32°16'S 148°39'E
in Ireland 18 E3 ..................................53°20'N 6°16'W
in Bay Ireland 18 E3 ..........................53°21'N 6°10'W
in City d. Ireland 18 E3 ......................53°24'N 6°18'W
o Ukraine 47 K4 ..................................50°25'N 25°43'E
ovnik Croatia 50 C6 ...........................42°39'N 18°06'E
ovytsya Ukraine 47 L4 .......................51°34'N 26°34'E
nka Russia 55 J4 ..................................69°22'N 86°11'E
ey England 8 C3 ...................................52°31'N 2°05'W
o r. Spain 45 B4 ..................................41°02'N 6°56'W
own Scotland 17 F2 ............................57°27'N 3°08'W
urspitze mt. Italy/Switz. 46 B1...........45°57'N 7°53'E
Otok i. Croatia 50 A7 .........................44°01'N 15°01'E
burg Germany 46 B4 ...........................51°28'N 6°47'E
än Qatar 95 H5 ....................................25°25'N 50°47'E
rton England 11 D3 .............................51°02'N 3°33'W
as U.S.A. 62 F4 ....................................35°53'N 101°59'W
barton Scotland 14 E3 ........................55°57'N 4°34'W
fries Scotland 15 F3 ............................55°04'N 3°36'W
fries and Galloway d. Scotland 20 D4 ... 55°09'N 3°46'W
yât Egypt 49 J3 ....................................31°25'N 31°49'E
ff Head Ireland 18 B3 .........................55°18'N 7°31'W
ny Point Ireland 18 E3 ........................53°52'N 6°14'W
újváros Hungary 46 H2........................46°59'N 18°56'E
ar Scotland 15 G4 ................................56°00'N 2°31'W
lane Scotland 15 F4 ............................56°11'N 3°58'W
ansby Head Scotland 17 F3...............58°39'N 3°01'W
hurch England 8 D3 ............................52°20'N 1°17'W
alk Ireland 18 E4 .................................54°00'N 6°24'W
alk Bay Ireland 18 E3 .........................53°57'N 6°13'W
lee Scotland 15 G4 ..............................56°28'N 2°58'W
lee d. Scotland 20 D5 ..........................56°29'N 2°59'W
onald Northern Ireland 14 D2 ............54°36'N 5°48'W
rum Bay Northern Ireland 14 D2 .......54°13'N 5°46'W
din New Zealand 109 G2 .....................45°53'S 170°30'E
ermline Scotland 15 F4 .......................56°04'N 3°27'W
annon Northern Ireland 14 C2............54°30'N 6°46'W
arvan Ireland 18 D2 ............................52°05'N 7°38'W
eness hd England 9 F1 .......................50°55'N 0°59'E
even Northern Ireland 14 C2 ..............54°55'N 6°55'W
un Malaysia 102 C4 .............................4°46'N 103°23'E
unab Sudan 94 E4 ...............................21°04'N 37°04'E
olme England 13 G2 ...........................53°18'N 0°28'W
uang China 98 E6 ................................40°07'N 94°40'E
erque France 44 E7 .............................51°02'N 2°22'E
ery Beacon hill England 11 D3 ...........51°10'N 3°35'W
irk France 44 E7 ..................................51°02'N 2°22'E
Laoghaire Ireland 18 E3 .....................53°17'N 6°08'W
Laoghaire-Rathdown d. Ireland 18 E3... 53°15'N 6°12'W
eer Ireland 18 E3 ................................53°50'N 6°23'W
by Northern Ireland 14 C3 .................55°00'N 6°24'W
nore East Ireland 18 E2 ......................52°09'N 6°59'W
hurry Northern Ireland 14 D2 ...........54°33'N 5°59'W
et Bay Scotland 17 F3 ........................58°37'N 3°24'W
et Head Scotland 17 F3 ......................58°41'N 3°23'W
on Scotland 14 E3 ...............................55°57'N 4°56'W
Scotland 15 G3 ....................................55°47'N 2°21'W
itable England 9 G2 ............................51°53'N 0°31'W
egan, Loch b. Scotland 16 C2 ............57°31'N 6°41'W
nce r. France 44 F3 .............................43°55'N 4°45'E
ngo Mexico 66 D5 ...............................24°02'N 104°43'W
ngo d. Mexico 66 D5 ...........................24°44'N 104°59'W
s U.S.A. 62 E4 .....................................37°16'N 107°52'W
an S. Africa 83 C2 ...............................29°51'S 31°02'E
n Germany 42 F3 .................................50°48'N 6°29'E
aman England 13 F3 ...........................54°47'N 1°35'W
am d. England 21 D4 ...........................54°42'N 2°09'W
am U.S.A. 63 K4 ...................................35°59'N 78°54'W
itor mt. Montenegro 50 C6 ................43°07'N 19°03'E
ess Scotland 16 E3 ..............................58°34'N 4°45'W
ess, Kyle of inlet Scotland 16 E3 ......58°34'N 4°49'W
s Albania 50 C5 ...................................41°19'N 19°27'E
ey Head Ireland 18 A1 ........................51°34'N 10°13'W
ey England 8 C2 ..................................51°41'N 2°21'W
anbe Tajikistan 96 C8 ........................38°38'N 68°51'E
eldorf Germany 46 B4 ........................51°13'N 6°47'E
n China 99 J3 ......................................26°13'N 107°32'E
e Turkey 51 I5 .....................................40°50'N 31°09'E
kovo Russia 47 P5 ...............................53°36'N 34°21'E
Scotland 17 F2 ....................................57°17'N 3°13'W
Cape Canada 61 L4 ............................66°39'N 61°16'W
. Wales 10 D4 ......................................52°33'N 3°56'W
church England 9 F2 ...........................51°01'N 0°59'E
ock England 8 C2 ................................51°59'N 2°26'W
nksk Ukraine 49 J6 ............................45°43'N 34°24'E
gdzhur, Khrebet mts Russia 55 O3 ...55°53'N 135°07'E
a r. Belarus 47 M6 ..............................55°33'N 28°13'E

England 9 E2 ........................................51°31'N 0°18'W
ton Scotland 15 G3 ............................55°38'N 2°41'W
. Scotland 15 F4 .................................56°20'N 3°20'W
Loch l. Scotland 14 E4 .......................56°23'N 4°15'W
gton England 13 F3 ............................54°47'N 1°21'W
gwold England 13 F3 ..........................54°07'N 1°11'W
Anglian Heights hills England 9 F3 ...52°03'N 0°15'E
and d. Scotland 20 C4 ........................55°59'N 4°15'W
ourne England 9 F1 .............................50°46'N 0°18'E
Cape New Zealand 109 G3 ...............39°40'S 178°33'E
China Sea N. Pacific Oc. 99 N4 ........31°00'N 127°22'E
Dunbartonshire d. Scotland 20 C4 ...55°58'N 4°12'W

Easter Island S. Pacific Oc. 116 C2 .........27°05'S 109°17'W
Eastern Desert Egypt 49 J2....................26°39'N 32°50'E
Eastern Ghats mts India 96 E3 ..............11°54'N 77°22'E
Easter Ross f. Scotland 16 E2 .................57°49'N 4°24'W
East Fen f. England 13 H2 .......................53°05'N 0°04'E
Eastfield England 13 G3...........................54°15'N 0°24'W
East Frisian Islands Germany 46 B5......53°45'N 7°00'E
East Grinstead England 9 E2 ..................51°08'N 0°01'W
East Kilbride Scotland 14 E3 ...................55°46'N 4°10'W
Eastleigh England 8 D1.............................50°58'N 1°22'W
East Linton Scotland 15 G3 .....................55°59'N 2°39'W
East Loch Tarbert inlet Scotland 16 C2...57°51'N 6°46'W
East London S. Africa 83 B1 ....................33°01'S 27°56'E
East Looe England 11 C2 .........................50°21'N 4°27'W
East Lothian d. Scotland 20 D4 ..............55°57'N 2°45'W
Eastmain Canada 61 K3 ...........................52°14'N 78°30'W
Eastmain r. Canada 61 K3 .......................52°14'N 78°24'W
Easton England 8 C1.................................50°33'N 2°26'W
East Renfrewshire d. Scotland 20 C4 .....55°46'N 4°21'W
East Riding of Yorkshire d. England 21 E3... 53°55'N 0°19'W
Eastry England 9 G2 .................................51°15'N 1°18'E
East Sea N. Pacific Oc. 104 B3 ...............39°13'N 133°37'E
East Siberian Sea Russia 55 P5 .............72°59'N 148°21'E
East Sussex d. England 21 F2 .................50°53'N 0°17'E
East Timor Asia 103 H2 ............................8°57'S 125°59'E
Eastwood England 13 F2 .........................53°01'N 1°18'W
Eaton Socon England 9 E3 ......................52°13'N 0°17'W
Eau Claire U.S.A. 63 H5 ...........................44°49'N 91°30'W
Eau Claire, Lac à l' l. Canada 61 K3.......56°13'N 74°07'W
Eauripik atoll Micronesia 103 K5.............6°43'N 143°04'E
Ebbw Vale Wales 10 D3 ...........................51°47'N 3°12'W
Eberswalde Germany 46 E5 .....................52°50'N 13°49'E
Ebinur Hu l. China 98 E6 ..........................44°46'N 82°51'E
Ebro r. Spain 45 F4 ...................................40°43'N 0°51'E
Ecclefechan Scotland 15 F3 ....................55°04'N 3°16'W
Eccleshall England 8 C3 ..........................52°52'N 2°15'W
Ech Chélif Algeria 84 E5 ...........................36°09'N 1°17'E
Écija Spain 45 C2 .......................................37°33'N 5°04'W
Eck, Loch l. Scotland 14 E4 .....................56°04'N 4°59'W
Eckington England 8 C3 ...........................52°04'N 2°07'W
Ecuador S. America 72 B6 ........................1°08'S 78°05'W
Eday i. Scotland 17 G4 ..............................59°11'N 2°50'W
Ed Da'ein Sudan 94 C2 .............................11°27'N 26°08'E
Ed Damazin Sudan 85 H3 .........................11°47'N 34°20'E
Ed Damer Sudan 85 H3 .............................17°26'N 33°58'E
Ed Debba Sudan 94 D3 .............................18°00'N 30°55'E
Ed Dueim Sudan 94 D2 .............................13°57'N 32°17'E
Eden r. England 12 D3 ..............................54°57'N 3°01'W
Edessa Greece 50 E5 ................................40°48'N 22°04'E
Edgeøya i. Arctic Oc. 54 D5......................77°32'N 22°45'E
Edinburgh Scotland 15 F3 ........................55°57'N 3°11'W
Edirne Turkey 50 G5 ..................................41°39'N 26°34'E
Edmonton Canada 60 G3 .........................53°33'N 113°33'W
Edmundston Canada 61 L2 ......................47°23'N 68°20'W
Edremit Turkey 50 G4 ................................39°35'N 27°00'E
Edson Canada 60 G3 ................................53°35'N 116°25'W
Edward, Lake Dem. Rep. Congo/Uganda 83 B4
....................................................................0°17'S 29°40'E
Edwards Plateau f. U.S.A. 62 F3 .............30°28'N 100°22'W
Éfaté i. Vanuatu 109 F5 ............................17°38'S 168°30'E
Effingham U.S.A. 63 I4 ..............................39°07'N 88°33'W
Eger Hungary 46 I2 ...................................47°54'N 20°22'E
Egilsay i. Scotland 17 G4 ..........................59°09'N 2°55'W
Egilsstaðir Iceland 43 Z2 ..........................65°16'N 14°25'W
Eğirdir Turkey 51 I3 ...................................37°51'N 30°51'E
Eğirdir Gölü l. Turkey 51 I3 .......................37°59'N 30°53'E
Eglinton Northern Ireland 14 B3 .............55°02'N 7°11'W
Egremont England 12 D3 ..........................54°29'N 3°32'W
Egvekinot Russia 55 T4 ............................66°20'N 179°17'W
Egypt Africa 85 G4 ....................................29°53'N 31°16'E
Eifel hills Germany 46 B4 ..........................50°10'N 6°39'E
Eigg i. Scotland 16 C1 ...............................56°54'N 6°10'W
Eighty Mile Beach f. Australia 108 B5 ....19°54'S 120°10'E
Eilat Israel 94 D4 .......................................29°33'N 34°56'E
Eilean Siar d. Scotland 20 B6 ..................58°15'N 6°33'W
Eindhoven Neth. 42 E4 .............................51°26'N 5°29'E
Eisenhüttenstadt Germany 46 F5 ...........52°09'N 14°38'E
Eishort, Loch inlet Scotland 16 D2 .........57°09'N 5°59'W
Ekibastuz Kazakhstan 98 D8 ...................51°46'N 75°27'E
Ekostrovskaya Imandra, Ozero l. Russia 43 H4
....................................................................67°29'N 32°23'E
Eksjö Sweden 43 C2 .................................57°40'N 14°59'E
Elazığ Turkey 51 M4 .................................38°39'N 39°15'E
Elba, Isola d' i. Italy 48 F5 ........................42°50'N 10°16'E
El'ban Russia 99 P8 ...................................50°03'N 136°26'E
Elbasan Albania 50 D5 .............................41°07'N 20°05'E
El Bayadh Algeria 48 D3 ...........................33°41'N 0°56'E
Elbe r. Germany 46 C5 ..............................53°53'N 9°05'E
Elbert, Mount U.S.A. 62 E4 ......................39°05'N 106°25'W
Elbistan Turkey 51 L4 ................................38°12'N 37°11'E
Elbląg Poland 46 H6 .................................54°10'N 19°24'E
El'brus mt. Russia 53 E2 ...........................43°22'N 42°25'E
Elburz Mountains Iran 95 G7 ...................36°52'N 49°43'E
El Callao Venezuela 67 L2 ........................7°17'N 61°47'W
Elche/Elx Spain 45 E3 ...............................38°16'N 0°41'W
Elda Spain 45 E3 ........................................38°29'N 0°47'W
El Dorado U.S.A. 63 H3 .............................33°13'N 92°36'W
Eldoret Kenya 85 H2 .................................0°31'N 35°15'E
El Eulma Algeria 48 E4 ..............................36°07'N 5°48'E
Eleuthera i. Bahamas 67 I6 .....................25°21'N 76°22'W
El Fasher Sudan 85 G3 ..............................13°36'N 25°20'E
El Geneina Sudan 85 G3 ...........................13°26'N 22°26'E
Elgin Scotland 17 F2 .................................57°39'N 3°19'W
El'ginsky Russia 55 P4 ..............................64°32'N 141°40'E
El Goléa Algeria 84 E5 ..............................30°34'N 2°58'E
Elgon, Mount Kenya/Uganda 85 H2........1°08'N 34°34'E
El Hierro i. Canary Islands 45 X1 ............27°40'N 17°56'W
Elhovo Bulgaria 50 G6 ..............................42°11'N 26°34'E
Elista Russia 53 E2 ....................................46°19'N 44°16'E
El Jadida Morocco 84 D5 ..........................33°12'N 8°27'W
Ełk Poland 47 J5 ........................................53°50'N 22°22'E
Elko U.S.A. 62 C5 .......................................40°51'N 115°46'W
Ellef Ringnes Island Canada 61 H5 ........78°38'N 101°56'W
Ellensburg U.S.A. 62 B6 ...........................46°59'N 120°32'W
Ellesmere England 8 C3 ...........................52°54'N 2°54'W
Ellesmere Island Canada 61 J5 ...............77°01'N 83°03'W
Ellesmere Port England 12 E2 ................53°17'N 2°54'W
Ellice r. Canada 60 H4 ...............................67°56'N 103°59'W
Ellon Scotland 17 G2 ................................57°22'N 2°04'W
Elmalı Turkey 51 H3 ..................................36°44'N 29°55'E
El Meghaïer Algeria 48 E3 ........................33°56'N 5°56'E
El Muglad Sudan 85 G3 .............................11°01'N 27°44'E
El Obeid Sudan 94 D2 ...............................13°10'N 30°11'E
El Oued Algeria 48 E3 ...............................33°21'N 6°54'E
El Paso U.S.A. 62 E3 .................................31°46'N 106°24'W
El Puerto de Santa María Spain 45 B2 ...36°36'N 6°13'W

El Salvador Central America 66 G3 .............13°22'N 88°59'W
El Tigre Venezuela 67 L2 ..............................8°52'N 64°16'W
Eluru India 96 F4 .............................................16°44'N 81°09'E
Elvas Portugal 45 B3 ......................................38°53'N 7°10'W
Elverum Norway 43 B3 ..................................60°53'N 11°33'E
Ely England 9 F3 ..............................................52°24'N 0°15'E
Ely, Isle of f. England 9 F3 ...........................52°27'N 0°14'E
Emba Kazakhstan 53 F2 ...............................48°47'N 58°07'E
Emden Germany 46 B5 ..................................53°22'N 7°13'E
Emerson Canada 62 G6 ................................49°02'N 97°11'W
Emi Koussi mt. Chad 85 F3 .........................19°46'N 18°34'E
Emirdağ Turkey 51 I4 ....................................39°01'N 31°09'E
Emmeloord Neth. 42 E5 ...............................52°43'N 5°45'E
Emmen Neth. 42 F5 ........................................52°47'N 6°54'E
Emory Peak U.S.A. 62 F2 .............................29°15'N 103°18'W
Ems r. Germany 46 B5 ...................................53°18'N 7°22'E
Endeh Indonesia 103 G2 ...............................8°47'S 121°38'E
Endicott Mountains U.S.A. 60 C4 .............67°50'N 152°33'W
Enfield England 9 E2 .......................................51°39'N 0°05'W
Engel's Russia 53 E3 ......................................51°29'N 46°06'E
England d. U.K. 21 E3 ......................................52°48'N 1°24'W
English Channel France/U.K. 9 E1 ..............49°59'N 1°24'W
Enköping Sweden 43 D2 ..............................59°38'N 17°06'E
En Nahud Sudan 85 G3 .................................12°42'N 28°25'E
Ennedi, Massif mts Chad 94 B3 .................16°59'N 22°58'E
Ennerdale Water l. England 12 D3 .............54°30'N 3°22'W
Ennis Ireland 18 C2 ........................................52°51'N 8°59'W
Enniscorthy Ireland 18 E2 ............................52°30'N 6°34'W
Enniskerry Ireland 10 A5 ..............................53°11'N 6°10'W
Enniskillen Northern Ireland 14 B2 ...........54°20'N 7°37'W
Ennistymon Ireland 18 B2 ...........................52°56'N 9°17'W
Enns r. Austria 46 F3 ......................................48°14'N 14°31'E
Enschede Neth. 42 F5 ....................................52°13'N 6°54'E
Ensenada Mexico 66 A7 ...............................31°52'N 116°37'W
Enshi China 99 J4 ............................................30°13'N 109°28'E
Enugu Nigeria 84 E2 .......................................6°24'N 7°31'E
Envira r. Brazil 72 B6 ......................................7°31'S 70°14'W
Épinal France 44 G6 .......................................48°11'N 6°27'E
Epping England 9 F2 .......................................51°42'N 0°07'E
Eppynt, Mynydd hills Wales 10 D4 ............52°05'N 3°28'W
Epsom England 9 E2 .......................................51°20'N 0°16'W
Epworth England 13 G2 .................................53°32'N 0°49'W
Eqlīd Iran 95 H6 ...............................................30°53'N 52°42'E
Equatorial Guinea Africa 84 E2 ...................3°00'N 8°36'E
Équeurdreville-Hainneville France 11 Z9 ...49°39'N 1°39'W
Erbeskopf hill Germany 42 G2 ....................49°43'N 7°04'E
Erciyes Dağı mt. Turkey 51 K4 ...................38°32'N 35°27'E
Erdemli Turkey 51 K3 .....................................36°36'N 34°19'E
Erdi f. Chad 94 B3 ...........................................19°02'N 21°36'E
Ereğli Konya Turkey 51 K3 ...........................37°30'N 34°03'E
Ereğli Zonguldak Turkey 51 I5 ....................41°17'N 31°25'E
Erfurt Germany 46 D4 ....................................50°59'N 11°02'E
Ergani Turkey 51 M4 ......................................38°15'N 39°46'E
Ergene r. Turkey 51 G5 ..................................40°59'N 26°22'E
Ericht r. Scotland 15 F4 .................................56°34'N 3°15'W
Ericht, Loch l. Scotland 17 E1 .....................56°48'N 4°25'W
Erie U.S.A. 63 J5 ...............................................42°07'N 80°06'W
Erie, Lake Canada/U.S.A. 61 J2 ..................42°14'N 80°53'W
Eriskay i. Scotland 16 B2 ..............................57°04'N 7°16'W
Eritrea Africa 85 H3 ........................................15°57'N 37°33'E
Erlangen Germany 46 D3 ..............................49°35'N 11°01'E
Ermenek Turkey 51 J3 ....................................36°37'N 32°54'E
Ermoupoli Greece 50 F3 ...............................37°26'N 24°56'E
Erode India 96 E3 ............................................11°21'N 77°43'E
Errachidia Morocco 84 D5 ...........................31°54'N 4°29'W
Er Rahad Sudan 85 H3 ...................................12°44'N 30°38'E
Errigal hill Ireland 18 C5 ................................55°02'N 8°07'W
Erris Head Ireland 18 A4 ...............................54°19'N 10°01'W
Errochty, Loch l. Scotland 17 E1 ................56°45'N 4°11'W
Erromango i. Vanuatu 109 F5......................18°49'S 168°58'E
Erzgebirge mts Czechia/Germany 46 E4 ...50°33'N 13°07'E
Erzincan Turkey 51 M4 .................................39°45'N 39°29'E
Erzurum Turkey 94 F7 ....................................39°53'N 41°17'E
Esbjerg Denmark 43 B1 ................................55°28'N 8°27'E
Escanaba U.S.A. 63 I6 ....................................45°45'N 87°03'W
Escárcega Mexico 66 F4 ...............................18°39'N 90°43'W
Esch-sur-Alzette Lux. 42 E2 ........................49°30'N 5°59'E
Eschweiler Germany 42 F3 ...........................50°49'N 6°18'E
Eşfahān Iran 95 H6 .........................................32°41'N 51°39'E
Esha Ness hd Scotland 17 H5 .....................60°30'N 1°37'W
Esk r. Scotland 15 F3 .......................................55°56'N 3°04'W
Eske, Lough l. Ireland 14 A2 ........................54°42'N 8°04'W
Eski Gediz Turkey 51 H4 ...............................39°03'N 29°25'E
Eskilstuna Sweden 43 D2 .............................59°22'N 16°32'E
Eskişehir Turkey 51 I4 ....................................39°47'N 30°31'E
Esla r. Spain 45 B4 ..........................................41°30'N 6°01'W
Eslāmābād-e Gharb Iran 95 G6 ................34°06'N 46°31'E
Esperance Australia 108 B3 .........................33°49'S 121°52'E
Espigüete mt. Spain 45 C5 ...........................42°57'N 4°47'W
Espírito Santo i. Vanuatu 109 F5...............15°15'S 166°35'E
Espoo Finland 43 F3 .......................................60°12'N 24°40'E
Esquel Argentina 73 B2 ................................42°55'S 71°20'W
Essen Germany 46 B4 ...................................51°28'N 7°03'E
Essequibo r. Guyana 72 D7 .........................6°23'N 58°36'W
Essex d. England 21 F2 ...................................51°51'N 0°42'E
Estados, Isla de los i. Argentina 73 C1 ....54°44'S 64°16'W
Estats, Pic d' mt. France/Spain 45 F5........42°40'N 1°24'E
Estevan Canada 60 H2 ...................................49°08'N 102°59'W
Estonia Europe 43 F2 .....................................58°44'N 25°26'E
Estrela, Serra da mts Portugal 45 B4 .......40°11'N 7°57'W
Estrella mt. Spain 45 D3 ...............................38°24'N 3°36'W
Eswatini Africa 83 C2 ....................................26°29'S 31°30'E
Étaples France 44 D7 .....................................50°31'N 1°39'E
Ethiopia Africa 85 H2 .....................................8°00'N 39°41'E
Ethiopian Highlands f. Ethiopia 85 H2 .....8°49'N 36°39'E
Etimesğut Turkey 51 J4 .................................39°56'N 32°39'E
Etive, Loch inlet Scotland 14 D4 ...............56°27'N 5°12'W
Etna, Mount vol. Italy 48 G4 ......................37°45'N 15°00'E
Etosha Pan f. Namibia 83 A3 ......................18°52'S 16°19'E
Ettelbruck Lux. 42 F2 .....................................49°51'N 6°06'E
Ettrick Forest Scotland 15 F3 .....................55°31'N 3°05'W
Ettrick Water r. Scotland 15 G3 ..................55°34'N 2°49'W
Etwall England 8 D3 ........................................52°53'N 1°36'W
Eugene U.S.A. 62 B5 .......................................44°04'N 123°05'W
Eugenia, Punta pt Mexico 66 A6 ...............27°51'N 115°04'W
Euphrates r. Asia 94 F6 .................................30°59'N 47°24'E
Eureka U.S.A. 62 B5 ........................................40°48'N 124°09'W
Europa, Picos de mts Spain 45 C5 ............43°07'N 5°01'W
Europe 34
Evans, Lac l. Canada 61 K3 ..........................50°49'N 77°07'W
Evanston U.S.A. 62 D5 ...................................41°17'N 110°56'W
Evansville U.S.A. 63 I4 ...................................37°59'N 87°32'W
Evaton S. Africa 83 B2 ...................................26°32'S 27°49'E
Everest, Mount China/Nepal 98 F3 ...........27°59'N 86°55'E
Everglades f. U.S.A. 63 J2 .............................26°15'N 81°02'W

Evesham England 8 D3 ..................................52°06'N 1°57'W
Evesham, Vale of f. England 8 D3 ..............52°05'N 1°57'W
Évora Portugal 45 B3 .....................................38°34'N 7°54'E
Évreux France 44 D6 .......................................49°01'N 1°09'E
Evvoia i. Greece 50 F4 ...................................38°19'N 24°14'E
Ewe, Loch b. Scotland 16 D2 .....................57°50'N 5°40'W
Exe r. England 11 D2 .......................................50°41'N 3°29'W
Exeter England 11 D2 .....................................50°43'N 3°32'W
Exminster England 11 D2 ..............................50°41'N 3°30'W
Exmoor hills England 11 D3 .........................51°10'N 3°46'W
Exmouth England 11 D2 ................................50°37'N 3°25'W
Exuma Cays is Bahamas 67 I5 ....................24°35'N 76°34'W
Exuma Sound str. Bahamas 67 I5 ..............24°17'N 75°59'W
Eyasi, Lake Tanzania 83 C4 .........................3°38'S 35°05'E
Eye P'boro. England 9 E3 ..............................52°37'N 0°11'W
Eye Suff. England 9 G3 ..................................52°19'N 1°09'E
Eyemouth Scotland 15 G3 ............................55°52'N 2°05'W
Eye Peninsula Scotland 16 C3 ....................58°14'N 6°14'W
Ezhva Russia 52 F4 .........................................61°48'N 50°45'E
Ezine Turkey 50 G4 .........................................39°46'N 26°19'E

# F

Faenza Italy 46 D1 ..........................................44°17'N 11°53'E
Făgăraş Romania 50 F7 .................................45°51'N 24°59'E
Fagatogo American Samoa 109 H5 ...........14°17'S 170°41'W
Fagersta Sweden 43 C2 ................................59°59'N 15°49'E
Fairbanks U.S.A. 60 D4 ..................................64°50'N 147°47'W
Fair Head Northern Ireland 14 C3 .............55°14'N 6°08'W
Fair Isle i. Scotland 17 H4 ............................59°34'N 1°38'W
Fairmont U.S.A. 63 H5 ...................................43°39'N 94°28'W
Fairweather, Mount Canada/U.S.A. 60 E3
....................................................................58°54'N 137°29'W
Fais i. Micronesia 103 K5................................9°45'N 140°33'E
Faisalabad Pakistan 96 D7 ...........................31°24'N 73°09'E
Fakaofo atoll Tokelau 109 H6 ......................9°23'S 171°08'W
Fakenham England 9 F3 ................................52°50'N 0°51'E
Fakfak Indonesia 103 I3 .................................2°55'S 132°17'E
Fal r. England 11 C2 ........................................50°14'N 4°58'W
Falcon Lake Mexico/U.S.A. 66 E6 .............26°53'N 99°20'W
Falkenberg Sweden 43 C2 ...........................56°55'N 12°31'E
Falkirk Scotland 15 F4 ....................................56°00'N 3°47'W
Falkirk d. Scotland 20 D4 ..............................55°59'N 3°48'W
Falkland Islands S. Atlantic Oc. 73 D1 ......50°55'S 59°36'W
Falköping Sweden 43 C2 ..............................58°10'N 13°33'E
Falmouth England 11 B2 ...............................50°09'N 5°04'W
Falmouth Bay England 11 B2 ......................50°06'N 5°04'W
Falso, Cabo c. Mexico 66 C5 .......................22°53'N 109°59'W
Falster i. Denmark 43 B1 ...............................54°49'N 11°58'E
Falun Sweden 43 C3 .......................................60°36'N 15°38'E
Famagusta Cyprus 51 J2 ...............................35°06'N 33°57'E
Fanad Head Ireland 14 B3 ...........................55°17'N 7°38'W
Fane r. Ireland 18 E3 .......................................53°57'N 6°22'W
Fannich, Loch l. Scotland 16 D2 ................57°39'N 5°03'W
Farafra Oasis Egypt 94 C5 ............................26°43'N 28°09'E
Farāh Afgh. 95 J6 .............................................32°23'N 62°07'E
Farallon de Pajaros vol. N. Mariana Is 103 K8
....................................................................20°32'N 144°55'E
Farasān, Jazā'ir is Saudi Arabia 94 F3......16°48'N 41°41'E
Fareham England 8 D1 ...................................50°51'N 1°11'W
Farewell, Cape New Zealand 109 G2........40°29'S 172°40'E
Fargo U.S.A. 62 G6 ..........................................46°52'N 96°49'W
Faridabad India 96 E6 ....................................28°25'N 77°19'E
Farnborough England 8 E2 ...........................51°17'N 0°45'W
Farndon England 12 E2 ..................................53°05'N 2°53'W
Farne Islands England 13 F4 .......................55°38'N 1°37'W
Farnham England 8 E2 ...................................51°13'N 0°48'W
Faro Portugal 45 B2 .......................................37°01'N 7°56'W
Fårö i. Sweden 43 D2 .....................................57°58'N 19°22'E
Faroe Islands Europe 34 D5 .........................62°00'N 7°00'W
Farrāshband Iran 95 H5 ................................28°52'N 52°05'E
Fasā Iran 95 H5 ................................................28°56'N 53°38'E
Fastiv Ukraine 47 M4 .....................................50°04'N 29°55'E
Fatehgarh India 96 E6 ....................................27°22'N 79°36'E
Faulquemont France 42 F2 ...........................49°03'N 6°36'E
Faversham England 9 F2 ...............................51°19'N 0°53'E
Faxaflói b. Iceland 43 X2 ...............................64°27'N 22°58'W
Fayetteville U.S.A. 63 K4 ...............................35°02'N 78°53'W
Fdérik Mauritania 84 C4 ................................22°42'N 12°44'W
Feale r. Ireland 18 B2 .....................................52°28'N 9°38'W
Fear, Cape U.S.A. 63 K3 .................................33°51'N 77°58'W
Fehmarn i. Germany 46 D6 ...........................54°29'N 11°07'E
Feira de Santana Brazil 72 F5 .....................12°12'S 38°57'W
Feldkirch Austria 46 C2 .................................47°15'N 9°36'E
Felixstowe England 9 G2 ...............................51°58'N 1°21'E
Femunden l. Norway 43 B3 ..........................62°05'N 11°48'E
Feniton England 11 D2 ...................................50°47'N 3°16'W
Feodosiya Ukraine 49 K6 ..............................45°02'N 35°22'E
Ferdows Iran 95 I6 ...........................................33°59'N 58°10'E
Fergus Falls town U.S.A. 62 G6 ..................46°17'N 96°07'W
Ferkessédougou Côte d'Ivoire 84 D2 .......9°35'N 5°13'W
Fermanagh f. Northern Ireland 18 D4 .......54°16'N 7°35'W
Fermanagh and Omagh d. Northern Ireland 21 B4
....................................................................54°27'N 7°45'W
Fermoy Ireland 18 C2 .....................................52°08'N 8°17'W
Ferndown England 8 D1 ................................50°48'N 1°54'W
Ferrara Italy 46 D1 ..........................................44°50'N 11°38'E
Ferrol Spain 45 A5 ...........................................43°29'N 8°13'W
Ferryhill England 13 F3 ..................................54°41'N 1°33'W
Fès Morocco 84 D5 ..........................................34°04'N 4°57'W
Fethaland, Point of Scotland 17 H5...........60°39'N 1°18'W
Fethard Ireland 18 D2 ....................................52°28'N 7°42'W
Fethiye Turkey 51 H3 ......................................36°37'N 29°06'E
Fetlar i. Scotland 17 I5 ...................................60°38'N 0°49'W
Feuilles, Rivière aux r. Canada 61 K3 .......58°46'N 70°13'W
Feyzābād Afgh. 95 L7 ....................................37°05'N 70°41'E
Fez Morocco 84 D5 .........................................34°04'N 4°57'W
Fezzan f. Libya 84 F4 .....................................25°00'N 14°00'E
Ffestiniog Wales 10 D4 ..................................52°58'N 3°56'W
Fianarantsoa Madagascar 83 D2 ...............21°27'S 47°07'E
Fife d. Scotland 20 D5 ....................................56°16'N 2°58'W
Fife Ness pt Scotland 15 G4 .........................56°16'N 2°35'W
Figeac France 44 E4 .......................................44°37'N 2°01'E
Figueira da Foz Portugal 45 A4 ..................40°10'N 8°51'W
Figueres Spain 45 G5 .....................................42°16'N 2°58'E
Figuig Morocco 48 C3 ....................................32°09'N 1°17'W
Fiji S. Pacific Oc. 109 G5 ...............................17°51'S 177°08'E
Filadelfia Paraguay 73 C4 ..............................22°22'S 60°03'W
Filey England 13 G3 ........................................54°13'N 0°18'W
Filton England 8 C2 .........................................51°30'N 2°35'W
Findhorn r. Scotland 17 F2 ...........................57°38'N 3°38'W
Fingal d. Ireland 18 E3 ...................................53°27'N 6°12'W
Finisterre, Cape Spain 45 A5 .......................42°53'N 9°15'W
Finland Europe 43 F3 .....................................63°43'N 26°54'E
Finland, Gulf of Europe 43 E2 .....................59°31'N 22°42'E

Finlay r. Canada 60 F3 ............... 56°41'N 124°49'W
Finn r. Ireland 18 D4 ............... 54°50'N 7°28'W
Finspång Sweden 43 C2 ............... 58°42'N 15°46'E
Finstown Scotland 17 F4 ............... 59°00'N 3°07'W
Fintona Northern Ireland 14 B2 ............... 54°29'N 7°19'W
Fionn Loch l. Scotland 16 D2 ............... 57°46'N 5°28'W
Fionnphort Scotland 14 C4 ............... 56°19'N 6°22'W
Fisher Strait Canada 61 J4 ............... 63°14'N 83°06'W
Fishguard Wales 10 C3 ............... 51°59'N 4°58'W
Fishguard Bay Wales 10 C4 ............... 52°01'N 4°58'W
Five Barrows Hill England 11 D3 ............... 51°07'N 3°49'W
Flagstaff U.S.A. 62 D4 ............... 35°12'N 111°39'W
Flamborough England 13 G3 ............... 54°07'N 0°07'W
Flamborough Head England 13 G3 ............... 54°07'N 0°03'W
Flannan Isles Scotland 16 B3 ............... 58°18'N 7°39'W
Flåsjön i. Sweden 43 C4 ............... 64°06'N 15°53'E
Flathead Lake U.S.A. 62 D6 ............... 47°52'N 114°03'W
Flat Holm i. Wales 11 D3 ............... 51°23'N 3°07'W
Fleet England 8 E2 ............... 51°17'N 0°50'W
Fleetwood England 12 D2 ............... 53°55'N 3°02'W
Flensburg Germany 46 C6 ............... 54°47'N 9°25'E
Flevoland d. Neth. 42 E5 ............... 52°17'N 5°00'E
Flinders r. Australia 108 D5 ............... 17°37'S 140°35'E
Flinders Island Australia 108 D3 ............... 39°56'S 148°04'E
Flinders Ranges mts Australia 108 C3 ............... 32°24'S 137°57'E
Flin Flon Canada 60 H3 ............... 54°46'N 101°51'W
Flint U.S.A. 63 J5 ............... 43°01'N 83°42'W
Flint Wales 10 D5 ............... 53°15'N 3°08'W
Flintshire d. Wales 21 D3 ............... 53°11'N 3°07'W
Florence Italy 48 F5 ............... 43°46'N 11°16'E
Florence U.S.A. 63 K3 ............... 34°11'N 79°45'W
Florencia Colombia 72 B7 ............... 1°36'N 75°36'W
Flores i. Indonesia 103 G2 ............... 8°29'S 121°14'E
Flores Sea Indonesia 102 F2 ............... 7°41'S 119°59'E
Florianópolis Brazil 73 E4 ............... 27°32'S 48°32'W
Florida d. U.S.A. 63 J3 ............... 30°12'N 83°39'W
Florida, Straits of Bahamas/U.S.A. 67 H5 ............... 23°56'N 81°35'W
Florida Keys is U.S.A. 63 J1 ............... 24°41'N 81°38'W
Florina Greece 50 D5 ............... 40°46'N 21°24'E
Florø Norway 43 A3 ............... 61°36'N 5°01'E
Flotta i. Scotland 17 F3 ............... 58°50'N 3°05'W
Fly r. P.N.G. 103 K2 ............... 8°18'S 142°36'E
Foča Bos. and Herz. 50 C6 ............... 43°29'N 18°45'E
Fochabers Scotland 17 F2 ............... 57°37'N 3°06'W
Focşani Romania 50 G7 ............... 45°42'N 27°11'E
Foggia Italy 49 G5 ............... 41°28'N 15°33'E
Fogo i. Cape Verde 84 B3 ............... 14°59'N 24°18'W
Foinaven hill Scotland 16 E3 ............... 58°25'N 4°53'W
Foix France 44 D3 ............... 42°58'N 1°36'E
Folkestone England 9 G2 ............... 51°05'N 1°10'E
Fonseca, Golfo de b. Central America 66 G3 ............... 13°03'N 88°12'W
Fontainebleau France 44 E6 ............... 48°25'N 2°43'E
Fontur pt Iceland 43 Z2 ............... 66°23'N 14°32'W
Førde Norway 43 A3 ............... 61°27'N 5°52'E
Fordingbridge England 8 D1 ............... 50°56'N 1°47'W
Foreland hd England 8 D1 ............... 50°41'N 1°04'W
Foreland Point England 11 D3 ............... 51°15'N 3°47'W
Forfar Scotland 17 G1 ............... 56°39'N 2°53'W
Forlì Italy 46 E1 ............... 44°14'N 12°02'E
Formby England 12 D2 ............... 53°34'N 3°04'W
Formentera i. Spain 45 F3 ............... 38°40'N 1°24'E
Formosa Argentina 73 D4 ............... 26°07'S 58°12'W
Forres Scotland 17 F2 ............... 57°37'N 3°37'W
Forssa Finland 43 E3 ............... 60°49'N 23°39'E
Fort Albany Canada 61 J3 ............... 52°13'N 81°41'W
Fortaleza Brazil 72 F6 ............... 3°43'S 38°32'W
Fort Augustus Scotland 16 E2 ............... 57°09'N 4°41'W
Fort Chipewyan Canada 60 G3 ............... 58°42'N 111°07'W
Fort Collins U.S.A. 62 E5 ............... 40°35'N 105°05'W
Fort-de-France Martinique 67 L3 ............... 14°37'N 61°05'W
Fortescue r. Australia 108 A4 ............... 21°02'S 116°06'E
Fort Frances Canada 61 I2 ............... 48°37'N 93°24'W
Fort Good Hope Canada 60 F4 ............... 66°16'N 128°39'W
Forth r. Scotland 14 F4 ............... 56°07'N 3°52'W
Forth, Firth of est. Scotland 15 F4 ............... 56°01'N 3°13'W
Fort Lauderdale U.S.A. 63 J2 ............... 26°04'N 80°11'W
Fort Liard Canada 60 F4 ............... 60°14'N 123°29'W
Fort McMurray Canada 60 G3 ............... 56°43'N 111°21'W
Fort McPherson Canada 60 E4 ............... 67°26'N 134°44'W
Fort Nelson Canada 60 F3 ............... 58°45'N 122°39'W
Fort Peck Reservoir U.S.A. 62 E6 ............... 47°47'N 106°55'W
Fort Pierce U.S.A. 63 J2 ............... 27°18'N 80°24'W
Fortrose Scotland 17 E2 ............... 57°35'N 4°08'W
Fort St John Canada 60 F3 ............... 56°15'N 120°49'W
Fort Severn Canada 61 J3 ............... 56°00'N 87°39'W
Fort-Shevchenko Kazakhstan 53 F2 ............... 44°29'N 50°17'E
Fort Simpson Canada 60 F4 ............... 61°52'N 121°22'W
Fort Smith Canada 60 G4 ............... 60°00'N 112°13'W
Fort Smith U.S.A. 63 H4 ............... 35°26'N 94°24'W
Fortuneswell England 8 C1 ............... 50°34'N 2°27'W
Fort Wayne U.S.A. 63 I5 ............... 41°04'N 85°08'W
Fort William Scotland 16 D1 ............... 56°49'N 5°06'W
Fort Worth U.S.A. 62 G3 ............... 32°46'N 97°19'W
Fort Yukon U.S.A. 60 D4 ............... 66°35'N 145°13'W
Foshan China 99 K2 ............... 23°03'N 113°06'E
Fossano Italy 46 B1 ............... 44°33'N 7°43'E
Fougères France 44 C6 ............... 48°21'N 1°12'W
Foula i. Scotland 17 G5 ............... 60°10'N 2°10'W
Foulness Point England 9 F2 ............... 51°37'N 0°57'E
Fouta Djallon f. Guinea 84 C3 ............... 11°26'N 12°34'W
Fowey r. England 11 C2 ............... 50°26'N 4°41'W
Foxe Basin g. Canada 61 K4 ............... 66°53'N 78°58'W
Foxe Channel Canada 61 J4 ............... 64°56'N 81°03'W
Foxe Peninsula Canada 61 K4 ............... 64°48'N 77°03'W
Foxford Ireland 18 B3 ............... 53°58'N 9°07'W
Fox Islands U.S.A. 60 B3 ............... 52°45'N 168°53'W
Foyle r. Ireland/U.K. 18 D4 ............... 54°53'N 7°26'W
Foyle, Lough inlet Ireland/U.K. 18 D5 ............... 55°07'N 7°07'W
Foz do Iguaçu Brazil 73 D4 ............... 25°30'S 54°32'W
Framlingham England 9 G3 ............... 52°13'N 1°21'E
France Europe 44 E5 ............... 46°57'N 2°11'E
Franceville Gabon 84 F1 ............... 1°37'S 13°37'E
Francistown Botswana 83 B2 ............... 21°10'S 27°29'E
Frankfort U.S.A. 63 J4 ............... 38°12'N 84°53'W
Frankfurt am Main Germany 46 C4 ............... 50°07'N 8°41'E
Frankfurt (Oder) Germany 46 G5 ............... 52°21'N 14°33'E
Franklin D. Roosevelt Lake resr U.S.A. 62 C6 ............... 48°16'N 118°09'W
Frantsa-Iosifa, Zemlya is Russia 54 G5 ............... 79°40'N 58°29'E
Fraser r. Canada 60 F2 ............... 49°19'N 121°38'W
Fraserburgh Scotland 17 G2 ............... 57°42'N 2°01'W
Fraser Island Australia 108 E4 ............... 25°12'S 153°11'E
Freckleton England 12 E2 ............... 53°45'N 2°52'W
Fredericia Denmark 43 B1 ............... 55°34'N 9°45'E
Fredericton Canada 61 L2 ............... 45°57'N 66°39'W
Frederikshavn Denmark 43 B2 ............... 57°27'N 10°32'E

Fredrikstad Norway 43 B2 ............... 59°13'N 10°56'E
Freeport Bahamas 67 I6 ............... 26°30'N 78°45'W
Freetown Sierra Leone 84 C2 ............... 8°28'N 13°12'W
Freiburg im Breisgau Germany 46 B3 ............... 48°00'N 7°50'E
Fréjus France 44 G3 ............... 43°26'N 6°45'E
Fremantle Australia 108 A3 ............... 32°05'S 115°42'E
French Guiana S. America 72 D7 ............... 3°56'N 53°03'W
French Polynesia is S. Pacific Oc. 114 B2 ............... 18°43'S 147°32'W
Freshwater England 8 D1 ............... 50°41'N 1°31'W
Fresno U.S.A. 62 C4 ............... 36°46'N 119°46'W
Frévent France 9 H1 ............... 50°16'N 2°17'E
Freyming-Merlebach France 42 F2 ............... 49°09'N 6°48'E
Fria Guinea 84 C3 ............... 10°24'N 13°35'W
Friedrichshafen Germany 46 C2 ............... 47°39'N 9°31'E
Friesland d. Neth. 42 E6 ............... 53°08'N 5°48'E
Frinton-on-Sea England 9 G2 ............... 51°50'N 1°15'E
Frisa, Loch l. Scotland 14 C4 ............... 56°34'N 6°06'W
Frisian Islands Europe 34 E4 ............... 54°00'N 7°00'E
Frizington England 12 D3 ............... 54°32'N 3°30'W
Frobisher Bay Canada 61 L4 ............... 63°18'N 67°31'W
Frodsham England 12 E2 ............... 53°18'N 2°44'W
Frohavet b. Norway 43 B3 ............... 63°52'N 9°12'E
Frome England 8 C2 ............... 51°14'N 2°19'W
Frome r. England 8 C1 ............... 50°41'N 2°05'W
Frome, Lake Australia 108 C3 ............... 30°43'S 139°48'E
Frøya i. Norway 43 B3 ............... 63°41'N 8°39'E
Fruges France 9 H1 ............... 50°31'N 2°08'E
Frýdek-Místek Czechia 46 H3 ............... 49°41'N 18°21'E
Fuenlabrada Spain 45 D4 ............... 40°17'N 3°47'W
Fuerteventura i. Canary Islands 45 Y2 ............... 28°36'N 14°04'W
Fujairah U.A.E. 95 H5 ............... 25°06'N 56°21'E
Fujian d. China 99 L3 ............... 25°52'N 117°59'E
Fuji-san vol. Japan 104 C3 ............... 35°22'N 138°43'E
Fukui Japan 104 C3 ............... 36°04'N 136°13'E
Fukuoka Japan 104 B2 ............... 33°35'N 130°24'E
Fukushima Japan 104 D3 ............... 37°45'N 140°28'E
Fulda Germany 46 C4 ............... 50°33'N 9°41'E
Fulford England 13 F2 ............... 53°56'N 1°04'W
Fulham England 9 E2 ............... 51°29'N 0°13'W
Fumay France 42 D2 ............... 49°59'N 4°42'E
Funafuti atoll Tuvalu 109 G6 ............... 8°25'S 179°13'E
Funchal Atlantic Oc. 84 C5 ............... 32°39'N 16°54'W
Fundy, Bay of b. Canada 61 L2 ............... 44°06'N 67°03'W
Fürth Germany 46 D3 ............... 49°29'N 10°57'E
Fushun China 99 M6 ............... 41°51'N 123°54'E
Fuxin China 99 M6 ............... 42°02'N 121°41'E
Fuyang China 99 L4 ............... 32°51'N 115°52'E
Fuyu China 99 M7 ............... 47°44'N 124°26'E
Fuzhou Fujian China 99 L3 ............... 26°07'N 119°21'E
Fuzhou Jiangxi China 99 L3 ............... 27°58'N 116°17'E
Fyn i. Denmark 43 B1 ............... 55°38'N 10°17'E

G

Gaalkacyo Somalia 85 I2 ............... 6°46'N 47°25'E
Gabès Tunisia 48 F3 ............... 33°53'N 10°07'E
Gabès, Golfe de g. Tunisia 48 F3 ............... 34°08'N 10°40'E
Gabon Africa 84 F1 ............... 0°56'S 11°32'E
Gaborone Botswana 83 B2 ............... 24°38'S 25°56'E
Gabrovo Bulgaria 50 F6 ............... 42°53'N 25°20'E
Gadsden U.S.A. 63 I3 ............... 34°03'N 86°04'W
Gaer Wales 10 D3 ............... 51°53'N 3°12'W
Gafsa Tunisia 48 E3 ............... 34°26'N 8°51'E
Gagarin Russia 47 P6 ............... 55°33'N 35°01'E
Gagnon Canada 61 L3 ............... 51°52'N 68°09'W
Gagra Georgia 51 N6 ............... 43°18'N 40°16'E
Gainesville U.S.A. 63 J2 ............... 29°36'N 82°20'W
Gainsborough England 13 G2 ............... 53°24'N 0°46'W
Gairdner, Lake Australia 108 C3 ............... 31°17'S 135°38'E
Gairloch Scotland 16 D2 ............... 57°44'N 5°42'W
Gair Loch b. Scotland 16 D2 ............... 57°43'N 5°44'W
Galapagos Islands Ecuador 68 B3 ............... 0°03'S 89°05'W
Galashiels Scotland 15 G3 ............... 55°37'N 2°49'W
Galaţi Romania 51 H7 ............... 45°27'N 28°03'E
Gala Water r. Scotland 15 G3 ............... 55°36'N 2°47'W
Galdhøpiggen mt. Norway 43 B3 ............... 61°38'N 8°19'E
Galich Russia 52 E3 ............... 58°22'N 42°20'E
Galilee, Sea of l. Israel 49 K3 ............... 32°49'N 35°37'E
Gallabat Sudan 94 E2 ............... 12°57'N 36°06'E
Galle Sri Lanka 96 F2 ............... 6°04'N 80°09'E
Galley Head Ireland 18 C1 ............... 51°32'N 8°57'W
Gallinas, Punta pt Colombia 67 J3 ............... 12°27'N 71°42'W
Gallipoli Italy 49 G5 ............... 40°03'N 18°00'E
Gallipoli Turkey 50 G5 ............... 40°25'N 26°39'E
Gällivare Sweden 43 E4 ............... 67°08'N 20°40'E
Gallup U.S.A. 62 E4 ............... 35°32'N 108°45'W
Galston Scotland 14 E3 ............... 55°36'N 4°23'W
Galtat Zemmour Western Sahara 84 C4 ............... 25°08'N 12°24'W
Galtee Mountains hills Ireland 18 C2 ............... 52°19'N 8°16'W
Galveston U.S.A. 63 H2 ............... 29°15'N 94°54'W
Galveston Bay U.S.A. 63 H2 ............... 29°19'N 94°46'W
Galway Ireland 18 B3 ............... 53°16'N 9°03'W
Galway d. Ireland 18 B3 ............... 53°22'N 9°06'W
Galway Bay Ireland 18 B3 ............... 53°12'N 9°16'W
Galway City d. Ireland 18 B3 ............... 53°16'N 9°03'W
Gambia r. Gambia 84 C3 ............... 13°28'N 16°35'W
Gâncâ Azerbaijan 53 E2 ............... 40°41'N 46°22'E
Gandadiwata, Bukit mt. Indonesia 102 F3 ............... 2°43'S 119°25'E
Gander Canada 61 M2 ............... 48°54'N 54°17'W
Gandhidham India 96 D5 ............... 23°06'N 70°08'E
Gandhinagar India 96 D5 ............... 23°14'N 72°44'E
Gandía Spain 45 E3 ............... 38°58'N 0°10'W
Ganges r. Bangl./India 96 H5 ............... 23°32'N 90°08'E
Ganges, Mouths of the Bangl./India 96 G5 ............... 21°17'N 88°23'E
Gangneung S. Korea 104 A3 ............... 37°46'N 128°52'E
Gannett Peak U.S.A. 62 E5 ............... 43°12'N 109°39'W
Gansu d. China 99 K3 ............... 40°01'N 97°56'E
Ganzhou China 99 K3 ............... 25°50'N 114°53'E
Gao Mali 84 D3 ............... 16°16'N 0°02'W
Gap France 44 G4 ............... 44°34'N 6°05'E
Gar China 98 E4 ............... 32°33'N 80°05'E
Gara, Lough l. Ireland 18 C3 ............... 53°57'N 8°28'W
Garabogaz Turkmenistan 53 F2 ............... 41°33'N 52°34'E
Garabogazköl b. Turkmenistan 53 F2 ............... 41°04'N 52°56'E
Garabogazköl Aýlagy b. Turkmenistan 53 F2 ............... 41°24'N 53°32'E
Garanhuns Brazil 72 F6 ............... 8°52'S 36°27'W
Garcia Sola, Embalse de resr Spain 45 C3 ............... 39°14'N 5°02'W
Gard r. France 44 F3 ............... 43°51'N 4°37'E
Garda, Lake Italy 46 D1 ............... 45°28'N 10°33'E
Garden City U.S.A. 62 F4 ............... 37°59'N 100°53'W
Gardēz Afghn. 95 K6 ............... 33°38'N 69°09'E
Garelochhead Scotland 14 E4 ............... 56°05'N 4°50'W

Garforth England 13 F2 ............... 53°48'N 1°23'W
Gargždai Lithuania 43 E1 ............... 55°43'N 21°24'E
Garissa Kenya 85 H1 ............... 0°25'S 39°40'E
Garmisch-Partenkirchen Germany 46 D2 ............... 47°30'N 11°06'E
Garonne r. France 44 C4 ............... 44°53'N 0°32'W
Garoowe Somalia 85 I2 ............... 8°23'N 48°28'E
Garoua Cameroon 84 F2 ............... 9°19'N 13°23'E
Garron Point Northern Ireland 14 D3 ............... 55°03'N 5°57'W
Garry r. Scotland 16 E2 ............... 57°04'N 4°46'W
Garry, Loch l. Scotland 17 E1 ............... 56°58'N 4°15'W
Garstang England 12 E2 ............... 53°54'N 2°46'W
Garvagh Northern Ireland 14 C2 ............... 54°59'N 6°41'W
Gary U.S.A. 63 I5 ............... 41°35'N 87°20'W
Gascony, Gulf of France 44 B3 ............... 43°43'N 2°00'W
Gascoyne r. Australia 108 A4 ............... 24°44'S 114°03'E
Gashua Nigeria 84 F3 ............... 12°51'N 11°04'E
Gaspé Canada 61 L2 ............... 48°48'N 64°32'W
Gaspé, Péninsule de pen. Canada 61 L2 ............... 48°35'N 65°31'W
Gastonia U.S.A. 63 J4 ............... 35°17'N 81°13'W
Gata, Cabo de c. Spain 45 D2 ............... 36°43'N 2°11'W
Gatehouse of Fleet Scotland 14 E2 ............... 54°53'N 4°11'W
Gateshead England 13 F3 ............... 54°57'N 1°36'W
Gatineau r. Canada 63 K6 ............... 45°27'N 75°42'W
Gävle Sweden 43 D3 ............... 60°41'N 17°08'E
Gaya India 96 G5 ............... 24°48'N 85°00'E
Gaya Niger 84 E3 ............... 11°54'N 3°27'E
Gaza Asia 49 J3 ............... 31°22'N 34°19'E
Gaza town Gaza 94 D6 ............... 31°31'N 34°26'E
Gaziantep Turkey 51 L3 ............... 37°03'N 37°21'E
Gdańsk Poland 46 H6 ............... 54°21'N 18°39'E
Gdańsk, Gulf of Poland/Russia 46 H6 ............... 54°32'N 19°12'E
Gdynia Poland 46 H6 ............... 54°31'N 18°33'E
Geal Charn hill Scotland 17 F2 ............... 57°12'N 3°30'W
Gedaref Sudan 85 H3 ............... 14°02'N 35°23'E
Gediz r. Turkey 51 G4 ............... 38°35'N 26°48'E
Geel Belgium 42 E4 ............... 51°09'N 5°00'E
Geelong Australia 108 D3 ............... 38°08'S 144°21'E
Gejiu China 99 I2 ............... 23°22'N 103°09'E
Gela Italy 48 F4 ............... 37°04'N 14°15'E
Gelderland d. Neth. 42 F5 ............... 52°04'N 6°08'E
Gelincik Dağı mt. Turkey 51 I4 ............... 38°03'N 30°42'E
Gelligaer Wales 10 D3 ............... 51°40'N 3°15'W
Gelsenkirchen Germany 46 B4 ............... 51°33'N 7°06'E
Gemlik Turkey 51 H5 ............... 40°25'N 29°09'E
General Santos Phil. 103 H5 ............... 6°08'N 125°15'E
Geneva Switz. 48 E6 ............... 46°13'N 6°09'E
Geneva, Lake France/Switz. 44 G5 ............... 46°22'N 6°16'E
Genil r. Spain 45 C2 ............... 37°42'N 5°18'W
Genk Belgium 42 E3 ............... 50°57'N 5°31'E
Genoa Italy 46 C1 ............... 44°24'N 8°56'E
Genoa, Gulf of Italy 48 D5 ............... 44°08'N 8°57'E
George r. Canada 61 L3 ............... 58°19'N 65°55'W
Georgetown Guyana 72 D7 ............... 6°49'N 58°09'W
George Town Malaysia 102 C5 ............... 5°26'N 100°17'E
Georgia Asia 53 E2 ............... 41°49'N 43°59'E
Georgia d. U.S.A. 63 J3 ............... 32°35'N 83°28'W
Georgian Bay Canada 61 J2 ............... 45°17'N 80°51'W
Georgina watercourse Australia 108 C4 ............... 24°54'S 139°35'E
Georgiyevka Kazakhstan 98 E7 ............... 49°16'N 81°34'E
Georgiyevsk Russia 53 E2 ............... 44°09'N 43°29'E
Gera Germany 46 E4 ............... 50°53'N 12°06'E
Geraldton Australia 108 A4 ............... 28°46'S 114°37'E
Gerede Turkey 51 J5 ............... 40°48'N 32°12'E
Gereshk Afghn. 95 J6 ............... 31°51'N 64°37'E
Gerlachovský štít mt. Slovakia 46 I3 ............... 49°10'N 20°07'E
Germany Europe 46 D4 ............... 51°18'N 10°22'E
Gevgelija North Macedonia 50 E5 ............... 41°09'N 22°30'E
Geyik Dağ mt. Turkey 51 J3 ............... 36°52'N 32°11'E
Geyve Turkey 51 I5 ............... 40°30'N 30°15'E
Ghadāmis Libya 84 E5 ............... 30°05'N 9°34'E
Ghaem Shahr Iran 95 H7 ............... 36°32'N 52°39'E
Ghaghara r. India 96 F6 ............... 25°42'N 84°51'E
Ghana Africa 84 D2 ............... 8°23'N 0°47'W
Ghardaïa Algeria 84 E5 ............... 32°20'N 3°49'E
Gharyān Libya 48 F3 ............... 32°11'N 13°01'E
Ghāt Libya 84 F4 ............... 25°10'N 10°13'E
Ghazaouet Algeria 48 C4 ............... 35°06'N 1°51'W
Ghaziabad India 96 E6 ............... 28°40'N 77°25'E
Ghaznī Afghn. 95 K6 ............... 33°33'N 68°27'E
Ghent Belgium 42 D3 ............... 51°03'N 3°43'E
Giant's Causeway f. Northern Ireland 14 C3 ............... 55°14'N 6°31'W
Gibraltar Gibraltar 45 C2 ............... 36°08'N 5°21'W
Gibraltar, Strait of Morocco/Spain 45 B1 ............... 35°50'N 6°05'W
Gibson Desert Australia 108 B4 ............... 24°46'S 123°25'E
Gien France 44 E5 ............... 47°41'N 2°38'E
Gießen Germany 46 C4 ............... 50°35'N 8°41'E
Gifu Japan 104 C3 ............... 35°25'N 136°46'E
Gigha i. Scotland 14 D3 ............... 55°41'N 5°46'W
Gijón/Xixón Spain 45 C5 ............... 43°32'N 5°39'W
Gila r. U.S.A. 62 D3 ............... 32°45'N 114°31'W
Gilgit Pakistan 96 D8 ............... 35°54'N 74°21'E
Gill, Lough l. Ireland 18 C4 ............... 54°15'N 8°25'W
Gillette U.S.A. 62 E5 ............... 44°18'N 105°29'W
Gillingham Dor. England 8 C2 ............... 51°02'N 2°17'W
Gillingham Medway England 9 F2 ............... 51°23'N 0°33'E
Gilwern Wales 10 D3 ............... 51°49'N 3°06'W
Gimbala, Jebel mt. Sudan 94 B2 ............... 13°00'N 24°20'E
Giresun Turkey 51 M5 ............... 40°55'N 38°23'E
Girona Spain 45 G4 ............... 41°58'N 2°49'E
Gironde est. France 44 C4 ............... 45°31'N 0°59'W
Girvan Scotland 14 E3 ............... 55°14'N 4°51'W
Gisborne New Zealand 109 H3 ............... 38°39'S 178°01'E
Gitega Burundi 85 G1 ............... 3°27'S 29°56'E
Giurgiu Romania 50 F6 ............... 43°54'N 25°57'E
Giza Egypt 85 H4 ............... 29°59'N 31°12'E
Gizhiga Russia 55 R4 ............... 62°01'N 160°28'E
Gjirokastër Albania 50 D5 ............... 40°04'N 20°09'E
Gjøvik Norway 43 B3 ............... 60°48'N 10°41'E
Gladstone Australia 108 E4 ............... 23°51'S 151°18'E
Glan r. Germany 42 G2 ............... 49°47'N 7°42'E
Glanton England 13 F4 ............... 55°25'N 1°53'W
Glasgow Scotland 14 E3 ............... 55°52'N 4°15'W
Glasgow U.S.A. 62 E6 ............... 48°10'N 106°34'W
Glass, Loch l. Scotland 17 E2 ............... 57°44'N 4°31'W
Glastonbury England 8 C2 ............... 51°09'N 2°43'W
Glazov Russia 52 F3 ............... 58°09'N 52°41'E
Glenarm Northern Ireland 14 D2 ............... 54°58'N 5°56'W
Glen Coe f. Scotland 16 D1 ............... 56°41'N 5°05'W
Glendale U.S.A. 62 D3 ............... 33°32'N 112°12'W
Glengad Head Ireland 18 D5 ............... 55°20'N 7°10'W
Glen Garry f. Scotland 16 D2 ............... 57°03'N 5°05'W
Glenluce Scotland 14 E2 ............... 54°53'N 4°49'W
Glen More f. Scotland 17 E2 ............... 57°09'N 4°44'W
Glen Moriston f. Scotland 16 E2 ............... 57°09'N 4°52'W
Glennallen U.S.A. 60 D4 ............... 62°09'N 145°32'W

Glenrothes Scotland 15 F4 ............... 56°12'N 3°°
Glen Shee f. Scotland 17 F1 ............... 56°48'N 3°°
Glinton England 9 E3 ............... 52°38'N 0°°
Gliwice Poland 46 H4 ............... 50°18'N 18°°
Głogów Poland 46 G4 ............... 51°40'N 16°°
Glomfjord Norway 43 C4 ............... 66°49'N 13°°
Glorieuses, Îles is Indian Oc. 83 D3 ............... 11°34'S 47°°
Glossop England 13 F2 ............... 53°27'N 1°°
Gloucester England 8 C2 ............... 51°52'N 2°°
Gloucestershire d. England 21 D3 ............... 51°49'N 2°°
Glusburn England 13 F2 ............... 53°54'N 1°°
Glyder Fawr hill Wales 10 C5 ............... 53°06'N 4°°
Glynneath Wales 10 D3 ............... 51°45'N 3°°
Gmünd Austria 46 F3 ............... 48°47'N 14°°
Gniezno Poland 46 G5 ............... 52°32'N 17°°
Goa d. India 96 D4 ............... 15°24'N 74°°
Goat Fell hill Scotland 14 D3 ............... 55°37'N 5°°
Gobabis Namibia 83 A2 ............... 22°27'S 18°°
Gobi des. China/Mongolia 99 J6 ............... 44°59'N 107°°
Gobowen England 8 B3 ............... 52°54'N 3°°
Goch Germany 42 F4 ............... 51°40'N 6°°
Godalming England 9 E2 ............... 51°11'N 0°°
Godavari r. India 96 F4 ............... 16°57'N 81°°
Godmanchester England 9 E3 ............... 52°19'N 0°°
Goes Neth. 42 C4 ............... 51°30'N 3°°
Goiânia Brazil 72 E5 ............... 16°41'S 49°°
Gökçeada i. Turkey 50 F5 ............... 40°12'N 25°°
Göksun Turkey 51 L4 ............... 38°02'N 36°°
Gölcük Turkey 51 H5 ............... 40°43'N 29°°
Gold Coast town Australia 108 E4 ............... 28°03'S 153°°
Golmud China 98 G5 ............... 36°21'N 94°°
Golpāyegān Iran 95 H6 ............... 33°23'N 50°°
Golspie Scotland 17 F2 ............... 57°58'N 3°°
Gómez Palacio Mexico 66 D6 ............... 25°35'N 103°°
Gonaïves Haiti 67 J4 ............... 19°27'N 72°°
Gonbad-e Kavus Iran 95 H7 ............... 37°14'N 55°°
Gonder Ethiopia 85 H3 ............... 12°39'N 37°°
Gondiya India 96 F5 ............... 21°28'N 80°°
Gongga Shan mt. China 99 I3 ............... 29°57'N 101°°
Good Hope, Cape of S. Africa 83 A1 ............... 34°22'S 18°°
Goodwick Wales 10 C4 ............... 52°00'N 4°°
Goole England 13 G2 ............... 53°42'N 0°°
Göppingen Germany 46 C3 ............... 48°43'N 9°°
Gora mt. Russia 54 H4 ............... 64°59'N 60°°
Gorakhpur India 96 F6 ............... 26°45'N 83°°
Gorebridge Scotland 15 F3 ............... 55°50'N 3°°
Gorey Ireland 18 E2 ............... 52°40'N 6°°
Gorgān Iran 95 H7 ............... 36°50'N 54°°
Gori Georgia 53 E2 ............... 41°59'N 44°°
Goris Armenia 95 G7 ............... 39°30'N 46°°
Gorizia Italy 46 E1 ............... 45°57'N 13°°
Görlitz Germany 46 F4 ............... 51°09'N 14°°
Gornji Vakuf Bos. and Herz. 50 B6 ............... 43°55'N 17°°
Gorno-Altaysk Russia 98 F8 ............... 51°59'N 85°°
Gornyak Russia 98 E8 ............... 50°59'N 81°°
Gorontalo Indonesia 103 G4 ............... 0°34'N 123°°
Gort Ireland 18 C3 ............... 53°04'N 8°°
Gorzów Wielkopolski Poland 46 F5 ............... 52°44'N 15°°
Gosberton England 9 E3 ............... 52°52'N 0°°
Gosford Australia 108 E3 ............... 33°25'S 151°°
Gosforth Cumb. England 12 D3 ............... 54°25'N 3°°
Gosforth T. and W. England 13 F4 ............... 55°00'N 1°°
Goshogawara Japan 104 D4 ............... 40°48'N 140°°
Gospić Croatia 50 A7 ............... 44°33'N 15°°
Gosport England 8 D1 ............... 50°48'N 1°°
Gostivar North Macedonia 50 D5 ............... 41°47'N 20°°
Gotha Germany 46 D4 ............... 50°57'N 10°°
Gothenburg Sweden 43 B2 ............... 57°43'N 11°°
Gotland i. Sweden 43 D2 ............... 57°36'N 18°°
Göttingen Germany 46 C4 ............... 51°32'N 9°°
Gouda Neth. 42 D5 ............... 52°00'N 4°°
Gouin, Réservoir resr Canada 61 K2 ............... 48°39'N 74°°
Goulburn Australia 108 D3 ............... 34°47'S 149°°
Gourdon France 44 D4 ............... 44°45'N 1°°
Governador Valadares Brazil 72 E5 ............... 18°49'S 41°°
Gower pen. Wales 10 C3 ............... 51°36'N 4°°
Gowna, Lough l. Ireland 18 D3 ............... 53°53'N 7°°
Göynük Turkey 51 I5 ............... 40°24'N 30°°
Grafham Water resr England 9 E3 ............... 52°18'N 0°°
Grafton Australia 108 E4 ............... 29°41'S 152°°
Grafton U.S.A. 62 G6 ............... 48°24'N 97°°
Grain England 9 F2 ............... 51°27'N 0°°
Grampian Mountains Scotland 17 E1 ............... 56°47'N 4°°
Granada Spain 45 D2 ............... 37°11'N 3°°
Gran Canaria i. Canary Islands 45 Y1 ............... 27°47'N 15°°
Gran Chaco f. Argentina/Paraguay 73 C4 ............... 27°08'S 62°°
Grand Bahama i. Bahamas 67 I6 ............... 26°34'N 78°°
Grand Canyon f. U.S.A. 62 D4 ............... 36°03'N 112°°
Grand Canyon town U.S.A. 62 D4 ............... 36°03'N 112°°
Grand Cayman i. Cayman Is 67 H4 ............... 19°23'N 81°°
Grande, Bahía b. Argentina 73 C1 ............... 50°40'S 68°°
Grande Prairie Canada 60 G3 ............... 55°11'N 118°°
Grandes, Salinas f. Argentina 73 C3 ............... 30°24'S 65°°
Grand Est d. France 42 E2 ............... 49°10'N 5°°
Grand Falls - Windsor Canada 61 M2 ............... 48°53'N 55°°
Grand Forks U.S.A. 62 G6 ............... 47°55'N 97°°
Grand Island U.S.A. 62 G5 ............... 40°56'N 98°°
Grand Junction U.S.A. 62 E4 ............... 39°04'N 108°°
Grândola Portugal 45 A3 ............... 38°11'N 8°°
Grand Rapids U.S.A. 63 I5 ............... 42°58'N 85°°
Grand Turk Turks and Caicos Is 67 J5 ............... 21°28'N 71°°
Grangemouth Scotland 15 F4 ............... 56°01'N 3°°
Grange-over-Sands England 12 E3 ............... 54°11'N 2°°
Gran Tarajal Canary Islands 45 Y2 ............... 28°12'N 14°°
Grantham England 13 G2 ............... 52°55'N 0°°
Grantown-on-Spey Scotland 17 F2 ............... 57°20'N 3°°
Grants Pass U.S.A. 62 B5 ............... 42°26'N 123°°
Grasse France 44 G3 ............... 43°39'N 6°°
Grassington England 13 F3 ............... 54°04'N 1°°
Grave, Pointe de pt France 44 C4 ............... 45°35'N 1°°
Gravelines France 9 H1 ............... 50°59'N 2°°
Gravesend England 9 F2 ............... 51°26'N 0°°
Grays England 9 F2 ............... 51°28'N 0°°
Graz Austria 46 F2 ............... 47°04'N 15°°
Great Abaco i. Bahamas 67 I6 ............... 26°08'N 77°°
Great Australian Bight g. Australia 108 B3 ............... 33°06'S 130°°
Great Baddow England 9 F2 ............... 51°43'N 0°°
Great Barrier Reef Australia 108 D5 ............... 11°25'S 144°°
Great Basin U.S.A. 62 C4 ............... 39°25'N 116°°
Great Bear Lake Canada 60 G4 ............... 66°03'N 119°°
Great Belt str. Denmark 46 D6 ............... 55°30'N 11°°
Great Bend U.S.A. 62 G4 ............... 38°23'N 98°°
Great Bernera i. Scotland 16 C3 ............... 58°14'N 6°°
Great Blasket Island Ireland 18 A2 ............... 52°06'N 10°°
Great Clifton England 12 D3 ............... 54°39'N 3°°
Great Cumbrae i. Scotland 14 E3 ............... 55°47'N 4°°

Dividing Range *mts* Australia 108 D3 .......37°30'S 144°27'E
Dunmow England 9 F2...........................51°52'N 0°22'E
ter Antilles *is* Caribbean Sea 67 H5 ....21°05'N 81°40'W
ter London *d.* England 21 E2 ...............51°30'N 0°11'W
ter Manchester *d.* England 21 D3........53°31'N 2°22'E
Exuma *i.* Bahamas 67 I5 ......................23°35'N 75°54'W
Falls *town* U.S.A. 62 D6 ....................47°30'N 111°17'W
Gonerby England 8 E3...........................52°56'N 0°40'W
cham England 13 F3.............................54°38'N 1°14'W
Harwood England 13 E2 ........................53°47'N 2°24'W
Inagua *i.* Bahamas 67 J5 ....................21°13'N 73°26'W
Karoo *f.* S. Africa 83 B1 ....................32°29'S 23°21'E
Linford England 8 E3............................52°04'N 0°46'W
Malvern England 8 C3...........................52°07'N 2°19'W
Namaqualand *f.* Namibia 83 A2.........26°29'S 16°25'E
Nicobar *i.* India 97 H2.........................7°06'N 94°08'E
Ormes Head Wales 10 D5 ....................53°21'N 3°52'W
Ouse *r.* England 9 F3...........................52°46'N 0°23'E
Plains *f.* N. America 56 E4 ................45°00'N 100°00'W
Rhos *hill* Wales 10 D4 ........................53°18'N 3°12'W
Rift Valley *f.* Africa 83 C4 ....................7°00'S 33°00'E
Salt Lake U.S.A. 62 D5 ......................40°58'N 112°26'W
Sand Sea *des.* Egypt/Libya 49 H2.......28°55'N 24°22'E
Sandy Desert Australia 108 B4.............20°35'S 123°36'E
Shelford England 9 F3...........................52°09'N 0°08'E
Slave Lake Canada 60 G4 .................61°26'N 114°35'W
Stour *r.* England 9 G2...........................51°20'N 1°14'E
Torrington England 11 C2 ....................50°57'N 4°08'W
Victoria Desert Australia 108 B4..........28°43'S 128°38'E
Whernside *hill* England 13 F3.............54°10'N 1°59'W
Yarmouth England 9 G3........................52°36'N 1°44'E
os, Sierra de *mts* Spain 45 C4...........40°08'N 5°43'W
e Europe 50 D4 ...................................39°03'N 21°56'E
ey U.S.A. 62 F5 ...................................40°25'N 109°43'W
r. U.S.A. 62 E4 ....................................38°12'N 109°53'W
Bay *town* U.S.A. 62 E5 ....................44°30'N 88°02'W
River *town* U.S.A. 62 E5 ................41°36'N 109°29'W
sboro U.S.A. 63 K4 ............................36°04'N 79°48'W
stone England 14 E2 ..........................54°43'N 1°44'W
stone Pond Scotland 16 D2 ...............57°56'N 5°40'W
ville Liberia 84 D2................................5°01'N 9°02'W
ville Miss. U.S.A. 63 H3 ....................33°22'N 91°01'W
ville U.S.A. 63 J3 ...............................34°50'N 82°27'W
wich England 9 E2...............................51°29'N 0°00'E
swald Germany 46 E6.........................54°05'N 13°24'E
ngen Neth. 42 F6 ................................53°13'N 6°34'E
ngen *d.* Neth. 42 F6 .........................53°16'N 6°40'E
e Eylandt *i.* Australia 108 C5.............13°58'S 137°09'E
er Speikkogel *mt.* Austria 46 F2........46°48'N 14°58'E
glockner *mt.* Austria 46 E2 ..............47°05'N 12°41'E
dhog *r.* Canada 61 J2 ......................49°40'N 81°56'W
ayy Russia 53 E2 ................................43°19'N 45°42'E
iądz Poland 46 H5 ..............................53°30'N 18°46'E
ard Bay Scotland 16 D2 ....................57°53'N 5°32'W
nayabo, Golfo de *b.* Cuba 67 I5 ......20°31'N 77°38'W
ajoz *r.* Spain 45 C2 ..........................37°51'N 4°51'W
alajara Mexico 66 D5 .......................20°40'N 103°24'W
alajara Spain 45 D4 ...........................40°38'N 3°09'W
alcanal *i.* Solomon Is 109 F6.............9°38'S 160°05'E
alope *r.* Spain 45 E4.........................41°15'N 0°02'W
alquivir *r.* Spain 45 B2 .....................36°48'N 6°21'W
alupe *i.* Mexico 66 C4 ....................29°09'N 118°23'W
alupe, Sierra de *mts* Spain 45 C3.....39°20'N 5°49'W
arrama, Sierra de *mts* Spain 45 C4....40°40'N 4°10'W
aloupe *i.* Central America 67 L4 .......16°30'N 61°29'W
ana *r.* Portugal/Spain 45 B2 ............37°11'N 7°24'W
ix Spain 45 D2 ....................................37°18'N 3°07'W
ra, Península de la *pen.* Colombia 72 B8
..........................................................11°59'N 71°45'W
*i.* N. Pacific Oc. 103 K6 ..................13°29'N 144°58'E
ajuato Mexico 66 D5 .........................21°01'N 101°15'W
ajuato *d.* Mexico 66 D5 ..................21°16'N 100°47'W
are Venezuela 67 K2 ..........................9°03'N 69°44'W
Cuba 67 H5 ........................................22°13'N 84°05'W
gdong *r.* China 99 K2.......................23°49'N 114°45'E
gxi Zhuangzu Zizhiqu *d.* China 99 J2
..........................................................23°52'N 108°27'E
gyuan China 99 J4..............................32°24'N 105°51'E
gzhou China 99 J4..............................23°09'N 113°21'E
pa *r.* Venezuela 67 L2 .......................9°53'N 62°26'W
tánamo Cuba 67 I5.............................20°07'N 75°13'W
ré *r.* Bolivia/Brazil 72 C5 ................11°57'S 65°04'W
, Sierra de *mts* Spain 45 E5.............42°15'N 0°20'W
la Portugal 45 B2 ...............................38°32'N 7°16'W
ave Mexico 66 C6 .............................25°33'N 108°30'W
emala Central America 66 F3 ...........15°43'N 90°16'W
emala City Guatemala 66 F3 ...........14°37'N 90°31'W
are *r.* Colombia 72 C7 ......................4°02'N 67°45'W
aquil Ecuador 72 B6 ...........................2°10'S 79°56'W
aquil, Golfo de *g.* Ecuador 68 B3 .....3°10'S 80°53'W
mas Mexico 66 B6 ...........................27°57'N 110°53'W
hou China 98 H6 ................................40°27'N 95°48'E
Ethiopia 85 H3 ....................................11°16'N 35°17'E
Dolgaya Russia 52 F5 ........................70°18'N 58°42'E
andsdalen *f.* Norway 43 B3...............61°58'N 9°20'E
kédou Guinea 84 C2 ............................8°33'N 10°11'W
na Algeria 48 E4 .................................36°27'N 7°29'E
nine Morocco 84 C4............................28°59'N 10°02'W
et France 44 E5 ...................................46°10'N 1°53'E
nsey *i.* Channel Is 11 Y9 ..................49°29'N 2°36'W
ro *d.* Nigeria 84 F2 ...........................11°47'N 100°48'W
a Highlands *mts* Guyana/Venezuela 72 C7
..........................................................6°18'N 63°41'W
ford England 9 E2...............................51°14'N 0°34'W
China 99 K3.........................................25°17'N 110°19'E
Africa 84 C3........................................10°50'N 11°28'W
Algeria 48 E4.......................................36°27'N 7°29'E
a, Gulf of Africa 84 C3 ......................2°31'N 4°26'E
-Bissau Africa 84 C3.........................11°54'N 14°45'W

Guînes France 42 A3 .............................50°52'N 1°52'E
Güiria Venezuela 67 L3........................10°33'N 62°19'W
Guisborough England 13 F3.................54°32'N 1°03'W
Guise France 42 C2...............................49°54'N 3°38'E
Guiyang China 99 J3............................26°33'N 106°39'E
Guizhou *d.* China 99 J3 .....................26°59'N 106°45'E
Gujarat *d.* India 96 D5 .......................22°51'N 72°32'E
Gujranwala Pakistan 96 D7 .................32°07'N 74°13'E
Gullane Scotland 15 G4........................56°02'N 2°50'W
Gulu Uganda 85 H2...............................2°44'N 32°17'E
Gumdag Turkmenistan 95 H7 ..............39°11'N 54°29'E
Gümüşhane Turkey 51 M5....................40°29'N 39°28'E
Guna India 96 E5.................................24°39'N 77°19'E
Guntur India 96 F4 ..............................16°19'N 80°26'E
Guri, Embalse de *resr* Venezuela 67 L2....7°38'N 62°47'W
Gusau Nigeria 84 E3............................12°15'N 6°37'E
Gushgy Turkmenistan 95 J7.................35°15'N 62°17'E
Güstrow Germany 46 E5......................53°48'N 12°11'E
Guwahati India 97 H6..........................26°09'N 91°46'E
Guyana S. America 72 D7 .....................5°59'N 59°59'W
Gwadar Pakistan 96 B6........................25°09'N 62°23'E
Gwalior India 96 E6.............................26°15'N 78°10'E
Gwangju S. Korea 99 N5 .....................35°09'N 126°54'E
Gwardafuy, Gees *c.* Somalia 85 J3.....11°49'N 51°16'E
Gweebarra Bay Ireland 18 C4.............54°53'N 8°30'W
Gweru Zimbabwe 83 B3......................19°27'S 29°50'E
Gwynedd *d.* Wales 21 C3 ...................53°00'N 4°02'W
Gydan Peninsula Russia 54 I5.............70°08'N 77°30'E
Gyöngyös Hungary 46 H2 ...................47°46'N 19°56'E
Győr Hungary 46 G2 ...........................47°41'N 17°39'E
Gypsumville Canada 60 I3 .................51°47'N 98°37'W
Gyumri Armenia 94 F8.........................40°47'N 43°51'E
Gyzylarbat Turkmenistan 54 G1..........38°59'N 56°17'E

H

Haapajärvi Finland 43 F3 .....................63°45'N 25°20'E
Haapsalu Estonia 43 E2 .......................58°56'N 23°33'E
Haarlem Neth. 42 D5............................52°22'N 4°38'E
Habbān Yemen 95 G2 ..........................14°20'N 47°05'E
Hachijo-jima *i.* Japan 104 C2 ...........33°07'N 139°50'E
Hachinohe Japan 104 D4.....................40°32'N 141°31'E
Ḥadd, Ra's al *pt* Oman 95 I4 ............22°30'N 59°50'E
Haddington Scotland 15 G3 .................55°58'N 2°46'W
Haderslev Denmark 43 B1....................55°15'N 9°29'E
Hadjer Hadid Chad 85 G3...................13°23'N 21°20'E
Had Kourt Morocco 45 C1 ..................34°31'N 5°48'W
Hadleigh England 9 F3.........................52°03'N 0°57'E
Ḥaḍramawt *f.* Yemen 95 G3 ..............15°07'N 47°48'E
Hadyach Ukraine 47 O4.......................50°22'N 33°59'E
Haeju N. Korea 99 N5..........................38°02'N 125°45'E
Hagar Nish Plateau *f.* Eritrea 94 E3....17°03'N 37°58'E
Hagåtña Guam 103 K6 ........................13°29'n 144°45'E
Hagen Germany 46 B4 .........................51°22'N 7°28'E
Hag's Head Ireland 18 B2....................52°56'N 9°29'W
Hague, Cap de la *c.* France 11 Z9 .....49°44'N 1°55'W
Haida Gwaii *is* Canada 60 E3............53°59'N 133°20'W
Haifa Israel 49 J3..................................32°50'N 34°58'E
Haikou China 99 K2.............................20°01'N 110°18'E
Ḥā'il Saudi Arabia 94 E5......................27°33'N 41°41'E
Hailsham England 9 F1 ........................50°52'N 0°15'E
Hainan *d.* China 99 J1 ........................19°09'N 109°33'E
Hainan *i.* China 99 J1 .........................18°51'N 110°29'E
Hainaut *d.* Belgium 42 D3 ..................50°29'N 4°00'E
Haines U.S.A. 60 E3.............................59°13'N 135°25'W
Hai Phong Vietnam 102 D8.................20°48'N 106°43'E
Haiti Central America 67 J4 .................19°19'N 73°30'W
Haiya Sudan 85 H3 ..............................18°20'N 36°23'E
Hakodate Japan 104 D4.......................41°47'N 140°44'E
Halabjah/Ḥełebce Iraq 95 G7..............35°11'N 45°56'E
Ḥalāniyāt, Juzur al *is* Oman 95 I3......17°30'N 56°11'E
Halden Norway 43 B2...........................59°07'N 11°25'E
Halesowen England 8 C3......................52°27'N 2°03'W
Halesworth England 9 G3.....................52°21'N 1°30'E
Halifax Canada 61 L2..........................44°39'N 63°36'W
Halifax England 13 F2 ..........................53°44'N 1°51'W
Halkirk Scotland 17 F3.........................58°31'N 3°29'W
Halladale *r.* Scotland 17 F3 ...............58°33'N 3°54'W
Hall Beach *town* Canada 61 J4...........68°42'N 81°17'W
Halle Belgium 42 D3............................50°44'N 4°14'E
Halle Germany 46 D4...........................51°29'N 11°59'E
Halls Creek *town* Australia 108 B5......18°17'S 127°40'E
Halmahera *i.* Indonesia 103 H4...........1°06'N 128°32'E
Halmstad Sweden 43 C2......................56°40'N 12°52'E
Halstead England 9 F2..........................51°57'N 0°39'E
Halton *d.* England 21 D3....................53°20'N 2°43'W
Haltwhistle England 13 E3...................54°58'N 2°27'W
Hamadan Iran 95 G6............................34°46'N 48°30'E
Hamah Syria 94 E7 ...............................35°08'N 36°45'E
Hamamatsu Japan 104 C2....................34°42'N 137°44'E
Hamar Norway 43 B3...........................60°48'N 11°05'E
Hambleton Hills England 13 F3...........54°19'N 1°14'W
Hamhŭng N. Korea 99 N5.....................39°55'N 127°33'E
Hami China 98 G6 ................................42°48'N 93°27'E
Hamilton Bermuda 67 L7.....................32°18'N 64°46'W
Hamilton Canada 61 K2.......................43°15'N 79°51'W
Hamilton New Zealand 109 G3............37°48'S 175°16'E
Hamilton Scotland 15 F3......................55°47'N 4°03'W
Ḥamīm, Wādī al *watercourse* Libya 49 H3....30°04'N 21°35'E
Hamina Finland 43 F3 ..........................60°34'N 27°12'E
Hamm Germany 46 B4..........................51°41'N 7°49'E
Hammamet, Golfe de *g.* Tunisia 48 F4....36°09'N 10°50'E
Hammerdal Sweden 43 C3....................63°35'N 15°21'E
Hammerfest Norway 43 E5...................70°40'N 23°40'E
Hampshire *d.* England 21 E2 ..............51°10'N 1°13'W
Hampshire Downs *hills* England 8 D2....51°20'N 1°35'W
Hamstreet England 9 F2.......................51°04'N 0°52'E
Hanamaki Japan 104 D3.......................39°23'N 141°07'E
Hancock U.S.A. 63 I6...........................47°08'N 88°36'W
Handa Island Scotland 16 D3...............58°23'N 5°13'W
Handan China 99 K5.............................36°35'N 114°32'E
Hangzhou China 99 M4.........................30°15'N 120°10'E
Hanna Canada 62 D7...........................51°38'N 111°56'W
Hannover Germany 46 C5....................52°23'N 9°44'E
Hanöbukten *b.* Sweden 46 F6............55°48'N 14°37'E
Hanoi Vietnam 102 D8.........................21°01'N 105°51'E
Hantsavichy Belarus 47 L5..................52°46'N 26°27'E
Hanzhong China 99 J4..........................33°04'N 107°03'E
Haparanda Sweden 43 F4.....................65°50'N 24°08'E
Happy Valley-Goose Bay *town* Canada 61 L3....53°19'N 60°07'W
Harare Zimbabwe 83 C3.......................17°49'S 31°04'E

Ḥarāsīs, Jiddat al *des.* Oman 95 I3......18°59'N 55°33'E
Harbin China 99 N7..............................45°40'N 126°37'E
Harderwijk Neth. 42 E5........................52°21'N 5°38'E
Haren Germany 42 G5 ..........................52°48'N 7°15'E
Hargeysa Somalia 85 I2 .........................9°32'N 44°05'E
Har Hu *l.* China 98 H5 ........................38°18'N 97°23'E
Hari Rūd *r.* Afgh./Iran 95 J7 .............36°50'N 60°58'E
Harlech Wales 10 C4.............................52°52'N 4°06'W
Harleston England 9 G3 .......................52°24'N 1°18'E
Harlingen Neth. 42 E6 ..........................53°10'N 5°25'E
Harlow England 9 F2.............................51°46'N 0°05'E
Harney Basin U.S.A. 62 C5...................43°23'N 119°55'W
Härnösand Sweden 43 D3 ....................62°38'N 17°56'E
Har Nuur *l.* Mongolia 98 G7...............48°02'N 93°23'E
Harpenden England 9 E2.......................51°49'N 0°21'W
Harray, Loch of *l.* Scotland 17 F4.......59°01'N 3°13'W
Harricanaw *r.* Canada 61 K3..............50°58'N 79°33'W
Harris, Sound of *str.* Scotland 16 B2....57°46'N 7°10'W
Harrisburg U.S.A. 63 K5 .......................40°17'N 76°54'W
Harrison, Cape Canada 61 M3.............54°56'N 57°42'W
Harrogate England 13 F2......................53°59'N 1°32'W
Hârşova Romania 51 G7........................44°41'N 27°57'E
Harstad Norway 43 D5..........................68°47'N 16°32'E
Harteigen *mt.* Norway 43 A3................60°12'N 7°05'E
Harter Fell *hill* England 12 E3.............54°29'N 2°52'W
Hart Fell *hill* Scotland 15 F3...............55°24'N 3°24'W
Hartford U.S.A. 63 L5...........................41°46'N 72°42'W
Hartland England 11 C2........................50°59'N 4°29'W
Hartland Point England 11 C3..............51°01'N 4°33'W
Hartlepool England 13 F3.....................54°41'N 1°13'W
Hartlepool *d.* England 21 E4...............54°40'N 1°15'W
Harwich England 9 G2..........................51°56'N 1°16'E
Haryana *d.* India 96 E6 ......................29°11'N 76°12'E
Haskovo Bulgaria 50 F5........................41°56'N 25°32'E
Haslemere England 8 E2.......................51°05'N 0°43'W
Hasselt Belgium 42 E3..........................50°56'N 5°20'E
Hassi Messaoud Algeria 84 E5.............31°41'N 6°10'E
Hässleholm Sweden 43 C2...................56°10'N 13°46'E
Hastings England 9 F1 ..........................50°51'N 0°35'E
Hatfield England 13 G2.........................53°35'N 0°59'W
Ha Tinh Vietnam 102 D7.......................18°18'N 105°55'E
Hatteras, Cape U.S.A. 63 K4................35°14'N 75°34'W
Hattiesburg U.S.A. 63 I3.......................31°23'N 89°19'W
Hat Yai Thailand 102 C5........................7°01'N 100°26'E
Haud *f.* Ethiopia 85 I2 ..........................8°37'N 44°15'E
Haugesund Norway 43 A2.....................59°24'N 5°18'E
Haukivesi *l.* Finland 43 G3 .................62°06'N 28°28'E
Haut Atlas *mts* Morocco 84 D5..........30°51'N 8°03'E
Haut-Folin *hill* France 44 F5...............46°59'N 4°01'E
Hauts-de-France *d.* France 42 B3.......50°14'N 2°43'E
Hauts Plateaux *f.* Algeria 48 C3.........33°42'N 0°42'W
Havana Cuba 67 H5..............................23°07'N 82°22'W
Havant England 8 E1............................50°51'N 0°59'W
Haverfordwest Wales 10 C3.................51°48'N 4°58'W
Haverhill England 9 F3 .........................52°05'N 0°26'E
Havre U.S.A. 62 E6 ..............................48°32'N 109°41'W
Havre-St-Pierre Canada 61 L3.............50°14'N 63°28'W
Hawaii *d.* U.S.A. 116 A3.....................19°35'N 155°17'W
Hawaiian Islands N. Pacific Oc. 116 A3....28°26'N 174°25'W
Hawarden Wales 10 D5.........................53°11'N 3°02'W
Hawes England 13 E3...........................54°18'N 2°12'W
Haweswater Reservoir England 12 E3....54°30'N 2°48'W
Hawick Scotland 15 G3.........................55°26'N 2°47'W
Hawke Bay New Zealand 109 G3.........39°24'S 177°23'E
Hawkhurst England 9 F2 ......................51°03'N 0°31'E
Haxby England 13 F3............................54°01'N 1°04'W
Hay Australia 108 D3............................34°31'S 144°48'E
Hay *r.* Canada 60 G4 ..........................60°48'N 115°47'W
Haydarābād Iran 94 G7..........................37°04'N 45°05'E
Haydon Bridge England 13 E3..............54°58'N 2°15'W
Hayle England 11 B2.............................50°11'N 5°25'W
Haymā' Oman 95 I3...............................19°54'N 56°13'E
Hay-on-Wye Wales 10 D4......................52°05'N 3°07'W
Hay River *town* Canada 60 G4............60°51'N 115°40'W
Hayshah, Sabkhat al *f.* Libya 49 G3....31°55'N 15°19'E
Haywards Heath England 9 E1 .............50°59'N 0°06'W
Hazarajat *f.* Afgh. 95 K6....................33°29'N 65°07'E
Hazebrouck France 42 B3.....................50°43'N 2°32'E
Heacham England 9 F3.........................52°54'N 0°30'E
Headcorn England 9 F2........................51°10'N 0°38'E
Heanor England 13 F2 ..........................53°01'N 1°21'W
Hearst Canada 63 J6.............................49°41'N 83°41'W
Heathfield England 9 F1 .......................50°58'N 0°16'E
Hebei *d.* China 99 L5..........................38°33'N 115°49'E
Hebron West Bank 49 J3.......................31°53'N 34°49'E
Hechi China 99 J2.................................24°38'N 108°04'E
Heckington England 9 E3.....................52°59'N 0°18'W
Hede Sweden 43 C3..............................62°25'N 13°32'E
Heerenveen Neth. 42 E5.......................52°58'N 5°56'E
Heerlen Neth. 42 E3..............................50°53'N 5°59'E
Hefei China 99 L4 .................................31°51'N 117°19'E
Hegang China 99 O7.............................47°13'N 130°13'E
Heidelberg Germany 46 C3...................49°24'N 8°41'E
Heighington England 13 G2..................53°13'N 0°27'W
Heilbronn Germany 46 C3.....................49°08'N 9°12'E
Heilen, Loch Scotland 17 F3.................58°36'N 3°17'W
Heilongjiang *d.* China 99 N7...............46°55'N 128°30'E
Heilong Jiang *r.* China 99 O7.............48°25'N 134°59'E
Heinola Finland 43 F3 ...........................61°12'N 26°02'E
Hekla *vol.* Iceland 43 Y1......................63°59'N 19°41'W
Helena U.S.A. 62 D6.............................46°36'N 112°01'W
Helensburgh Scotland 14 E4................56°00'N 4°44'W
Helgoländer Bucht *g.* Germany 46 C6....54°10'N 8°14'E
Hellín Spain 45 E3.................................38°31'N 1°41'W
Helmand *r.* Afgh. 95 J6.......................31°13'N 61°35'E
Helmond Neth. 42 E4 ...........................51°28'N 5°40'E
Helmsdale Scotland 17 F3....................58°07'N 3°39'W
Helmsdale *r.* Scotland 17 F3..............58°07'N 3°38'W
Helmsley England 13 F3........................54°15'N 1°04'W
Helsingborg Sweden 43 C2..................56°03'N 12°42'E
Helsingør Denmark 46 E7.....................56°02'N 12°36'E
Helsinki Finland 43 F3 ..........................60°10'N 24°57'E
Helston England 11 B2..........................50°06'N 5°16'W
Helvellyn *hill* England 12 D3 ...............54°32'N 3°01'W
Hemel Hempstead England 9 E2..........51°46'N 0°28'W
Henan *d.* China 99 K4.........................33°59'N 112°54'E
Henares *r.* Spain 45 D4.......................40°25'N 3°29'W
Hendon England 9 E2............................51°35'N 0°13'W
Henfield England 9 E1...........................50°56'N 0°16'W
Hengelo Neth. 42 F5.............................52°16'N 6°48'E
Hengoed Wales 10 D3 ..........................51°39'N 3°14'W
Hengyang China 99 K3.........................26°53'N 112°32'E
Henichesk Ukraine 49 J6......................46°10'N 34°48'E
Henley-on-Thames England 8 E2.........51°32'N 0°54'W
Hennef Germany 42 G3.........................50°47'N 7°18'E

Henrietta Maria, Cape Canada 61 J3 ....55°21'N 82°13'W
Henzada Myanmar 97 I4.......................17°36'N 95°26'E
Herāt Afgh. 95 J6..................................34°22'N 62°11'E
Hereford England 8 C3..........................52°03'N 2°43'W
Herefordshire *d.* England 21 D3.........52°07'N 2°40'W
Herm *i.* Channel Is 11 Y9 ...................49°28'N 2°26'W
Herma Ness *hd* Scotland 17 I5...........60°51'N 0°54'W
Hermosillo Mexico 66 B6.....................29°04'N 110°58'W
Herne Germany 42 G4...........................51°32'N 7°13'E
Herne Bay *town* England 9 G2.............51°22'N 1°08'E
Herning Denmark 43 B2........................56°08'N 8°58'E
Hertford England 9 E2...........................51°48'N 0°05'W
Hertfordshire *d.* England 21 F2...........51°55'N 0°09'E
Hesdin France 9 H1...............................50°22'N 2°03'E
Heswall England 12 D2.........................53°20'N 3°06'W
Hetton England 13 E3............................54°01'N 2°03'W
Hexham England 13 E3.........................54°58'N 2°07'W
Heysham England 12 E3........................54°02'N 2°54'W
Heywood England 13 E2........................53°36'N 2°13'W
Heze China 99 L5 .................................35°17'N 115°32'E
Hidaka-sanmyaku *mts* Japan 104 D4....42°49'N 142°38'E
Hidalgo *d.* Mexico 66 E5.....................20°35'N 99°07'W
Hidalgo del Parral Mexico 66 C6.........26°56'N 105°41'W
Higashi-suidō *str.* Japan 104 A2........33°55'N 129°23'E
Higham Ferrers England 9 E3...............52°18'N 0°36'W
Highbridge England 8 C2......................51°13'N 2°59'W
Highclere England 8 D2........................51°20'N 1°22'W
Highland *d.* Scotland 20 C5................57°38'N 4°59'W
High Peak *hills* England 13 F2.............53°23'N 1°54'W
High Seat *hill* England 13 E3...............54°24'N 2°18'W
Highworth England 8 D2.......................51°38'N 1°43'W
High Wycombe England 8 E2................51°38'N 0°45'W
Hiiumaa *i.* Estonia 43 E2....................58°50'N 22°24'E
Hijaz *f.* Saudi Arabia 94 E5.................26°08'N 37°01'E
Hilāl, Ra's al *pt* Libya 49 H3...............32°54'N 22°09'E
Hildesheim Germany 46 C5..................52°09'N 9°57'E
Hillah Iraq 94 F6...................................32°27'N 44°24'E
Hillerød Denmark 43 C1.......................55°56'N 12°18'E
Hillside Scotland 17 G1.........................56°45'N 2°29'W
Hillswick Scotland 17 H5......................60°29'N 1°29'W
Hilpsford Point England 12 D3.............54°02'N 3°12'W
Hilversum Neth. 42 E5..........................52°13'N 5°11'E
Himachal Pradesh *d.* India 96 E7.......31°59'N 77°23'E
Himalaya *mts* Asia 96 E7..................33°06'N 76°46'E
Hinckley England 8 D3..........................52°33'N 1°23'W
Hinderwell England 13 G3....................54°32'N 0°46'W
Hindhead England 8 E2.........................51°07'N 0°44'W
Hindley England 12 E2..........................53°32'N 2°35'W
Hindu Kush *mts* Afgh./Pakistan 95 K6....34°58'N 67°52'E
Hinnøya *i.* Norway 43 C5....................68°37'N 15°58'E
Hirosaki Japan 104 D4..........................40°36'N 140°28'E
Hiroshima Japan 104 B2........................34°22'N 132°27'E
Hirson France 42 D2.............................49°55'N 4°05'E
Hirwaun Wales 10 D3............................51°44'N 3°31'W
Hispaniola *i.* Caribbean Sea 67 J5......20°18'N 72°57'W
Hitachi Japan 104 D3............................36°35'N 140°39'E
Hitchin England 9 E2.............................51°57'N 0°17'W
Hitra *i.* Norway 43 B3..........................63°31'N 8°49'E
Hjälmaren *l.* Sweden 43 C2.................59°14'N 15°51'E
Hjørring Denmark 43 B2........................57°28'N 10°01'E
Hlybokaye Belarus 47 L6......................55°08'N 27°40'E
Hobart Australia 108 D1.......................42°52'S 147°19'E
Hobro Denmark 43 B2...........................56°38'N 9°48'E
Ho Chi Minh City Vietnam 102 D6.......10°45'N 106°42'E
Hochschwab *mt.* Austria 46 F2............47°38'N 15°09'E
Hoddesdon England 9 E2......................51°46'N 0°01'W
Hodeidah Yemen 94 F2.........................14°50'N 42°54'E
Hódmezővásárhely Hungary 46 I2........46°25'N 20°21'E
Hodna, Chott el *f.* Algeria 48 D4.........35°27'N 4°55'E
Hodnet England 8 C3............................52°51'N 2°35'W
Hoek van Holland Neth. 42 D4.............51°58'N 4°08'E
Hof Germany 46 D4...............................50°19'N 11°55'E
Höfn Iceland 43 Z2................................64°16'N 15°13'W
Hofsjökull *ice cap* Iceland 43 Y2.........64°49'N 18°52'W
Hohhot China 99 K6.............................40°43'N 111°44'E
Hokkaidō *i.* Japan 104 D4...................43°33'N 143°27'E
Holbæk Denmark 43 B1........................55°43'N 11°44'E
Holbeach England 9 F3 .........................52°48'N 0°01'E
Holbeach Marsh England 9 F3..............52°51'N 0°02'E
Holderness *pen.* England 13 G2..........53°52'N 0°08'E
Holguín Cuba 67 I5................................20°54'N 76°14'W
Hollabrunn Austria 46 G3.....................48°34'N 16°05'E
Holland Fen *f.* England 9 E3................52°59'N 0°11'W
Hollesley Bay England 9 G3..................52°02'N 1°28'E
Hollington England 9 F1........................50°53'N 0°33'E
Hollingworth England 13 F2.................53°28'N 1°59'W
Holme-on-Spalding-Moor England 13 G2....53°50'N 0°47'W
Holmfirth England 13 F2.......................53°34'N 1°47'W
Holstebro Denmark 43 B2....................56°21'N 8°37'E
Holsworthy England 11 C2...................50°49'N 4°21'W
Holt England 9 G3.................................52°55'N 1°05'E
Holyhead Wales 10 C5..........................53°19'N 4°38'W
Holyhead Bay Wales 10 C5..................53°22'N 4°40'W
Holy Island England 13 F4...................55°41'N 1°47'W
Holy Island Wales 10 C5......................53°15'N 4°41'W
Holywell Wales 10 D5...........................53°17'N 3°13'W
Homāyunshahr Iran 95 H6....................32°59'N 50°23'E
Homburg Germany 42 G2......................49°19'N 7°20'E
Home Bay Canada 61 L4......................68°52'N 67°27'W
Homs Syria 94 E6.................................34°44'N 36°44'E
Homyel'/Gomel' Belarus 47 N5...........52°25'N 31°01'E
Honduras Central America 66 G3..........14°47'N 86°43'W
Honduras, Gulf of Belize/Honduras 66 G4
..........................................................16°20'N 87°30'W
Hønefoss Norway 43 B3........................60°10'N 10°14'E
Hong Kong China 99 K2.......................22°16'N 114°11'E
Hong Kong *d.* China 99 K2.................22°21'N 114°13'E
Honiara Solomon Is 109 E6...................9°26'S 159°57'E
Honiton England 11 D2.........................50°48'N 3°11'W
Honley England 13 F2 ...........................53°36'N 1°48'W
Honshū *i.* Japan 104 B3......................35°42'N 133°20'E
Hood, Mount *vol.* U.S.A. 62 B6...........45°23'N 121°42'W
Hood Point Australia 108 A3................34°19'S 119°33'E
Hoogeveen Neth. 42 F5.........................52°43'N 6°30'E
Hook England 8 E2................................51°17'N 0°58'W
Hook Head Ireland 18 E2......................52°07'N 6°56'W
Hoorn Neth. 42 E5.................................52°39'N 5°04'E
Hope, Loch *l.* Scotland 17 E3..............58°27'N 4°39'W
Hope, Point U.S.A. 60 B4......................68°21'N 166°49'W
Hopedale Canada 61 L3........................55°27'N 60°00'W
Hörby Sweden 46 E6.............................55°51'N 13°40'E
Horley England 9 E2..............................51°10'N 0°10'W
Hormuz, Strait of Iran/Oman 95 I5.......26°35'N 56°59'E
Horn *c.* Iceland 43 X2..........................66°28'N 22°29'W
Horn, Cape Chile 73 C1.........................56°04'S 67°17'W
Hornavan *l.* Sweden 43 D4..................66°11'N 17°44'E
Horncastle England 13 G2....................53°12'N 0°07'W

Hornepayne Canada 63 J6 .......... 49°13'N 84°47'W
Hornsea England 13 G2 .......... 53°55'N 0°10'W
Horodnya Ukraine 47 N4 .......... 51°53'N 31°36'E
Horodok Ukraine 47 J3 .......... 49°47'N 23°39'E
Horrabridge England 11 C2 .......... 50°31'N 4°06'W
Horsens Denmark 43 B1 .......... 55°52'N 9°51'E
Horsham Australia 108 D3 .......... 36°43'S 142°13'E
Horsham England 9 E2 .......... 51°04'N 0°19'W
Horten Norway 43 B2 .......... 59°25'N 10°28'E
Horwich England 12 E2 .......... 53°36'N 2°33'W
Hotan China 98 E5 .......... 37°07'N 80°02'E
Houffalize Belgium 42 E3 .......... 50°08'N 5°48'E
Houghton le Spring England 13 F3 .......... 54°50'N 1°28'W
Houghton Regis England 9 E2 .......... 51°54'N 0°31'W
Hourn, Loch inlet Scotland 16 D2 .......... 57°08'N 5°42'W
Houston U.S.A. 63 G2 .......... 29°43'N 95°19'W
Hovd Mongolia 98 G7 .......... 47°59'N 91°41'E
Hove England 9 E1 .......... 50°50'N 0°10'W
Hoveton England 9 G3 .......... 52°43'N 1°25'E
Hövsgöl Nuur l. Mongolia 99 I8 .......... 50°59'N 100°42'E
Howden England 13 G2 .......... 53°45'N 0°52'W
Hoy i. Scotland 17 F3 .......... 58°50'N 3°16'W
Høyanger Norway 43 A3 .......... 61°13'N 6°04'E
Hoyerswerda Germany 46 F4 .......... 51°27'N 14°16'E
Höytiäinen l. Finland 43 G3 .......... 62°46'N 29°43'E
Hradec Králové Czechia 46 F4 .......... 50°13'N 15°50'E
Hrebinka Ukraine 47 O4 .......... 50°06'N 32°26'E
Hrodna Belarus 47 J5 .......... 53°41'N 23°49'E
Hsinchu Taiwan 99 M2 .......... 24°48'N 120°58'E
Huaibei China 99 L4 .......... 33°57'N 116°51'E
Huainan China 99 L4 .......... 32°36'N 117°02'E
Huambo Angola 83 A3 .......... 12°46'S 15°44'E
Huancayo Peru 72 B5 .......... 12°03'S 75°11'W
Huang He r. China 99 L5 .......... 37°46'N 118°57'E
Huangshi China 99 L4 .......... 30°10'N 115°08'E
Huascarán, Nevado de mt. Peru 72 B6 .......... 9°09'S 77°36'W
Hubballi India 96 E4 .......... 15°18'N 75°15'E
Hubei d. China 99 K4 .......... 31°09'N 113°06'E
Hucknall England 13 F2 .......... 53°02'N 1°12'W
Huddersfield England 13 F2 .......... 53°39'N 1°47'W
Hudiksvall Sweden 43 D3 .......... 61°43'N 17°06'E
Hudson r. U.S.A. 63 L5 .......... 40°54'N 73°56'W
Hudson Bay sea Canada 61 J3 .......... 59°05'N 86°00'W
Hudson Strait Canada 61 K4 .......... 63°31'N 74°25'W
Huê Vietnam 102 D7 .......... 16°26'N 107°33'E
Huelva Spain 45 B2 .......... 37°16'N 6°55'W
Huércal-Overa Spain 45 E2 .......... 37°23'N 1°55'W
Huesca Spain 45 E5 .......... 42°09'N 0°25'W
Huizhou China 99 K2 .......... 23°05'N 114°25'E
Hull Canada 63 K6 .......... 45°27'N 75°45'W
Hulun Buir China 99 L7 .......... 49°04'N 119°46'E
Hulun Nur l. China 99 L7 .......... 48°32'N 117°11'E
Ḥulwān Egypt 49 J2 .......... 29°55'N 31°18'E
Humber, Mouth of the England 13 H2 .......... 53°33'N 0°06'E
Humboldt r. U.S.A. 62 C5 .......... 40°04'N 118°36'W
Humphreys Peak U.S.A. 62 D4 .......... 35°21'N 111°40'W
Húnaflói b. Iceland 43 X2 .......... 65°46'N 20°50'W
Hunan d. China 99 K3 .......... 27°26'N 111°22'E
Hungarian Plain f. Hungary 49 G6 .......... 46°30'N 19°00'E
Hungary Europe 46 H2 .......... 47°01'N 18°59'E
Hungerford England 8 D2 .......... 51°25'N 1°31'W
Hunish, Rubha pt Scotland 16 C2 .......... 57°42'N 6°24'W
Hunmanby England 13 G3 .......... 54°11'N 0°19'W
Hunsrück hills Germany 46 B3 .......... 49°47'N 7°00'E
Hunstanton England 9 F3 .......... 52°56'N 0°30'E
Huntingdon England 9 E3 .......... 52°20'N 0°11'W
Huntington U.S.A. 63 J4 .......... 38°25'N 82°18'W
Huntly Scotland 17 G2 .......... 57°27'N 2°47'W
Huntsville Ala. U.S.A. 63 I3 .......... 34°46'N 86°34'W
Huntsville Tex. U.S.A. 63 G3 .......... 30°42'N 95°34'W
Hurghada Egypt 49 J2 .......... 27°12'N 33°48'E
Huron U.S.A. 62 G5 .......... 44°23'N 98°13'W
Huron, Lake Canada/U.S.A. 61 J2 .......... 44°39'N 82°23'W
Hurstpierpoint England 9 E1 .......... 50°56'N 0°11'W
Husum Germany 46 C6 .......... 54°29'N 9°04'E
Hutton Rudby England 13 F3 .......... 54°27'N 1°17'W
Huzhou China 99 M4 .......... 30°50'N 120°08'E
Hvannadalshnúkur vol. Iceland 43 Y2 .......... 64°01'N 16°41'W
Hvar i. Croatia 50 B6 .......... 43°08'N 16°33'E
Hyargas Nuur l. Mongolia 98 G7 .......... 49°02'N 93°18'E
Hyderabad India 96 E4 .......... 17°21'N 78°25'E
Hyderabad Pakistan 96 C6 .......... 25°21'N 68°23'E
Hyères France 44 F3 .......... 43°07'N 6°08'E
Hyrynsalmi Finland 43 G4 .......... 64°40'N 28°29'E
Hythe Hants. England 8 D1 .......... 50°52'N 1°24'W
Hythe Kent England 9 G2 .......... 51°04'N 1°05'E
Hyvinkää Finland 43 F3 .......... 60°38'N 24°51'E

## I

Ialomiţa r. Romania 50 G7 .......... 44°43'N 27°51'E
Iar Connaught f. Ireland 18 B3 .......... 53°21'N 9°19'W
Iaşi Romania 49 I6 .......... 47°10'N 27°35'E
Ibadan Nigeria 84 E2 .......... 7°24'N 3°55'E
Ibagué Colombia 72 B7 .......... 4°24'N 75°13'W
Ibar r. Kosovo/Serbia 50 D6 .......... 43°43'N 20°45'E
Ibb Yemen 94 F2 .......... 14°03'N 44°09'E
Ibiza Spain 45 F3 .......... 38°54'N 1°27'E
Ibiza i. Spain 45 F3 .......... 39°10'N 1°39'E
Ibrā' Oman 95 I4 .......... 22°41'N 58°33'E
Ibstock England 8 D3 .......... 52°42'N 1°24'W
Ica Peru 72 B5 .......... 14°04'S 75°43'W
Iceland Europe 43 X2 .......... 64°42'N 18°19'W
Ichinoseki Japan 104 D3 .......... 38°55'N 141°07'E
Icklesham England 9 F1 .......... 50°55'N 0°40'E
Idaho d. U.S.A. 62 D5 .......... 44°08'N 114°08'W
Idaho Falls town U.S.A. 62 D5 .......... 43°32'N 112°01'W
Idar-Oberstein Germany 42 G2 .......... 49°42'N 7°18'E
Idfū Egypt 49 J1 .......... 24°55'N 32°49'E
Idi mt. Greece 50 F2 .......... 35°13'N 24°47'E
Idlib Syria 51 L2 .......... 35°56'N 36°38'E
Ieper Belgium 42 B3 .......... 50°51'N 2°53'E
Iešjávri l. Norway 43 F5 .......... 69°39'N 24°28'E
Igan Malaysia 102 E4 .......... 2°51'N 111°44'E
Iggesund Sweden 43 D3 .......... 61°39'N 17°05'E
İğneada Burnu pt Turkey 51 H5 .......... 41°53'N 28°03'E
Igoumenitsa Greece 50 D4 .......... 39°30'N 20°17'E
Iguaçu r. Brazil 73 D4 .......... 25°36'S 54°35'W
Iisalmi Finland 43 F3 .......... 63°34'N 27°11'E
IJmuiden Neth. 42 D5 .......... 52°27'N 4°37'E
IJssel r. Neth. 42 E5 .......... 52°35'N 5°50'E
IJsselmeer l. Neth. 42 E5 .......... 52°48'N 5°22'E
IJzer r. Belgium 9 H2 .......... 51°09'N 2°44'E
Ikahauk Canada 60 F5 .......... 71°55'N 125°05'W
Ikaria i. Greece 50 G3 .......... 37°39'N 26°13'E

Iki i. Japan 104 A2 .......... 33°45'N 129°39'E
Ilagan Phil. 103 G7 .......... 17°06'N 121°53'E
Ilchester England 8 C2 .......... 51°00'N 2°41'W
Ilebo Dem. Rep. Congo 83 B4 .......... 4°21'S 20°36'E
Île-de-France d. France 42 B1 .......... 48°39'N 2°36'E
Ilford England 9 F2 .......... 51°33'N 0°05'E
Ilfracombe England 11 C3 .......... 51°12'N 4°07'W
Ilhéus Brazil 72 F5 .......... 14°46'S 39°02'W
Iligan Phil. 103 G5 .......... 8°13'N 124°15'E
Ilkeston England 8 D3 .......... 52°58'N 1°18'W
Ilkley England 13 F2 .......... 53°56'N 1°49'W
Illinois d. U.S.A. 63 I4 .......... 39°52'N 89°07'W
Illinois r. U.S.A. 63 H4 .......... 38°56'N 90°30'W
Illizi Algeria 84 E4 .......... 26°29'N 8°30'E
Ilminster England 8 C1 .......... 50°56'N 2°54'W
Iloilo Phil. 103 G6 .......... 10°41'N 122°32'E
Ilorin Nigeria 84 E2 .......... 8°30'N 4°34'E
Ilovlya Russia 53 E2 .......... 49°19'N 43°59'E
Imatra Finland 43 G3 .......... 61°11'N 28°47'E
Immingham England 13 G2 .......... 53°37'N 0°13'W
Imola Italy 46 D1 .......... 44°21'N 11°42'E
Imperatriz Brazil 72 E6 .......... 5°33'S 47°26'W
Imphal India 97 H5 .......... 24°46'N 93°56'E
İmroz Turkey 50 F5 .......... 40°10'N 25°55'E
Inarijärvi l. Finland 43 F5 .......... 68°57'N 27°37'E
Inchard, Loch b. Scotland 16 D3 .......... 58°27'N 5°04'W
Incheon S. Korea 99 N5 .......... 37°28'N 126°39'E
Inchkeith i. Scotland 15 F4 .......... 56°02'N 3°08'W
Indalsälven r. Sweden 43 D3 .......... 62°32'N 17°24'E
Independence U.S.A. 63 H4 .......... 39°07'N 94°26'W
Inderbor Kazakhstan 53 F2 .......... 48°33'N 51°44'E
India Asia 96 E5 .......... 22°00'N 79°00'E
Indiana d. U.S.A. 63 I5 .......... 40°09'N 86°01'W
Indianapolis U.S.A. 63 I4 .......... 39°46'N 86°10'W
Indian Ocean 117 G2
Indigirka r. Russia 55 P5 .......... 71°28'N 149°53'E
Indonesia Asia 102 E2 .......... 4°12'S 112°00'E
Indore India 96 E5 .......... 22°40'N 75°53'E
Indre r. France 44 D5 .......... 47°14'N 0°12'E
Indus r. China/Pakistan 96 C5 .......... 23°56'N 67°38'E
Indus, Mouths of the Pakistan 96 C5 .......... 24°36'N 66°36'E
Inebolu Turkey 51 J5 .......... 41°58'N 33°45'E
İnegöl Turkey 51 H5 .......... 40°04'N 29°30'E
Infiernillo, Presa resr Mexico 66 D4 .......... 18°41'N 101°57'W
Infiesto Spain 45 C5 .......... 43°21'N 5°20'W
Ingatestone England 9 F2 .......... 51°40'N 0°23'E
Ingleborough hill England 13 E3 .......... 54°10'N 2°24'W
Ingleton England 13 E3 .......... 54°09'N 2°28'W
Ingoldmells England 13 H2 .......... 53°12'N 0°20'E
Ingolstadt Germany 46 D3 .......... 48°46'N 11°27'E
Inhambane Mozambique 83 C2 .......... 23°47'S 35°31'E
Inhul r. Ukraine 47 N2 .......... 46°58'N 31°58'E
Inhulets' r. Ukraine 47 O2 .......... 46°41'N 32°49'E
Inishbofin i. Ireland 18 A3 .......... 53°38'N 10°14'W
Inisheer i. Ireland 18 B3 .......... 53°04'N 9°30'W
Inishmaan i. Ireland 18 B3 .......... 53°05'N 9°33'W
Inishmore i. Ireland 18 B3 .......... 53°09'N 9°47'W
Inishmurray i. Ireland 18 C4 .......... 54°26'N 8°40'W
Inishowen pen. Ireland 18 D5 .......... 55°13'N 7°17'W
Inishowen Head Ireland 14 C3 .......... 55°14'N 6°55'W
Inishtrahull i. Ireland 18 D5 .......... 55°26'N 7°13'W
Inishtrahull Sound str. Ireland 14 B3 .......... 55°27'N 7°28'W
Inishturk i. Ireland 18 A3 .......... 53°42'N 10°08'W
Inn r. Europe 46 D2 .......... 46°55'N 10°29'E
Inner Mongolia d. China 99 I6 .......... 40°12'N 103°26'E
Inner Sound str. Scotland 16 D2 .......... 57°21'N 5°57'W
Innsbruck Austria 46 D2 .......... 47°16'N 11°24'E
Inny r. Ireland 18 D3 .......... 53°33'N 7°50'W
Inowrocław Poland 46 H5 .......... 52°48'N 18°16'E
In Salah Algeria 84 E4 .......... 27°13'N 2°25'E
Insch Scotland 17 G2 .......... 57°20'N 2°37'W
Inta Russia 52 F4 .......... 65°59'N 60°00'E
International Falls town U.S.A. 63 H6 .......... 48°36'N 93°25'W
Inukjuak Canada 61 K3 .......... 58°28'N 78°04'W
Inuvialuit f. Canada 60 F4 .......... 69°10'N 128°00'W
Inuvik Canada 60 E4 .......... 68°24'N 133°43'W
Inveraray Scotland 14 D4 .......... 56°14'N 5°04'W
Inverbervie Scotland 17 G1 .......... 56°51'N 2°17'W
Invercargill New Zealand 109 F1 .......... 46°25'S 168°22'E
Inverclyde d. Scotland 20 C4 .......... 55°54'N 4°44'W
Invergordon Scotland 17 E2 .......... 57°42'N 4°10'W
Inverkeithing Scotland 15 F4 .......... 56°02'N 3°24'W
Inverness Scotland 17 E2 .......... 57°29'N 4°13'W
Inverurie Scotland 17 G2 .......... 57°17'N 2°22'W
Ioannina Greece 50 D4 .......... 39°40'N 20°51'E
Iona i. Scotland 14 C4 .......... 56°19'N 6°25'W
Ionian Islands Greece 50 C4 .......... 39°26'N 19°33'E
Ionian Sea Greece/Italy 50 C4 .......... 38°11'N 18°29'E
Ios i. Greece 50 F3 .......... 36°44'N 25°22'E
Iowa d. U.S.A. 63 H5 .......... 42°12'N 92°47'W
Iowa City U.S.A. 63 H5 .......... 41°40'N 91°32'W
Ipoh Malaysia 102 C4 .......... 4°40'N 101°04'E
Ipswich England 9 G3 .......... 52°03'N 1°09'E
Iput' r. Russia 47 N5 .......... 52°30'N 31°37'E
Iputs' r. Belarus 47 N5 .......... 52°26'N 31°04'E
Iqaluit Canada 61 L4 .......... 63°45'N 68°36'W
Iquique Chile 73 B4 .......... 20°14'S 70°07'W
Iquitos Peru 72 B6 .......... 3°50'S 73°13'W
Iraklion Greece 50 F2 .......... 35°19'N 25°08'E
Iran Asia 95 H5 .......... 31°28'N 55°05'E
Iran, Pegunungan mts Indonesia 102 E4 .......... 1°47'N 114°46'E
Iranian Plateau f. Iran 86 D3 .......... 32°00'N 55°00'E
Irapuato Mexico 66 D5 .......... 20°41'N 101°23'W
Iraq Asia 94 F6 .......... 32°50'N 42°21'E
Irbid Jordan 94 E6 .......... 32°34'N 35°51'E
Ireland Europe 18 D3 .......... 53°33'N 7°43'W
Ireland's Eye i. Ireland 18 E3 .......... 53°24'N 6°03'W
Iringa Tanzania 83 C4 .......... 7°48'S 35°43'E
Iriri r. Brazil 72 D6 .......... 3°52'S 52°37'W
Irish Sea Ireland/U.K. 18 F3 .......... 53°40'N 5°11'W
Irkutsk Russia 55 L3 .......... 52°11'N 104°09'E
Iron Mountain U.S.A. 63 I6 .......... 45°49'N 88°04'W
Ironwood U.S.A. 63 H6 .......... 46°28'N 90°09'W
Irosin Phil. 103 G6 .......... 12°42'N 124°01'E
Irrawaddy r. Myanmar 97 I4 .......... 15°48'N 95°05'E
Irrawaddy, Mouths of the Myanmar 97 H4 .......... 15°35'N 94°02'E
Irsha r. Ukraine 47 M4 .......... 50°46'N 29°35'E
Irthing r. England 12 E3 .......... 54°55'N 2°49'W
Irtysh r. Kazakhstan/Russia 54 H4 .......... 61°07'N 68°50'E
Irún Spain 45 E5 .......... 43°20'N 1°48'W
Irvine Scotland 14 E3 .......... 55°37'N 4°40'W
Irvinestown Northern Ireland 14 B2 .......... 54°28'N 7°38'W
Isabela Phil. 103 G5 .......... 6°40'N 121°59'E
Isabelia, Cordillera mts Nicaragua 67 G3 .......... 13°13'N 85°59'W
Ísafjörður Iceland 43 X2 .......... 66°05'N 23°10'W

Isar r. Germany 46 E3 .......... 48°49'N 12°59'E
Isbister Scotland 17 H5 .......... 60°36'N 1°19'W
Ise Japan 104 C2 .......... 34°29'N 136°43'E
Ise-wan b. Japan 104 D4 .......... 34°17'N 140°58'E
Ishikari-wan b. Japan 104 D4 .......... 43°17'N 140°58'E
Ishim r. Kazakhstan/Russia 54 I3 .......... 57°43'N 71°13'E
Ishinomaki Japan 104 D3 .......... 38°25'N 141°17'E
Isiro Dem. Rep. Congo 83 B5 .......... 2°46'N 27°36'E
İskenderun Turkey 51 L3 .......... 36°34'N 36°08'E
İskenderun Körfezi b. Turkey 51 K3 .......... 36°38'N 35°54'E
İskûr r. Bulgaria 50 F6 .......... 43°44'N 24°27'E
Isla r. Ang. Scotland 17 F1 .......... 56°32'N 3°22'W
Isla r. Mor. Scotland 17 F2 .......... 57°31'N 2°47'W
Islamabad Pakistan 96 D7 .......... 33°42'N 73°08'E
Islandmagee pen. Northern Ireland 14 D2 .......... 54°50'N 5°41'W
Islas Malvinas is S. Atlantic Oc. 73 D1 .......... 50°55'S 59°36'W
Islay i. Scotland 14 C3 .......... 55°48'N 6°20'W
Isle of Anglesey d. Wales 21 C3 .......... 53°18'N 4°23'W
Isle of Wight d. England 21 E2 .......... 50°41'N 1°18'W
Isles of Scilly d. England 21 B1 .......... 49°55'N 6°17'W
Isna Egypt 49 J2 .......... 25°17'N 32°33'E
Isparta Turkey 51 I3 .......... 37°46'N 30°32'E
Israel Asia 49 J3 .......... 32°12'N 34°48'E
Istanbul Turkey 51 H5 .......... 41°07'N 28°58'E
Istra pen. Croatia 46 E1 .......... 45°12'N 13°53'E
Itabuna Brazil 72 F5 .......... 14°47'S 39°17'W
Itaituba Brazil 72 D6 .......... 4°16'S 56°00'W
Itajaí Brazil 73 E4 .......... 26°52'S 48°41'W
Italy Europe 48 F5 .......... 41°46'N 14°35'E
Itambé, Pico de mt. Brazil 72 E5 .......... 18°23'S 43°20'W
Itapetininga Brazil 73 E4 .......... 23°35'S 48°03'W
Itiquira r. Brazil 72 D5 .......... 17°18'S 56°20'W
Iul'tin Russia 55 T4 .......... 67°51'N 178°47'W
Ivalo Finland 43 F5 .......... 68°39'N 27°32'E
Ivano-Frankivs'k Ukraine 47 K3 .......... 48°55'N 24°43'E
Ivanovo Russia 52 E3 .......... 56°59'N 40°59'E
Ivatsevichy Belarus 47 K5 .......... 52°43'N 25°21'E
Ivdel' Russia 52 G4 .......... 60°38'N 60°26'E
Ivittuut Greenland 61 N4 .......... 61°13'N 48°10'W
Ivory Coast Africa 84 D2 .......... 7°35'N 4°22'W
Ivybridge England 11 D2 .......... 50°23'N 3°55'W
Iwaki Japan 104 D3 .......... 37°03'N 140°53'E
Iwo Nigeria 84 E2 .......... 7°38'N 4°10'E
Ixworth England 9 F3 .......... 52°18'N 0°50'E
Izabal, Lago de l. Guatemala 66 G4 .......... 15°36'N 89°08'W
Izhevsk Russia 52 F3 .......... 56°48'N 53°10'E
Izhma Russia 52 F4 .......... 65°01'N 53°56'E
Izmayil Ukraine 49 I6 .......... 45°21'N 28°51'E
İzmir Turkey 50 G4 .......... 38°24'N 27°10'E
İzmir Körfezi g. Turkey 50 G4 .......... 38°30'N 26°44'E
İzmit Turkey 51 H5 .......... 40°46'N 29°56'E
Izu-shotō is Japan 104 C2 .......... 34°24'N 139°14'E
Izyum Ukraine 53 D2 .......... 49°13'N 37°16'E

## J

Jabalón r. Spain 45 C3 .......... 38°53'N 4°05'W
Jabalpur India 96 E5 .......... 23°10'N 79°57'E
Jablah Syria 51 K2 .......... 35°21'N 35°56'E
Jaca Spain 45 E5 .......... 42°34'N 0°33'W
Jackson U.S.A. 63 H3 .......... 32°19'N 90°12'W
Jacksonville U.S.A. 63 J3 .......... 30°18'N 81°42'W
Jacmel Haiti 67 J4 .......... 18°16'N 72°32'W
Jacobabad Pakistan 96 C6 .......... 28°15'N 68°29'E
Jādū Libya 48 F3 .......... 31°58'N 12°04'E
Jaén Spain 45 D2 .......... 37°46'N 3°47'W
Jaffna Sri Lanka 96 E2 .......... 9°41'N 79°59'E
Jagdalpur India 96 F4 .......... 19°04'N 82°07'E
Jahrom Iran 95 H5 .......... 28°31'N 53°33'E
Jaipur India 96 E6 .......... 26°51'N 75°50'E
Jaisalmer India 96 D6 .......... 26°52'N 70°56'E
Jajce Bos. and Herz. 50 B7 .......... 44°21'N 17°16'E
Jakarta Indonesia 102 D2 .......... 6°07'S 106°48'E
Jakobstad Finland 43 E3 .......... 63°40'N 22°42'E
Jalālābād Afgh. 95 L6 .......... 34°26'N 70°28'E
Jalandhar India 96 E7 .......... 31°18'N 75°40'E
Jalgaon India 96 E5 .......... 21°01'N 75°41'E
Jalisco d. Mexico 66 D4 .......... 19°59'N 104°18'W
Jalna India 96 E4 .......... 19°49'N 75°57'E
Jalón r. Spain 45 E4 .......... 41°47'N 1°02'W
Jālū Libya 85 G4 .......... 29°03'N 21°33'E
Jamaica Central America 67 I4 .......... 18°30'N 77°19'W
Jamaica Channel Haiti/Jamaica 67 I4 .......... 18°29'N 75°24'W
Jambi Indonesia 102 C3 .......... 1°37'S 103°37'E
James r. U.S.A. 62 G5 .......... 42°50'N 97°15'W
James Bay Canada 61 J3 .......... 53°23'N 80°25'W
James Shoal S. China Sea 102 E4 .......... 3°58'N 112°21'E
Jamestown U.S.A. 62 G6 .......... 46°53'N 98°43'W
Jammu India 96 D7 .......... 32°42'N 74°56'E
Jammu and Kashmir d. India 96 E7 .......... 33°33'N 75°10'E
Jamnagar India 96 D5 .......... 22°26'N 70°06'E
Jampur Pakistan 96 D6 .......... 29°37'N 70°41'E
Jämsänkoski Finland 43 F3 .......... 61°56'N 25°11'E
Jamshedpur India 96 G5 .......... 22°46'N 86°12'E
Jandía hill Canary Islands 45 Y2 .......... 28°06'N 14°21'W
Jan Mayen i. Arctic Oc. 34 D6 .......... 72°00'N 8°00'W
Japan Asia 104 C3 .......... 34°48'N 133°17'E
Japan, Sea of N. Pacific Oc. 104 B3 .......... 39°13'N 133°37'E
Japurá r. Brazil 72 C6 .......... 3°05'S 64°45'W
Jardines de la Reina, Archipiélago de los is Cuba 67 I5 .......... 20°46'N 79°01'W
Järpen Sweden 43 C3 .......... 63°22'N 13°28'E
Järvenpää Finland 43 F3 .......... 60°29'N 25°06'E
Jasper Canada 60 G3 .......... 52°53'N 118°05'W
Jastrzębie-Zdrój Poland 46 H3 .......... 49°57'N 18°35'E
Java i. Indonesia 102 D2 .......... 8°12'S 107°16'E
Java Sea Indonesia 102 E3 .......... 4°56'S 110°49'E
Jawhar Somalia 85 I2 .......... 2°43'N 45°27'E
Jaya, Puncak mt. Indonesia 103 J3 .......... 4°03'S 137°12'E
Jayapura Indonesia 103 K3 .......... 2°34'S 140°42'E
Jāzān Saudi Arabia 94 F3 .......... 16°56'N 42°30'E
Jaz Mūrīān, Hāmūn-e l. Iran 95 I5 .......... 27°23'N 58°47'E
Jebel Abyad Plateau f. Sudan 94 C3 .......... 19°25'N 28°59'E
Jedburgh Scotland 15 G3 .......... 55°29'N 2°33'W
Jeddah Saudi Arabia 94 E4 .......... 21°30'N 39°08'E
Jefferson City U.S.A. 63 H4 .......... 38°37'N 92°11'W
Jelenia Góra Poland 46 F4 .......... 50°55'N 15°44'E
Jelgava Latvia 43 E2 .......... 56°39'N 23°44'E
Jember Indonesia 102 E2 .......... 8°05'S 113°45'E
Jena Germany 46 D4 .......... 50°56'N 11°36'E
Jendouba Tunisia 48 E4 .......... 36°28'N 8°47'E
Jeonju S. Korea 99 N5 .......... 35°51'N 127°09'E
Jequié Brazil 72 E5 .......... 13°48'S 40°00'W
Jequitinhonha r. Brazil 72 E5 .......... 15°51'S 38°52'W

Jérémie Haiti 67 J4 .......... 18°38'N 74°
Jerez de la Frontera Spain 45 B2 .......... 36°41'N 6°
Jerid, Chott el f. Tunisia 48 E3 .......... 33°38'N 8°
Jersey i. Channel Is 11 Z8 .......... 49°16'N 2°
Jerusalem Israel/West Bank 49 K3 .......... 31°47'N 35°
Jesup U.S.A. 63 J3 .......... 31°34'N 81°
Jhang Pakistan 95 L6 .......... 31°17'N 72°
Jhansi India 96 E6 .......... 25°27'N 78°
Jharkhand d. India 96 G5 .......... 23°36'N 85°
Jiamusi China 99 O7 .......... 46°47'N 130°
Ji'an China 99 K3 .......... 27°09'N 114°
Jiangmen China 99 K2 .......... 22°35'N 113°
Jiangsu d. China 99 L4 .......... 33°10'N 119°
Jiangxi d. China 99 L3 .......... 27°21'N 115°
Jiaozuo China 99 K5 .......... 35°12'N 113°
Jiaxing China 99 M4 .......... 30°46'N 120°
Jiayi Taiwan 99 M2 .......... 23°29'N 120°
Jiehkkevárri mt. Norway 43 D5 .......... 69°28'N 19°
Jieyang China 99 L2 .......... 23°34'N 116°
Jihlava Czechia 46 F3 .......... 49°24'N 15°
Jilf al Kabīr, Hadabat al f. Egypt 94 C4 .......... 23°12'N 25°
Jilib Somalia 85 I2 .......... 0°30'N 42°
Jilin China 99 N6 .......... 43°53'N 126°
Jilin d. China 99 N6 .......... 43°33'N 125°
Jīma Ethiopia 85 H2 .......... 7°40'N 36°
Jiménez Mexico 66 D6 .......... 27°08'N 104°
Jinan China 99 L5 .......... 36°38'N 117°
Jingdezhen China 99 L3 .......... 29°21'N 117°
Jinghong China 99 I2 .......... 21°57'N 100°
Jingmen China 99 K4 .......... 31°00'N 112°
Jingzhou China 99 K4 .......... 30°17'N 112°
Jinhua China 99 L3 .......... 29°12'N 119°
Jining Nei Mongol China 99 K6 .......... 40°54'N 113°
Jining Shandong China 99 L5 .......... 35°22'N 116°
Jinja Uganda 85 H2 .......... 0°28'N 33°
Jinjiang China 99 L2 .......... 24°49'N 118°
Jinzhou China 99 M6 .......... 41°02'N 121°
Jiparaná r. Brazil 72 C6 .......... 8°09'S 62°
Jiu r. Romania 50 E6 .......... 43°47'N 23°
Jiujiang China 99 L3 .......... 29°43'N 116°
Jiwani Pakistan 95 J5 .......... 25°07'N 61°
Jixi China 99 O7 .......... 45°13'N 130°
João Pessoa Brazil 72 F6 .......... 7°05'S 34°
Jodhpur India 96 D6 .......... 26°16'N 73°
Joensuu Finland 43 G3 .......... 62°36'N 29°
Jōetsu Japan 104 C3 .......... 37°10'N 138°
Johannesburg S. Africa 83 B2 .......... 26°09'S 27°
John o'Groats Scotland 17 F3 .......... 58°38'N 3°
Johnston Wales 10 C3 .......... 51°45'N 4°
Johnstone Scotland 14 E3 .......... 55°50'N 4°
Johor Bahru Malaysia 102 C4 .......... 1°29'N 103°
Jokkmokk Sweden 43 D4 .......... 66°37'N 19°
Jolo i. Phil. 103 G5 .......... 5°57'N 121°
Jones Sound str. Canada 61 J5 .......... 75°58'N 88°
Jönköping Sweden 43 C2 .......... 57°46'N 14°
Jonquière Canada 61 K2 .......... 48°25'N 71°
Joplin U.S.A. 63 H4 .......... 37°12'N 94°
Jordan Asia 94 E6 .......... 31°17'N 36°
Jörn Sweden 43 E4 .......... 65°03'N 20°
Jos Nigeria 84 E2 .......... 9°55'N 8°
Joseph Bonaparte Gulf Australia 108 B5 .......... 14°08'S 128°
Juan Fernández, Archipiélago is S. Pacific Oc. 68 B2 .......... 33°24'S 80°
Juàzeiro do Norte Brazil 72 F6 .......... 7°11'S 39°
Juba South Sudan 85 H2 .......... 4°53'N 31°
Jubaland Somalia 85 I2 .......... 0°45'N 39°
Jubba r. Somalia 85 I1 .......... 0°15'S 42°
Júcar r. Spain 45 E3 .......... 39°09'N 0°
Juchitán Mexico 66 E4 .......... 16°29'N 95°
Judenburg Austria 46 F2 .......... 47°11'N 14°
Juist i. Germany 42 G6 .......... 53°40'N 7°
Juliaca Peru 72 B5 .......... 15°28'S 70°
Junction City U.S.A. 62 G4 .......... 39°03'N 96°
Juneau U.S.A. 60 E3 .......... 58°19'N 134°
Jungfrau mt. Switz. 46 B2 .......... 46°33'N
Junggar Pendi basin China 98 F7 .......... 45°02'N 87°
Jura mts France/Switz. 44 F4 .......... 45°38'N
Jura i. Scotland 14 C4 .......... 56°02'N 5°
Jura, Sound of str. Scotland 14 D3 .......... 55°51'N 5°
Jurbarkas Lithuania 43 J7 .......... 55°05'N 22°
Jūrmala Latvia 47 J7 .......... 56°57'N 2°
Juruá r. Brazil 72 C6 .......... 2°39'S 65°
Juruena r. Brazil 72 D5 .......... 7°21'S 58°
Jutaí r. Brazil 72 C6 .......... 2°45'S 66°
Jutland pen. Denmark 43 B2 .......... 56°13'N
Juventud, Isla de la i. Cuba 67 H5 .......... 21°27'N 82°
Jyväskylä Finland 43 F3 .......... 62°14'N 25°

## K

K2 mt. China/Pakistan 98 D5 .......... 35°52'N
Kabaena i. Indonesia 103 G2 .......... 5°15'S 12
Kabalo Dem. Rep. Congo 83 B4 .......... 6°02'S 2
Kābul Afgh. 95 K6 .......... 34°30'N 6
Kabwe Zambia 83 B3 .......... 14°27'S 2
Kachchh, Gulf of India 96 C5 .......... 22°35'N 6
Kachug Russia 55 L3 .......... 53°54'N 10
Kadapa India 96 E3 .......... 14°29'N 7
Kadavu i. Fiji 109 G5 .......... 19°00'S 17
Kadıköy Turkey 51 H5 .......... 40°59'N 2
Kadirli Turkey 51 L3 .......... 37°22'N 3
Kadugli Sudan 85 G3 .......... 11°01'N 2
Kaduna Nigeria 84 E3 .......... 10°30'N
Kadzherom Russia 52 F4 .......... 64°42'N 5
Kaesŏng N. Korea 99 N5 .......... 37°58'N 12
Kafireas, Akra pt Greece 50 F4 .......... 38°10'N 2
Kaga Bandoro C.A.R. 85 F2 .......... 6°57'N 1
Kagoshima Japan 104 B2 .......... 31°34'N 13
Kahramanmaraş Turkey 51 L3 .......... 37°35'N 3
Kai, Kepulauan is Indonesia 103 I2 .......... 5°26'S 13
Kaifeng China 99 K4 .......... 34°43'N 11
Kaimana Indonesia 103 I3 .......... 3°42'S 13
Kairouan Tunisia 48 F4 .......... 35°41'N 1
Kaiserslautern Germany 46 B3 .......... 49°27'N
Kaiyuan China 99 I2 .......... 23°40'N 10
Kajaani Finland 43 F4 .......... 64°13'N 2
Kakhovs'ke Vodoskhovyshche resr Ukraine 47 O2 .......... 47°00'N 34
Kakinada India 96 F4 .......... 16°57'N 8
Kaktovik U.S.A. 60 D5 .......... 70°04'N 14
Kakuma Kenya 85 H2 .......... 3°40'N 3
Kalaburagi India 96 E4 .......... 17°20'N 7
Kalach-na-Donu Russia 53 E2 .......... 48°42'N 4
Kalahari Desert Africa 83 B2 .......... 23°28'S 2
Kalajoki Finland 43 E4 .......... 64°15'N 2

...naria Greece 50 E5 ............... 40°36'N 22°57'E
...nata Greece 50 E3 ............... 37°02'N 22°07'E
... Afgh. 95 K6 ............... 32°05'N 66°58'E
...ik Turkey 51 J5 ............... 40°05'N 33°26'E
...nie Dem. Rep. Congo 83 B4 ......... 5°56'S 29°08'E
...orlie Australia 108 B3 ......... 30°50'S 121°30'E
...kra, Nos pt Bulgaria 51 H6 ....... 43°22'N 28°28'E
...antan f. Indonesia 102 E3 ....... 2°10'S 111°35'E
...ngrad Russia 46 I6 ............... 54°42'N 20°31'E
...kavichy Belarus 47 M5 ......... 52°08'N 29°15'E
...bell U.S.A. 62 D6 ............... 48°11'N 114°19'W
... Poland 46 H4 ............... 51°46'N 18°05'E
...ilven r. Sweden 43 E4 ......... 65°51'N 20°38'E
...resi l. Finland 43 F3 ......... 62°47'N 27°47'E
...ön l. Sweden 43 C3 ......... 63°37'N 13°00'E
...ar Sweden 43 D2 ............... 56°40'N 16°22'E
... U.S.A. 60 C4 ............... 64°20'N 158°52'W
...dborg Denmark 43 B1 ......... 55°41'N 11°06'E
...h Ukraine 47 K3 ............... 49°02'N 24°22'E
...r. Russia 52 F3 ............... 56°01'N 53°46'E
...ishi Japan 104 D3 ............... 39°16'N 141°53'E
...n Turkey 51 J4 ............... 39°22'N 33°43'E
...hatka Peninsula Russia 55 Q3 .... 56°10'N 159°12'E
...n', Gory mts Russia 55 K4 ....... 66°00'N 95°00'E
...nskoye Russia 55 R4 ......... 62°33'N 166°10'E
...nsk-Ural'skiy Russia 52 G3 ..... 56°28'N 61°48'E
...na Dem. Rep. Congo 83 B4 ........ 8°44'S 24°57'E
...n'-Kashyrs'kyy Ukraine 47 K4 .... 51°37'N 24°58'E
...oops Canada 60 F3 ......... 50°41'N 120°21'W
...ala Uganda 85 H2 ............... 0°20'N 32°34'E
...en Neth. 42 E5 ............... 52°33'N 5°55'E
...ông Cham Cambodia 102 D6 ....... 11°59'N 105°26'E
...ôt Cambodia 102 C6 ......... 10°36'N 104°12'E
...yanets'-Podil's'kyy Ukraine 47 L3 ... 48°41'N 26°35'E
...shin Russia 53 E3 ............... 50°06'N 45°25'E
...ga Dem. Rep. Congo 83 B4 ....... 5°51'S 22°22'E
...n Russia 52 E3 ............... 55°30'N 47°28'E
...awa Japan 104 C3 ......... 36°34'N 136°39'E
...ipuram India 96 E3 ......... 12°51'N 79°43'E
...hār Afgh. 95 K6 ......... 31°37'N 65°47'E
...alaksha Russia 43 H4 ......... 67°10'N 32°23'E
...alakshskiy Zaliv g. Russia 43 H4 ... 66°38'N 33°25'E
...ra Turkey 51 I5 ......... 41°04'N 30°08'E
... Sri Lanka 96 F2 ......... 7°19'N 80°34'E
...l Turkey 51 L4 ......... 39°14'N 37°23'E
...roo Island Australia 108 C3 ..... 35°48'S 137°11'E
...var Iran 95 G6 ......... 34°29'N 47°51'E
...henjunga mt. India/Nepal 96 G6 .... 27°41'N 88°12'E
...ling China 97 J7 ......... 30°03'N 101°56'E
...an, Kepulauan is Indonesia 102 F2 ... 5°26'S 115°13'E
...rttivaq str. Greenland 61 P5 ..... 70°31'N 24°44'W
...qsualujjuaq Canada 61 L3 ..... 58°35'N 65°45'W
...qsujuaq Canada 61 K4 ......... 61°34'N 71°56'W
...nar China 98 F3 ......... 28°30'N 89°33'E
...Poluostrov pen. Russia 52 E4 .... 66°50'N 44°50'E
...Nos, Mys c. Russia 52 E4 ....... 68°00'N 43°00'E
...anpää Finland 43 E3 ......... 61°49'N 22°25'E
...kee U.S.A. 63 I5 ......... 41°07'N 87°51'W
...n Guinea 84 D3 ......... 10°23'N 9°19'W
...r India 96 F3 ......... 20°16'N 81°32'E
...Nigeria 84 E3 ......... 12°01'N 8°31'E
...r India 96 F6 ......... 26°27'N 80°24'E
...s d. U.S.A. 62 G4 ......... 38°35'N 98°34'W
...s r. U.S.A. 62 H4 ......... 39°07'N 94°40'W
...s City U.S.A. 63 H4 ......... 39°11'N 94°45'W
...Russia 55 K3 ......... 56°10'N 95°43'E
...nari Burkina Faso 84 E3 ....... 12°29'N 1°03'E
...n atoll Kiribati 109 H6 ....... 2°44'S 171°42'W
...Botswana 83 B2 ......... 24°58'S 25°21'E
...iung Taiwan 99 M2 ......... 22°39'N 120°20'E
...veld f. Namibia 83 A3 ......... 17°41'S 12°33'E
...k Senegal 84 C3 ......... 16°09'N 16°04'W
...vár Hungary 46 G2 ......... 46°22'N 17°48'E
...kasing Canada 61 J2 ......... 49°26'N 82°26'W
...ik Turkey 51 J5 ......... 41°11'N 32°38'E
...tak Kazakhstan 54 H2 ......... 49°55'N 60°09'E
...ni Pakistan 96 C5 ......... 24°51'N 67°03'E
...nda Kazakhstan 54 I2 ......... 49°52'N 73°04'E
...nskiy Zaliv b. Russia 55 R3 ..... 59°32'N 164°48'E
...ran 95 H7 ......... 35°45'N 50°54'E
...elong i. Indonesia 103 H4 ....... 4°22'N 126°43'E
...ram Range mts Asia 96 D8 ....... 36°18'N 74°54'E
...um Desert Turkmenistan 54 G2 .... 38°58'N 60°05'E
...n Turkey 51 J3 ......... 37°11'N 33°13'E
...ay China 98 E7 ......... 45°31'N 84°54'E
...n Russia 96 G6 ......... 34°14'N 46°16'E
...nar Turkey 51 J3 ......... 37°43'N 33°33'E
...urg Namibia 83 A2 ......... 28°01'S 18°45'E
...ea Russia 54 I3 ......... 74°13'N 71°44'E
...uk Russia 54 I3 ......... 53°43'N 78°03'E
...l Iraq 94 F6 ......... 36°36'N 44°01'E
...g Hungary 46 I2 ......... 47°19'N 20°52'E
...sa Congo 54 D4 ......... 39°21'N 21°55'E
...Estonia 43 E2 ......... 58°59'N 22°45'E
...nali Bulgaria 50 F5 ......... 41°39'N 25°22'E
...le Sudan 85 H3 ......... 18°31'N 31°49'E
..., Lake resr Zambia/Zimbabwe 83 B3 ... 17°37'S 27°17'E
...o Bulgaria 50 F6 ......... 42°39'N 24°48'E
...y Vary Czechia 46 E4 ......... 50°14'N 12°53'E
...am Sweden 43 C2 ......... 56°11'N 14°52'E
...rona Sweden 43 C2 ......... 59°20'N 14°33'E
...ona Sweden 43 C2 ......... 56°12'N 15°38'E
...uhe Germany 46 C3 ......... 49°01'N 8°24'E
...ad Sweden 43 C2 ......... 59°23'N 13°31'E
...y l. Norway 43 A2 ......... 59°11'N 5°15'E
...taka d. India 96 E4 ......... 15°37'N 75°29'E
...pat Bulgaria 50 G6 ......... 42°39'N 25°19'E
... Eritrea 85 H3 ......... 17°41'N 38°23'E
...hos i. Greece 50 G2 ......... 35°36'N 27°10'E
...nisi Greece 50 G2 ......... 35°30'N 27°13'E
...aka Turkey 50 G4 ......... 38°27'N 27°06'E
...la Finland 43 F3 ......... 62°53'N 24°48'E
...Turkey 51 H5 ......... 40°54'N 29°11'E
...Russia 53 G3 ......... 53°01'N 60°37'E
...skoye Russia 55 M3 ......... 51°30'N 114°25'E
...Zambia 83 C3 ......... 10°12'S 31°12'E
...Uganda 85 H2 ......... 0°10'N 30°05'E
...Iran 95 H6 ......... 33°58'N 51°30'E

Kashi China 98 D5 ............... 39°29'N 76°03'E
Kashiwazaki Japan 104 C3 ....... 37°22'N 138°34'E
Käshmar Iran 95 I7 ......... 35°10'N 58°22'E
Kashmir Asia 96 E8 ......... 35°00'N 77°00'E
Kasos i. Greece 50 G2 ......... 35°23'N 26°52'E
Kassala Sudan 85 H3 ......... 15°24'N 36°20'E
Kassel Germany 46 C4 ......... 51°19'N 9°30'E
Kasserine Tunisia 48 E4 ......... 35°11'N 8°50'E
Kastamonu Turkey 51 J5 ......... 41°22'N 33°46'E
Kastelli Greece 50 E2 ......... 35°30'N 23°38'E
Kastoria Greece 50 D5 ......... 40°31'N 21°16'E
Kastsyukovichy Belarus 47 O5 ..... 53°21'N 32°09'E
Katerini Greece 50 E5 ......... 40°16'N 22°31'E
Kate's Needle mt. Canada/U.S.A. 60 E3 ... 57°02'N 132°02'W
Katha Myanmar 97 I5 ......... 24°11'N 96°20'E
Katherine Australia 108 C5 ....... 14°28'S 132°18'E
Kathmandu Nepal 96 G6 ......... 27°42'N 85°18'E
Katima Mulilo Namibia 83 B3 ....... 17°32'S 24°15'E
Kati Thanda-Lake Eyre (North) Australia 108 C4
......... 28°24'S 137°16'E
Kati Thanda-Lake Eyre (South) Australia 108 C4
......... 28°30'S 137°25'E
Katni India 96 F5 ......... 23°50'N 80°23'E
Katowice Poland 46 H4 ......... 50°16'N 19°01'E
Kätrīnā, Jabal mt. Egypt 49 J2 ..... 28°31'N 33°58'E
Katrine, Loch l. Scotland 14 E4 ... 56°15'N 4°34'W
Katrineholm Sweden 43 D2 ....... 58°59'N 16°14'E
Katsina Nigeria 84 E3 ......... 12°59'N 7°36'E
Kattegat str. Denmark/Sweden 43 B2 ... 56°49'N 11°21'E
Kauhajoki Finland 43 E3 ......... 62°25'N 22°11'E
Kaunas Lithuania 43 E1 ......... 54°54'N 23°55'E
Kaura-Namoda Nigeria 84 E3 ....... 12°37'N 6°35'E
Kavala Greece 50 F5 ......... 40°56'N 24°23'E
Kavarna Bulgaria 51 H6 ......... 43°26'N 28°19'E
Kavīr, Dasht-e des. Iran 95 H6 ..... 34°36'N 54°41'E
Kawasaki Japan 104 C3 ......... 35°32'N 139°43'E
Kawm Umbū Egypt 49 J1 ......... 24°28'N 32°55'E
Kayes Mali 84 C3 ......... 14°26'N 11°27'W
Kayseri Turkey 51 K4 ......... 38°43'N 35°29'E
Kazach'ye Russia 55 O5 ......... 70°45'N 136°09'E
Kazakhstan Asia 54 H2 ......... 49°18'N 82°53'E
Kazan' Russia 52 E3 ......... 55°47'N 49°07'E
Kazanlak Bulgaria 50 F6 ......... 42°37'N 25°23'E
Kazbek mt. Georgia/Russia 53 E2 ... 42°45'N 44°34'E
Käzerün Iran 95 H5 ......... 29°37'N 51°39'E
Kazym-Mys Russia 52 G4 ......... 64°43'N 65°36'E
Kea i. Greece 50 F3 ......... 37°38'N 24°24'E
Keady Northern Ireland 14 C2 ..... 54°15'N 6°42'W
Kearney U.S.A. 62 G5 ......... 40°43'N 99°05'W
Keban Baraji resr Turkey 51 M4 ..... 38°53'N 38°55'E
Kebkabiya Sudan 94 B2 ......... 13°37'N 24°06'E
Kebnekaise mt. Sweden 43 D4 ....... 67°55'N 18°31'E
Kebock Head Scotland 16 C3 ....... 58°03'N 6°21'W
Keçiören Turkey 51 J5 ......... 40°00'N 32°50'E
Kecskemét Hungary 46 H2 ......... 46°55'N 19°42'E
Keetmanshoop Namibia 83 A2 ....... 26°35'S 18°09'E
Keewatin Canada 63 H6 ......... 49°46'N 94°34'W
Keflavík Iceland 43 X2 ......... 64°00'N 22°34'W
Kegworth England 8 D2 ......... 52°50'N 1°17'W
Keighley England 13 F2 ......... 53°52'N 1°55'W
Keitele l. Finland 43 F3 ......... 62°52'N 26°00'E
Keith Scotland 17 G2 ......... 57°33'N 2°57'W
Kelifskiy Uzboy f. Turkmenistan 95 J7 ... 38°07'N 63°33'E
Kelkit r. Turkey 51 L5 ......... 40°51'N 36°26'E
Kellett, Cape Canada 60 F5 ....... 71°59'N 125°59'W
Kells Ireland 18 E3 ......... 53°44'N 6°52'W
Kelmė Lithuania 47 J6 ......... 55°38'N 22°56'E
Kélo Chad 84 F2 ......... 9°18'N 15°49'E
Kelowna Canada 60 G2 ......... 49°53'N 119°29'W
Kelso Scotland 15 G3 ......... 55°36'N 2°26'W
Keluang Malaysia 102 C4 ......... 1°59'N 103°19'E
Kelvedon England 9 F2 ......... 51°50'N 0°42'E
Kem' Russia 52 D4 ......... 64°57'N 34°34'E
Kemerovo Russia 54 J3 ......... 55°23'N 86°01'E
Kemi Finland 43 F4 ......... 65°46'N 24°33'E
Kemijärvi Finland 43 F4 ......... 66°43'N 27°23'E
Kemijärvi l. Finland 43 F4 ....... 66°35'N 27°25'E
Kemijoki r. Finland 43 F4 ......... 65°47'N 24°32'E
Kemnay Scotland 17 G2 ......... 57°14'N 2°27'W
Kempston England 9 E3 ......... 52°07'N 0°30'W
Kempten Germany 46 D2 ......... 47°43'N 10°18'E
Kenai U.S.A. 60 C4 ......... 60°35'N 151°16'W
Kendal England 12 E3 ......... 54°20'N 2°45'W
Kendari Indonesia 103 G3 ......... 3°59'S 122°35'E
Kendawangan Indonesia 102 E3 ..... 2°30'S 110°14'E
Kengtung Myanmar 97 I5 ......... 21°18'N 99°38'E
Kenilworth England 8 D3 ......... 52°21'N 1°35'W
Kénitra Morocco 84 D5 ......... 34°16'N 6°33'W
Kenmare Ireland 18 B1 ......... 51°53'N 9°35'W
Kenmare River inlet Ireland 18 A1 ... 51°43'N 10°03'W
Kennet r. England 8 D2 ......... 51°27'N 0°57'W
Kenora Canada 61 I2 ......... 49°47'N 94°30'W
Kent d. England 21 F2 ......... 51°12'N 0°37'E
Kent r. England 12 E3 ......... 54°15'N 2°48'W
Kentucky d. U.S.A. 63 J4 ......... 37°24'N 84°54'W
Kentucky r. U.S.A. 63 I4 ......... 38°41'N 85°10'W
Kenya Africa 85 H2 ......... 0°59'N 37°32'E
Kenya, Mount Kenya 85 H1 ......... 0°08'S 37°18'E
Kerala d. India 96 E3 ......... 11°31'N 75°51'E
Kerch Ukraine 49 K6 ......... 45°22'N 36°29'E
Kerema P.N.G. 108 D6 ......... 7°56'S 145°48'E
Keren Eritrea 94 E3 ......... 15°46'N 38°28'E
Kerinci, Gunung vol. Indonesia 102 C3 ... 1°42'S 101°15'E
Kerki Turkmenistan 95 K7 ......... 37°51'N 65°13'E
Kerkyra Greece 50 C4 ......... 39°37'N 19°55'E
Kerma Sudan 94 D3 ......... 19°37'N 30°26'E
Kermadec Islands S. Pacific Oc. 109 H3 ... 30°19'S 178°19'W
Kermān Iran 95 I5 ......... 30°17'N 57°04'E
Kermān Desert Iran 95 I5 ......... 28°27'N 59°19'E
Kermānshāh Iran 95 G6 ......... 34°19'N 47°02'E
Kerry d. Ireland 18 B2 ......... 52°09'N 9°28'W
Kerry Head Ireland 18 B2 ......... 52°25'N 9°57'W
Keşan Turkey 50 G5 ......... 40°51'N 26°37'E
Kesennuma Japan 104 D3 ......... 38°54'N 141°33'E
Kessingland England 9 G3 ......... 52°25'N 1°43'E
Keswick England 12 D3 ......... 54°36'N 3°07'W
Ketapang Indonesia 102 E3 ....... 1°50'S 110°00'E
Ketchikan U.S.A. 60 E3 ......... 55°20'N 131°38'W
Kettering England 8 E3 ......... 52°24'N 0°44'W
Keweenaw Bay U.S.A. 63 I6 ....... 46°52'N 88°26'W
Key, Lough l. Ireland 18 C4 ....... 54°01'N 8°15'W
Keynsham England 8 C2 ......... 51°25'N 2°30'W
Khabarovsk Russia 55 O2 ......... 48°30'N 135°08'E
Khadyzhensk Russia 51 M7 ......... 44°25'N 39°32'E

Khambhat, Gulf of India 96 D4 ..... 19°59'N 71°29'E
Khānābād Afgh. 95 K7 ......... 36°42'N 69°09'E
Khandwa India 96 E5 ......... 21°49'N 76°21'E
Khanewal Pakistan 95 L6 ......... 30°19'N 71°59'E
Khanka, Lake China/Russia 99 O6 ... 44°54'N 132°45'E
Khanpur Pakistan 96 D6 ......... 28°37'N 70°41'E
Khantayskoye, Ozero l. Russia 55 K4 ... 68°25'N 91°57'E
Khanty-Mansiysk Russia 52 G4 ..... 61°05'N 69°01'E
Kharagpur India 96 G5 ......... 22°20'N 87°20'E
Kharkiv Ukraine 47 Q3 ......... 49°59'N 36°16'E
Khartoum Sudan 85 H3 ......... 15°32'N 32°32'E
Khasavyurt Russia 53 E2 ......... 43°14'N 46°35'E
Khāsh Iran 95 J5 ......... 28°12'N 61°14'E
Khashm el Girba Sudan 85 H3 ..... 14°56'N 35°51'E
Khatanga Russia 55 L5 ......... 71°57'N 102°24'E
Khatangskiy Zaliv b. Russia 55 L5 ... 73°19'N 107°17'E
Khayelitsha S. Africa 83 A1 ....... 34°05'S 18°39'E
Khenchela Algeria 48 E4 ......... 35°26'N 7°10'E
Khenifra Morocco 48 B3 ......... 32°58'N 5°37'W
Kherson Ukraine 49 J6 ......... 46°39'N 32°37'E
Kheta r. Russia 55 L5 ......... 71°55'N 102°04'E
Khimki Russia 47 Q6 ......... 55°53'N 37°26'E
Khmel'nyts'kyy Ukraine 47 L3 ..... 49°25'N 26°59'E
Khon Kaen Thailand 102 C7 ....... 16°27'N 102°52'E
Khorinsk Russia 99 J8 ......... 52°09'N 109°48'E
Khorramābād Iran 95 G6 ......... 33°27'N 48°19'E
Khorugh Tajikistan 95 L7 ......... 37°29'N 71°35'E
Khoshgort Russia 52 G4 ......... 62°22'N 65°43'E
Khouribga Morocco 48 B3 ......... 32°53'N 6°55'W
Khowst Afgh. 95 K6 ......... 33°22'N 69°59'E
Khromtau Kazakhstan 53 F3 ....... 50°10'N 58°22'E
Khūjand Tajikistan 98 B6 ......... 40°15'N 69°38'E
Khulna Bangl. 97 G5 ......... 22°50'N 89°33'E
Khunsar Iran 95 H6 ......... 33°10'N 50°17'E
Khust Ukraine 47 J3 ......... 48°10'N 23°18'E
Khvoy Iran 94 F7 ......... 38°33'N 44°58'E
Khyber Pass Afgh./Pakistan 95 L6 ... 34°08'N 71°12'E
Kiantajärvi l. Finland 43 G4 ....... 64°58'N 29°06'E
Kičevo North Macedonia 50 D5 ..... 41°30'N 20°58'E
Kidderminster England 8 C3 ....... 52°23'N 2°15'W
Kidsgrove England 13 E2 ......... 53°05'N 2°14'W
Kidwelly Wales 10 C3 ......... 51°44'N 4°18'W
Kiel Germany 46 D6 ......... 54°19'N 10°08'E
Kiel Canal Germany 43 B1 ......... 54°10'N 9°27'E
Kielce Poland 46 I4 ......... 50°51'N 20°37'E
Kielder Water resr England 13 E4 ... 55°12'N 2°34'W
Kieler Bucht b. Germany 46 D6 ..... 54°27'N 10°41'E
Kiev Ukraine 47 N4 ......... 50°26'N 30°34'E
Kigali Rwanda 85 H1 ......... 1°59'S 30°05'E
Kigoma Tanzania 83 B4 ......... 4°51'S 29°40'E
Kii-suidō str. Japan 104 B2 ....... 33°57'N 134°49'E
Kikinda Serbia 50 D7 ......... 45°50'N 20°28'E
Kikori P.N.G. 108 D6 ......... 7°22'S 144°14'E
Kikwit Dem. Rep. Congo 83 A4 ..... 5°03'S 18°50'E
Kilbrannan Sound str. Scotland 14 D3 ... 55°31'N 5°27'W
Kilcoole Ireland 10 A5 ......... 53°06'N 6°03'W
Kilcormac Ireland 18 D3 ......... 53°10'N 7°44'W
Kilcullen Ireland 18 E3 ......... 53°08'N 6°45'W
Kildare Ireland 18 E3 ......... 53°09'N 6°55'W
Kildare d. Ireland 18 E3 ......... 53°17'N 6°47'W
Kilimanjaro vol. Tanzania 83 C4 ... 3°03'S 37°21'E
Kilis Turkey 51 L3 ......... 36°43'N 37°07'E
Kilkee Ireland 18 B2 ......... 52°41'N 9°38'W
Kilkeel Northern Ireland 14 D2 ..... 54°04'N 5°59'W
Kilkenny Ireland 18 D2 ......... 52°39'N 7°15'W
Kilkenny d. Ireland 18 D2 ......... 52°31'N 7°14'W
Kilkis Greece 50 E5 ......... 40°59'N 22°52'E
Killala Bay Ireland 18 B4 ......... 54°16'N 9°08'W
Killarney Ireland 18 B2 ......... 52°03'N 9°30'W
Killeen U.S.A. 62 G3 ......... 31°08'N 97°44'W
Killin Scotland 14 E4 ......... 56°28'N 4°19'W
Killorglin Ireland 18 B2 ......... 52°06'N 9°47'W
Killybegs Ireland 18 C4 ......... 54°38'N 8°27'W
Kilmallock Ireland 18 C2 ......... 52°24'N 8°35'W
Kilmarnock Scotland 14 E3 ....... 55°37'N 4°30'W
Kilmelford Scotland 14 D4 ......... 56°16'N 5°28'W
Kilmichael Point Ireland 18 E2 ..... 52°44'N 6°08'W
Kilrea Northern Ireland 14 C2 ..... 54°57'N 6°33'W
Kilrush Ireland 18 B2 ......... 52°38'N 9°29'W
Kilsyth Scotland 15 E3 ......... 55°59'N 4°03'W
Kilwinning Scotland 14 E3 ......... 55°40'N 4°42'W
Kimberley S. Africa 83 B2 ......... 28°44'S 24°46'E
Kimberley Plateau f. Australia 108 B5 ... 17°26'S 127°05'E
Kimch'aek N. Korea 99 N6 ......... 40°41'N 129°12'E
Kinabalu, Gunung mt. Malaysia 102 F5 ... 6°04'N 116°33'E
Kinder Scout hill England 13 F2 ... 53°23'N 1°52'W
Kindersley Canada 62 F7 ......... 51°28'N 109°10'W
Kindu Dem. Rep. Congo 83 B4 ..... 2°57'S 25°53'E
Kineshma Russia 52 E3 ......... 57°27'N 42°07'E
King Abdullah Economic City Saudi Arabia 94 E4
......... 22°24'N 39°05'E
King Island Australia 108 D3 ..... 39°50'S 143°58'E
Kingman U.S.A. 62 D4 ......... 35°14'N 114°02'W
Kingsbridge England 11 D2 ....... 50°17'N 3°47'W
Kingsclere England 8 D2 ......... 51°19'N 1°14'W
Kingscourt Ireland 18 E3 ......... 53°54'N 6°48'W
King's Lynn England 9 F3 ......... 52°45'N 0°24'E
Kingsmill Group is Kiribati 109 G6 ... 1°37'S 175°52'E
Kingsnorth England 9 F2 ......... 51°07'N 0°52'E
Kings Peak U.S.A. 62 D5 ......... 40°45'N 110°23'W
Kingston Canada 61 K2 ......... 44°14'N 76°30'W
Kingston Jamaica 67 I4 ......... 18°00'N 76°47'W
Kingston upon Hull England 13 G2 ... 53°45'N 0°20'W
Kingston upon Thames England 9 E2 ... 51°25'N 0°18'W
Kingstown St Vincent 67 L3 ....... 13°10'N 61°15'W
Kingsville U.S.A. 62 G2 ......... 27°27'N 97°47'W
Kingswood England 8 C2 ......... 51°28'N 2°30'W
Kings Worthy England 8 D2 ....... 51°06'N 1°18'W
Kington England 8 B3 ......... 52°12'N 3°02'W
Kingussie Scotland 17 E2 ......... 57°05'N 4°03'W
King William Island Canada 61 I4 ... 69°10'N 97°45'W
Kinlochbervie Scotland 16 D3 ..... 58°28'N 5°03'W
Kinlochleven Scotland 16 E1 ....... 56°43'N 4°58'W
Kinloss Scotland 17 F2 ......... 57°38'N 3°34'W
Kinna Sweden 43 C2 ......... 57°31'N 12°40'E
Kinnegad Ireland 18 D3 ......... 53°27'N 7°06'W
Kinross Scotland 15 F4 ......... 56°12'N 3°25'W
Kinsale Ireland 18 C1 ......... 51°42'N 8°31'W
Kinshasa Dem. Rep. Congo 83 A4 ... 4°22'S 15°23'E
Kintore Scotland 17 G2 ......... 57°14'N 2°21'W
Kintyre pen. Scotland 14 D3 ....... 55°30'N 5°39'W
Kinubbin Northern Ireland 14 D2 ... 54°30'N 5°28'W
Kiribati Pacific Oc. 109 H6 ....... 6°00'S 164°59'W

Kirkby in Ashfield England 13 F2 ... 53°06'N 1°16'W
Kirkby Lonsdale England 12 E3 ..... 54°12'N 2°36'W
Kirkbymoorside England 13 G3 ..... 54°16'N 0°56'W
Kirkby Stephen England 13 E3 ..... 54°29'N 2°21'W
Kirkcaldy Scotland 15 F4 ......... 56°07'N 3°09'W
Kirkcolm Scotland 14 D2 ......... 54°58'N 5°05'W
Kirkconnel Scotland 15 E3 ......... 55°23'N 4°00'W
Kirkcudbright Scotland 15 E2 ..... 54°50'N 4°03'W
Kirkenes Norway 43 H5 ......... 69°43'N 30°01'E
Kirkham England 12 E2 ......... 53°47'N 2°52'W
Kirkintilloch Scotland 14 E3 ....... 55°56'N 4°09'W
Kirkkonummi Finland 43 F3 ....... 60°07'N 24°27'E
Kirkland Lake town Canada 61 J2 ... 48°10'N 80°02'W
Kırklareli Turkey 50 G5 ......... 41°44'N 27°13'E
Kirkük Iraq 94 F7 ......... 35°24'N 44°24'E
Kirkwall Scotland 17 G3 ......... 58°59'N 2°58'W
Kirov Russia 47 P6 ......... 54°04'N 34°20'E
Kirov Russia 52 E3 ......... 59°52'N 30°59'E
Kirovsk Russia 43 H4 ......... 67°37'N 33°40'E
Kirriemuir Scotland 17 F1 ......... 56°41'N 3°00'W
Kirs Russia 52 F3 ......... 59°20'N 52°13'E
Kırşehir Turkey 51 K4 ......... 39°09'N 34°09'E
Kirtlington England 8 D2 ......... 51°52'N 1°16'W
Kirton in Lindsey England 13 G2 ... 53°29'N 0°35'W
Kiruna Sweden 43 E4 ......... 67°51'N 20°14'E
Kisangani Dem. Rep. Congo 83 B5 ... 0°34'N 25°11'E
Kislovodsk Russia 49 L5 ......... 43°55'N 42°44'E
Kismaayo Somalia 85 I1 ......... 0°19'S 42°31'E
Kisoro Uganda 85 G1 ......... 1°17'S 29°45'E
Kisumu Kenya 85 H2 ......... 0°04'S 34°47'E
Kita-Kyūshū Japan 104 B2 ......... 33°52'N 130°50'E
Kitami Japan 104 D4 ......... 43°49'N 143°53'E
Kitimat Canada 60 F3 ......... 54°03'N 128°39'W
Kittilä Finland 43 F4 ......... 67°38'N 24°54'E
Kitwe Zambia 83 B3 ......... 12°48'S 28°12'E
Kiuruvesi Finland 43 F3 ......... 63°39'N 26°38'E
Kivu, Lake Dem. Rep. Congo/Rwanda 83 B4 ... 1°55'S 29°00'E
Kizel Russia 52 F3 ......... 59°03'N 57°39'E
Kızıl Daği mt. Turkey 51 M4 ....... 39°57'N 38°12'E
Kızılırmak r. Turkey 51 K5 ....... 41°49'N 35°54'E
Kladno Czechia 46 F4 ......... 50°09'N 14°08'E
Klagenfurt am Wörthersee Austria 46 F2 ... 46°38'N 14°19'E
Klaipėda Lithuania 43 E1 ......... 55°43'N 21°09'E
Klamath r. U.S.A. 62 B5 ......... 41°27'N 124°02'W
Klamath Falls town U.S.A. 62 B5 ... 42°15'N 121°46'W
Klang Malaysia 102 C4 ......... 3°02'N 101°25'E
Klazienaveen Neth. 42 F5 ......... 52°44'N 6°59'E
Kleve Germany 42 F4 ......... 51°47'N 6°08'E
Klimovo Russia 47 O5 ......... 52°23'N 32°12'E
Klin Russia 52 D3 ......... 56°20'N 36°43'E
Klintsy Russia 47 O5 ......... 52°45'N 32°15'E
Kłodzko Poland 46 G4 ......... 50°26'N 16°39'E
Klyuchevskaya, Sopka vol. Russia 55 R3 ... 56°01'N 160°41'E
Knaresborough England 13 F3 ..... 54°01'N 1°28'W
Knighton Wales 10 D4 ......... 52°20'N 3°03'W
Knin Croatia 50 B7 ......... 44°03'N 16°12'E
Knockaboy hill Ireland 18 B1 ..... 51°48'N 9°26'W
Knockadoon Head Ireland 18 D1 ... 51°53'N 7°52'W
Knockalongy hill Ireland 18 C4 ... 54°12'N 8°46'W
Knock Hill Scotland 17 G2 ......... 57°35'N 2°46'W
Knocklayd hill Northern Ireland 14 C3 ... 55°10'N 6°15'W
Knockmealdown Mountains hills Ireland 18 C2
......... 52°14'N 8°04'W
Knottingley England 13 F2 ......... 53°42'N 1°15'W
Knowle England 8 D3 ......... 52°23'N 1°44'W
Knoxville U.S.A. 63 J4 ......... 35°59'N 83°56'W
Knutsford England 13 E2 ......... 53°18'N 2°22'W
Kōbe Japan 104 C2 ......... 34°41'N 135°11'E
Koblenz Germany 46 B4 ......... 50°21'N 7°35'E
Kobroör i. Indonesia 103 I2 ....... 6°07'S 134°30'E
Kobryn Belarus 47 K5 ......... 52°12'N 24°20'E
Kočani North Macedonia 50 E5 ..... 41°55'N 22°23'E
Kochi India 96 E2 ......... 9°55'N 76°14'E
Kōchi Japan 104 B2 ......... 33°33'N 133°32'E
Kochubey Russia 53 E2 ......... 44°23'N 46°33'E
Kodiak U.S.A. 60 C3 ......... 57°46'N 152°30'W
Kodiak Island U.S.A. 60 C3 ....... 57°26'N 153°20'W
Kōfu Japan 104 C3 ......... 35°39'N 138°34'E
Køge Denmark 43 C1 ......... 55°27'N 12°11'E
Kohat Pakistan 95 L6 ......... 33°37'N 71°30'E
Kokand Uzbekistan 98 C6 ......... 40°31'N 70°57'E
Kokkola Finland 43 E3 ......... 63°51'N 23°08'E
Kokshetau Kazakhstan 54 H3 ....... 53°17'N 69°23'E
Kola Russia 43 H5 ......... 68°52'N 33°03'E
Kolaka Indonesia 103 G3 ......... 4°03'S 121°38'E
Kola Peninsula Russia 52 D4 ....... 67°29'N 34°49'E
Kolding Denmark 43 B1 ......... 55°30'N 9°28'E
Kolguyev, Ostrov i. Russia 52 E4 ... 69°07'N 49°03'E
Kolhapur India 96 D4 ......... 16°40'N 74°19'E
Kolkata India 96 G5 ......... 22°32'N 88°21'E
Kollam India 96 E2 ......... 8°53'N 76°36'E
Kołobrzeg Poland 46 F6 ......... 54°11'N 15°35'E
Kolomna Russia 53 D3 ......... 55°05'N 38°47'E
Kolomyya Ukraine 47 K3 ......... 48°32'N 25°02'E
Koluli Eritrea 94 E3 ......... 14°24'N 40°20'E
Kolvitskoye, Ozero l. Russia 43 H4 ... 67°05'N 33°30'E
Kolwezi Dem. Rep. Congo 83 B3 ... 10°42'S 25°28'E
Kolyma r. Russia 55 R4 ......... 69°22'N 161°24'E
Kolymskiy, Khrebet mts Russia 55 R4 ... 66°50'N 167°12'E
Komatsu Japan 104 C3 ......... 36°23'N 136°28'E
Komotini Greece 50 F5 ......... 41°07'N 25°24'E
Komsomolets, Ostrov i. Russia 55 K6 ... 80°42'N 94°20'E
Komsomol's'k Ukraine 47 O3 ....... 49°01'N 33°39'E
Komsomol'sk-na-Amure Russia 55 O3 ... 50°36'N 136°55'E
Kong Christian IX Land f. Greenland 61 O4
......... 66°49'N 37°44'W
Kongsberg Norway 43 B2 ......... 59°40'N 9°39'E
Kongsvinger Norway 43 C3 ......... 60°12'N 12°01'E
Konin Poland 46 H5 ......... 52°14'N 18°15'E
Konosha Russia 52 E4 ......... 60°58'N 40°15'E
Konotop Ukraine 47 O4 ......... 51°14'N 33°12'E
Konstanz Germany 46 C2 ......... 47°40'N 9°10'E
Konya Turkey 51 J3 ......... 37°52'N 32°29'E
Konzhakovskiy Kamen', Gora mt. Russia 52 F3
......... 59°37'N 59°08'E
Köping Sweden 43 D2 ......... 59°31'N 16°00'E
Koprivnica Croatia 50 G2 ......... 46°10'N 16°50'E
Korçë Albania 50 D5 ......... 40°37'N 20°47'E
Korčula i. Croatia 50 B6 ......... 42°54'N 16°56'E
Korea Bay China/N. Korea 99 M5 ... 39°05'N 124°25'E
Korea Strait Japan/S. Korea 104 A2 ... 34°12'N 128°36'E
Körfez Turkey 51 H5 ......... 40°47'N 29°42'E
Korinthiakos Kolpos str. Greece 50 E4 ... 38°16'N 22°11'E
Kōriyama Japan 104 D3 ......... 37°24'N 140°22'E
Korkuteli Turkey 51 I3 ......... 37°04'N 30°11'E

Korla China 98 F6...41°39'N 86°08'E
Köroğlu Tepesi mt. Turkey 51 J5...40°30'N 32°01'E
Korosten' Ukraine 47 M4...50°57'N 28°39'E
Koro Toro Chad 85 F3...16°05'N 18°30'E
Korsakov Russia 55 P2...46°38'N 142°45'E
Kortrijk Belgium 42 C3...50°49'N 3°16'E
Koryakskiy Khrebet mts Russia 55 S4...62°59'N 177°49'E
Koryazhma Russia 52 E4...61°19'N 47°12'E
Kos i. Greece 50 G3...36°46'N 27°07'E
Kościerzyna Poland 46 G6...54°07'N 17°59'E
Kosciuszko, Mount Australia 108 D3...36°28'S 148°15'E
Košice Slovakia 46 I3...48°43'N 21°16'E
Kosovo Europe 50 D6...42°35'N 21°00'E
Kosovska Mitrovica Kosovo 50 D6...42°52'N 20°52'E
Kostanay Kazakhstan 54 H3...53°12'N 63°40'E
Kosti Sudan 85 H3...13°09'N 32°38'E
Kostomuksha Russia 52 D4...64°34'N 30°33'E
Kostroma Russia 52 E3...57°46'N 40°58'E
Kostrzyn nad Odrą Poland 46 F5...52°35'N 14°39'E
Koszalin Poland 46 G6...54°11'N 16°11'E
Kota India 96 E6...25°10'N 75°52'E
Kota Bharu Malaysia 102 C5...6°08'N 102°16'E
Kotabumi Indonesia 102 C3...4°51'S 104°55'E
Kota Kinabalu Malaysia 102 F5...5°58'N 116°05'E
Kotel'nich Russia 52 E3...58°18'N 48°20'E
Kotel'nyy Russia 55 O5...76°00'N 137°59'E
Kotel'nyy, Ostrov i. Russia 55 O5...75°07'N 139°31'E
Kotlas Russia 52 E4...61°16'N 46°38'E
Kötlutangi pt Iceland 43 Y1...63°24'N 18°45'W
Kotuy r. Russia 55 L5...71°55'N 102°06'E
Kotzebue U.S.A. 60 B4...66°53'N 162°32'W
Kotzebue Sound str. U.S.A. 60 B4...66°33'N 163°11'W
Koundâra Guinea 84 C3...12°30'N 13°19'W
Kouvola Finland 43 F3...60°52'N 26°42'E
Kovel' Ukraine 47 K4...51°13'N 24°43'E
Kovrov Russia 52 E3...56°22'N 41°19'E
Kowloon China 102 E8...22°20'N 114°13'E
Koyang S. Korea 99 N5...37°38'N 126°49'E
Kozan Turkey 51 K3...37°28'N 35°48'E
Kozani Greece 50 D5...40°18'N 21°48'E
Kozelets' Ukraine 47 N4...50°55'N 31°07'E
Kozhikode India 96 E3...11°15'N 75°45'E
Kozyatyn Ukraine 47 M3...49°42'N 28°49'E
Krabi Thailand 102 B5...8°05'N 98°56'E
Krâchéh Cambodia 102 D6...12°27'N 106°03'E
Kragujevac Serbia 50 D7...44°01'N 20°55'E
Kraków Poland 46 H4...50°03'N 19°56'E
Kraljevo Serbia 49 H5...43°43'N 20°41'E
Kramfors Sweden 43 D3...62°56'N 17°48'E
Kranj Slovenia 46 F2...46°15'N 14°21'E
Krasino Russia 52 F5...70°44'N 54°28'E
Krasnoborsk Russia 52 E4...61°33'N 45°56'E
Krasnodar Russia 53 D2...45°02'N 38°59'E
Krasnohrad Ukraine 47 P3...49°22'N 35°28'E
Krasnokamsk Russia 52 F3...58°05'N 55°45'E
Krasnoperekops'k Ukraine 51 J7...45°57'N 33°49'E
Krasnotur'insk Russia 52 G3...59°47'N 60°13'E
Krasnoufimsk Russia 52 F3...56°36'N 57°46'E
Krasnoyarsk Russia 55 K3...56°03'N 92°50'E
Krasnyy Luch Ukraine 53 D2...48°08'N 38°55'E
Krefeld Germany 46 B4...51°20'N 6°33'E
Kremenchuk Ukraine 47 O3...49°04'N 33°25'E
Kremenchuts'ka Vodoskhovyshche resr Ukraine 47 O3
...49°18'N 32°42'E
Kretinga Lithuania 46 I6...55°53'N 21°14'E
Krishna r. India 96 F4...16°01'N 80°53'E
Kristiansand Norway 43 A2...58°08'N 7°59'E
Kristianstad Sweden 43 C2...56°02'N 14°10'E
Kristiansund Norway 43 A3...63°07'N 7°45'E
Kristinehamn Sweden 43 C2...59°19'N 14°07'E
Krk i. Croatia 50 A7...45°02'N 14°47'E
Kropotkin Russia 53 E2...45°26'N 40°34'E
Kropyvnyts'kyy Ukraine 47 O3...48°30'N 32°16'E
Krosno Poland 47 I3...49°41'N 21°46'E
Kruševac Serbia 50 D6...43°35'N 21°19'E
Krychaw Belarus 47 N5...53°44'N 31°43'E
Krymsk Russia 51 L7...44°55'N 37°59'E
Krytiko Pelagos sea Greece 50 F3...36°11'N 25°24'E
Kryvyy Rih Ukraine 47 O2...47°54'N 33°21'E
Ksabi Algeria 84 D4...28°54'N 0°47'W
Ksar el Boukhari Algeria 48 D4...35°52'N 2°45'E
Ksar el Kebir Morocco 48 B4...35°01'N 5°54'W
Kuala Lumpur Malaysia 102 C4...3°06'N 101°42'E
Kuala Terengganu Malaysia 102 C5...5°19'N 103°07'E
Kuantan Malaysia 102 C4...3°50'N 103°21'E
Kuban' r. Russia 51 L7...45°19'N 37°22'E
Kuching Malaysia 102 E4...1°32'N 110°20'E
Kugluktuk Canada 60 G4...67°46'N 115°07'W
Kuhmo Finland 43 G4...64°07'N 29°30'E
Kuito Angola 83 A3...12°23'S 16°57'E
Kujū-san vol. Japan 104 B2...33°05'N 131°16'E
Kül r. Iran 95 I5...27°04'N 55°44'E
Kulandy Kazakhstan 53 F2...46°03'N 59°32'E
Kuldīga Latvia 43 E2...56°58'N 21°59'E
Kŭlob Tajikistan 95 K7...37°54'N 69°51'E
Kul'sary Kazakhstan 53 F2...46°56'N 54°00'E
Kulunda Russia 98 D8...52°33'N 78°56'E
Kulundinskoye, Ozero l. Russia 98 D8...53°08'N 79°54'E
Kumamoto Japan 104 B2...32°47'N 130°43'E
Kumanovo North Macedonia 50 D6...42°08'N 21°43'E
Kumasi Ghana 84 D2...6°42'N 1°38'W
Kumbakonam India 96 E3...10°58'N 79°23'E
Kumertau Russia 53 F3...52°44'N 55°46'E
Kumla Sweden 43 C2...59°07'N 15°10'E
Kumo Nigeria 84 F3...10°06'N 11°11'E
Kunashir, Ostrov i. Russia 104 E4...44°13'N 146°23'E
Kungur Russia 52 F3...57°27'N 56°54'E
Kunlun Shan mts China 98 D5...36°11'N 78°01'E
Kunming China 99 I3...25°02'N 102°44'E
Kuohijärvi l. Finland 43 F3...61°12'N 24°53'E
Kuopio Finland 43 F3...62°53'N 27°41'E
Kupa r. Croatia/Slovenia 50 B7...45°28'N 16°25'E
Kupang Indonesia 103 G1...10°12'S 123°35'E
Kupiškis Lithuania 43 F1...55°49'N 24°59'E
Kup"yans'k Ukraine 53 D2...49°42'N 37°37'E
Kuqa China 98 E6...41°38'N 83°01'E
Kurdistan f. Asia 94 F7...37°00'N 43°30'E
Kuressaare Estonia 43 E2...58°16'N 22°29'E
Kurgan Russia 54 H3...55°28'N 65°23'E
Kurikka Finland 43 E3...62°37'N 22°25'E
Kuril Islands Russia 55 P2...46°04'N 148°33'E
Kuril'sk Russia 55 P2...45°13'N 147°52'E
Kuril Trench f. N. Pacific Oc. 117 I4...41°44'N 146°31'E
Kurmuk Sudan 85 H3...10°31'N 34°16'E
Kurnool India 96 E4...15°49'N 77°59'E
Kursk Russia 53 D3...51°45'N 36°12'E
Kuršumlija Serbia 50 D6...43°08'N 21°17'E

Kurume Japan 104 B2...33°18'N 130°31'E
Kurunegala Sri Lanka 96 F2...7°30'N 80°19'E
Kuşadası Turkey 50 G3...37°52'N 27°15'E
Kushiro Japan 104 D4...42°59'N 144°23'E
Kuskokwim Mountains U.S.A. 60 C4...64°24'N 155°17'W
Kütahya Turkey 51 H4...39°25'N 29°58'E
Kutaisi Georgia 53 E2...42°16'N 42°43'E
Kutno Poland 46 H5...52°14'N 19°22'E
Kuujjuaq Canada 61 L3...58°10'N 68°13'W
Kuusamo Finland 43 G4...65°58'N 29°09'E
Kuwait Asia 95 G5...29°22'N 47°08'E
Kuwait town Kuwait 95 G5...29°18'N 47°55'E
Kuybyshevskoye Vodokhranilische resr Russia 52 E3
...54°55'N 49°00'E
Kuytun China 98 E6...44°20'N 84°55'E
Kuznetsk Russia 53 E3...53°07'N 46°37'E
Kvaløya i. Norway 43 D5...69°38'N 18°30'E
KwaMashu S. Africa 83 C2...29°44'S 30°59'E
KwaNobuhle S. Africa 83 B1...33°48'S 25°24'E
Kwilu r. Angola/Dem. Rep. Congo 83 A4...3°23'S 17°22'E
Kwoka mt. Indonesia 103 I3...0°38'S 132°28'E
Kyakhta Russia 55 L3...50°21'N 106°30'E
Kyangwali Uganda 85 H2...1°15'N 30°45'E
Kyle of Lochalsh Scotland 16 D2...57°17'N 5°43'W
Kyle of Tongue inlet Scotland 17 E3...58°28'N 4°27'W
Kyllini mt. Greece 50 E3...37°56'N 22°24'E
Kyoga, Lake Uganda 85 H2...1°28'N 32°53'E
Kyōto Japan 104 C2...34°59'N 135°46'E
Kyparissia Greece 50 E3...37°15'N 21°41'E
Kyrenia Cyprus 51 J2...35°20'N 33°19'E
Kyrgyzstan Asia 98 C6...41°47'N 74°37'E
Kyrta Russia 52 F4...64°04'N 57°40'E
Kythira i. Greece 50 E3...36°16'N 22°55'E
Kythnos i. Greece 50 F3...37°26'N 24°27'E
Kyūshū i. Japan 104 B2...31°30'N 131°45'E
Kyustendil Bulgaria 50 E6...42°17'N 22°41'E
Kyyivs'ke Vodoskhovyshche resr Ukraine 47 N4
...50°54'N 30°30'E
Kyzyl Russia 55 K3...51°43'N 94°24'E
Kyzylorda Kazakhstan 54 H2...44°51'N 65°30'E

## L

Laâyoune Western Sahara 84 C4...27°09'N 13°12'W
Labé Guinea 84 C3...11°20'N 12°18'W
Labrador f. Canada 61 L3...54°04'N 62°29'W
Labrador City Canada 61 L3...52°59'N 66°54'W
Labrador Sea Canada/Greenland 61 M4...60°07'N 56°06'W
Labytnangi Russia 52 G4...66°42'N 66°18'E
Laccadive Sea Asia 96 D2...10°00'N 73°00'E
Laceby England 13 G2...53°32'N 0°10'W
Lachlan r. Australia 108 D3...34°21'S 143°57'E
La Crosse U.S.A. 63 H5...43°48'N 91°12'W
Ladakh d. India 96 E7...34°05'N 77°10'E
Ladhar Bheinn mt. Scotland 16 D2...57°05'N 5°35'W
Ladoga, Lake Russia 54 D4...60°48'N 31°37'E
Ladybank Scotland 15 F4...56°17'N 3°08'W
Ladybower Reservoir England 13 F2...53°23'N 1°45'W
Ladysmith S. Africa 83 B2...28°34'S 29°47'E
Lae P.N.G. 108 D6...6°43'S 147°00'E
Læsø i. Denmark 43 B2...57°15'N 11°05'E
Lafayette U.S.A. 63 H3...30°14'N 92°03'W
Lagan r. Northern Ireland 14 D2...54°37'N 5°54'W
Lagan' Russia 53 E2...45°25'N 47°18'E
Laggan, Loch l. Scotland 17 E1...56°56'N 4°31'W
Laghouat Algeria 84 E5...33°42'N 2°53'E
La Gomera i. Canary Islands 45 X2...28°14'N 17°18'W
Lagos Nigeria 84 E2...6°26'N 3°20'E
Lagos Portugal 45 A2...37°06'N 8°41'W
La Grande U.S.A. 62 C6...45°19'N 118°02'W
La Grande 2, Réservoir Canada 61 K3...53°52'N 76°54'W
La Grande 3, Réservoir Canada 61 K3...53°36'N 75°18'W
La Grande 4, Réservoir Canada 61 K3...54°13'N 73°17'W
La Gran Sabana f. Venezuela 67 L2...5°13'N 61°40'W
Lahad Datu Malaysia 102 F5...5°02'N 118°20'E
Lahat Indonesia 102 C3...3°46'S 103°34'E
Lahij Yemen 94 F2...13°02'N 44°50'E
Lāhījān Iran 95 G7...37°11'N 49°56'E
Lahore Pakistan 96 D7...31°33'N 74°23'E
Lahti Finland 43 F3...60°59'N 25°41'E
Laidon, Loch l. Scotland 17 E1...56°39'N 4°39'W
Laihia Finland 43 E3...62°58'N 22°01'E
Lainioälven r. Sweden 43 E4...67°22'N 22°39'E
Lake City U.S.A. 63 J3...30°10'N 82°39'W
Lake District f. England 12 D3...54°30'N 3°10'W
Lakeland U.S.A. 63 J2...27°59'N 81°58'W
Lakki Pakistan 95 L6...32°35'N 70°58'E
Lakonikos Kolpos b. Greece 50 E3...36°32'N 22°42'E
Laksefjorden str. Norway 43 F5...70°52'N 27°00'E
Lakshadweep d. India 96 D3...10°35'N 73°13'E
Lakshadweep is India 96 D3...10°50'N 72°11'E
La Línea de la Concepción Spain 45 C2...36°10'N 5°21'W
La Louvière Belgium 42 D3...50°28'N 4°11'E
La Mancha f. Spain 45 D3...39°15'N 2°58'W
Lamar U.S.A. 62 F4...38°06'N 102°38'W
La Martre, Lac l. Canada 60 G4...63°19'N 118°02'W
Lambay Island Ireland 18 E3...53°29'N 5°59'W
Lambourn England 8 D2...51°30'N 1°32'W
Lambourn Downs hills England 8 D2...51°32'N 1°32'W
Lamego Portugal 45 B4...41°06'N 7°48'W
Lämerd Iran 95 H5...27°22'N 53°08'E
Lamia Greece 50 E4...38°54'N 22°25'E
Lamlash Scotland 14 D3...55°32'N 5°08'W
Lammermuir Hills Scotland 15 G3...55°49'N 2°50'W
Lampang Thailand 102 B7...18°16'N 99°32'E
Lampeter Wales 10 C4...52°07'N 4°05'W
Lanark Scotland 15 F3...55°40'N 3°47'W
Lancashire d. England 21 D3...53°51'N 2°51'W
Lancaster England 12 E3...54°03'N 2°48'W
Lancaster Canal England 12 E3...54°03'N 2°48'W
Lancaster Sound str. Canada 61 J5...74°15'N 89°18'W
Landeck Austria 46 D2...47°08'N 10°34'E
Landes f. France 44 C4...44°48'N 0°55'W
Landguard Point England 9 G2...51°56'N 1°19'E
Land's End England 11 B2...50°03'N 5°46'W
Landshut Germany 46 E3...48°33'N 12°10'E
Landskrona Sweden 46 E6...55°53'N 12°50'E
Lanesborough Ireland 18 D3...53°40'N 7°59'W
Langavat, Loch l. Na h-E. S. Scotland 16 C2
...57°48'N 6°59'W
Langavat, Loch l. Na h-E. S. Scotland 16 C3
...58°02'N 6°49'W

Langeland i. Denmark 43 B1...55°02'N 10°55'E
Langeoog i. Germany 42 G6...53°46'N 7°36'E
Langholm Scotland 15 G3...55°09'N 2°59'W
Langøya i. Norway 43 C5...68°44'N 14°27'E
Langport England 8 C2...51°02'N 2°50'W
Langres France 44 F5...47°52'N 5°20'E
Langsa Indonesia 102 B4...4°25'N 97°57'E
Langstrothdale Chase hills England 13 E3...54°13'N 2°18'W
Languedoc f. France 44 E3...43°10'N 1°57'E
Lanivet England 11 C2...50°26'N 4°46'W
Länkäran Azerbaijan 95 G7...38°45'N 48°51'E
Lannion France 44 B6...48°44'N 3°27'W
Lansing U.S.A. 63 J5...42°44'N 84°33'W
Lanzarote i. Canary Islands 45 Z2...29°09'N 13°35'W
Lanzhou China 99 I5...36°04'N 103°43'E
Laoag Phil. 102 G7...18°14'N 120°36'E
Lao Cai Vietnam 102 C8...22°26'N 103°59'E
Laois d. Ireland 18 D2...52°57'N 7°23'W
Laojunmiao China 98 H5...39°46'N 97°33'E
Laon France 44 E6...49°34'N 3°38'E
Laos Asia 102 C7...19°30'N 103°01'E
La Palma i. Canary Islands 45 X2...28°33'N 17°44'W
La Palma Panama 67 I2...8°21'N 78°11'W
La Palma del Condado Spain 45 B2...37°23'N 6°33'W
La Paragua Venezuela 67 L2...6°50'N 63°19'W
La Paz Bolivia 72 C5...16°30'S 68°10'W
La Paz Mexico 66 B5...24°08'N 110°17'W
La Pérouse Strait Japan/Russia 104 D5...45°35'N 141°33'E
Lapland f. Europe 43 D4...67°12'N 18°37'E
La Plata Argentina 73 D3...34°55'S 57°58'W
La Plata, Río de str. Argentina/Uruguay 73 D3
...34°39'S 57°53'W
Lappajärvi l. Finland 43 E3...63°07'N 23°41'E
Lappeenranta Finland 43 G3...61°03'N 28°11'E
Laptev Sea Russia 55 N5...76°05'N 125°40'E
Lapua Finland 43 E3...62°58'N 23°00'E
Larache Morocco 48 B4...35°12'N 6°09'W
Laramie U.S.A. 62 E5...41°20'N 105°36'W
Laredo U.S.A. 62 G2...27°30'N 99°30'W
Largs Scotland 14 E3...55°48'N 4°52'W
La Rioja Argentina 73 C4...29°25'S 66°51'W
Larisa Greece 50 E4...39°38'N 22°25'E
Larkana Pakistan 96 C6...27°31'N 68°15'E
Larnaca Cyprus 51 J2...34°55'N 33°38'E
Larne Northern Ireland 14 D2...54°51'N 5°49'W
Larne Lough inlet Northern Ireland 14 D2...54°49'N 5°47'W
La Rochelle France 44 C5...46°10'N 1°09'W
La Roche-sur-Yon France 44 C5...46°40'N 1°25'W
La Ronge Canada 60 H3...55°06'N 105°17'W
Larvik Norway 43 B2...59°03'N 10°05'E
La Sagra f. Spain 45 D4...40°05'N 3°56'W
La Sagra mt. Spain 45 D2...37°58'N 2°35'W
La Sarre Canada 61 K2...48°48'N 79°12'W
Las Cruces U.S.A. 62 E3...32°19'N 106°47'W
La Serena Chile 73 B4...29°53'S 71°16'W
Las Marismas marsh Spain 45 B2...37°07'N 6°35'W
Las Palmas de Gran Canaria Canary Islands 45 Y2
...28°06'N 15°26'W
La Spezia Italy 46 C1...44°07'N 9°49'E
Las Tórtolas, Cerro mt. Chile 73 C4...29°56'S 69°52'W
Las Tunas Cuba 67 I5...20°57'N 76°57'W
Las Vegas U.S.A. 62 C4...36°10'N 115°09'W
Las Villuercas mt. Spain 45 C3...39°29'S 5°23'W
Latacunga Ecuador 72 B7...0°58'S 78°37'W
Latheron Scotland 17 F3...58°17'N 3°22'W
Latina Italy 48 F5...41°28'N 12°54'E
Latvia Europe 43 E2...56°47'N 23°49'E
Lauchhammer Germany 46 E4...51°30'N 13°46'E
Launceston Australia 108 D2...41°27'S 147°09'E
Launceston England 11 C2...50°38'N 4°21'W
Laurencekirk Scotland 17 G1...56°50'N 2°28'W
Lausanne Switz. 48 E6...46°32'N 6°39'E
Laut i. Indonesia 102 F3...3°39'S 116°18'E
Laval France 44 C6...48°04'N 0°46'W
Lavenham England 9 F3...52°06'N 0°48'E
Lawton U.S.A. 62 G3...34°37'N 98°24'W
Lawz, Jabal al mt. Saudi Arabia 49 K2...28°39'N 35°18'E
Laxey Isle of Man 12 C3...54°14'N 4°24'W
Laxford, Loch inlet Scotland 16 D3...58°25'N 5°06'W
Lázaro Cárdenas Baja Calif. Mexico 66 A7
...30°30'N 115°56'W
Lázaro Cárdenas Michoacán Mexico 66 D4
...17°57'N 102°12'W
Leader Water r. Scotland 15 G3...55°36'N 2°40'W
Leane, Lough l. Ireland 18 B2...52°02'N 9°34'W
Leatherhead England 9 E2...51°17'N 0°19'W
Lebanon Asia 49 K3...33°17'N 35°20'E
Lebork Poland 46 G6...54°32'N 17°45'E
Lecce Italy 49 G5...40°20'N 18°11'E
Lech r. Austria/Germany 46 D2...47°32'N 10°40'E
Lechlade-on-Thames England 8 D2...51°42'N 1°41'W
Le Croisy France 9 G1...50°13'N 1°38'E
Ledbury England 8 C3...52°02'N 2°25'W
Lee r. Ireland 18 C1...51°54'N 8°25'W
Leeds England 13 F2...53°48'N 1°33'W
Leek England 13 E2...53°07'N 2°01'W
Leeming England 13 F3...54°18'N 1°33'W
Lee Moor England 11 C2...50°26'N 4°01'W
Leer Germany 42 G6...53°15'N 7°28'E
Leeuwarden Neth. 42 E6...53°12'N 5°48'E
Leeuwin, Cape Australia 108 A3...34°23'S 115°09'E
Leeward Islands Caribbean Sea 67 L4...18°59'N 64°04'W
Lefkada i. Greece 50 D4...38°45'N 20°35'E
Legaspi Phil. 103 G6...13°08'N 123°43'E
Legnica Poland 46 G4...51°13'N 16°10'E
Leh India 96 E7...34°09'N 77°36'E
Le Havre France 44 D6...49°30'N 0°06'E
Leiah Pakistan 95 L6...30°58'N 70°58'E
Leicester England 8 D3...52°38'N 1°08'W
Leicester d. England 21 E3...52°39'N 1°07'W
Leicestershire d. England 21 E3...52°37'N 0°59'W
Leichhardt r. Australia 108 C5...17°35'S 139°44'E
Leiden Neth. 42 D5...52°10'N 4°30'E
Leigh England 12 E2...53°30'N 2°31'W
Leighton Buzzard England 8 E2...51°55'N 0°40'W
Leinster f. Ireland 18 E2...52°37'N 6°47'W
Leinster, Mount hill Ireland 18 E2...52°37'N 6°47'W
Leipzig Germany 46 E4...51°21'N 12°23'E
Leiston England 9 G3...52°13'N 1°35'E
Leith Scotland 15 F3...55°59'N 3°10'W
Leith Hill England 9 E2...51°11'N 0°22'W
Leitrim d. Ireland 18 C4...54°19'N 8°13'W
Leixlip Ireland 18 E3...53°22'N 6°29'W
Leizhou Bandao pen. China 99 J2...21°03'N 109°41'E
Lek r. Neth. 42 D4...51°54'N 4°34'E

Leka Norway 43 B4...65°05'N 11°40'E
Leksozero, Ozero l. Russia 43 G3...63°51'N 30°30'E
Lelystad Neth. 42 E5...52°32'N 5°28'E
Le Mans France 44 D6...48°00'N 0°12'E
Lena r. Russia 55 N5...72°20'N 126°45'E
Lens France 42 C4...50°26'N 2°49'E
Lensk Russia 55 M4...60°44'N 114°55'E
Leoben Austria 46 F2...47°23'N 15°06'E
Leominster England 8 C3...52°14'N 2°44'W
León Mexico 66 D5...21°07'N 101°40'W
León Spain 45 C5...42°36'N 5°34'W
Le Puy-en-Velay France 44 E4...45°03'N 3°53'E
Lerum Sweden 43 C2...57°46'N 12°18'E
Lerwick Scotland 17 H5...60°09'N 1°09'W
Lesbos i. Greece 50 F4...39°09'N 26°24'E
Les Cayes Haiti 67 J4...18°14'N 73°46'W
Leshan China 99 I3...29°37'N 103°47'E
Leskovac Serbia 50 D6...42°59'N 21°57'E
Lesotho Africa 83 B2...29°38'S 28°17'E
Les Pieux France 11 Z9...49°31'N 1°48'W
Les Sables-d'Olonne France 44 C5...46°30'N 1°47'W
Lesser Antilles is Caribbean Sea 67 K3...12°28'N 67°05'W
Lesser Slave Lake Canada 60 G3...55°28'N 115°34'W
Lestijärvi l. Finland 43 F3...63°30'N 24°45'E
Leszno Poland 46 G4...51°51'N 16°35'E
Letchworth Garden City England 9 E2...51°59'N 0°13'W
Lethbridge Canada 62 D6...49°41'N 112°49'W
Leti, Kepulauan is Indonesia 103 H2...8°18'S 127°40'E
Letterkenny Ireland 18 D4...54°57'N 7°44'W
Leuchars Scotland 15 G4...56°23'N 2°53'W
Leuser, Gunung mt. Indonesia 102 B4...3°46'N 97°09'E
Leuven Belgium 42 D3...50°52'N 4°42'E
Levadeia Greece 50 E4...38°26'N 22°52'E
Leven England 13 G2...53°54'N 0°18'W
Leven Scotland 15 G4...56°12'N 2°59'W
Leven, Loch inlet Scotland 16 D1...56°41'N 5°06'W
Leven, Loch l. Scotland 15 F4...56°12'N 3°20'W
Levens England 12 E3...54°16'N 2°47'W
Leverkusen Germany 46 B4...51°03'N 6°59'E
Lewes England 9 F1...50°52'N 0°01'E
Lewis, Isle of i. Scotland 16 C3...58°09'N 6°40'W
Lexington U.S.A. 63 J4...38°02'N 84°30'W
Leyburn England 13 F3...54°19'N 1°50'W
Leyland England 12 E2...53°42'N 2°42'W
Leyte i. Phil. 103 G6...11°05'N 124°40'E
Lezhë Albania 50 C5...41°46'N 19°39'E
L'gov Russia 47 P4...51°39'N 35°15'E
Lhargarbo China 98 G4...32°15'N 91°50'E
Lhasa China 98 G3...29°39'N 91°06'E
Lhazê China 98 F3...29°08'N 87°39'E
Lhokseumawe Indonesia 102 B5...5°09'N 97°09'E
L'Hospitalet de Llobregat Spain 45 G4...41°22'N 2°06'E
Lianshan China 99 M6...40°41'N 120°48'E
Lianyungang China 99 L4...34°37'N 119°10'E
Liaoning d. China 99 M6...41°30'N 122°48'E
Liaoyuan China 99 N6...42°54'N 125°09'E
Liard r. Canada 60 F4...61°51'N 121°18'W
Libenge Dem. Rep. Congo 83 A5...3°37'N 18°40'E
Liberal U.S.A. 62 F4...37°03'N 100°56'W
Liberec Czechia 46 F4...50°45'N 15°03'E
Liberia Africa 84 C2...6°52'N 9°56'W
Libin Belgium 42 E2...49°59'N 5°16'E
Libourne France 44 C4...44°55'N 0°14'W
Libreville Gabon 84 E2...0°28'N 9°27'E
Libya Africa 84 F4...26°07'N 16°10'E
Libyan Desert Egypt/Libya 85 G4...24°51'N 25°42'E
Libyan Plateau f. Egypt/Libya 49 I3...30°59'N 25°40'E
Lichfield England 8 D3...52°41'N 1°49'W
Lichinga Mozambique 83 C3...13°17'S 35°14'E
Lida Belarus 47 K5...53°53'N 25°18'E
Liddel r. Scotland 15 G3...55°04'N 2°57'W
Lidköping Sweden 43 C2...58°30'N 13°10'E
Liechtenstein Europe 44 H5...47°07'N 9°33'E
Liège Belgium 42 E3...50°38'N 5°34'E
Liège d. Belgium 42 E3...50°29'N 5°39'E
Lieksa Finland 43 G3...63°19'N 30°00'E
Lienz Austria 46 E2...46°50'N 12°46'E
Liepāja Latvia 43 E2...56°31'N 21°01'E
Liévin France 42 B3...50°25'N 2°48'E
Liffey r. Ireland 18 E3...53°21'N 6°15'W
Lifford Ireland 18 D4...54°50'N 7°29'W
Ligurian Sea France/Italy 44 H3...43°30'N 8°40'E
Likasi Dem. Rep. Congo 83 B3...10°58'S 26°47'E
Lilla Edet Sweden 43 C2...58°08'N 12°08'E
Lille Belgium 42 D4...51°14'N 4°49'E
Lille France 44 E7...50°38'N 3°04'E
Lillehammer Norway 43 B3...61°06'N 10°27'E
Lilleshall England 8 C3...52°44'N 2°23'W
Lillestrøm Norway 43 B2...59°59'N 11°05'E
Lilongwe Malawi 83 C3...13°57'S 33°48'E
Lima Peru 72 B5...12°04'S 77°03'W
Limassol Cyprus 51 J2...34°41'N 33°03'E
Limavady Northern Ireland 14 C3...55°03'N 6°58'W
Limburg d. Belgium 42 E4...51°04'N 5°28'E
Limburg d. Neth. 42 E4...51°15'N 5°55'E
Limerick Ireland 18 C2...52°40'N 8°38'W
Limerick d. Ireland 18 C2...52°29'N 8°55'W
Limingen l. Norway 43 C4...64°48'N 13°35'E
Limnos i. Greece 50 F4...39°51'N 25°16'E
Limoges France 44 D4...45°50'N 1°16'E
Limousin f. France 44 D4...45°34'N 1°36'E
Limoux France 44 E3...43°04'N 2°14'E
Limpopo r. S. Africa/Zimbabwe 83 C2...25°13'S 33°32'E
Linares Spain 45 D3...38°06'N 3°38'W
Lincoln England 13 G2...53°14'N 0°33'W
Lincoln U.S.A. 62 G5...40°51'N 96°41'W
Lincolnshire d. England 21 E3...53°14'N 0°07'W
Lincolnshire Wolds hills England 13 G2...53°30'N 0°10'W
Lindesnes c. Norway 43 A2...58°00'N 7°04'E
Lindfield England 9 E1...51°01'N 0°06'W
Lindi Tanzania 83 C4...9°59'S 39°42'E
Lindos Greece 51 H3...36°05'N 28°05'E
Line Islands Kiribati 116 B3...5°19'N 161°49'W
Linfen China 99 K5...36°05'N 111°31'E
Lingen Germany 46 B5...52°32'N 7°20'E
Lingfield England 9 E2...51°11'N 0°01'W
Lingga, Kepulauan is Indonesia 102 D3...0°02'S 104°34'E
Linhares Brazil 73 E5...19°27'S 40°04'W
Linköping Sweden 43 C2...58°25'N 15°38'E
Linlithgow Scotland 15 F3...55°58'N 3°37'W
Linney Head Wales 10 B3...51°37'N 5°16'W
Linnhe, Loch inlet Scotland 14 D4...56°37'N 5°25'W
Linqing China 99 L5...36°49'N 115°42'E
Linxia China 99 I5...35°31'N 103°08'E
Linz Austria 46 F3...48°19'N 14°18'E
Lions, Gulf of France 44 E3...43°00'N 4°00'E
Lipari, Isole is Italy 48 F4...38°35'N 14°50'E

...sk Russia 53 D3 .............................52°37'N 39°36'E
...ook England 8 E2 ..........................51°04'N 0°48'W
...va Romania 50 D4 ..........................46°05'N 21°43'E
...ovsk Kazakhstan 53 G3 .....................52°28'N 62°30'E
...a Dem. Rep. Congo 83 B5 ..................2°10'N 21°32'E
...on Portugal 45 A3 .........................38°44'N 9°08'W
...rn and Castlereagh d. Northern Ireland 21 B4
.......................................54°31'N 6°04'W
...nnor Bay Ireland 18 B2 ....................52°55'N 9°26'W
...ard England 11 C2 ........................50°27'N 4°28'W
...ore Australia 108 E4 .......................28°47'S 153°19'E
...ore Ireland 18 D2 .........................52°08'N 7°56'W
...skea Northern Ireland 14 B2 ...............54°15'N 7°26'W
...England 9 F3 .............................51°03'N 0°53'E
...wel Ireland 18 B2 ........................52°26'N 9°29'W
...ania Europe 47 J6 .........................55°29'N 23°45'E
...Abaco i. Bahamas 67 I6 ...................26°54'N 77°50'W
...Andaman i. India 97 H3 ...................10°38'N 92°31'E
...Belt str. Denmark 43 B1 ..................55°15'N 9°47'E
...borough England 13 E2 ....................53°39'N 2°06'W
...Cayman i. Cayman Is 67 H4 ..............19°42'N 80°04'W
...hampton England 9 E1 .....................50°49'N 0°32'W
...Inagua Island Bahamas 67 J5 ............21°31'N 72°59'W
...Karoo f. S. Africa 83 B1 ..................33°43'S 20°46'E
...Minch str. Scotland 16 B2 ................57°32'N 7°00'W
...Ouse r. England 9 F3 .....................52°30'N 0°22'E
...Rock town U.S.A. 63 H3 .................34°46'N 92°18'W
...nshui China 99 I3 ........................26°40'N 104°48'E
...ou China 99 J2 ...........................24°21'N 109°22'E
...pool Canada 63 N5 ........................44°02'N 64°43'W
...pool England 12 E2 .......................53°25'N 2°59'W
...gston Scotland 15 F3 ......................55°54'N 3°31'W
...gstone Zambia 83 B3 .......................17°52'S 25°52'E
...no Italy 48 F5 ............................43°32'N 10°18'E
...d England 11 B1 ..........................49°58'N 5°12'W
...d Point England 11 B1 ....................49°57'N 5°17'W
...iana Slovenia 46 F4 .......................46°03'N 14°30'E
...gan r. Sweden 43 D3 ......................62°18'N 17°23'E
...gby Sweden 43 C2 ........................56°51'N 13°59'E
...al Sweden 43 D3 ..........................61°50'N 16°06'E
...rth Wales 10 C4 ..........................52°12'N 4°18'W
...adarn Fawr Wales 10 C4 ..................52°24'N 4°04'W
...eris Wales 10 C5 ..........................53°07'N 4°08'W
...leilo Wales 10 D3 .........................51°53'N 3°59'W
...lovery Wales 10 D3 .......................51°59'N 3°48'W
...rindod Wells Wales 10 D4 .................52°14'N 3°23'W
...ludno Wales 10 C5 ........................53°19'N 3°50'W
...lwrog Wales 10 C5 ........................53°05'N 4°19'W
...ysul Wales 10 C4 .........................52°03'N 4°18'W
...gwad Wales 10 C3 ........................51°52'N 4°09'W
...lli Wales 10 C3 ...........................51°41'N 4°10'W
...s Spain 45 C5 .............................43°25'N 4°44'W
...air Caereinion Wales 10 D4 ................52°39'N 3°20'W
...airfechan Wales 10 C5 ....................53°15'N 3°58'W
...airpwllgwyngyll Wales 10 C5 ..............53°13'N 4°12'W
...air-yn-neubwll Wales 10 C5 ...............53°16'N 4°33'W
...yllin Wales 10 D3 .........................52°46'N 3°16'W
...adog Wales 10 D3 ........................51°56'N 3°53'W
...efni Wales 10 C5 ..........................53°15'N 4°19'W
...eler Wales 10 C5 .........................52°02'N 4°22'W
...elynin Wales 10 C4 .......................52°39'N 4°07'W
...oed Wales 10 C4 .........................53°18'N 4°05'W
...ollen Wales 10 D4 ........................52°58'N 3°10'W
...urig Wales 10 D4 .........................52°24'N 3°36'W
...dloes Wales 10 D4 ........................52°27'N 3°32'W
...wchaiarn Wales 10 D4 ....................52°32'N 3°17'W
...yfni Wales 10 C5 .........................53°03'N 4°17'W
...s f. Col./Venez. 72 C7 .....................5°54'N 69°50'W
...umney Wales 11 D3 ........................51°31'N 3°07'W
...wst Wales 10 D5 ..........................53°08'N 3°48'W
...annan Wales 10 D5 .......................53°11'N 3°36'W
...armi r. Wales 10 D3 .......................51°33'N 3°22'W
...wit Major Wales 11 D3 ....................51°25'N 3°29'W
...ynda Wales 10 C5 ........................53°05'N 4°17'W
...ynog Wales 10 D4 ........................52°32'N 3°27'W
...bydder Wales 10 C4 ......................52°04'N 4°09'W
...Wales 10 D5 .............................53°06'N 3°00'W
...na Spain 45 B3 ...........................41°36'N 0°38'E
...na Spain 45 B3 ...........................38°15'N 6°01'W
...Peninsula Wales 10 C4 ...................52°51'N 4°34'W
...George, Mount Canada 60 F3 .............57°50'N 124°57'W
...minster Canada 60 G3 ....................53°17'N 110°00'W
...illaco, Volcán vol. Chile 73 C4 ............24°42'S 68°33'W
...mba Swaziland 83 C2 .....................26°26'S 31°12'E
...o Angola 83 A2 ...........................12°24'S 13°32'E
...aline Scotland 14 D4 .....................56°32'N 5°47'W
...oisdale Scotland 16 B2 ....................57°09'N 7°19'W
...gelly Scotland 15 F4 ......................56°08'N 3°18'W
...gilphead Scotland 14 D4 ..................56°02'N 5°26'W
...nver Scotland 16 D3 ......................58°09'N 5°14'W
...maben Scotland 15 F3 .....................55°08'N 3°26'W
...maddy Scotland 16 B2 ....................57°36'N 7°10'W
...nagar mt. Scotland 17 F1 .................56°58'N 3°15'W
...ranza Scotland 14 D3 .....................55°42'N 5°17'W
...y, Loch l. Scotland 16 E1 .................56°56'N 4°58'W
...erbie Scotland 15 F3 ......................55°07'N 3°21'W
...on England 9 G3 .........................52°32'N 1°29'E
...noye Pole Russia 52 D4 ...................60°44'N 33°34'E
...ar Kenya 85 H2 ...........................3°06'N 35°34'E
...Poland 46 H4 ............................51°46'N 19°28'E
...en is Norway 43 C5 .......................68°06'N 12°44'E
...n, Mount Canada 60 D4 ..................60°40'N 140°02'W
...erheads Scotland 15 G5 ...................42°28'N 2°26'W
...oño Spain 45 D5 .........................42°28'N 2°23'W
...r. France 44 B5 ...........................47°17'N 2°07'W
...Ecuador 72 B6 ...........................4°00'S 79°14'W
...n Spain 45 C2 ............................37°10'N 4°09'W
...h tekojärvi resr Finland 43 F4 .............67°56'N 27°35'E
...en Belgium 42 E2 .........................51°06'N 4°00'E
...ia Nigeria 84 E2 ..........................7°49'N 6°44'E
...nd r. Denmark 43 B1 .....................54°47'N 11°21'E
...Bulgaria 50 E6 ...........................43°49'N 23°14'E
...n Dem. Rep. Congo 83 B5 ................0°47'N 24°17'E
...ook i. Indonesia 102 F2 ...................9°07'S 116°13'E
...e Togo 84 E2 .............................6°09'N 1°13'E
...nel Belgium 42 E4 ........................51°14'N 5°19'E
...ond, Loch l. Scotland 14 E4 ..............56°04'N 4°37'W
...za Poland 47 J5 ..........................52°42'N 22°05'E
...on Canada 61 J2 ..........................42°59'N 81°14'W
...on Canada 61 J2 ..........................42°59'N 81°14'W
...onderry Northern Ireland 14 B2 ...........54°59'N 7°20'W
...onderry, Cape Australia 108 B5 ...........13°47'S 126°53'E
...Loch inlet Scotland 14 E4 .................56°06'N 4°51'W

Longa, Proliv str. Russia 55 S5 ..............70°10'N 178°17'E
Long Ashton England 8 C2 ..................51°26'N 2°39'W
Long Beach town U.S.A. 62 C3 ...............33°47'N 118°20'W
Long Bennington England 8 E3 ...............52°59'N 0°46'W
Long Eaton England 8 D3 ...................52°54'N 1°16'W
Longford Ireland 18 D3 .....................53°44'N 7°48'W
Longford d. Ireland 18 D3 ...................53°45'N 7°41'W
Longhorsley England 13 F4 .................55°15'N 1°46'W
Longhoughton England 13 F4 ...............55°26'N 1°37'W
Long Island Bahamas 67 I5 .................23°18'N 75°06'W
Long Island U.S.A. 63 L5 ....................40°49'N 72°36'W
Longlac Canada 61 J2 ......................49°47'N 86°33'W
Longridge England 12 E2 ...................53°50'N 2°36'W
Long Stratton England 9 G3 ................52°29'N 1°14'E
Longton England 12 E2 .....................53°44'N 2°48'W
Longtown England 12 E4 ...................55°00'N 2°58'W
Longuyon France 42 F2 .....................49°27'N 5°37'E
Longview U.S.A. 62 G3 .....................32°32'N 94°44'W
Long Xuyên Vietnam 102 D6 ...............10°20'N 105°25'E
Longyearbyen Arctic Oc. 54 C5 .............77°59'N 15°44'E
Lons-le-Saunier France 44 F5 ..............46°41'N 5°33'E
Lookout, Cape U.S.A. 63 K3 ...............34°37'N 76°33'W
Loop Head Ireland 18 B2 ...................52°33'N 9°56'W
Lop Nur f. China 98 G6 ....................40°28'N 90°20'E
Lopphavet b. Norway 43 E5 ................70°21'N 21°03'E
Loralai Pakistan 95 K6 .....................30°21'N 68°43'E
Lorca Spain 45 E2 ..........................37°41'N 1°41'W
Lord Howe Island Australia 109 E3 ........31°26'S 158°57'E
Lorient France 44 B5 .......................47°45'N 3°22'W
Lorn, Firth of est. Scotland 14 D4 ..........56°15'N 5°54'W
Los Ángeles Chile 73 B3 ....................37°28'S 72°21'W
Los Angeles U.S.A. 62 C3 ..................34°01'N 118°15'W
Los Mochis Mexico 66 C6 ..................25°48'N 108°59'W
Los Roques, Islas is Venezuela 67 K3 ......11°55'N 66°39'W
Lossie r. Scotland 17 F2 ....................57°43'N 3°17'W
Lossiemouth Scotland 17 F2 ...............57°43'N 3°17'W
Lostwithiel England 11 C2 .................50°24'N 4°40'W
Lot r. France 44 D4 ........................44°19'N 0°20'E
Loth Scotland 17 G4 .......................59°12'N 2°41'W
Lotta r. Finland/Russia 43 G5 ..............68°40'N 30°14'E
Louangnamtha Laos 102 C8 ...............21°03'N 101°29'E
Louangphabang Laos 102 C7 ..............19°54'N 102°10'E
Loughborough England 8 D3 ...............52°46'N 1°12'W
Loughor r. Wales 10 C3 ....................51°42'N 4°03'W
Loughrea Ireland 18 C3 ....................53°12'N 8°35'W
Loughton England 9 F2 ....................51°39'N 0°04'E
Louisiana d. U.S.A. 63 H3 ..................30°40'N 91°56'W
Louisville U.S.A. 63 I4 ......................38°15'N 85°46'W
Loukhi Russia 43 H4 .......................66°04'N 33°03'E
Lourdes France 44 C3 ......................43°06'N 0°02'E
Louth England 13 G2 ......................53°22'N 0°01'W
Louth d. Ireland 18 E3 .....................53°53'N 6°31'W
Lovech Bulgaria 50 F6 .....................43°09'N 24°42'E
Lovozero Russia 52 D4 .....................68°01'N 34°59'E
Lowell U.S.A. 63 L5 .........................42°39'N 71°19'W
Lower Lough Erne l. Northern Ireland 14 B2
.......................................54°29'N 7°51'W
Lowestoft England 9 G3 ...................52°29'N 1°45'E
Loyal, Loch l. Scotland 17 E3 ..............58°25'N 4°22'W
Loyauté, Îles is New Caledonia 109 F4 .....20°23'S 167°17'E
Loyne, Loch l. Scotland 16 D2 .............57°06'N 5°05'W
Loznica Serbia 50 C7 .......................44°33'N 19°15'E
Lozova Ukraine 53 D2 ......................49°26'N 35°56'E
Lu'an China 99 L4 .........................31°45'N 116°32'E
Luanda Angola 83 A4 .......................8°50'S 13°14'E
Luarca Spain 45 B5 ........................43°32'N 6°31'W
Luau Angola 83 B3 ........................10°42'S 22°15'E
Lubango Angola 83 A3 .....................14°55'S 13°30'E
Lubartów Poland 47 J4 ....................51°28'N 22°37'E
Lubbock U.S.A. 62 F3 ......................33°38'N 101°51'W
Lübeck Germany 46 D5 .....................53°52'N 10°42'E
Lübecker Bucht b. Germany 46 D6 .........54°03'N 10°47'E
Lubin Poland 46 G4 ........................51°24'N 16°13'E
Lublin Poland 47 J4 ........................51°14'N 22°35'E
Lubnaig, Loch l. Scotland 14 E4 ...........56°18'N 4°19'W
Lubny Ukraine 47 O4 ......................50°01'N 33°00'E
Lubuklinggau Indonesia 102 C3 ...........3°23'S 102°56'E
Lubumbashi Dem. Rep. Congo 83 B3 ......11°40'S 27°29'E
Lubutu Dem. Rep. Congo 83 B4 ...........0°44'S 26°35'E
Lucan Ireland 10 A5 .......................53°21'N 6°27'W
Luce Bay Scotland 14 E2 ...................54°47'N 4°52'W
Lucena Phil. 103 G6 ........................13°56'N 121°36'E
Lucena Spain 45 C2 ........................37°25'N 4°29'W
Lučenec Slovakia 46 H3 ....................48°21'N 19°41'E
Lucerne Switz. 46 C2 .......................47°03'N 8°18'E
Lucknow India 96 F6 ......................26°51'N 80°58'E
Lüderitz Namibia 83 A2 ....................26°40'S 15°09'E
Ludgershall England 8 D2 .................51°15'N 1°37'W
Ludhiana India 96 E7 ......................30°54'N 75°53'E
Ludlow England 8 C3 ......................52°22'N 2°43'W
Ludvika Sweden 43 C3 .....................60°09'N 15°12'E
Ludwigsburg Germany 46 C3 ..............48°54'N 9°12'E
Ludwigshafen am Rhein Germany 46 C3
.......................................49°28'N 8°26'E
Ludwigslust Germany 46 D5 ...............53°20'N 11°30'E
Luena Angola 83 A3 .......................11°47'S 19°54'E
Lufeng China 99 L2 .......................22°58'N 115°41'E
Lufkin U.S.A. 63 H3 ........................31°21'N 94°44'W
Luga Russia 43 G2 .........................58°43'N 29°51'E
Luga r. Russia 43 G2 .......................59°40'N 28°18'E
Lugano Switz. 46 C2 .......................46°01'N 8°57'E
Lugg r. Wales 10 E4 ........................52°02'N 2°38'W
Lugo Spain 45 B5 ..........................43°01'N 7°33'W
Lugoj Romania 50 D7 ......................45°42'N 21°55'E
Luhans'k Ukraine 53 D2 ...................48°33'N 39°19'E
Luichart, Loch l. Scotland 16 E2 ...........57°37'N 4°48'W
Luing i. Scotland 14 D4 ....................56°14'N 5°39'W
Łuków Poland 47 J4 .......................51°56'N 22°24'E
Luleå Sweden 43 E4 ........................65°35'N 22°10'E
Luleälven r. Sweden 43 E4 .................65°35'N 22°03'E
Lüleburgaz Turkey 50 G5 ..................41°25'N 27°21'E
Lumberton U.S.A. 63 K3 ..................34°36'N 79°05'W
Lunan Bay Scotland 17 G1 ................56°39'N 2°30'W
Lund Sweden 43 C1 ........................55°42'N 13°12'E
Lundy i. England 11 C3 ....................51°11'N 4°39'W
Lune r. England 12 E3 .....................54°03'N 2°49'W
Lüneburg Germany 46 D5 .................53°15'N 10°25'E
Lunéville France 44 G6 ....................48°36'N 6°30'E
Luninyets Belarus 47 L5 ...................52°14'N 26°48'E
Luoyang China 99 K4 .....................34°38'N 112°27'E
Lure France 44 G5 .........................47°41'N 6°30'E
Lurgainn, Loch l. Scotland 16 D3 ..........58°02'N 5°14'W
Lurgan Northern Ireland 14 C2 ............54°27'N 6°19'W
Lusaka Zambia 83 B3 ......................15°23'S 28°16'E
Lushnjë Albania 50 C5 .....................40°57'N 19°42'E
Lut, Dasht-e des. Iran 95 I6 ...............30°47'N 58°45'E
Lutherstadt Wittenberg Germany 46 E4 ....51°52'N 12°39'E

Luton England 9 E2 .......................51°53'N 0°25'W
Luton d. England 21 E2 ....................51°54'N 0°25'W
Luts'k Ukraine 47 K4 .......................50°45'N 25°21'E
Lutterworth England 8 D3 .................52°27'N 1°12'W
Luxor Egypt 85 H4 ........................25°43'N 32°39'E
Luxembourg Europe 42 F2 ................49°49'N 6°01'E
Luxembourg town Lux. 42 F2 .............49°36'N 6°08'E
Luza Russia 52 E4 .........................60°38'N 47°15'E
Luziânia Brazil 72 E5 ......................16°17'S 47°53'W
Luzon i. Phil. 103 G7 ......................15°24'N 122°02'E
Luzon Strait Phil. 102 G8 ..................20°19'N 121°07'E
L'viv Ukraine 47 K3 ........................49°50'N 24°02'E
Lycksele Sweden 43 D4 ....................64°36'N 18°41'E
Lydd England 9 F1 .........................50°57'N 0°55'E
Lydford England 11 C2 ....................50°39'N 4°06'W
Lydney England 8 C2 ......................51°44'N 2°32'W
Lyepyel' Belarus 47 M6 ....................54°53'N 28°42'E
Lyme Bay England 8 C1 ...................50°39'N 2°59'W
Lyme Regis England 8 C1 .................50°43'N 2°56'W
Lymington England 8 D1 ..................50°45'N 1°33'W
Lynchburg U.S.A. 63 K4 ..................37°24'N 79°09'W
Lyndhurst England 8 D1 ..................50°52'N 1°35'W
Lynmouth England 11 D3 ................51°14'N 3°50'W
Lynn Lake town Canada 60 H3 ...........56°51'N 101°03'W
Lynton England 11 D3 ....................51°14'N 3°50'W
Lyon France 44 F4 .........................45°45'N 4°52'E
Lyon r. Scotland 17 F1 .....................56°37'N 3°58'W
Lys'va Russia 52 F3 ........................58°08'N 57°48'E
Lysychans' Ukraine 53 D2 .................48°55'N 38°26'E
Lysyye Gory Russia 53 E3 .................51°31'N 44°49'E
Lytchett Minster England 8 C1 ............50°44'N 2°03'W
Lytham St Anne's England 12 D2 .........53°45'N 3°02'W

## M

Ma'ān Jordan 94 E6 .......................30°12'N 35°43'E
Ma'arrat an Nu'mān Syria 51 L2 .........35°39'N 36°40'E
Maas r. Neth. 42 D4 .......................51°43'N 4°53'E
Maaseik Belgium 42 E4 ....................51°05'N 5°48'E
Maastricht Neth. 42 E3 ....................50°51'N 5°42'E
Mabalane Mozambique 83 C2 ...........23°50'S 32°37'E
Mablethorpe England 13 H2 .............53°20'N 0°16'E
Macao China 99 K2 .......................22°15'N 113°34'E
Macapá Brazil 72 D7 .......................0°03'N 51°02'W
Macassar Strait Indonesia 102 F3 .........3°55'S 117°24'E
Macclesfield England 13 E2 ...............53°16'N 2°07'W
MacDonnell Ranges mts Australia 108 C4 ...23°33'S 131°18'E
Macduff Scotland 17 G2 ..................57°40'N 2°30'W
Macedo de Cavaleiros Portugal 45 B4 .....41°32'N 6°57'W
Maceió Brazil 72 F6 ........................9°36'S 35°40'W
Macgillycuddy's Reeks mts Ireland 18 B1 ...51°57'N 9°52'W
Mach Pakistan 96 C6 ......................29°52'N 67°20'E
Machala Ecuador 72 B6 ....................3°17'S 79°57'W
Machilipatnam India 96 F4 ...............16°11'N 81°10'E
Machrihanish Scotland 14 D3 ............55°25'N 5°44'W
Machynlleth Wales 10 D4 ................52°35'N 3°51'W
Mackay Australia 108 D4 .................21°10'S 149°11'E
Mackay, Lake Australia 108 B4 ..........22°36'S 128°28'E
Mackenzie r. Canada 60 E4 ..............69°15'N 134°11'W
Mackenzie King Island Canada 60 G5 ...77°42'N 111°56'W
Mackenzie Mountains Canada 60 E4 .....65°04'N 133°03'W
MacLeod, Lake Australia 108 A4 .........24°08'S 113°43'E
Mâcon France 44 F5 .......................46°19'N 4°50'E
Macon U.S.A. 63 J3 .......................32°53'N 83°37'W
Macroom Ireland 18 C1 ...................51°54'N 8°58'W
Madadeni S. Africa 83 C2 .................27°45'S 30°02'E
Madagascar Africa 83 D3 .................19°57'S 46°27'E
Madeira r. Brazil 72 C6 ....................3°23'S 58°47'W
Madeira is N. Atlantic Oc. 84 C5 .........33°15'N 16°57'W
Madeley England 8 C3 .....................52°38'N 2°26'W
Madera Mexico 66 C6 .....................29°11'N 108°11'W
Madhya Pradesh d. India 96 E5 ..........23°32'N 78°56'E
Madinat ath Thawrah Syria 51 M2 .......35°51'N 38°33'E
Madison U.S.A. 63 I5 ......................43°04'N 89°23'W
Madona Latvia 47 L7 ......................56°51'N 26°13'E
Madrakah, Ra's c. Oman 95 I3 ...........19°01'N 57°51'E
Madre, Laguna lagoon Mexico 66 E6 .....25°06'N 97°37'W
Madre, Sierra mts C. America 56 F2 ......15°00'N 90°00'W
Madre de Dios r. Peru 72 C5 ..............10°59'S 66°07'W
Madre del Sur, Sierra mts Mexico 66 D4
.......................................18°07'N 101°24'W
Madre Occidental, Sierra mts Mexico 66 C6
.......................................28°46'N 108°51'W
Madre Oriental, Sierra mts Mexico 66 D6
.......................................26°41'N 101°44'W
Madrid Spain 45 D4 .......................40°26'N 3°40'W
Madura i. Indonesia 102 E2 ...............7°02'S 113°11'E
Madurai India 96 E2 .......................9°55'N 78°07'E
Maebashi Japan 104 C3 ...................36°23'N 139°04'E
Maesteg Wales 10 D3 .....................51°36'N 3°40'W
Maestra, Sierra mts Cuba 67 I4 ...........19°54'N 77°33'W
Mafia Island Tanzania 83 C4 .............7°48'S 39°52'E
Mafraq Jordan 94 E6 ......................32°20'N 36°13'E
Magadan Russia 55 Q3 ...................59°38'N 151°00'E
Magdalena r. Colombia 72 B8 ...........11°06'N 74°52'W
Magdalena Mexico 66 B7 .................30°38'N 110°59'W
Magdeburg Germany 46 D5 ..............52°07'N 11°38'E
Magellan, Strait of Chile 73 B1 ..........53°42'S 71°59'W
Magerøya i. Norway 43 F5 ................70°59'N 25°40'E
Maggiorasca, Monte mt. Italy 46 C1 .....44°33'N 9°30'E
Maggiore, Lake Italy 46 C1 ...............45°56'N 8°36'E
Maghera Northern Ireland 14 C2 .........54°50'N 6°40'W
Magherafelt Northern Ireland 14 C2 .....54°45'N 6°36'W
Maghull England 12 E2 ...................53°31'N 2°57'W
Magilligan Point Northern Ireland 14 C3 ...55°11'N 6°58'W
Magnitogorsk Russia 53 F3 ...............53°24'N 59°08'E
Magway Myanmar 97 H5 .................20°09'N 94°56'E
Mahābād Iran 95 G7 ......................36°44'N 45°41'E
Mahagi Dem. Rep. Congo 85 H2 .........2°16'N 30°55'E
Mahajanga Madagascar 83 D3 ..........15°45'S 46°21'E
Mahalevona Madagascar 83 D3 .........15°24'S 49°53'E
Maharashtra d. India 96 E4 ...............19°24'N 75°18'E
Mahé i. Seychelles 85 J1 ..................4°36'S 55°24'E
Mahilyow/Mogilëv Belarus 47 N5 .......53°55'N 30°20'E
Mahón Spain 45 H3 .......................39°53'N 4°17'E
Mahrāt, Jabal mt. Yemen 95 H3 .........17°07'N 51°07'E
Maicao Colombia 67 J3 ...................11°25'N 72°33'W
Maidenhead England 8 E2 ...............51°31'N 0°43'W
Maidstone England 9 F2 ..................51°16'N 0°31'E
Maiduguri Nigeria 84 F3 ..................11°50'N 13°08'E
Main r. Northern Ireland 14 C2 ...........54°43'N 6°18'W
Mai-Ndombe, Lac l. Dem. Rep. Congo 83 A4
.......................................2°15'S 18°22'E
Maine d. U.S.A. 63 M6 ...................45°20'N 69°21'W
Mainland i. Orkn. Scotland 17 F4 ........59°04'N 3°15'W

Mainland i. Shetl. Scotland 17 H5 ........60°21'N 1°17'W
Mainz Germany 46 C4 ....................50°00'N 8°16'E
Maiquetía Venezuela 67 K3 ..............10°32'N 66°56'W
Maíz, Islas del is Nicaragua 67 H3 .......12°10'N 83°02'W
Maizuru Japan 104 C3 ....................35°28'N 135°24'E
Maja Jezercë mt. Albania 50 C6 ..........42°26'N 19°52'E
Majene Indonesia 102 F3 ..................3°30'S 118°54'E
Major, Puig mt. Spain 45 G3 .............39°48'N 2°49'E
Majorca i. Spain 45 G3 ....................39°57'N 2°43'E
Makale Indonesia 102 F3 ..................3°06'S 119°52'E
Makarska Croatia 50 B6 ...................43°18'N 17°02'E
Makassar Indonesia 102 F2 ...............5°06'S 119°27'E
Makat Kazakhstan 53 F2 ..................47°37'N 53°14'E
Makgadikgadi f. Botswana 83 B2 .........20°45'S 25°35'E
Makhachkala Russia 53 E2 ...............42°59'N 47°30'E
Makhanda S. Africa 83 B1 ................33°19'S 26°32'E
Makira i. Solomon Is 109 F5 ..............10°38'S 161°38'E
Makran f. Iran/Pakistan 95 J5 ............26°29'N 60°27'E
Makurdi Nigeria 84 E2 ....................7°43'N 8°33'E
Mala, Punta pt Panama 67 H2 ...........7°27'N 80°00'W
Malabar Coast f. India 96 D3 .............12°16'N 74°30'E
Malabo Equat. Guinea 84 E2 .............3°45'N 8°46'E
Malacca, Strait of Indonesia/Malaysia 102 B5
.......................................5°41'N 98°38'E
Maladzyechna Belarus 47 L6 .............54°18'N 26°52'E
Málaga Spain 45 C2 .......................36°43'N 4°25'W
Malahide Ireland 18 E3 ...................53°27'N 6°09'W
Malaita i. Solomon Is 109 F6 .............8°58'S 161°09'E
Malakal South Sudan 85 H2 ..............9°30'N 31°40'E
Malakula i. Vanuatu 109 F5 ..............16°15'S 167°19'E
Malang Indonesia 102 E2 .................7°56'S 112°46'E
Malanje Angola 83 A4 .....................9°33'S 16°23'E
Mälaren l. Sweden 43 D2 ................59°27'N 17°13'E
Malatya Turkey 51 M4 ....................38°20'N 38°20'E
Malawi Africa 83 C3 .......................11°32'S 33°43'E
Mälāyer Iran 95 G6 ........................34°17'N 48°48'E
Malaysia Asia 102 C4/E4 .................3°39'N 108°45'E
Malbork Poland 46 H6 ....................54°02'N 19°02'E
Maldives Indian Oc. 96 D2 ...............6°09'N 72°23'E
Maldon England 9 F2 ......................51°44'N 0°40'E
Male Maldives 96 D1 ......................4°18'N 73°29'E
Maleas, Akra c. Greece 50 E3 ............36°26'N 23°12'E
Malgomaj l. Sweden 43 D4 ...............64°44'N 16°15'E
Mali Africa 84 D3 ..........................13°54'N 5°34'W
Malili Indonesia 103 G3 ...................2°37'S 121°07'E
Malin Head Ireland 18 D5 ................55°23'N 7°24'W
Mallaig Scotland 16 D2 ...................57°00'N 5°50'W
Mallawī Egypt 49 J2 ......................27°43'N 30°50'E
Mallow Ireland 18 C2 .....................52°08'N 8°39'W
Malmberget Sweden 43 E4 ..............67°10'N 20°40'E
Malmédy Belgium 42 F3 .................50°26'N 6°02'E
Malmesbury England 8 C2 ...............51°35'N 2°06'W
Malmö Sweden 43 C1 ....................55°36'N 13°01'E
Måløy Norway 43 A3 ......................61°56'N 5°07'E
Malozemel'skaya Tundra f. Russia 52 F4 ...67°50'N 50°00'E
Malpas England 12 E2 ....................53°01'N 2°46'W
Malpelo, Isla de i. N. Pacific Oc. 68 B4 ...3°59'N 81°34'W
Malta Europe 48 F4 .......................35°49'N 14°18'E
Maltby England 13 F2 .....................53°25'N 1°12'W
Malton England 13 G3 ....................54°08'N 0°48'W
Malvern Hills England 8 C3 ..............52°05'N 2°20'W
Malyy Anyuy r. Russia 55 R4 ............68°27'N 161°01'E
Mama r. Russia 55 P4 .....................66°28'N 143°13'E
Mamelodi S. Africa 83 B2 ................25°42'S 28°23'E
Mamuju Indonesia 102 F3 ...............2°40'S 118°51'E
Man, Isle of i. Irish Sea 14 E2 ...........54°16'N 4°41'W
Manacor Spain 45 G3 ....................39°34'N 3°14'E
Manado Indonesia 103 G3 ..............1°33'N 124°52'E
Managua Nicaragua 67 G3 ..............12°07'N 86°17'W
Manama Bahrain 95 H5 ..................26°12'N 50°35'E
Mananjary Madagascar 83 D2 ..........21°14'S 48°20'E
Manaus Brazil 72 D6 ......................3°04'S 60°00'W
Manavgat Turkey 51 I3 ...................36°48'N 31°26'E
Manchester England 13 E2 ..............53°29'N 2°15'W
Manchuria f. China 99 M7 ..............46°27'N 123°48'E
Mand r. Iran 95 H5 ........................21°42'N 83°15'E
Mandala, Puncak mt. Indonesia 103 K3 ...4°43'S 140°21'E
Mandalay Myanmar 97 I5 ...............21°59'N 96°06'E
Mandalgovĭ Mongolia 99 J7 .............45°42'N 106°19'E
Mangalia Romania 51 H6 .................43°49'N 28°34'E
Mangaluru India 96 D3 ...................12°53'N 74°51'E
Mangaung S. Africa 83 B2 ...............29°09'S 26°16'E
Mangoky r. Madagascar 83 D2 ..........23°25'S 45°25'E
Mangole i. Indonesia 103 H3 ...........1°51'S 125°49'E
Mangotsfield England 8 C2 ..............51°29'N 2°31'W
Manicouagan, Réservoir Canada 61 L3 ...51°18'N 68°18'W
Maniitsoq Greenland 61 M4 .............65°26'N 52°55'W
Manila Phil. 103 G6 .......................14°34'N 120°59'E
Manipur d. India 97 H5 ..................24°53'N 93°56'E
Manisa Turkey 50 G4 .....................38°36'N 27°25'E
Manitoba d. Canada 60 I3 ...............53°40'N 98°06'W
Manitoba, Lake Canada 60 I3 ...........51°34'N 99°04'W
Manizales Colombia 72 B7 ..............5°00'N 75°30'W
Manmad India 96 D5 .....................20°15'N 74°30'E
Mannheim Germany 46 C3 ..............49°29'N 8°28'E
Manningtree England 9 G2 ..............51°57'N 1°04'E
Manokwari Indonesia 103 I3 ............0°52'S 134°06'E
Manorbier Wales 10 C3 ..................51°39'N 4°48'W
Manorhamilton Ireland 18 C4 ...........54°18'N 8°11'W
Manra i. Kiribati 109 H6 ..................4°26'S 171°13'W
Manresa Spain 45 F4 .....................41°43'N 1°50'E
Mansa Zambia 83 B3 ......................11°11'S 28°53'E
Mansel Island Canada 61 K4 ............62°05'N 79°35'W
Mansfield England 13 F2 .................53°09'N 1°12'W
Mansfield U.S.A. 63 J5 ....................40°45'N 82°32'W
Manston England 8 C1 ...................50°56'N 2°16'W
Mantua Italy 46 D1 ........................45°09'N 10°47'E
Manukau New Zealand 109 G3 .........36°58'S 174°50'E
Manzanares Spain 45 D3 ................39°00'N 3°21'W
Manzhouli China 99 L7 ...................49°20'N 117°29'E
Maoke, Pegunungan mts Indonesia 103 J3 ...3°34'S 135°25'E
Mapinhane Mozambique 83 C2 .........22°17'S 35°06'E
Maputo Mozambique 83 C2 .............25°56'S 32°34'E
Marabá Brazil 72 E6 .......................5°23'S 49°08'W
Maracaibo Venezuela 72 B8 .............10°40'N 71°38'W
Maracaibo, Lake inlet Venezuela 72 B7 ...9°45'N 71°36'W
Maracaju, Serra de hills Brazil 73 D4 .....21°59'S 55°53'W
Maracay Venezuela 72 C8 ................10°16'N 67°35'W
Marādah Libya 85 F4 ......................29°12'N 19°12'E
Maradi Niger 84 E3 ........................13°31'N 7°07'E
Marāgheh Iran 95 G7 .....................37°23'N 46°14'E
Marajó, Ilha de i. Brazil 72 E6 ...........0°45'S 50°38'W
Marand Iran 95 G7 .......................38°26'N 45°46'E
Marañón r. Peru 72 B6 ....................4°25'S 73°30'W
Marathon Canada 63 I6 ..................48°43'N 86°23'W
Marathonas Greece 50 E4 ...............38°09'N 23°58'E
Marazion England 11 B2 .................50°07'N 5°28'W

Marbella Spain 45 C2 ..................................36°31′N 4°52′W
Marburg Germany 46 C4 ...............................50°48′N 8°46′E
Marburg S. Africa 83 C1 ................................30°43′S 30°32′E
March England 9 F3 .....................................52°33′N 0°05′E
Marche-en-Famenne Belgium 42 E3 ..............50°14′N 5°21′E
Marchtrenk Austria 46 F3 .............................48°12′N 14°07′E
Mardan Pakistan 95 L6 .................................34°14′N 72°04′E
Mar del Plata Argentina 73 D3 .....................37°59′S 57°35′W
Mardin Turkey 94 M1 ...................................37°18′N 40°46′E
Maree, Loch l. Scotland 16 D2 .....................57°38′N 5°21′W
Maresfield England 9 F1 ...............................50°59′N 0°05′E
Margarita, Isla de i. Venezuela 72 C8 ...........11°06′N 63°53′W
Margate England 9 G2 ..................................51°23′N 1°23′E
Margery Hill England 13 F2 ..........................53°28′N 1°43′W
Mārgow, Dasht-e des. Afgh. 95 J6 ...............30°27′N 62°22′E
Marhanets' Ukraine 47 P2 .............................47°40′N 34°37′E
Marías, Islas is Mexico 66 C5 .......................21°25′N 106°33′W
Maria van Diemen, Cape New Zealand 109 G3
                                                       34°29′S 172°38′E
Ma'rib Yemen 95 G3 .....................................15°32′N 45°26′E
Maribor Slovenia 46 F2 .................................46°32′N 15°40′E
Marie-Galante i. Guadeloupe 67 L4 ...............15°56′N 61°14′W
Mariehamn Finland 43 D3 .............................60°06′N 19°57′E
Mariental Namibia 83 A2 ...............................24°39′S 17°58′E
Mariestad Sweden 43 C2 ...............................58°43′N 13°50′E
Marijampolė Lithuania 47 J6 .........................54°33′N 23°22′E
Marília Brazil 73 E4 ......................................22°13′S 49°57′W
Mar"ina Horka Belarus 47 M5 ......................53°31′N 28°08′E
Maringá Brazil 73 D4 ....................................23°27′S 51°59′W
Maritime Alps mts France/Italy 44 G4 ...........44°16′N 6°56′E
Maritsa r. Bulgaria 50 G5 ..............................41°43′N 26°20′E
Mariupol' Ukraine 49 K6 ..............................47°06′N 37°33′E
Marka Somalia 85 I2 .....................................1°43′N 44°44′E
Markermeer l. Neth. 42 E5 ............................52°34′N 5°14′E
Market Deeping England 9 E3 ......................52°41′N 0°19′W
Market Drayton England 8 C3 ......................52°54′N 2°29′W
Market Harborough England 8 E3 ................52°29′N 0°55′W
Markethill Northern Ireland 14 C2 ...............54°17′N 6°31′W
Market Rasen England 13 G2 ........................53°23′N 0°20′W
Market Warsop England 13 F2 ......................53°12′N 1°09′W
Market Weighton England 13 G2 ..................53°52′N 0°40′W
Markha r. Russia 55 M4 ................................63°29′N 118°52′E
Marlborough England 8 D2 ...........................51°25′N 1°44′W
Marlborough Downs hills England 8 D2 ........51°29′N 1°48′W
Marlow England 8 E2 ...................................51°34′N 0°46′W
Marmande France 44 D4 ...............................44°31′N 0°10′E
Marmara, Sea of g. Turkey 51 H5 ................40°43′N 28°20′E
Marmaris Turkey 51 H3 ................................36°50′N 28°15′E
Marne r. France 44 E6 ..................................48°49′N 2°25′E
Marne-la-Vallée France 44 E6 ........................48°51′N 2°36′E
Maromokotro mt. Madagascar 83 D3 ...........14°01′S 48°58′E
Marondera Zimbabwe 83 C3 .........................18°13′S 31°34′E
Maroni r. French Guiana 72 D7 .....................5°44′N 54°01′W
Maroua Cameroon 84 F3 ..............................10°37′N 14°19′E
Marple England 13 E2 ...................................53°24′N 2°04′W
Marquesas Islands French Polynesia 114 B2
                                                       8°39′S 139°15′W
Marquette U.S.A. 63 I6 .................................46°32′N 87°25′W
Marra, Jebel mt. Sudan 85 G3 .......................12°54′N 24°11′E
Marrakesh Morocco 84 D5 ............................31°39′N 7°58′W
Marra Plateau f. Sudan 85 G3 .......................13°24′N 24°25′E
Marsá al 'Alam Egypt 49 J2 ...........................25°04′N 34°50′E
Marsa al Burayqah Libya 85 F5 ......................30°22′N 19°35′E
Marsabit Kenya 85 H2 ..................................2°20′N 37°59′E
Marsala Italy 48 F4 .......................................37°48′N 12°26′E
Marsá Maţrūḩ Egypt 85 G5 ..........................31°20′N 27°16′E
Marseille France 44 F3 .................................43°18′N 5°23′E
Marsfjället mt. Sweden 43 C4 ........................65°06′N 15°23′E
Märsta Sweden 43 D2 ..................................59°37′N 17°53′E
Martaban Myanmar 97 I4 ..............................16°34′N 97°34′E
Martaban, Gulf of Myanmar 97 I4 ................16°20′N 96°57′E
Martapura Indonesia 102 C3 ........................4°20′S 104°21′E
Martin Slovakia 46 H3 ..................................49°04′N 18°55′E
Martinique i. Central America 67 L3 ..............14°36′N 60°56′W
Martin Vaz, Islas is S. Atlantic Ocean 68 E2
                                                       20°30′S 28°51′W
Martock England 8 C1 ..................................50°58′N 2°46′W
Martok Kazakhstan 53 F3 ..............................50°43′N 56°28′E
Mary Turkmenistan 95 J7 ..............................37°34′N 61°52′E
Maryborough Australia 108 E4 ......................25°32′S 152°41′E
Maryland d. U.S.A. 63 K4 ..............................38°39′N 76°30′W
Maryport England 12 D3 ..............................54°43′N 3°30′W
Masan S. Korea 99 N5 ...................................35°14′N 128°36′E
Masbate Phil. 103 G6 ....................................12°20′N 123°37′E
Masbate i. Phil. 103 G6 .................................12°20′N 123°36′E
Mascara Algeria 48 D4 ..................................35°23′N 0°08′E
Maseru Lesotho 83 B2 ..................................29°19′S 27°29′E
Mashhad Iran 95 I7 .......................................36°18′N 59°35′E
Mashkel, Hamun-i- f. Pakistan 96 B6 ............28°15′N 63°02′E
Maşīrah, Jazīrat i. Oman 95 I4 ......................20°16′N 58°58′E
Maşīrah, Khalīj b. Oman 95 I3 ......................19°47′N 58°22′E
Masjed Soleymān Iran 95 G6 ........................31°57′N 49°18′E
Mask, Lough l. Ireland 18 B3 ........................53°37′N 9°21′W
Mason City U.S.A. 63 H5 ...............................43°09′N 93°12′W
Massachusetts d. U.S.A. 63 L5 .......................42°23′N 72°18′W
Massachusetts Bay U.S.A. 63 L5 ....................42°25′N 70°51′W
Massakory Chad 84 F3 ..................................12°59′N 15°43′E
Massif Central mts France 44 E4 ....................45°16′N 3°25′E
Mastung Pakistan 95 K5 ...............................29°45′N 66°56′E
Masuda Japan 104 B2 ...................................34°40′N 131°52′E
Masvingo Zimbabwe 83 C2 ...........................20°04′S 30°48′E
Matadi Dem. Rep. Congo 83 A4 ....................5°50′S 13°29′E
Matagami Canada 63 K6 ...............................49°46′N 77°38′W
Matam Senegal 84 C3 ...................................15°40′N 13°16′W
Matamoros Mexico 66 E6 .............................25°50′N 97°34′W
Matanzas Cuba 67 H5 ..................................23°04′N 81°34′W
Matara Sri Lanka 96 F2 .................................5°58′N 80°29′E
Mataram Indonesia 102 F2 ...........................8°35′S 116°10′E
Mataró Spain 45 G4 .....................................41°32′N 2°27′E
Matä'utu Wallis and Futuna Is 109 H5 ...........13°17′S 176°07′W
Matehuala Mexico 62 F1 ...............................23°40′N 100°38′W
Mathura India 96 E6 .....................................27°26′N 77°43′E
Matlock England 13 F2 .................................53°08′N 1°33′W
Maţraḩ Oman 95 I4 ......................................23°37′N 58°32′E
Matsue Japan 104 B3 ....................................35°28′N 133°03′E
Matsumoto Japan 104 C3 .............................36°15′N 137°58′E
Matsusaka Japan 104 C2 ...............................34°34′N 136°33′E
Matsuyama Japan 104 B2 ..............................33°49′N 132°46′E
Matterhorn mt. Italy/Switz. 46 B1 ................45°59′N 7°40′E
Maturín Venezuela 72 C7 ..............................9°44′N 63°10′W
Maubeuge France 42 C3 ...............................50°17′N 3°58′E
Mauchline Scotland 14 E3 ............................55°31′N 4°23′W
Maughold Head Isle of Man 12 C3 ...............54°18′N 4°19′W
Maug Islands N. Mariana Is 103 L8 ...............20°02′N 145°16′E
Maumere Indonesia 103 G2 ..........................8°40′S 122°13′E
Maun Botswana 83 B3 ..................................19°57′S 23°25′E

Mauritania Africa 84 C3 ...............................19°51′N 11°35′W
Mauritius country Indian Oc. 79 E1 ...............20°10′S 58°00′E
May, Isle of i. Scotland 15 G4 .......................56°11′N 2°33′W
Maya r. Russia 55 O3 ....................................60°26′N 134°33′E
Mayaguana i. Bahamas 67 J5 ........................22°23′N 72°56′W
Mayagüez Puerto Rico 67 K4 ........................18°12′N 67°08′W
Mayamey Iran 95 I7 ......................................36°27′N 55°40′E
Mayar hill Scotland 17 F1 .............................56°51′N 3°15′W
Maybole Scotland 14 E3 ...............................55°21′N 4°41′W
Mayen Germany 42 G3 .................................50°19′N 7°13′E
Mayenne r. France 44 C5 ..............................47°30′N 0°32′W
Maykop Russia 53 E2 ....................................44°36′N 40°07′E
Mayo Canada 60 E4 ......................................63°37′N 135°54′W
Mayo d. Ireland 18 B3 ..................................53°46′N 9°13′W
Mayotte i. Africa 83 D3 ................................12°59′S 45°09′E
Mazār-e Sharīf Afgh. 95 K7 ..........................36°43′N 67°07′E
Mazatlán Mexico 66 C5 ................................23°14′N 106°27′W
Mažeikiai Lithuania 43 E2 ............................56°18′N 22°22′E
Mazyr Belarus 47 M5 ....................................52°03′N 29°15′E
Mbabane Swaziland 83 C2 ............................26°20′S 31°09′E
Mbandaka Dem. Rep. Congo 83 A4 .............0°00′S 18°17′E
M'banza Congo Angola 83 A4 ......................6°14′S 14°17′E
Mbarara Uganda 85 H1 ................................0°35′S 30°37′E
Mbeya Tanzania 83 C4 .................................8°53′S 33°26′E
Mbuji-Mayi Dem. Rep. Congo 83 B4 ...........6°06′S 23°36′E
McClintock Channel Canada 60 H5 .............71°10′N 101°39′W
McClure Strait Canada 60 G5 .......................74°09′N 114°57′W
McCook U.S.A. 62 F5 ....................................40°14′N 100°39′W
McGrath U.S.A. 60 C4 ..................................62°52′N 155°37′W
McKinley, Mount U.S.A. 60 C4 ....................63°05′N 150°20′W
Mdantsane S. Africa 83 B1 ...........................32°58′S 27°48′E
Mead, Lake resr U.S.A. 62 D4 ........................36°12′N 114°24′W
Mealasta Island Scotland 16 B3 ....................58°05′N 7°10′W
Meall a' Bhuiridh mt. Scotland 16 E1 ...........56°37′N 4°51′W
Meath d. Ireland 18 E3 .................................53°41′N 6°35′W
Meaux France 44 E6 .....................................48°58′N 2°53′E
Mecca Saudi Arabia 94 E4 ............................21°25′N 39°47′E
Mechelen Belgium 42 D4 .............................51°01′N 4°29′E
Mecheria Algeria 48 D3 ................................33°33′N 0°19′W
Meckenheim Germany 42 G3 .......................50°37′N 7°02′E
Medan Indonesia 102 B4 ..............................3°38′N 98°40′E
Medellín Colombia 72 B7 .............................6°13′N 75°35′W
Meden r. England 13 G2 ...............................53°25′N 0°59′W
Medenine Tunisia 48 F4 ...............................33°21′N 10°31′E
Medetsiz Tepe mt. Turkey 51 K3 ..................37°24′N 34°37′E
Mediaş Romania 50 F8 .................................46°10′N 24°22′E
Medicine Hat Canada 60 G3 ........................50°03′N 110°41′W
Medina Saudi Arabia 94 E4 ..........................24°31′N 39°32′E
Medina del Campo Spain 45 C4 ...................41°19′N 4°54′W
Mediterranean Sea World 48 H3 .................33°25′N 32°44′E
Mednogorsk Russia 53 F3 ............................51°19′N 57°35′E
Medvezh'yegorsk Russia 52 D4 ....................62°55′N 34°29′E
Medway d. England 21 F2 ............................51°22′N 0°34′E
Medway r. England 9 F2 ...............................51°21′N 0°27′E
Meerut India 96 E6 ......................................29°02′N 77°45′E
Megara Greece 50 E4 ....................................38°00′N 23°21′E
Meghalaya d. India 97 H6 ............................25°36′N 91°22′E
Mehrestän Iran 95 J6 ....................................30°59′N 61°31′E
Meiktila Myanmar 97 I5 ................................20°50′N 95°53′E
Meiningen Germany 46 D4 ..........................50°34′N 10°25′E
Meißen Germany 46 E4 ................................51°10′N 13°28′E
Meizhou China 99 L2 ...................................24°17′N 116°09′E
Mek'elē Ethiopia 94 E2 ................................13°31′N 39°28′E
Meknès Morocco 84 D5 ...............................33°53′N 5°30′W
Mekong r. Asia 97 K3 ...................................10°53′N 105°14′E
Mekong, Mouths of the Vietnam 102 D5 ...9°03′N 106°31′E
Melaka Malaysia 102 C4 ...............................2°11′N 102°17′E
Melanesia is Pacific Oc. 106 F3 ...................10°00′S 165°00′E
Melbourn England 9 F3 ................................52°05′N 0°02′E
Melbourne Australia 108 D3 ........................37°49′S 144°59′E
Melbourne U.S.A. 63 J2 ...............................28°01′N 80°43′W
Melby Scotland 17 H5 ..................................60°18′N 1°40′W
Melfi Chad 84 F3 ..........................................11°03′N 18°00′E
Melilla N. Africa 48 D4 .................................35°18′N 2°57′W
Melitopol' Ukraine 47 P2 .............................46°51′N 35°22′E
Melksham England 8 C2 ...............................51°22′N 2°08′W
Melrhir, Chott f. Algeria 84 E5 .....................34°15′N 6°23′E
Melrose Scotland 15 G3 ...............................55°36′N 2°43′W
Meltham England 13 F2 ...............................53°36′N 1°51′W
Melton Mowbray England 8 E3 ...................52°46′N 0°53′W
Melun France 44 E6 ......................................48°32′N 2°39′E
Melvich Scotland 17 F3 ................................58°33′N 3°55′W
Melville Canada 60 H3 .................................50°56′N 102°49′W
Melville Bay Greenland 61 L4 .......................76°00′N 64°00′W
Melville Island Australia 108 C5 ...................11°37′S 130°55′E
Melville Island Canada 60 H5 ......................75°14′N 109°26′W
Melville Peninsula Canada 61 J4 ..................68°00′N 84°12′W
Melvin, Lough l. Ireland/U.K. 18 C4 ............54°25′N 8°09′W
Memberamo r. Indonesia 103 J3 ..................1°32′S 137°52′E
Memmingen Germany 46 D3 ........................47°59′N 10°11′E
Memphis U.S.A. 63 H4 .................................35°09′N 90°04′W
Mena Ukraine 47 O4 ....................................51°31′N 32°14′E
Menai Bridge Wales 10 C5 ...........................53°13′N 4°10′W
Menai Strait Wales 10 C5 .............................53°09′N 4°17′W
Mende France 44 E4 .....................................44°31′N 3°30′E
Mendī Ethiopia 85 H2 .................................9°49′N 35°03′E
Mendenine Tunisia 48 F4 .............................33°21′N 10°31′E
Mendip Hills England 8 C2 ..........................51°19′N 2°46′W
Mendoza Argentina 73 C3 ...........................32°53′S 68°50′W
Menongue Angola 83 A3 .............................14°38′S 17°41′E
Mentawai, Kepulauan is Indonesia 102 B3 ...3°17′S 99°55′E
Mentok Indonesia 102 C3 ............................2°01′S 105°12′E
Menzel Bourguiba Tunisia 48 E4 ..................37°09′N 9°46′E
Meppel Neth. 42 F5 .....................................52°42′N 6°11′E
Meppen Germany 42 G5 ..............................52°41′N 7°18′E
Merano Italy 46 D2 ......................................46°41′N 11°10′E
Merauke Indonesia 103 K2 ..........................8°31′S 140°25′E
Mere England 8 C2 ......................................51°05′N 2°16′W
Merefa Ukraine 47 Q3 .................................49°49′N 36°04′E
Mergui Myanmar 97 I3 .................................12°27′N 98°37′E
Mergui Archipelago is Myanmar 97 I3 .........11°38′N 97°41′E
Mérida Mexico 66 G5 ..................................20°59′N 89°37′W
Mérida Spain 45 B3 .....................................38°56′N 6°20′W
Mérida, Cordillera de mts Venezuela 67 J2
                                                       7°59′N 71°35′W
Meridian U.S.A. 63 I3 ...................................32°23′N 88°40′W
Merowe Sudan 85 H3 ...................................18°27′N 31°51′E
Merowe Dam resr Sudan D3 .........................18°30′N 31°55′E
Merrick hill Scotland 14 E3 ...........................55°08′N 4°28′W
Mersch Lux. 42 F2 ........................................49°45′N 6°07′E
Mersey est. England 12 E2 ............................53°21′N 2°56′W
Merseyside d. England 21 D3 ........................53°32′N 3°04′W
Mersin Turkey 51 K3 .....................................36°49′N 34°37′E
Merthyr Tydfil Wales 10 D3 ..........................51°45′N 3°23′W
Merthyr Tydfil d. Wales 21 D2 ......................51°44′N 3°20′W
Mértola Portugal 45 B2 ................................37°38′N 7°39′W
Merzifon Turkey 51 K5 .................................40°52′N 35°27′E
Merzig Germany 42 F2 .................................49°27′N 6°39′E

Mesolongi Greece 50 D4 .............................38°22′N 21°26′E
Mesopotamia f. Iraq 85 I5 ...........................35°42′N 42°19′E
Messina Italy 48 G4 ......................................38°11′N 15°33′E
Messiniakos Kolpos b. Greece 50 E3 ...........36°51′N 22°03′E
Mesta r. Bulgaria 50 F5 .................................41°26′N 24°02′E
Meta r. Col./Venez. 72 C7 ............................6°10′N 67°24′W
Metheringham England 13 G2 ....................53°08′N 0°24′W
Methwold England 9 F3 ..............................52°31′N 0°33′E
Metković Croatia 50 B6 ...............................43°03′N 17°40′E
Metz France 44 G6 .......................................49°07′N 6°11′E
Meuse r. Belgium/France 42 E4 ...................51°08′N 5°51′E
Mevagissey England 11 C2 ...........................50°16′N 4°47′W
Mexborough England 13 F2 ........................53°30′N 1°17′W
Mexicali Mexico 66 A7 ................................32°39′N 115°28′W
Mexico Central America 66 C5 ....................31°47′N 114°01′W
México d. Mexico 66 E4 ...............................19°38′N 99°46′W
Mexico, Gulf of Mexico/U.S.A. 66 F5 .........25°00′N 90°00′W
Mexico City Mexico 66 E4 ...........................19°24′N 99°12′W
Meymaneh Afgh. 95 J7 ................................35°56′N 64°45′E
Mezen' Russia 52 E4 ....................................65°50′N 44°18′E
Mezen' r. Russia 52 E4 .................................66°10′N 43°58′E
Mezha r. Russia 47 N6 .................................55°43′N 31°30′E
Mezquital r. Mexico 66 C5 ..........................21°52′N 105°29′W
Miami U.S.A. 63 J2 .......................................25°41′N 80°18′W
Miāndoāb Iran 95 G7 ..................................36°58′N 46°07′E
Miandrivazo Madagascar 83 D3 ..................19°30′S 45°29′E
Mīāneh Iran 95 G7 .......................................37°24′N 47°40′E
Mianwali Pakistan 95 L6 ..............................32°32′N 71°34′E
Miass Russia 52 G3 ......................................54°58′N 60°05′E
Michigan d. U.S.A. 63 I5 ..............................46°12′N 88°00′W
Michigan, Lake U.S.A. 63 I5 .........................43°02′N 87°18′W
Michipicoten Island Canada 63 I6 ...............47°41′N 85°48′W
Michipicoten River town Canada 63 J6 .......47°57′N 84°50′W
Michoacán d. Mexico 66 D4 ........................18°21′N 102°59′W
Michurinsk Russia 53 E3 ..............................52°55′N 40°30′E
Micronesia is Pacific Oc. 117 I3 ...................11°40′N 147°31′E
Micronesia, Federated States of N. Pacific Oc. 103 K5
                                                       3°37′N 153°49′E
Mid and East Antrim d. Northern Ireland 20 B4
                                                       54°53′N 6°14′W
Middlesbrough England 13 F3 .....................54°34′N 1°14′W
Middlesbrough d. England 21 E4 .................54°33′N 1°14′W
Middleton England 12 E2 .............................53°33′N 2°12′W
Middleton in Teesdale England 13 E3 .........54°38′N 2°05′W
Middleton St George England 13 F3 ...........54°31′N 1°28′W
Middlewich England 13 E2 ...........................53°12′N 2°27′W
Midhurst England 8 E1 .................................50°59′N 0°44′W
Midi, Canal du France 44 E3 ........................43°14′N 2°22′E
Midland U.S.A. 62 F3 ...................................32°01′N 101°58′W
Midleton Ireland 18 C1 ................................51°55′N 8°10′W
Midlothian d. Scotland 20 D5 ......................55°50′N 3°06′W
Mid Ulster d. Northern Ireland 21 B4 .........54°39′N 6°44′W
Miekojärvi l. Finland 43 F4 ..........................66°34′N 24°25′E
Mielec Poland 47 I4 ......................................50°17′N 21°26′E
Miercurea Ciuc Romania 50 F8 ...................46°22′N 25°48′E
Mikhaylovka Russia 53 E3 ...........................50°04′N 43°15′E
Mikhaylovskiy Russia 98 D8 ........................51°40′N 79°45′E
Mikkeli Finland 43 F3 ...................................61°41′N 27°17′E
Mikun' Russia 52 F4 .....................................62°22′N 50°05′E
Milan Italy 46 C1 ..........................................45°28′N 9°11′E
Milas Turkey 51 G3 ......................................37°18′N 27°46′E
Milborne Port England 8 C1 ........................50°58′N 2°28′W
Mildenhall England 9 F3 ..............................52°21′N 0°30′E
Mildura Australia 108 D3 .............................34°12′S 142°11′E
Miles City U.S.A. 62 E6 ................................46°25′N 105°47′W
Milford Haven Wales 10 B3 .........................51°43′N 5°02′W
Milk r. U.S.A. 62 E6 ......................................48°03′N 106°19′W
Millars r. Spain 45 E3 ...................................39°57′N 0°04′W
Millau France 44 E4 .....................................44°06′N 3°05′E
Mille Lacs lakes U.S.A. 63 H6 ......................46°14′N 93°39′W
Milleur Point Scotland 14 D3 ......................55°01′N 5°07′W
Millom England 12 D3 .................................54°13′N 3°16′W
Millport Scotland 14 E3 ...............................55°45′N 4°56′W
Milnthorpe England 12 E3 ...........................54°14′N 2°46′W
Milos i. Greece 50 F3 ...................................36°39′N 24°25′E
Milton Keynes England 8 E3 ........................52°01′N 0°44′W
Milton Keynes d. England 21 E3 ..................52°05′N 0°44′W
Milwaukee U.S.A. 63 I5 ................................43°01′N 87°55′W
Mimizan France 44 C4 ..................................44°12′N 1°14′W
Mīnāb Iran 95 I5 ..........................................27°09′N 57°04′E
Minas Indonesia 97 J1 .................................0°52′N 101°30′E
Minatitlán Mexico 66 F4 ..............................18°01′N 94°33′W
Mindanao i. Phil. 103 H5 .............................7°48′N 125°06′E
Mindelo Cape Verde 84 B3 .........................16°52′N 24°59′W
Mindoro i. Phil. 103 G6 ...............................13°05′N 120°52′E
Mindoro Strait Phil. 102 F6 .........................12°47′N 119°59′E
Minehead England 11 D3 .............................51°12′N 3°28′W
Mingäçevir Azerbaijan 53 E2 .......................40°46′N 47°03′E
Mingulay i. Scotland 16 B1 ..........................56°49′N 7°37′W
Minna Nigeria 84 E2 ....................................9°38′N 6°32′E
Minneapolis U.S.A. 63 H5 ...........................44°55′N 93°18′W
Minnesota d. U.S.A. 63 H6 ..........................47°08′N 92°44′W
Minnesota r. U.S.A. 63 H5 ...........................44°55′N 93°11′W
Miño r. Portugal/Spain 45 A4 ......................41°36′N 8°45′W
Minorca i. Spain 45 G4 ................................40°06′N 3°51′E
Minot U.S.A. 62 F6 .......................................48°13′N 101°18′W
Minsk Belarus 47 L5 .....................................53°53′N 27°34′E
Minsterley England 8 C3 ..............................52°38′N 2°55′W
Mintlaw Scotland 17 H2 ..............................57°31′N 1°59′W
Miranda de Ebro Spain 45 D5 ....................42°42′N 2°56′W
Mirandela Portugal 45 B4 ...........................41°29′N 7°10′W
Mirbāţ Oman 95 H3 ....................................17°02′N 54°43′E
Miri Malaysia 102 E4 ...................................4°27′N 114°01′E
Mirim, Lagoa l. Brazil/Uruguay 73 D3 .........32°40′S 52°59′W
Mirnyy Russia 55 M4 ..................................62°25′N 114°10′E
Mirpur Khas Pakistan 96 C6 ........................25°32′N 69°04′E
Mirzapur India 96 F6 ...................................25°06′N 82°39′E
Miskitos, Cayos is Nicaragua 67 H3 ............14°24′N 82°44′W
Miskolc Hungary 46 I3 ................................48°06′N 20°48′E
Misoöl i. Indonesia 103 I3 ...........................1°53′S 130°06′E
Mişrātah Libya 85 F5 ...................................32°21′N 15°04′E
Missinaibi r. Canada 61 J3 ...........................50°45′N 81°31′W
Mississippi d. U.S.A. 63 I3 ...........................32°33′N 89°45′W
Mississippi r. U.S.A. 63 I2 ............................29°07′N 89°06′W
Mississippi Delta U.S.A. 63 I2 .....................29°05′N 89°06′W
Missoula U.S.A. 62 D6 .................................46°52′N 113°59′W
Missouri d. U.S.A. 63 H4 ..............................38°27′N 92°10′W
Missouri r. U.S.A. 63 H4 ...............................38°50′N 90°09′W
Mistassini, Lac l. Canada 61 K3 ...................51°01′N 73°48′W
Mistissini Canada 61 K3 ..............................50°25′N 73°48′W
Mitchell r. Australia 108 D5 .........................15°14′S 141°37′E
Mitchell U.S.A. 62 G5 ..................................43°42′N 98°02′W
Mitchell, Mount U.S.A. 63 J4 ......................35°46′N 82°16′W
Mitchelstown Ireland 18 C2 ........................52°16′N 8°16′W
Mito Japan 104 D3 ......................................36°23′N 140°28′E
Mitsiwwa Eritrea 85 H3 ...............................15°36′N 39°27′E

Mittimatalik Canada 61 K5 .........................72°35′N 77°
Mitumba, Chaîne des mts Dem. Rep. Congo 83 B3
                                                       11°46′S 25°
Miyako Japan 104 D3 ...................................39°38′N 141°
Miyazaki Japan 104 B2 .................................31°54′N 131°
Mizdah Libya 48 F3 ......................................31°25′N 12°
Mizen Head Cork Ireland 18 B1 ...................51°26′N 9°
Mizen Head Wick. Ireland 18 E2 .................52°51′N 6°
Mizoram d. India 97 H5 ...............................23°27′N 92°
Mjölby Sweden 43 C2 ..................................58°20′N 15°
Mława Poland 46 I5 ......................................53°07′N 20°
Mljet i. Croatia 50 B6 ...................................42°44′N 17°
Mmabatho S. Africa 83 B2 ...........................25°47′S 25°
Mobile U.S.A. 63 I3 ......................................30°40′N 88°
Mobile Bay U.S.A. 63 I3 ...............................30°24′N 88°
Mobridge U.S.A. 62 F6 .................................45°32′N 100°
Moçambique Mozambique 83 D3 ..............15°05′S 40°
Mocha Yemen 94 F2 .....................................13°20′N 43°
Mocuba Mozambique 83 C3 ........................16°53′S 36°
Modbury England 11 D2 ..............................50°21′N 3°
Modena Italy 46 D1 ......................................44°39′N 10°
Moelfre Wales 10 C5 .....................................53°21′N 4°
Moel Sych hill Wales 10 D4 ..........................52°53′N 3°
Moffat Scotland 15 F3 ..................................55°20′N 3°
Mogadishu Somalia 85 I2 .............................2°04′N 45°
Mohawk r. U.S.A. 63 L5 ................................42°46′N 73°
Mohyliv Podil's'kyy Ukraine 47 L3 ..............48°27′N 27°
Mo i Rana Norway 43 C4 ..............................66°19′N 14°
Mold Wales 10 D5 ........................................53°10′N 3°
Moldova Europe 49 I6 ..................................46°59′N 28°
Moldoveanu, Vârful mt. Romania 50 F7 ......45°36′N 24°
Molopo watercourse Botswana/S. Africa 83 B2
                                                       28°32′S 20°
Moluccas is Indonesia 103 H3 .....................0°30′S 125°
Molucca Sea Indonesia 103 H3 ...................1°08′S 125°
Mombasa Kenya 85 H1 ................................3°59′S 39°
Møn i. Denmark 43 C1 .................................55°00′N 12°
Mona, Isla i. Puerto Rico 67 K4 ...................18°04′N 67°
Monach, Sound of str. Scotland 16 B2 ........57°33′N 7°
Monach Islands Scotland 16 B2 ..................57°32′N 7°
Monaco Europe 44 G3 .................................43°44′N 7°
Monadhliath Mountains Scotland 17 E2 ......57°04′N 4°
Monaghan Ireland 18 E4 .............................54°15′N 6°
Monaghan d. Ireland 18 E4 .........................54°10′N 6°
Mona Passage str. Dom. Rep./Puerto Rico 67 K4
                                                       18°10′N 68°
Monar, Loch l. Scotland 16 D2 ...................57°25′N 5°
Monbetsu Japan 104 D4 ..............................44°21′N 143°
Monchegorsk Russia 43 H4 .........................67°57′N 32°
Mönchengladbach Germany 42 F4 .............51°12′N 6°
Monclova Mexico 66 D6 ..............................26°53′N 101°
Moncton Canada 61 L2 ...............................46°04′N 64°
Mondego r. Portugal 45 A4 .........................40°10′N 8°
Mondoví Italy 46 B1 ....................................44°23′N 7°
Moneymore Northern Ireland 14 C2 ...........54°41′N 6°
Monforte de Lemos Spain 45 B5 ................42°32′N 7°
Monga Dem. Rep. Congo 83 B5 ..................4°11′N 22°
Mongolia Asia 99 I7 .....................................46°59′N 103°
Mongora Pakistan 95 L6 ..............................34°46′N 72°
Mongu Zambia 83 B3 ..................................15°15′S 23°
Moniaive Scotland 15 F3 ..............................55°12′N 3°
Monmouth Wales 10 E3 ...............................51°49′N 2°
Monmouthshire d. Wales 21 D2 .................51°47′N 2°
Monnow r. U.K. 8 C2 ...................................51°48′N 2°
Monroe U.S.A. 63 H3 ...................................32°30′N 92°
Monrovia Liberia 84 C2 ...............................6°20′N 10°
Mons Belgium 42 C3 ...................................50°27′N 3°
Montana Bulgaria 50 E6 ..............................43°25′N 23°
Montana d. U.S.A. 62 E6 ..............................46°44′N 109°
Montargis France 44 E5 ...............................47°59′N 2°
Montauban France 44 D4 ............................44°01′N 1°
Montbéliard France 44 G5 ...........................47°30′N 6°
Mont-de-Marsan France 44 C3 ...................43°53′N 0°
Monte-Carlo Monaco 44 G3 .......................43°44′N 7°
Montego Bay town Jamaica 67 I4 ...............18°28′N 77°
Montélimar France 44 F4 .............................44°33′N 4°
Montemorelos Mexico 66 E6 ......................25°11′N 99°
Montenegro Europe 50 C6 ..........................43°01′N 19°
Montería Colombia 72 B7 ...........................8°43′N 75°
Monterrey Mexico 66 D6 .............................25°42′N 100°
Montes Claros Brazil 72 E5 ..........................16°43′S 43°
Montevideo Uruguay 73 D3 ........................34°52′S 56°
Monte Vista U.S.A. 62 E4 .............................37°34′N 106°
Montgomery U.S.A. 63 I3 ............................32°23′N 86°
Montgomery Wales 10 D4 ...........................52°34′N 3°
Mont-Joli Canada 63 M6 .............................48°35′N 68°
Montmagny Canada 63 L6 ...........................46°59′N 70°
Montpelier U.S.A. 63 L5 ...............................44°16′N 72°
Montpellier France 44 E3 .............................43°37′N 3°
Montréal Canada 61 K2 ...............................45°32′N 73°
Montreuil France 9 G1 .................................50°28′N 1°
Montrose Scotland 17 G1 ............................56°43′N 2°
Montserrat i. Central America 67 L4 ............16°44′N 62°
Monywa Myanmar 97 I5 ..............................22°05′N 95°
Monza Italy 46 C1 ........................................45°35′N 9°
Monzón Spain 45 F4 ....................................41°55′N 0°
Moore, Lake Australia 108 A4 .....................29°43′S 117°
Moose r. Canada 61 J3 ................................51°20′N 80°
Moose Jaw Canada 60 H3 ...........................50°26′N 105°
Moosomin Canada 62 F7 .............................50°09′N 101°
Moosonee Canada 61 J3 .............................51°16′N 80°
Mopti Mali 84 D3 .........................................14°30′N 4°
Mora Sweden 43 C3 .....................................61°00′N 14°
Morar, Loch l. Scotland 16 D1 .....................56°57′N 5°
Moray d. Scotland 20 D5 .............................57°30′N 3°
Moray Firth b. Scotland 17 E2 .....................57°31′N 4°
Morbach Germany 42 G2 ............................49°48′N 7°
Morden Canada 60 I2 ..................................49°12′N 98°
More, Loch l. Scotland 16 E3 .......................58°18′N 4°
Morecambe England 12 E3 ..........................54°04′N 2°
Morecambe Bay England 12 D3 ..................54°07′N 3°
Moree Australia 108 D4 ...............................29°28′S 149°
Morehead P.N.G. 103 K2 .............................8°44′S 141°
Morelia Mexico 66 D4 .................................19°39′N 101°
Morelos d. Mexico 66 E4 .............................18°47′N 98°
Morena, Sierra mts Spain 45 B2 ..................37°57′N 6°
Moretonhampstead England 11 D2 ............50°40′N 3°
Morgan City U.S.A. 63 H2 ............................29°41′N 91°
Mori Japan 104 D4 ......................................42°06′N 140°
Morioka Japan 104 D3 ................................39°42′N 141°
Moriston r. Scotland 16 E2 ..........................57°11′N 4°
Morlaix France 44 B6 ...................................48°35′N 3°
Morley England 13 F2 ..................................53°45′N 1°
Morocco Africa 84 D5 .................................31°57′N 6°

ogoro Tanzania 83 C4 .................................6°47'S 37°40'E
o Gulf Phil. 103 G5 ...............................6°59'N 123°21'E
ombe Madagascar 83 D2 ...................21°46'S 43°21'E
ón Mongolia 99 I7 ..............................49°28'N 100°08'E
ondava Madagascar 83 D2 ..................20°18'S 44°17'E
ón de la Frontera Spain 45 C2 ...........37°08'N 5°27'W
oni Comoros 83 D3 ...........................11°39'S 43°14'E
otai i. England 103 H4 .......................2°23'N 128°27'E
peth England 13 F4 ...........................55°10'N 1°41'W
riston Wales 10 D3 .............................51°40'N 3°56'W
ro, Punta pt Chile 73 B4 ...................27°07'S 70°59'W
osquillo, Golfo de b. Colombia 67 I2....9°33'N 75°39'W
shansk Russia 53 E3 .........................53°27'N 41°49'E
e Bay England 11 C3 ........................51°10'N 4°14'W
iehoe England 11 C3 ..........................51°11'N 4°12'W
ern f. Scotland 16 D1 ........................56°36'N 5°53'W
borough England 13 F2 ....................53°20'N 1°22'W
ul Russia 52 F3 ..................................55°45'N 37°38'E
cow U.S.A. 62 C6 ............................46°44'N 116°58'W
rau Germany 42 G3 ..........................50°22'N 7°36'E
elle r. France 44 G6 ..........................49°27'N 6°22'E
hi Tanzania 83 C4 ...............................3°23'S 37°02'E
øen Norway 43 C4 ............................65°51'N 13°12'E
quitos, Golfo de los b. Panama 67 H2   8°56'N 81°17'W
s Norway 43 B2 ................................59°26'N 10°39'E
soró Brazil 72 F6 ..............................5°08'S 37°15'W
sel Bay town S. Africa 83 B1 .............34°11'S 22°08'E
aganem Algeria 48 D4 .....................35°55'N 0°06'E
ar Bos. and Herz. 50 B6 ..................43°20'N 17°49'E
ul Iraq 94 F7 ....................................36°18'N 43°05'E
vatnet l. Norway 43 B2 ....................59°51'N 8°06'E
la Sweden 43 C2 .............................58°32'N 15°07'E
erwell Scotland 15 F3 ......................55°48'N 3°59'W
il Spain 45 D2 .................................36°45'N 3°31'W
ins France 44 E5 ..............................46°34'N 3°20'E
mein Myanmar 97 I4 .........................16°30'N 97°40'E
ndou Chad 84 F2 ..............................8°36'N 16°05'E
nt Gambier town Australia 108 D3...37°52'S 140°48'E
nt Isa town Australia 108 C4 ...........20°45'S 139°29'E
ntmellick Ireland 18 D3 ...................53°07'N 7°20'W
ntrath Ireland 18 D3 ........................53°00'N 7°28'W
nt's Bay England 11 B2 ....................50°05'S 9°29'W
ntsorrel England 8 D3 ......................52°44'N 1°08'W
rdi, Dépression du f. Chad 94 B3.....18°01'N 21°56'E
ne r. Northern Ireland 14 B2 ...........54°50'N 7°28'W
ne Mountains Northern Ireland 14 C2
......................................................54°06'N 6°11'W
sa i. Scotland 17 H5 .......................60°00'N 1°11'W
scron Belgium 42 C3 .......................50°44'N 3°13'E
ton France 42 E2 .............................49°37'N 5°05'E
r. Ireland 18 B4 .............................54°07'N 9°08'W
mbe Ethiopia 85 H2 ........................3°32'N 39°03'E
ale Atlas mts Morocco 48 B3 ..........32°25'N 5°37'W
noq Uzbekistan 53 F2 .....................43°45'N 58°53'E
mbique Africa 83 C3 ......................20°09'S 34°14'E
mbique Channel Africa 83 D2 ........20°15'S 40°16'E
ken Tunisia 51 H3 ...........................35°43'N 10°35'E
nsk Russia 47 Q5 ............................53°17'N 36°36'E
ara Tanzania 83 C3 .........................10°19'S 40°09'E
bungo Indonesia 102 C3 .................1°27'S 102°08'E
Wenlock England 8 C3 ...................52°36'N 2°33'W
i. Scotland 16 C1 ...........................56°50'N 6°14'W
kish Mountain Ireland 14 A3 ..........55°06'N 8°00'W
kle Roe i. Scotland 17 H5 ..............60°21'N 1°25'W
anjiang China 99 N6 .......................44°32'N 129°34'E
urnu Turkey 51 I5 ..........................40°27'N 31°13'E
da Mozambique 83 C3 ....................11°38'S 39°34'E
a Turkey 51 H3 ...............................37°12'N 28°21'E
ammad Qol Sudan 94 E4 ...............20°54'N 37°07'E
hausen/Thüringen Germany 46 D4...51°13'N 10°27'E
os Finland 43 F4 .............................64°48'N 25°58'E
e Bheag Ireland 18 E2 ...................52°42'N 6°58'W
kirk Scotland 15 E3 ........................55°31'N 4°04'W
neag hill Scotland 16 C3 ................58°22'N 6°18'W
acheve Ukraine 47 J3 .....................48°27'N 22°43'E
alla Yemen 95 G2 ...........................14°34'N 49°06'E
nje, Mount Malawi 83 C3 ...............15°54'S 35°35'E
le Germany 46 E4 ...........................51°52'N 12°15'E
acén mt. Spain 45 D2 ......................37°02'N 3°18'W
ouse France 44 E4 ..........................47°45'N 7°20'E
i. Scotland 14 D4 ...........................56°27'N 5°58'W
Sound of str. Scotland 14 C4 ..........56°37'N 6°01'W
aghareirk Mountains Ireland 18 B2..52°22'N 9°17'W
aghcleevaun hill Ireland 10 A5 ........53°06'N 6°24'W
Head Scotland 17 G4 .....................59°23'N 2°53'W
ngar Ireland 18 D3 .........................53°31'N 7°20'W
of Galloway Scotland 14 C2 ...........54°38'N 4°52'W
of Kintyre hd Scotland 14 D3 .........55°17'N 5°50'W
of Oa hd Scotland 14 C3 ................55°35'N 6°20'W
an Pakistan 96 D7 ..........................30°12'N 71°35'E
bai India 96 D4 ..............................18°56'N 72°51'E
bles Wales 10 C3 ...........................51°34'N 4°00'W
i. Indonesia 103 G2 .......................5°02'S 122°30'E
a r. Russia 52 E3 ............................55°34'N 42°04'E
om Russia 52 F3 .............................68°57'N 33°07'E
na India 96 D4 ...............................42°19'N 140°58'E
ay r. Australia 108 C3 ....................35°22'S 139°18'E
ay Bridge Australia 108 C3 ............35°07'S 139°17'E
umbidgee r. Australia 108 D3 ........34°42'S 143°13'E
Libya 84 F4 ....................................25°54'N 13°55'E
zuschlag Austria 46 F2 ..................47°37'N 15°41'E
ala mt. Bulgaria 50 E6 ...................42°11'N 23°35'E
cat Oman 95 I4 ..............................23°36'N 58°35'E
grave Ranges mts Australia 108 C4..26°17'S 131°01'E
kogee U.S.A. 63 G4 ........................35°47'N 95°23'W
mar Sudan 94 E3 ...........................18°13'N 34°00'E
soma Tanzania 83 C4 ......................1°32'S 33°47'E
selburgh Scotland 15 F3 .................55°57'N 3°03'W
afakemalpaşa Turkey 51 H5 ...........40°02'N 28°23'E

Mūţ Egypt 85 G4 ...............................25°28'N 28°58'E
Mut Turkey 51 J3 ..............................36°39'N 33°26'E
Mutare Zimbabwe 83 C3 ...................18°58'S 32°39'E
Mutis, Gunung mt. Indonesia 103 G2......9°35'S 124°14'E
Mutsu Japan 104 D4 .........................41°17'N 141°10'E
Mutuali Mozambique 83 C3 ..............14°52'S 37°01'E
Muyezerskiy Russia 52 D4 ................63°57'N 32°01'E
Muzaffargarh Pakistan 95 L6 ............30°03'N 71°14'E
Muzaffarpur India 96 G6 ...................26°05'N 85°28'E
Mwanza Tanzania 83 C4 .....................2°30'S 32°56'E
Mwene-Ditu Dem. Rep. Congo 83 B4...7°01'S 23°27'E
Mweru, Lake Dem. Rep. Congo/Zambia 83 B4
......................................................8°57'S 28°46'E
Myanmar Asia 97 I5 ..........................22°37'N 95°02'E
Mykolayiv Ukraine 49 J6 ..................46°57'N 32°02'E
Myla Russia 52 F4 .............................65°27'N 50°52'E
Myronivka Ukraine 47 N3 ..................49°39'N 30°59'E
Myrtle Beach town U.S.A. 63 K3 ........33°43'N 78°54'W
Mysuru India 96 E3 ...........................12°16'N 76°36'E
My Tho Vietnam 102 D6 ....................10°20'N 106°23'E
Mytilini Greece 50 G4 .......................39°07'N 26°33'E
Mzuzu Malawi 83 C3 .........................11°27'S 34°00'E

# N

Naas Ireland 18 E3 ...........................53°13'N 6°40'W
Naberezhnyye Chelny Russia 52 F3............55°42'N 52°21'E
Nabeul Tunisia 48 F4 ........................36°29'N 10°45'E
Nacala Mozambique 83 D3 ................14°34'S 40°40'E
Nador Morocco 48 C4 ......................35°11'N 2°56'W
Nadvoitsy Russia 52 D4 ....................63°54'N 34°17'E
Nadym Russia 54 I4 ..........................65°29'N 72°34'E
Næstved Denmark 43 B1 ...................55°14'N 11°46'E
Nafplio Greece 50 E3 ........................37°34'N 22°49'E
Naga Phil. 103 G6 .............................13°35'N 123°11'E
Nagaland d. India 97 H6 ....................26°03'N 94°37'E
Nagano Japan 104 C3 .......................36°38'N 138°11'E
Nagaoka Japan 104 C3 ......................37°26'N 138°51'E
Nagaon India 97 H6 ..........................26°19'N 92°42'E
Nagasaki Japan 104 A2 .....................32°46'N 129°52'E
Nagercoil India 96 E2 .........................8°10'N 77°28'E
Nagha Kalat Pakistan 95 K5 ..............27°23'N 65°13'E
Nagorno-Karabakh i. Azerbaijan 53 E2....40°00'N 46°30'E
Nagoya Japan 104 C3 .......................35°10'N 136°53'E
Nagpur India 96 E5 ...........................21°09'N 79°05'E
Nagurskoye Russia 54 F6 ..................80°31'N 47°36'E
Nagykanizsa Hungary 46 G2 .............46°28'N 16°59'E
Naha Japan 99 N3 ............................26°12'N 127°39'E
Nahāvand Iran 95 G6 ........................34°12'N 48°22'E
Na h-Eileanan Siar d. Scotland 20 B5..57°54'N 6°48'W
Nailsworth England 8 C2 ..................51°42'N 2°13'W
Nain Canada 61 L3 ...........................56°31'N 61°31'W
Nā'īn Iran 95 H6 ...............................32°50'N 53°03'E
Nairn Scotland 17 F2 ........................57°35'N 3°52'W
Nairn r. Scotland 17 F2 .....................57°35'N 3°52'W
Nairobi Kenya 85 H1 ..........................1°17'S 36°48'E
Najafābād Iran 95 H6 ........................32°37'N 51°20'E
Najd f. Saudi Arabia 94 F5 ................26°14'N 40°21'E
Najrān Saudi Arabia 94 F3 ................17°34'N 44°17'E
Nakhodka Russia 55 O2 ....................42°48'N 132°54'E
Nakhon Ratchasima Thailand 102 C6....14°57'N 102°08'E
Nakhon Sawan Thailand 102 C7 ........15°40'N 100°06'E
Nakhon Si Thammarat Thailand 102 B5...8°25'N 99°58'E
Nakina Canada 61 J2 ........................50°10'N 86°43'W
Nakonde Zambia 83 C3 .......................9°21'S 32°42'E
Nakskov Denmark 43 B1 ....................54°49'N 11°09'E
Nakuru Kenya 85 H1 ..........................0°16'S 36°05'E
Nal'chik Russia 53 E2 .......................43°29'N 43°38'E
Nālūt Libya 84 F5 ..............................31°49'N 10°57'E
Namak, Kavīr-e f. Iran 95 I6 .............34°26'N 57°32'E
Namakzar-e Shadad f. Iran 95 I6 .......30°44'N 58°01'E
Namangan Uzbekistan 98 C6 .............40°59'N 71°38'E
Nam Co l. China 98 G4 .....................30°42'N 90°35'E
Nam Đinh Vietnam 102 D8 ................20°22'N 106°11'E
Namib Desert Namibia 83 A2 ............25°21'S 15°06'E
Namibe Angola 83 A3 .......................15°11'S 12°10'E
Namibia Africa 83 A2 ........................23°22'S 15°55'E
Namlea Indonesia 103 H3 ...................3°14'S 127°05'E
Namp'o N. Korea 99 N5 ....................38°43'N 125°23'E
Nampula Mozambique 83 C3 ............15°10'S 39°13'E
Namsos Norway 43 B4 ......................64°28'N 11°31'E
Namur Belgium 42 D3 .......................50°28'N 4°52'E
Namur d. Belgium 42 D3 ...................50°16'N 4°53'E
Nan Thailand 102 C7 ........................18°47'N 100°47'E
Nanaimo Canada 62 B6 ....................49°10'N 123°56'W
Nanao Japan 104 C3 ........................37°03'N 136°58'E
Nanchang China 99 L3 .....................28°42'N 115°58'E
Nanchong China 99 J4 .....................30°46'N 106°04'E
Nancy France 44 G6 ...........................48°42'N 6°11'E
Nan Ling mts China 99 K2 ................24°59'N 111°08'E
Nanning China 99 J2 ........................22°49'N 108°24'E
Nanortalik Greenland 61 N4 .............60°09'N 45°15'W
Nanping China 99 L3 ........................26°41'N 118°08'E
Nantes France 44 C5 .........................47°13'N 1°33'W
Nantes à Brest, Canal de France 44 B5...47°42'N 2°07'W
Nantong China 99 M4 .......................31°59'N 120°56'E
Nantucket Island U.S.A. 63 M5 .........41°17'N 69°59'W
Nantwich England 13 E2 ...................53°04'N 2°31'W
Nant-y-moch Reservoir Wales 10 D4....52°28'N 3°54'W
Nanyang China 99 K4 .......................33°01'N 112°35'E
Nao, Cabo de la c. Spain 45 F3 .........38°44'N 0°15'E
Napaimiut U.S.A. 60 C4 ....................61°38'N 158°24'W
Napier New Zealand 109 G2 ..............39°30'S 176°53'E
Naples Italy 48 F5 ..............................40°51'N 14°15'E
Narberth Wales 10 C3 .......................51°48'N 4°45'W
Narbonne France 44 E3 .......................43°11'N 3°01'E
Narborough Leics. England 8 D3 .......52°34'N 1°13'W
Narborough Norf. England 9 F3 .........52°41'N 0°35'E
Nares Strait Canada/Greenland 61 K5...79°12'N 71°28'W
Narmada r. India 96 D5 ....................21°43'N 73°06'E
Narodnaya, Gora mt. Russia 52 F4 ....65°01'N 60°06'E
Naro-Fominsk Russia 47 Q6 .............55°22'N 36°45'E
Närpes Finland 43 E3 ........................62°29'N 21°21'E
Narva Estonia 43 G2 .........................59°22'N 28°11'E
Narvik Norway 43 D5 ........................68°26'N 17°25'E
Nar'yan-Mar Russia 52 F4 .................67°40'S 53°10'E
Naryn Kyrgyzstan 98 D6 ...................41°19'N 75°56'E
Nashik India 96 D5 ...........................20°00'N 73°52'E
Nashville U.S.A. 63 I4 .......................36°11'N 86°46'W
Näsijärvi l. Finland 43 E3 ...................61°35'N 23°44'E
Nassau Bahamas 67 I6 ......................25°05'N 77°23'W
Nassau i. Cook Is 109 I5 ...................11°32'S 165°22'W
Nasser, Lake resr Egypt 85 H4 ..........23°09'N 33°02'E
Nässjö Sweden 43 C2 ........................57°39'N 14°43'E

Nata Botswana 83 B2 ........................20°12'S 26°10'E
Natal Brazil 72 F6 ...............................5°44'S 35°10'W
Natchez U.S.A. 63 H3 .......................31°35'N 91°24'W
Natron, Lake Tanzania 83 C4 ..............2°18'S 36°02'E
Natuna, Kepulauan is Indonesia 102 D4....4°12'N 107°23'E
Natuna Besar i. Indonesia 102 D4 .......4°04'N 108°28'E
Naujaat Canada 61 J4 .......................66°32'N 86°08'W
Nauru S. Pacific Oc. 109 F6 ...............0°30'S 166°56'E
Navalmoral de la Mata Spain 45 C3...39°53'N 5°32'W
Navan Ireland 18 E3 ..........................53°39'N 6°41'W
Navapolatsk Belarus 47 M6 ..............55°32'N 28°40'E
Naver r. Scotland 17 E3 .....................58°31'N 4°13'W
Naver, Loch l. Scotland 17 E3 ............58°17'N 4°24'W
Navlya Russia 47 P5 ..........................52°49'N 34°31'E
Navojoa Mexico 66 C6 ......................27°04'N 109°32'W
Nawabshah Pakistan 96 C6 ...............26°13'N 68°25'E
Naxçıvan Azerbaijan 95 G7 ...............39°13'N 45°24'E
Naxos i. Greece 50 F3 .......................37°02'N 25°35'E
Nayarit d. Mexico 66 D5 ...................22°07'N 104°45'W
Nay Pyi Taw Myanmar 97 I4 .............19°44'N 96°13'E
Nazareth Israel 49 K3 .......................32°40'N 35°18'E
Nazas r. Mexico 66 D6 ......................25°34'N 104°55'W
Nazilli Turkey 51 H3 ..........................37°55'N 28°19'E
Nazrēt Ethiopia 85 H2 .......................8°32'N 39°15'E
Nazwá Oman 95 I4 ...........................22°56'N 57°31'E
N'dalatando Angola 83 A4 ..................9°18'S 14°56'E
Ndélé C.A.R. 85 F2 .............................8°24'N 20°38'E
Ndeni i. Solomon Is 109 F5 ..............10°41'S 166°07'E
N'Djaména Chad 84 F3 .....................12°08'N 15°03'E
Ndola Zambia 83 B3 .........................12°57'S 28°39'E
Neagh, Lough l. Northern Ireland 14 C2....54°40'N 6°24'W
Nea Liosia Greece 50 E4 ...................38°04'N 23°42'E
Neapoli Greece 50 E3 .......................36°31'N 23°04'E
Neath Wales 10 D3 ...........................51°39'N 3°48'W
Neath r. Wales 10 D3 ........................51°39'N 3°49'W
Neath Port Talbot d. Wales 21 D2 .....51°43'N 3°49'W
Nebitdag Turkmenistan 95 H7 ...........39°27'N 54°17'E
Neblina, Pico da mt. Brazil 72 C7 .......0°49'N 66°13'W
Nebraska d. U.S.A. 62 F5 ..................41°30'N 100°06'W
Neckar r. Germany 44 H6 ..................49°31'N 8°27'E
Needham Market England 9 G3 .........52°09'N 1°03'E
Needles U.S.A. 62 D3 .......................34°50'N 114°36'W
Neftekamsk Russia 52 F3 ..................56°06'N 54°14'E
Nefyn Wales 10 C4 ...........................52°56'N 4°31'W
Negotin Serbia 50 E7 ........................44°13'N 22°33'E
Negra, Punta pt Peru 68 B3 ................6°05'S 81°21'W
Negro r. Argentina 73 C2 ..................41°01'S 62°48'W
Negro r. Brazil 72 C6 ..........................3°08'S 59°57'W
Negro, Cabo c. Morocco 45 C1 .........35°41'N 5°17'W
Negros i. Phil. 103 G5 .........................9°43'N 122°50'E
Neijiang China 99 J3 .........................29°35'N 105°04'E
Nei Mongol Zizhiqu d. China 99 I6 ....40°12'N 103°26'E
Neiße r. Germany/Poland 46 F5 .........52°04'N 14°46'E
Neiva Colombia 72 B7 .........................2°55'N 75°15'W
Nek'emtē Ethiopia 85 H2 ....................9°06'N 36°32'E
Neksø Denmark 46 F6 .......................55°03'N 15°08'E
Nelidovo Russia 47 O7 ......................56°14'N 32°47'E
Nellore India 96 E3 ...........................14°29'N 79°59'E
Nelson Canada 60 G2 .......................49°29'N 117°17'W
Nelson r. Canada 61 I3 .....................56°58'N 92°45'W
Nelson England 13 E2 .......................53°50'N 2°13'W
Nelson New Zealand 109 G2 .............41°17'S 173°15'E
Nelspruit S. Africa 83 C2 ...................25°28'S 30°59'E
Neman Russia 47 J6 ..........................55°02'N 22°02'E
Neman r. Russia 47 J6 .......................55°03'N 22°14'E
Nementcha, Monts des mts Algeria 48 E3...34°48'N 6°23'E
Nemuro Japan 104 E4 .......................43°17'N 145°30'E
Nenagh Ireland 18 C2 .......................52°52'N 8°12'W
Nene r. England 9 F3 .........................52°49'N 0°13'E
Nenjiang China 99 N7 .......................49°04'N 125°12'E
Nepal Asia 96 F6 ..............................28°59'N 82°06'E
Nephin hill Ireland 18 B4 ..................54°01'N 9°22'W
Neris r. Lithuania 43 F1 .....................54°55'N 23°53'E
Ness r. Scotland 17 E2 ......................57°29'N 4°14'W
Ness, Loch l. Scotland 17 E2 .............57°10'N 4°37'W
Neston England 12 D2 .......................53°17'N 3°04'W
Nestos r. Greece 50 F5 ......................40°51'N 24°48'E
Netherlands Europe 42 E5 .................52°13'N 5°33'E
Netley Abbey England 8 D1 ..............50°52'N 1°19'W
Nettilling Lake Canada 61 K4 ...........66°30'N 70°39'W
Neubrandenburg Germany 46 F5 .......53°33'N 13°15'E
Neufchâteau Belgium 42 E2 ..............49°51'N 5°27'E
Neum Bos. and Herz. 50 B6 ..............42°55'N 17°37'E
Neumünster Germany 46 C6 .............54°05'N 9°59'E
Neunkirchen Germany 46 B4 ............49°21'N 7°11'E
Neuquén Argentina 73 C3 .................38°57'S 68°03'W
Neuruppin Germany 46 E5 ................52°56'N 12°48'E
Neustrelitz Germany 46 E5 ...............53°22'N 13°04'E
Neuwied Germany 46 B4 ..................50°26'N 7°28'E
Nevada d. U.S.A. 62 C4 ....................39°03'N 117°06'W
Nevada, Sierra mts Spain 45 D2 .......37°04'N 3°20'W
Nevada, Sierra mts U.S.A. 62 B5 .......40°07'N 121°00'W
Nevel' Russia 47 M7 .........................56°01'N 29°55'E
Nevers France 44 E5 .........................47°00'N 3°09'E
Nevinnomyssk Russia 49 L5 .............44°38'N 41°56'E
Nevis, Loch inlet Scotland 16 D2 ......57°00'N 5°42'W
Nevşehir Turkey 51 K4 ......................38°37'N 34°43'E
New Addington England 9 E2 ...........51°21'N 0°01'W
New Alresford England 8 D2 .............51°05'N 1°10'W
Newark U.S.A. 63 L5 ........................40°44'N 74°24'W
Newark-on-Trent England 13 G2 .......53°04'N 0°48'W
New Bern U.S.A. 63 K4 .....................35°05'N 77°03'W
Newbiggin-by-the-Sea England 13 F4....55°11'N 1°31'W
Newbridge Ireland 18 E3 ..................53°11'N 6°48'W
Newbridge Wales 10 D3 ...................51°40'N 3°09'W
New Britain i. P.N.G. 108 D6 ...............5°42'S 148°56'E
New Brunswick d. Canada 61 L2 .......46°41'N 66°28'W
Newburgh Scotland 15 F4 .................56°21'N 3°14'W
Newbury England 8 D2 .....................51°24'N 1°19'W
New Caledonia is S. Pacific Oc. 109 F4...21°41'S 164°27'E
Newcastle Australia 108 E3 ..............32°56'S 151°44'E
Newcastle Northern Ireland 14 D2 ....54°13'N 5°53'W
Newcastle Scotland 15 G3 ................55°11'N 2°49'W
Newcastle Emlyn Wales 10 C4 ..........52°02'N 4°28'W
Newcastleton Scotland 15 G3 ...........55°11'N 2°49'W
Newcastle-under-Lyme England 13 E2...53°01'N 2°13'W
Newcastle upon Tyne England 13 F3....54°59'N 1°37'W
Newcastle West Ireland 18 B2 ..........52°27'N 9°03'W
New Cumnock Scotland 14 E3 ...........55°23'N 4°11'W
New Delhi India 96 E6 .......................28°36'N 77°12'E
Newent England 8 C2 .......................51°56'N 2°24'W
New Forest nature res. England 8 D1...50°52'N 1°35'W
Newfoundland i. Canada 61 M2 ........48°30'N 56°04'W
Newfoundland and Labrador d. Canada 61 M3
......................................................55°44'N 56°53'W
New Galloway Scotland 14 E3 ...........55°05'N 4°08'W
New Georgia Sound str. Solomon Is 108 E6...7°21'S 156°36'E
New Glasgow Canada 63 N6 .............45°35'N 62°35'W

New Guinea i. Indonesia/P.N.G. 103 K2...5°26'S 140°49'E
New Hampshire d. U.S.A. 63 L5 ........44°02'N 71°34'W
Newhaven England 9 F1 ....................50°48'N 0°03'E
New Haven U.S.A. 63 L5 ...................41°18'N 72°56'W
New Ireland i. P.N.G. 108 E6 ...............3°33'S 152°14'E
New Jersey d. U.S.A. 63 L4 ...............39°57'N 74°26'W
New Liskeard Canada 63 K6 .............47°31'N 79°41'W
Newmarket England 9 F3 ..................52°15'N 0°25'E
Newmarket-on-Fergus Ireland 18 C2....52°46'N 8°53'W
New Mexico d. U.S.A. 62 E3 .............34°32'N 105°55'W
New Milton England 8 D1 .................50°45'N 1°40'W
Newnham England 8 C2 ....................51°48'N 2°27'W
New Orleans U.S.A. 63 H2 ................29°58'N 90°03'W
New Pitsligo Scotland 17 G2 ............57°36'N 2°12'W
Newport Ess. England 9 F2 ...............51°59'N 0°13'E
Newport I. o. W. England 8 D1 ..........50°42'N 1°17'W
Newport New. Wales 10 E3 ..............51°35'N 2°59'W
Newport Pem. Wales 10 C4 ..............52°01'N 4°50'W
Newport Tel. Wre. England 8 C3 .......52°46'N 2°22'W
Newport d. Wales 21 D2 ...................51°35'N 2°59'W
Newport Bay Wales 10 C4 ................52°02'N 4°53'W
Newport News U.S.A. 63 K4 .............37°00'N 76°26'W
Newport Pagnell England 8 E3 ..........52°05'N 0°43'W
New Providence i. Bahamas 67 I6 .....25°03'N 77°25'W
Newquay England 11 B2 ...................50°25'N 5°04'W
New Quay Wales 10 C4 ....................52°13'N 4°22'W
New Romney England 9 F1 ...............50°59'N 0°56'E
New Ross Ireland 18 E2 ....................52°23'N 6°57'W
Newry Northern Ireland 14 C2 ..........54°10'N 6°19'W
Newry Canal Northern Ireland 14 C2....54°16'N 6°21'W
Newry, Mourne and Down d. Northern Ireland 21 B4
......................................................54°10'N 6°18'W
New Siberian Islands Russia 55 P5 .....76°08'N 149°21'E
New South Wales d. Australia 108 D3...32°42'S 146°22'E
Newton Abbot England 11 D2 ...........50°32'N 3°37'W
Newton Aycliffe England 13 F3 .........54°37'N 1°34'W
Newtonbutler Northern Ireland 14 B2...54°10'N 7°21'W
Newtonhill Scotland 17 G2 ...............57°02'N 2°09'W
Newton-le-Willows England 12 E2 .....53°27'N 2°38'W
Newton Mearns Scotland 14 E3 ........55°46'N 4°20'W
Newtonmore Scotland 17 E2 ............57°04'N 4°07'W
Newton St Cyres England 11 D2 .......50°46'N 3°35'W
Newton Stewart Scotland 14 E2 ........54°58'N 4°29'W
Newtown Wales 10 D4 ......................52°31'N 3°19'W
Newtownabbey Northern Ireland 14 D2...54°39'N 5°54'W
Newtownards Northern Ireland 14 D2...54°35'N 5°41'W
Newtown St Boswells Scotland 15 G3...55°35'N 2°40'W
Newtownstewart Northern Ireland 14 B2...54°43'N 7°22'W
New York U.S.A. 63 L5 ......................40°41'N 73°59'W
New York d. U.S.A. 63 K5 ..................42°43'N 75°14'W
New Zealand Oceania 109 G2 ...........42°54'S 174°10'E
Neyrīz Iran 95 H5 .............................29°12'N 54°19'E
Neyshābūr Iran 95 I7 ........................36°12'N 58°46'E
Ngaoundéré Cameroon 84 F2 .............7°19'N 13°34'E
Ngerulmud Palau 103 I5 ....................7°30'N 134°39'E
Nguigmi Niger 84 F3 ........................14°14'N 13°05'E
Ngulu atoll Micronesia 103 J5 .............8°28'N 137°37'E
Nha Trang Vietnam 102 D6 ...............12°11'N 109°11'E
Niamey Niger 84 E3 .........................13°31'N 2°07'E
Niangara Dem. Rep. Congo 83 B5 .......3°40'N 27°52'E
Nias i. Indonesia 102 B4 ....................1°11'N 97°04'E
Nicaragua Central America 67 G3 .....13°13'N 85°57'W
Nicaragua, Lake Nicaragua 67 G3 ....11°31'N 85°17'W
Nice France 44 G3 ............................43°42'N 7°17'E
Nicobar Islands India 97 H2 ...............8°00'N 93°59'E
Nicosia Cyprus 51 J2 ........................35°10'N 33°22'E
Nicoya, Golfo de b. Costa Rica 67 H2....9°42'N 84°48'W
Nidd r. England 13 F3 .......................54°01'N 1°13'W
Nidzica Poland 46 I5 .........................53°22'N 20°26'E
Niedersachsen d. Germany 42 G5 .....52°43'N 8°53'E
Nienburg Germany 46 C5 ..................52°38'N 9°13'E
Niers r. Germany 42 E4 .....................51°42'N 5°57'E
Nieuwpoort Belgium 42 C4 ...............51°08'N 2°45'E
Nieves, Pico de las mt. Canary Islands 45 Y1
......................................................27°57'N 15°34'W
Niğde Turkey 51 K3 ..........................37°59'N 34°41'E
Niger Africa 84 E3 ............................17°03'N 10°05'E
Niger r. Africa 84 E2 .........................4°17'N 6°05'E
Nigeria Africa 84 E2 ...........................9°09'N 7°54'E
Nigg Bay Scotland 17 E2 ..................57°43'N 4°05'W
Niigata Japan 104 C3 .......................37°55'N 139°03'E
Nijmegen Neth. 42 E4 ......................51°50'N 5°52'E
Nikel' Russia 43 G5 ..........................69°24'N 30°13'E
Nikol'sk Russia 52 E3 .......................59°32'N 45°27'E
Nikopol' Ukraine 47 P2 .....................47°34'N 34°24'E
Niksar Turkey 51 L5 .........................40°35'N 36°57'E
Nikšić Montenegro 50 C6 ..................42°46'N 18°56'E
Nikumaroro atoll Kiribati 109 H6 ........4°43'S 174°31'W
Nile r. Africa 85 H5 ...........................30°11'N 31°06'E
Nile Delta Egypt 94 D6 .....................30°50'N 31°00'E
Nilgiri Hills India 96 E3 .....................11°08'N 76°28'E
Nîmes France 44 F3 ..........................43°51'N 4°22'E
Ningbo China 99 M3 ........................29°54'N 121°34'E
Ningxia Huizu Zizhiqu d. China 99 J5...37°11'N 105°28'E
Niobrara r. U.S.A. 62 G5 ...................42°46'N 98°02'W
Nioro Mali 84 D3 ..............................15°14'N 9°36'W
Niort France 44 C5 ...........................46°20'N 0°28'W
Nipigon Canada 61 J2 ......................49°00'N 88°17'W
Nipigon, Lake Canada 61 J2 .............49°43'N 88°33'W
Nipissing, Lake Canada 63 K6 ..........46°15'N 79°39'W
Niš Serbia 50 D6 ..............................43°19'N 21°54'E
Nith r. Scotland 15 F3 .......................55°02'N 3°36'W
Nitra Slovakia 46 H3 .........................48°19'N 18°05'E
Niue i. S. Pacific Oc. 109 I5 ..............19°03'S 169°45'W
Nivelles Belgium 42 D3 ....................50°36'N 4°20'E
Nizamabad India 96 E4 .....................18°40'N 78°07'E
Nizhnekamsk Russia 52 F3 ...............55°38'N 51°55'E
Nizhneudinsk Russia 55 K3 ..............54°55'N 98°58'E
Nizhnevartovsk Russia 54 I4 .............60°56'N 76°38'E
Nizhniy Tagil Russia 52 F3 ................57°56'N 59°56'E
Nizhniy Novgorod Russia 52 E3 ........56°17'N 43°54'E
Nizhnyaya Tura Russia 52 F3 .............58°37'N 59°48'E
Nizhnyaya Tunguska r. Russia 55 J4...65°47'N 87°59'E
Nizhyn Ukraine 47 N4 .......................51°02'N 31°53'E
Nizip Turkey 51 L3 ............................36°59'N 37°48'E
Nkongsamba Cameroon 84 E2 ...........4°58'N 9°57'E
Nobeoka Japan 104 B2 .....................32°34'N 131°41'E
Nogales Mexico 66 B7 ......................31°19'N 110°57'W
Nogent-le-Rotrou France 44 D6 ........48°19'N 0°49'E
Nohfelden Germany 42 G2 ................49°35'N 7°08'E
Noirmoutier, Île de i. France 44 B5 ....46°58'N 2°16'W
Nok Kundi Pakistan 95 I5 .................28°49'N 62°50'E
Nolinsk Russia 52 F3 ........................57°33'N 49°57'E
Nome U.S.A. 60 B4 ...........................64°32'N 165°28'W
Nonthaburi Thailand 102 C6 .............13°51'N 100°32'E
Noord-Brabant d. Neth. 42 E4 ...........51°32'N 5°01'E
Noord-Holland d. Neth. 42 D5 ...........52°46'N 4°54'E

Nordaustlandet i. Arctic Oc. 54 D5.........79°36'N 22°37'E
Norden Germany 42 G6.........53°36'N 7°12'E
Norderney i. Germany 42 G6.........53°44'N 7°19'E
Norderstedt Germany 46 D5.........53°44'N 10°00'E
Nordhausen Germany 46 D4.........51°30'N 10°47'E
Nordhorn Germany 42 G5.........52°26'N 7°05'E
Nordrhein-Westfalen d. Germany 42 G4...51°04'N 7°25'E
Nore r. Ireland 18 E2.........52°25'N 6°58'W
Norfolk d. England 21 F3.........52°44'N 0°59'E
Norfolk U.S.A. 63 K4.........36°53'N 76°16'W
Norfolk Broads f. England 9 G3...52°43'N 1°28'E
Norfolk Island S. Pacific Oc. 109 F4...28°59'S 167°59'E
Noril'sk Russia 55 K4.........69°19'N 88°08'E
Normandy f. France 44 C6.........48°53'N 0°32'W
Normanton Australia 108 D5.........17°41'S 141°05'E
Norra Storfjället mts Sweden 43 C4...65°53'N 15°07'E
Norrköping Sweden 43 D2.........58°36'N 16°12'E
Norrtälje Sweden 43 D2.........59°45'N 18°41'E
Norseman Australia 108 B3.........32°14'S 121°47'E
Northallerton England 13 F3.........54°20'N 1°26'W
North America 56
North American Basin f. Atlantic Oc. 116 D3
.........30°00'N 60°00'W
Northampton England 8 E3.........52°14'N 0°54'W
Northamptonshire d. England 21 E3...52°12'N 0°57'W
North Ayrshire d. Scotland 20 C4...55°44'N 4°44'W
North Battleford Canada 60 H3...52°46'N 108°17'W
North Bay town Canada 61 K2...46°19'N 79°28'W
North Berwick Scotland 15 G4...56°04'N 2°43'W
North Cape New Zealand 109 G3...34°25'S 173°03'E
North Cape Norway 43 F5.........71°10'N 25°47'E
North Carolina d. U.S.A. 63 K4...36°13'N 79°52'W
North Cave England 13 G2.........53°47'N 0°39'W
North Channel U.K. 14 C3.........55°23'N 6°13'W
North China Plain f. China 86 G3...34°30'N 117°00'E
North Dakota d. U.S.A. 62 F6...47°19'N 100°24'W
North Dorset Downs hills England 8 C1...50°46'N 2°32'W
North Downs hills England 9 E2...51°14'N 0°58'W
North East Lincolnshire d. England 21 E3...53°37'N 0°13'W
Northern Dvina r. Russia 52 E4...64°31'N 40°33'E
Northern Ireland d. U.K. 21 B4...54°38'N 6°49'W
Northern Mariana Islands N. Pacific Oc. 103 K7
.........17°15'N 143°32'E
Northern Territory d. Australia 108 C5...17°40'S 133°30'E
North Esk r. Scotland 17 G1...56°45'N 2°26'W
North European Plain f. Europe 34 G4...56°00'N 27°00'E
North Foreland c. England 9 G2...51°23'N 1°27'E
North Frisian Islands Germany 46 C6...54°52'N 8°02'E
North Harris f. Scotland 16 C2...57°59'N 6°48'W
North Hykeham England 13 G2...53°11'N 0°35'W
North Island New Zealand 109 G3...38°11'S 173°23'E
North Korea Asia 99 N6.........40°01'N 126°59'E
North Lanarkshire d. Scotland 20 D4...55°53'N 3°57'W
North Lincolnshire d. England 21 E3...53°39'N 0°30'W
North Macedonia Europe 50 D5...41°31'N 21°46'E
North Platte U.S.A. 62 F5.........41°09'N 100°46'W
North Platte r. U.S.A. 62 F5...41°10'N 100°48'W
North Ronaldsay i. Scotland 17 G4...59°24'N 2°26'W
North Ronaldsay Firth str. Scotland 17 G4...59°20'N 2°29'W
North Saskatchewan r. Canada 60 H3...53°13'N 105°11'W
North Sea Europe 34 E4.........56°00'N 4°00'E
North Shields England 13 F4...55°01'N 1°27'W
North Siberian Lowland f. Russia 55 L5...73°26'N 103°17'E
North Somercotes England 13 H2...53°27'N 0°09'E
North Somerset d. England 21 D2...51°24'N 2°48'W
North Sunderland England 13 F4...55°35'N 1°39'W
North Tidworth England 8 D2...51°14'N 1°40'W
North Tyne r. England 13 E3...54°59'N 2°08'W
North Ugie r. Scotland 17 H2...57°32'N 1°55'W
North Uist i. Scotland 16 B2...57°37'N 7°26'W
Northumberland d. England 21 E4...55°13'N 2°00'W
Northumberland Strait Canada 63 N6...46°50'N 64°43'W
North Walsham England 9 G3...52°49'N 1°23'E
North West Cape Australia 108 A4...21°49'S 114°12'E
Northwest Territories d. Canada 60 H4...63°48'N 105°17'W
Northwich England 12 E3.........53°16'N 2°31'W
North York Moors f. England 13 G3...54°23'N 0°50'W
North Yorkshire d. England 21 E4...54°12'N 1°59'W
Norton England 13 G3.........54°08'N 0°47'W
Norton Fitzwarren England 11 D3...51°02'N 3°08'W
Norton Sound str. U.S.A. 60 B4...63°58'N 163°01'W
Norway Europe 43 B3.........62°46'N 10°30'E
Norway House Canada 60 I3...53°56'N 97°52'W
Norwegian Sea N. Atlantic Oc. 34 D5...66°00'N 2°00'E
Norwich England 9 G3.........52°38'N 1°18'E
Noshiro Japan 104 D4.........40°12'N 140°01'E
Nosovaya Russia 52 F4.........68°15'N 54°35'E
Noss, Isle of i. Scotland 17 H5...60°09'N 1°00'W
Nottingham England 8 D3.........52°57'N 1°09'W
Nottingham d. England 21 E3...52°58'N 1°10'W
Nottinghamshire d. England 21 E3...53°03'N 0°59'W
Nouâdhibou Mauritania 84 C4...21°04'N 17°00'W
Nouâdhibou, Râs c. Mauritania 84 C4...20°51'N 17°04'W
Nouakchott Mauritania 84 C3...18°06'N 15°58'W
Nouméa New Caledonia 109 F4...22°18'S 166°26'E
Noup Head Scotland 17 F4...59°20'N 3°04'W
Nova Gradiška Croatia 50 B7...45°16'N 17°23'E
Novara Italy 46 C1.........45°27'N 8°37'E
Nova Scotia d. Canada 61 L2...43°53'N 65°45'W
Novaya Sibir', Ostrov i. Russia 55 P5...75°04'N 148°22'E
Novaya Zemlya is Russia 54 G5...71°41'N 55°45'E
Nové Zámky Slovakia 46 H2...47°59'N 18°09'E
Novi Pazar Serbia 50 D6.........43°08'N 20°30'E
Novi Sad Serbia 50 C7.........45°16'N 19°51'E
Novoanninskiy Russia 53 E3...50°32'N 42°41'E
Novodvinsk Russia 52 E4...64°25'N 40°50'E
Novo Hamburgo Brazil 73 E4...29°40'S 51°09'W
Novohrad-Volyns'kyy Ukraine 47 L4...50°36'N 27°37'E
Novokuznetsk Russia 54 J3...53°45'N 87°09'E
Novo Mesto Slovenia 46 F1...45°48'N 15°10'E
Novomoskovsk Russia 53 D3...54°01'N 38°19'E
Novomoskovs'k Ukraine 47 P3...48°38'N 35°14'E
Novooleksiyivka Ukraine 51 K8...46°14'N 34°39'E
Novorossiysk Russia 53 D2...44°43'N 37°47'E
Novosibirsk Russia 54 J3...55°03'N 83°02'E
Novovolyns'k Ukraine 47 K4...50°43'N 24°11'E
Novyy Port Russia 54 I4...68°13'N 73°02'E
Nowshera Pakistan 95 L6.........34°00'N 72°01'E
Nowy Sącz Poland 46 I3.........49°38'N 20°42'E
Noyabr'sk Russia 54 I4.........63°13'N 75°32'E
Nuajaat town Canada 61 J4...66°32'N 86°08'W
Nu'aym f. Oman 95 I4.........23°14'N 55°59'E
Nuba Mountains Sudan 94 D2...11°28'N 30°33'E
Nubian Desert Sudan 85 H4...21°00'N 33°20'E
Nudo Coropuna mt. Peru 72 B5...15°29'S 72°43'W
Nuevo Casas Grandes Mexico 66 C7...30°23'N 107°56'W
Nuevo Laredo Mexico 66 E6...27°29'N 99°31'W

Nuevo León d. Mexico 66 E6...25°51'N 99°56'W
Nui atoll Tuvalu 109 G6...7°12'S 177°12'E
Nuku'alofa Tonga 109 H4...21°07'S 175°12'W
Nukufetau atoll Tuvalu 109 G6...8°03'S 178°25'E
Nukunonu atoll Tokelau 109 H6...9°05'S 171°50'W
Nukus Uzbekistan 54 G2...42°27'N 59°36'E
Nullarbor Plain f. Australia 108 B3...31°01'S 129°03'E
Numazu Japan 104 C3.........35°05'N 138°52'E
Nunatsiavut f. Canada 61 L3...56°30'N 62°30'W
Nunavut d. Canada 61 I4...66°30'N 89°54'W
Nunivak Island U.S.A. 60 B3...59°58'N 166°18'W
Nuneaton England 8 D3.........52°31'N 1°28'W
Nuoro Italy 48 E5.........40°19'N 9°20'E
Nuqrah Saudi Arabia 94 F5...25°36'N 41°26'E
Nuremberg Germany 46 D3...49°27'N 11°04'E
Nurmes Finland 43 G3.........63°33'N 29°07'E
Nur-Sultan Kazakhstan 54 I3...51°09'N 71°27'E
Nushki Pakistan 95 K5.........29°34'N 66°02'E
Nuuk Greenland 61 M4.........64°11'N 51°45'W
Nyagan' Russia 52 G4.........62°09'N 65°24'E
Nyala Sudan 85 G3.........12°03'N 24°55'E
Nyasa, Lake Africa 83 C4...9°59'S 34°05'E
Nyborg Denmark 43 B1.........55°19'N 10°47'E
Nybro Sweden 43 C2.........56°44'N 15°55'E
Nyíregyháza Hungary 47 I2...47°57'N 21°43'E
Nykarleby Finland 43 E3.........63°31'N 22°33'E
Nykøbing Falster Denmark 43 B1...54°46'N 11°53'E
Nyköping Sweden 43 D2...58°45'N 17°01'E
Nynäshamn Sweden 43 D2...58°54'N 17°57'E
Nyrob Russia 52 F4.........60°43'N 56°42'E
Nyurba Russia 55 M4.........63°17'N 118°17'E
Nyzhn'ohirs'kyy Ukraine 51 K7...45°27'N 34°45'E

## O

Oadby England 8 D3.........52°36'N 1°05'W
Oahe, Lake U.S.A. 62 F5...44°49'N 100°32'W
Oakengates England 8 C3...52°42'N 2°26'W
Oakham England 8 E3.........52°40'N 0°44'W
Oakland U.S.A. 62 B4.........37°50'N 122°15'W
Oaxaca Mexico 66 E4.........17°05'N 96°40'W
Oaxaca d. Mexico 66 E4...17°22'N 96°30'W
Ob' r. Russia 52 G4.........66°47'N 69°08'E
Oban Scotland 14 D4.........56°25'N 5°28'W
Obi i. Indonesia 103 H3...1°33'S 127°41'E
Obihiro Japan 104 D4.........42°55'N 143°11'E
Obninsk Russia 52 D3.........55°04'N 36°38'E
Oboyan' Russia 47 Q4...51°13'N 36°16'E
Obozerskiy Russia 52 E4...63°28'N 40°19'E
Obshchiy Syrt f. Russia 53 F3...51°20'N 52°00'E
Obskaya Guba str. Russia 54 I4...67°13'N 72°49'E
Ob''yachevo Russia 52 E4...61°13'N 49°37'E
Occidental, Cordillera mts Colombia 72 B7
.........1°36'N 77°47'W
Occidental, Cordillera mts Peru 72 B5...16°07'S 71°46'W
Ocean Falls town Canada 60 F3...52°21'N 127°41'W
Oceania 106
Oceanside U.S.A. 62 C3...33°12'N 117°23'W
Ocher Russia 52 F3.........57°55'N 54°44'E
Ochil Hills Scotland 15 F4...56°12'N 3°49'W
Oda, Jebel mt. Sudan 85 H4...20°20'N 36°39'E
Ódáðahraun f. Iceland 43 Y2...64°48'N 17°17'W
Ōdate Japan 104 D4.........40°16'N 140°34'E
Ödemiş Turkey 51 H4.........38°13'N 27°58'E
Odense Denmark 43 B1.........55°24'N 10°23'E
Oder r. Germany 46 C4...51°43'N 9°56'E
Odesa Ukraine 49 J6.........46°28'N 30°39'E
Odessa U.S.A. 62 F3.........31°50'N 102°20'W
Odintsovo Russia 47 Q6...55°40'N 37°18'E
Odisha d. India 96 F5.........20°57'N 84°15'E
Odra r. Germany/Poland 46 H3...49°54'N 18°19'E
Offaly d. Ireland 18 D3...53°15'N 7°35'W
Offenbach am Main Germany 46 C4...50°06'N 8°46'E
Offenburg Germany 46 B3...48°29'N 7°57'E
Ogadēn f. Ethiopia 85 I2...7°09'N 45°27'E
Ōgaki Japan 104 C3.........35°21'N 136°37'E
Ogbomoso Nigeria 84 E2...8°08'N 4°14'E
Ogden U.S.A. 62 D5.........41°14'N 111°57'W
Ogilvie r. Canada 60 E4...65°50'N 137°13'W
Oglio r. Italy 46 D1.........45°01'N 10°40'E
Ogoki r. Canada 63 I7...51°40'N 85°58'W
Ogulin Croatia 50 A7.........45°16'N 15°14'E
Ohio d. U.S.A. 63 J5.........40°27'N 82°28'W
Ohio r. U.S.A. 63 I4.........37°05'N 89°12'W
Ohrid North Macedonia 50 D5...41°07'N 20°49'E
Ohrid, Lake Albania/North Macedonia 50 D5
.........41°02'N 20°43'E
Oich r. Scotland 16 E2...57°09'N 4°40'W
Oich, Loch l. Scotland 16 E2...57°04'N 4°46'W
Oise r. France 44 E6.........48°59'N 2°04'E
Ōita Japan 104 B2.........33°13'N 131°37'E
Oiti mt. Greece 50 E4...38°48'N 22°16'E
Ojinaga Mexico 66 D6...29°33'N 104°25'W
Ojos del Salado, Cerro mt. Argentina/Chile 73 C4
.........27°06'S 68°35'W
Oka r. Russia 52 D3.........56°20'N 43°59'E
Okanogan r. U.S.A. 62 C6...48°06'N 119°41'W
Okavango Delta f. Botswana 83 B3...19°42'S 23°02'E
Okaya Japan 104 C3.........36°03'N 138°04'E
Okayama Japan 104 B2...34°39'N 133°55'E
Okeechobee, Lake U.S.A. 63 J2...26°56'N 81°00'W
Okehampton England 11 C2...50°44'N 4°00'W
Okha India 96 C5.........22°26'N 69°08'E
Okha Russia 55 P3.........53°33'N 143°01'E
Okhotsk Russia 55 P3...59°23'N 143°22'E
Okhotsk, Sea of Japan/Russia 104 D4...44°58'N 144°06'E
Okhtyrka Ukraine 47 P4...50°19'N 34°54'E
Okinawa i. Japan 99 N3...26°27'N 127°58'E
Oki-shotō is Japan 104 B3...36°07'N 133°26'E
Oklahoma d. U.S.A. 62 G4...35°41'N 97°24'W
Oklahoma City U.S.A. 62 G4...35°31'N 97°31'W
Okovskiy Les f. Russia 52 D3...56°10'N 34°02'E
Oksskolten mt. Norway 43 C4...66°01'N 14°20'E
Oktyabr'skiy Russia 53 F3...54°28'N 53°28'E
Oktyabr'skiy Russia 52 F3...61°05'N 43°07'E
Oktyabr'skoye Russia 52 G4...62°27'N 66°02'E
Oktyabr'skoy Revolyutsii, Ostrov i. Russia 55 K5
.........79°30'N 96°42'E
Öland i. Sweden 43 D2...56°57'N 17°02'E
Olbia Italy 48 E5.........40°55'N 9°30'E
Old Crow Canada 60 E4...67°36'N 139°54'W
Oldenburg Germany 46 C5...53°08'N 8°13'E
Oldenzaal Neth. 42 F5...52°19'N 6°56'E
Oldham England 13 E2...53°33'N 2°07'W
Old Head of Kinsale Ireland 18 C1...51°36'N 8°31'W

Old Leake England 13 H2...53°02'N 0°06'E
Oldmeldrum Scotland 17 G2...57°20'N 2°19'W
Olean U.S.A. 63 K5.........42°05'N 78°26'W
Olekma r. Russia 55 N4...60°15'N 121°07'E
Olekminsk Russia 55 N4...60°24'N 120°21'E
Oleksandriya Ukraine 47 O3...48°41'N 33°07'E
Olenek Russia 55 M5.........72°58'N 119°45'E
Olenek r. Russia 55 M4...68°28'N 112°26'E
Olenekskiy Zaliv b. Russia 55 N5...73°22'N 121°09'E
Oléron, Île d' i. France 44 C4...45°55'N 1°20'W
Olevs'k Ukraine 47 L4...51°13'N 27°39'E
Olney England 8 E3.........52°09'N 0°42'W
Olomouc Czechia 46 G3...49°35'N 17°16'E
Olonets Russia 52 D4...60°58'N 32°59'E
Oloron-Ste-Marie France 44 C3...43°12'N 0°36'W
Olsztyn Poland 46 I5.........53°47'N 20°29'E
Olt r. Romania 50 F7.........44°22'N 24°07'E
Olympia U.S.A. 62 B6...47°02'N 122°53'W
Olympos Cyprus 51 J2...34°56'N 32°51'E
Olympus, Mount Greece 50 E5...40°05'N 22°21'E
Olympus, Mount U.S.A. 62 B6...47°45'N 123°47'W
Olyutorskiy Zaliv b. Russia 55 R3...59°51'N 168°08'E
Omagh Northern Ireland 14 B2...54°36'N 7°17'W
Omaha U.S.A. 62 G5.........41°17'N 95°58'W
Oman Asia 95 H3.........18°15'N 53°34'E
Oman, Gulf of Asia 95 I5...25°37'N 56°49'E
Ombersley England 8 C3...52°16'N 2°14'W
Omdurman Sudan 85 H3...15°38'N 32°28'E
Ommen Neth. 42 F5...52°32'N 6°25'E
Omolon r. Russia 55 Q4...68°44'N 158°43'E
Omono r. Japan 104 D3...39°41'N 140°04'E
Omsk Russia 54 I3.........55°00'N 73°22'E
Omsukchan Russia 55 Q4...62°25'N 155°43'E
Ōmuta Japan 104 B2.........33°02'N 130°28'E
Onchan Isle of Man 12 C3...54°11'N 4°27'W
Ondjiva Angola 83 A3...17°04'S 15°44'E
Onega Russia 52 D4...63°55'N 38°02'E
Onega r. Russia 52 D4...63°58'N 38°00'E
Onega, Lake Russia 52 D4...62°05'N 35°21'E
Oneşti Romania 50 G8...46°16'N 26°46'E
Ongole India 96 F4.........15°32'N 80°02'E
Onitsha Nigeria 84 E2...6°08'N 6°48'E
Ono-i-Lau i. Fiji 109 H4...20°39'S 178°45'W
Ontario d. Canada 61 I3...51°51'N 91°22'W
Ontario, Lake Canada/U.S.A. 61 K2...43°31'N 77°57'W
Ontong Java Atoll Solomon Is 109 E6...5°24'S 159°34'E
Oosterschelde est. Neth. 42 C4...51°38'N 3°35'E
Oost-Vlaanderen d. Belgium 42 C3...50°56'N 3°44'E
Opala Dem. Rep. Congo 83 B4...0°36'S 24°22'E
Opava Czechia 46 G3...49°56'N 17°54'E
Opochka Russia 43 G2...56°43'N 28°41'E
Opole Poland 46 G4...50°40'N 17°56'E
Oporto Portugal 45 A4...41°11'N 8°36'W
Oradea Romania 47 I2...47°04'N 21°57'E
Oran Algeria 84 D5...35°42'N 0°38'W
Orange France 44 F4...44°09'N 4°49'E
Orange r. Namibia/S. Africa 83 A2...28°36'S 16°28'E
Orange, Cabo c. Brazil 72 D7...4°22'N 51°17'W
Oranmore Ireland 18 C3...53°16'N 8°55'W
Orchila, Isla i. Venezuela 67 K3...11°45'N 66°09'W
Orchy r. Scotland 14 D4...56°24'N 5°01'W
Ord, Mount hill Australia 108 B5...17°19'S 125°29'E
Ordu Turkey 51 L5.........40°59'N 37°53'E
Örebro Sweden 43 C2...59°16'N 15°14'E
Oregon d. U.S.A. 62 B5...43°43'N 120°32'W
Orel Russia 53 D3.........52°58'N 36°05'E
Orenburg Russia 53 F3...51°46'N 55°05'E
Orford Ness hd England 9 G3...52°05'N 1°35'E
Orhei Moldova 47 M2...47°22'N 28°50'E
Oriental, Cordillera mts Bolivia 72 C5...16°47'S 66°35'W
Oriental, Cordillera mts Colombia 72 B7...7°42'N 72°45'W
Oriental, Cordillera mts Peru 72 B5...10°29'S 74°41'W
Orillia Canada 63 K5...44°36'N 79°25'W
Orinoco r. Col./Venez. 72 C7...8°35'N 61°50'W
Orinoco Delta Venezuela 72 C7...9°22'N 60°44'W
Oristano Italy 48 E4...39°55'N 8°35'E
Orivesi l. Finland 43 G3...62°14'N 29°27'E
Orizaba Mexico 66 E4...18°53'N 97°06'W
Örkelljunga Sweden 46 E7...56°17'N 13°17'E
Orkney d. Scotland 20 D6...58°59'N 2°42'W
Orkney Islands Scotland 17 F4...59°06'N 3°20'W
Orléans France 44 D5...47°55'N 1°54'E
Ormoc Phil. 103 G6...11°00'N 124°37'E
Ormskirk England 12 E2...53°34'N 2°53'W
Orne r. France 44 C6...49°16'N 0°14'W
Örnsköldsvik Sweden 43 D3...63°18'N 18°43'E
Oronsay i. Scotland 14 C4...56°01'N 6°12'W
Orrin r. Scotland 16 E2...57°29'N 4°40'W
Orrin Reservoir Scotland 16 E2...57°30'N 4°45'W
Orsha Belarus 47 N6...54°30'N 30°26'E
Orsk Russia 53 F3.........51°07'N 58°33'E
Orşova Romania 50 E7...44°42'N 22°25'E
Oruro Bolivia 72 C5...17°59'S 67°09'W
Osa, Península de pen. Costa Rica 67 H2...8°34'N 83°32'W
Ōsaka Japan 104 C2...34°42'N 135°30'E
Oshakati Namibia 83 A3...17°45'S 15°43'E
Oshawa Canada 61 K2...43°54'N 78°51'W
O-shima i. Japan 104 C2...34°44'N 139°28'E
Osijek Croatia 50 C7...45°35'N 18°42'E
Osjön l. Sweden 43 C3...63°54'N 16°26'E
Oskarshamn Sweden 43 D2...57°16'N 16°26'E
Oslo Norway 43 B2...59°55'N 10°46'E
Osmancık Turkey 51 K5...40°58'N 34°48'E
Osmaniye Turkey 51 L3...37°04'N 36°15'E
Osnabrück Germany 46 C5...52°17'N 8°04'E
Osorno Chile 73 B2...40°35'S 73°09'W
Osorno Spain 45 C5...42°24'N 4°21'W
Oss Neth. 42 E4...51°45'N 5°32'E
Ossa mt. Greece 50 E4...39°48'N 22°41'E
Ossa, Mount Australia 108 D2...41°54'S 146°12'E
Ostend Belgium 42 B4...51°13'N 2°55'E
Österdalälven r. Sweden 43 C3...61°40'N 13°15'E
Østerdalen f. Norway 43 B3...62°05'N 10°36'E
Östersund Sweden 43 C3...63°11'N 14°39'E
Ostrava Czechia 46 H3...49°50'N 18°17'E
Ostróda Poland 46 H5...53°42'N 19°59'E
Ostrov Russia 43 G2...57°21'N 28°21'E
Ostrowiec Świętokrzyski Poland 47 I4...50°56'N 21°24'E
Ostrów Mazowiecka Poland 47 I5...52°48'N 21°53'E
Ostrów Wielkopolski Poland 46 G4...51°39'N 17°49'E
Ostrzeszów Poland 46 G4...51°25'N 17°56'E
Osŭm r. Bulgaria 50 F6...43°42'N 24°51'E
Osumi-kaikyo str. Japan 104 B2...30°50'N 130°52'E
Ōsumi-shotō is Japan 104 B2...30°32'N 130°36'E
Osuna Spain 45 C2...37°14'N 5°06'W

Oswestry England 8 B3...52°51'N 3°
Otaru Japan 104 D4...43°12'N 140°
Otjiwarongo Namibia 83 A2...20°28'S 16°
Otley England 13 F2...53°54'N 1°
Otranto Italy 50 C5...40°09'N 18°
Otranto, Strait of Albania/Italy 50 C5...40°36'N 18°
Otta Norway 43 B3...61°46'N 9°
Ottawa Canada 61 K2...45°25'N 75°
Ottawa r. Canada 61 K2...45°28'N 74°
Ottawa Islands Canada 61 J3...59°57'N 80°
Otter r. England 11 D2...50°38'N 3°
Otterburn England 13 E4...55°14'N 2°
Ottery r. England 11 C2...50°39'N 4°
Ottignies Belgium 42 D3...50°39'N 4°
Otukpo Nigeria 84 E2...7°13'N 8°
Ouachita r. U.S.A. 63 H3...31°50'N 91°
Ouagadougou Burkina Faso 84 D3...12°22'N 1°
Ouargla Algeria 84 E5...31°58'N 5°
Ouarzazate Morocco 84 D5...30°56'N 6°
Oudenaarde Belgium 42 C3...50°51'N 3°
Ouesso Congo 84 F2...1°36'N 16°
Ouezzane Morocco 48 B3...34°46'N 5°
Oughter, Lough l. Ireland 18 D4...54°01'N 7°
Ouistreham France 44 C6...49°17'N 0°
Oujda Morocco 84 D5...34°44'N 1°
Oulainen Finland 43 F4...64°16'N 24°
Oulton England 9 G3...52°30'N 1°
Oulu Finland 43 F4...65°01'N 25°
Oulujärvi l. Finland 43 F4...64°17'N 27°
Oundle England 9 E3...52°29'N 0°
Oupeye Belgium 42 E3...50°42'N 5°
Ourense Spain 45 B5...42°21'N 7°
Ouse r. E. Sussex England 9 F1...50°48'N 0°
Ouse r. E. Yorks. England 13 G2...53°44'N 0°
Outer Hebrides is Scotland 16 B2...57°53'N 7°
Outokumpu Finland 43 G3...62°43'N 29°
Out Skerries is Scotland 17 I5...60°26'N 0°
Ovamboland f. Namibia 83 A3...17°50'S 15°
Overijssel d. Neth. 42 F5...52°25'N 6°
Overton Wales 10 E4...52°58'N 2°
Övertorneå Sweden 43 E4...66°24'N 23°
Oviedo Spain 45 C5...43°22'N 5°
Ovruch Ukraine 47 M4...51°20'N 28°
Owando Congo 84 F1...0°29'S 15°
Owen Stanley Range mts P.N.G. 108 D6...8°59'S 147°
Owyhee r. U.S.A. 62 C5...43°48'N 117°
Öxarfjörður b. Iceland 43 Y2...66°12'N 16°
Oxelösund Sweden 43 D2...58°40'N 17°
Oxford England 8 D2...51°45'N 1°
Oxfordshire d. England 21 E2...51°54'N 1°
Oxnard U.S.A. 62 C3...34°12'N 119°
Oxted England 9 F2...51°15'N 0°
Oyama Japan 104 C3...36°18'N 139°
Oykel r. Scotland 16 E2...57°55'N 4°
Ozark Plateau f. U.S.A. 63 H4...36°58'N 93°
Ozarks, Lake of the U.S.A. 63 H4...38°14'N 93°
Ózd Hungary 46 I3...48°13'N 20°
Ozernovskiy Russia 55 Q3...51°30'N 156°

## P

Paamiut Greenland 61 N4...62°01'N 49°
Pabbay i. Na h-E. S. Scotland 16 B1...56°51'N 7°
Pabbay i. Na h-E. S. Scotland 16 B2...57°46'N 7°
Pabianice Poland 46 H4...51°40'N 19°
Pachuca Mexico 66 E5...20°09'N 98°
Pacific Ocean 116 B3
Padang Indonesia 102 C3...0°58'S 100°
Paderborn Germany 46 C4...51°43'N 8°
Padiham England 13 E2...53°48'N 2°
Padre Island U.S.A. 62 G2...26°57'N 97°
Padstow England 11 C2...50°32'N 4°
Padua Italy 46 D1...45°24'N 11°
Pag i. Croatia 50 A7...44°31'N 14°
Pagadian Phil. 103 G5...7°50'N 123°
Pagai Selatan i. Indonesia 102 C3...2°58'S 100°
Pagai Utara i. Indonesia 102 C3...2°36'S 100°
Pagan i. N. Mariana Is 103 L7...18°08'N 145°
Page U.S.A. 62 D4...36°55'N 111°
Paget, Mount S. Atlantic Oc. 73 F1...54°23'S 36°
Paignton England 11 D2...50°26'N 3°
Päijänne l. Finland 43 F3...61°30'N 25°
Painswick England 8 C2...51°47'N 2°
Paisley Scotland 14 E3...55°51'N 4°
Pakanbaru Indonesia 102 C4...0°34'N 101°
Pakaraima Mountains S. America 67 L1...3°47'N 63°
Pakistan Asia 96 C6...28°01'N 64°
Pakokku Myanmar 97 I5...21°21'N 95°
Pakxé Laos 102 D7...15°04'N 105°
Palana Russia 55 Q3...59°05'N 159°
Palangkaraya Indonesia 102 E3...2°18'S 113°
Palatka Russia 55 Q4...60°08'N 150°
Palau N. Pacific Oc. 103 I5...7°23'N 134°
Palawan i. Phil. 102 F5...8°50'N 117°
Palembang Indonesia 102 C3...2°56'S 104°
Palencia Spain 45 C5...42°01'N 4°
Palermo Italy 48 F4...38°07'N 13°
Pali India 96 D6...25°46'N 73°
Palikir Fed. States of Micronesia 115 I3...6°55'N 158°
Palk Strait India/Sri Lanka 96 E2...9°36'N 79°
Palma de Mallorca Spain 45 G3...39°35'N 2°
Palmas Brazil 72 E5...10°20'S 48°
Palmas, Cape Liberia 84 D2...4°22'N 7°
Palmerston atoll Cook Is 109 I5...18°01'S 163°
Palmerston North New Zealand 109 G2...40°22'S 175°
Palmira Colombia 72 B7...3°31'N 76°
Palopo Indonesia 102 G3...3°01'S 120°
Palos, Cabo de c. Spain 45 E2...37°37'N 0°
Palu Indonesia 102 F3...0°54'S 119°
Pamiers France 44 D3...43°07'N 1°
Pamirs mts Asia 95 L7...38°39'N 72°
Pampas f. Argentina 73 C3...38°35'S 64°
Pamplona Spain 45 E5...42°49'N 1°
Panaji India 96 D4...15°28'N 73°
Panama Central America 67 H2...8°22'N 81°
Panama, Gulf of Panama 67 I2...7°38'N 79°
Panama, Isthmus of f. C. America 56 F2...9°00'N 80°
Panama Canal Panama 67 I2...9°07'N 79°
Panamá City Panama 67 I2...8°56'N 79°
Panama City U.S.A. 63 I3...30°10'N 85°
Panay i. Phil. 103 G6...11°10'N 122°
Pančevo Serbia 50 D7...44°52'N 20°
Panevėžys Lithuania 43 F1...55°44'N 24°
Pangkalanbuun Indonesia 102 E3...2°40'S 111°

kalpinang Indonesia 102 D3.............2°08'S 106°06'E
nirtung Canada 61 L4.............66°03'N 65°48'W
gur Pakistan 95 J5.............26°58'N 64°07'E
elleria, Isola di i. Italy 48 F4.............36°47'N 12°04'E
nihua China 99 I3.............26°35'N 101°43'E
Stour i. Scotland 17 H5.............60°21'N 1°42'W
Westray i. Scotland 17 G4.............59°22'N 2°52'W
nburg Germany 42 G6.............53°05'N 7°24'E
os Cyprus 51 J2.............34°47'N 32°25'E
a, Gulf of P.N.G. 108 D6.............8°34'S 144°45'E
a New Guinea Oceania 108 D6.............6°05'S 146°34'E
ngland 11 C2.............50°21'N 4°42'W
el Islands S. China Sea 102 E7.............16°46'N 112°39'E
gui r. Brazil 72 D5.............22°06'S 57°57'W
guay r. Argentina/Paraguay 73 D4.............27°12'S 58°39'W
guay S. America 73 D4.............22°45'S 58°44'W
ou Benin 84 E2.............9°22'N 2°36'E
naribo Suriname 72 D7.............5°51'N 55°17'W
á Argentina 73 E4.............31°44'S 60°31'W
á r. S. America 73 D3.............33°52'S 59°12'W
aguá Brazil 73 E4.............25°32'S 48°33'W
aíba r. Brazil 72 D5.............20°04'S 51°00'W
gul Mare, Vârful mt. Romania 50 E7.............45°21'N 23°33'E
is, Serra dos hills Brazil 72 C5.............11°28'S 63°12'W
are Indonesia 102 F3.............4°01'S 119°40'E
Península de pen. Venezuela 67 L3.............10°43'N 62°58'W
a, Serra mts Brazil 67 L1.............2°57'N 64°55'W
France 44 E6.............48°52'N 2°21'E
a Italy 46 D1.............44°48'N 10°19'E
íba Brazil 72 E6.............2°56'S 41°45'W
íba r. Brazil 72 E6.............3°02'S 41°51'W
ssos mt. Greece 50 E4.............38°32'N 22°38'E
Estonia 43 F2.............58°23'N 24°30'E
amisus mts Afgh. 95 J7.............35°06'N 61°20'E
i. Greece 50 E4.............37°06'N 25°08'E
tt r. England 13 E3.............51°08'N 3°00'W
Cape Canada 61 F5.............70°12'N 124°31'W
Islands Canada 60 G5.............76°50'N 111°03'W
a r. Poland 46 F5.............54°11'N 15°34'E
enay France 44 C5.............46°39'N 0°15'W
Mountains Ireland 18 B3.............54°39'N 9°39'W
ena U.S.A. 62 C3.............34°11'N 118°08'W
ni Romania 47 L2.............47°15'N 26°44'E
Pakistan 95 J5.............29°33'N 63°31'E
u Germany 46 E3.............48°34'N 13°25'E
Fundo Brazil 73 D4.............28°18'S 52°24'W
vy Belarus 47 L6.............55°07'N 26°50'E
Colombia 72 B7.............1°11'N 77°17'W
onia f. Argentina 73 B1.............51°44'S 71°19'W
way England 8 C2.............51°32'N 2°34'W
son U.S.A. 63 I5.............40°54'N 74°09'W
n Myanmar 97 H4.............16°45'N 94°44'E
India 96 D6.............25°35'N 85°16'E
Albania 50 C5.............40°40'N 19°39'E
, Lagoa dos l. Brazil 73 D3.............30°39'S 50°58'W
de Minas Brazil 73 E3.............18°36'S 46°30'W
kos Kolpos b. Greece 50 D4.............38°15'N 21°26'E
s Greece 50 D4.............38°14'N 21°45'E
gton England 13 G2.............53°41'N 0°01'W
ance 44 C3.............43°18'N 0°22'W
Afonso Brazil 72 F6.............9°20'S 38°13'W
Italy 46 C1.............45°11'N 9°09'E
dar Kazakhstan 54 I3.............52°18'N 77°02'E
nrad Ukraine 47 P3.............48°31'N 35°53'E
vskaya Russia 49 K6.............46°09'N 39°47'E
on Myanmar 97 I4.............16°16'N 95°41'E
hoy, Khrebet hills Russia 52 G4.............69°17'N 62°13'E
y U.S.A. 62 D5.............32°19'S 58°05'W
ndú Uruguay 73 D3.............32°19'S 58°05'W
dzhik Bulgaria 50 F6.............42°12'N 24°20'E
r. Canada 60 G3.............58°54'N 111°50'W
haven England 9 E1.............50°48'N 0°00'W
River town Canada 60 G3.............56°15'N 117°17'W
Mount U.S.A. 62 E4.............38°26'N 109°13'W
r. U.S.A. 63 I3.............30°10'N 89°37'W
osovo 50 D6.............42°39'N 20°17'E
ra Russia 52 F4.............65°09'N 53°54'E
ra r. Russia 52 F4.............68°13'N 53°54'E
rskoye More sea Russia 52 F4.............69°00'N 55°00'E
U.S.A. 62 F3.............31°23'N 103°30'W
Juan Caballero Paraguay 73 D4.............22°29'S 55°44'W
e Scotland 15 F3.............55°39'N 3°12'W
. Canada 60 E4.............68°03'N 134°26'W
e Isle of Man 12 C3.............54°13'N 4°41'W
us Bay New Zealand 109 G2.............43°20'S 172°49'E
ell Bay England 9 G2.............51°19'N 1°21'E
ongan Indonesia 102 C4.............6°54'S 109°38'E
Mont mt. France 44 G4.............44°16'N 6°43'E
g i. Indonesia 103 G3.............1°15'S 123°29'E
Finland 43 F2.............66°47'N 23°59'E
as Brazil 73 D3.............31°46'S 52°19'W
as, Rio das r. Brazil 73 D4.............27°35'S 51°24'W
a Mozambique 83 D3.............12°59'S 40°32'E
a Zambia 83 B3.............16°33'S 27°22'E
a Tanzania 83 C4.............5°25'S 39°46'E
rey Wales 10 C3.............51°41'N 4°17'W
roke England 23 K6.............45°49'N 77°06'W
roke Wales 10 C3.............51°40'N 4°55'W
roke Dock Wales 10 C3.............51°41'N 4°57'W
rokeshire d. Wales 21 C2.............51°55'N 4°48'W
ury England 9 F2.............51°09'N 0°19'E
Nevada, Cerro mt. Mexico 66 E5.............23°46'N 99°50'W
nda de Bracamonte Spain 45 C4.............40°55'N 5°11'W
th Wales 11 D3.............51°26'N 3°10'W
, Golfo de g. Chile 73 B2.............47°18'S 75°35'W
ne Wales 10 C3.............51°45'N 4°34'W
ebury England 13 E2.............53°30'N 2°19'W
e Hill England 13 E2.............53°07'N 3°18'E
eton U.S.A. 62 C6.............45°39'N 118°48'W
uik Scotland 15 F3.............55°50'N 3°13'W
sular Malaysia 102 C4.............3°59'N 102°43'E
idge England 8 C3.............52°43'N 2°07'W
nes Hills England 13 F3.............53°41'N 1°55'W
sylvania d. U.S.A. 63 K5.............41°18'N 78°00'W
y Icecap Canada 61 L4.............67°10'N 66°02'W
yn Mawr pt Wales 10 C4.............52°51'N 4°43'W
h England 12 E3.............54°40'N 2°45'W
e England 11 B2.............50°21'N 5°06'W
icola U.S.A. 63 I3.............30°27'N 87°13'W
cton Canada 62 C6.............49°30'N 119°35'W
e Point England 11 B2.............50°35'N 5°00'W
and Firth str. Scotland 17 F3.............58°43'N 3°16'W
and Hills Scotland 15 F3.............55°43'N 3°30'W

Pentland Skerries is Scotland 17 G3.............58°41'N 2°54'W
Penygadair hill Wales 10 D4.............52°42'N 3°55'W
Pen-y-Ghent hill England 13 E3.............54°10'N 2°15'W
Penza Russia 53 E3.............53°12'N 45°01'E
Penzance England 11 B2.............50°07'N 5°32'W
Penzhinskaya Guba b. Russia 55 R4.............62°05'N 163°30'E
Peoria U.S.A. 63 I5.............40°41'N 89°37'W
Peregrebnoye Russia 52 G4.............62°59'N 65°11'E
Pereira Colombia 72 B7.............4°45'N 75°41'W
Périgueux France 44 D4.............45°11'N 0°43'E
Perija, Sierra de mts Venezuela 67 J2.............9°09'N 73°12'W
Perito Moreno Argentina 73 B2.............46°36'S 71°02'W
Perlas, Punta de pt Nicaragua 67 H3.............12°24'N 83°31'W
Perm' Russia 52 F3.............58°01'N 56°14'E
Pernik Bulgaria 50 E6.............42°36'N 23°02'E
Péronne France 42 B2.............49°56'N 2°56'E
Perpignan France 44 E3.............42°42'N 2°54'E
Perranporth England 11 B2.............50°21'N 5°09'W
Pershore England 8 C3.............52°07'N 2°04'W
Perth Australia 108 A3.............31°56'S 115°47'E
Perth Scotland 15 F4.............56°24'N 3°26'W
Perth and Kinross d. Scotland 20 C5.............56°37'N 4°07'W
Peru S. America 72 B5.............5°50'S 77°14'W
Perugia Italy 48 F5.............43°07'N 12°23'E
Pervomays'k Ukraine 47 N3.............48°03'N 30°51'E
Pescara Italy 48 F5.............42°27'N 14°12'E
Pesebre, Punta pt Canary Islands 45 Y2.............28°07'N 14°29'W
Peshawar Pakistan 96 D7.............34°01'N 71°40'E
Peshkopi Albania 50 D5.............41°41'N 20°26'E
Peterborough Canada 61 K2.............44°18'N 78°20'W
Peterborough England 9 E3.............52°34'N 0°14'W
Peterborough d. England 21 E3.............52°36'N 0°16'W
Peterhead Scotland 17 H2.............57°31'N 1°47'W
Peterlee England 13 F3.............54°46'N 1°20'W
Petersfield England 8 E2.............51°00'N 0°56'W
Petersville U.S.A. 60 C4.............62°33'N 150°50'W
Petit Mécatina r. Canada 61 M3.............50°40'N 59°25'W
Petrich Bulgaria 50 E5.............41°24'N 23°12'E
Petropavlovsk Kazakhstan 54 H3.............54°51'N 69°06'E
Petropavlovsk-Kamchatskiy Russia 55 Q3
.............53°01'N 158°44'E
Petroşani Romania 50 E7.............45°25'N 23°23'E
Petrozavodsk Russia 52 D4.............61°48'N 34°19'E
Petworth England 9 E1.............50°59'N 0°36'W
Pevensey England 9 F1.............50°49'N 0°21'E
Pewsey England 8 D2.............51°20'N 1°46'W
Pforzheim Germany 46 C3.............48°53'N 8°42'E
Phan Thiết Vietnam 102 D6.............10°55'N 108°06'E
Phatthalung Thailand 102 C5.............7°39'N 100°06'E
Phayao Thailand 102 B7.............19°10'N 99°57'E
Phet Buri Thailand 102 B6.............13°06'N 99°56'E
Philadelphia U.S.A. 63 K4.............39°57'N 75°10'W
Philippeville Belgium 42 D3.............50°12'N 4°33'E
Philippines Asia 103 G6.............15°36'N 122°55'E
Phitsanulok Thailand 102 C7.............16°50'N 100°18'E
Phnom Penh Cambodia 102 C6.............11°33'N 104°57'E
Phoenix U.S.A. 62 D3.............33°31'N 112°07'W
Phoenix Islands Kiribati 109 H6.............2°43'S 173°22'W
Phôngsali Laos 102 C8.............21°41'N 102°08'E
Phrae Thailand 102 C7.............18°07'N 100°12'E
Phuket Thailand 102 B5.............7°53'N 98°23'E
Piacenza Italy 46 C1.............45°03'N 9°42'E
Piatra Neamţ Romania 47 L2.............46°56'N 26°22'E
Piave r. Italy 46 E1.............45°32'N 12°44'E
Picardy f. France 44 D6.............49°47'N 1°35'E
Pickering England 13 G3.............54°15'N 0°47'W
Pickering, Vale of f. England 13 G3.............54°13'N 0°45'W
Picos Brazil 72 E6.............7°05'S 41°20'W
Piedras Negras Mexico 66 D6.............28°40'N 100°34'W
Pieksämäki Finland 43 F3.............62°18'N 27°10'E
Pielinen l. Finland 43 G3.............63°14'N 29°41'E
Pierre U.S.A. 62 F5.............44°23'N 100°23'W
Pietermaritzburg S. Africa 83 C2.............29°36'S 30°23'E
Pietrosa mt. Romania 47 K2.............47°34'N 24°41'E
Pihlajavesi l. Finland 43 G3.............61°45'N 28°46'E
Pijijiapan Mexico 66 F4.............15°46'N 93°14'W
Piła Poland 46 H5.............53°09'N 16°45'E
Pilbara f. Australia 108 A4.............22°45'S 117°00'E
Pimperne England 8 C1.............50°53'N 2°08'W
Pinang i. Malaysia 102 B5.............5°21'N 100°11'E
Pınarbaşı Turkey 51 L4.............38°44'N 36°25'E
Pinar del Río Cuba 67 H5.............22°25'N 83°43'W
Pindus Mountains Greece 50 D4.............39°56'N 21°03'E
Pine Bluff U.S.A. 63 H3.............34°16'N 92°02'W
Pinega r. Greece 50 E4.............64°41'N 43°24'E
Pineios r. Greece 50 E4.............39°53'N 22°43'E
Pingdingshan China 99 K4.............33°45'N 113°18'E
Pingxiang Guangxi China 99 J2.............22°03'N 106°50'E
Pingxiang Jiangxi China 99 K3.............27°42'N 113°52'E
Pinsk Belarus 47 L5.............52°08'N 26°06'E
Pionerskiy Russia 52 G4.............61°08'N 62°51'E
Piotrków Trybunalski Poland 46 H4.............51°25'N 19°41'E
Pipmuacan, Réservoir Canada 63 L6.............49°37'N 70°33'W
Piraeus Greece 50 E3.............37°56'N 23°38'E
Pirot Serbia 50 E6.............43°09'N 22°34'E
Pisa Italy 48 F5.............43°42'N 10°24'E
Písek Czechia 46 F3.............49°19'N 14°10'E
Pisuerga r. Spain 45 C4.............41°34'N 4°50'W
Pisz Poland 47 I5.............53°38'N 21°48'E
Pitcairn Island S. Pacific Oc. 116 B2.............25°03'S 130°06'W
Pitcairn Islands S. Pacific Oc. 116 B2.............23°35'S 126°31'W
Piteå Sweden 43 E4.............65°19'N 21°30'E
Piteşti Romania 50 F7.............44°52'N 24°53'E
Pitlochry Scotland 17 F1.............56°42'N 3°44'W
Pittsburgh U.S.A. 63 J5.............40°26'N 79°59'W
Piz Bernina mt. Italy/Switz. 46 C2.............46°23'N 9°54'E
Plasencia Spain 45 B4.............40°02'N 6°05'W
Platinum U.S.A. 60 B3.............58°59'N 161°48'W
Platte r. U.S.A. 62 G5.............41°04'N 95°53'W
Plauen Germany 46 E4.............50°30'N 12°08'E
Plavsk Russia 47 Q6.............53°42'N 37°18'E
Playa Blanca Canary Islands 45 Z2.............28°52'N 13°50'W
Plenty, Bay of g. New Zealand 109 G3.............37°37'S 176°59'E
Plesetsk Russia 52 E4.............62°43'N 40°18'E
Pleven Bulgaria 50 F6.............43°25'N 24°37'E
Płock Poland 46 H5.............52°33'N 19°43'E
Pločno mt. Bos. and Herz. 50 B6.............43°36'N 17°35'E
Ploieşti Romania 50 G7.............44°56'N 26°02'E
Plomb du Cantal mt. France 44 E4.............45°03'N 2°46'E
Plovdiv Bulgaria 50 F6.............42°10'N 24°44'E
Plungė Lithuania 47 I6.............55°55'N 21°51'E
Plymouth England 11 C2.............50°22'N 4°08'W
Plymouth d. England 21 C2.............50°24'N 4°08'W
Plympton England 11 C2.............50°23'N 4°03'W
Plymstock England 11 C2.............50°21'N 4°06'W
Plynlimon hill Wales 10 D4.............52°28'N 3°47'W

Plzeň Czechia 46 E3.............49°45'N 13°23'E
Pô Burkina Faso 84 D3.............11°12'N 1°08'W
Po r. Italy 46 E1.............45°02'N 12°11'E
Pobeda, Gora mt. Russia 55 P4.............65°12'N 145°54'E
Pocatello U.S.A. 62 D5.............42°54'N 112°25'W
Pochep Russia 47 O5.............52°56'N 33°27'E
Pocklington England 13 G2.............53°56'N 0°47'W
Poços de Caldas Brazil 73 E4.............21°48'S 46°31'W
Podgorica Montenegro 50 C6.............42°27'N 19°17'E
Podkamennaya Tunguska r. Russia 55 K4.............61°36'N 90°08'E
Podol'sk Russia 52 D3.............55°25'N 37°34'E
Pohang S. Korea 104 A3.............36°01'N 129°22'E
Pointe-à-Pitre Guadeloupe 72 C8.............16°15'N 61°32'W
Pointe-Noire Congo 84 F1.............4°44'S 11°53'E
Poitiers France 44 D5.............46°35'N 0°20'E
Pokaran India 96 D6.............26°53'N 71°57'E
Pokrovs'k Ukraine 49 K6.............48°17'N 37°10'E
Poland Europe 46 H4.............52°07'N 19°27'E
Polatlı Turkey 51 J4.............39°35'N 32°08'E
Polatsk Belarus 47 M6.............55°29'N 28°47'E
Polegate England 9 F1.............50°49'N 0°15'E
Pol-e Khomri Afgh. 95 K7.............35°56'N 68°46'E
Polis Cyprus 51 J2.............35°01'N 32°25'E
Pollaphuca Reservoir Ireland 18 E3.............53°08'N 6°30'W
Polokwane S. Africa 83 B2.............23°54'S 29°27'E
Polperro England 11 C2.............50°20'N 4°31'W
Poltava Ukraine 47 P3.............49°36'N 34°34'E
Polygyros Greece 50 E5.............40°23'N 23°27'E
Polykastro Greece 50 E5.............40°59'N 22°34'E
Polynesia is Pacific Oc. 116 B2.............8°00'S 170°00'E
Pombal Portugal 45 A3.............39°55'N 8°37'W
Ponce Puerto Rico 67 K4.............18°00'N 66°37'W
Ponferrada Spain 45 B5.............42°33'N 6°36'W
Ponta do Sol Cape Verde 84 B3.............17°10'N 25°05'W
Ponta Grossa Brazil 73 D4.............25°03'S 50°07'W
Pont-à-Mousson France 42 F1.............48°54'N 6°03'E
Pontardawe Wales 10 D3.............51°43'N 3°51'W
Pontefract England 13 F2.............53°41'N 1°18'W
Ponteland England 13 F4.............55°03'N 1°44'W
Pontevedra Spain 45 A5.............42°27'N 8°39'W
Pontianak Indonesia 102 D3.............0°03'S 109°18'E
Pontoise France 44 E6.............49°03'N 2°06'E
Pontycymer Wales 10 D3.............51°37'N 3°35'W
Pontypool Wales 10 D3.............51°42'N 3°02'W
Pontypridd Wales 10 D3.............51°36'N 3°20'W
Poole England 8 D1.............50°43'N 1°59'W
Poole Bay England 8 D1.............50°40'N 1°55'W
Pooley Bridge England 12 E3.............54°37'N 2°49'W
Poopó, Lago de l. Bolivia 72 C5.............18°50'S 67°05'W
Popigay r. Russia 55 L5.............72°56'N 106°10'E
Poplar Bluff U.S.A. 63 H4.............36°47'N 90°23'W
Popocatépetl, Volcán vol. Mexico 66 E4.............19°02'N 98°38'W
Poprad Slovakia 46 I3.............49°04'N 20°18'E
Porbandar India 96 C5.............21°39'N 69°40'E
Pori Finland 43 E3.............61°29'N 21°48'E
Porlock England 11 D3.............51°13'N 3°36'W
Poronaysk Russia 55 P2.............49°16'N 143°03'E
Porsangerfjorden str. Norway 43 F5.............70°19'N 25°18'E
Porsangerhalvøya pen. Norway 43 F5.............70°45'N 25°01'E
Porsgrunn Norway 43 B2.............59°08'N 9°39'E
Porsuk r. Turkey 51 I4.............39°41'N 31°58'E
Portadown Northern Ireland 14 C2.............54°25'N 6°26'W
Portaferry Northern Ireland 14 D2.............54°23'N 5°32'W
Portage la Prairie Canada 60 I2.............49°58'N 98°19'W
Portalegre Portugal 45 B3.............39°18'N 7°25'W
Port Angeles U.S.A. 62 B6.............48°06'N 123°25'W
Port Arthur U.S.A. 63 H2.............29°51'N 93°58'W
Port Askaig Scotland 14 C3.............55°51'N 6°06'W
Port Augusta Australia 108 C3.............32°29'S 137°45'E
Port-au-Prince Haiti 67 J4.............18°33'N 72°19'W
Portavogie Northern Ireland 14 D2.............54°27'N 5°26'W
Port Blair India 97 H3.............11°41'N 92°42'E
Port-de-Paix Haiti 67 J4.............19°57'N 72°50'W
Port Elizabeth S. Africa 83 B1.............33°57'S 25°37'E
Port Ellen Scotland 14 C3.............55°38'N 6°11'W
Port Erin Isle of Man 12 C3.............54°05'N 4°45'W
Port-Gentil Gabon 84 E1.............0°46'S 8°49'E
Port Glasgow Scotland 14 E3.............55°56'N 4°41'W
Port Harcourt Nigeria 84 E2.............4°46'N 7°01'E
Porthcawl Wales 11 D3.............51°29'N 3°42'W
Port Hedland Australia 108 A4.............20°23'S 118°37'E
Porthleven England 11 B2.............50°04'N 5°19'W
Porthmadog Wales 10 C4.............52°56'N 4°08'W
Port Hope Simpson Canada 61 M3.............52°31'N 55°47'W
Portimão Portugal 45 A2.............37°08'N 8°32'W
Port Isaac Bay England 11 C2.............50°36'N 4°49'W
Portishead England 8 C2.............51°29'N 2°46'W
Portknockie Scotland 17 G2.............57°42'N 2°51'W
Portland Australia 108 C3.............38°21'S 141°34'E
Portland Me. U.S.A. 63 L5.............43°41'N 70°17'W
Portland Oreg. U.S.A. 62 B6.............45°29'N 122°38'W
Portland, Isle of pen. England 8 C1.............50°33'N 2°25'W
Portlaoise Ireland 18 D3.............53°02'N 7°18'W
Portlethen Scotland 17 G2.............57°04'N 2°08'W
Port Lincoln Australia 108 C3.............34°43'S 135°49'E
Port Louis Mauritius 79 E1.............20°10'S 57°30'E
Port Macquarie Australia 108 E3.............31°25'S 152°53'E
Port Moresby P.N.G. 108 D6.............9°28'S 147°13'E
Portnahaven Scotland 14 C3.............55°41'N 6°30'W
Porto Alegre Brazil 73 D3.............30°03'S 51°11'W
Porto Esperidião Brazil 72 D5.............15°50'S 58°32'W
Port of Ness Scotland 16 C3.............58°30'N 6°14'W
Port of Spain Trinidad and Tobago 67 L3.............10°37'N 61°30'W
Portoguaro Italy 46 E1.............45°46'N 12°50'E
Porto-Novo Benin 84 E2.............6°30'N 2°40'E
Porto Santana Brazil 72 D6.............0°01'S 51°09'W
Porto-Vecchio France 44 H2.............41°35'N 9°16'E
Porto Velho Brazil 72 C6.............8°47'S 63°54'W
Portoviejo Ecuador 72 A6.............1°06'S 80°28'W
Portpatrick Scotland 14 D2.............54°51'N 5°07'W
Port Pirie Australia 108 C3.............33°10'S 138°02'E
Portree Scotland 16 C2.............57°25'N 6°12'W
Portrush Northern Ireland 14 C3.............55°12'N 6°39'W
Port Said Egypt 85 H5.............31°16'N 32°18'E
Portsmouth England 8 D1.............50°48'N 1°06'W
Portsmouth d. England 21 E2.............50°50'N 1°04'W
Portsmouth U.S.A. 63 J4.............38°44'N 82°59'W
Portsoy Scotland 17 G2.............57°41'N 2°41'W
Portstewart Northern Ireland 14 C3.............55°11'N 6°43'W
Port Sudan Sudan 85 H3.............19°36'N 37°12'E
Port Talbot Wales 10 D3.............51°36'N 3°48'W
Portugal Europe 45 B3.............39°41'N 7°57'W
Portumna Ireland 18 C3.............53°06'N 8°13'W
Port Vila Vanuatu 109 F5.............17°44'S 168°17'E
Port William Scotland 14 E2.............54°46'N 4°35'W
Posadas Argentina 73 D4.............27°23'S 55°52'W
Poso Indonesia 103 G3.............1°24'S 120°47'E

Potenza Italy 49 F5.............40°38'N 15°48'E
Poti Georgia 53 E2.............42°09'N 41°40'E
Potiskum Nigeria 84 F3.............11°42'N 11°04'E
Potosí Bolivia 72 C5.............19°36'S 65°47'W
Potsdam Germany 46 E5.............52°24'N 13°04'E
Poulton-le-Fylde England 12 E2.............53°51'N 2°59'W
Poûthĭsăt Cambodia 102 C6.............12°32'N 103°57'E
Powell, Lake resr U.S.A. 62 D4.............37°34'N 110°37'W
Powick England 8 C3.............52°10'N 2°15'W
Powys d. Wales 21 D3.............52°23'N 3°25'W
Poyang Hu l. China 99 L3.............29°05'N 116°22'E
Požarevac Serbia 50 D7.............44°37'N 21°11'E
Poza Rica Mexico 66 E5.............20°35'N 97°26'W
Poznań Poland 46 G5.............52°25'N 16°56'E
Pozoblanco Spain 45 C3.............38°23'N 4°50'W
Prabumulih Indonesia 102 C3.............3°26'S 104°13'E
Prachuap Khiri Khan Thailand 102 B6.............11°49'N 99°49'E
Prague Czechia 46 F4.............50°04'N 14°26'E
Praia Cape Verde 84 B3.............14°55'N 23°29'W
Prapat Indonesia 102 B4.............2°41'N 98°57'E
Prawle Point England 11 D2.............50°12'N 3°44'W
Preparis Island Cocos Is 97 H3.............14°51'N 93°39'E
Přerov Czechia 46 G3.............49°27'N 17°27'E
Presidente Prudente Brazil 73 D4.............22°10'S 51°23'W
Prešov Slovakia 46 I3.............48°59'N 21°16'E
Prespa, Lake Europe 50 D5.............40°52'N 21°03'E
Presque Isle town U.S.A. 63 M6.............46°41'N 68°01'W
Prestatyn Wales 10 D5.............53°20'N 3°24'W
Presteigne Wales 10 D4.............52°16'N 3°00'W
Preston Dor. England 8 C1.............50°39'N 2°25'W
Preston Lancs. England 12 E2.............53°46'N 2°42'W
Prestonpans Scotland 15 G3.............55°58'N 2°59'W
Prestwick Scotland 14 E3.............55°30'N 4°37'W
Pretoria S. Africa 83 B2.............25°44'S 28°13'E
Preveza Greece 50 D4.............38°57'N 20°45'E
Prievidza Slovakia 46 H3.............48°47'N 18°38'E
Prijedor Bos. and Herz. 50 B7.............44°59'N 16°43'E
Prijepolje Serbia 50 C6.............43°23'N 19°39'E
Prilep North Macedonia 50 D5.............41°21'N 21°33'E
Primorsko-Akhtarsk Russia 51 M8.............46°03'N 38°10'E
Prince Albert Canada 60 H3.............53°12'N 105°44'W
Prince Alfred, Cape Canada 60 F5.............74°20'N 124°47'W
Prince Charles Island Canada 61 K4.............67°48'N 76°12'W
Prince Edward Island d. Canada 61 L2.............46°41'N 63°09'W
Prince Edward Islands Indian Oc. 117 F1.............47°00'S 37°00'E
Prince George Canada 60 F3.............53°55'N 122°46'W
Prince of Wales Island Australia 108 D5.............10°43'S 142°09'E
Prince of Wales Island Canada 61 I5.............72°27'N 99°08'W
Prince of Wales Island U.S.A. 60 E3.............55°30'N 132°45'W
Prince Patrick Island Canada 60 G5.............76°57'N 118°47'W
Prince Rupert Canada 60 E3.............54°19'N 130°19'W
Princes Risborough England 8 E2.............51°43'N 0°50'W
Príncipe i. São Tomé and Príncipe 84 E2.............1°39'N 7°22'E
Pripet r. Ukraine 47 N4.............51°16'N 30°16'E
Pripet Marshes Belarus/Ukraine 47 K4.............51°39'N 24°34'E
Pristina Kosovo 50 D6.............42°40'N 21°10'E
Privas France 44 F4.............44°44'N 4°36'E
Prizren Kosovo 50 D6.............42°13'N 20°43'E
Probolinggo Indonesia 102 E2.............7°47'S 113°13'E
Probus England 11 C2.............50°18'N 4°57'W
Providence U.S.A. 63 L5.............41°50'N 71°25'W
Providence, Cape New Zealand 109 F2.............46°01'S 166°28'E
Providencia, Isla de i. Caribbean Sea 67 H3.............13°21'N 81°20'W
Provins France 44 E6.............48°34'N 3°18'E
Provo U.S.A. 62 D5.............40°17'N 111°41'W
Prudhoe Bay town U.S.A. 60 D5.............70°18'N 148°10'W
Prüm Germany 42 F3.............50°13'N 6°25'E
Pruszków Poland 46 I5.............52°10'N 20°49'E
Prut r. Europe 47 M1.............45°28'N 28°12'E
Pryluky Ukraine 47 O4.............50°35'N 32°24'E
Przemyśl Poland 47 J3.............49°47'N 22°46'E
Psara i. Greece 50 F4.............38°37'N 25°35'E
Psebay Russia 51 N7.............44°07'N 40°47'E
Psel r. Russia/Ukraine 47 P4.............51°05'N 35°15'E
Pskov Russia 43 G2.............57°49'N 28°19'E
Pskov, Lake Estonia/Russia 43 F2.............58°02'N 27°56'E
Pucallpa Peru 72 B6.............8°22'S 74°35'W
Pudozh Russia 52 D4.............61°49'N 36°22'E
Pudsey England 13 F2.............53°48'N 1°40'W
Puducherry India 96 E3.............11°57'N 79°48'E
Puebla Mexico 66 E4.............19°02'N 98°12'W
Puebla d. Mexico 66 E4.............18°04'N 98°39'W
Pueblo U.S.A. 62 F4.............38°17'N 104°38'W
Puente-Genil Spain 45 C2.............37°23'N 4°46'W
Puerto Ángel Mexico 66 E4.............15°42'N 96°31'W
Puerto de la Estaca Canary Islands 45 X1.............27°47'N 17°54'W
Puerto del Rosario Canary Islands 45 Z2.............28°30'N 13°52'W
Puerto Deseado Argentina 73 C2.............47°45'S 65°55'W
Puertollano Spain 45 C3.............38°41'N 4°06'W
Puerto Montt Chile 73 B2.............41°27'S 72°58'W
Puerto Natales Chile 73 B1.............51°35'S 72°24'W
Puerto Peñasco Mexico 66 B7.............31°19'N 113°32'W
Puerto Princesa Phil. 102 F5.............9°45'N 118°45'E
Puerto Rico i. Central America 67 K4.............17°45'N 66°34'W
Puerto Vallarta Mexico 66 C5.............20°40'N 105°14'W
Pula Croatia 46 E1.............44°53'N 13°51'E
Pulborough England 9 E1.............50°57'N 0°30'W
Pune India 96 D4.............18°32'N 73°57'E
Puning China 99 L2.............23°17'N 116°09'E
Punjab d. India 96 E7.............30°17'N 75°18'E
Punta Arenas Chile 73 B1.............53°09'S 70°57'W
Punta Gorda Nicaragua 67 H3.............11°32'N 83°46'W
Punto Fijo Venezuela 67 J3.............11°39'N 70°11'W
Pur r. Russia 54 I4.............67°33'N 77°53'E
Purari r. P.N.G. 108 D6.............7°46'S 144°54'E
Purbeck, Isle of pen. England 8 C1.............50°39'N 2°01'W
Puri India 96 G4.............19°48'N 85°55'E
Purmerend Neth. 42 D5.............52°31'N 4°57'E
Purus r. Brazil/Peru 72 C6.............3°42'S 61°28'W
Pustoshka Russia 47 M7.............56°20'N 29°22'E
Putian China 99 L3.............25°26'N 119°00'E
Puting, Tanjung pt Indonesia 102 E3.............3°35'S 111°50'E
Putrajaya Malaysia 102 C4.............2°55'N 101°39'E
Puttalam Sri Lanka 96 E2.............8°01'N 79°50'E
Putumayo r. Colombia 72 B6.............3°25'S 70°03'W
Puvurnituq Canada 61 K4.............60°02'N 77°17'W
Puy de Dôme mt. France 44 E4.............45°46'N 2°58'E
Puy de Sancy mt. France 44 E4.............45°31'N 2°49'E
Pwllheli Wales 10 C4.............52°53'N 4°25'W
Pyaozero, Ozero l. Russia 43 G4.............66°11'N 30°47'E
Pyasina r. Russia 55 J5.............73°35'N 86°19'E
Pyatigorsk Russia 53 E2.............44°02'N 43°03'E
Pyay Myanmar 97 I4.............18°48'N 95°13'E
Pyhäjoki r. Finland 43 F4.............64°28'N 24°15'E
Pyhäselkä l. Finland 43 G3.............62°31'N 29°41'E

Pyinmana Myanmar 97 I4 ...............19°44'N 96°13'E
Pyle Wales 11 D3...........................51°32'N 3°42'W
Pylos Greece 50 D3.......................36°55'N 21°42'E
P'yŏngyang N. Korea 99 N5..........39°01'N 125°44'E
Pyramid Lake U.S.A. 62 C5...........40°09'N 119°37'W
Pyrenees mts Europe 45 G5...........42°30'N 2°00'E
Pyrgos Greece 50 D3.....................37°40'N 21°27'E
Pyryatyn Ukraine 47 O4...............50°14'N 32°30'E

## Q

Qā'en Iran 95 I6............................33°42'N 59°05'E
Qamanittuaq Canada 61 I4............64°17'N 95°43'W
Qamdo China 98 H4......................31°13'N 97°08'E
Qarshi Uzbekistan 95 K7................38°52'N 65°48'E
Qasigiannguit Greenland 61 M4......68°48'N 51°11'W
Qatar Asia 95 H5...........................25°25'N 51°57'E
Qattara Depression f. Egypt 85 G4....29°48'N 27°00'E
Qazax Azerbaijan 53 E2.................41°06'N 45°21'E
Qazvīn Iran 95 G7.........................36°17'N 49°58'E
Qeshm Iran 95 I5..........................26°57'N 56°15'E
Qiemo China 98 F5.......................38°05'N 85°33'E
Qijiaojing China 98 G6..................43°25'N 91°38'E
Qilian Shan mts China 98 H5...........39°21'N 97°06'E
Qinā Egypt 85 H4..........................26°08'N 32°45'E
Qingdao China 99 M5...................36°05'N 120°24'E
Qinghai d. China 98 H5..................36°07'N 96°31'E
Qinghai Hu l. China 99 I5...............36°49'N 100°06'E
Qinhuangdao China 99 L5.............39°56'N 119°38'E
Qinzhou China 99 J2....................21°57'N 108°31'E
Qionghai China 99 K1..................13°13'N 110°29'E
Qiqihar China 99 M7....................47°13'N 123°58'E
Qom Iran 95 H6...........................34°38'N 50°51'E
Qo'ng'irot Uzbekistan 53 F2..........43°04'N 58°51'E
Qornet es Saouda mt. Lebanon 51 L2...34°18'N 36°06'E
Quang Ngai Vietnam 102 D7.........15°04'N 108°50'E
Quantock Hills England 11 D3........51°10'N 3°15'W
Quanzhou China 99 K3.................25°57'N 111°05'E
Quba Azerbaijan 53 E2..................41°22'N 48°31'E
Quchan Iran 95 I7.........................36°59'N 58°29'E
Québec Canada 61 K2....................46°48'N 71°15'W
Québec d. Canada 61 K3................54°45'N 74°31'W
Queenborough England 9 F2.........51°25'N 0°45'E
Queen Charlotte Islands Canada 60 E3.... 53°59'N 133°20'W
Queen Charlotte Sound str. Canada 60 F3
                                                      51°24'N 129°09'W
Queen Elizabeth Islands Canada 61 I4....76°31'N 107°31'W
Queen Maud Gulf Canada 60 H4......68°13'N 102°08'W
Queensland d. Australia 108 D4.......22°37'S 144°17'E
Quelimane Mozambique 83 C3.......17°53'S 36°53'E
Querétaro Mexico 66 D5.................20°37'N 100°22'W
Querétaro d. Mexico 66 E5.............20°51'N 99°50'W
Quetta Pakistan 96 C7...................30°14'N 67°03'E
Quetzaltenango Guatemala 66 F3...14°50'N 91°30'W
Quezon City Phil. 103 G6...............14°36'N 121°01'E
Quibala Angola 83 A3....................10°44'S 14°59'E
Quibdó Colombia 72 B7................5°39'N 76°38'W
Quimper France 44 A5...................47°59'N 4°06'W
Quintana Roo d. Mexico 66 G4......18°44'N 88°47'W
Quito Ecuador 72 B6....................0°14'S 78°30'W
Quoich, Loch l. Scotland 16 D2.......57°03'N 5°18'W
Quoile r. Northern Ireland 14 D2.....54°21'N 5°42'W
Quy Nhơn Vietnam 102 D6...........13°44'N 109°13'E
Quzhou China 99 L3.....................28°57'N 118°52'E

## R

Raahe Finland 43 F4......................64°41'N 24°29'E
Raalte Neth. 42 F5........................52°23'N 6°17'E
Raasay i. Scotland 16 C2................57°23'N 6°02'W
Raasay, Sound of str. Scotland 16 C2....57°26'N 6°06'W
Raba Indonesia 102 F2..................8°32'S 118°46'E
Rabat Morocco 84 D5...................34°01'N 6°47'W
Rābigh Saudi Arabia 94 E4.............22°50'N 39°00'E
Race, Cape Canada 61 M2.............46°38'N 53°09'W
Rach Gia Vietnam 102 D5.............9°59'N 105°06'E
Radom Poland 46 I4.....................51°24'N 21°09'E
Radomsko Poland 46 H4...............51°04'N 19°27'E
Radstock England 8 C2................51°17'N 2°27'W
Rafhā' Saudi Arabia 94 F5.............29°33'N 43°25'E
Rafsanjān Iran 95 I6.....................30°24'N 55°59'E
Raglan Wales 10 E3......................51°46'N 2°51'W
Ragusa Italy 48 F4........................36°55'N 14°44'E
Rahachow Belarus 47 N5...............53°05'N 30°03'E
Rahimyar Khan Pakistan 96 C6.......28°22'N 70°19'E
Raichur India 96 E4.....................16°13'N 77°18'E
Rainier, Mount vol. U.S.A. 62 B6....46°54'N 121°44'W
Raipur India 96 F5.......................21°14'N 81°39'E
Rajahmundry India 96 F4..............17°00'N 81°52'E
Rajanpur Pakistan 96 C6...............29°05'N 70°24'E
Rajasthan d. India 96 D6...............26°40'N 73°31'E
Rajkot India 96 D5.......................22°14'N 70°53'E
Rajshahi Bangl. 96 G5..................24°22'N 88°36'E
Rakhiv Ukraine 47 K3...................48°03'N 24°12'E
Rakitnoye Russia 47 P4................50°50'N 35°50'E
Rakvere Estonia 43 F2...................59°21'N 26°22'E
Raleigh U.S.A. 63 K4.....................35°47'N 78°37'W
Rame Head England 11 C2............50°19'N 4°15'W
Rāmhormoz Iran 95 G6.................31°10'N 49°35'E
Râmnicu Vâlcea Romania 50 F7......45°07'N 24°22'E
Ramsbottom England 13 E2...........53°39'N 2°19'W
Ramsey England 9 E3....................52°27'N 0°06'W
Ramsey Isle of Man 12 C3.............54°19'N 4°23'W
Ramsey Bay Isle of Man 12 C3........54°20'N 4°22'W
Ramsey Island Wales 10 B3............51°51'N 5°22'W
Ramsgate England 9 G2.................51°20'N 1°25'E
Rancagua Chile 73 B3....................34°11'S 70°44'W
Ranchi India 96 G5.......................23°22'N 85°20'E
Randers Denmark 43 B2.................56°27'N 10°03'E
Rangoon Myanmar 97 I4...............16°49'N 96°08'E
Rangpur Bangl. 97 G6..................25°46'N 89°16'E
Rankin Inlet Canada 61 I4.............62°52'N 92°03'W
Rannoch, Loch l. Scotland 17 E4.....56°41'N 4°23'W
Rannoch Moor f. Scotland 16 E1.....56°38'N 4°46'W
Ranong Thailand 102 B5...............9°57'N 98°38'E
Rantauprapat Indonesia 102 B4.....2°06'N 99°47'E
Raoul Island Indian Oc. 109 H4......29°16'S 177°57'W
Rapallo Italy 46 C1......................44°21'N 9°14'E
Raphoe Ireland 14 B2..................54°52'N 7°35'W
Rapid City U.S.A. 62 F5.................44°04'N 103°14'W
Ras Dejen mt. Ethiopia 85 H3.........13°12'N 38°23'E
Rasht Iran 95 G7..........................37°16'N 49°34'E
Raskoh mts Pakistan 95 K5............28°54'N 65°26'E

Ras Tannūrah Saudi Arabia 95 H5............26°38'N 50°10'E
Rat Buri Thailand 102 B6......................13°31'N 99°50'E
Rathdrum Ireland 18 E2.......................52°56'N 6°14'W
Rathenow Germany 46 E5....................52°37'N 12°20'E
Rathfriland Northern Ireland 14 C2........54°14'N 6°09'W
Rathkeale Ireland 18 C2.......................52°31'N 8°56'W
Rathlin Island Northern Ireland 14 C3.....55°17'N 6°10'W
Rathluirc Ireland 18 C2.........................52°21'N 8°41'W
Ratne Ukraine 47 K4.............................51°40'N 24°32'E
Rattray Head Scotland 17 H2.................57°37'N 1°49'W
Rättvik Sweden 43 C3..........................60°53'N 15°08'E
Rauma Finland 43 E3...........................61°08'N 21°31'E
Raunds England 9 E3...........................52°20'N 0°32'W
Ravenna Italy 46 E1.............................44°25'N 12°13'E
Ravensthorpe Australia 108 B3..............33°34'S 120°01'E
Rawaki i. Kiribati 109 H6.......................3°42'S 170°40'W
Rawalpindi Pakistan 96 D7....................33°38'N 73°08'E
Rawicz Poland 46 G4...........................51°37'N 16°51'E
Rawlins U.S.A. 62 E5............................41°48'N 107°13'W
Rawson Argentina 73 C2.......................43°15'S 65°06'W
Rawtenstall England 13 E2....................53°42'N 2°17'W
Rayleigh England 9 F2..........................51°35'N 0°36'E
Razgrad Bulgaria 50 G6........................43°32'N 26°30'E
Ré, Île de i. France 44 C5......................46°10'N 1°22'W
Reading England 8 E2..........................51°27'N 0°58'W
Reading d. England 21 E2.....................51°27'N 0°59'W
Rebiana Sand Sea des. Libya 94 B4........24°42'N 21°18'E
Reboly Russia 43 G3............................63°50'N 30°48'E
Rechytsa Belarus 47 N5........................52°22'N 30°26'E
Recife Brazil 72 F6...............................8°02'S 34°48'W
Red r. U.S.A. 63 H3..............................31°05'N 91°44'W
Red Bluff U.S.A. 62 B5.........................40°11'N 122°14'W
Redcar England 13 F3...........................54°37'N 1°03'W
Redcar and Cleveland d. England 21 E4....54°33'N 1°02'W
Red Deer Canada 60 G3........................52°16'N 113°49'W
Redding U.S.A. 62 B5...........................40°36'N 122°29'W
Redditch England 8 D3.........................52°19'N 1°56'W
Redhill England 9 E2............................51°14'N 0°10'W
Red Lake town Canada 61 I3..................51°01'N 93°50'W
Red Lakes U.S.A. 63 H6........................48°03'N 94°44'W
Redruth England 11 B2.........................50°14'N 5°14'W
Red Sea Africa/Asia 94 E4.....................26°30'N 34°42'E
Red Wharf Bay Wales 10 C5..................53°19'N 4°11'W
Ree, Lough l. Ireland 18 D3...................53°32'N 7°59'W
Reggane Algeria 84 E4..........................26°46'N 0°09'E
Reggio di Calabria Italy 49 G4................38°06'N 15°39'E
Reggio nell'Emilia Italy 46 D1................44°41'N 10°38'E
Regina Canada 60 H3...........................50°27'N 104°37'W
Regensburg Germany 46 E3...................49°01'N 12°06'E
Reidh, Rubha pt Scotland 16 D2............57°52'N 5°51'W
Reigate England 9 E2............................51°14'N 0°12'W
Reims France 44 F6..............................49°15'N 4°03'E
Reindeer Lake Canada 60 H3.................57°24'N 102°23'W
Reinosa Spain 45 C5.............................42°59'N 4°07'W
Reiphólsfjöll hill Iceland 43 X2..............65°41'N 22°00'W
Reliance Canada 60 H4.........................62°43'N 109°06'W
Relizane Algeria 48 D4..........................35°44'N 0°40'E
Rena Norway 43 B3..............................61°08'N 11°22'E
Renfrewshire d. Scotland 20 C4..............55°52'N 4°31'W
Reni Ukraine 51 H7...............................45°27'N 28°18'E
Rennell i. Solomon Is 109 F5..................11°40'S 160°18'E
Rennes France 44 C6............................48°07'N 1°41'W
Reno r. Italy 46 E1................................44°35'N 12°17'E
Reno U.S.A. 62 C4...............................39°32'N 119°48'W
Republican r. U.S.A. 62 G4....................39°06'N 96°52'W
Resistencia Argentina 73 D4..................27°24'S 58°59'W
Reşiţa Romania 50 D7..........................45°18'N 21°53'E
Resolute Canada 61 I5..........................74°41'N 94°46'W
Resolution Island Canada 61 L4.............61°34'N 64°52'W
Retford England 13 G2..........................53°19'N 0°57'W
Rethel France 42 D2.............................49°31'N 4°23'E
Rethymno Greece 50 F2.......................35°21'N 24°28'E
Réunion i. Indian Oc. 117 G2.................20°00'S 55°00'E
Reus Spain 45 F4..................................41°09'N 1°06'E
Reutlingen Germany 46 C3....................48°30'N 9°12'E
Rewa India 96 F5.................................24°32'N 81°18'E
Reykjavík Iceland 43 X2........................64°08'N 21°55'W
Reynosa Mexico 66 E6..........................26°04'N 98°17'W
Rēzekne Latvia 43 F2............................56°31'N 27°20'E
Rhayader Wales 10 D4..........................52°18'N 3°31'W
Rheine Germany 42 G5.........................52°17'N 7°28'E
Rheinland-Pfalz d. Germany 42 G2.........49°46'N 7°27'E
Rhine r. Europe 46 B4...........................51°53'N 6°03'E
Rhins of Galloway, The pen. Scotland 14 D2
                                                                   54°55'N 5°07'W
Rhode Island d. U.S.A. 63 L5..................41°40'N 71°35'W
Rhodes Greece 51 H3...........................36°26'N 28°13'E
Rhodes i. Greece 51 H3.........................36°15'N 28°10'E
Rhodope Mountains Bulgaria/Greece 50 E5
                                                                   41°52'N 23°41'E
Rhondda f. Wales 10 D3........................51°38'N 3°25'W
Rhondda Cynon Taff d. Wales 21 D2........51°36'N 3°23'W
Rhône r. France/Switz. 44 F3.................43°37'N 4°40'E
Rhyl Wales 10 D5.................................53°19'N 3°29'W
Riau, Kepulauan is Indonesia 102 C4.......0°34'N 104°11'E
Ribble r. England 13 E2.........................53°45'N 2°45'W
Ribe Denmark 43 B1.............................55°20'N 8°46'E
Ribeirão Preto Brazil 73 E4....................21°12'S 47°48'W
Ribnita Moldova 47 M2.........................47°46'N 29°00'E
Richfield U.S.A. 62 D4...........................38°47'N 112°05'W
Richland U.S.A. 62 C6...........................46°19'N 119°17'W
Richmond England 13 F3......................54°24'N 1°44'W
Richmond U.S.A. 63 K4.........................37°34'N 77°28'W
Riesa Germany 46 E4............................51°19'N 13°17'E
Rifstangi pt Iceland 43 Y2......................66°33'N 16°13'W
Rīga Latvia 43 F2.................................56°56'N 24°07'E
Riga, Gulf of Estonia/Latvia 43 E2...........57°24'N 23°45'E
Rigside Scotland 15 F3..........................55°36'N 3°47'W
Riihimäki Finland 43 F3........................60°44'N 24°47'E
Rijeka Croatia 50 A7.............................45°20'N 14°26'E
Rimini Italy 48 F5.................................44°04'N 12°34'E
Rimouski Canada 61 L2.........................48°27'N 68°32'W
Rimsdale, Loch l. Scotland 17 E3............58°17'N 4°10'W
Ringkøbing Denmark 43 B2...................56°05'N 8°15'E
Ringvassøya i. Norway 43 D5................69°55'N 18°56'E
Ringwood England 8 D1.......................50°51'N 1°47'W
Riobamba Ecuador 72 B6......................1°41'S 78°42'W
Río Branco Brazil 72 C5........................10°01'S 67°48'W
Río Cuarto Argentina 73 C3...................33°08'S 64°21'W
Rio de Janeiro Brazil 73 E4....................22°55'S 43°17'W
Río Gallegos Argentina 73 C1................51°39'S 69°15'W
Rio Grande town Brazil 73 D3................32°04'S 52°08'W
Rio Grande r. Mexico/U.S.A. 67 E6.........25°57'N 97°10'W
Riohacha Colombia 72 B8......................11°32'N 72°58'W
Rio Verde Brazil 72 D5..........................17°48'S 50°55'W
Ripley England 13 F2............................53°03'N 1°24'W
Ripon England 13 F3............................54°08'N 1°32'W

Risca Wales 10 D3.....................................51°37'N 3°06'W
Rishton England 13 E2...............................53°46'N 2°25'W
Riva del Garda Italy 46 D1..........................45°53'N 10°50'E
Riverside U.S.A. 62 C3...............................33°57'N 117°24'W
Rivière-du-Loup Canada 61 L2....................47°50'N 69°32'W
Rivne Ukraine 47 L4...................................50°37'N 26°14'E
Riyadh Saudi Arabia 95 G4.........................24°43'N 46°41'E
Rize Turkey 51 N5.....................................41°02'N 40°32'E
Rizhao China 99 L5...................................35°19'N 119°33'E
Rjuvbrokkene mt. Norway 43 A2................59°11'N 7°10'E
Roadford Reservoir England 11 C2..............50°41'N 4°13'W
Roanne France 44 F5.................................46°03'N 4°05'E
Roanoke U.S.A. 63 K4...............................37°16'N 79°58'W
Roanoke r. U.S.A. 63 K4.............................36°02'N 76°22'W
Robertsfors Sweden 43 E4..........................64°12'N 20°52'E
Roberval Canada 61 K2...............................48°31'N 72°14'W
Robson, Mount Canada 60 G3....................53°07'N 119°06'W
Roca, Cabo da c. Portugal 45 A3.................38°47'N 9°29'W
Rocha Uruguay 73 D3................................34°30'S 54°19'W
Rochdale England 13 E2.............................53°37'N 2°10'W
Rochefort Belgium 42 E3............................50°10'N 5°13'E
Rochefort France 44 C4.............................45°57'N 0°58'W
Rochester England 9 F2..............................51°23'N 0°30'E
Rochester Minn. U.S.A. 63 H5.....................44°02'N 92°27'W
Rochester N. Y. U.S.A. 63 K5.......................43°09'N 77°38'W
Rochford England 9 F2..............................51°35'N 0°42'E
Rockford U.S.A. 63 I5.................................42°17'N 89°04'W
Rockhampton Australia 108 E4...................23°23'S 150°34'E
Rockingham Forest England 9 E3................52°31'N 0°32'W
Rocky Mountains Canada/U.S.A. 60 F3........40°57'N 107°58'W
Rodel Scotland 16 C2................................57°45'N 6°58'W
Rodez France 44 E4...................................44°22'N 2°34'E
Roe r. Northern Ireland 14 C3......................55°06'N 6°58'W
Roermond Neth. 42 E4...............................51°12'N 5°59'E
Roeselare Belgium 42 C3............................50°56'N 3°08'E
Rokiškis Lithuania 43 F1.............................55°57'N 25°35'E
Rolla U.S.A. 63 H4.....................................37°56'N 91°46'W
Roma i. Indonesia 103 H2...........................7°31'S 127°25'E
Romain, Cape U.S.A. 63 K3.........................32°59'N 79°27'W
Roman Romania 47 L2................................46°56'N 26°55'E
Romania Europe 49 H6...............................46°07'N 24°36'E
Romanzof, Cape U.S.A. 60 B4......................61°49'N 166°06'W
Rombas France 42 F2.................................49°15'N 6°05'E
Rome Italy 48 F5.......................................41°54'N 12°30'E
Romford England 9 F2...............................51°35'N 0°11'E
Romney Marsh f. England 9 F2...................51°03'N 0°54'E
Romny Ukraine 47 O4................................50°45'N 33°28'E
Romsey England 8 D1................................50°59'N 1°30'W
Rona i. Scotland 16 D3...............................57°33'N 5°57'W
Rona i. Scotland 16 D4...............................59°07'N 5°49'W
Ronas Hill Scotland 17 H5...........................60°32'N 1°27'W
Ronda Spain 45 C2....................................36°45'N 5°10'W
Rondonópolis Brazil 72 D5..........................16°29'S 54°38'W
Rønne Denmark 43 C1................................55°06'N 14°43'E
Ronse Belgium 42 C3.................................50°45'N 3°36'E
Roosendaal Neth. 42 D4.............................51°31'N 4°28'E
Roque de los Muchachos vol. Canary Islands 45 X2
                                                                             28°45'N 17°51'W
Roquefort France 44 C4..............................44°02'N 0°19'W
Roraima, Mount Guyana 72 C7....................5°15'N 60°44'W
Røros Norway 43 B3...................................62°34'N 11°23'E
Rosario Argentina 73 C3.............................32°56'S 60°41'W
Roscoff France 44 B6.................................48°43'N 3°59'W
Roscommon Ireland 18 C3..........................53°38'N 8°11'W
Roscommon d. Ireland 18 C3.......................53°49'N 8°16'W
Roscrea Ireland 18 D2................................52°57'N 7°48'W
Roseau Dominica 67 L4...............................15°17'N 61°23'W
Roseburg U.S.A. 62 B5................................43°13'N 123°21'W
Roseires Reservoir Sudan 94 D2...................11°33'N 34°31'E
Rosenheim Germany 46 E2..........................47°51'N 12°08'E
Roşiori de Vede Romania 50 F7....................44°07'N 25°00'E
Roslavl' Russia 47 O5..................................53°57'N 32°51'E
Rossan Point Ireland 18 C4..........................54°42'N 8°48'W
Rossel Island P.N.G. 108 E5.........................11°24'S 154°10'E
Rossington England 13 F2............................53°29'N 1°03'W
Rosslare Harbour Ireland 18 E2....................52°15'N 6°20'W
Rosso Mauritania 84 C3...............................16°29'N 15°47'W
Ross of Mull pen. Scotland 14 C4.................56°18'N 6°19'W
Ross-on-Wye England 8 C2..........................51°55'N 2°35'W
Rossosh' Russia 53 D3.................................50°12'N 39°33'E
Røssvatnet l. Norway 43 C4..........................65°46'N 14°19'E
Rostock Germany 46 E6................................54°05'N 12°07'E
Rostov-na-Donu Russia 53 D2.......................47°13'N 39°44'E
Roswell U.S.A. 62 F3....................................33°21'N 104°30'W
Rota i. N. Mariana Is 103 L6..........................14°09'N 145°17'E
Rote i. Indonesia 103 G1..............................10°29'S 123°24'E
Rothbury England 13 F4...............................55°19'N 1°54'W
Rother r. England 8 E1.................................50°57'N 0°32'W
Rotherham England 13 F2............................53°26'N 1°21'W
Rothes Scotland 17 F2.................................57°32'N 3°12'W
Rothesay Scotland 14 D3.............................55°50'N 5°03'W
Rothwell England 8 E3.................................52°25'N 0°48'W
Rotterdam Neth. 42 D4................................51°55'N 4°30'E
Rotuma i. Fiji 109 G5...................................12°29'S 177°05'E
Roubaix France 44 E7..................................50°42'N 3°10'E
Rouen France 44 D6....................................49°26'N 1°06'E
Round Hill England 13 F3.............................54°21'N 1°05'W
Round Mountain Australia 108 E3................30°24'S 152°15'E
Rousay i. Scotland 17 F4..............................59°11'N 3°08'W
Rouyn-Noranda Canada 63 K6.....................48°14'N 79°02'W
Rovaniemi Finland 43 F4..............................66°29'N 25°42'E
Rovigo Italy 46 D1......................................45°04'N 11°47'E
Rovinj Croatia 46 E1...................................45°05'N 13°38'E
Royale, Isle i. U.S.A. 63 I6............................48°02'N 88°38'W
Royal Leamington Spa England 8 D3...........52°17'N 1°32'W
Royal Tunbridge Wells England 9 F2.............51°08'N 0°16'E
Royal Wootton Bassett England 8 D2...........51°32'N 1°54'W
Royan France 44 C4....................................45°38'N 1°01'W
Royston England 9 E3.................................52°03'N 0°01'W
Royton England 13 E2.................................53°34'N 2°07'W
Ruabon Wales 10 D4...................................52°59'N 3°02'W
Rub' al Khāli des. Asia 95 G3........................19°01'N 46°30'E
Rubtsovsk Russia 54 J3................................51°33'N 81°09'E
Rudnaya Pristan' Russia 99 O6.....................44°21'N 135°51'E
Rudnyy Kazakhstan 54 H3............................52°57'N 63°07'E
Rufiji r. Tanzania 83 C4................................8°02'S 39°17'E
Rugby England 8 D3....................................52°22'N 1°16'W
Rugby U.S.A. 62 F6.....................................48°20'N 100°01'W
Rugeley England 8 D3..................................52°46'N 1°55'W
Rügen i. Germany 46 E6...............................54°23'N 13°27'E
Ruhr r. Germany 42 F4.................................51°26'N 6°43'E
Rukwa, Lake Tanzania 83 C4.........................8°09'S 32°25'E
Rum i. Scotland 16 C1.................................56°59'N 6°22'W
Ruma Serbia 50 C7.....................................45°00'N 19°50'E
Rum Cay i. Bahamas 67 J5...........................23°42'N 74°48'W
Runcorn England 12 E2...............................53°20'N 2°42'W
Rundu Namibia 83 A3.................................17°54'S 19°47'E

Ruoqiang China 98 F5.......................38°58'N 88
Ruse Bulgaria 50 F6............................43°49'N 25
Rushden England 8 E3.........................52°17'N 0°
Russia Asia/Europe 54 I4....................57°12'N 40
Ruteng Indonesia 102 G2..................8°33'S 120
Ruthin Wales 10 D5..............................53°07'N 3°
Rutland d. England 21 E3..................52°42'N 0°
Rutland Water resr England 8 E3.......52°39'N 0°
Ruza Russia 47 Q6................................55°42'N 36
Ruzayevka Russia 53 E3......................54°03'N 44
Ružomberok Slovakia 46 H3..............49°05'N 19
Rwanda Africa 85 G1..........................2°16'S 29
Ryan, Loch b. Scotland 14 D3.............55°01'N 5°
Ryazan' Russia 53 D3..........................54°37'N 39
Rybachiy, Poluostrov f. Russia 52 D4....69°40'N 32
Rybinsk Russia 52 D3..........................58°03'N 38
Rybinskoye Vodokhranilishche resr Russia 52 D3
                                                                   58°21'N 38
Rybnik Poland 46 H4.........................50°06'N 18
Ryde England 8 D1..............................50°44'N 1°
Rye England 9 F1.................................50°57'N 0°
Rye r. England 13 G3............................54°10'N 0°
Rye Bay England 9 F1...........................50°55'N 0°
Ryōtsu Japan 104 C3..........................38°04'N 138
Ryukyu Islands Japan 99 M2...............24°13'N 124°
Rzeszów Poland 47 J4.........................50°02'N 22
Rzhev Russia 52 D3.............................56°16'N 34

## S

Saale r. Germany 46 D4......................51°57'N 11
Saarbrücken Germany 46 B3...............49°15'N 6°
Saaremaa i. Estonia 43 E2...................58°14'N 22
Saarland d. Germany 42 F2.................49°28'N 6
Saarlouis Germany 42 F2....................49°20'N 6°
Sab' Ābār Syria 51 L1..........................33°42'N 37
Šabac Serbia 50 C7.............................44°46'N 19
Sabadell Spain 45 G4..........................41°33'N 2
Sabah d. Malaysia 102 F5...................5°27'N 116
Sabana, Archipiélago de is Cuba 67 H5....23°18'N 80°
Sabhā Libya 84 F4...............................26°55'N 14
Sabinas Mexico 66 D6........................27°52'N 101°
Sabine r. U.S.A. 63 H3.........................29°41'N 94
Sable, Cape Canada 61 L2...................43°25'N 65°
Sable, Cape U.S.A. 63 J2......................25°08'N 81°
Sable Island Canada 61 M2.................43°57'N 59°
Şabyā Saudi Arabia 94 F3....................17°07'N 42
Sabzevār Iran 95 I7..............................36°13'N 57
Sacramento U.S.A. 62 B4....................38°34'N 121°
Sacramento Mountains U.S.A. 62 E3....34°23'N 106°
Sado r. Portugal 45 A3........................38°25'N 8°
Sadoga-shima i. Japan 104 C3............37°56'N 138
Säffle Sweden 43 C2...........................59°08'N 12
Saffron Walden England 9 F3...............52°02'N 0
Safi Morocco 84 D5............................32°22'N 9°
Safonovo Russia 47 O6.......................55°07'N 33
Safonovo Russia 52 G4.......................65°41'N 48
Sagar India 96 E5................................23°50'N 78
Sagres Portugal 45 A2........................37°01'N 8°
Sahand, Kūh-e mt. Iran 95 G7..............37°38'N 46
Sahara des. Africa 84 E4.....................19°01'N 4°
Saidpur Bangl. 96 G6..........................25°46'N 88
Saimaa l. Finland 43 G3.......................61°15'N 28
St Abb's Head Scotland 15 G3...............55°55'N 2°
St Agnes England 11 B2.......................50°19'N 5°
St Agnes i. England 11 A1....................49°53'N 6°
St Albans England 9 E2.......................51°45'N 0°
St Aldhelm's Head England 8 C1..........50°35'N 2°
St-Amand-les-Eaux France 42 C3.........50°26'N 3°
St-Amand-Montrond France 44 E5.......46°44'N 2
St Andrews Scotland 15 G4.................56°20'N 2°
St Anne Channel Is 11 Z9....................49°43'N 2°
St Ann's Head Wales 10 B3..................51°41'N 5°
St Anthony Canada 61 M3..................51°20'N 55°
St Asaph Wales 10 D5.........................53°15'N 3°
St Austell England 11 C2.....................50°20'N 4°
St Austell Bay England 11 C2...............50°19'N 4°
St-Barthélemy i. Central America 67 L4....17°54'N 62°
St Bees England 12 D3........................54°30'N 3
St Bees Head England 12 D3................54°31'N 3°
St Brelade Channel Is 11 Z8.................49°11'N 2°
St Bride's Bay Wales 10 B3...................51°48'N 5°
St-Brieuc France 44 B6........................48°31'N 2°
St Catherine's Point England 8 D1........50°34'N 1°
St Clears Wales 10 C3..........................51°49'N 4°
St Cloud U.S.A. 63 H6.........................45°34'N 94°
St Columb Major England 11 C2...........50°26'N 4°
St David's Wales 10 B3........................51°53'N 5°
St David's Head Wales 10 B3................51°54'N 5°
St-Dié France 44 G6............................48°17'N 6
St-Dizier France 44 F6.........................48°39'N 4
Saintes France 44 C4..........................45°45'N 0°
St-Étienne France 44 F4.......................45°26'N 4°
Saintfield Northern Ireland 14 D2.........54°27'N 5°
St Gallen Switz. 46 C2.........................47°26'N 9°
St-Gaudens France 44 D3....................43°07'N 0°
St George's Grenada 67 L3..................12°04'N 61°
St George's Channel Ireland/U.K. 18 E1....51°58'N 6°
St Germans England 11 C2..................50°24'N 4°
St Govan's Head Wales 10 C3...............51°36'N 4°
St Helena i. Atlantic Oc. 78 B2.............16°00'S 5°
St Helena Bay S. Africa 83 A1...............32°43'S 18
St Helens England 12 E2.....................53°27'N 2°
St Helens, Mount vol. U.S.A. 62 B6.......46°08'N 122°
St Helier Channel Is 11 Z8...................49°11'N 2°
St Ives Cambs. England 9 E3................52°20'N 0°
St Ives Corn. England 11 B2.................50°13'N 5°
St Ives Bay England 11 B2...................50°13'N 5°
St-Jean, Lac l. Canada 63 L6.................48°15'N 66°
Saint John Canada 61 L2....................45°16'N 66°
Saint John r. U.S.A. 63 M6..................45°46'N 66°
St John's Antigua 67 L4.......................17°05'N 61°
St John's Canada 61 M2......................47°28'N 52°
St John's Point Northern Ireland 14 D2....54°13'N 5°
St John's Town of Dalry Scotland 14 E3....55°06'N 4°
St Joseph U.S.A. 63 H4........................39°48'N 94°
St Joseph, Lake Canada 63 H7..............50°59'N 90°
St Just England 11 B2..........................50°08'N 5°
St Keverne England 11 B2....................50°03'N 5°
St Kilda i. Scotland 16 A2....................57°49'N 8°
St Kitts and Nevis Central America 67 L4....17°17'N 62°
St Lawrence inlet Canada 61 L2.............48°18'N 69°
St Lawrence, Gulf of Canada 61 L2........48°20'N 61°
St Lawrence Island U.S.A. 60 B4............63°05'N 170°

France 44 C6................................49°07′N 1°05′W
uis Senegal 84 C3....................16°00′N 16°29′W
uis U.S.A. 63 H4.......................38°43′N 90°14′W
cia Central America 67 L3...........13°57′N 60°53′W
agnus Bay Scotland 17 H5...........60°24′N 1°37′W
alo France 44 B6........................48°39′N 2°00′W
alo, Golfe de g. France 44 B6.......48°48′N 2°16′W
argaret's Hope Scotland 17 G3.....58°49′N 2°57′W
artin Channel Is 11 Y9...............49°26′N 2°33′W
artin Channel Is 11 Z8...............49°27′N 2°33′W
artin i. Central America 67 L4......18°08′N 62°59′W
artin's i. England 11 A1..............49°58′N 6°17′W
ary's i. England 11 A1...............49°53′N 6°17′W
atthew Island U.S.A. 60 A4.........60°27′N 172°49′W
aurice r. Canada 63 L6..............46°22′N 72°32′W
awes England 11 B2...................50°09′N 5°01′W
oritz Switz. 46 C2.....................46°30′N 9°50′E
aire France 44 B5......................47°17′N 2°13′W
ots England 9 E3......................52°14′N 0°16′W
klaas Belgium 42 D4.................51°10′N 4°08′E
ner France 42 B3......................50°45′N 2°16′E
en Channel Is 11 Z8...................49°14′N 2°12′W
ul U.S.A. 63 H5.........................44°57′N 93°05′W
er Port Channel Is 11 Y9.............49°28′N 2°32′W
tersburg Russia 54 E3................59°56′N 30°18′E
tersburg U.S.A. 63 J2................27°45′N 82°42′W
rre and Miquelon is N. America 61 M2
                                          46°42′N 56°29′W
l-sur-Ternoise France 9 H1...........50°23′N 2°20′E
ten Austria 46 F3.....................48°12′N 15°38′E
entin France 44 E6....................49°51′N 3°17′E
mpson Channel Is 11 Y9.............49°29′N 2°33′W
cent and the Grenadines Central America 67 L3
                                          12°50′N 60°52′W
h Belgium 42 F3.......................50°17′N 6°07′E
ndel Germany 42 G2...................49°28′N 7°09′E
n i. N. Mariana Is 103 L7.............15°15′N 145°49′E
na Japan 104 C3.......................35°51′N 139°39′E
nulkki hill Finland 43 F4..............66°57′N 25°48′E
a, Nevado mt. Bolivia 72 C5.........18°09′S 68°52′W
Morocco 45 D1.........................34°37′N 3°23′W
a Saudi Arabia 94 F5...................29°56′N 40°05′E
awea, Lake U.S.A. 62 F6..............47°45′N 102°15′W
ya r. Turkey 51 I5......................41°07′N 30°38′E
a Japan 104 C3........................38°54′N 139°49′E
lin i. Russia 55 P2......................48°10′N 142°40′E
zerbaijan 53 E2.........................41°12′N 47°11′E
a Japan 104 D3.........................35°44′N 140°13′E
Cape Verde 84 B3.....................16°49′N 22°59′W
weden 43 D2...........................59°55′N 16°36′E
o r. Argentina 73 E2...................32°27′S 60°49′W
o r. Mexico 66 E6......................26°45′N 99°26′W
h Oman 95 H3..........................17°02′N 54°10′E
anca Spain 45 C4......................40°58′N 5°39′W
ati i. Indonesia 103 I3.................1°05′S 130°53′E
r i. Indonesia 102 E2.................6°08′S 120°30′E
inkai Lithuania 47 K6................54°18′N 25°23′E
mbe England 11 D2....................50°14′N 3°46′W
australia 108 D3.......................38°06′S 147°06′E
ngland 13 E2............................53°26′N 2°19′W
urst England 9 F1.....................50°59′N 0°30′E
aard Russia 52 G4.....................31°07′N 66°43′E
India 96 E3.............................11°37′N 78°08′E
aad England 13 E2....................44°54′N 122°58′W
o Italy 48 F5.............................40°40′N 14°47′E
o, Golfo di g. Italy 48 F5.............40°25′N 14°43′E
d England 13 E2.......................53°29′N 2°18′W
Turkey 51 H4...........................38°29′N 28°08′E
rsk Belarus 47 L5.....................52°47′N 27°32′E
s U.S.A. 62 B4.........................36°41′N 121°39′W
ngland 8 D2............................51°04′N 1°48′W
ury U.S.A. 63 K4.......................38°22′N 75°36′W
ury Plain f. England 8 C2.............51°15′N 2°03′W
Canada 61 K4...........................56°15′N 75°42′W
r U.S.A. 62 C6.........................45°52′N 116°45′W
 Arm Canada 62 C7...................44°46′N 119°17′W
 River Mountains U.S.A. 62 C5......44°46′N 115°01′W
inland 43 E2.............................60°23′N 23°08′E
Russia 53 E2............................46°28′N 41°33′E
U.S.A. 62 D3............................33°22′N 112°17′W
England 11 C2...........................50°24′N 4°13′W
ats Scotland 14 E3....................55°38′N 4°47′W
Islands Ireland 18 E2.................52°07′N 6°36′W
Mexico 66 D6............................25°25′N 101°01′W
ake City U.S.A. 62 D5.................40°42′N 111°54′W
Sea l. U.S.A. 62 C3...................33°28′N 115°58′W
lor Brazil 72 F5.........................12°57′S 38°25′W
en r. China/Myanmar 97 I5..........24°06′N 98°35′E
Azerbaijan 53 E1......................39°35′N 48°58′E
rg Austria 46 E3........................47°48′N 13°03′E
ter Germany 46 D5....................52°10′N 10°24′E
ndağ Turkey 51 K3....................36°04′N 35°58′E
ni Japan 104 D4.......................42°08′N 142°54′E
a Russia 53 F3.........................53°11′N 50°09′E
inda Indonesia 102 F3................0°29′S 117°11′E
rā′ Iraq 94 F6..........................34°12′N 43°54′E
 Dem. Rep. Congo 83 B4.............4°38′S 26°20′E
alpur India 96 F5.....................21°27′N 83°59′E
s Indonesia 102 D4...................1°22′N 109°19′E
r Ukraine 47 J3........................49°31′N 23°12′E
r Belgium/France 42 D3..............50°17′N 4°06′E
France 9 G1............................50°38′N 1°45′E
 S. Pacific Oc. 109 H5................13°58′S 173°23′W
 Greece 50 F5..........................37°49′N 26°44′E
hraki i. Greece 50 F5.................40°24′N 25°33′E
t Indonesia 102 E3...................2°34′S 112°55′E
n Turkey 51 L5.........................41°17′N 36°19′E
England 13 E2..........................53°43′N 1°21′W
Yemen 94 F3............................15°23′N 44°11′E
daj Iran 95 G7..........................35°16′N 46°58′E
ndrés, Isla de i. Caribbean Sea 67 H3
                                          12°33′N 81°41′W
ngelo U.S.A. 62 F3....................31°28′N 100°23′W
ntonio U.S.A. 62 G2..................29°25′N 98°27′W
ntonio, Cabo c. Cuba 67 H5.........21°51′N 84°55′W
enedicto, Isla i. Mexico 66 B4......19°19′N 110°47′W
emente, Monte mt. Chile 73 B2.....46°35′S 73°27′W
ristóbal Venezuela 72 B7.............7°45′N 72°15′W
ristóbal de la Laguna Canary Islands 45 X2
                                          28°28′N 16°19′W
 Spíritu Cuba 67 I5....................21°56′N 79°26′W
 Island Scotland 14 D3...............55°16′N 5°35′W
n Malaysia 102 F5.....................5°51′N 118°05′E

Sandane Norway 43 A3................61°47′N 6°14′E
Sandanski Bulgaria 50 E5.............41°34′N 23°16′E
Sanday i. Scotland 17 G4.............59°15′N 2°29′W
Sanday Sound str. Scotland 17 G4..59°12′N 2°34′W
Sandbach England 13 E2..............53°09′N 2°22′W
Sandhurst England 8 E2..............51°21′N 0°48′W
San Diego U.S.A. 62 C3................32°43′N 117°05′W
Sandıklı Turkey 51 I4...................38°28′N 30°16′E
Sandnes Norway 43 A2................58°51′N 5°44′E
Sandnessjøen Norway 43 C4..........66°01′N 12°39′E
Sandoway Myanmar 97 H4............18°27′N 94°22′E
Sandown England 8 D1................50°40′N 1°09′W
Sandpoint U.S.A. 62 C6...............48°16′N 116°33′W
Sandray i. Scotland 16 B1............56°54′N 7°30′W
Sandviken Sweden 43 D3..............60°37′N 16°46′E
Sandwich England 9 G2................51°16′N 1°20′E
Sandy England 9 E3....................52°08′N 0°18′W
Sandy Cape Australia 108 E4.........24°42′S 153°15′E
Sandy Lake town Canada 61 I3.......53°03′N 93°18′W
San Felipe Mexico 66 B7..............31°02′N 114°50′W
San Fernando Phil. 102 G7............16°38′N 120°18′E
San Fernando Spain 45 B2.............36°28′N 6°11′W
San Fernando de Apure Venezuela 72 C7....7°49′N 67°28′W
San Francisco U.S.A. 62 B4...........37°45′N 122°25′W
San Francisco de Paula, Cabo c. Argentina 73 C2
                                          49°42′S 67°40′W
Sangir, Kepulauan is Indonesia 103 G4....2°15′N 124°57′E
Sangkulirang Indonesia 102 F4.......0°55′N 117°58′E
Sangli India 96 D4......................16°53′N 74°38′E
Sangre de Cristo Range mts U.S.A. 62 E4..38°19′N 106°01′W
San Jorge, Golfo de g. Argentina 73 C2....45°57′S 65°55′W
San José Costa Rica 67 H2.............9°57′N 84°02′W
San Jose U.S.A. 62 B4..................37°18′N 121°57′W
San José, Isla i. Mexico 66 B5........24°54′N 110°33′W
San José del Cabo Mexico 66 C5......23°04′N 109°44′W
San Juan Argentina 73 C3.............31°33′S 68°31′W
San Juan r. Costa Rica/Nicaragua 67 H3..10°47′N 83°44′W
San Juan Puerto Rico 67 K4...........18°26′N 66°04′W
San Juan U.S.A. 62 D4.................37°15′N 110°30′W
San Juan Mountains U.S.A. 62 E4....37°35′N 107°17′W
Şanlıurfa Turkey 51 M3.................37°09′N 38°49′E
San Lorenzo Spain 45 D5..............42°14′N 2°58′W
Sanlúcar de Barrameda Spain 45 B2..36°46′N 6°21′W
San Luis Obispo U.S.A. 62 B4.........35°18′N 120°40′W
San Luis Potosí Mexico 66 D5.........22°10′N 100°57′W
San Luis Potosí d. Mexico 66 D5......22°51′N 100°48′W
San Marcos U.S.A. 62 G2.............29°51′N 97°56′W
San Marino Europe 48 F5...............43°58′N 12°27′E
San Marino San Marino 48 F5.........43°57′N 12°27′E
San Matías, Golfo g. Argentina 73 C2..41°20′S 64°35′W
San Miguel r. Bolivia 72 C5............13°52′S 63°54′W
San Miguel El Salvador 66 G3.........13°43′N 88°11′W
San Miguel de Tucumán Argentina 73 C4..26°48′S 65°16′W
Sanming China 99 L3...................26°11′N 117°38′E
San Pablo Phil. 103 G6................14°04′N 121°18′E
San Pedro de Ycumandyyú Paraguay 73 D4
                                          24°08′S 57°08′W
San Pedro, Sierra de mts Spain 45 B3.....39°31′N 7°15′W
San Pedro Sula Honduras 66 G4......15°28′N 88°01′W
Sanquhar Scotland 15 F3..............55°22′N 3°56′W
San Quintín, Cabo c. Mexico 62 C3..30°23′N 116°01′W
Sanremo Italy 44 G3...................43°49′N 7°47′E
San Salvador i. Bahamas 67 J5........24°07′N 74°27′W
San Salvador El Salvador 66 G3.......13°43′N 89°11′W
San Salvador de Jujuy Argentina 73 C4....24°10′S 65°20′W
San Sebastián Spain 45 D5............43°19′N 1°59′W
San Sebastián de la Gomera Canary Islands 45 X2
                                          28°05′N 17°06′W
Santa Ana El Salvador 66 G3..........14°00′N 89°31′W
Santa Ana U.S.A. 62 C3................33°45′N 117°56′W
Santa Barbara U.S.A. 62 C3...........34°27′N 119°43′W
Santa Clara Cuba 67 I5.................22°24′N 79°56′W
Santa Cruz Bolivia 72 C5..............17°47′S 63°12′W
Santa Cruz de la Palma Canary Islands 45 X2
                                          28°41′N 17°46′W
Santa Cruz de Tenerife Canary Islands 45 X2
                                          28°27′N 16°15′W
Santa Cruz Islands Solomon Is 109 F5....10°46′S 167°21′E
Santa Fé Argentina 73 C3.............31°37′S 60°42′W
Santa Fe U.S.A. 62 E4.................35°42′N 105°57′W
Santa Isabel i. Solomon Is 109 E6....7°54′S 159°11′E
Santa Margarita, Isla i. Mexico 66 B5..24°25′N 111°50′W
Santa Maria Brazil 73 D4..............29°41′S 53°48′W
Santa Maria U.S.A. 62 B3..............34°58′N 120°26′W
Santa Maria di Leuca, Capo c. Italy 50 C4..39°47′N 18°21′E
Santa Marta Colombia 72 B8..........11°16′N 74°12′W
Santander Spain 45 D5.................43°28′N 3°48′W
Santarém Brazil 72 D6..................2°27′S 54°43′W
Santarém Portugal 45 A3...............39°15′N 8°41′W
Santa Rosa Argentina 73 C3...........36°37′S 64°17′W
Santa Rosalía Mexico 66 B6...........27°21′N 112°18′W
Santiago i. Cape Verde 84 B3.........15°19′N 23°45′W
Santiago Chile 73 B3...................33°28′S 70°39′W
Santiago Dom. Rep. 67 J4.............19°29′N 70°41′W
Santiago de Compostela Spain 45 A5..42°53′N 8°32′W
Santiago de Cuba Cuba 67 I5.........20°00′N 75°49′W
Sant Jordi, Golf de g. Spain 45 F4...40°49′N 0°56′E
Santo André Brazil 73 E4..............23°38′S 46°30′W
Santo Antão i. Cape Verde 84 B3.....17°01′N 25°21′W
Santo Domingo Dom. Rep. 67 K4.....18°31′N 69°52′W
Santoña Spain 45 D5...................43°27′N 3°27′W
Santos Brazil 73 E4.....................23°58′S 46°20′W
São Francisco r. Brazil 72 E5.........10°19′S 36°31′W
São José do Rio Preto Brazil 73 E4...20°49′S 49°22′W
São Luís Brazil 72 E6..................2°35′S 44°18′W
Saône r. France 44 F4.................45°44′N 4°49′E
São Paulo Brazil 73 E4................23°35′S 46°43′W
São Tomé São Tomé and Príncipe 84 E2....0°19′N 6°44′E
São Tomé i. São Tomé and Príncipe 84 E2....0°21′N 6°35′E
São Tomé, Cabo de c. Brazil 73 E4...22°00′S 40°59′W
São Tomé and Príncipe Africa 84 E2..1°00′N 7°04′E
São Vicente, Cabo de c. Portugal 45 A2....37°01′N 8°59′W
Sapporo Japan 104 D4................43°04′N 141°20′E
Sapri Italy 49 G5......................40°04′N 15°38′E
Saqqaq Greenland 61 M5..............70°01′N 51°56′W
Saqqez Iran 95 G7.....................36°12′N 46°15′E
Sarāb Iran 95 G7........................37°55′N 47°31′E
Sara Buri Thailand 102 C6.............14°29′N 100°57′E
Sarajevo Bos. and Herz. 50 C6.......43°51′N 18°25′E
Sarandë Albania 50 D4.................39°53′N 20°01′E
Saransk Russia 53 E3..................54°11′N 45°12′E
Sarapul Russia 52 F3...................56°30′N 53°48′E
Sarasota U.S.A. 63 J2..................27°19′N 82°33′W
Saratov Russia 53 E3...................51°34′N 45°59′E
Saravan Iran 95 J5.....................27°20′N 62°25′E
Sarawak d. Malaysia 102 E4...........1°46′N 111°53′E
Saray Turkey 51 G5....................41°26′N 27°55′E

Sardinia i. Italy 48 E5..................40°16′N 8°04′E
Sarektjåkkå mt. Sweden 43 D4.......67°27′N 17°43′E
Sar-e Pol Afgh. 95 K7..................36°15′N 65°57′E
Sargodha Pakistan 96 D7..............32°01′N 72°41′E
Sarh Chad 85 F2.......................9°07′N 18°23′E
Sārī Iran 95 H7..........................36°33′N 53°03′E
Sarigan i. N. Mariana Is 103 L7.......16°42′N 145°48′E
Sarıyer Turkey 51 H5..................41°10′N 29°03′E
Sark i. Channel Is 11 Y9..............49°24′N 2°24′W
Şarkışla Turkey 51 L4..................39°21′N 36°25′E
Şarköy Turkey 50 G5..................40°37′N 27°06′E
Särna Sweden 43 C3...................61°42′N 13°08′E
Sarny Ukraine 47 L4...................51°20′N 26°37′E
Saros Körfezi b. Turkey 50 G5........40°34′N 26°36′E
Sarov Russia 53 E3.....................54°56′N 43°20′E
Sarpsborg Norway 43 B2..............59°17′N 11°08′E
Sarrebourg France 44 G6..............48°44′N 7°03′E
Sarreguemines France 42 G2.........49°07′N 7°04′E
Sarria Spain 45 B5......................42°47′N 7°24′W
Sarthe r. France 44 C5.................47°34′N 0°31′W
Sasebo Japan 104 A2..................33°09′N 129°44′E
Saskatchewan d. Canada 60 H3......53°08′N 106°03′W
Saskatchewan r. Canada 60 H3.......53°40′N 100°27′W
Saskatoon Canada 60 H3..............52°08′N 106°39′W
Sassandra Côte d'Ivoire 84 D2........4°57′N 6°05′W
Sassari Italy 48 E5.....................40°43′N 8°34′E
Sassnitz Germany 46 E6...............54°31′N 13°38′E
Satka Russia 52 F3.....................55°04′N 58°58′E
Satpura Range mts India 96 D5.......21°47′N 74°23′E
Satu Mare Romania 47 J2.............47°47′N 22°53′E
Sauðárkrókur Iceland 43 Y2............65°45′N 19°40′W
Saudi Arabia Asia 94 F4...............23°41′N 44°13′E
Sault Sainte Marie Canada 61 J2.....46°31′N 84°20′W
Saumlakki Indonesia 103 I2...........8°00′S 131°20′E
Saundersfoot Wales 10 C3............51°43′N 4°42′W
Saurimo Angola 83 B3.................9°39′S 20°25′E
Sava r. Europe 50 D7...................44°50′N 20°28′E
Savai'i i. Samoa 109 H5...............13°25′S 172°39′W
Savannah U.S.A. 63 J3................32°04′N 81°07′W
Savannah r. U.S.A. 63 J3..............32°02′N 80°53′W
Savannakhét Laos 102 C7.............16°32′N 104°46′E
Save r. Mozambique/Zimbabwe 83 C2....20°56′S 35°03′E
Savinskiy Russia 52 E4................62°56′N 40°09′E
Savona Italy 46 C1.....................44°19′N 8°29′E
Savu Sea Indonesia 103 G2...........9°51′S 121°22′E
Sawel Mountain hill Northern Ireland 14 B2
                                          54°49′N 7°02′W
Sawhāj Egypt 49 J2...................26°31′N 31°38′E
Sawston England 9 F3.................52°07′N 0°10′E
Sawtry England 9 E3...................52°26′N 0°17′W
Sawu i. Indonesia 103 G1.............10°32′S 121°58′E
Saxilby England 13 G2.................53°16′N 0°40′W
Saxmundham England 9 G3..........52°13′N 1°29′E
Sayhūt Yemen 95 H3..................15°15′N 51°19′E
Saynshand Mongolia 99 K6............44°46′N 110°12′E
Scafell Pike hill England 12 D3.......54°27′N 3°13′W
Scalasaig Scotland 14 C4.............56°04′N 6°11′W
Scalby England 13 G3..................54°18′N 0°27′W
Scalloway Scotland 17 H5.............60°08′N 1°17′W
Scalp hill Ireland 18 C2................52°59′N 8°29′W
Scalpay i. High. Scotland 16 D2......57°18′N 5°59′W
Scalpay i. Na h-E. S. Scotland 16 C2..57°52′N 6°39′W
Scalp Mountain hill Ireland 14 B3.....55°06′N 7°22′W
Scampton England 13 G2.............53°18′N 0°34′W
Scandinavia f. Europe 34 F5...........65°00′N 18°00′E
Scapa Flow inlet Scotland 17 F3......58°54′N 3°08′W
Scarba i. Scotland 14 D4..............56°10′N 5°45′W
Scarborough England 13 G3..........54°17′N 0°24′W
Scarp i. Scotland 16 B3................58°01′N 7°11′W
Schaffhausen Switz. 46 C2............47°42′N 8°38′E
Schagen Neth. 42 D5..................52°47′N 4°48′E
Schefferville Canada 61 L3............54°47′N 66°48′W
Scheldt r. Belgium 42 D4..............51°21′N 4°15′E
Schiehallion mt. Scotland 17 E1.......56°40′N 4°06′W
Schiermonnikoog i. Neth. 42 F6.......53°31′N 6°17′E
Schleswig Germany 46 C6.............54°31′N 9°33′E
Schwäbische Alb mts Germany 46 C2....47°59′N 8°43′E
Schwaner, Pegunungan mts Indonesia 102 E3
                                          0°46′S 112°26′E
Schwarzer Mann hill Germany 42 F3..50°15′N 6°21′E
Schwedt/Oder Germany 46 F5........53°04′N 14°18′E
Schweinfurt Germany 46 D4..........50°03′N 10°13′E
Schwerin Germany 46 D5..............53°38′N 11°25′E
Scilly, Isles of England 11 A1.........49°53′N 6°17′W
Scioto r. U.S.A. 63 J4..................38°44′N 82°59′W
Scole England 9 G3.....................52°22′N 1°09′E
Scone Scotland 15 F4..................56°25′N 3°24′W
Scotland d. U.K. 20 D5.................57°01′N 3°53′W
Scottish Borders d. Scotland 20 D4..55°40′N 2°44′W
Scottsbluff U.S.A. 62 F5...............41°54′N 103°41′W
Scourie Scotland 16 D3................58°21′N 5°09′W
Scranton U.S.A. 63 K5.................41°25′N 75°39′W
Scridain, Loch inlet Scotland 14 C4...56°21′N 6°11′W
Scunthorpe England 13 G2............53°35′N 0°39′W
Scuol Switz. 46 D2......................46°48′N 10°18′E
Scutari, Lake Albania/Montenegro 50 C6....42°14′N 19°12′E
Seaford England 9 F1..................50°46′N 0°06′E
Seaham England 13 F3................54°50′N 1°20′W
Seamer England 13 G3................54°14′N 0°26′W
Seascale England 12 D3...............54°24′N 3°29′W
Seaton Cumb. England 12 D3........54°40′N 3°31′W
Seaton Dev. England 11 D2..........50°42′N 3°04′W
Seaton Delaval England 13 F4........55°04′N 1°31′W
Seattle U.S.A. 62 B6..................47°36′N 122°20′W
Sebastián Vizcaíno, Bahía b. Mexico 66 B6
                                          28°08′N 114°45′W
Sebeş Romania 50 E7..................45°58′N 23°34′E
Şebinkarahisar Turkey 51 M5.........40°17′N 38°25′E
Secunderabad India 96 E4............17°25′N 78°27′E
Sedan France 44 F6....................49°42′N 4°57′E
Sedbergh England 12 E3..............54°19′N 2°31′W
Segezha Russia 52 D4.................63°45′N 34°19′E
Segorbe Spain 45 E3...................39°51′N 0°28′W
Segovia Spain 45 C4....................40°57′N 4°06′W
Segura r. Spain 45 E3..................38°06′N 0°38′W
Segura, Sierra de mts Spain 45 D2...37°59′N 2°46′W
Seiland i. Norway 43 E5...............70°28′N 23°18′E
Seinäjoki Finland 43 E3...............62°47′N 22°51′E
Seine r. France 44 D6..................49°26′N 0°15′E
Seine, Baie de b. France 44 C6.......49°29′N 0°12′W
Sekondi Ghana 84 D2..................4°58′N 1°43′W
Selaru i. Indonesia 103 I2.............8°13′S 130°57′E
Selatan, Tanjung pt Indonesia 102 E3..4°09′S 114°38′E
Selattyn England 8 B3.................52°54′N 3°05′W
Selawik U.S.A. 60 B4..................66°36′N 160°16′W

Selby England 13 F2...................53°47′N 1°04′W
Selkirk Canada 60 I3...................50°09′N 96°53′W
Selkirk Scotland 15 G3................55°33′N 2°50′W
Sellindge England 9 F2................51°06′N 0°59′E
Selsey England 8 E1....................50°44′N 0°47′W
Selsey Bill hd England 8 E1...........50°43′N 0°49′W
Selvas f. Brazil 72 B6..................6°29′S 71°47′W
Selwyn Mountains Canada 60 E4....64°16′N 131°38′W
Selwyn Range hills Australia 108 C4..21°14′S 139°54′E
Semarang Indonesia 102 E2..........6°55′S 110°29′E
Semenivka Ukraine 47 O5.............52°10′N 32°35′E
Seminoe Reservoir U.S.A. 62 E5......42°06′N 106°51′W
Semipalatinsk Kazakhstan 54 J3......50°25′N 80°19′E
Semnān Iran 95 H7....................35°30′N 53°21′E
Semois r. Belgium/France 42 D2......49°53′N 4°45′E
Sendai Japan 104 D3..................38°15′N 140°53′E
Senegal Africa 84 C3...................14°29′N 14°41′W
Sénégal r. Mauritania 84 C3..........16°00′N 16°31′W
Senja i. Norway 43 D5.................69°20′N 17°14′E
Sennar Sudan 85 H3...................13°31′N 33°36′E
Sens France 44 E6......................48°12′N 3°17′E
Seoul S. Korea 99 N5...................37°32′N 127°00′E
Sepik r. P.N.G. 103 K3.................3°53′S 144°33′E
Sept-Îles Canada 61 L3................50°13′N 66°23′W
Serang Indonesia 102 D2..............6°04′S 106°09′E
Serbia Europe 50 D6...................44°01′N 20°55′E
Şereflikoçhisar Turkey 51 J4..........38°56′N 33°33′E
Seremban Malaysia 102 C4............2°41′N 101°54′E
Seret r. Ukraine 47 K3.................48°36′N 25°51′E
Sergino Russia 52 G4..................62°30′N 65°39′E
Sergiyev Posad Russia 52 D3.........56°19′N 38°08′E
Serik Turkey 51 I3......................36°57′N 31°07′E
Serov Russia 52 G3....................59°38′N 60°34′E
Serowe Botswana 83 B2...............22°24′S 26°42′E
Serpukhov Russia 53 D3..............54°55′N 37°25′E
Serra da Mesa, Represa resr Brazil 72 E5....14°17′S 48°30′W
Serres Greece 50 E5...................41°06′N 23°33′E
Serui Indonesia 103 J3................1°52′S 136°17′E
Sestroretsk Russia 43 G3.............60°05′N 29°57′E
Sète France 44 E3......................43°24′N 3°42′E
Sete Lagoas Brazil 72 E5.............19°28′S 44°13′W
Setesdal f. Norway 43 A2.............59°15′N 7°23′E
Sétif Algeria 84 E5....................36°11′N 5°25′E
Seto-naikai sea Japan 104 B2........33°38′N 132°17′E
Settat Morocco 84 D5..................32°58′N 7°36′W
Settle England 13 E3...................54°04′N 2°17′W
Setúbal Portugal 45 A3................38°32′N 8°53′W
Setúbal, Baía de b. Portugal 45 A3...38°20′N 9°02′W
Seul, Lac l. Canada 63 H7.............50°21′N 92°29′W
Sevan Armenia 53 E2..................40°33′N 44°58′E
Sevastopol′ Ukraine 49 J5.............44°36′N 33°31′E
Seven Heads Ireland 18 C1............51°34′N 8°42′W
Sevenoaks England 9 F2...............51°16′N 0°12′E
Severn r. Canada 61 J3................55°59′N 87°36′W
Severn r. U.K. 8 C2....................51°51′N 2°21′W
Severnaya Zemlya is Russia 55 L6....80°09′N 103°23′E
Severnyy Russia 52 G4................67°36′N 64°13′E
Severnyy, Ostrov i. Russia 54 F5.....75°00′N 58°00′E
Severo-Kuril′sk Russia 55 Q3.........50°40′N 156°06′E
Sevier Lake U.S.A. 62 D4.............38°56′N 113°09′W
Seville Spain 45 C2....................37°24′N 5°58′W
Seward U.S.A. 60 D4..................60°09′N 149°24′W
Seward Peninsula U.S.A. 60 B4......65°29′N 164°05′W
Seychelles Indian Oc. 79 E2..........4°40′S 55°43′E
Seydişehir Turkey 51 I3...............37°25′N 31°52′E
Seyðisfjörður Iceland 43 Z2...........65°16′N 14°02′W
Seyhan r. Turkey 51 K3...............36°44′N 34°54′E
Seym r. Russia/Ukraine 47 P4........51°16′N 34°16′E
Seymchan Russia 55 Q4...............62°50′N 152°20′E
Sfântu Gheorghe Romania 50 F7.....45°52′N 25°48′E
Sfax Tunisia 48 F3.....................34°45′N 10°45′E
Sgurr Alasdair hill Scotland 16 C2...57°12′N 6°13′W
Sgurr Dhomhnuill hill Scotland 16 D1..56°45′N 5°27′W
Sgurr Mòr mt. Scotland 16 D2........57°42′N 5°01′W
Shaanxi d. China 99 J4.................34°43′N 108°13′E
Shadrinsk Russia 52 G3...............56°07′N 63°37′E
Shaftesbury England 8 C2.............51°00′N 2°12′W
Shahr-e Kord Iran 95 H6...............32°19′N 50°49′E
Shahreẓā Iran 95 H6..................32°00′N 51°52′E
Shāhrūd Iran 95 H7...................36°24′N 54°56′E
Shakhovskaya Russia 47 P7...........56°02′N 35°30′E
Shakhty Russia 53 E2.................47°42′N 40°12′E
Shakhun′ya Russia 52 E3.............57°40′N 46°36′E
Shalkar Kazakhstan 53 F2.............47°47′N 59°39′E
Shandong d. China 99 L4.............36°22′N 117°45′E
Shandong Bandao pen. China 99 M5..37°05′N 121°02′E
Shanghai China 99 M4................31°15′N 121°29′E
Shangqiu China 99 L4.................34°24′N 115°38′E
Shanklin England 8 D1................50°38′N 1°10′W
Shannon r. Ireland 18 C2.............52°40′N 8°38′W
Shannon, Mouth of the Ireland 18 B2..52°31′N 9°51′W
Shantarskiye Ostrova is Russia 55 O3..55°20′N 137°22′E
Shantou China 99 L2..................23°24′N 116°42′E
Shanxi d. China 99 K5.................38°03′N 111°48′E
Shaoguan China 99 K2................24°48′N 113°37′E
Shaoxing China 99 M4................30°01′N 120°38′E
Shaoyang China 99 K3................27°14′N 111°30′E
Shap England 12 E3...................54°32′N 2°41′W
Shapinsay i. Scotland 17 G4..........59°02′N 2°48′W
Shaqrā′ Saudi Arabia 94 G5..........25°15′N 45°16′E
Sharjah U.A.E. 95 I5...................25°21′N 55°23′E
Shark Bay Australia 108 A4............25°17′S 113°32′E
Shasta, Mount vol. U.S.A. 62 B5......41°23′N 122°10′W
Shchigry Russia 47 Q4.................51°52′N 36°56′E
Shebelē Wenz, Wabē r. Ethiopia/Somalia 85 I2
                                          0°10′N 42°46′E
Sheberghān Afgh. 95 K7..............36°42′N 65°45′E
Sheboygan U.S.A. 63 I5...............43°45′N 87°43′W
Sheelin, Lough l. Ireland 18 D3......53°49′N 7°19′W
Sheep Haven b. Ireland 14 B3........55°12′N 7°55′W
Sheerness England 9 F2...............51°26′N 0°46′E
Sheffield England 13 F2...............53°23′N 1°28′W
Shelby U.S.A. 62 D6...................48°29′N 111°48′W
Shelikhova, Zaliv g. Russia 55 Q4....60°40′N 157°23′E
Shelikof Strait U.S.A. 60 C3..........57°27′N 155°17′W
Shenyang China 99 M6...............41°46′N 123°24′E
Shenzhen China 99 K2................22°33′N 114°09′E
Shepetivka Ukraine 47 L4.............50°11′N 27°04′E
Sheppey, Isle of i. England 9 F2......51°23′N 0°50′E
Shepshed England 8 D3..............52°46′N 1°18′W
Shepton Mallet England 8 C2.........51°11′N 2°33′W
Sherborne England 8 C1..............50°57′N 2°31′W
Sherbrooke Canada 61 K2............45°24′N 71°54′W
Shereiq Sudan 94 D3..................18°42′N 33°40′E
Sheridan U.S.A. 62 E5................44°48′N 106°55′W
Sheringham England 9 G3............52°57′N 1°13′E
's-Hertogenbosch Neth. 42 E4........51°41′N 5°19′E

# 200  Index

Sherwood Forest England 13 F2......53°04'N 1°07'W
Shetland d. Scotland 20 E7......60°14'N 0°57'W
Shetland Islands Scotland 17 I5......60°36'N 0°47'W
Shetpe Kazakhstan 53 F2......44°09'N 52°17'E
Sheyenne r. U.S.A. 62 G6......47°03'N 96°50'W
Shiant Islands Scotland 16 C2......57°53'N 6°25'W
Shibām Yemen 95 G3......15°59'N 48°57'E
Shiel, Loch l. Scotland 16 D1......56°47'N 5°35'W
Shieldaig Scotland 16 D2......57°31'N 5°39'W
Shifnal England 8 C3......52°40'N 2°22'W
Shihezi China 98 F6......44°14'N 86°03'E
Shijiazhuang China 99 K5......38°00'N 114°32'E
Shikarpur India 96 E3......14°14'N 75°18'E
Shikarpur Pakistan 95 K5......27°56'N 68°42'E
Shikoku i. Japan 104 B2......33°08'N 133°49'E
Shikoku-sanchi mts Japan 104 B2......33°26'N 132°53'E
Shildon England 13 F3......54°38'N 1°39'W
Shilega Russia 52 E4......64°04'N 40°58'E
Shillong India 97 H6......25°33'N 91°53'E
Shimonoseki Japan 104 B2......33°57'N 130°57'E
Shin, Loch l. Scotland 17 E3......58°09'N 4°38'W
Shingū Japan 104 C2......33°43'N 136°00'E
Shining Tor hill England 13 E2......53°16'N 2°00'W
Shipley England 13 F2......53°50'N 1°47'W
Shipston on Stour England 8 D3......52°04'N 1°37'W
Shirane-san mt. Japan 104 C3......35°40'N 138°13'E
Shīrāz Iran 95 H5......29°37'N 52°31'E
Shire r. Malawi 83 C3......17°41'S 35°19'E
Shivamogga India 96 E3......13°54'N 75°31'E
Shizuishan China 99 J5......38°58'N 106°27'E
Shizuoka Japan 104 C2......34°58'N 138°23'E
Shklow Belarus 47 N6......54°13'N 30°17'E
Shkodër Albania 50 C6......42°04'N 19°31'E
Shona, Eilean i. Scotland 16 D1......56°48'N 5°53'W
Sho'rchi Uzbekistan 95 K7......37°59'N 67°46'E
Shostka Ukraine 47 O4......51°51'N 33°29'E
Shpola Ukraine 47 N3......49°01'N 31°23'E
Shreveport U.S.A. 63 H3......32°29'N 93°46'W
Shrewsbury England 8 C3......52°42'N 2°45'W
Shropshire d. England 21 D3......52°45'N 2°38'W
Shuangjiang China 99 H2......23°28'N 99°49'E
Shubarkudyk Kazakhstan 53 F3......49°08'N 56°50'E
Shumagin Islands U.S.A. 60 C3......55°09'N 161°01'W
Shumen Bulgaria 50 G6......43°16'N 26°56'E
Shuqrah Yemen 95 G2......13°24'N 45°40'E
Shūshtar Iran 95 G6......32°01'N 48°49'E
Shwebo Myanmar 97 I5......22°34'N 95°43'E
Shwegyin Myanmar 97 I4......17°56'N 96°52'E
Shymkent Kazakhstan 54 I2......42°19'N 69°38'E
Siahan Range mts Pakistan 95 J5......27°13'N 63°38'E
Šiauliai Lithuania 43 E1......55°56'N 23°19'E
Šibenik Croatia 50 A6......43°44'N 15°54'E
Siberia f. Russia 55 M4......65°18'N 115°57'E
Siberut i. Indonesia 102 B3......1°23'S 98°41'E
Sibi Pakistan 95 K5......29°30'N 67°55'E
Sibiu Romania 50 F7......45°48'N 24°09'E
Sibolga Indonesia 102 B4......1°40'N 98°48'E
Sibsey England 13 H2......53°02'N 0°01'E
Sibu Malaysia 102 E4......2°17'N 111°51'E
Sibut C.A.R. 85 F2......5°44'N 19°05'E
Sichuan d. China 99 I4......30°05'N 103°11'E
Sicily i. Italy 48 F4......38°21'N 14°09'E
Sidi Bel Abbès Algeria 84 D5......35°12'N 0°38'W
Sidi Kacem Morocco 84 B3......34°12'N 5°39'W
Sidlaw Hills Scotland 15 F4......56°26'N 3°21'W
Sidmouth England 11 D2......50°41'N 3°14'W
Sidney U.S.A. 62 F5......41°12'N 103°09'W
Sidon Lebanon 49 K3......33°33'N 35°23'E
Siedlce Poland 47 J5......52°10'N 22°17'E
Siegen Germany 46 C4......50°52'N 8°01'E
Sierra Leone Africa 84 C2......8°35'N 11°58'W
Sighetu Marmaţiei Romania 47 J2......47°56'N 23°54'E
Sighişoara Romania 50 F8......46°14'N 24°47'E
Siglufjörður Iceland 43 Y2......66°08'N 18°52'W
Sigüenza Spain 45 D4......41°05'N 2°37'W
Siguiri Guinea 84 D3......11°28'N 9°10'W
Sihanoukville Cambodia 102 C6......10°38'N 103°34'E
Siilinjärvi Finland 43 F3......63°05'N 27°40'E
Siirt Turkey 94 F7......37°55'N 41°58'E
Sikar India 96 E6......27°31'N 75°13'E
Sikasso Mali 84 D3......11°19'N 5°40'W
Sikeston U.S.A. 63 I4......36°51'N 89°34'W
Sikhote-Alin' mts Russia 55 O2......43°58'N 133°53'E
Sikkim d. India 96 G6......27°31'N 88°27'E
Sil r. Spain 45 B5......42°28'N 7°42'W
Siletiteniz, Ozero l. Kazakhstan 98 C8......53°11'N 72°53'E
Silifke Turkey 51 J3......36°22'N 33°56'E
Siling Co l. China 98 F4......31°47'N 88°41'E
Silistra Bulgaria 50 G7......44°07'N 27°16'E
Silivri Turkey 51 H5......41°04'N 28°16'E
Siljan l. Sweden 43 C3......60°53'N 14°44'E
Šilutė Lithuania 47 I6......55°21'N 21°28'E
Silver City U.S.A. 62 E3......32°45'N 108°19'W
Silverstone England 8 D3......52°05'N 1°02'W
Silverton England 11 D2......50°49'N 3°29'W
Simav Turkey 51 H4......39°05'N 28°58'E
Simēn mts Ethiopia 94 E2......13°16'N 37°50'E
Simeulue i. Indonesia 102 B4......2°41'N 96°08'E
Simferopol' Ukraine 49 J5......44°57'N 34°07'E
Simojärvi l. Finland 43 F4......66°01'N 27°15'E
Simpson Desert Australia 108 C4......24°59'S 136°50'E
Simrishamn Sweden 46 F6......55°33'N 14°21'E
Sinai pen. Egypt 85 H4......29°13'N 33°47'E
Sinaloa d. Mexico 66 C6......25°42'N 108°11'W
Sincelejo Colombia 72 B7......9°17'N 75°24'W
Sinclair's Bay Scotland 17 F3......58°30'N 3°07'W
Sindor Russia 52 F4......62°52'N 51°54'E
Sines Portugal 45 A2......37°58'N 8°52'W
Singa Sudan 94 D2......13°09'N 33°55'E
Singapore Asia 102 C4......1°27'N 104°32'E
Singapore town Singapore 102 C4......1°19'N 103°51'E
Singaraja Indonesia 102 F2......8°06'S 115°06'E
Singida Tanzania 83 C4......4°50'S 34°45'E
Singkawang Indonesia 102 D4......0°57'N 108°59'E
Sinj Croatia 50 B6......43°42'N 16°38'E
Sinkat Sudan 94 E3......18°45'N 36°49'E
Sinop Turkey 51 K6......42°02'N 35°08'E
Sint Maarten i. Neth. Antilles 67 L4......18°02'N 63°04'W
Sion Mills Northern Ireland 14 B2......54°47'N 7°28'W
Sioux City U.S.A. 62 G5......42°32'N 96°23'W
Sioux Falls town U.S.A. 62 G5......43°32'N 96°43'W
Sioux Lookout Canada 61 I3......50°06'N 91°56'W
Siping China 99 M6......43°04'N 124°24'E
Sipura i. Indonesia 102 B3......2°12'S 99°42'E
Sira r. Norway 43 A2......58°16'N 6°24'E
Siret r. Romania 50 H7......45°25'N 28°02'E

Sīrjān Iran 95 I5......29°27'N 55°40'E
Sirte Libya 85 F5......31°09'N 16°40'E
Sirte, Gulf of Libya 85 F5......31°11'N 18°03'E
Şirvan Azerbaijan 53 E1......39°56'N 48°56'E
Sisak Croatia 50 B7......45°29'N 16°23'E
Sisimiut Greenland 61 M4......66°56'N 53°40'W
Sisophon Cambodia 102 C6......13°34'N 102°59'E
Sīstān, Daryācheh-ye marsh Afgh./Iran 95 J6......31°33'N 61°10'E
Sisteron France 44 F4......44°12'N 5°57'E
Siteia Greece 50 G2......35°12'N 26°06'E
Sitka U.S.A. 60 E3......57°03'N 135°18'W
Sittard Neth. 42 E3......50°59'N 5°51'E
Sittingbourne England 9 F2......51°20'N 0°44'E
Sittwe Myanmar 97 H5......20°08'N 92°54'E
Sivas Turkey 51 L4......39°43'N 37°00'E
Siverek Turkey 51 M3......37°44'N 39°21'E
Sivrihisar Turkey 51 I4......39°27'N 31°32'E
Sīwah Egypt 85 G4......29°09'N 25°30'E
Skadovs'k Ukraine 51 J8......46°07'N 32°54'E
Skagen Denmark 43 B2......57°43'N 10°35'E
Skagerrak str. Denmark/Norway 43 B2......57°27'N 8°13'E
Skagway U.S.A. 60 E3......59°29'N 135°18'W
Skara Sweden 43 C2......58°23'N 13°26'E
Skarżysko-Kamienna Poland 46 I4......51°07'N 20°53'E
Skegness England 13 H2......53°09'N 0°20'E
Skellefteå Sweden 43 E4......64°45'N 20°58'E
Skellefteälven r. Sweden 43 E4......64°42'N 21°07'E
Skelmersdale England 12 E2......53°33'N 2°46'W
Skerries Ireland 18 E3......53°35'N 6°06'W
Ski Norway 43 B2......59°43'N 10°50'E
Skibbereen Ireland 18 B1......51°33'N 9°16'W
Skiddaw hill England 12 D3......54°39'N 3°09'W
Skien Norway 43 B2......59°12'N 9°36'E
Skikda Algeria 84 E5......36°54'N 6°57'E
Skipton England 13 E2......53°58'N 2°01'W
Skive Denmark 43 B2......56°34'N 9°02'E
Skokholm Island Wales 10 B3......51°41'N 5°16'W
Skomer Island Wales 10 B3......51°44'N 5°20'W
Skopje North Macedonia 50 D5......41°59'N 21°27'E
Skövde Sweden 43 C2......58°23'N 13°51'E
Skovorodino Russia 55 N3......54°05'N 123°52'E
Skye i. Scotland 16 C2......57°21'N 6°20'W
Skyros i. Greece 50 F4......38°53'N 24°35'E
Slagelse Denmark 43 B1......55°24'N 11°22'E
Slamet vol. Indonesia 102 D2......7°14'S 109°10'E
Slaney r. Ireland 18 E2......52°25'N 6°34'W
Slatina Romania 50 F7......44°26'N 24°22'E
Slave r. Canada 60 G4......61°17'N 113°31'W
Slave Lake town Canada 60 G3......55°17'N 114°47'W
Slavonski Brod Croatia 50 C7......45°10'N 18°01'E
Slavyansk-na-Kubani Russia 51 M7......45°16'N 38°08'E
Slawharad Belarus 47 N5......53°27'N 31°00'E
Sleaford England 9 E3......53°00'N 0°24'W
Sleat, Sound of str. Scotland 16 D2......57°02'N 5°53'W
Sleights England 13 G3......54°27'N 0°40'W
Slieve Anierin hill Ireland 14 B2......54°05'N 7°59'W
Slieve Beagh Ireland/U.K. 14 B2......54°20'N 7°12'W
Slievecallan hill Ireland 18 B2......52°51'N 9°16'W
Slieve Car hill Ireland 18 B4......54°04'N 9°40'W
Slieve Donard hill Northern Ireland 14 D2......54°11'N 5°55'W
Slievenamon hill Ireland 18 D2......52°26'N 7°34'W
Slieve Snaght hill Ireland 18 D5......55°11'N 7°20'W
Sligo Ireland 18 C4......54°17'N 8°28'W
Sligo d. Ireland 18 C4......54°07'N 8°30'W
Sligo Bay Ireland 18 C4......54°18'N 8°55'W
Sliven Bulgaria 50 G6......42°41'N 26°19'E
Slobozia Romania 50 G7......44°34'N 27°23'E
Slonim Belarus 47 K5......53°05'N 25°19'E
Slough England 9 E2......51°31'N 0°36'W
Slough d. England 21 E2......51°30'N 0°35'W
Slovakia Europe 46 H3......48°45'N 19°35'E
Slovenia Europe 46 F1......46°09'N 14°47'E
Slov"yans'k Ukraine 53 D2......48°51'N 37°37'E
Slovyechna r. Belarus 47 M4......51°39'N 29°43'E
Sluch r. Ukraine 47 L4......51°37'N 26°39'E
Słupsk Poland 46 G6......54°27'N 17°02'E
Slutsk Belarus 47 L5......53°01'N 27°32'E
Slyne Head Ireland 18 A3......53°24'N 10°14'W
Slyudyanka Russia 99 I8......51°28'N 103°36'E
Smallwood Reservoir Canada 61 L3......54°01'N 64°50'W
Smarhon' Belarus 47 L6......54°29'N 26°25'E
Smila Ukraine 47 N3......49°12'N 31°54'E
Smoky r. Canada 60 G3......56°08'N 117°20'W
Smøla i. Norway 43 A3......63°23'N 7°59'E
Smolensk Russia 53 D3......54°47'N 32°04'E
Smolikas mt. Greece 50 D5......40°05'N 20°56'E
Smolyan Bulgaria 50 F5......41°35'N 24°41'E
Snæfell mt. Iceland 43 Z2......64°48'N 15°35'W
Snaefell hill Isle of Man 12 C3......54°16'N 4°28'W
Snaith England 13 F2......53°41'N 1°01'W
Snake r. U.S.A. 62 C6......46°13'N 118°59'W
Snåsa Norway 43 C4......64°15'N 12°23'E
Sneek Neth. 42 E6......53°02'N 5°40'E
Snettisham England 9 F3......52°53'N 0°30'E
Snežnik mt. Slovenia 46 F1......45°35'N 14°26'E
Śniardwy, Jezioro l. Poland 47 I5......53°46'N 21°42'E
Snizort, Loch b. Scotland 16 C2......57°33'N 6°28'W
Snøtinden mt. Norway 43 C4......66°38'N 13°57'E
Snov r. Ukraine 47 N4......51°32'N 31°32'E
Snowdon mt. Wales 10 C5......53°04'N 4°04'W
Soay i. Scotland 16 C2......57°09'N 6°15'W
Sobradinho, Barragem de resr Brazil 72 E5......10°14'S 42°24'W
Sobral Brazil 72 E6......3°41'S 40°19'W
Sochi Russia 53 D2......43°36'N 39°44'E
Society Islands is French Polynesia 116 B2......17°22'S 152°28'W
Socorro, Isla i. Mexico 66 B4......18°51'N 110°58'W
Socotra i. Yemen 95 H2......12°34'N 54°30'E
Sodankylä Finland 43 F4......67°25'N 26°34'E
Söderhamn Sweden 43 D3......61°18'N 17°04'E
Södertälje Sweden 43 D2......59°12'N 17°38'E
Sodo Ethiopia 85 H2......6°49'N 37°42'E
Södra Kvarken str. Finland/Sweden 43 D3......60°19'N 19°02'E
Sofia Bulgaria 50 E6......42°41'N 23°19'E
Sognefjorden inlet Norway 43 A3......61°05'N 5°33'E
Soham England 9 F3......52°20'N 0°20'E
Soignies Belgium 42 D3......50°35'N 4°04'E
Soissons France 44 E6......49°23'N 3°20'E
Söke Turkey 50 G3......37°45'N 27°23'E
Sokhumi Georgia 53 E2......43°00'N 41°02'E
Sokoto Nigeria 84 E3......13°05'N 5°15'E
Sokoto r. Nigeria 84 E3......11°23'N 4°09'E
Solapur India 96 E4......17°41'N 75°55'E
Solihull England 8 D3......52°25'N 1°47'W

Solikamsk Russia 52 F3......59°42'N 56°44'E
Sol'-Iletsk Russia 53 F3......51°06'N 54°58'E
Sollefteå Sweden 43 D3......63°10'N 17°17'E
Solomon Islands S. Pacific Oc. 109 F6......7°13'S 157°49'E
Solomon Sea S. Pacific Oc. 108 E6......7°01'S 152°18'E
Solway Firth est. Scotland 15 F2......54°48'N 3°33'W
Solwezi Zambia 83 B3......12°10'S 26°26'E
Soma Turkey 50 G4......39°11'N 27°36'E
Somalia Africa 85 I2......3°56'N 46°23'E
Sombor Serbia 50 C7......45°47'N 19°07'E
Somerset d. England 21 D2......51°04'N 2°56'W
Somerset Island Canada 61 I5......73°19'N 93°22'W
Somerton England 8 C2......51°03'N 2°44'W
Sommen l. Sweden 43 C2......58°00'N 15°17'E
Sønderborg Denmark 46 C6......54°55'N 9°48'E
Sondrio Italy 46 C2......46°10'N 9°52'E
Songea Tanzania 83 C3......10°39'S 35°38'E
Songkhla Thailand 102 C5......7°10'N 100°35'E
Songyuan China 99 M7......45°05'N 124°53'E
Son La Vietnam 102 C8......21°20'N 103°57'E
Sonora d. Mexico 66 B6......29°42'N 110°36'W
Sonora r. Mexico 66 B6......28°47'N 111°54'W
Soria Spain 45 D4......41°47'N 2°26'W
Soroca Moldova 49 I6......48°09'N 28°17'E
Sorochinsk Russia 53 F3......52°21'N 52°59'E
Sorol atoll Micronesia 103 K5......8°10'N 140°22'E
Sorong Indonesia 103 I3......0°54'S 131°17'E
Soroti Uganda 85 H2......1°42'N 33°37'E
Sørøya i. Norway 43 E5......70°34'N 22°32'E
Sorraia r. Portugal 45 A3......38°02'N 8°50'W
Sorsele Sweden 43 D4......65°31'N 17°33'E
Sortavala Russia 43 G3......61°42'N 30°41'E
Soshanguve S. Africa 83 B2......25°31'S 28°06'E
Sosna r. Russia 47 R5......52°41'N 38°54'E
Sosneado mt. Argentina 73 C3......34°44'S 69°59'W
Sosnogorsk Russia 52 F4......63°36'N 53°53'E
Sosnovka Russia 52 E4......66°30'N 40°34'E
Sosnowiec Poland 46 H4......50°17'N 19°08'E
Sos'va Russia 52 G3......59°08'N 61°48'E
Souk Ahras Algeria 48 E4......36°17'N 7°59'E
Souk el Arbaâ du Rharb Morocco 45 C1......34°40'N 5°58'W
Souris r. Canada 62 G6......49°41'N 99°40'W
Sousse Tunisia 48 F4......35°47'N 10°39'E
Soustons France 44 C3......43°45'N 1°20'W
South Africa Africa 83 B1......30°06'S 24°04'E
Southam England 8 D3......52°15'N 1°23'W
South America 72
Southampton England 8 D1......50°55'N 1°24'W
Southampton d. England 21 D2......50°56'N 1°24'W
Southampton Island Canada 61 J4......64°31'N 85°04'W
South Anston England 13 F2......53°22'N 1°13'W
South Australia d. Australia 108 C3......30°27'S 132°43'E
South Ayrshire d. Scotland 20 C4......55°09'N 4°47'W
South Bank England 13 F3......54°35'N 1°10'W
South Bend U.S.A. 63 I5......41°40'N 86°13'W
South Carolina d. U.S.A. 63 J3......34°02'N 80°47'W
South Cave England 13 G2......53°46'N 0°36'W
South China Sea N. Pacific Oc. 102 F6......12°00'N 117°49'E
South Dakota d. U.S.A. 62 F5......44°27'N 100°14'W
South Dorset Downs hills England 8 C1......50°42'N 2°37'W
South Downs hills England 8 E1......50°53'N 0°28'W
South Dublin d. Ireland 18 E3......53°16'N 6°24'W
South East Cape Australia 108 D2......43°38'S 146°55'E
Southend-on-Sea England 9 F2......51°33'N 0°43'E
Southend-on-Sea d. England 21 F2......51°33'N 0°42'E
Southern Alps/Ka Tiritiri o te Moana mts New Zealand 109 G2......43°26'S 170°28'E
Southern Ocean 116 E1
Southern Uplands hills Scotland 14 E3......55°14'N 4°32'W
Southery England 9 F3......52°32'N 0°24'E
South Esk r. Scotland 17 G1......56°43'N 2°33'W
South Georgia and South Sandwich Islands S. Atlantic Oc. 73 F1......53°50'S 36°30'W
South Gloucestershire d. England 21 D2......51°33'N 2°27'W
South Harris pen. Scotland 16 B2......57°50'N 6°55'W
South Island New Zealand 109 G2......44°24'S 172°31'E
South Kirkby England 13 F2......53°36'N 1°19'W
South Korea Asia 99 N5......35°32'N 128°04'E
South Lanarkshire d. Scotland 20 D4......55°38'N 3°49'W
Southminster England 9 F2......51°40'N 0°50'E
South Molton England 11 D3......51°01'N 3°50'W
South Nahanni r. Canada 60 F4......61°03'N 123°18'W
South Ockendon England 9 F2......51°31'N 0°18'E
South Ossetia d. Georgia 53 E2......42°40'N 44°06'E
South Platte r. U.S.A. 62 F5......41°08'N 100°42'W
Southport Australia 108 E4......27°56'S 153°23'E
Southport England 12 D2......53°39'N 3°00'W
South Ronaldsay i. Scotland 17 G3......58°47'N 2°54'W
South Saskatchewan r. Canada 60 H3......53°09'N 105°08'W
South Shields England 13 F3......54°59'N 1°26'W
South Sudan Africa 85 G2......7°01'N 30°00'E
South Tyne r. England 13 E3......54°59'N 2°08'W
South Uist i. Scotland 16 B2......57°17'N 7°22'W
South Walls pen. Scotland 17 F3......58°47'N 3°08'W
Southwell England 13 G2......53°05'N 0°58'W
Southwold England 9 G3......52°19'N 1°41'E
South Woodham Ferrers England 9 F2......51°39'N 0°37'E
South Wootton England 9 F3......52°46'N 0°26'E
South Yorkshire d. England 21 E2......53°28'N 1°16'W
Sovetsk Russia 47 I6......55°05'N 21°53'E
Sovetskiy Russia 52 G4......61°26'N 63°30'E
Soweto S. Africa 83 B2......26°15'S 27°50'E
Sozh r. Europe 47 N4......51°57'N 30°49'E
Spain Europe 45 D4......40°26'N 3°48'W
Spalding England 9 E3......52°47'N 0°09'W
Sparks U.S.A. 62 C4......39°32'N 119°46'W
Sparti Greece 50 E3......37°04'N 22°26'E
Spartivento, Capo c. Italy 48 E4......37°55'N 16°04'E
Spas-Demensk Russia 47 P6......54°25'N 34°03'E
Spatha, Akra pt Greece 50 E2......35°41'N 23°44'E
Spencer Gulf est. Australia 108 C3......34°54'S 136°27'E
Spennymoor England 13 F3......54°42'N 1°35'W
Sperrin Mountains hills Northern Ireland 14 B2......54°49'N 7°09'W
Spey r. Scotland 17 F2......57°39'N 3°06'W
Speyer Germany 44 H6......49°19'N 8°24'E
Spijkenisse Neth. 42 D4......51°50'N 4°19'E
Spilsby England 13 H2......53°10'N 0°06'E
Spitsbergen i. Arctic Oc. 54 C5......78°37'N 16°06'E
Split Croatia 50 B6......43°31'N 16°27'E
Spofforth England 13 F2......53°57'N 1°27'W
Spokane U.S.A. 62 C6......47°38'N 117°22'W
Spratly Islands S. China Sea 102 E6......10°01'N 114°21'E
Spree r. Germany 46 E5......52°32'N 13°13'E
Springfield Ill. U.S.A. 63 I4......39°48'N 89°39'W
Springfield Mass. U.S.A. 63 L5......42°05'N 72°35'W

Springfield Mo. U.S.A. 63 H4......37°16'N 93°
Sprowston England 9 G3......52°39'N 1°
Spurn Head England 13 H2......53°34'N 0°
Srebrenica Bos. and Herz. 50 C7......44°07'N 19°
Srednekolymsk Russia 55 Q4......67°32'N 153°
Sretensk Russia 55 N3......52°08'N 117°
Sri Aman Malaysia 102 E4......1°12'N 11°
Sri Jayewardenepura Kotte Sri Lanka 96 E2......6°56'N 79°
Sri Lanka Asia 96 F2......7°29'N 80°
Srinagar India 96 D7......34°08'N 74°
Stadskanaal Neth. 42 F5......52°59'N 6°
Staffa i. Scotland 14 C4......56°26'N 6°
Stafford England 8 C3......52°48'N 2°
Staffordshire d. England 21 D3......52°52'N 2°
Staines-upon-Thames England 9 E2......51°26'N 0°
Stalbridge England 8 C1......50°57'N 2°
Stalham England 9 G3......52°46'N 1°
Stalowa Wola Poland 47 J4......50°34'N 22°
Stamford England 9 E3......52°39'N 0°
Stamford Bridge England 13 G2......53°59'N 0°
Standish England 12 E2......53°35'N 2°
Stanley England 13 F3......54°52'N 1°
Stanley Falkland Is 73 D1......51°43'S 57°
Stanley, Mount Dem. Rep. Congo/Uganda 83 B5......0°25'N 29°
Stannington England 13 F4......55°06'N 1°
Stanovoy Khrebet mts Russia 55 N3......57°21'N 120°
Stansted Mountfitchet England 9 F2......51°54'N 0°
Stanton England 9 F3......52°19'N 0°
Staraya Russa Russia 52 D3......57°59'N 31°
Stara Zagora Bulgaria 50 F6......42°26'N 25°
Stargard Szczeciński Poland 46 F5......53°20'N 15°
Starogard Gdański Poland 46 H5......53°58'N 18°
Starokostyantyniv Ukraine 47 L3......49°45'N 27°
Start Bay England 11 D2......50°18'N 3°
Start Point England 11 D2......50°13'N 3°
Staryya Darohi Belarus 47 M5......53°02'N 28°
Staryy Oskol Russia 53 D3......51°18'N 37°
Stavanger Norway 43 A2......58°58'N 5°
Staveley England 13 F2......53°16'N 1°
Stavropol' Russia 53 E2......45°03'N 41°
Stavropol'skaya Vozvyshennost' hills Russia 53 E2......45°05'N 42°
Steenwijk Neth. 42 F5......52°47'N 6°
Steep Holm i. England 8 B2......51°20'N 3°
Stefansson Island Canada 60 H5......73°21'N 105°
Steinfurt Germany 42 G5......52°09'N 2°
Steinkjer Norway 43 B4......64°01'N 11°
Stenness, Loch of l. Scotland 17 F4......59°00'N 3°
Sterling U.S.A. 62 F5......40°39'N 103°
Sterlitamak Russia 53 F3......53°36'N 55°
Stevenage England 9 E2......51°54'N 0°
Stewart Canada 60 F3......55°57'N 129°
Stewart r. Canada 60 E4......63°18'N 139°
Stewart Island/Rakiura New Zealand 109 F2......47°09'S 16°
Stewarton Scotland 14 E3......55°41'N 4°
Steyning England 9 E1......50°53'N 0°
Steyr Austria 46 F3......48°03'N 14°
Stikine r. Canada 60 E3......56°41'N 132°
Stilton England 9 E3......52°29'N 0°
Stinchar r. Scotland 14 D3......55°06'N 5°
Stirling Scotland 15 F4......56°07'N 3°
Stirling d. Scotland 20 C5......56°17'N 4°
Stjørdalshalsen Norway 43 B3......63°28'N 10°
Stob Choire Claurigh mt. Scotland 16 E1......56°50'N 4°
Stockholm Sweden 43 D2......59°20'N 18°
Stockport England 13 E2......53°24'N 2°
Stockton U.S.A. 62 B4......37°57'N 121°
Stockton-on-Tees England 13 F3......54°34'N 1°
Stockton-on-Tees d. England 21 E4......54°33'N 1°
Stœng Trêng Cambodia 102 D6......13°28'N 105°
Stoer, Point of Scotland 16 D3......58°16'N 5°
Stoke-on-Trent England 13 E2......53°00'N 2°
Stoke-on-Trent d. England 21 D3......53°01'N 2°
Stokesay England 8 C3......52°26'N 2°
Stokesley England 13 F3......54°28'N 1°
Stolin Belarus 47 L4......51°53'N 26°
Stone England 8 C3......52°54'N 2°
Stonehaven Scotland 17 G1......56°58'N 2°
Stony Rapids town Canada 60 H3......59°15'N 105°
Stora Lulevatten l. Sweden 43 D4......67°09'N 19°
Storavan l. Sweden 43 D4......65°40'N 18°
Stornoway Scotland 16 C3......58°13'N 6°
Storrington England 9 E1......50°55'N 0°
Storsjön l. Sweden 43 C3......63°13'N 14°
Storskrymten mt. Norway 43 B3......62°22'N 9°
Storuman Sweden 43 D4......65°05'N 17°
Storuman l. Sweden 43 D4......65°11'N 16°
Stotfold England 9 E3......52°01'N 0°
Stour r. Dor. England 8 D1......50°44'N 1°
Stour r. Kent England 9 G2......51°18'N 1°
Stour r. Warwicks. England 8 D3......52°11'N 1°
Stourbridge England 8 C3......52°27'N 2°
Stourport-on-Severn England 8 C3......52°20'N 2°
Stowbtsy Belarus 47 L5......53°28'N 26°
Stowmarket England 9 F3......52°11'N 0°
Stow-on-the-Wold England 8 D2......51°56'N 1°
Strabane Northern Ireland 14 B2......54°50'N 7°
Stradbroke England 9 G3......52°19'N 1°
Stralsund Germany 46 E6......54°18'N 13°
Stranda Norway 43 A3......62°18'N 6°
Strangford Lough inlet Northern Ireland 14 D2......54°28'N 5°
Stranraer Scotland 14 D2......54°54'N 5°
Strasbourg France 44 G6......48°35'N 7°
Stratford-upon-Avon England 8 D3......52°11'N 1°
Strathaven Scotland 15 E3......55°41'N 4°
Strathbeg, Loch of l. Scotland 17 H2......57°37'N 1°
Strathbogie f. Scotland 17 G2......57°26'N 2°
Strathmore r. Scotland 16 E3......58°25'N 4°
Strathy Point Scotland 17 E3......58°36'N 4°
Strathspey f. Scotland 17 F2......57°15'N 3°
Stratton England 11 C2......50°50'N 4°
Stratton St Margaret England 8 D2......51°35'N 1°
Straubing Germany 46 E3......48°53'N 12°
Straumnes pt Iceland 43 X2......66°26'N 23°
Streatley England 8 D2......51°32'N 1°
Street England 8 C2......51°07'N 2°
Strelka Russia 55 Q4......61°52'N 152°
Stretham England 9 F3......52°21'N 0°
Strimonas r. Greece 50 E5......40°48'N 23°
Stroma, Island of Scotland 17 F3......58°42'N 3°
Stromboli, Isola i. Italy 48 F4......38°45'N 15°
Stromness Scotland 17 F3......58°58'N 3°
Strömsund Sweden 43 C3......63°52'N 15°

say i. Scotland 17 G4 .......... 59°08'N 2°33'W
say Firth str. Scotland 17 G4 ....... 59°06'N 2°50'W
d England 8 C2 .......... 51°45'N 2°13'W
r Denmark 43 B2.......... 56°29'N 8°36'E
r. Northern Ireland 14 B2 .......... 54°43'N 7°21'W
na r. Bulgaria 50 E5 .......... 41°23'N 23°26'E
nble Head Wales 10 B4.......... 52°02'N 5°08'W
nica North Macedonia 50 E5.......... 41°26'N 22°38'E
Ukraine 47 J3.......... 49°15'N 23°51'E
ey England 8 D3 .......... 52°16'N 1°54'W
no Russia 47 R6.......... 54°54'N 38°05'E
y England 9 G2 .......... 51°18'N 1°07'E
Stony Desert Australia 108 D4......28°20'S 141°15'E
gart Germany 46 C3 .......... 48°47'N 9°10'E
. Belarus/Ukraine 47 L5 .......... 52°08'N 26°35'E
n Sudan 85 H3 .......... 19°06'N 37°18'E
ava Romania 47 L2.......... 47°40'N 26°16'E
r. Ireland 18 C3.......... 53°16'N 8°03'W
Bolivia 72 C5.......... 19°06'S 65°18'W
k Ukraine 51 K7.......... 44°51'N 34°59'E
n Africa 85 G3.......... 13°34'N 30°02'E
ury England 61 J2 .......... 46°29'N 80°59'W
ury England 9 F3 .......... 52°03'N 0°44'E
f. South Sudan 85 G2.......... 7°43'N 29°41'E
ty mts Czechia/Poland 46 F4 .......... 50°46'N 15°50'E
Egypt 85 H4.......... 29°58'N 32°33'E
Gulf of Egypt 85 H4 .......... 28°03'N 33°33'E
Canal Egypt 49 J3.......... 30°47'N 32°19'E
lk d. England 21 F3 .......... 52°10'N 0°52'E
Oman 95 I4 .......... 24°22'N 56°44'E
Germany 46 D4 .......... 50°36'N 10°42'E
ng China 99 J4.......... 30°29'N 105°33'E
. Ireland 18 D2.......... 52°20'N 7°23'W
ou China 99 K4 .......... 31°42'N 113°20'E
oumi Indonesia 102 D2.......... 6°58'S 106°53'E
dana Indonesia 102 D3 .......... 1°12'S 109°59'E
nichi Russia 47 P6.......... 54°07'N 35°22'E
ur Pakistan 96 C6.......... 27°42'N 68°55'E
. Norway 43 A3 .......... 61°09'N 4°55'E
esi i. Indonesia 103 H3 .......... 2°12'S 125°58'E
a Romania 51 H7.......... 45°09'N 29°39'E
na Peru 72 A6.......... 4°56'S 80°41'W
Wales 11 D3.......... 51°24'N 3°13'W
Archipelago is Phil. 103 G5......6°55'N 122°00'E
Sea N. Pacific Oc. 102 F5 .......... 8°20'N 119°46'E
stra i. Indonesia 102 B4.......... 3°05'N 98°12'E
a i. Indonesia 102 G2.......... 9°49'S 120°11'E
awa i. Indonesia 102 F2.......... 8°54'S 118°45'E
urgh Scotland 17 H4.......... 59°52'N 1°17'W
urgh Head Scotland 17 H4.......... 59°51'N 1°16'W
ner Isles Scotland 16 D3.......... 58°01'N 5°30'W
gayit Azerbaijan 53 E2.......... 40°35'N 49°40'E
Ukraine 47 P4.......... 50°55'N 34°48'E
t, Loch inlet Scotland 16 D1.......... 56°40'N 5°51'W
a, Selat str. Indonesia 102 C2.......... 6°32'S 104°55'E
erland England 13 F3 .......... 54°54'N 1°23'W
svall Sweden 43 D3.......... 62°24'N 17°17'E
urlu Turkey 51 K5 .......... 40°11'N 34°22'E
järvet f. Finland 43 G4 .......... 66°14'N 28°04'E
enjoki Finland 43 F3 .......... 62°37'N 27°07'E
arvi Russia 52 D4.......... 62°06'N 32°22'E
ior U.S.A. 63 H6.......... 46°41'N 92°01'W
ior, Lake Canada/U.S.A. 61 J2......47°46'N 87°14'W
sh Shuyūkh Iraq 95 G6.......... 30°51'N 46°20'E
n China 99 L4.......... 33°55'N 118°18'E
man 95 I4 .......... 22°34'N 59°31'E
Pakistan 95 K5.......... 28°29'N 66°19'E
aya Indonesia 102 E2 .......... 7°13'S 112°45'E
arta Indonesia 102 E2 .......... 7°31'S 110°52'E
India 96 B5.......... 21°11'N 72°53'E
adranagar India 96 D5.......... 22°42'N 71°41'E
t Russia 54 I4.......... 61°13'N 73°22'E
ao Phil. 103 H5.......... 9°48'N 125°29'E
Thailand 102 C6.......... 14°52'N 103°32'E
ame S. America 72 D7.......... 4°05'N 56°22'W
y d. England 21 E2.......... 51°15'N 0°29'W
ey i. Iceland 43 X1.......... 63°18'N 20°36'W
ngerd Iran 95 G6.......... 31°37'N 48°04'E
ari Turkey 51 M5.......... 40°10'N 38°04'E
man Russia 55 P4.......... 62°47'N 148°02'E
luk Turkey 51 H4.......... 39°55'N 28°09'E
erland f. Scotland 17 E3.......... 58°16'N 4°24'W
r. India/Pakistan 96 D6.......... 29°24'N 71°08'E
rton England 9 E3.......... 52°54'N 0°06'W
n England 9 E3.......... 52°23'N 0°07'E
n Bridge England 9 F3.......... 52°46'N 0°11'E
n Coldfield England 8 D3.......... 52°34'N 1°49'W
n Ashfield England 13 F2.......... 53°08'N 1°16'W
Fiji 109 G5.......... 18°07'S 178°28'E
rov Russia 47 Q6.......... 54°07'N 36°31'E
tki Poland 47 J6.......... 54°06'N 22°14'E
rrow atoll Cook Is 109 I5 .......... 13°11'S 162°57'W
ou Anhui China 99 L5.......... 33°34'N 116°59'E
ou Jiangsu China 99 M4 .......... 31°18'N 120°40'E
Japan 104 C3.......... 37°26'N 137°15'E
ka Japan 104 C3.......... 34°53'N 136°35'E
ard is Arctic Oc. 54 C5 .......... 79°47'N 16°13'E
a r. Russia 47 P4.......... 51°44'N 34°57'E
Sweden 43 C3.......... 62°02'N 14°23'E
dborg Denmark 43 B1.......... 55°04'N 10°37'E
ograd Russia 49 L6.......... 45°02'N 42°51'E
gorsk Russia 43 G3.......... 61°07'N 28°51'E
núkar vol. Iceland 43 Y2.......... 64°25'N 17°09'W
y Czechia 46 G3.......... 49°45'N 16°28'E
vods'k Ukraine 47 O3.......... 49°03'N 33°15'E
odnyy Russia 55 N3.......... 51°23'N 128°04'E
lahorsk Belarus 47 M5.......... 52°38'N 29°46'E
lincote England 8 D3.......... 52°46'N 1°33'W
ham England 9 F3.......... 52°39'N 0°41'E
ns Island atoll American Samoa 109 H5
.......... 11°01'S 171°03'W
opmund Namibia 83 A2 .......... 22°41'S 14°32'E
e r. England 13 F3.......... 54°05'N 1°21'E
age England 8 D1.......... 50°36'N 1°58'W
ley England 9 F2.......... 51°24'N 0°11'E
River town Canada 62 F7.......... 52°06'N 101°16'W
sea d. England 21 E2.......... 51°15'N 0°29'W
sea d. Wales 21 D2.......... 51°39'N 3°57'W
sea Bay Wales 10 D3.......... 51°34'N 3°54'W
iland Africa 83 C2.......... 26°29'S 31°30'E
twater r. U.S.A. 62 E5.......... 42°27'N 106°55'W
nica Poland 46 E5.......... 50°50'N 16°29'E
win Poland 46 F5.......... 53°47'N 15°47'E
Current Canada 60 H3.......... 50°17'N 107°47'W

Swilly, Lough inlet Ireland 18 D5......55°15'N 7°34'W
Swindon England 8 D2..........51°33'N 1°47'W
Swindon d. England 21 E2..........51°35'N 1°45'W
Swineshead England 9 E3..........52°57'N 0°10'W
Świnoujście Poland 46 F5..........53°54'N 14°15'E
Switzerland Europe 48 E6..........46°44'N 8°18'E
Swords Ireland 18 E3..........53°27'N 6°13'W
Sybil Point Ireland 18 A2..........52°11'N 10°28'W
Sychevka Russia 47 P6..........55°49'N 34°17'E
Sydney Australia 108 E3..........33°54'S 151°11'E
Sydney Canada 61 L2..........46°06'N 60°08'W
Syktyvkar Russia 52 F4..........61°41'N 50°48'E
Sylarna mt. Norway/Sweden 43 C3..........63°01'N 12°12'E
Sylt i. Germany 43 B1..........54°49'N 8°15'E
Syracuse U.S.A. 63 K5..........43°04'N 76°11'W
Syr Darya r. Asia 98 A7..........46°05'N 60°55'E
Syria Asia 94 E6..........35°25'N 39°17'E
Syrian Desert Asia 94 E6..........32°02'N 39°22'E
Syros i. Greece 50 F3..........37°27'N 24°53'E
Syzran' Russia 53 E3..........53°10'N 48°29'E
Szczecin Poland 46 F5..........53°26'N 14°34'E
Szczecinek Poland 46 G5..........53°42'N 16°42'E
Szczytno Poland 46 I5..........53°34'N 20°59'E
Szeged Hungary 46 I2..........46°15'N 20°09'E
Székesfehérvár Hungary 46 H2..........47°12'N 18°25'E
Szekszárd Hungary 46 H2..........46°22'N 18°42'E
Szolnok Hungary 46 I2..........47°10'N 20°12'E
Szombathely Hungary 46 G2..........47°15'N 16°38'E

T

Ṭabas Iran 95 I6..........33°35'N 56°52'E
Tabasco d. Mexico 66 F4..........18°03'N 92°59'W
Tábor Czechia 46 F3..........49°24'N 14°42'E
Tabora Tanzania 83 C4..........5°00'S 32°47'E
Tabrīz Iran 95 G7..........38°04'N 46°17'E
Tabūk Saudi Arabia 94 E5..........28°22'N 36°38'E
Täby Sweden 43 D2..........59°27'N 18°04'E
Tacheng China 98 E7..........46°43'N 83°01'E
Tacloban Phil. 103 H6..........11°12'N 125°01'E
Tacna Peru 72 B5..........18°01'S 70°15'W
Tacoma U.S.A. 62 B6..........47°15'N 122°27'W
Tacuarembó Uruguay 73 D3..........31°42'S 55°59'W
Tadcaster England 13 F2..........53°53'N 1°16'W
Tadjoura Djibouti 94 F2..........11°46'N 42°48'E
Tadmur Syria 94 E6..........34°34'N 38°17'E
Taf r. Wales 10 C3..........51°47'N 4°27'W
Taganrog Russia 49 K6..........47°14'N 38°55'E
Taganrog, Gulf of Russia/Ukraine 49 K6......47°00'N 38°31'E
Tagbilaran Phil. 103 G5..........9°38'N 123°53'E
Tagula Island P.N.G. 108 E5..........11°33'S 153°23'E
Tagus r. Portugal 45 A3..........38°59'N 8°56'W
Tahat, Mont mt. Algeria 84 E4..........23°18'N 5°37'E
Tahiti i. French Polynesia 114 B2..........17°49'S 149°15'W
Taichung Taiwan 99 M2..........24°09'N 120°42'E
Tain Scotland 17 E2..........57°49'N 4°03'W
Tainan Taiwan 99 M2..........23°01'N 120°13'E
Tainaro, Akra pt Greece 50 E3..........36°23'N 22°29'E
Taipei Taiwan 99 M3..........25°04'N 121°33'E
Taiping Malaysia 102 C4..........4°55'N 100°42'E
Taitung Taiwan 99 M2..........22°45'N 121°08'E
Taivalkoski Finland 43 G4..........65°34'N 28°12'E
Taivaskero hill Finland 43 F5..........68°04'N 24°02'E
Taiwan Asia 99 M2..........23°34'N 121°32'E
Taiwan Strait China/Taiwan 99 L2..........23°49'N 119°16'E
Taiyuan China 99 K5..........37°48'N 112°38'E
Taizhou China 99 M3..........28°39'N 121°32'E
Ta'izz Yemen 94 F2..........13°35'N 43°59'E
Tajikistan Asia 87 E3..........38°54'N 71°08'E
Tak Thailand 102 B7..........16°51'N 99°08'E
Takamatsu Japan 104 B2..........34°19'N 134°03'E
Takaoka Japan 104 C3..........36°45'N 137°01'E
Taklimakan Desert China 98 E5..........38°25'N 80°50'E
Talagang Pakistan 95 L6..........32°55'N 72°29'E
Talaud, Kepulauan is Indonesia 103 H4......4°05'N 127°24'E
Talavera de la Reina Spain 45 C3..........39°58'N 4°49'W
Talca Chile 73 B3..........35°26'S 71°39'W
Talcahuano Chile 73 B3..........36°44'S 73°07'W
Taldykorgan Kazakhstan 54 I2..........44°59'N 78°22'E
Talgarth Wales 10 D3..........51°59'N 3°14'W
Taliabu i. Indonesia 103 G3..........1°47'S 124°43'E
Tallahassee U.S.A. 63 I3..........30°26'N 84°17'W
Tallinn Estonia 43 F2..........59°27'N 24°45'E
Taloyoak Canada 62 I4..........69°27'N 93°22'W
Talsi Latvia 43 E2..........57°15'N 22°35'E
Taltson r. Canada 60 G4..........61°24'N 112°43'W
Tamale Ghana 84 D2..........9°25'N 0°51'W
Tamanrasset Algeria 84 E4..........22°48'N 5°33'E
Tamar r. England 11 C2..........50°29'N 4°13'W
Tamaulipas d. Mexico 66 E5..........22°41'N 99°13'W
Tambacounda Senegal 84 C3..........13°47'N 13°40'W
Tambelan, Kepulauan is Indonesia 102 D4
..........1°03'N 107°03'E
Tambov Russia 53 E3..........52°43'N 41°26'E
Tambre r. Spain 45 A5..........42°49'N 8°51'W
Tâmega r. Portugal 45 A4..........41°05'N 8°17'W
Tamiahua, Laguna de lagoon Mexico 66 E5..21°39'N 97°36'W
Tamil Nadu d. India 96 E3..........11°11'N 78°08'E
Tamiš r. Serbia 50 D7..........44°50'N 20°39'E
Tampa U.S.A. 63 J2..........27°57'N 82°29'W
Tampere Finland 43 E3..........61°30'N 23°48'E
Tampico Mexico 66 E5..........22°16'N 97°52'W
Tamsweg Austria 46 E2..........47°08'N 13°47'E
Tamworth Australia 108 E3..........31°06'S 150°56'E
Tamworth England 8 D3..........52°38'N 1°41'W
Tana r. Kenya 85 I1..........2°31'S 40°30'E
Tana, Lake Ethiopia 85 H3..........11°59'N 37°16'E
Tanafjorden inlet Norway 43 G5..........70°32'N 28°12'E
Tanami Desert Australia 108 C5..........19°26'S 131°26'E
Tanaro r. Italy 46 C1..........45°01'N 8°47'E
Tando Adam Pakistan 96 C6..........25°43'N 68°40'E
Tandragee Northern Ireland 14 C2..........54°21'N 6°24'W
Tanega-shima i. Japan 104 B2..........30°28'N 130°58'E
Tanga Tanzania 83 C4..........5°06'S 39°05'E
Tanganyika, Lake Africa 83 B4..........5°00'S 29°26'E
Tangier Morocco 84 D5..........35°47'N 5°49'W
Tangshan China 99 L5..........39°34'N 118°13'E
Tanimbar, Kepulauan is Indonesia 103 I2......7°29'S 131°40'E
Tanjay Phil. 103 G5..........9°29'N 123°09'E
Tanjungpandan Indonesia 102 D3..........2°46'S 107°37'E
Tanjungredeb Indonesia 102 F4..........2°11'N 117°27'E
Tank Pakistan 95 L6..........32°14'N 70°29'E
Tanna i. Vanuatu 109 F5..........19°32'S 169°14'E
Tanout Niger 84 E3..........14°56'N 8°53'E

Ṭanṭā Egypt 85 H5..........30°47'N 31°00'E
Tanzania Africa 83 C4..........6°14'S 34°03'E
Taonan China 99 M7..........45°12'N 122°48'E
Taourirt Morocco 48 C3..........34°25'N 2°55'W
Tapachula Mexico 66 F3..........14°56'N 92°15'W
Tapajós r. Brazil 72 D6..........2°23'S 54°48'W
Tapi r. India 96 D5..........21°13'N 72°58'E
Taquarí r. Brazil 72 D5..........19°05'S 57°22'W
Tar r. Ireland 18 D2..........52°17'N 7°50'W
Tara r. Bos. and Herz./Montenegro 50 C6...43°20'N 18°53'E
Tarakan Indonesia 102 F4..........3°20'N 117°37'E
Taranaki, Mount vol. New Zealand 109 G3
..........39°18'S 174°03'E
Tarancón Spain 45 D4..........40°01'N 3°00'W
Taransay i. Scotland 16 B2..........57°55'N 7°02'W
Taranto Italy 49 G5..........40°28'N 17°14'E
Taranto, Gulf of Italy 49 G5..........40°07'N 17°20'E
Tarbat Ness pt Scotland 17 F2..........57°52'N 3°46'W
Tarbert A. and B. Scotland 14 D3..........55°58'N 5°50'W
Tarbert A. and B. Scotland 14 D3..........55°52'N 5°25'W
Tarbert Na h-E. S. Scotland 16 C2..........57°54'N 6°48'W
Tarbes France 44 D3..........43°14'N 0°05'E
Târgoviște Romania 50 F7..........44°56'N 25°27'E
Târgu Jiu Romania 50 E7..........45°03'N 23°17'E
Târgu Mureș Romania 47 K2..........46°32'N 24°34'E
Târgu Secuiesc Romania 50 G8..........46°00'N 26°08'E
Tarija Bolivia 73 C4..........21°36'S 64°47'W
Tarim Yemen 95 G3..........16°08'N 49°23'E
Tarim Basin China 98 E5..........39°41'N 80°53'E
Tarleton England 12 E2..........53°41'N 2°50'W
Tarn r. France 44 D4..........44°05'N 1°03'E
Tarnica mt. Poland 47 J3..........49°05'N 22°46'E
Tarnobrzeg Poland 47 I4..........50°34'N 21°40'E
Tarnów Poland 46 I4..........50°01'N 20°59'E
Tarragona Spain 45 F4..........41°07'N 1°15'E
Tarsus Turkey 51 K3..........36°54'N 34°53'E
Tartu Estonia 43 F2..........58°23'N 26°43'E
Ṭarṭūs Syria 51 K2..........34°54'N 35°53'E
Tashk, Daryācheh-ye l. Iran 95 H5..........29°42'N 53°29'E
Tashkent Uzbekistan 54 H2..........41°16'N 69°15'E
Tasiilaq Greenland 61 O4..........65°37'N 37°42'W
Tasikmalaya Indonesia 102 D2..........7°19'S 108°17'E
Tasmania d. Australia 108 D2..........42°27'S 145°20'E
Tasman Sea S. Pacific Oc. 108 G2..........40°31'S 170°54'E
Tatabánya Hungary 46 H2..........47°34'N 18°26'E
Tatarbunary Ukraine 51 H7..........45°50'N 29°37'E
Tatarsk Russia 54 I3..........55°13'N 75°59'E
Tatarskiy Proliv str. Russia 55 P3..........50°29'N 141°05'E
Tatvan Turkey 94 F7..........38°29'N 42°17'E
Taunggyi Myanmar 97 I5..........20°49'N 97°05'E
Taunton England 11 D3..........51°01'N 3°06'W
Taunus hills Germany 46 B4..........50°10'N 7°59'E
Taupo, Lake New Zealand 109 G3..........38°48'S 175°55'E
Tauragė Lithuania 47 J6..........55°15'N 22°17'E
Taurus Mountains Turkey 51 J3..........37°00'N 32°09'E
Tavda Russia 52 G3..........58°05'N 65°19'E
Taverham England 9 G3..........52°41'N 1°12'E
Tavira Portugal 45 B2..........37°08'N 7°38'W
Tavistock England 11 C2..........50°33'N 4°08'W
Tavşanlı Turkey 51 H4..........39°32'N 29°28'E
Tavy r. England 11 C2..........50°27'N 4°09'W
Taw r. England 11 C3..........51°04'N 4°03'W
Tawau Malaysia 102 F4..........4°16'N 117°54'E
Tawe r. Wales 10 D3..........51°37'N 3°55'W
Tawitawi i. Phil. 102 F5..........5°14'N 119°57'E
Tay r. Scotland 15 F4..........56°23'N 3°24'W
Tay, Firth of est. Scotland 15 F4..........56°25'N 3°07'W
Tay, Loch l. Scotland 14 E4..........56°30'N 4°11'W
Taymā' Saudi Arabia 94 E5..........27°39'N 38°28'E
Taymura r. Russia 55 K4..........63°43'N 98°05'E
Taymyr, Ozero l. Russia 55 L5..........74°20'N 101°51'E
Taymyr Peninsula Russia 55 J5..........73°54'N 89°12'E
Tây Ninh Vietnam 102 D6..........11°17'N 106°07'E
Tayport Scotland 15 G4..........56°27'N 2°53'W
Taytay Phil. 102 F6..........10°49'N 119°30'E
Taz r. Russia 54 J4..........66°34'N 78°36'E
Taza Morocco 48 C3..........34°16'N 3°56'W
Tbilisi Georgia 53 E2..........41°42'N 44°48'E
Tczew Poland 46 H6..........54°06'N 18°48'E
Te Anau, Lake New Zealand 109 F2..........45°18'S 167°48'E
Tébessa Algeria 84 E5..........35°23'N 8°12'E
Tebingtinggi Indonesia 102 B4..........3°19'N 99°08'E
Tecuci Romania 50 G7..........45°51'N 27°26'E
Tedzhen Turkmenistan 95 J7..........37°22'N 60°25'E
Tees r. England 13 F3..........54°35'N 1°15'W
Tees Bay England 13 F3..........54°41'N 1°09'W
Tegal Indonesia 102 D2..........6°51'S 109°07'E
Tegucigalpa Honduras 66 G3..........14°05'N 87°12'W
Tehrān Iran 95 H7..........35°39'N 51°23'E
Tehuantepec, Gulf of Mexico 66 F4..........15°47'N 94°53'W
Teide, Pico del vol. Canary Islands 45 X2...28°16'N 16°37'W
Teifi r. Wales 10 C4..........52°05'N 4°40'W
Teign r. England 11 D2..........50°32'N 3°35'W
Teignmouth England 11 D2..........50°33'N 3°30'W
Te Ike-a-Māui i. New Zealand 109 G3..........38°11'S 173°23'E
Teith r. Scotland 14 E4..........56°09'N 3°59'W
Tekirdağ Turkey 50 G5..........40°59'N 27°30'E
Telangana d. India 96 E4..........18°00'N 79°00'E
Tel Aviv-Yafo Israel 49 J3..........32°04'N 34°46'E
Teles Pires r. Brazil 72 D6..........7°20'S 58°03'W
Telford England 8 C3..........52°41'N 2°27'W
Telford and Wrekin d. England 21 D3..........52°43'N 2°29'W
Telpoziz, Gora mt. Russia 52 F4..........63°54'N 59°09'E
Tembenchi r. Russia 55 K4..........64°35'N 99°49'E
Teme r. England 8 C3..........52°10'N 2°13'W
Temirtau Kazakhstan 54 I3..........50°03'N 72°57'E
Temple Ewell England 9 G2..........51°09'N 1°16'E
Templemore Ireland 18 D2..........52°48'N 7°50'W
Temryuk Russia 51 L6..........45°17'N 37°23'E
Temuco Chile 73 B3..........38°44'S 72°35'W
Tenasserim Myanmar 97 I3..........12°02'N 98°58'E
Tenbury Wells England 8 C3..........52°19'N 2°35'W
Ten Degree Channel India 97 H2..........9°57'N 92°51'E
Tendō Japan 104 D3..........38°21'N 140°22'E
Tenerife i. Canary Islands 45 X2..........28°28'N 16°39'W
Tengiz d. Kazakhstan 54 H3..........50°09'N 68°23'E
Tennessee d. U.S.A. 63 I4..........36°12'N 85°01'W
Tennessee r. U.S.A. 63 I4..........37°08'N 88°25'W
Tenterden England 9 F2..........51°04'N 0°41'E
Tentudía mt. Spain 45 B3..........38°03'N 6°19'W
Teófilo Otoni Brazil 72 E5..........17°52'S 41°32'W
Tepic Mexico 66 D5..........21°31'N 104°55'W
Teplice Czechia 46 E4..........50°38'N 13°50'E
Terebovlya Ukraine 47 K3..........49°18'N 25°42'E
Teresina Brazil 72 E6..........5°07'S 42°44'W
Terme Turkey 51 L5..........41°12'N 36°59'E

Términos, Laguna de lagoon Mexico 66 F4
..........18°30'N 91°37'W
Termiz Uzbekistan 95 K7..........37°15'N 67°17'E
Tern r. England 8 C3..........52°40'N 2°40'W
Ternate Indonesia 103 H4..........0°49'N 127°20'E
Terneuzen Neth. 42 C4..........51°19'N 3°50'E
Terni Italy 48 F5..........42°33'N 12°39'E
Ternopil' Ukraine 47 K3..........49°33'N 25°36'E
Terrace Canada 60 F3..........54°32'N 128°37'W
Terrassa Spain 45 G4..........41°34'N 2°00'E
Terre Haute U.S.A. 63 I4..........39°28'N 87°24'W
Terrington Marsh England 9 F3..........52°47'N 0°16'E
Terschelling i. Neth. 42 E6..........53°27'N 5°28'E
Teseney Eritrea 94 E3..........15°07'N 36°39'E
Teslin Canada 60 E4..........60°12'N 132°39'W
Test r. England 8 D1..........50°56'N 1°29'W
Tetas, Punta pt Chile 73 B4..........23°28'S 70°34'W
Tetbury England 8 C2..........51°38'N 2°09'W
Tete Mozambique 83 C3..........16°10'S 33°36'E
Tetney England 13 G2..........53°29'N 0°01'W
Tétouan Morocco 84 D5..........35°34'N 5°23'W
Tetovo North Macedonia 50 D6..........42°00'N 20°58'E
Teuco r. Argentina 73 C4..........25°39'S 60°11'W
Teviot r. Scotland 15 G3..........55°36'N 2°26'W
Teviothead Scotland 15 G3..........55°20'N 2°56'W
Te Waipounamu i. New Zealand 109 G2......44°24'S 172°31'E
Tewkesbury England 8 C2..........51°59'N 2°09'W
Texarkana U.S.A. 63 H3..........33°25'N 94°03'W
Texas d. U.S.A. 62 G3..........31°58'N 99°13'W
Texel i. Neth. 42 D6..........53°09'N 4°46'E
Texoma, Lake U.S.A. 62 G3..........33°59'N 96°53'W
Tezpur India 97 H6..........26°36'N 92°49'E
Thabana Ntlenyana mt. Lesotho 83 B2......29°29'S 29°16'E
Thai Binh Vietnam 102 D8..........20°24'N 106°19'E
Thailand Asia 102 C7..........16°14'N 101°59'E
Thailand, Gulf of Asia 102 C6..........11°08'N 101°16'E
Thai Nguyên Vietnam 102 D8..........21°31'N 105°52'E
Thal Desert Pakistan 95 L6..........31°25'N 71°33'E
Thame England 8 E2..........51°45'N 0°58'W
Thame r. England 8 D2..........51°38'N 1°10'W
Thames est. England 9 F2..........51°30'N 0°31'E
Thames r. England 9 F2..........51°27'N 0°21'E
Thandwe Myanmar 97 H4..........18°27'N 94°22'E
Thanet, Isle of pen. England 9 G2..........51°22'N 1°17'E
Thanh Hoa Vietnam 102 D7..........19°47'N 105°49'E
Thar Desert India/Pakistan 96 C6..........25°48'N 69°50'E
Thasos i. Greece 50 F5..........40°40'N 24°31'E
Thatcham England 8 D2..........51°24'N 1°16'W
Thaton Myanmar 97 I4..........16°54'N 97°23'E
Thaxted England 9 F2..........51°57'N 0°21'E
The Bahamas Central America 67 I6..........24°55'N 77°44'W
The Calf hill England 13 E3..........54°22'N 2°31'W
The Cheviot hill England 13 E4..........55°29'N 2°09'W
The Cuillin Scotland 16 C2..........57°14'N 6°17'W
The Fens f. England 9 E3..........52°42'N 0°08'W
The Gambia Africa 84 C3..........13°22'N 16°25'W
The Great Oasis Egypt 94 D4..........24°52'N 30°42'E
The Gulf Asia 95 H5..........28°03'N 50°06'E
The Hague Neth. 42 D5..........52°05'N 4°18'E
Thelon r. Canada 60 I4..........64°17'N 96°18'W
The Marsh England 9 F3..........52°50'N 0°10'E
The Minch str. Scotland 16 C3..........58°02'N 6°02'W
The Mullet b. Ireland 18 A4..........54°10'N 10°07'W
The Naze pt England 9 G2..........51°52'N 1°17'E
The Needles f. England 8 D1..........50°40'N 1°37'W
The North Sound str. Scotland 17 G4......59°17'N 2°43'W
Theodore Roosevelt r. Brazil 72 C6......7°35'S 60°21'W
The Old Man of Coniston hill England 12 D3
..........54°22'N 3°07'W
The Pas Canada 60 H3..........53°49'N 101°16'W
Thermaïkos Kolpos g. Greece 50 E5..........40°11'N 22°54'E
The Solent str. England 8 D1..........50°45'N 1°23'W
The Sound est. England 11 C2..........50°21'N 4°09'W
Thessaloniki Greece 50 E5..........40°38'N 22°57'E
The Storr hill Scotland 16 C2..........57°31'N 6°11'W
Thet r. England 9 F3..........52°24'N 0°45'E
Thetford England 9 F3..........52°25'N 0°45'E
The Trossachs hills Scotland 14 E4..........56°13'N 4°26'E
The Wash b. England 9 F3..........52°55'N 0°11'E
The Weald f. England 9 F2..........51°05'N 0°18'E
Thiers France 44 E4..........45°51'N 3°33'E
Thiès Senegal 84 C3..........14°48'N 16°56'W
Thimphu Bhutan 97 G6..........27°29'N 89°42'E
Thionville France 44 G6..........49°22'N 6°10'E
Thira i. Greece 50 F3..........36°27'N 25°27'E
Thirlmere resr England 12 D3..........54°33'N 3°04'W
Thirsk England 13 F3..........54°14'N 1°20'W
Thiruvananthapuram India 96 E2..........8°30'N 76°57'E
Thisted Denmark 43 B2..........56°57'N 8°41'E
Thomastown Ireland 18 D2..........52°31'N 7°07'W
Thompson Canada 60 I3..........55°48'N 97°55'W
Thornaby-on-Tees England 13 F3..........54°32'N 1°17'W
Thornbury England 8 C2..........51°36'N 2°31'W
Thorne England 13 G2..........53°37'N 0°58'W
Thornhill Scotland 15 F3..........55°15'N 3°46'W
Thornton England 12 D2..........53°52'N 3°00'W
Thrakiko Pelagos sea Greece 50 F5..........40°22'N 24°46'E
Thrapston England 9 E3..........52°24'N 0°32'W
Thuin Belgium 42 D3..........50°20'N 4°17'E
Thule Greenland 61 K5..........77°28'N 69°11'W
Thunder Bay town Canada 61 J2..........48°26'N 89°15'W
Thurles Ireland 18 D2..........52°41'N 7°49'W
Thurrock d. England 21 F2..........51°31'N 0°22'E
Thursby England 12 D3..........54°51'N 3°03'W
Thurso Scotland 17 F3..........58°36'N 3°31'W
Thurso r. Scotland 17 F3..........58°36'N 3°31'W
Thurso Bay Scotland 17 F3..........58°37'N 3°31'W
Tianjin China 99 L5..........39°04'N 117°15'E
Tianshui China 99 J4..........34°30'N 105°37'E
Tiaret Algeria 48 D4..........35°20'N 1°19'E
Tibati Cameroon 84 F2..........6°26'N 12°35'E
Tibesti mts Chad 85 F4..........20°53'N 17°03'E
Tibet, Plateau of f. China 98 E4..........33°48'N 84°16'E
Tiburón, Isla i. Mexico 66 B6..........29°08'N 112°29'W
Ticehurst England 9 F2..........51°03'N 0°25'E
Tidjikja Mauritania 84 C3..........18°31'N 11°26'W
Tiel Neth. 42 E4..........51°52'N 5°25'E
Tielt Belgium 42 C3..........50°59'N 3°20'E
Tienen Belgium 42 D3..........50°48'N 4°57'E
Tien Shan mts China/Kyrgyzstan 98 D6......40°48'N 76°25'E
Tierra del Fuego i. Argentina/Chile 73 C1...54°11'S 68°48'W
Tiétar r. Spain 45 C3..........39°56'N 5°54'W
Tigre r. Venezuela 72 C7..........9°26'N 62°25'W
Tigris r. Iraq/Syria 95 G6..........30°59'N 47°25'E
Tihāmah f. Saudi Arabia 85 I3..........17°18'N 42°25'E
Tijuana Mexico 66 A7..........32°29'N 117°02'W
Tikhoretsk Russia 53 E2..........45°52'N 40°06'E

Tikhvin Russia 52 D3 .....59°39'N 33°32'E
Tikrīt Iraq 94 F6 .....34°33'N 43°37'E
Tiksi Russia 55 N5 .....71°38'N 128°36'E
Tilburg Neth. 42 E4 .....51°33'N 5°05'E
Tilbury England 9 F2 .....51°28'N 0°22'E
Tilehurst England 8 D2 .....51°27'N 1°02'W
Tillabéri Niger 84 E3 .....14°13'N 1°29'E
Tillicoultry Scotland 15 F4 .....56°09'N 3°44'W
Til'tim Russia 52 G4 .....65°12'N 63°13'E
Ṭīmā Egypt 49 J2 .....26°53'N 31°25'E
Timanskiy Kryazh f. Russia 52 F4 .....65°00'N 50°00'E
Timashëvsk Russia 53 D2 .....45°37'N 38°56'E
Timbuktu Mali 84 D3 .....16°46'N 2°59'W
Timiş r. Romania 50 D7 .....45°27'N 20°52'E
Timişoara Romania 50 D7 .....45°45'N 21°14'E
Timmins Canada 61 J2 .....48°29'N 81°21'W
Timor i. East Timor/Indonesia 103 H2 .....8°49'S 126°02'E
Timor-Leste Asia 103 H2 .....
Timor Sea Australia/Indonesia 108 B5 .....11°23'S 126°22'E
Timrå Sweden 43 D3 .....62°30'N 17°20'E
Tindouf Algeria 84 D4 .....27°42'N 8°07'W
Tinian i. N. Mariana Is 103 L6 .....14°58'N 145°41'E
Tinos i. Greece 50 F3 .....37°40'N 25°12'E
Tintagel England 11 C2 .....50°40'N 4°45'W
Tinto hill Scotland 15 F3 .....55°36'N 3°40'W
Tipperary Ireland 18 C2 .....52°28'N 8°10'W
Tipperary d. Ireland 18 D2 .....52°43'N 7°54'W
Tiptree England 9 F2 .....51°49'N 0°45'E
Tirana Albania 50 C5 .....41°19'N 19°49'E
Tiraspol Moldova 47 M6 .....46°51'N 29°37'E
Tiree i. Scotland 14 C4 .....56°30'N 6°57'W
Tirga Mòr hill Scotland 16 C2 .....57°59'N 6°59'W
Tiruchchirappalli India 96 E3 .....10°49'N 78°41'E
Tiruppur India 96 E3 .....11°06'N 77°18'E
Tisa r. Serbia 50 D7 .....45°08'N 20°17'E
Tisza r. Hungary 47 I2 .....46°09'N 20°04'E
Titicaca, Lake Bolivia/Peru 72 C5 .....15°49'S 69°40'W
Tiverton England 11 D2 .....50°54'N 3°29'W
Tizi Ouzou Algeria 48 D4 .....36°41'N 4°05'E
Tiznit Morocco 84 D4 .....29°41'N 9°43'W
Tiztoutine Morocco 45 D1 .....34°58'N 3°09'W
Tlaxcala Mexico 66 E4 .....19°21'N 98°13'W
Tlaxcala d. Mexico 66 E4 .....19°35'N 98°20'W
Tlemcen Algeria 84 D5 .....34°54'N 1°19'W
Toamasina Madagascar 83 D3 .....18°09'S 49°22'E
Toba, Danau l. Indonesia 102 B4 .....2°32'N 98°59'E
Tobago i. Trinidad and Tobago 67 L3 .....11°17'N 60°38'W
Tobelo Indonesia 103 H4 .....1°44'N 127°57'E
Tobermory Scotland 16 C1 .....56°38'N 6°04'W
Toboali Indonesia 102 D3 .....2°59'S 106°30'E
Tobol r. Kazakhstan/Russia 54 H3 .....58°10'N 68°13'E
Tobol'sk Russia 54 H3 .....58°14'N 68°16'E
Tocantins r. Brazil 72 E6 .....1°49'S 49°13'W
Todmorden England 13 E2 .....53°43'N 2°06'W
Toft Scotland 17 H5 .....60°28'N 1°13'W
Togian, Kepulauan is Indonesia 103 G3 .....0°06'S 121°53'E
Togo Africa 84 E2 .....8°27'N 1°11'E
Tok U.S.A. 60 D4 .....63°21'N 143°01'W
Tokat Turkey 51 L5 .....40°19'N 36°32'E
Tokelau is S. Pacific Oc. 109 H6 .....8°30'S 171°28'W
Tokushima Japan 104 B2 .....34°04'N 134°34'E
Tōkyō Japan 104 C3 .....35°40'N 139°46'E
Tōkyō d. Japan 104 C3 .....35°22'N 139°03'E
Toledo Spain 45 C3 .....39°52'N 4°01'W
Toledo U.S.A. 63 J5 .....41°39'N 83°33'W
Toledo, Montes de mts Spain 45 C3 .....39°39'N 4°54'W
Toledo Bend Reservoir U.S.A. 63 H3 .....31°38'N 93°43'W
Toliara Madagascar 83 D2 .....23°22'S 43°39'E
Tolitoli Indonesia 103 G4 .....1°05'N 120°50'E
Tollesbury England 9 F2 .....51°45'N 0°50'E
Tolsta Head Scotland 16 C3 .....58°21'N 6°10'W
Toluca Mexico 66 E4 .....19°18'N 99°39'W
Tol'yatti Russia 53 E3 .....53°31'N 49°26'E
Tomakomai Japan 104 D4 .....42°38'N 141°36'E
Tomanivi mt. Fiji 109 G5 .....17°37'S 178°00'E
Tomaszów Lubelski Poland 47 J4 .....50°28'N 23°25'E
Tomaszów Mazowiecki Poland 46 I4 .....51°32'N 20°01'E
Tombigbee r. U.S.A. 63 I3 .....31°11'N 87°57'W
Tombua Angola 83 A3 .....15°50'S 11°50'E
Tomelloso Spain 45 D3 .....39°09'N 3°00'W
Tomini, Teluk g. Indonesia 102 G3 .....0°21'S 120°54'E
Tomsk Russia 54 J3 .....56°30'N 85°01'E
Tomtabacken hill Sweden 43 C2 .....57°30'N 14°29'E
Tonbridge England 9 F2 .....51°12'N 0°17'E
Tondano Indonesia 103 G4 .....1°21'N 124°56'E
Tønder Denmark 46 C6 .....54°57'N 8°52'E
Tone r. England 8 C2 .....51°04'N 2°56'W
Tonelagee hill Ireland 10 A5 .....53°03'N 6°23'W
Tonga S. Pacific Oc. 109 H5 .....20°05'S 173°45'W
Tongatapu Group is Tonga 109 H4 .....21°07'S 174°45'W
Tongeren Belgium 42 E3 .....50°47'N 5°28'E
Tonghua China 99 N6 .....41°43'N 125°57'E
Tongking, Gulf of China/Vietnam 99 J2 .....20°29'N 108°15'E
Tongliao China 99 M6 .....43°31'N 122°14'E
Tongling China 99 L4 .....30°55'N 117°52'E
Tongue Scotland 17 E3 .....58°29'N 4°25'W
Tônlé Sab, Bœng l. Cambodia 102 C6 .....13°04'N 103°51'E
Tonopah U.S.A. 62 C4 .....38°04'N 117°14'W
Tønsberg Norway 43 B2 .....59°17'N 10°23'E
Toowoomba Australia 108 E4 .....27°33'S 151°58'E
Topeka U.S.A. 63 G4 .....39°04'N 95°36'W
Topozero, Ozero l. Russia 43 H4 .....65°42'N 32°00'E
Topsham England 11 D2 .....50°41'N 3°28'W
Torbat-e Heydarīyeh Iran 95 I7 .....35°13'N 59°06'E
Torbat-e Jām Iran 95 J7 .....35°15'N 60°34'E
Torbay d. England 11 D2 .....50°26'N 3°34'W
Tor Bay England 11 D2 .....50°25'N 3°32'W
Tordesillas Spain 45 C4 .....41°31'N 4°59'W
Torenberg hill Neth. 42 E5 .....52°14'N 5°52'E
Torfaen d. Wales 21 D2 .....51°44'N 3°05'W
Tormes r. Spain 45 B4 .....41°18'N 6°27'W
Torneälven r. Sweden 43 F4 .....65°49'N 24°09'E
Torneträsk l. Sweden 43 D5 .....68°23'N 18°56'E
Tornio Finland 43 F4 .....65°50'N 24°11'E
Toronto Canada 61 K2 .....43°40'N 79°23'W
Toropets Russia 47 N7 .....56°30'N 31°38'E
Torpoint England 11 C2 .....50°22'N 4°12'W
Torquay England 11 D2 .....50°28'N 3°30'W
Torre mt. Portugal 45 B4 .....40°20'N 7°35'W
Torrecerredo mt. Spain 45 C5 .....43°12'N 4°49'W
Torremolinos Spain 45 C2 .....36°36'N 4°30'W
Torrens, Lake Australia 108 C3 .....30°32'S 137°28'E
Torreón Mexico 66 D6 .....25°31'N 103°27'W
Torres Islands Vanuatu 109 F5 .....13°08'S 166°17'E
Torres Strait Australia 108 D6 .....9°50'S 142°11'E
Torres Vedras Portugal 45 A3 .....39°06'N 9°15'W

Torrevieja Spain 45 E2 .....37°59'N 0°40'W
Torridge r. England 11 C2 .....50°59'N 4°11'W
Torridon Scotland 16 D2 .....57°33'N 5°31'W
Torridon, Loch b. Scotland 16 D2 .....57°37'N 5°50'W
Tortosa Spain 45 F4 .....40°50'N 0°32'E
Toruń Poland 46 H5 .....53°01'N 18°37'E
Tory Island Ireland 18 C5 .....55°16'N 8°13'W
Torzhok Russia 52 D3 .....57°02'N 34°57'E
Tosno Russia 43 G2 .....59°33'N 30°54'E
Tosya Turkey 51 K5 .....40°59'N 34°04'E
Totland England 8 D1 .....50°41'N 1°32'W
Tot'ma Russia 52 E3 .....59°59'N 42°46'E
Totnes England 11 D2 .....50°26'N 3°41'W
Totton England 8 D1 .....50°55'N 1°29'W
Tottori Japan 104 B3 .....35°29'N 134°14'E
Toubkal, Jebel mt. Morocco 84 D5 .....31°03'N 7°57'W
Touggourt Algeria 84 E5 .....33°06'N 6°04'E
Toulon France 44 F3 .....43°08'N 5°56'E
Toulouse France 44 D3 .....43°37'N 1°26'E
Toungoo Myanmar 97 I4 .....18°55'N 96°25'E
Touraine f. France 44 D4 .....47°14'N 0°21'E
Tournai Belgium 42 C3 .....50°36'N 3°24'E
Tournon-sur-Rhône France 44 F4 .....45°04'N 4°50'E
Tours France 44 D5 .....47°23'N 0°42'E
Tove r. England 8 E2 .....52°05'N 0°50'W
Towcester England 8 E2 .....52°08'N 0°59'W
Townsville Australia 108 D5 .....19°15'S 146°49'E
Towori, Teluk b. Indonesia 103 G3 .....2°02'S 121°57'E
Toyama Japan 104 C3 .....36°41'N 137°13'E
Toyama-wan b. Japan 104 C3 .....36°54'N 137°14'E
Toyota Japan 104 C3 .....35°05'N 137°10'E
Tozeur Tunisia 48 E3 .....33°55'N 8°07'E
Trabzon Turkey 51 M5 .....40°59'N 39°44'E
Trafalgar, Cabo c. Spain 45 B2 .....36°11'N 6°02'W
Tralee Ireland 18 B2 .....52°16'N 9°42'W
Tralee Bay Ireland 18 B2 .....52°18'N 9°57'W
Tramore Ireland 18 D2 .....52°10'N 7°09'W
Tranås Sweden 43 C2 .....58°02'N 14°59'E
Trangan i. Indonesia 103 I2 .....6°35'S 134°16'E
Transnistria Europe 47 M2 .....47°45'N 29°03'E
Transylvanian Alps mts Romania 47 J1 .....45°35'N 24°40'E
Trapani Italy 48 F4 .....38°01'N 12°31'E
Traunsee l. Austria 46 F2 .....47°54'N 13°47'E
Traverse City U.S.A. 63 I5 .....44°46'N 85°37'W
Travnik Bos. and Herz. 50 B7 .....44°14'N 17°40'E
Trawsfynydd, Llyn resr Wales 10 D4 .....52°55'N 3°59'W
Tredegar Wales 10 D3 .....51°46'N 3°15'W
Tregaron Wales 10 D4 .....52°13'N 3°56'W
Treig, Loch l. Scotland 16 E1 .....56°48'N 4°44'W
Trelleborg Sweden 43 C1 .....55°22'N 13°10'E
Tremadog Bay Wales 10 C4 .....52°52'N 4°16'W
Trenčín Slovakia 46 H3 .....48°53'N 18°02'E
Trent r. England 13 G2 .....53°38'N 0°43'W
Trento Italy 46 D2 .....46°04'N 11°08'E
Trenton U.S.A. 63 L5 .....40°13'N 74°47'W
Treorchy Wales 10 D3 .....51°39'N 3°30'W
Tresco i. England 11 A1 .....49°57'N 6°19'W
Tres Puntas, Cabo c. Argentina 73 C2 .....47°08'S 65°53'W
Treviso Italy 46 E1 .....45°40'N 12°15'E
Trevose Head England 11 B2 .....50°33'N 5°06'W
Trier Germany 46 B3 .....49°45'N 6°38'E
Trieste Italy 46 E1 .....45°39'N 13°46'E
Trikala Greece 50 D4 .....39°33'N 21°46'E
Trim Ireland 18 E3 .....53°33'N 6°47'W
Trincomalee Sri Lanka 96 F2 .....8°37'N 81°13'E
Trindade, Ilha da i. S. Atlantic Ocean 68 E2 .....20°31'S 29°19'W
Tring England 8 E2 .....51°48'N 0°39'W
Trinidad i. Trinidad and Tobago 67 L3 .....10°27'N 61°13'W
Trinidad U.S.A. 62 F4 .....37°11'N 104°30'W
Trinidad and Tobago Central America 67 L3 .....10°49'N 61°00'W
Tripoli Greece 50 E3 .....37°31'N 22°23'E
Tripoli Lebanon 49 K3 .....34°26'N 35°52'E
Tripoli Libya 84 F5 .....32°52'N 13°08'E
Tripolitania f. Libya 48 F3 .....30°39'N 13°17'E
Tripura d. India 97 H5 .....23°36'N 91°35'E
Tristan da Cunha i. Atlantic Oc. 116 E2 .....38°00'S 12°00'W
Trnava Slovakia 46 G3 .....48°22'N 17°36'E
Trobriand Islands P.N.G. 108 E6 .....8°33'S 151°09'E
Troisdorf Germany 42 G3 .....50°49'N 7°09'E
Trois-Rivières Canada 61 K2 .....46°21'N 72°35'W
Troitsk Russia 53 G3 .....54°08'N 61°36'E
Trollhättan Sweden 43 C2 .....58°16'N 12°18'E
Tromsø Norway 43 D5 .....69°39'N 18°57'E
Trondheim Norway 43 B3 .....63°25'N 10°22'E
Troon Scotland 14 E3 .....55°32'N 4°40'W
Trostan hill Northern Ireland 14 C3 .....55°03'N 6°09'W
Troup Head Scotland 17 G2 .....57°42'N 2°18'W
Trout Lake Canada 63 H7 .....51°15'N 93°06'W
Trowbridge England 8 C2 .....51°19'N 2°12'W
Troyes France 44 F6 .....48°18'N 4°05'E
Trubchevsk Russia 47 O5 .....52°35'N 33°47'E
Trujillo Peru 72 B6 .....8°07'S 79°02'W
Truro Canada 61 L2 .....45°22'N 63°13'W
Truro England 11 B2 .....50°16'N 5°03'W
Tsaratanana, Massif du mts Madagascar 83 D3 .....13°44'S 48°59'E
Tsetserleg Mongolia 99 I7 .....47°19'N 101°29'E
Tshchikskoye Vodokhranilishche resr Russia 51 M7 .....45°07'N 39°28'E
Tsimlyanskoye Vodokhranilishche resr Russia 53 E2 .....48°00'N 43°00'E
Tsna r. Belarus 47 L5 .....52°09'N 27°01'E
Tsu Japan 104 C2 .....34°43'N 136°31'E
Tsuchiura Japan 104 D3 .....36°04'N 140°12'E
Tsugarū-kaikyō str. Japan 104 D4 .....41°16'N 140°21'E
Tsumeb Namibia 83 A3 .....19°14'S 17°43'E
Tsumis Park Namibia 83 A2 .....23°47'S 17°31'E
Tsuruga Japan 104 C3 .....35°38'N 136°04'E
Tsushima is Japan 104 A2 .....34°24'N 129°23'E
Tuam Ireland 18 C3 .....53°31'N 8°51'W
Tuamotu Archipelago is French Polynesia 116 B2 .....14°29'S 142°50'W
Tuapse Russia 53 D2 .....44°06'N 39°04'E
Tuban Indonesia 102 E2 .....6°55'S 112°02'E
Tubbercurry Ireland 18 C4 .....54°03'N 8°43'W
Tübingen Germany 46 C3 .....48°31'N 9°04'E
Tubruq Libya 85 G5 .....32°04'N 23°57'E
Tucson U.S.A. 62 D3 .....32°14'N 110°55'W
Tucumcari U.S.A. 62 F4 .....35°12'N 103°44'W
Tucuruí Brazil 72 E6 .....3°42'S 49°40'W
Tucuruí, Represa resr Brazil 72 E6 .....4°26'S 49°40'W
Tudela Spain 45 E5 .....42°04'N 1°36'W
Tuela r. Portugal 45 B4 .....41°38'N 7°08'W

Tuguegarao Phil. 103 G7 .....17°37'N 121°43'E
Tui Spain 45 A5 .....42°03'N 8°38'W
Tukangbesi, Kepulauan is Indonesia 103 G2 .....5°40'S 123°55'E
Tukums Latvia 43 E2 .....56°58'N 23°07'E
Tula Russia 53 D3 .....54°12'N 37°37'E
Tulcea Romania 51 H7 .....45°10'N 28°48'E
Tul'chyn Ukraine 47 M3 .....48°41'N 28°50'E
Tulít'a Canada 60 F4 .....64°55'N 125°31'W
Tullamore Ireland 18 D3 .....53°17'N 7°30'W
Tulle France 44 D4 .....45°16'N 1°46'E
Tullow Ireland 18 E2 .....52°48'N 6°44'W
Tullybrack hill Northern Ireland 14 B2 .....54°23'N 7°52'W
Tulsa U.S.A. 62 G4 .....36°09'N 95°58'W
Tumaco Colombia 72 B7 .....1°48'N 78°49'W
Tumakuru India 96 E3 .....13°19'N 77°06'E
Tumba, Lac l. Dem. Rep. Congo 83 A4 .....0°52'S 18°05'E
Tummel r. Scotland 17 F1 .....56°39'N 3°40'W
Tummel, Loch l. Scotland 17 F1 .....56°42'N 3°58'W
Tump Pakistan 95 J5 .....26°06'N 62°26'E
Tumucumaque, Serra hills Brazil 72 D7 .....1°59'N 56°09'W
Tunceli Turkey 51 M4 .....39°06'N 39°33'E
Tundzha r. Bulgaria 50 G5 .....41°39'N 26°33'E
Tunis Tunisia 48 F4 .....36°46'N 10°16'E
Tunisia Africa 48 E3 .....34°52'N 9°24'E
Tunja Colombia 72 B7 .....5°30'N 73°22'W
Tunnsjøen l. Norway 43 C4 .....64°42'N 13°24'E
Tuolumne r. U.S.A. 62 B4 .....37°36'N 121°10'W
Tura Russia 55 L4 .....64°16'N 100°15'E
Turabah Saudi Arabia 94 F4 .....21°14'N 41°37'E
Turbat Pakistan 96 B6 .....26°01'N 63°07'E
Turbo Colombia 67 I2 .....8°05'N 76°43'W
Turda Romania 47 J2 .....46°34'N 23°47'E
Turgutlu Turkey 50 G4 .....38°29'N 27°42'E
Turhal Turkey 51 L5 .....40°23'N 36°04'E
Turia r. Spain 45 E3 .....39°26'N 0°18'W
Turin Italy 46 B1 .....45°04'N 7°41'E
Turinsk Russia 52 G3 .....58°04'N 63°42'E
Turkana, Lake Ethiopia/Kenya 85 H2 .....3°59'N 35°57'E
Turkey Asia/Europe 51 I4 .....39°19'N 34°21'E
Turkmenabat Turkmenistan 54 H1 .....39°05'N 63°34'E
Turkmenbaşy Turkmenistan 53 F2 .....40°02'N 52°59'E
Turkmenistan Asia 87 D4 .....40°00'N 60°00'E
Turks and Caicos Islands Central America 67 J5 .....21°59'N 71°36'W
Turks Islands Turks and Caicos Is 67 J5 .....21°25'N 71°09'W
Turku Finland 43 E3 .....60°27'N 22°15'E
Turnhout Belgium 42 D4 .....51°19'N 4°57'E
Turnu Măgurele Romania 50 F6 .....43°45'N 24°51'E
Turpan China 98 F6 .....42°52'N 89°12'E
Turquino, Pico mt. Cuba 67 I5 .....20°02'N 76°51'W
Turriff Scotland 17 G2 .....57°32'N 2°28'W
Tuscaloosa U.S.A. 63 I3 .....33°11'N 87°30'W
Tutbury England 8 D3 .....52°51'N 1°41'W
Tuticorin India 96 E2 .....8°48'N 78°08'E
Tuttlingen Germany 46 C2 .....47°59'N 8°49'E
Tutuila i. American Samoa 109 H5 .....14°16'S 170°33'W
Tuvalu S. Pacific Oc. 109 G6 .....7°24'S 178°20'E
Tuxford England 13 G2 .....53°14'N 0°54'W
Tuxpan Mexico 66 E5 .....20°58'N 97°22'W
Tuxtla Gutiérrez Mexico 66 F4 .....16°46'N 93°08'W
Tuz, Lake Turkey 51 J4 .....38°42'N 33°24'E
Tuzla Bos. and Herz. 50 C7 .....44°33'N 18°42'E
Tver' Russia 52 D3 .....56°50'N 35°54'E
Tweed r. U.K. 13 E4 .....55°45'N 2°06'W
Twin Falls town U.S.A. 62 D5 .....42°35'N 114°27'W
Twyford England 8 E2 .....51°29'N 0°52'W
Tyler U.S.A. 63 G3 .....32°20'N 95°18'W
Tynda Russia 55 N3 .....55°07'N 124°44'E
Tyne r. Scotland 15 G4 .....56°00'N 2°36'W
Tyne and Wear d. England 20 E4 .....54°56'N 1°16'W
Tynemouth England 13 F4 .....55°01'N 1°25'W
Tynset Norway 43 B3 .....62°16'N 10°45'E
Tyre Lebanon 49 K3 .....33°15'N 35°14'E
Tyrrhenian Sea France/Italy 48 F5 .....40°13'N 10°15'E
Tyumen' Russia 54 H3 .....57°09'N 65°28'E
Tywi r. Wales 10 C3 .....51°48'N 4°20'W

# U

Uaupés Brazil 72 C6 .....0°06'S 67°02'W
Ubangi r. C.A.R./Dem. Rep. Congo 85 F1 .....0°25'S 17°44'E
Úbeda Spain 45 D3 .....38°01'N 3°22'W
Uberaba Brazil 73 E4 .....19°46'S 47°53'W
Uberlândia Brazil 72 E5 .....18°56'S 48°14'W
Ubon Ratchathani Thailand 102 C7 .....15°14'N 104°53'E
Ucayali r. Peru 72 B6 .....4°28'S 73°29'W
Uchur r. Russia 55 O3 .....58°29'N 131°17'E
Uckfield England 9 F1 .....50°58'N 0°06'E
Uda r. Russia 55 N3 .....54°41'N 135°18'E
Udaipur India 96 D5 .....24°35'N 73°47'E
Uddevalla Sweden 43 B2 .....58°21'N 11°57'E
Uddjaure l. Sweden 43 D4 .....65°56'N 17°52'E
Udine Italy 46 E2 .....46°04'N 13°14'E
Udon Thani Thailand 102 C7 .....17°22'N 102°50'E
Udupi India 96 D3 .....13°20'N 74°46'E
Ueda Japan 104 C3 .....36°24'N 138°15'E
Uele r. Dem. Rep. Congo 83 B5 .....3°32'N 25°16'E
Uelzen Germany 46 D5 .....52°58'N 10°34'E
Ufa Russia 53 F3 .....54°44'N 55°58'E
Uganda Africa 85 H2 .....2°34'N 32°37'E
Uglegorsk Russia 55 P2 .....49°02'N 142°02'E
Uig Scotland 16 C2 .....57°36'N 6°21'W
Uíge Angola 83 A4 .....7°36'S 15°05'E
Uinta Mountains U.S.A. 62 D5 .....40°36'N 110°69'W
Ukhta Russia 52 F4 .....63°33'N 53°46'E
Ukiah U.S.A. 62 B4 .....39°09'N 123°13'W
Ukmergė Lithuania 47 K6 .....55°15'N 24°46'E
Ukraine Europe 47 N3 .....49°23'N 31°18'E
Ulaangom Mongolia 98 G7 .....49°57'N 92°03'E
Ulanhot China 99 M7 .....46°04'N 122°03'E
Ulan-Khol Russia 53 E2 .....45°26'N 46°51'E
Ulan-Ude Russia 55 L3 .....51°49'N 107°38'E
Uliastay Mongolia 98 H7 .....47°36'N 96°48'E
Ulithi atoll Micronesia 103 J6 .....10°07'N 139°40'E
Uljin S. Korea 104 A3 .....36°59'N 129°23'E
Ullapool Scotland 16 D2 .....57°54'N 5°10'W
Ullswater l. England 12 E3 .....54°34'N 2°54'W
Ullŭng-do i. S. Korea 104 B3 .....37°30'N 130°55'E
Ulm Germany 46 C3 .....48°25'N 9°59'E
Ulsan S. Korea 104 A3 .....35°34'N 129°19'E
Ulster Canal Ireland/U.K. 14 B2 .....54°12'N 7°01'W
Uludağ mt. Turkey 51 H5 .....40°06'N 29°17'E
Ulundi S. Africa 83 C2 .....28°19'S 31°25'E
Uluru/Ayers Rock hill Australia 108 C4 .....25°20'S 131°00'E

Ulva i. Scotland 14 C4 .....56°28'N 6°...W
Ulverston England 12 D3 .....54°12'N 3°...
Ul'yanovsk Russia 53 E3 .....54°18'N 48...
Uman' Ukraine 47 N3 .....48°45'N 30...
Umba Russia 52 D4 .....66°41'N 34...
Umboi i. P.N.G. 108 D6 .....5°42'S 147...
Umeå Sweden 43 E3 .....63°50'N 20...
Umeälven r. Sweden 43 D3 .....63°50'N 20...
Umm Keddada Sudan 94 C2 .....13°35'N 26...
Umm Ruwaba Sudan 94 D2 .....12°52'N 31...
Umm Sa'ad Libya 85 G5 .....31°34'N 25...
Umtata S. Africa 83 B1 .....31°35'S 28...
Umuarama Brazil 73 D4 .....23°46'S 53...
Una r. Bos. and Herz./Croatia 50 B7 .....45°16'N 16...
'Unayzah Saudi Arabia 94 F5 .....26°05'N 43...
Unecha Russia 47 O5 .....52°51'N 32...
Ungava, Péninsule d' pen. Canada 61 K4 .....60°46'N 74°...
Ungava Bay Canada 61 L3 .....59°16'N 67...
Unimak Island U.S.A. 60 B3 .....54°58'N 164°...
United Arab Emirates Asia 95 H4 .....23°30'N 52...
United Kingdom Europe 20 .....54°35'N 1°...
United States of America N. America 62 G4 .....38°59'N 99°...
Unst i. Scotland 17 I5 .....60°46'N 0°...
Upa r. Russia 47 Q6 .....54°01'N 36...
Upavon England 8 D2 .....51°18'N 1°...
Upemba, Lac l. Dem. Rep. Congo 83 B4 .....8°39'S 26...
Upernavik Greenland 61 M5 .....72°48'N 56...
Upington S. Africa 83 B2 .....28°28'S 21...
Upolu i. Samoa 109 H5 .....14°04'S 171°...
Upper Klamath Lake U.S.A. 62 B5 .....42°22'N 121...
Upper Lough Erne l. Northern Ireland 14 B2 .....54°15'N 7°...
Upper Tean England 8 D3 .....52°57'N 1°...
Uppingham England 8 E3 .....52°35'N 0°...
Uppsala Sweden 43 D2 .....59°51'N 17°...
Upton upon Severn England 8 C3 .....52°04'N 2°...
Ural r. Kazakhstan/Russia 53 F2 .....46°55'N 51°...
Ural Mountains Russia 54 H4 .....66°50'N 63...
Ural'sk Kazakhstan 53 F3 .....51°11'N 51°...
Uranium City Canada 60 H3 .....59°31'N 108°...
Ure r. England 13 F3 .....54°05'N 1°...
Urengoy Russia 54 I4 .....65°55'N 78...
Urganch Uzbekistan 54 H2 .....41°32'N 60...
Urie r. Scotland 17 G2 .....57°16'N 2°...
Urla Turkey 50 G4 .....38°17'N 26...
Urmia, Lake Iran 94 G7 .....37°35'N 45°...
Uruapan Mexico 66 D4 .....19°25'N 102°...
Urubamba r. Peru 72 B5 .....10°46'S 73°...
Uruguaiana Brazil 73 D4 .....29°45'S 57°...
Uruguay r. Argentina/Brazil/Uruguay 73 D4 .....33°52'S 58...
Uruguay S. America 73 D3 .....32°45'S 55°...
Ürümqi China 98 F6 .....43°44'N 87°...
Urziceni Romania 50 G7 .....44°43'N 26...
Usa r. Russia 52 F4 .....66°00'N 57...
Uşak Turkey 51 H4 .....38°40'N 29...
Ushuaia Argentina 73 C1 .....54°46'S 68°...
Usinsk Russia 52 F4 .....66°01'N 57°...
Usk Wales 10 E3 .....51°42'N 2°...
Usk r. Wales 10 E3 .....51°34'N 2°...
Usk Reservoir Wales 10 D3 .....51°56'N 3°...
Usogorsk Russia 52 E4 .....63°26'N 48...
Usol'ye-Sibirskoye Russia 55 L3 .....52°45'N 103°...
Ussuriysk Russia 55 O2 .....43°48'N 131...
Ust'-Ilimsk Russia 55 L3 .....58°02'N 102...
Ust'-Ilych Russia 52 F4 .....62°33'N 56...
Ústí nad Labem Czechia 46 F4 .....50°40'N 14...
Ust'-Kamchatsk Russia 55 S3 .....56°15'N 162...
Ust'-Kamenogorsk Kazakhstan 54 J2 .....49°52'N 82°...
Ust'-Kara Russia 52 G4 .....69°13'N 64...
Ust'-Kulom Russia 52 F4 .....61°41'N 53...
Ust'-Kut Russia 55 L3 .....56°45'N 105°...
Ust'-Maya Russia 55 O4 .....60°27'N 134...
Ust'-Olenek Russia 55 M5 .....72°55'N 119...
Ust'-Tsil'ma Russia 52 F4 .....65°26'N 52...
Ustyurt Plateau f. Kazakhstan/Uzbekistan 53 F2 .....43°29'N 56...
Utah d. U.S.A. 62 D4 .....39°34'N 111°...
Utena Lithuania 47 K6 .....55°30'N 25...
Utica U.S.A. 63 K5 .....43°06'N 75°...
Utiel Spain 45 E3 .....39°34'N 1°...
Utqiagvik U.S.A. 60 C5 .....71°18'N 156°...
Utrecht Neth. 42 E5 .....52°07'N 5°...
Utrecht d. Neth. 42 E5 .....52°07'N 5°...
Utrera Spain 45 C2 .....37°11'N 5°...
Utsunomiya Japan 104 C3 .....36°34'N 139°...
Utta Russia 53 E2 .....46°23'N 46...
Uttaradit Thailand 102 C7 .....17°37'N 100°...
Uttarakhand d. India 96 E7 .....30°11'N 79°...
Uttar Pradesh d. India 96 E6 .....27°37'N 79°...
Uttoxeter England 8 D3 .....52°54'N 1°...
Uusikaupunki Finland 43 E3 .....60°48'N 21°...
Uwajima Japan 104 B2 .....33°13'N 132°...
Uxbridge England 9 E2 .....51°33'N 0°...
Uyuni, Salar de f. Bolivia 73 C4 .....20°13'S 67°...
Uzbekistan Asia 87 D4 .....40°00'N 60°...
Uzhhorod Ukraine 47 J3 .....48°37'N 22°...
Užice Serbia 50 C6 .....43°51'N 19°...
Uzlovaya Russia 53 D3 .....53°59'N 38°...
Uzunköprü Turkey 50 G5 .....41°15'N 26°...

# V

Vaal r. S. Africa 83 B2 .....29°05'S 23°...
Vaasa Finland 43 E3 .....63°06'N 21°...
Vác Hungary 47 H2 .....47°47'N 19°...
Vadodara India 96 D5 .....22°16'N 73°...
Vadsø Norway 43 G5 .....70°05'N 29°...
Vaduz Liechtenstein 46 C2 .....47°08'N 9°...
Værøy i. Norway 43 C4 .....67°39'N 12°...
Vaganski Vrh mt. Croatia 50 A7 .....44°22'N 15°...
Váh r. Slovakia 46 H2 .....47°46'N 18°...
Vaiaku Tuvalu 109 G6 .....8°28'S 179°...
Vaitupu i. Tuvalu 109 G6 .....7°27'S 178°...
Valdai Hills Russia 34 H4 .....57°10'N 33°...
Valdepeñas Spain 45 D3 .....38°46'N 3°...
Valdés, Península pen. Argentina 73 C2 .....42°31'S 63°...
Valdez U.S.A. 60 D4 .....61°07'N 146°...
Valdivia Chile 73 B3 .....39°50'S 73°...
Val-d'Or Canada 61 K2 .....48°06'N 77°...
Valdosta U.S.A. 63 J3 .....30°51'N 83°...

...res f. Norway 43 B3 ....................60°56'N 9°13'E
...nce France 44 F4 .......................44°56'N 4°54'E
...ncia Spain 45 E3 ........................39°29'N 0°21'W
...ncia Venezuela 72 C8 ...............10°10'N 67°59'W
...ncia, Golfo de g. Spain 45 F3 ........39°28'N 0°21'E
...ncia de Alcántara Spain 45 B3 .......39°25'N 7°14'W
...aciennes France 44 E7 ..................50°21'N 3°32'E
...of Glamorgan d. Wales 21 D2 .....51°26'N 3°21'E
...a Venezuela 72 B7 .......................9°14'N 70°35'W
...Mont mt. France 44 D3 .............42°48'N 1°05'E
...co, Golfe de g. France 44 H2 .......41°40'N 8°50'E
...vo Serbia 50 C7 ...........................44°17'N 19°55'E
...Latvia 43 F2 ...............................57°46'N 26°00'E
...akoski Finland 43 F3 ...................61°15'N 24°03'E
...nswaard Neth. 42 E4 ..................51°21'N 5°27'E
...dolid Spain 45 C4 .........................41°39'N 4°43'W
...de la Pascua Venezuela 67 K2 .......9°10'N 65°57'W
...dupar Colombia 72 B8 .................10°30'N 73°16'W
...tta Malta 48 F4 ............................35°54'N 14°30'E
...y Wales 11 D2 .............................53°17'N 4°34'W
...raíso Chile 73 B3 ........................33°03'S 71°36'W
...Tanjung c. Indonesia 103 J2 ........8°26'S 137°40'E
...nila Finland 43 E3 ......................61°20'N 22°56'E
...urkey 94 F7 ..................................38°30'N 43°22'E
...Lake Turkey 94 F7 ......................38°37'N 42°47'E
...dzor Armenia 53 E2 .....................40°49'N 44°28'E
...ouver Canada 60 F2 .....................49°16'N 123°08'W
...ouver Island Canada 60 F2 ..........49°28'N 125°39'W
...rn l. Sweden 43 C2 ......................59°05'N 13°36'E
...rsborg Sweden 43 C2 ..................58°23'N 12°20'E
...aindrano Madagascar 83 D2 .......23°22'S 47°34'E
...nea P.N.G. 103 K3 .........................2°42'S 141°20'E
...näs Sweden 43 D3 .......................63°55'N 19°46'E
...nes France 44 B5 ........................47°39'N 2°45'W
...a Finland 43 F3 .............................60°18'N 24°57'E
...a Levu i. Fiji 109 G5 ...................16°10'S 179°40'E
...u S. Pacific Oc. 109 F5 .............16°05'S 167°04'E
...Diemen Gulf Australia 103 I1 ......11°54'S 132°00'E
...nasi India 96 F4 ...........................25°20'N 83°04'E
...agerfjorden str. Norway 43 G5 ....70°04'N 29°07'E
...din Croatia 46 G2 ........................46°19'N 16°22'E
...erg Sweden 43 C2 .......................57°07'N 12°16'E
...ar r. North Macedonia 50 E5 .......41°07'N 22°32'E
...na Lithuania 47 K6 .......................54°13'N 24°35'E
...se Italy 46 C1 ...............................45°49'N 8°50'E
...us Finland 43 F3 ..........................62°19'N 27°54'E
...a Bulgaria 51 G6 ..........................43°12'N 27°54'E
...amo Sweden 43 C2 .....................57°11'N 14°03'E
...alota Hungary 46 H2 ....................47°12'N 18°08'E
...rdalälven r. Sweden 43 C3 ...........60°32'N 15°07'E
...vrvik Sweden 43 C2 .....................57°45'N 16°39'E
...ra India 96 E3 ..............................12°56'N 79°07'E
...say i. Sweden 43 D3 ....................61°03'N 42°05'E
...say i. Scotland 16 B1 ...................56°56'N 7°38'W
...an City Europe 35 F3 ...................41°54'N 12°27'E
...jökull ice cap Iceland 43 Y2 .........64°28'N 16°37'W
...rn l. Sweden 43 C2 ......................58°05'N 14°21'E
...u Group is Tonga 109 H5 .............18°24'S 174°21'W
...avysk Belarus 47 K5 .....................53°09'N 24°27'E
...Sweden 43 C2 ...............................56°53'N 14°49'E
...ach, Ostrov i. Russia 52 F5 ..........69°59'N 59°05'E
...r r. Germany 42 F5 ......................52°37'N 6°43'E
...dam Neth. 42 F6 ..........................53°06'N 6°53'E
...endaal Neth. 42 E5 ......................52°01'N 5°33'E
...i. Norway 43 B4 ...........................65°39'N 11°53'E
...Denmark 43 B1 .............................55°43'N 9°32'E
...Germany 42 F4 .............................51°53'N 6°59'E
...North Macedonia 50 D5 ...............41°42'N 21°47'E
...-Málaga r. Spain 45 C2 ...............36°47'N 4°06'W
...s r. Brazil 72 E5 ..........................17°13'S 44°49'W
...a Morava canal Serbia 50 D7 ......44°43'N 21°03'E
...aya r. Russia 52 F5 ......................57°50'N 28°15'E
...aya r. Russia 55 S4 .....................64°32'N 176°06'E
...ye Luki Russia 52 D3 ...................56°20'N 30°31'E
...y Novgorod Russia 52 E4 .............56°20'N 30°31'E
...y Ustyug Russia 52 E4 .................60°46'N 46°18'E
...o Tarnovo Bulgaria 50 F6 ...........43°05'N 25°39'E
...ra r. Russia 55 N4 ........................55°36'N 31°12'E
...re India 96 E3 ...............................12°56'N 79°07'E
...rôme France 44 D5 ......................47°48'N 1°04'E
...zuela S. America 67 K2 ...............7°35'N 66°30'W
...zuela, Golfo de g. Venezuela 72 B8

11°32'N 71°03'W
...te Italy 46 E1 ................................45°26'N 12°20'E
...e, Gulf of Europe 46 E1 ...............45°19'N 12°43'E
...ay Neth. 42 E4 ..............................51°31'N 5°58'E
...r Latvia/Lithuania 43 E2 ..............56°24'N 21°33'E
...nor England 8 D1 .........................50°36'N 1°12'W
...spils Latvia 43 E2 ........................57°23'N 21°36'E
...Spain 45 E2 ...................................37°15'N 1°52'W
...cruz Mexico 66 E4 ........................19°11'N 96°09'W
...cruz d. Mexico 66 E5 ....................20°54'N 97°46'W
...lli Italy 46 C1 ...............................45°19'N 8°26'E
...alsøra Norway 43 B3 ...................63°47'N 11°29'E
...e r. Brazil 72 D5 ..........................21°10'S 51°58'W
...a 62 D3 .........................................33°33'N 111°39'W
...un France 44 F6 ...........................49°10'N 5°24'E
...Spain 45 B4 ...................................41°56'N 7°25'W
...nnevilyuysk Russia 55 N4 ............63°26'N 120°12'E
...oyansk Russia 55 O4 ...................67°32'N 133°27'E
...oyanskiy Khrebet mts Russia 55 N5

70°07'N 128°50'E
...ont d. U.S.A. 63 L5 .......................44°03'N 72°42'W
...a Greece 50 E4 ............................40°32'N 22°13'E
...na Italy 46 D1 ...............................45°26'N 10°59'E
...illes France 44 E6 ........................48°48'N 2°08'E
...Cap c. Senegal 84 C3 ..................14°44'N 17°31'W
...ers Belgium 42 E3 ........................50°35'N 5°52'E
...ood England 8 D1 ........................50°53'N 1°52'W
...aya, Gora mt. Russia 53 F3 .........54°34'N 57°59'E
...al France 44 E6 ...........................47°38'N 6°09'E
...rälen is Norway 43 C5 .................68°43'N 13°59'E
...jorden str. Norway 43 C4 ............67°40'N 13°54'E
...annaeyjar is Iceland 43 X1 ..........63°24'N 20°13'W
...arhorn hd Iceland 43 Z2 ..............64°17'N 14°00'W
...vius vol. Italy 46 F5 ......................40°50'N 14°26'E
...prém Hungary 46 G2 ....................47°06'N 17°54'E
...ga Russia 52 E3 ...........................57°52'N 45°48'E

Victoria d. Australia 108 D3 ..............36°56'S 144°52'E
Victoria r. Australia 108 C5 ..............15°23'S 130°17'E
Victoria Canada 60 F2 ......................48°25'N 123°22'W
Victoria Seychelles 79 E2 ..................4°38'S 55°28'E
Victoria, Lake Africa 83 C4 .................0°59'S 32°51'E
Victoria U.S.A. 62 G2 .......................28°49'N 96°59'W
Victoria, Mount Myanmar 97 H5 .....21°11'N 93°56'E
Victoria, Mount P.N.G. 108 D6 ...........8°49'S 147°30'E
Victoria Falls Zambia/Zimbabwe 83 B3 ...17°49'S 25°42'E
Victoria Island Canada 60 H5 ...........70°42'N 106°38'W
Viedma Argentina 73 C2 ...................40°50'S 63°00'W
Viedma, Lago l. Argentina 73 B2 .......49°35'S 72°49'W
Vienna Austria 46 G3 .......................48°12'N 16°23'E
Vienne France 44 F4 ........................45°31'N 4°53'E
Vienne r. France 44 D4 .....................47°13'N 0°05'E
Vierzon France 44 E5 .......................47°14'N 2°04'E
Vieste Italy 50 B5 .............................41°53'N 16°11'E
Vietnam Asia 102 D7 .......................19°20'N 104°48'E
Vignemale mt. France 44 C3 ............42°46'N 0°09'W
Vigo Spain 45 A5 ..............................42°14'N 8°43'W
Vijayapura India 96 E4 ......................16°49'N 75°48'E
Vijayawada India 96 F4 ....................16°33'N 80°39'E
Vík Iceland 43 Y1 .............................63°26'N 19°02'W
Vikna i. Norway 43 B4 ......................64°53'N 10°50'E
Vilagarcía Spain 45 A5 .....................42°36'N 8°45'W
Vilaine r. France 44 B5 .....................47°35'N 2°16'W
Vila Real Portugal 45 B4 ...................41°18'N 7°44'W
Vilcabamba, Cordillera mts Peru 72 B5 ...12°30'S 73°27'W
Vilhelmina Sweden 43 D4 ................64°37'N 16°41'E
Vilhena Brazil 72 C5 .........................12°42'S 60°07'W
Viljandi Estonia 43 F2 ......................58°22'N 25°35'E
Vilkaviškis Lithuania 47 J6 ...............54°39'N 23°03'E
Vil'kitskogo, Proliv str. Russia 55 K5 ...77°30'N 98°42'E
Villach Austria 46 E2 ........................46°37'N 13°51'E
Villahermosa Mexico 66 F4 ..............18°00'N 92°53'W
Villa Insurgentes Mexico 66 B6 .......25°16'N 111°47'W
Villarrobledo Spain 45 D3 ................39°16'N 2°36'W
Villavicencio Colombia 72 B7 .............4°07'N 73°36'W
Villefranche-sur-Saône France 44 F4 ...45°59'N 4°44'E
Villena Spain 45 E3 .........................38°38'N 0°51'W
Villeneuve-sur-Lot France 44 D4 ......44°25'N 0°42'E
Villeurbanne France 44 F4 ................45°46'N 4°54'E
Vilnius Lithuania 43 F1 .....................54°40'N 25°16'E
Vilvoorde Belgium 42 D3 ..................50°55'N 4°27'E
Vilyuy r. Russia 55 N4 .......................64°24'N 126°28'E
Vindelälven r. Sweden 43 D3 ...........63°56'N 19°51'E
Vinh Vietnam 102 D7 .......................18°38'N 105°42'E
Vinkovci Croatia 50 C7 ......................45°17'N 18°49'E
Vinnytsya Ukraine 47 M3 .................49°14'N 28°30'E
Viranşehir Turkey 51 M3 ...................37°13'N 39°47'E
Virden Canada 62 F6 .......................49°51'N 100°56'W
Vire France 44 C6 ............................48°50'N 0°53'W
Virginia d. U.S.A. 63 K4 ....................37°47'N 78°01'W
Virgin Islands (U.K.) Central America 67 L4

18°37'N 64°37'W
Virgin Islands (U.S.A.) Central America 67 L4

18°14'N 64°53'W
Virovitica Croatia 50 B7 ....................45°50'N 17°23'E
Virton Belgium 42 E2 .......................49°34'N 5°33'E
Vis i. Croatia 50 B6 ..........................43°05'N 16°06'E
Visaginas Lithuania 47 L6 ................55°35'N 26°26'E
Visby Sweden 43 D2 ........................57°38'N 18°18'E
Viscount Melville Sound str. Canada 60 G5

73°50'N 112°57'W
Viseu Portugal 45 B4 .......................40°40'N 7°55'W
Vishakhapatnam India 96 F4 ...........17°42'N 83°22'E
Vistula r. Poland 46 H5 .....................54°18'N 18°55'E
Viterbo Italy 48 F5 ...........................42°24'N 12°07'E
Viti Levu i. Fiji 109 G5 .......................18°05'S 177°19'E
Vitim r. Russia 55 M3 .......................59°26'N 112°35'E
Vitória Brazil 73 E4 ...........................20°19'S 40°21'W
Vitória da Conquista Brazil 72 E5 .....14°50'S 40°47'W
Vitoria-Gasteiz Spain 45 D5 .............42°51'N 2°39'W
Vitsyebsk Belarus 47 N6 ..................55°12'N 30°10'E
Vittel France 44 F6 ...........................48°12'N 5°57'E
Vizianagaram India 96 F4 ................18°08'N 83°31'E
Vlaams-Brabant d. Belgium 42 D3 ...50°56'N 4°36'E
Vlaardingen Neth. 42 D4 ..................51°54'N 4°21'E
Vlădeasa, Vârful mt. Romania 47 J2 ...46°45'N 22°50'E
Vladikavkaz Russia 53 E2 ................43°02'N 44°41'E
Vladimir Russia 52 E3 ......................56°08'N 40°24'E
Vladivostok Russia 55 O2 .................43°07'N 131°56'E
Vlieland i. Neth. 42 D6 ......................53°16'N 4°57'E
Vlissingen Neth. 42 C4 .....................51°27'N 3°34'E
Vlorë Albania 50 C5 .........................40°28'N 19°30'E
Vltava r. Czechia 46 F4 .....................50°19'N 14°29'E
Voe Scotland 17 H5 ..........................60°21'N 1°16'W
Vohimena, Tanjona c. Madagascar 83 D2

25°36'S 45°12'E
Volda Norway 43 A3 ........................62°08'N 6°05'E
Volga r. Russia 53 E2 .......................45°47'N 47°34'E
Volga Uplands hills Russia 34 I4 ......53°15'N 45°45'E
Volgodonsk Russia 53 E2 ................47°32'N 42°08'E
Volgograd Russia 53 E2 ...................48°44'N 44°30'E
Völklingen Germany 42 F2 ...............49°15'N 6°51'E
Volodymyr-Volyns'kyy Ukraine 47 K4 ...50°51'N 24°20'E
Vologda Russia 52 D3 ......................59°13'N 39°54'E
Volos Greece 50 E4 ..........................39°22'N 22°57'E
Vol'sk Russia 53 E3 ..........................52°02'N 47°22'E
Volta, Lake resr Ghana 84 E2 .............6°23'N 0°05'E
Volta Redonda Brazil 73 E4 ..............22°30'S 44°07'W
Volzhskiy Russia 53 E2 .....................53°24'N 50°05'E
Voreioi Sporades is Greece 50 E4 .....39°15'N 23°27'E
Vorkuta Russia 52 G4 .......................67°29'N 64°05'E
Voronezh Russia 53 D3 ....................51°38'N 39°12'E
Vorskla r. Russia 47 P3 .....................48°55'N 34°08'E
Vosges mts France 44 G5 .................47°46'N 6°41'E
Voss Norway 43 A3 ..........................60°38'N 6°27'E
Vostochnyy Sayan mts Russia 55 K3 ...54°43'N 94°48'E
Votkinsk Russia 52 F3 ......................57°03'N 53°58'E
Vouziers France 44 D2 .....................49°24'N 4°42'E
Voznesens'k Ukraine 47 N2 .............47°33'N 31°21'E
Vranje Serbia 50 D6 .........................42°33'N 21°54'E
Vratsa Bulgaria 50 E6 ......................43°12'N 23°33'E
Vrbas r. Bos. and Herz. 50 B7 ..........45°07'N 17°31'E
Vršac Serbia 50 D7 ..........................45°07'N 21°17'E
Vuktyl Russia 52 F4 ..........................63°52'N 57°19'E
Vung Tau Vietnam 102 D6 ................10°22'N 107°05'E
Vuollerim Sweden 43 E4 ..................66°26'N 20°37'E
Vyaz'ma Russia 47 P6 ......................55°13'N 34°18'E
Vyborg Russia 43 G3 ........................60°42'N 28°46'E
Vychegda r. Russia 53 E4 .................61°15'N 46°28'E
Vygozero, Ozero l. Russia 52 D4 ......64°40'N 35°00'E
Vyrnwy, Lake Wales 10 D4 ...............52°46'N 3°29'W
Vyshniy-Volochek Russia 52 D3 .......57°35'N 34°33'E
Vytegra Russia 52 D4 .......................61°00'N 36°26'E

# W

Wa Ghana 84 D3 ............................10°04'N 2°30'W
Wabasca r. Canada 60 G3 ...............58°18'N 115°23'W
Wabash r. U.S.A. 63 I4 .....................37°50'N 88°01'W
Wabush Canada 61 L3 .....................52°51'N 66°49'W
Waco U.S.A. 62 G3 ...........................31°34'N 97°08'W
Wad Pakistan 96 C6 .........................27°20'N 66°30'E
Waddān Libya 84 F4 .........................29°09'N 16°09'E
Waddenzee str. Neth. 42 D5 .............52°51'N 4°51'E
Waddington England 13 G2 ..............53°10'N 0°32'W
Waddington, Mount Canada 60 F3 ....51°21'N 125°18'W
Wadebridge England 11 C2 ..............50°31'N 4°50'W
Wadhurst England 9 F2 .....................51°04'N 0°20'E
Wadi Halfa Sudan 85 H4 ...................21°48'N 31°20'E
Wad Madani Sudan 85 H3 ...............14°22'N 33°30'E
Wagga Wagga Australia 108 D3 .......35°08'S 147°23'E
Wāhāt Jālū Libya 49 H2 ....................29°14'N 21°04'E
Wahpeton U.S.A. 62 G6 ...................46°15'N 96°50'W
Waigeo i. Indonesia 103 I3 .................0°11'S 130°59'E
Wainfleet All Saints England 13 H2 ...53°06'N 0°14'E
Waingapu Indonesia 102 G2 ..............9°38'S 120°15'E
Waini Point Guyana 72 D7 ..................8°22'N 59°44'W
Wainwright U.S.A. 60 C5 ...................70°39'N 159°51'W
Wakasa-wan b. Japan 104 C3 ..........35°45'N 135°36'E
Wakayama Japan 104 C2 .................34°13'N 135°10'E
Wakefield England 13 F2 ..................53°41'N 1°30'W
Wakkanai Japan 104 D5 ...................45°24'N 141°40'E
Wałbrzych Poland 46 G4 ..................50°46'N 16°18'E
Wałcz Poland 46 G5 ........................53°17'N 16°29'E
Wales d. U.K. 21 D3 ..........................52°04'N 3°41'W
Wallasey England 12 D2 ...................53°26'N 3°04'W
Wallingford England 8 E2 .................51°36'N 1°08'W
Wallis and Futuna is S. Pacific Oc. 109 H5

13°24'S 177°57'W
Walls Scotland 17 H5 .......................60°14'N 1°33'W
Walney, Isle of i. England 12 D3 .......54°04'N 3°16'W
Walsall England 8 D3 .......................52°35'N 1°59'W
Waltham on the Wolds England 8 E3 ...52°49'N 0°49'W
Walton-on-Thames England 9 E2 .....51°23'N 0°25'W
Walvis Bay town Namibia 83 A2 .......22°58'S 14°30'E
Wandsworth England 9 E2 ...............51°27'N 0°12'W
Wantage England 8 D2 ....................51°35'N 1°25'W
Wanzhou China 99 J4 ......................30°47'N 108°22'E
Warangal India 96 E4 .......................17°59'N 79°35'E
Warboys England 9 E3 .......................52°24'N 0°05'W
Warburton watercourse Australia 108 C4 ...27°54'S 137°19'E
Ward Hill Scotland 17 F3 ..................58°54'N 3°22'W
Ward's Stone hill England 12 E3 ......54°02'N 2°38'W
Wareham England 8 C1 ...................50°41'N 2°07'W
Waremme Belgium 42 E3 .................50°42'N 5°15'E
Warlingham England 9 E2 ................51°19'N 0°03'W
Warminster England 8 C2 ................51°12'N 2°11'W
Warrego r. Australia 108 D3 .............30°24'S 145°21'E
Warrenpoint Northern Ireland 14 C2 ...54°06'N 6°15'W
Warri Nigeria 84 E2 ............................5°35'N 5°45'E
Warrington England 12 E2 ................53°23'N 2°36'W
Warrington d. England 21 D3 ...........53°24'N 2°33'W
Warsaw Poland 46 I5 .......................52°15'N 21°01'E
Warta r. Poland 46 F5 .......................52°35'N 14°37'E
Warwick England 8 D3 .....................52°17'N 1°35'W
Warwickshire d. England 21 E3 ........52°19'N 1°32'W
Washington England 13 F3 ..............54°54'N 1°31'W
Washington U.S.A. 63 K4 .................38°54'N 77°01'W
Washington d. U.S.A. 62 B6 .............47°36'N 120°19'W
Washington, Mount U.S.A. 63 L5 ......44°18'N 71°18'W
Waskaganish Canada 61 K3 .............51°28'N 78°46'W
Wast Water l. England 12 D3 ............54°26'N 3°18'W
Watampone Indonesia 102 G3 ...........4°31'S 120°21'E
Watchet England 11 D3 ....................51°11'N 3°20'W
Waterford Ireland 18 D2 ...................52°15'N 7°07'W
Waterford d. Ireland 18 D2 ...............52°10'N 7°53'W
Watergate Bay England 11 B2 ..........50°27'N 5°05'W
Waterlooville England 8 D1 ..............50°53'N 1°02'W
Water of Saughs r. Scotland 17 G1 ...56°47'N 2°37'W
Watertown U.S.A. 62 G5 ..................44°53'N 97°07'W
Watford England 9 E2 ......................51°39'N 0°23'W
Watlington England 8 D2 .................51°39'N 1°01'W
Watson Lake town Canada 60 F4 .....60°04'N 128°42'W
Watten, Loch l. Scotland 17 F3 .........58°29'N 3°21'W
Watton England 9 F3 ........................52°34'N 0°50'E
Wau South Sudan 85 G2 ...................7°40'N 27°59'E
Wausau U.S.A. 63 I5 ........................44°58'N 89°37'W
Waveney r. England 9 G3 .................52°29'N 1°41'E
Wear r. England 13 F3 .....................54°54'N 1°22'W
Wedmore England 8 C2 ...................51°14'N 2°49'W
Weener Germany 42 G6 ...................53°10'N 7°21'E
Weert Neth. 42 E4 ...........................51°15'N 5°43'E
Weifang China 99 L5 .......................36°42'N 119°03'E
Weihai China 99 M5 ........................37°30'N 122°07'E
Weinan China 99 J4 ........................34°27'N 109°33'E
Weipa Australia 103 K1 ....................12°37'S 141°55'E
Weldiya Ethiopia 85 H3 ....................11°49'N 39°36'E
Welkom S. Africa 83 B2 ...................27°59'S 26°44'E
Welland r. England 8 E3 ..................52°52'N 0°03'W
Wellesley Islands Australia 108 C5 ...16°18'S 139°33'E
Wellingborough England 8 E3 ..........52°18'N 0°42'W
Wellington New Zealand 109 G2 ......41°18'S 174°46'E
Wellington Som. England 11 D2 .......50°59'N 3°13'W
Wellington Tel. Wre. England 8 C3 ....52°42'N 2°31'W
Wells England 8 C2 ..........................51°13'N 2°39'W
Wells, Lake Australia 108 B4 ............26°40'S 123°16'E
Wells-next-the-Sea England 9 F3 .....52°57'N 0°51'E
Wels Austria 46 F3 ..........................48°10'N 14°01'E
Welshpool Wales 10 D4 ...................52°40'N 3°09'W
Welwyn Garden City England 9 E2 ...51°48'N 0°12'W
Wem England 8 C3 ..........................52°51'N 2°44'W
Wembley England 9 E2 ....................51°33'N 0°18'W
Wemyss Bay town Scotland 14 E3 ...55°53'N 4°53'W
Wenchi Ghana 84 D2 ........................7°45'N 2°07'W
Wendo Ethiopia 85 H2 ......................6°35'N 38°25'E
Wendover England 8 E2 ...................51°46'N 0°44'W
Wenlock Edge f. England 8 C3 .........52°27'N 2°49'W
Wensleydale f. England 13 E3 .........54°09'N 2°02'W
Wensum r. England 9 G3 .................52°37'N 1°20'E
Wenzhou China 99 M3 .....................27°59'N 120°41'E
Wesel Germany 42 F4 ......................51°40'N 6°38'E
Weser r. Germany 44 C5 ...................52°58'N 8°31'E
Wessel, Cape Australia 108 C5 ........11°03'S 136°46'E
Wessel Islands Australia 108 C5 ......11°19'S 136°26'E
West Australian Basin f. Indian Oc. 117 H2

17°42'S 102°36'E
West Bank Asia 49 K3 ......................31°52'N 35°19'E
West Bengal d. India 96 G5 ..............22°34'N 87°20'E
West Berkshire d. England 21 E2 ......51°28'N 1°20'W
West Bridgford England 8 D3 ...........52°56'N 1°08'W

West Bromwich England 8 D3 ..........52°31'N 1°59'W
Westbury England 8 C2 ....................51°15'N 2°11'W
West Calder Scotland 15 F3 .............55°51'N 3°34'W
West Dunbartonshire d. Scotland 20 C4 ...55°59'N 4°31'W
Western Australia d. Australia 108 B4 ...24°24'S 121°53'E
Western Desert Egypt 49 I2 ..............26°42'N 29°45'E
Western Dvina r. Europe 47 N6 .........55°28'N 30°54'E
Western Ghats mts India 96 D3 ........14°19'N 74°54'E
Western Isles d. Scotland 20 B5 .......57°54'N 6°48'W
Western Sahara Africa 84 C4 ...........22°14'N 15°05'W
Wester Ross f. Scotland 16 D2 .........57°39'N 5°20'W
Westerschelde est. Neth. 42 C4 ........51°27'N 3°27'E
West Falkland i. Falkland Is 73 C1 .....51°16'S 61°32'W
West Fen f. Cambs. England 9 F3 ......52°32'N 0°00'E
West Fen f. Lincs. England 8 E3 ........53°04'N 0°05'W
West Frisian Islands Neth. 42 D6 ......53°11'N 4°37'E
Westhill Scotland 17 G2 ...................57°09'N 2°17'W
West Kirby England 12 D2 ................53°22'N 3°11'W
West Lavington England 8 D2 ...........51°17'N 1°59'W
West Linton Scotland 15 F3 ..............55°45'N 3°21'W
West Loch Roag b. Scotland 16 C3 ...58°15'N 6°57'W
West Lothian d. Scotland 20 D4 ........55°54'N 3°31'W
West Malling England 9 F2 ...............51°18'N 0°25'E
Westmeath d. Ireland 18 D3 .............53°34'N 7°24'W
West Mersea England 9 F2 ..............51°47'N 0°56'E
West Midlands d. England 21 E3 .......52°28'N 1°49'W
Weston-super-Mare England 8 C2 ....51°21'N 2°59'W
West Palm Beach town U.S.A. 63 J2 ...26°40'N 80°09'W
Westport Ireland 18 B3 ....................53°48'N 9°31'W
Westray i. Scotland 17 F4 .................59°18'N 3°02'W
Westray Firth str. Scotland 17 F4 ......59°16'N 3°07'W
West Siberian Plain f. Russia 54 J4 ...62°39'N 80°21'E
West Sussex d. England 21 E2 ..........51°00'N 0°18'W
West-Terschelling Neth. 42 E6 ..........53°22'N 5°13'E
West Virginia d. U.S.A. 63 J4 ............38°45'N 80°27'W
West-Vlaanderen d. Belgium 42 B3 ...50°59'N 2°56'E
Westward Ho! England 11 C3 ...........51°02'N 4°14'W
West Yorkshire d. England 21 D3 ......53°46'N 2°04'W
Wetar i. Indonesia 103 H2 .................7°49'S 126°13'E
Wetherby England 13 F2 ..................53°56'N 1°23'W
Wetzlar Germany 44 H7 ...................50°34'N 8°30'E
Wexford Ireland 18 E2 ......................52°20'N 6°28'W
Wexford d. Ireland 18 E2 ..................52°37'N 6°32'W
Wexford Bay Ireland 18 E2 ...............52°25'N 6°19'W
Weybridge England 9 E2 ..................51°22'N 0°27'W
Weyburn Canada 62 F6 ....................49°40'N 103°52'W
Weymouth England 8 C1 .................50°36'N 2°27'W
Whalsay i. Scotland 17 I5 .................60°21'N 0°57'W
Whangarei New Zealand 109 G3 .....35°43'S 174°19'E
Wharfe r. England 13 F2 ..................53°50'N 1°08'W
Wheeler Peak Nev. U.S.A. 62 D4 ......38°57'N 114°17'W
Wheeler Peak N. M. U.S.A. 62 E4 .....36°33'N 105°24'W
Whernside hill England 13 E3 ..........54°14'N 2°24'W
Whitburn Scotland 15 F3 .................55°52'N 3°41'W
Whitby England 13 G3 .....................54°29'N 0°37'W
Whitchurch England 8 C3 ................52°58'N 2°41'W
Whitchurch Wales 11 D3 .................51°31'N 3°13'W
White r. U.S.A. 63 H3 ......................33°59'N 91°09'W
White, Lake Australia 108 B4 ...........21°03'S 129°07'E
Whitecourt Canada 60 G3 ...............54°08'N 115°43'W
Whitehaven England 12 D3 .............54°33'N 3°35'W
Whitehead Northern Ireland 14 D2 ...54°45'N 5°42'W
Whitehill England 8 E2 ....................51°06'N 0°52'W
Whitehorse Canada 60 E4 ..............60°44'N 135°06'W
White Nile r. Sudan/South Sudan/Uganda 85 H3

15°38'N 32°30'E
White Sea Russia 52 D4 ..................65°51'N 36°58'E
White Volta r. Burkina Faso/Ghana 84 D2 ...9°07'N 1°10'W
Whitfield England 9 G2 .....................51°09'N 1°17'E
Whithorn Scotland 14 E2 .................54°44'N 4°25'W
Whitland Wales 10 C3 .....................51°49'N 4°37'W
Whitley Bay town England 13 F4 .......55°03'N 1°27'W
Whitney, Mount U.S.A. 62 C4 ..........36°35'N 118°16'W
Whitsand Bay England 11 C2 ..........50°20'N 4°20'W
Whitstable England 9 G2 .................51°22'N 1°01'E
Whittlesey England 9 E3 ..................52°34'N 0°08'W
Whyalla Australia 108 C3 .................33°03'S 137°31'E
Wichita U.S.A. 62 G4 ......................37°42'N 97°20'W
Wichita Falls town U.S.A. 62 G3 ......33°55'N 98°29'W
Wick Scotland 17 F3 ........................58°26'N 3°06'W
Wick r. Scotland 17 F3 .....................58°26'N 3°05'W
Wickford England 9 F2 .....................51°37'N 0°31'E
Wickham England 8 D1 ....................50°54'N 1°11'W
Wickham Market England 9 G3 ........52°09'N 1°22'E
Wicklow Ireland 18 E2 .....................52°59'N 6°02'W
Wicklow d. Ireland 18 E3 .................53°02'N 6°27'W
Wicklow Head Ireland 18 F2 ............52°58'N 5°59'W
Wicklow Mountains Ireland 18 E2 ....52°53'N 6°34'W
Widecombe in the Moor England 11 D2 ...50°34'N 3°49'W
Wide Firth str. Scotland 17 F4 ..........59°01'N 3°02'W
Widnes England 12 E2 ....................53°21'N 2°44'W
Wieluń Poland 46 H4 .......................51°13'N 18°34'E
Wiener Neustadt Austria 46 G2 ........47°49'N 16°15'E
Wiesbaden Germany 46 C4 .............50°05'N 8°14'E
Wiesmoor Germany 42 G6 ...............53°25'N 7°45'E
Wigan England 12 E2 ......................53°33'N 2°38'W
Wight, Isle of i. England 8 D1 ..........50°39'N 1°07'W
Wigston England 8 D3 .....................52°35'N 1°06'W
Wigton England 12 D3 .....................54°50'N 3°10'W
Wigtown Scotland 14 E2 ..................54°52'N 4°27'W
Wigtown Bay Scotland 14 E2 ...........54°48'N 4°19'W
Wijchen Neth. 42 E4 .......................51°48'N 5°43'E
Wildhorn mt. Switz. 46 B2 ...............46°22'N 7°22'E
Wilhelm, Mount P.N.G. 108 D6 ..........5°46'S 144°52'E
Wilhelmshaven Germany 46 C5 .......53°32'N 8°08'E
Willebroek Belgium 42 D4 ...............51°03'N 4°22'E
William, Mount Australia 108 D3 .......37°19'S 142°35'E
Williams Lake town Canada 60 F3 ....52°08'N 122°09'W
Willingdon England 9 F1 ...................50°46'N 0°15'E
Williston U.S.A. 62 F6 ......................48°10'N 103°37'W
Williston Lake Canada 60 F3 ............55°51'N 123°43'W
Williton England 11 D3 .....................51°10'N 3°19'W
Wills, Lake Australia 108 B4 .............21°20'S 128°37'E
Wilmington Del. U.S.A. 63 K4 ...........39°43'N 75°33'W
Wilmington N. C. U.S.A. 63 K3 .........34°13'N 77°58'W
Wilmslow England 13 E2 .................53°20'N 2°14'W
Wilson's Promontory pen. Australia 108 D3

38°55'S 146°27'E
Wilton England 8 D2 ........................51°05'N 1°52'W
Wiltshire d. England 21 E2 ...............51°24'N 1°53'W
Wiltz Lux. 42 E2 ..............................49°58'N 5°56'E
Wimbledon England 9 E2 .................51°25'N 0°13'W
Wimborne Minster England 8 D1 .....50°48'N 1°59'W
Wimereux France 9 G1 ....................50°46'N 1°37'E
Wincanton England 8 C2 .................51°03'N 2°25'W
Winchester England 8 D2 ................51°04'N 1°19'W
Windermere England 12 E3 .............54°23'N 2°54'W

Windermere *l.* England 12 E3 ...... 54°18'N 2°57'W
Windhoek Namibia 83 A2 ...... 22°34'S 17°04'E
Windrush *r.* England 8 D2 ...... 51°43'N 1°25'W
Windsor Canada 63 J5 ...... 42°18'N 83°01'W
Windsor England 9 E2 ...... 51°29'N 0°37'W
Windsor and Maidenhead *d.* England 21 E2
...... 51°28'N 0°40'W
Windward Islands Caribbean Sea 67 L4 ...... 15°42'N 60°03'W
Windward Passage *str.* Cuba/Haiti 67 J4 ...... 19°40'N 74°11'W
Wingate England 13 F3 ...... 54°44'N 1°23'W
Winisk *r.* Canada 61 J3 ...... 55°01'N 85°22'W
Winkleigh England 11 D2 ...... 50°51'N 3°57'W
Winnebago, Lake U.S.A. 63 I5 ...... 44°00'N 88°28'W
Winnemucca U.S.A. 62 C5 ...... 40°59'N 117°44'W
Winnipeg Canada 60 I2 ...... 49°53'N 97°10'W
Winnipeg, Lake Canada 60 I3 ...... 51°31'N 96°40'W
Winnipegosis, Lake Canada 60 H3 ...... 53°05'N 100°40'W
Winsford England 12 E3 ...... 53°12'N 2°31'W
Winslow England 8 E2 ...... 51°57'N 0°53'W
Winslow U.S.A. 62 D4 ...... 35°02'N 110°42'W
Winston-Salem U.S.A. 63 J4 ...... 36°07'N 80°17'W
Winterswijk Neth. 42 F4 ...... 51°58'N 6°42'E
Winterthur Switz. 44 C2 ...... 47°30'N 8°43'E
Winterton England 13 G2 ...... 53°39'N 0°36'W
Wirksworth England 13 F2 ...... 53°05'N 1°34'W
Wirral *pen.* England 12 D2 ...... 53°22'N 3°07'W
Wisbech England 9 F3 ...... 52°40'N 0°10'E
Wisconsin *d.* U.S.A. 63 I5 ...... 44°30'N 89°32'W
Wishaw Scotland 15 F3 ...... 55°46'N 3°55'W
Wismar Germany 46 D5 ...... 53°53'N 11°28'E
Witham England 9 F2 ...... 51°48'N 0°38'E
Witham *r.* England 9 F3 ...... 52°56'N 0°05'E
Witheridge England 11 D2 ...... 50°55'N 3°42'W
Withernsea England 13 H2 ...... 53°44'N 0°02'E
Witney England 8 D2 ...... 51°47'N 1°29'W
Wittenberge Germany 46 D5 ...... 52°59'N 11°45'E
Wittlich Germany 42 F2 ...... 49°59'N 6°53'E
Wittmund Germany 42 G6 ...... 53°35'N 7°47'E
Wiveliscombe England 11 D3 ...... 51°03'N 3°19'W
Wivenhoe England 9 F2 ...... 51°51'N 0°58'E
Wkra *r.* Poland 46 I5 ...... 52°27'N 20°45'E
Władysławowo Poland 46 H6 ...... 54°47'N 18°25'E
Włocławek Poland 46 H5 ...... 52°39'N 19°05'E
Wokam *i.* Indonesia 103 I2 ...... 5°45'S 134°31'E
Woking England 9 E2 ...... 51°19'N 0°34'W
Wokingham England 8 E2 ...... 51°25'N 0°50'W
Wokingham *d.* England 21 E2 ...... 51°24'N 0°53'W
Wolfsberg Austria 46 F2 ...... 46°50'N 14°51'E
Wolfsburg Germany 46 D5 ...... 52°25'N 10°48'E
Wollaston Lake Canada 60 H3 ...... 58°16'N 103°22'W
Wollongong Australia 108 E3 ...... 34°25'S 150°51'E
Wolsingham England 13 F3 ...... 54°44'N 1°53'W
Wolvega Neth. 42 F5 ...... 52°53'N 6°00'E
Wolverhampton England 8 C3 ...... 52°35'N 2°08'W
Wombwell England 13 F2 ...... 53°31'N 1°24'W
Wŏnsan N. Korea 99 N5 ...... 39°09'N 127°27'E
Woodbridge England 9 G3 ...... 52°06'N 1°19'E
Woodcote England 8 D2 ...... 51°32'N 1°04'W
Woodhall Spa England 13 G2 ...... 53°09'N 0°13'W
Woodlark Island P.N.G. 108 E6 ...... 8°58'S 152°47'E
Woods, Lake of the Canada/U.S.A. 61 I2 ...... 49°22'N 94°50'W
Woodstock England 8 D2 ...... 51°51'N 1°21'W
Wooler England 13 E4 ...... 55°33'N 2°01'W
Worcester England 8 C3 ...... 52°12'N 2°13'W
Worcester S. Africa 83 A1 ...... 33°38'S 19°27'E
Worcester U.S.A. 63 L5 ...... 42°16'N 71°48'W
Worcestershire *d.* England 21 D3 ...... 52°12'N 2°12'W
Wörgl Austria 46 E2 ...... 47°29'N 12°05'E
Workington England 12 D3 ...... 54°39'N 3°32'W
Worksop England 13 F2 ...... 53°19'N 1°07'W
Worms Germany 46 H4 ...... 49°38'N 8°21'E
Worms Head Wales 10 C3 ...... 51°34'N 4°21'W
Worth England 9 E2 ...... 51°07'N 0°09'W
Worthing England 9 E1 ...... 50°49'N 0°22'W
Wowoni *i.* Indonesia 103 G3 ...... 4°09'S 123°13'E
Wragby England 13 G2 ...... 53°17'N 0°18'W
Wrangel Island Russia 55 T5 ...... 71°07'N 178°56'W
Wrangell U.S.A. 60 E3 ...... 56°28'N 132°22'W
Wrangle England 13 H2 ...... 53°02'N 0°07'E
Wrath, Cape Scotland 16 D3 ...... 58°38'N 5°00'W
Wreake *r.* England 8 D3 ...... 52°42'N 1°06'W
Wrexham Wales 10 E5 ...... 53°03'N 2°59'W
Wrexham *d.* Wales 21 D3 ...... 53°01'N 2°49'W
Wrigley Canada 60 F4 ...... 63°12'N 123°24'W
Wrocław Poland 46 G4 ...... 51°06'N 17°02'E
Wuhai China 99 J5 ...... 39°36'N 106°53'E
Wuhan China 99 K4 ...... 30°37'N 114°18'E
Wuhu China 99 L4 ...... 31°21'N 118°25'E
Wuppertal Germany 42 G4 ...... 51°16'N 7°09'E
Würzburg Germany 46 C3 ...... 49°48'N 9°55'E
Wuvulu Island P.N.G. 103 K3 ...... 1°43'S 142°50'E
Wuwei China 99 I5 ...... 37°52'N 102°38'E

Wuxi China 99 M4 ...... 31°31'N 120°18'E
Wuzhou China 99 K2 ...... 23°28'N 111°22'E
Wye England 9 F2 ...... 51°11'N 0°56'E
Wye *r.* Wales 10 E3 ...... 51°37'N 2°40'W
Wylye *r.* England 8 D2 ...... 51°04'N 1°48'W
Wymondham England 9 G3 ...... 52°34'N 1°07'E
Wyndham Australia 108 B5 ...... 15°29'S 128°05'E
Wynyard Canada 62 F7 ...... 51°46'N 104°12'W
Wyoming *d.* U.S.A. 62 E5 ...... 42°57'N 107°30'W
Wythall England 8 D3 ...... 52°23'N 1°53'W

**X**

Xai-Xai Mozambique 83 C2 ...... 25°02'S 33°41'E
Xankändi Azerbaijan 53 E2 ...... 39°49'N 46°46'E
Xanthi Greece 50 F5 ...... 41°09'N 24°53'E
Xiamen China 99 L2 ...... 24°29'N 118°11'E
Xi'an China 99 J4 ...... 34°12'N 108°59'E
Xiangkhoang Laos 102 C7 ...... 19°21'N 103°25'E
Xiangtan China 99 K3 ...... 27°52'N 112°47'E
Xiangyang China 99 K4 ...... 32°03'N 112°07'E
Xichang China 99 I3 ...... 27°55'N 102°11'E
Xigazê China 98 F3 ...... 29°17'N 88°45'E
Xi Jiang *r.* China 99 K2 ...... 22°23'N 113°20'E
Xilinhot China 99 L6 ...... 43°54'N 116°08'E
Xingtai China 99 K5 ...... 37°01'N 114°33'E
Xingu *r.* Brazil 72 D6 ...... 1°37'S 52°12'W
Xining China 99 I5 ...... 36°35'N 101°40'E
Xinjiang Uygur Zizhiqu *d.* China 98 D6 ...... 40°15'N 78°50'E
Xintai China 99 L5 ...... 35°55'N 117°45'E
Xinxiang China 99 K5 ...... 35°14'N 113°54'E
Xinyang China 99 K4 ...... 32°08'N 114°04'E
Xixón Spain 45 C5 ...... 43°32'N 5°39'W
Xizang Zizhiqu *d.* China 98 F4 ...... 31°26'N 88°12'E
Xun Jiang *r.* China 99 K2 ...... 23°27'N 111°25'E
Xuwen China 102 E8 ...... 20°18'N 110°09'E
Xuzhou China 99 L4 ...... 34°12'N 117°14'E

**Y**

Yablonovyy Khrebet *mts* Russia 55 L3 ...... 50°48'N 108°47'E
Yakima U.S.A. 62 B6 ...... 46°36'N 120°29'W
Yakumo Japan 104 D4 ...... 42°15'N 140°15'E
Yaku-shima *i.* Japan 104 B2 ...... 30°15'N 130°36'E
Yakutsk Russia 55 N4 ...... 61°59'N 129°40'E
Yala Thailand 102 C5 ...... 6°32'N 101°17'E
Yalova Turkey 51 H5 ...... 40°39'N 29°17'E
Yalta Ukraine 51 K7 ...... 44°30'N 34°11'E
Yamagata Japan 104 D3 ...... 38°15'N 140°20'E
Yamal Peninsula Russia 54 H5 ...... 70°40'N 69°23'E
Yambol Bulgaria 50 G6 ...... 42°29'N 26°30'E
Yamoussoukro Côte d'Ivoire 84 D2 ...... 6°48'N 5°15'W
Yamuna *r.* India 96 F6 ...... 25°26'N 81°57'E
Yana *r.* Russia 55 O5 ...... 71°09'N 135°57'E
Yanbu' al Baḥr Saudi Arabia 94 E4 ...... 24°05'N 38°06'E
Yancheng China 99 M4 ...... 33°22'N 120°09'E
Yangon Myanmar 97 I4 ...... 16°49'N 96°08'E
Yangquan China 99 K5 ...... 37°52'N 113°33'E
Yangzhou China 99 L4 ...... 32°23'N 119°25'E
Yanji China 99 N6 ...... 42°54'N 129°31'E
Yanskiy Zaliv *g.* Russia 55 O5 ...... 71°55'N 135°13'E
Yantai China 99 M5 ...... 37°30'N 121°21'E
Yaoundé Cameroon 84 F2 ...... 3°51'N 11°30'E
Yap *i.* Micronesia 103 J5 ...... 9°30'N 138°12'E
Yapen *i.* Indonesia 103 J3 ...... 1°46'S 136°12'E
Yaqui *r.* Mexico 66 B6 ...... 27°36'N 110°36'W
Yare *r.* England 9 G3 ...... 52°35'N 1°38'E
Yaren Nauru 115 J2 ...... 0°33'S 166°54'E
Yarm England 13 F3 ...... 54°30'N 1°21'W
Yarmouth Canada 61 L2 ...... 43°50'N 66°07'W
Yarmouth England 8 D1 ...... 50°42'N 1°30'W
Yarono Russia 52 G4 ...... 68°11'N 69°23'E
Yaroslavl' Russia 52 D3 ...... 57°37'N 39°53'E
Yartsevo Russia 47 O6 ...... 55°04'N 32°41'E
Yasawa Group *is* Fiji 109 G5 ...... 16°56'S 177°18'E
Yasyel'da *r.* Belarus 47 L5 ...... 52°08'N 26°27'E
Yatağan Turkey 51 H3 ...... 37°20'N 28°09'E
Yate England 8 C2 ...... 51°32'N 2°25'W
Yatton England 8 C2 ...... 51°23'N 2°49'W
Yavari *r.* Brazil/Peru 72 B6 ...... 4°18'S 69°59'W
Yaví, Cerro *mt.* Venezuela 72 C7 ...... 5°32'N 65°58'W
Yawatahama Japan 104 B2 ...... 33°27'N 132°26'E
Yazd Iran 95 H6 ...... 31°53'N 54°21'E
Yealmpton England 11 D2 ...... 50°21'N 3°59'W
Yekaterinburg Russia 52 G3 ...... 56°53'N 60°35'E
Yelets Russia 53 D3 ...... 52°36'N 38°29'E
Yell *i.* Scotland 17 H5 ...... 60°35'N 1°06'W
Yellowknife Canada 60 G4 ...... 62°29'N 114°19'W

Yellow Sea N. Pacific Oc. 99 N5 ...... 35°28'N 125°29'E
Yellowstone *r.* U.S.A. 62 F6 ...... 47°59'N 103°59'W
Yell Sound *str.* Scotland 17 H5 ...... 60°37'N 1°15'W
Yemen Asia 95 G3 ...... 14°48'N 45°46'E
Yenisey *r.* Russia 55 J5 ...... 70°22'N 82°59'E
Yeniseysk Russia 55 K3 ...... 58°27'N 92°13'E
Yeovil England 8 C1 ...... 50°56'N 2°38'W
Yerevan Armenia 53 E2 ...... 40°11'N 44°32'E
Yereymentau Kazakhstan 98 C8 ...... 51°36'N 73°08'E
Yershov Russia 53 E3 ...... 51°20'N 48°18'E
Yeşilırmak *r.* Turkey 51 L5 ...... 41°27'N 36°36'E
Yes Tor *hill* England 11 C2 ...... 50°41'N 4°01'W
Yevpatoriya Ukraine 49 J6 ...... 45°12'N 33°22'E
Yeysk Russia 53 D2 ...... 46°43'N 38°17'E
Yibin China 99 I3 ...... 28°46'N 104°36'E
Yichang China 99 K4 ...... 30°41'N 111°19'E
Yichun China 99 N7 ...... 47°37'N 128°52'E
Yıldızeli Turkey 51 L4 ...... 39°53'N 36°35'E
Yinchuan China 99 J5 ...... 38°26'N 106°18'E
Yingkou China 99 M6 ...... 40°40'N 122°15'E
Yining China 98 E6 ...... 43°54'N 81°22'E
Yiyang China 99 K3 ...... 28°37'N 112°16'E
Yli-Kitka *l.* Finland 43 G4 ...... 66°10'N 28°46'E
Ylitornio Finland 43 E4 ...... 66°20'N 23°41'E
Y Llethr *hill* Wales 10 D4 ...... 52°49'N 3°59'W
Ylöjärvi Finland 43 E3 ...... 61°34'N 23°36'E
Yogyakarta Indonesia 102 E2 ...... 7°47'S 110°23'E
Yokohama Japan 104 C3 ...... 35°26'N 139°37'E
Yongzhou China 99 K3 ...... 26°25'N 111°35'E
Yonne *r.* France 44 E6 ...... 48°23'N 2°58'E
York England 13 F2 ...... 53°58'N 1°05'W
York *d.* England 21 E3 ...... 53°57'N 1°04'W
York, Cape Australia 108 D5 ...... 10°41'S 142°36'E
York, Cape Canada 61 J5 ...... 73°47'N 87°15'W
York, Vale of *f.* England 13 F3 ...... 54°13'N 1°32'W
Yorkshire Wolds *hills* England 13 G2 ...... 53°53'N 0°35'W
Yorkton Canada 60 H3 ...... 51°12'N 102°27'W
Yoshkar-Ola Russia 52 E3 ...... 56°38'N 47°54'E
Youghal Ireland 18 D1 ...... 51°58'N 7°51'W
Yozgat Turkey 51 K4 ...... 39°49'N 34°47'E
Yrgyz Kazakhstan 54 H2 ...... 48°36'N 61°18'E
Yser *r.* France 42 B4 ...... 50°54'N 2°37'E
Ystad Sweden 43 C1 ...... 55°26'N 13°49'E
Ystalyfera Wales 10 D3 ...... 51°46'N 3°47'W
Ystwyth *r.* Wales 10 C4 ...... 52°24'N 4°05'W
Ysyk-Köl *l.* Kyrgyzstan 98 D6 ...... 42°25'N 77°12'E
Ythan *r.* Scotland 17 G2 ...... 57°22'N 2°01'W
Yūbari Japan 104 D4 ...... 43°04'N 141°59'E
Yucatán *d.* Mexico 66 G5 ...... 20°35'N 89°05'W
Yucatán *pen.* Mexico 66 F4 ...... 19°17'N 90°15'W
Yucatan Channel Cuba/Mexico 67 G5 ...... 22°16'N 86°56'W
Yueyang China 99 K3 ...... 29°23'N 113°07'E
Yukon *d.* Canada 60 E4 ...... 63°23'N 135°52'W
Yukon *r.* Canada/U.S.A. 60 B4 ...... 62°44'N 164°41'W
Yuma U.S.A. 62 D3 ...... 32°43'N 114°38'W
Yunak Turkey 51 I4 ...... 38°48'N 31°44'E
Yungas *f.* Bolivia 72 C5 ...... 16°51'S 65°20'W
Yunnan *d.* China 99 I2 ...... 24°45'N 101°07'E
Yushu China 98 H4 ...... 32°59'N 96°59'E
Yuxi China 99 I2 ...... 24°20'N 102°33'E
Yuzhno-Kuril'sk Russia 104 E4 ...... 44°04'N 145°49'E
Yuzhno-Sakhalinsk Russia 55 P2 ...... 46°57'N 142°39'E
Yuzhnoukrayinsk Ukraine 47 N2 ...... 47°50'N 31°11'E
Yuzhnyy, Ostrov *i.* Russia 54 G5 ...... 72°00'N 54°00'E

**Z**

Zaandam Neth. 42 D5 ...... 52°26'N 4°51'E
Zabid Yemen 94 F2 ...... 14°11'N 43°15'E
Zacatecas Mexico 66 D5 ...... 22°46'N 102°38'W
Zacatecas *d.* Mexico 66 D5 ...... 23°56'N 102°42'W
Zadar Croatia 50 A7 ...... 44°07'N 15°14'E
Zafra Spain 45 B3 ...... 38°26'N 6°25'W
Zagreb Croatia 50 A7 ...... 45°48'N 15°58'E
Zagros Mountains Iran 95 G6 ...... 34°02'N 47°10'E
Zāhedān Iran 95 J5 ...... 29°30'N 60°52'E
Zahlé Lebanon 49 K3 ...... 33°50'N 35°55'E
Zaječar Serbia 50 E6 ...... 43°54'N 22°16'E
Zākhū/Zaxo Iraq 94 F7 ...... 37°08'N 42°42'E
Zakynthos Greece 50 D3 ...... 37°47'N 20°54'E
Zakynthos *i.* Greece 50 D3 ...... 37°45'N 20°42'E
Zalaegerszeg Hungary 46 G2 ...... 46°51'N 16°53'E
Zalău Romania 47 J2 ...... 47°11'N 23°04'E
Zambezi *r.* Africa 83 C3 ...... 15°41'S 30°25'E
Zambia Africa 83 B3 ...... 14°13'S 27°30'E
Zamboanga Phil. 103 G5 ...... 6°56'N 122°05'E
Zamora Spain 45 C4 ...... 41°31'N 5°44'W
Zamość Poland 47 J4 ...... 50°43'N 23°16'E
Zanjān Iran 95 G7 ...... 36°40'N 48°27'E

Zanzibar Tanzania 83 C4 ...... 6°08'S 39°[...]
Zanzibar Island Tanzania 83 C4 ...... 6°17'S 39°[...]
Zaoyang China 99 K4 ...... 32°10'N 112[...]
Zaozhuang China 99 L4 ...... 34°52'N 117[...]
Zapadnaya Dvina Russia 47 O7 ...... 56°16'N 32[...]
Zapadnyy Sayan *f.* Russia 55 J3 ...... 51°41'N 88[...]
Zapolyarnyy Russia 43 G5 ...... 69°26'N 30[...]
Zaporizhzhya Ukraine 47 P2 ...... 47°50'N 35[...]
Zara Turkey 51 L4 ...... 39°54'N 37[...]
Zaragoza Spain 45 E4 ...... 41°40'N 0°[...]
Zarand Iran 95 I6 ...... 30°49'N 56[...]
Zaraza Venezuela 67 K2 ...... 9°21'N 65[...]
Zaria Nigeria 84 E3 ...... 11°07'N 7[...]
Żary Poland 46 F4 ...... 51°38'N 15[...]
Zarzis Tunisia 48 F3 ...... 33°30'N 11[...]
Zawiercie Poland 46 H4 ...... 50°29'N 19[...]
Zawīlah Libya 85 G2 ...... 26°08'N 15[...]
Zaysan Kazakhstan 98 E7 ...... 47°27'N 84[...]
Zaysan, Lake Kazakhstan 54 J2 ...... 48°05'N 83[...]
Zealand *i.* Denmark 43 B1 ...... 55°23'N 11[...]
Zeebrugge Belgium 42 C4 ...... 51°20'N 3[...]
Zeeland *d.* Neth. 42 C4 ...... 51°31'N 3[...]
Zeil, Mount Australia 108 C4 ...... 23°24'S 132[...]
Zelenodol'sk Russia 52 E3 ...... 55°49'N 48[...]
Zelenograd Russia 47 Q7 ...... 56°00'N 37[...]
Zémio C.A.R. 85 G2 ...... 5°00'N 25[...]
Zenica Bos. and Herz. 50 B7 ...... 44°11'N 17[...]
Zerah, Gowd-e *f.* Afgh. 95 J5 ...... 29°50'N 62[...]
Zeya Russia 55 N3 ...... 53°47'N 126[...]
Zêzere *r.* Portugal 45 A3 ...... 39°28'N 8°[...]
Zgierz Poland 46 H4 ...... 51°51'N 19[...]
Zhalpaktal Kazakhstan 53 E2 ...... 49°40'N 49[...]
Zhambyl Kazakhstan 98 C6 ...... 42°50'N 71[...]
Zhanaozen Kazakhstan 53 F2 ...... 43°18'N 52[...]
Zhangjiakou China 99 K6 ...... 40°41'N 114[...]
Zhangping China 99 L3 ...... 25°21'N 117[...]
Zhangshu China 99 L3 ...... 28°04'N 115[...]
Zhanjiang China 99 K2 ...... 21°10'N 110[...]
Zhaotong China 99 I3 ...... 27°22'N 103[...]
Zhashkiv Ukraine 47 N3 ...... 49°15'N 30[...]
Zhejiang *d.* China 99 M3 ...... 29°21'N 120[...]
Zheleznogorsk Russia 47 P5 ...... 52°19'N 35[...]
Zhengzhou China 99 K4 ...... 34°41'N 113[...]
Zhenjiang China 99 L4 ...... 32°10'N 119[...]
Zheshart Russia 52 E4 ...... 62°04'N 49[...]
Zhezkazgan Kazakhstan 54 H2 ...... 47°45'N 67[...]
Zhitikara Kazakhstan 53 G3 ...... 52°08'N 62[...]
Zhlobin Belarus 47 N5 ...... 52°54'N 30[...]
Zhmerynka Ukraine 47 M3 ...... 49°03'N 28[...]
Zhob Pakistan 95 K6 ...... 31°21'N 69[...]
Zhongshan China 99 K2 ...... 22°31'N 113[...]
Zhovti Vody Ukraine 47 O3 ...... 48°21'N 33[...]
Zhukovskiy Russia 47 R6 ...... 55°35'N 38[...]
Zhuzhou China 99 K3 ...... 27°49'N 113[...]
Zhytkavichy Belarus 47 L5 ...... 52°13'N 27[...]
Zhytomyr Ukraine 47 M4 ...... 50°15'N 28[...]
Zibo China 99 L5 ...... 36°47'N 118[...]
Zielona Góra Poland 46 F4 ...... 51°57'N 15[...]
Zīghan Libya 49 H2 ...... 25°27'N 22[...]
Zigong China 99 I3 ...... 29°24'N 104[...]
Žilina Slovakia 46 H3 ...... 49°14'N 18[...]
Zillah Libya 49 G2 ...... 28°32'N 17[...]
Zima Russia 98 I8 ...... 53°54'N 101[...]
Zimbabwe Africa 83 B3 ...... 22°06'S 30[...]
Zimmi Sierra Leone 84 C2 ...... 7°16'N 11[...]
Zimnicea Romania 50 F6 ...... 43°40'N 25[...]
Zinder Niger 84 E3 ...... 13°48'N 8[...]
Zlatoust Russia 52 F3 ...... 55°10'N 59[...]
Zlín Czechia 46 G3 ...... 49°13'N 17[...]
Zmiyevka Russia 47 Q5 ...... 52°40'N 36[...]
Znam"yanka Ukraine 47 O3 ...... 48°43'N 32[...]
Znojmo Czechia 46 G3 ...... 48°51'N 16[...]
Zolochiv Ukraine 47 K3 ...... 49°48'N 24[...]
Zolotonosha Ukraine 47 O3 ...... 49°42'N 32[...]
Zonguldak Turkey 51 I5 ...... 41°27'N 31[...]
Zouar Chad 85 F4 ...... 20°27'N 16[...]
Zouérat Mauritania 84 C4 ...... 22°46'N 12[...]
Zrenjanin Serbia 50 D7 ...... 45°23'N 20[...]
Zugdidi Georgia 53 E2 ...... 42°30'N 41[...]
Zugspitze *mt.* Austria/Germany 46 D2 ...... 47°26'N 10[...]
Zuid-Holland *d.* Neth. 42 D4 ...... 51°57'N 4[...]
Zújar *r.* Spain 45 C3 ...... 39°01'N 5[...]
Zülpich Germany 42 F3 ...... 50°42'N 6[...]
Zunyi China 99 J3 ...... 27°40'N 106[...]
Zürich Switz. 44 C2 ...... 47°23'N 8[...]
Zutphen Neth. 42 F5 ...... 52°09'N 6[...]
Zuwārah Libya 48 F3 ...... 32°56'N 12[...]
Zvishavane Zimbabwe 83 C2 ...... 20°17'S 30[...]
Zvolen Slovakia 46 H3 ...... 48°35'N 19[...]
Zvornik Bos. and Herz. 50 C7 ...... 44°24'N 19[...]
Zwickau Germany 46 E4 ...... 50°43'N 12[...]
Zwolle Neth. 42 F5 ...... 52°30'N 6[...]
Zyryanovsk Kazakhstan 98 E7 ...... 49°46'N 84[...]